Yanomami Warfare

Yanomami Warfare

∎ A POLITICAL HISTORY

R. BRIAN FERGUSON

SCHOOL OF AMERICAN RESEARCH PRESS ∎ SANTA FE ∎ NEW MEXICO

School of American Research Press
Post Office Box 2188
Santa Fe, New Mexico 87504-2188
Distributed by the University of Washington Press

Director of Publications: Joan K. O'Donnell
Editor: Jane Kepp
Art Director: Deborah Flynn Post
Maps: Carol Cooperrider
Typographer: Tseng Information Systems
Printer: Thomson-Shore

Library of Congress Cataloging-in-Publication Data:

Ferguson, R. Brian.
Yanomami warfare : a political history / R. Brian Ferguson.
p. cm.
Includes bibliographical references and index.
ISBN 0-933452-38-1 (cloth). -- ISBN 0-933452-41-1 (paper)
1. Yanomamo Indians--Warfare. 2. Yanomamo Indians--History.
I. Title.
F2520. 1.Y3F47 1995
980'.004982--dc20   94-12130
                                                          CIP

Cover photo: Menowa from Mahikora-teri, Upper Orinoco,
Southern Venezuela, 1971. Photo © Timothy Asch.

To Tim Trumpler

the kind of guy who liked to bend the rules

Contents

Maps

Funeral oration at the cremation of Fusiwe, killed in war near the far upper Orinoco, c. 1948

▎It rained but the fire did not go out. "Sha, sha, wah! Sha, sha, wah!" went the water on the flames. They cried out; they placed the possessions before the corpse; they wept. I watched from my shelter, crying. With me were Yariwe and Konokama, both crying.

▎"Your father has gone away," said Morokaima to Miramawe. "Never will he return."

▎"Brother of mine, you have left me," said Konokama. "When you meet our father tell him: Let us go back to our *shapono* [village], because over there, they are alone. You are a shaman and now you forgot your *hekura* [spirit], your garden, your *shapono*. You have died and no one has been able to avenge you still."

▎"Brother, you have gone away," said Shamawe. "I will stay. Remember that wherever you used to go, I would go too. I never left you alone. You guided us. Now we have no one to guide us. Why did you leave us alone?"

▎Kumaiwe, embracing Miramawe, said: "The songs of the *hekura* that your father was going to teach you, you will never learn. His enemies consumed him. He always said that when you were bigger he would teach you to be *hekura* [shaman]. Now he has gone away. Who will teach you those songs?"

▎"Brother, brother," said weeping Nakishewe. "You went to the garden, went to hunt. We went with you. You never scolded me. You were good with everyone. Now you have left me. When our father died I did not suffer so because I knew I still had another father: you. . . . Now you also have gone."

—Helena Valero, *Yo Soy Napëyoma*

Preface

Case Study

This book is part of a broader effort to develop a uniform theory of war. Over the past decade I have elaborated an explanation intended to address the multidimensional nature of war in a theoretically consistent way. Most of my work deals with war among nonstate peoples, although I have applied aspects of the theory to issues of modern warfare (Ferguson 1988a, 1989a). At its most general level, this work has produced two complementary approaches.

One (Ferguson 1990a) concerns war as a total social fact—a condition of society with causes and effects ramifying through all domains of cultural organization. I have expanded and elaborated that broadly sketched approach in a series of comparative studies using Amazonian material and dealing with interlocking aspects of the sociocultural system: ecological adaptation (Ferguson 1989b, 1989c), social organization (1988b), politics (n.d.*a*), and sociocultural evolution (1993). All those findings inform the present work.

The other basic approach was actually developed first, in a case study of indigenous warfare on the Pacific Northwest Coast (1984a). This approach aims at answering a narrow yet fundamental question: why do wars occur? Why does actual fighting happen when and where it does? That is the question addressed in this monograph.

The subject here is warfare among the Yanomami. These inhabitants of the rugged Brazil-Venezuela border region are a challenge to any anthropological explanation of war. Their legendary fierceness, their popular reputation as perhaps the most violent people on earth (e.g., Booth 1989:1138; Lumsden and Wilson 1983:139; O'Hanlon 1988: back cover), makes the Yanomami question virtually inescapable for a student of war. Even though I had never seen a Yanomami—my own field research was in Puerto Rico on an entirely different subject—any

Studies every recorded case of
Yanimano warfare.

time I discussed warfare I was asked, "What about the Yanomami?" Un-satisfied with existing explanations of their conflict, I set out to apply the two approaches, to see if they worked in this supremely puzzling case.

In a separate article (Ferguson 1992a), I applied the general model of war as a total social fact to the Yanomami of the Orinoco-Mavaca area. That article describes how these particular Yanomami have been pushed into an extreme conflict mode by interacting circumstances related to the intense and highly changeable Western presence in their area. It con-cludes that the historical encounter has resulted in a lowered threshold for war—a warlike disposition that makes violence more likely. These findings will turn up in many discussions to come.

This book addresses the question, Why do actual wars occur? Its goal is to show the underlying tensions that structure reported instances of Yanomami warfare. In attempting to find answers, I adopt four basic positions that go directly against strong currents in the anthropology of war. First, I believe that to understand the occurrence of war, the primary evidence must be recorded behavior rather than actors' stated understandings. Second, this behavior must be examined in concrete his-torical context rather than as a generalized cultural war pattern. Third, the existence and variation of actual Yanomami warfare in historical context is explainable largely by reference to changing circumstances of Western contact, which, contrary to established opinion, has been im-portant to the Yanomami for centuries. And fourth, warfare is motivated primarily by actors' concerns with their material well-being.

Probably most anthropologists concerned with war would reject some or all of these points. Moreover, many would reject a priori the possibility of an explanation of war that applies across cultures. I see theories as tools, instruments for building a better understanding. In that sense, the acid test of a theory is whether it is useful—whether through the application of the theory we achieve a deeper knowledge of a sub-ject. This monograph is a test of that sort.

It is equally important to make clear what this book is not. It is not a general portrayal of the Yanomami. Anyone who wishes to understand the richness of Yanomami culture should consult the bibliography for more appropriate works. The current study is, in contrast, deliberately one-dimensional. The analytical model developed in the next chapters is a world away from the Yanomami's own views on life and death. Nevertheless, the model does account for observed variations in war-fare—what the Yanomami actually do.

Alcida Ramos (1987) has discussed how different researchers' inter-ests and orientations "reflect on" their portrayals of the Yanomami;

Etic not an
Emic point of view

Not what they believe.

elsewhere (1990:4) she noted that any portrayal of them, or of any indigenous people, has potential political implications. Both points are
made particularly pressing by the ongoing struggle over preservation of
Yanomami territory in Brazil and Venezuela. This book examines the
Yanomami in order to better understand the nature of war. But it can
also contribute to our understanding of who the Yanomami are by de-
mythologizing them, by taking them out of an imaginary, timeless isolation and integrating them within a changing social universe. We shall
see that the current assault on the Yanomami is only the latest in a long
and sad history, although this time the results could be terminal. And
we will see that the Yanomami are not particularly warlike on their own,
although they can be so in certain circumstances.

At the outset, several acknowledgments are in order. The arguments
in this book have been worked out over several years in communica-
tion with many friends and colleagues, including Bruce Albert, Patricia
Antoniello, Timothy Asch, Bill Balée, Jane Bennett Ross, Brian Burk-
halter, Anne Marie Cantwell, Charlotte Cerf, Janet Chernela, Karen
Colvard, Jeff English, Eugenia Georges, Ken Good, Jonathan Haas,
Carol Henderson, Peter Kincl, Eglée López-Zent, William Manson, Joan
O'Donnell, Sandra Prado, Barbara Price, Bonnie Quern, Alcida Ramos,
Dolores Shapiro, Janet Siskind, William Smole, Leslie Sponsel, Alaka
Wali, Joel Wallman, Neil Whitehead, Stanford Zent, and all the partici-
pants in the H. F. Guggenheim/School of American Research Advanced
Seminar that led to the book *War in the Tribal Zone.*

Morton Fried set me to looking at the impact of Western contact on
war. Marvin Harris and Robert Murphy both encouraged me to pursue
my ideas on war and on the Yanomami in particular. Rutgers-Newark
librarians Carolyn Foote and Wanda Gawienowski offered invaluable
assistance in obtaining obscure sources. Joan K. O'Donnell, director of
publications at the School of American Research, provided expertise
and an occasional prod in seeing this long project through. Jane Kepp,
editor *extraordinaire,* made countless improvements in both substantive
arguments and style.

My wife, Leslie, suffered through this project and was my first
reader. Although this time wasn't as bad as the dissertation on Puerto
Rico, it was not fun, and her patience and support made it possible.
Finally, I want to acknowledge Bruiser, one of our cats, now gone, who
sat with me every day while I worked and held all my papers down.

I have not used diacritical marks on Yanomami words in this book
except in the bibliography. Their use in original sources is highly variable, and I am already asking enough of my readers without also asking

them to worry about pronunciation. I have standardized the spelling of names of particular local groups, generally going with the most widely used spelling in English language sources. Unless otherwise noted, all translations in the text are my own.

Finally, I feel I should apologize to the Yanomami for using the personal names of individuals. To do so, especially when the person is dead, is considered a serious insult (see Chagnon 1977:10–11). But since these names are already in print, I do not see sufficient reason for inventing pseudonyms.

Yanomami Warfare

PART I

Theory

1

Yanomami and the Study of War

The Yanomami people occupy a special place in Western thought. Their ancestral homeland, the mountainous country between Brazil and Venezuela, is the last major region of the New World to be explored and mapped by Europeans. The source of the Orinoco River in the Parima highlands (map 1) was not reached by outsiders until 1951. For centuries, this rugged frontier has been the stuff of legends, the land of the fabled Lake Parimé and El Dorado. The rapids and waterfalls that defeated Spanish and Portuguese invaders enabled the Yanomami to escape the holocaust that obliterated most Amazonian peoples. To the outside world, the Yanomami have remained shadowy figures, subjects of considerable fantasy.

Their protective isolation has diminished in recent decades, as Yanomami moved downstream to lowland areas and as roads, airstrips, military bases, and mining operations entered their territory. Wholesale destruction of Yanomami people and culture has ensued, especially in Brazil. At the same time, however, the Yanomami have become well known as the largest group of relatively unacculturated indigenous people remaining in lowland South America—indeed, in the entire hemisphere (CCPY 1979:1; Colchester 1985a:1; Smole 1976:218). Dozens of anthropologists and other investigators have written about the Yanomami. One result of all this attention is that Yanomami ethnocide cannot pass unnoticed. The devastation has triggered international campaigns to protect and preserve Yanomami territory (Anthropology Resource Center 1981; Colchester 1985a; *Cultural Survival Quarterly*, no. 1, 1989; and see Albert 1992; Chagnon 1992a, 1992b; Arvelo-Jiménez and Cousins 1992).

Much of the credit for raising global consciousness about the Yanomami belongs to Napoleon Chagnon, whose textbook, *Yanomamö: The Fierce People,* has been read by hundreds of thousands of college students. In it and other publications, Chagnon (1967, 1974, 1977, 1983) has portrayed Yanomami men as embroiled in virtually endless warfare over women, status, and revenge.[1] In his more recent works, Chagnon (1983, 1988, 1990a, 1990b; Chagnon and Irons 1979) has invoked a sociobiological or "evolutionary biological" paradigm to explain Yanomami warfare, attributing it to "reproductive striving." For years, Chagnon has debated the causes of Yanomami warfare with Marvin Harris (1974, 1977, 1979, 1984) and others, who have explained Yanomami conflict as a culturally evolved adaptive response to the limited availability of nutritionally crucial game resources. I will discuss these and other explanations in the concluding chapter of this book.

Recently, it is the image of fierceness itself that has come under attack as both an inaccurate representation of Yanomami life and a potential rationale for ethnocide (Albert 1989; Booth 1989; Carneiro da Cunha 1989; Lizot 1989; Ramos 1987; cf. Chagnon 1989a, 1992a:90, 208). Academic attention is shifting away from Yanomami warfare as a theoretical issue and toward Yanomami survival as a political cause. For the Yanomami this is certainly a promising change, but it does have one drawback. Intentionally or not, the recent focus on the Yanomami lets stand the illusion that they enjoyed a pristine isolation until very recently (see Booth 1989:1139; Brooke 1993a). In fact, Western encroachment on Yanomami lands since the 1940s is only the latest of several waves of state expansion to afflict the Yanomami. I believe that only by putting Yanomami society in historical perspective can we understand their warfare, and only by understanding the causes of their warfare can we understand what Western contact has meant to them and how they have acted as agents in shaping their own history.

Although some Yanomami really have been engaged in intensive warfare and other kinds of bloody conflict, this violence is not an expression of Yanomami culture itself. It is, rather, a product of specific historical situations: the Yanomami make war not because Western influence is absent but because it is present, and present in certain specific forms. All Yanomami warfare *that we know about* occurs within what Neil Whitehead and I call a "tribal zone," an extensive area beyond state administrative control, inhabited by nonstate people who must react to the far-flung effects of the state presence (Ferguson and Whitehead 1992a; Ferguson 1992b). In this book I explore one ethnohistorical incarnation of a tribal zone over a span of some 350 years. More concretely, my aim is to identify specific variables and patterns related to the expansion and contraction of nearby state systems that explain variations in the form and intensity of violence—including long periods of peace—among all Yanomami groups.

I hope to show that the occurrence of warfare among different Yanomami groups almost invariably follows identifiable changes in the Western presence—including the presence of anthropologists—and that without those changes there is little or no war. I also hope to explain the causality of this temporal connection by showing that the patterning of who attacks whom is primarily a result of antagonistic interests in the acquisition of steel tools and other Western manufactures.

General Perspectives

The anthropology of war has grown tremendously as a research area since the mid-1960s (Ferguson 1984b; Ferguson with Farragher 1988; Haas 1990). Ecological approaches have been developed, supported, criticized, and qualified. Social structural approaches have been statistically elaborated and confirmed, but with limited impact on nonstatistical research. In recent years, theoretical approaches to war have grown in number and diversity. At present, none of the new approaches seems likely to lead to any new consensus or even to reach a level of acceptance comparable to that of the older theories they seek to supplant. For all the attention paid to war, generally accepted understandings about it remain limited.

In my opinion, there are at least two serious obstacles to a deepening anthropological knowledge of war. One stems from the fact that most theorizing is done from very limited perspectives that deal with narrowly restricted aspects of war. There is nothing wrong with such theorizing in itself—indeed, this book is just such an exercise. Rather, the problem is that too often contending theorists have each portrayed his or her particular research interest as if it were the whole story, as if the positing of psychological, institutional, and material bases of war were somehow incompatible. Our knowledge has grown, but it has grown as a stack of two-dimensional images rather than by encompassing war as a three-dimensional phenomenon.

Broader synthesis was raised as a possibility in Ferguson (1984b) and attempted in Ferguson (1990a). The latter study approached war as a total social fact, seeking to provide a logically and theoretically coherent framework for synthesizing existing research findings from diverse perspectives and at the same time providing a means of addressing the multitude of causes and effects associated with war as a state or condition of a given society. In another work (Ferguson 1992a), I applied that model to the Yanomami of the Orinoco-Mavaca area, who have been so well researched by Napoleon Chagnon, Jacques Lizot, and others. Because of the wealth of information available about these particular Yanomami, they are also the main group studied in this book—the focus of part III. But the goals of that article and this book, although mutually supporting, are quite distinct.

The article explored the multiple ways in which Western contact has disrupted Orinoco-Mavaca social life, fomenting not just war but a range of interpersonal hostilities and creating, at times, an appearance of pervasive violence. Along with competition over Western manufactures, the article discussed the shattering impact of introduced diseases and the consequences of contact-related game depletions. It followed the ramifications of these infrastructural changes into the patterning of social, economic, and political organization—which themselves respond directly to the Western presence. Finally, the cognitive and valuational dimensions of these changes were described. All these points will come up again in this book, but my focus here is different.

Where the previous work (and see Ferguson 1993) tried to understand the total impact of change in relation to violence—that is, What makes the Orinoco-Mavaca Yanomami seem fierce or warlike?—this book is, in different ways, both more broadly and more narrowly defined. More broadly, it deals with *all* Yanomami, to the limits of available information, and not just those of the Orinoco-Mavaca area. More narrowly, it is concerned with overall changes in local societies only as they may inform one central question: How can we explain the actual occurrence of war?

I argue that the actual practice of war among the Yanomami is explainable largely as a result of antagonisms related to scarce, coveted, and unequally distributed Western manufactured goods. Other correlates of contact, however important in themselves, are of secondary concern here. I may thus seem guilty of the sort of limited perspective I just criticized. But again, the problem with limited perspectives is not so much their narrowness of research interests as their failure to recognize the possibility of multiple, compatible approaches. The analysis to be developed here dovetails with the broader questions of my earlier work; they inform each other.

The total transformation of local society that occurred in the Orinoco-Mavaca area lowers the threshold of war, the point at which conflict turns violent. Political disputes that would be resolved without violence in other cultures or even among other Yanomami groups instead gave rise to bloodshed along the Orinoco and Mavaca rivers. Understanding this threshold effect is necessary to explain why certain wars take place. But it in no way contradicts the present and more narrow explanation of the causes of war because the factors that led to this bellicose transformation are the same contact circumstances that give rise to war, along with the fact of war itself. Thus, raising or lowering the threshold is a feedback effect. It must be taken into consideration to understand variations in war proneness, but it does not change the patterning of hostilities and collective violence.

The second obstacle to developing a better anthropological understanding of war is more germane to the approach taken in this book. In the past, anthropologists have usually approached warfare as a general cultural pattern, an aspect of society abstracted from the actual practice of war. Theories sought to explain why a given people had a certain kind of warfare, but not why particular wars happened when and where they did. The theory developed here is intended to apply to the actual practice of war—why organized groups of men actually go off on specific occasions with intent to kill. Spatial and temporal variations in this practice of war are central to my explanation.

I propose that wars occur when those who make the decision to fight estimate that it is in their material interests to do so (Ferguson 1990a: 30). Why start with this motivational hypothesis, which would probably be rejected by the great majority of researchers in the topic? In previous work (1984b: 23–24), I described how the question of "economic motivation" in war, which during the 1940s led to excellent ethnohistorical studies of North American Indian warfare, was abandoned in favor of a new doctrine that culture determines warriors' motivation. The entire question of why people go to war was shunted off the research agenda, relegated to minor significance as mere proximate causation. With strikingly little discussion, at least in print, it became anthropological dogma that people are ready and willing to go to war for any purpose that their culture valorizes.

All theories about culture rest on some psychological premises. For the past forty years, most anthropological studies of war, including but not limited to ecological approaches, have rested on the assumption that the cognitive logic of a particular culture provides the motivation for its members to go to war. This assumption goes hand in hand with the ahistorical use of illustrative case material: cultural values are expressed in a general cultural pattern, with limited reference to actual practice and its variations over time and space. Such illustrative use of evidence is capable of supporting almost any argument, and one result is the profusion of apparently incompatible theories.

The material motivation hypothesis I propose is the capstone of a large structure of inference, deduction, and not a little speculation—as will be demonstrated in the following pages. Starting out with this somewhat heretical idea leads to a critical reevaluation of our received wisdom about why wars occur. Previously (1984a), I attempted such a reevaluation of warfare on the Pacific Northwest Coast, particularly that of the Kwakiutl, long the virtual archetype of nonmaterially induced warfare (Codere 1950). This time, of course, the case is the Yanomami. But before getting to the Yanomami material, the structure of the broader theory must be described.

Interests and Objectives

I begin that broader theory (Ferguson 1984b:38) with a minimal specification of the material interests involved in war: (1) maintenance or improvement of existing consumption standards; (2) energetic efficiency, or, more specifically, maintenance of labor requirements within acceptable levels; and (3) protection against life-threatening hazards, either environmental or human. Number 3 may encompass potential threats to numbers 1 and 2.

These interests, I propose (Ferguson 1990a:30), find expression in six basic types of strategic objectives: (1) to increase access to a resource by eliminating a competitor; (2) to capture movable valuables; (3) to impose an exploitative relationship on another independent group; (4) to conquer and incorporate another group; (5) to use external conflict as a means of enhancing the decision-makers' position within their own society; and (6) to forestall attacks by others. Objectives 5 and especially 4 are most applicable to war in hierarchically organized societies (chiefdoms and states), so this book will be concerned primarily with 1, 2, 3, and 6.

This concern does not imply a "psychologistic approach" to war, nor does it confuse ultimate and proximate causation (see Kroeber and Fontana 1986:164). It is, instead, a recognition that ultimate causes must work through proximate mechanisms, and an assertion that theories about ultimate causes should be able to show how these result in actual motivation and behavior. In a sentence, the ultimate causes of war are the processes that generate the circumstances that structure the incentives that lead people to decide on war.[2]

This emphasis on material motivation in war requires clarification. I must make clear that I do not assert or believe that all human action is ultimately derived from these few material motives. Absolutely not. War is a special case in human affairs because, unlike most other spheres of activity, war typically involves major hazards and costs in lives, resources, effort, and emotions. It is true that all over the world, young men with no combat experience often look forward to battle as an exciting challenge or even a game, but it is rare to see that attitude reported among the seasoned adults who usually make the decisions. Those who have witnessed the shattered families, the infected wounds and permanent disfigurements, the panicked flights, the fear and the weeping are usually very reluctant to open new hostilities. With these costs in mind, if the decision to go to war does not have a compelling material rationale, then from a material perspective, it would be a profoundly irrational decision.[3]

I should clarify that I do not maintain that only material incentives are sufficient to motivate an individual to kill. Not at all. A wide range of human emotions can culminate in lethal violence. But material interests are different from other grounds for violence in a very important way. In intergroup relations, material interests tend to be more collective in nature. An individual may be insulted, a family may want revenge, but an entire village can experience material deprivation. This collective impact, combined with the spatial patterning of crucial material parameters—resource distributions, trade routes, foci of state expansion—makes for a *structured* pattern of antagonisms that is lacking for most other deadly grudges. That is why material interests are far more likely to lead to war.

It is true that a host of other motivations will be involved in any decision to attack, and some of these will have no connection to any possible material benefit. Yet many of the reported nonmaterial motivations for war, I would argue, are moral rationalizations for material interests. Although I am concerned primarily with motivation as it is expressed in action, in this book I also give attention to the thought processes involved, developing some general positions sketched out in previous work (Ferguson 1984b:38–41). One conclusion is that it would be exceptional, among the Yanomami and perhaps any group, to find a decision to fight emically conceptualized in terms of pure, naked material interest. Material objectives are often stated by actors themselves, but along with so many other expressed reasons for going to war that it would seem arbitrary to single them out. War makers do not talk like materialists, and I believe they do not think like materialists.

My position is that people's perceived material interests strongly influence their evaluations of their broader social relationships. In their interpretation of a relationship and of events taking place within its context, material interests go through a conversion into moral idioms. "Wants" are translated into "rights." Always, it seems, "*they* started it" with some act that is characterized as a grave moral affront. (It is one of the depressing constants of human history that those setting off for war believe they are morally justified in their actions.) But even to speak of this as "morality" may be overly abstract. The offending acts seem to be thought of in very concrete terms: specific persons and what they did or said—usually an "insult." In many cases of war among neighbors, the conversion of material needs into highly charged and very personal terms is all the more imperative because combat involves violent action against individuals who previously had been joined together in a long-standing social relationship (see Netting 1974).

The way in which actors evaluate the deeds and words of others depends on the current political character of relations between groups. What actually happened is often less significant than whether relations were previously on good or bad terms. Much can be overlooked between friends, and little may be tolerated from enemies. Moreover, the most overt and provocative acts usually occur in situations where relations are already strained. Situated in context, any act may stand for or symbolize the broader relationship that exists between groups and thus may serve as a trigger for fighting. That broader relationship, I assert, is largely structured by material interests; but material interests may be superficially eclipsed by even trivial affairs when antagonism becomes confrontation.

Other considerations further obscure the significance of material interests in decisions for war. My initial formulation of the material incentive position referred to "those who decide on war." This phrase calls attention to the political structure (see Ferguson 1988a, 1990a). In most Amazonian societies, leadership is strongly consensual (Ferguson n.d.*a*). Amazonian leaders seek to persuade others by skillful oratory that invokes the highest moral principles and values. They extol bravery and chastise cowardice, exhort vengeance, vilify suspected sorcerers and thieves, and so on. Often this oratory takes place within the context of a history of violent conflict that lowers the threshold for war, making members of a society quicker to perceive an insult and readier to respond violently.

What all this means is that the material motivation hypothesis cannot be evaluated adequately using informants' (emic) accounts and explanations, since almost any act of war will have a great number of rationales that can be elicited. Perhaps something important would be revealed if anthropologists in the field pressed informants about the material interests involved in war. To my knowledge, no one has attempted that for the Yanomami. But I suspect that insults and provocations would still loom large in any recounting because they truly are important to the actors. Moreover, accurate elicitation of underlying interests and conflicts related to trade in Western manufactures may be especially difficult because the informant may be manipulating the anthropologist, who is perceived primarily as a source of trade goods.

An Etic Behavioral Approach

How then can the hypothesis be evaluated? As an alternative to relying on informants' explanations, I have developed an etic behavioral approach to identifying the objectives in war (Ferguson 1984a:270–71, 1984b:41). Variations in the behavior of war—who attacks and who is attacked, periods of relative peace and periods of intense fighting— are related to a set of contextual variables identified by the outside analyst as pertaining to the material conditions of life. If these variables are sufficient to explain the variations in warfare—that is, if there is a consistent pattern in which people behave *as if* they were pursuing the identified material interests—then it is reasonable to assume that the posited material motivation is indeed determining their actions, unless one can offer a reasonable alternative explanation for the observed variation (see Cannon 1992).[4]

To make such an analysis, one must assemble a large number of cases with sufficient contextual information to substantiate the posited patterns. This entails constructing a historical record—the who, what, when, and where of war. While this is a laborious and at times frustratingly uncertain task, my experience is that a usable chronology can be put together from published sources about reasonably well studied peoples. The objective, usually unattainable, should be completeness. But the reconstructed history should at least mention *all* cases of warfare that can be situated by time and place, so that the reader can assess the general validity of the analysis.

That is the method employed in my study of Northwest Coast warfare (Ferguson 1984b). In the present work, I try to expand on this approach in three ways. First, I devote more effort to constructing a formal analytical model (chapters 2 and 3), which is then tested in a piecemeal but repetitive and cumulative fashion against the patchy information assembled in the histories of conflicts. Second, I view warfare as one manifestation of political history. Uniform application of factors identified as causing war also helps explain other kinds of political behavior, including division and relocation of local groups, alliance, factionalism, and nonlethal combats. Third, I examine human behavior not only to assess the causes of war but also to make inferences about the strategies and tactics employed in war.

My historical reconstruction and theoretical explanation jointly emphasize circumstances of Western contact (as do other works [Ferguson 1984a, 1984b, 1990a, 1990b, 1992b; Ferguson and Whitehead 1992a, 1992b]). It is important to clarify that I do not take state expansion in general or Western contact in particular to be the sole cause of war among nonstate peoples. In the Americas, as elsewhere, there is abundant evidence of war—occasionally quite brutal war—long before Columbus. (Warfare not related to expanding states is discussed in Ferguson 1983, 1984a, 1984b, 1989c, 1990a, and 1993.) The point is not that the West invented war, but that Western expansion regularly transformed, frequently intensified, and sometimes generated war among nonstate peoples at its periphery.

The military impact of states expanding into nonstate areas is examined at a global level in Ferguson and Whitehead (1992b; and see Blick 1988; Schmidt 1990). The case studies collected there document the many ways in which state expansion transforms and generates warfare among indigenous people. They also show that the influence of states typically extends far beyond their frontiers into a "tribal zone" that is rife with conflict of various sorts. One conclusion of that work is that few ethnographically or historically known cases can be said to exemplify precontact, or "pristine," warfare. Thus, historical reconstruction is more than a method, more than a means of accumulating sufficient cases to test a model. A historical perspective, or, more specifically, an understanding of the history of state penetration, is an essential aspect of the explanation itself.

The need to address the role of state expansion is also argued in another work about warfare throughout Amazonia (Ferguson 1990b). That paper seeks to demonstrate a simple point: that virtually all his-

torically known Amazonian warfare has been demonstrably affected
—transformed, intensified, or even generated—by the presence or proximity of Westerners. I call this general impact "warrification."

My earlier paper also frames the theoretical problem that is the subject of this book. The wars of the Yanomami clearly do not fall under two
of my three headings (1990b:243–47) of types of warrification: wars
waged under the direct control or deliberate influence of Europeans and
wars related to major demographic disruption and dislocation. My third
heading, however, does apply to the Yanomami: warfare related to conflict over Western manufactures, especially iron or steel cutting tools.

In some cases the relationship between war and Western manufactures is straightforward, as when warfare consists of raiding to plunder
the tools or when major monopolists of trade in Western goods openly
make war to protect their privileged position. But other cases are more
complicated and embedded in the social fabric, involving quarrels and
factionalism even among coresidents. A good amount of Yanomami
raiding, we shall see, is openly directed at plunder, especially in those
situations where the possessors of Western goods are Westerners themselves, other non-Yanomami, or distant Yanomami. Much Yanomami
warfare, however, and most of the fighting reported by recent ethnographers as occurring between related local groups, is not so simply explained. These wars fall into the "more complicated" category.

This book attempts to elucidate those complications, to show how
competing interests in Western manufactures weave through social relationships to structure social conflicts that lead to war. In the process,
materially based antagonisms are transformed into moral imperatives
to kill. Specifying all the linkages and arranging them into a workable
analytic model are the tasks of chapters 2 and 3.

I should emphasize at this point that the model to be developed here
is not intended as a general explanation of warfare in Amazonia or elsewhere. It is instead an application of a more general approach to one
ethnohistorical situation. Application of the general perspective and detailed model building for other cases must begin with the empirical
realities of those situations.

Building the model means starting from scratch, since the objects
of contention—the introduced Western manufactures—have been excluded from consideration in anthropological theory. The following section lays the groundwork for the model by surveying what is known
about the social character and consequences of trade in Western manufactures throughout Amazonia. It also forms a bridge, picking up where

the discussion left off in Ferguson (1990b) and connecting it to the subject of the present book.

Amazonian Trade in Western Manufactures

Machetes, axes, and knives are in great demand among indigenous Amazonian peoples. The reason is clear. Various studies show that steel edges bring an increase in work efficiency of 300 percent to 1,000 percent, depending on circumstances and method of calculation (Carneiro 1979a, 1979b; Colchester 1984:294–95; Hames 1979:219–20; Up de Graff 1985; Whitehead 1988a:50). Throughout Amazonia, steel spread through indigenous trade networks and replaced stone tools decades or even generations before any anthropologist, and often before any Western observer at all, arrived on the scene (Balée 1988:168; Carneiro 1979a:21, 1983:70; Dumont 1976:43; Hahn 1981:89; Lapointe 1970:43; Oberem 1985:352; Oberg 1953:17; Thomas 1982:22–24; Yde 1965:24–25). Thus there is reason to pay special attention to cutting tools.[5]

Steel tools, however, are only part of the situation. Indigenous people typically come to need, or at least want, a wide variety of Western manufactures, including metal pots and griddles, fishhooks and line, shotguns and ammunition, clothing, matches, medicines, and sometimes foodstuffs. Nor is the demand entirely utilitarian. Combs, mirrors, and glass beads are avidly sought. Frequently, the expanding demand for Western goods is an open-ended process leading to the assimilation of native peoples into the lowest levels of Western society (Arhem 1981:53; Arvelo-Jiménez 1971:27–29; Gillin 1936:5–17; Goldman 1963:69; Harner 1973:17–31; Jackson 1983:62; Lapointe 1970:20–21; Murphy and Steward 1956; Oberem 1985:352; Rivière 1969:40; Siskind 1973a:33, 170; Whitten 1976:13).

Anthropology has paid little attention to the impact of steel tools and introduced manufactures on indigenous societies. In one sense this is difficult to understand. Our discipline divides the history of human existence into ages of stone, bronze, and iron, but it treats as insignificant, or at least uninteresting, the fact that virtually the entire universe of nonstate societies has jumped recently from stone to steel. Two studies stand out as exceptions: Sharp (1974) for Australia and Salisbury (1962) for New Guinea. Although these well-known studies both document extensive social change as a consequence of the acquisition of

Western manufactures, the leads they offer have received little follow-up by other anthropologists.[6]

In another sense, however, this sustained lack of interest in the impact of Western goods is not at all difficult to comprehend. It follows a long-standing disciplinary commitment to reconstruct portraits of indigenous peoples free of outside "contamination" (see Ferguson and Whitehead 1992a:2). But despite little direct focus on the topic, observations scattered throughout the extensive literature on Amazonia are sufficient to allow some generalizations about the significance of exogenous manufactures.

We know that indigenous peoples in Amazonia have made great efforts to obtain Western manufactures, making long journeys and relocating settlements to get access to sources (Arhem 1981:53; Arvelo-Jiménez 1971:18–27; Bamberger 1979:132–33; Colson 1973:10; Coppens 1971:33–36; Hemming 1978:6–10, 436–37; Lapointe 1970:20; Maybury-Lewis 1974:52; Myers 1974:153; Oberg 1953:98; Rausch 1984:69; Rivière 1969:15; Thomas 1972:11; Whitehead 1988a:19; Yde 1965:3–4, 14, 238; Yost and Kelly 1983:202). They have also gone to war to get tools, raiding Westerners and other Indians to plunder their steel, or accepting the manufactures as payment for mercenary service or slave raiding for the Westerners (Balée 1988:162–64, 168; Edmundson 1922:100; Hahn 1981:88–89; Hemming 1987:299–300; Holmberg 1969:14, 159; Isaac 1977:142; Kracke 1978:10; Metraux 1963:386; Morey and Marwitt 1975:441, 447; Morey and Metzger 1974:102; Murphy 1960:29–30; Murphy and Quain 1955:14; Nimuendajú 1967:3; Siskind 1973a:43; Stearman 1984:643–44; Stocks 1983:82; Taylor 1981:650–51; Wagley 1983:39; Whitehead 1988a, 1990a, 1990b). In short, indigenous people value steel and other Western items so highly that they are willing to kill and risk death to get them.

It is also clear that the entry of Western manufactures into indigenous exchange networks is accompanied by various sorts of violent and nonviolent conflict. In an earlier paper (Ferguson 1990b:245–47), I described numerous instances of such conflict but made no attempt to analyze just how and why the introduction of the Western items caused so much trouble. To carry out such an analysis, I must start by looking at general characteristics of exchange (see Lathrap 1982).

Trade can be difficult, even hazardous, in Amazonia. Just to be possible over a distance, it must be built into stable social relationships, often formalized as trade partnerships (Harner 1973:125–33; Thomas

1972:35, 1982:124; Whitten 1976:216–19). Exchange of important items tends toward exclusivity, in that *A* normally will receive item *X* only from *B* (although that tendency must be qualified in various ways to describe specific cases) (Colson 1973; Gregor 1977:309–10; Jackson 1983:64; Murphy and Quain 1955:18–19; Oberg 1953:41; Roth 1985:163–64; Thomas 1972:34–35, 1982:124). Material exchanges are accompanied by a host of social interactions and relationships—intermarriage, political-military alliance, religious community, and so forth (Arvelo-Jiménez and Biord Castillo 1989:11; Boomert 1987:36–38; Harner 1973:116–25; Jackson 1983:124; Lapointe 1970:20–21; Morey and Metzger 1974:103; Oberg 1953:52; Thomas 1982:124–26). For these reasons, in relatively unacculturated situations trade typically does not involve market relationships, and trade equivalencies may differ strikingly from cash market values (Coppens 1971; Thomas 1972). This kind of exchange is fixed firmly in the context of a deliberately stabilized and multidimensional social relationship.

The introduction of Western manufactures brings a categorical asymmetry into exchange relationships. Western products go in one direction, indigenous goods or services go in the other. Generally, people in Amazonia pay for Western manufactures with great amounts of labor in various forms. Game and other forest products are brought to those who reciprocate with steel. So are garden foods, especially the ubiquitous manioc flour. People seeking Western goods also produce traditional products with high labor costs, such as canoes, blowguns, manioc graters, and trained hunting dogs (Aspelin 1975:chapter 6; Bancroft 1769:263–64; Colson 1973:59; Coppens 1971; Dumont 1978:152; Farabee 1918:51; Fock 1963:239; Harner 1973:127–30; im Thurn 1967:272–73; Kloos 1977:16; Morey and Metzger 1974:103; Rivière 1969:51–54; Thomas 1972:10–15; Vickers 1981:58; Whitten 1976: 217; Yde 1965:34, 248–49). In some situations, people put themselves directly at the service of those who can supply the precious items, as do the polyethnic Maku of northwest Amazonia, who offer themselves as servants, sexual partners, and political-military supporters to Tukanoans (Jackson 1983:154–62; Milton 1984:9; Whiffen 1915:60).[7]

That sociopolitical inequality can accompany unequal access to sources of Western manufactures is easy to understand: other things being equal, middlemen are in a position to set conditions and make demands. The Western goods they control are extraordinarily desired, they are scarce, and they are available only through a few restricted points. If people are willing to risk death in a raid or relocate their village in order to obtain Western manufactures, they will also be willing to make other sacrifices for them. Those who control the flow of steel very literally control the means of production.

That control is reinforced by other inequalities that accompany different positions in trade networks. Unequal access to critical technology in itself confers a kind of status (Dumont 1978:133; Holmberg 1969: 275; Maybury-Lewis 1974:21, 195–96; Murphy 1960:39, 42, 121–25). Status is often accompanied by the direct political support of Westerners, who seek to promote their preferred *capitán* (Dumont 1978:37–38; Golob 1982:115; Kracke 1978:51–52; Price 1981:697), and by military inequality, as Western backing provides important tactical advantages (Golob 1982:126; Maybury-Lewis 1974:211; Wagley 1983:35; Whitten 1976:13; and see Hemming 1978, 1987, for all of these points). Those who control the flow of Western manufactures are thus in position to impose very favorable terms of trade (see Emmanuel 1972)— in this context, the going rate of exchange of indigenous products and effort for Western manufactures. For example, how much manioc flour equals one machete?

My idea here is that the introduction of Western manufactures alters the nature of indigenous exchange from a state of roughly balanced reciprocity to one that is fundamentally exploitative.[8] This posited exploitation is potentially measurable as an unequal flow of realized labor time towards the source of Western goods and as a parallel imbalance in claims on persons, in terms of wives, bride service, and political and military support. But it must be immediately emphasized that all these posited relationships apply in the earlier phases of acquisition of Western goods. They are expected to weaken or perhaps disappear as "traditional," highly socialized trading relationships are replaced by more marketlike situations with multiple sources of Western items.

Unfortunately, the balance of trade between villages rarely receives anthropological attention, and I found no direct evidence in the general literature on Amazonia to directly support or refute this proposal. As will be seen in chapter 2, substantial support for the idea of exploitative exchange does exist in the detailed Yanomami ethnography. In chapter 3, exploitation by middlemen and other antagonisms related to differential access to sources of Western manufactures are argued to be the basis for violent conflict.

Maps

Map 1 ▪ The Yanomami area in southern Venezuela and northern Brazil.

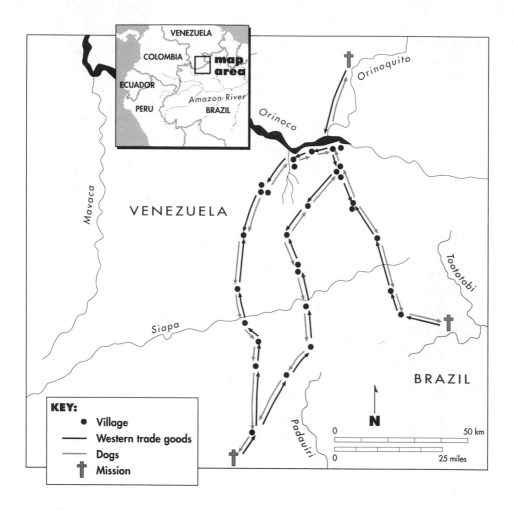

Map 2 ▪ Trade between Yanomami on the Orinoco and those on tributaries of the Río Negro (redrawn from Good 1984).

Map 3 ▪ Distribution of Yanomami language groups, about 1983 (based on Colchester 1985a:3). The Yanomami around the Apiau and Ajarani rivers may speak a distinct language but are considered in this book along with the Yanomam in chapter 8.

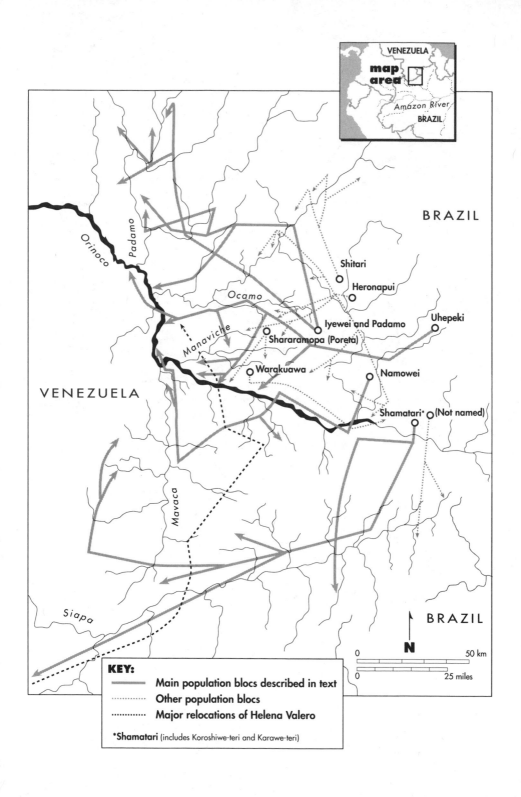

VENEZUELA

map area

Amazon River

BRAZIL

BRAZIL

Orinoco

Padamo

Ocamo

Manaviche

VENEZUELA

Mavaca

Siapa

Shitari

Heronapui

Uhepeki

Iyewei and Padamo

Shararamopa (Poreta)

Warakuawa

Namowei

Shamatari* (Not named)

N

0   50 km

0   25 miles

KEY:

Main population blocs described in text

Other population blocs

Major relocations of Helena Valero

*Shamatari (includes Koroshiwe-teri and Karawe-teri)

Map 4 ▪ Main movements of western Yanomamo population blocs. The years covered and sources for each group are as follows: Shamatari (including Kohoroshiwe-teri and Karawe-teri), Namowei, and the unnamed group, 1880–1966 (Chagnon 1966:148, 1977:43; Valero 1984: map 1); Iyewei and Padamo, 1920–1976 (Hames 1983:12); Warakuawa (or Poreta), Shitari, Heronapui, and Uhepeki, years unspecified (Lizot 1988:522); Valero's travels (Valero 1984: map 2).

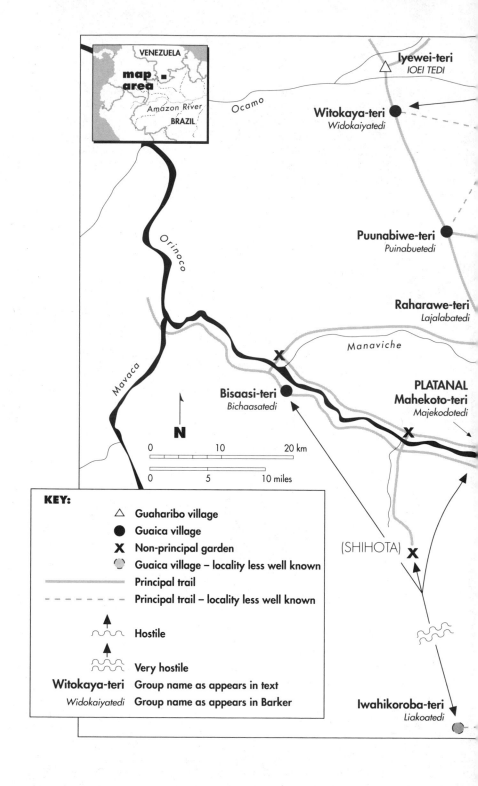

VENEZUELA

map
area

Amazon River

BRAZIL

Ocamo

Iyewei-teri
IOEI TEDI

Witokaya-teri
Widokaiyatedi

Orinoco

Puunabiwe-teri
Puinabuetedi

Raharawe-teri
Lajalabatedi

Manaviche

Bisaasi-teri
Bichaasatedi

PLATANAL
Mahekoto-teri
Majekodotedi

Mavaca

N

0   10   20 km

0   5   10 miles

(SHIHOTA) X

Iwahikoroba-teri
Liakoatedi

KEY:

△ Guaharibo village

● Guaica village

X Non-principal garden

◍ Guaica village – locality less well known

——— Principal trail

– – – Principal trail – locality less well known

〜〜 Hostile

〜〜 Very hostile

Witokaya-teri Group name as appears in text

Widokaiyatedi Group name as appears in Barker

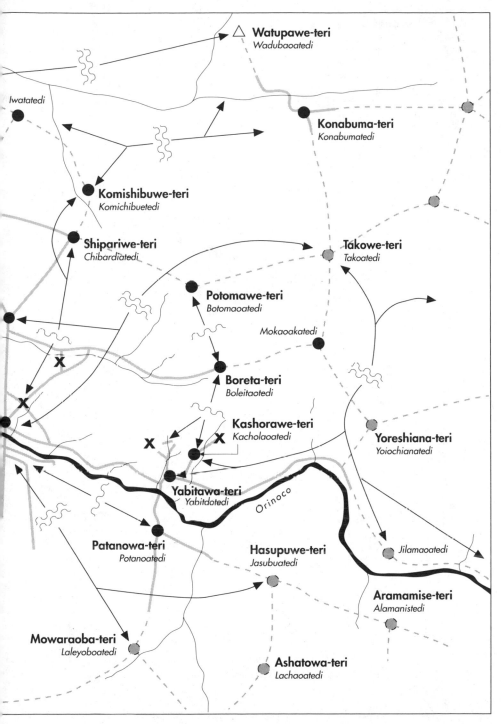

Map 5 ▪ Missionary James Barker's 1953 political map (redrawn from Barker 1953: following p. 436, original drawn by H. Dupouy).

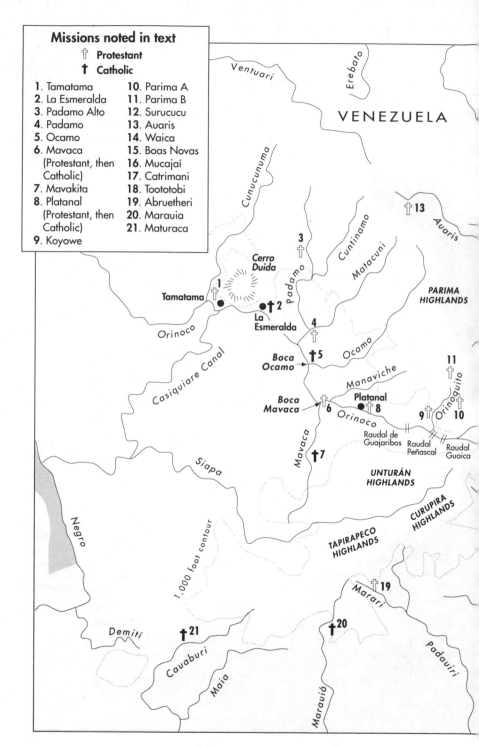

Map 6 ▪ Locations of religious missions in the central Yanomami area.

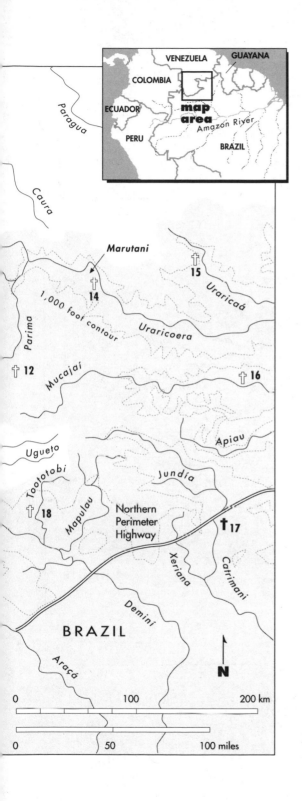

Map 7 ▪ Principal villages of the Orinoco-Mavaco area in the late 1960s (based on Chagnon 1977:43; Cocco 1972:24).

2

The Problem of Western Goods

This chapter presents the first half of the explanatory model—the half that deals with the significance of steel tools and other Western manufactures and the problems involved in securing access to them. It discusses more closely, and using Yanomami case material, many of the points raised in the previous chapter.

The Infrastructural Impact of Western Contact

Western manufactures are not introduced in a vacuum. They are a manifestation of contact usually accompanied by other effects, which combine to produce major societal disruption. The degree of the disruption strongly conditions people's readiness to use violence in both individual and group confrontations. This overall impact of contact is the subject of my article on the Orinoco-Mavaca Yanomami (Ferguson 1992a), but some sort of connection between general contact-related disruption and violence has been suspected for many years (Albert 1990b:558–59; Bennett Ross 1971:16–20; Colchester n.d.; Davis and Mathews 1976; Smole 1976:31). Before going into the details of introduced Western manufactures, I will outline the other major infrastructural changes commonly brought on by increasing Western contact, and their effects.

First and foremost are the introduced epidemic diseases, which take a tremendous toll in Yanomami communities connected to the outside world (Albert 1990; CCYP 1989a; Chagnon and Melancon 1983; Colchester 1985b; Comité 1983; Early and Peters 1990; Ramos and Taylor

1979). Detailed information from the Orinoco-Mavaca area (Ferguson 1992a:203–204) indicates that even in this violent region, deaths caused by disease run three or four times higher than those attributed to war (Chagnon 1966:62; Eguillor García 1984:52–53). Deaths in war themselves vary dramatically among Yanomami communities (a fact I attribute to varying contact circumstances), ranging from 12 percent to 40 percent of the deaths of adult males in recently studied communities (Albert 1989:637; Chagnon 1983:79; Cocco 1972:393; Early and Peters 1990:72; Hames 1983:420; Lizot 1989:30). All this dying disrupts family organization and marriage ties, shocking a social order based upon bonds of kinship.

Despite the mortal hazards associated with the proximity of Westerners, the lure of their trade goods and other advantages draw many Yanomami toward the intruders—and once established alongside a mission or other post, they become relatively fixed in place. This increased fixity has two major implications for levels of violence. First, it works against what is probably the major alternative to war in recently observed Amazonian societies: movement, or the quick relocation away from potential threats (Ferguson 1989b:195–96). (We will see, however, that movement remains the way in which many wars finally end.)

Second, being anchored to a Western outpost or settlement leads to game depletion. Recently studied Yanomami who do not live close to a Westerner spend a great part of the year—20 percent to 40 percent or even more—on trek in the forest (Barandiaran 1967:39–40; Fuentes 1980:31–33; Good 1989:90). At least some missionaries have actively discouraged forest trekking (Jank 1977:85–86, 177; Lizot 1976: 12; Vareschi 1959:169), and strategic considerations also argue against leaving a source of steel (that is, the Western settlement) unguarded. As a result, time spent on trek by outpost villagers is reduced or even eliminated (Colchester 1984:299; Eguillor García 1984:219), and game animals in the vicinity of Yanomami settlements tied to Westerners are depleted (Chagnon 1977:148; Colchester and Semba 1985:17; Comité 1983:27; Lizot 1976:205; Saffirio and Hames 1983:37–38; Saffirio and Scaglion 1982; Salazar 1967:92; Smole 1976:163–67, 175–76).[1]

There are some major factors that complicate the issue of game depletion and its impact, especially an increased reliance on river resources (Cocco 1972:174, 378; Colchester 1984:299; Good 1989:64; Lizot 1977:509, 1988:504) and on food provided by the resident Westerners (Cocco 1972:176; Colchester 1981a:56–57; Comité 1983:54;

Salazar 1967:222). Nevertheless, one social consequence of game depletion is a reduction in the reciprocal sharing of meat in villages anchored to a Western outpost (Cocco 1972:365; Saffirio and Hames 1983:39–41; Seitz 1963:141). (In some cases, missionaries actually discourage sharing in order to promote individual autonomy [Montgomery 1970:157].) Following Good (1989:131–40) and others, I argue that reduction of game availability and meat sharing serves to loosen Yanomami ties of solidarity (Ferguson 1992a:206) and, in combination with the impact of disease and other deaths, to increase a tendency toward atomization and anomie that is conducive to greater reliance on violence in interpersonal relationships.

The expression and impact of disease and war mortality, settlement anchoring, and game depletion are highly variable. In their more concentrated forms, and in concert with contact-related changes in social organization, they can contribute heavily to the development of an aggressive, "warlike" disposition (Ferguson 1992a:208–25) and markedly lower the threshold for violence. That is what occurred in the Orinoco-Mavaca area and apparently in other locales that are less well described (see parts II and III). But although these factors are important for understanding Yanomami warfare, they are secondary to the antagonisms generated by Western manufactured goods. It is these antagonisms, I hope to show, that explain most of the variation in the intensity and direction of Yanomami fighting.

Western Manufactures

The Yanomami have long depended on iron and steel tools. All ethnographically described Yanomami had begun using metal tools long before any anthropologist arrived. Except for one deliberate experiment conducted by an anthropologist (Carneiro 1979a, 1979b), I have found no outsider's account from any period reportedly witnessing Yanomami using stone axes, although some Yanomami interviewed in the 1960s recall a time when they used stone axes found in ancient gardens. More striking, perhaps, I have never found any report of a Yanomami who knew how to make stone axes or who said that an ancestor had made them. The Yanomami ax usually found at "first contact" is the *haowe,* made not of stone but from a broken piece of machete hafted on wood (Albert 1988:95; Chagnon 1977:34; Cocco 1972:181; Lizot 1976:7; Smole 1976:112).

Experiments conducted by anthropologists in different parts of the world indicate that steel cutting tools are three to ten times more efficient than tools of stone. Carneiro's experiment among the Yanomami (1979a, 1979b) shows that efficiency is directly affected by the diameter and hardness of trees. In the Orinoco-Mavaca area, he calculated that a steel ax was seven to ten times more efficient than a stone ax for clearing gardens. Although this huge difference was probably diminished by greater skill with stone axes in the past and alternative clearing techniques—more burning, pulling with lianas, having one falling tree take down others—the advantage is still enormous.[2] (Another observer reported that using steel cut by half the time needed to make arrows [Montgomery 1970:156].) As indicators of the importance of steel, one informant recalled a time when the people of an entire village took turns using their one metal edge (Chagnon 1977:34), and another remembered a village growing larger because people wanted access to one common piece of steel (Fuentes in Colchester 1984:296). When steel is especially scarce, one machete or an ax can be a treasure.[3]

Yanomami villages show a great ability to absorb steel when it is available. Peters (1973:115) reports a minimum standard of at least one ax, machete, and knife per family. Chagnon (1977:82) and Smole (1976:193) both indicate that one ax is needed per adult, since women use axes in wood gathering. Villages with good access to sources of Western tools have even higher per capita levels of cutting tools and other items (Lizot 1971:45; Saffirio and Hames 1983:20). As Western goods become more available, Yanomami become more discriminating about their quality (Smole, personal communication). They may also discover new uses for steel, as did those who began tipping their arrows with pieces of machetes (Fuentes 1980:46).

Some idea of the total demand comes from the Orinoco-Mavaca area, where, at the unusually bountiful Salesian mission of Santa María de los Guaicas, there were distributed between 1957 and 1978 more than ten thousand machetes, more than two thousand axes, close to a million fishhooks, and comparable quantities of many other items that were regularly traded far into the interior (Chagnon 1972a:66; Cocco 1972:378; Peña Vargas 1981:37; Smole 1976:238). Other Western manufactures commonly provided to the Yanomami in recent years include shotguns, ammunition, medicines, beads, clothes, fabric, pots, matches, fishing line, lamps, batteries (Albert 1988; Colchester 1985a: 10–11; Peña Vargas 1981:40; Peters 1973:115–17; Saffirio and Hames 1983:14–16, 19, 43), dugout canoes manufactured by other Indians

(Chagnon 1977:9), and even outboard motors (Peña Vargas 1981:40).

How do Western manufactures enter the circuits of Yanomami use and exchange? Little information is available for earlier times, even for the rubber boom of the late nineteenth and early twentieth centuries. What exists is cited in the historical chapters later in this book, but it is not enough to form a clear picture. About all that can be said is that both peaceful trade and pillage were involved, and that obtaining steel generally involved more direct physical danger and labor effort than it does at present.

In recent and contemporary times, most Western manufactures enter Yanomami networks as gifts or payments from missionaries, scientists, government agents, or other Westerners.[4] A large gift—on the order of 25 machetes along with other items—can accompany initial direct contact with a village (Chagnon 1974:29–31; Seitz 1963:190), although prestations are often much smaller. As contact becomes more routine, regular payments develop. Some eastern Yanomami have hunted for animal pelts to trade for Western items, and some have traveled downstream to work as farmhands (Peters 1973:113–14). Several groups produce manioc flour for trade (Ramos 1972:32; Saffirio and Hames 1983:17; Smole 1976:103), and others, bananas (Chagnon 1977:144).

The most common way of obtaining Western goods, however, is through direct service to Westerners residing in Yanomami territory. Resident Westerners pay Yanomami for goods such as game, crops, and firewood, and for their service as laborers, informants, translators, guides, and servants.[5] Except for supplying passing travelers, most work for the outsiders requires being close to them, and the Yanomami regularly reported to do such work generally live or are allowed to reside temporarily in villages near the Western residence (Albert 1988: 102–103; Chagnon 1972a:66, 1977:7–12, 1983:17, 32; Cocco 1972: 377; Good 1991:27–28, 89; Jank 1977:59–63; Peters 1973:51, 113– 15, 167–68; Ramos 1972:10, 27; Salazar 1967:76; Shapiro 1972:29, 42; Smole 1976:192; Soares Diniz 1969:4). This simple fact has great implications for this study.

I must emphasize that not all Yanomami wish to live near Westerners. Along with the major advantages to be described, proximity to Westerners also has enormous drawbacks. In earlier times, there was the very real danger of being captured or killed by raiders or press gangs. Often the danger was such that Yanomami tried to avoid any contact with Westerners and withdrew into more inaccessible areas, although even in times of active raiding by Westerners, some Yanomami dared to approach them to obtain steel. In recent decades, the prime hazard of proximity has been greater exposure to diseases—a hazard partly mitigated by Western medicine. Along with that danger, I argue, often goes increased warfare, ecological stress, and other decidedly negative circumstances.

The combination of risks and benefits associated with proximity to Westerners results in a marked ambivalence on the part of the Yanomami. According to Saffirio and Hames (1983:5), "all Yanomama recognize disease as the worst dimension of contact with whites, yet some actively seek contact and the mortal risk associated with it, while others actively avoid contact believing the material benefits (e.g., steel tools) are not worth the potentially deadly results." In the past, I will argue, the overwhelmingly negative aspects of direct contact drove the Yanomami deep into the mountains and made them wary of early efforts to coax them out. The continuing hazards of direct contact may explain why many have chosen to remain "isolated."

The last century, however, has seen a consistent pattern of long-distance movements out of the highlands or in the direction of Westerners or both—movements ethnographers have recognized as efforts to improve access to Western manufactures (Albert 1988:98; Colchester 1985a:10–11; Peters 1973:62–63; Saffirio 1985:24, 91–93; Shapiro 1972:25–29; Smole 1976:51–52; and see parts II and III). In the Orinoco-Mavaca area, this pattern has led, since the mid-1940s, to repeated village relocations from the highlands to the lowland rivers —areas otherwise avoided by Yanomami because of heat and insects —in order to gain direct, sustained contact with Westerners (Chagnon 1966:35; Cocco 1972:18, 32, 114; Hames 1983:405–14; Smole 1976: 47–48). As Chagnon put it (1977:161): "The Yanomamo traditionally avoid larger rivers and have only moved to them in the very recent past because of the allure of exotic trade goods, such as steel tools, fish-hooks, fish line, matches, aluminum cooking pots, and other desirable items. No Yanomamo would tolerate the discomfort of living near the bug-infested rivers unless there were powerful incentives, such as trade goods, to attract them there."

Movement, Trade, and Marriage

Moving long distances to draw nearer to sources of Western goods raises logistical problems for Yanomami. Long-distance relocation of settlements is a much more difficult undertaking than are the short village movements associated with subsistence demands. The key problem is that of establishing a new garden.

Even with steel tools, clearing forest and preparing a new garden is the most arduous vital task required of Yanomami men. Plantains, the staple food of most Yanomami, grow from cuttings, and since larger cuttings bear fruit faster, it is desirable to start new gardens with cuttings weighing up to 10 pounds. Moreover, one garden isn't enough. A new garden begins producing within a year, but its yield is irregular at first. As it matures and provides a more regular supply of a wide variety of crops, it is often extended in area. Within a few years, transitional regrowth and declining soil fertility set in, and the old garden fades to become only an occasional source of crops. At the same time, game and firewood become harder to find in the immediate environs of the settlement, and insect infestations increase. For these reasons, Yanomami frequently have three or four gardens in various stages of preparation or use, usually within a half-day's walk of each other (Biocca 1971; Chagnon 1977:34–35; Good 1989:43–61; Harris 1971:478–82; Lizot 1988:506–509; Smole 1976:105–106).

The burden of transporting cuttings and the need to rely on food from older gardens while new ones mature together mean that the costs of establishing a new garden increase dramatically with distance. It is very difficult to start one beyond reasonable walking distance from some "donor" garden. Moves over longer distances from old sites are accomplished by relying on a nearby ally to provide cuttings, food, and often labor (Biocca 1971:209–10; Chagnon 1977:35), or by establishing an intermediate garden as a staging area for a move to a more desired location (Chagnon 1977:78). These constraints on long-distance village movement are important for understanding war.

Relocation of villages is not the only means of drawing nearer to sources of Western manufactures. Another way is for an individual, family, or small group to move into another village that already enjoys better access. Among the Yanomami—as among many Amazonian peoples (Ferguson 1988b:139)—the flexibility of kinship and residence rules allows wide latitude for relocation. Many ethnographic descriptions of village life mention temporary or long-term residents who came from elsewhere, a pattern that is particularly pronounced in villages near to Westerners (Early and Peters 1990:66; Eguillor García 1984:54–56; Good 1991:206; Ramos 1972:41).

Moving into another village, getting a domestic space in the collective house (*shabono*), being supported while establishing one's own garden, and being included in redistributions of game obviously require acceptance by established residents. This acceptance is gained through the idiom of kinship. According to Chagnon (1977:87), "New individuals are incorporated into the community by an extension of kinship ties. Unless one is incorporated into the village in this fashion, there is no basis for social behavior vis-à-vis others" (see also Chagnon 1966:102; Good 1991:79–80; Lizot 1988:558). Chagnon goes on to observe that the primary means of establishing kin ties is through marriage (although neighboring Yanomami also typically have other ties of affinity or descent that they may activate opportunistically). We will see shortly that intervillage marriage is a highly political affair.

A third way to get access to Western manufactures, and the one that is most significant for the rest of this chapter, is through trade. Understanding the patterns and social implications of trade requires first understanding the practicalities of travel.

Until recently, most Yanomami have been "foot Indians," without experience in making or managing canoes. Yanomami men cover trails at a rapid pace (Good 1991:87, 92); one estimate put walking speed at a quick 8 kilometers per hour (Anduze 1960:82). Smole (1976:84) estimated that men alone could travel 15 miles or more in a day, but only a fraction of that if accompanied by their families (see also Good 1991:62). In the lower-lying areas of Yanomami territory, foot travel is seasonal because heavy rains expand the swamps, making passage difficult or impossible. In the Orinoco-Mavaca area, the season for overland travel is September through April; February is the peak time for movement (Chagnon 1967:117, 1977:20). In the Parima highlands, flooding is not such a problem, and traveling lacks this pronounced seasonality (Smole 1976:81–82).

Travel follows established trails, a subject that is very poorly described. Trails connect neighboring villages and link villages to gardens. They are quite straight (Good 1991:92; Smole 1976:79). The Yanomami "take the most direct route to their destination, regardless of the terrain" (Chagnon 1977:19). Because of the village-to-village orientation of trails, travel to distant points often involves passing through or close to other villages, and that can be hazardous. Yanomami certainly recognize the danger of using trails that pass near hostile intermediary villages (e.g., Biocca 1971:266–67; Lizot 1985:81). During violent times in the Orinoco-Mavaca area, men rarely went beyond the villages of their immediate neighbors (Barker 1953:469), while in the more peaceful highlands men traveled widely (Smole 1976:82–84). Two narratives of life among the Yanomami (Biocca 1971; Valero 1984) show again and again that during both war and peace, although travel through unmarked forest is possible, the layout of trails does very strongly determine possibilities of quotidian travel.[6]

Trade in Western manufactures is structured by these constraints on travel. Items obtained directly from Westerners are passed along from village to village (Albert 1988:95; Barker 1953:469; Chagnon 1974:11; Cocco 1972:378; Smole 1976:102). Villages separated from Western sources by a few other villages acting as middlemen may receive few, poor-quality tools (Barandiaran and Walalam 1983:191; Chagnon 1974:35, 1977:34, 1983:39; Lizot 1976:7).

One of the most informative discussions of trade comes from an unpublished manuscript by Kenneth Good (1984:6–7). Since it reveals many key aspects of trade at once, I quote it at length.

> Despite the fact that little visiting is done to distant subsistence territories, large blocks of Yanomami settlements are integrated by an extensive nexus of intervillage trading. Presently, the most common articles of exchange are Western goods by communities residing near the Orinoco River and other points of foreign settlement and hunting dogs by the communities living in more remote areas. . . . Thus, Western goods arrive to communities well beyond the limits of visitation by the original owners. Many villages I visited had previously never been contacted by a non-Yanomami, but all possessed axes, machetes, aluminum pots and clothing, granted in a very worn state and few in number.
>
> The principal basis for intervillage interaction and maintenance of friendly terms with neighboring communities is the exchange of goods. Visits to another village occur almost exclusively for purposes of trade. If a Yanomami consistently refuses to give upon request it is understood that this person does not wish to maintain friendly relations with the requester. . . .
>
> A machete acquired for a dog is used for a while and then traded to another village for another dog. That village will in turn use the machete for an additional period of time and re-trade it to a more distant village and replace the dog it had given. Likewise, the communities living nearer to the source of manufactured goods will trade the dog it acquired to communities living at the source of goods and replace the items it gave up. They usually acquire newer items and again use them until they

are worn and trade them off. They frequently acquire a pup for a single machete, raise it until full grown and then trade it north for a machete, large pot and an ax. So goods are only temporarily possessed and the flow is constant.

While trading is most often done for the purpose of filling a momentary shortage, an important result of intervillage exchange is the development and maintenance of friendly relationships. The importance of this exchange is even greater than consanguineal relationships, for without trade even kin ties deteriorate. The village-to-village patterning of trade that Good describes is illustrated in the accompanying sketch-map redrawn from one in his paper (map 2).

Good points out the extremely important connection between trade and alliance. Village-to-village trade imparts a strong spatial element to political ties, which are also conditioned by historical connections and the current ties of kinship between settlements. Proximity along established trails intensifies political relations, at least in the politically charged Orinoco-Mavaca area, about which Chagnon (1977:118) writes: "No two villages that are within comfortable walking distance from each other can maintain such a relationship [neutrality] indefinitely: They must become allies, or hostility is likely to develop between them" (see also Chagnon and Hames 1980:35). Thus it seems reasonable to speak of Yanomami "geopolitics."

Monopolists, Middlemen, and Exchange

When Western manufactures are scarce and available locally through only one or a very few sources, Yanomami make a great effort to monopolize any visiting Westerners and to prevent them from going on to another village (Albert 1988:102–103; Chagnon 1974:7–15, 163–71, 1977:79, 152–53, 1983:18; Peña Vargas 1981:30; Shapiro 1972:33, 43). In some of the most common reports from contact situations, Yanomami or other Indians tell the Westerners that if they travel to more isolated villages, the "savages" there will kill them (e.g., Gheerbrant 1954: 139–46; Good 1991:89; Steinvorth de Goetz 1969:113; Vinci 1959: 53, 110).[7]

The advantages of monopolistic access to a Westerner are two. First, the monopolizers can obtain Western manufactures for their own use because Westerners hand out goods to people around them. If a Westerner moves away, a village loses the source of highly desired items. Second, a monopoly over a source of Western manufactures gives a village an advantage in trading with other, uncontacted villages.

Yanomami who have secure access to Western providers do not normally hoard goods, which would be to waste the goodwill created by generosity and, in some situations, virtually to invite an attack. Hoarding would be self-destructive (see Ferguson 1983). Instead, they actualize the goods' exchange value by trading them to more remote peoples (Smole 1976:193). For example, in 1965 Chagnon (1972a:66) observed that although the mission at Santa María de los Guaicas had dispensed some three thousand machetes in the previous eight years, only about thirty remained in Iyewei-teri, the Yanomami village alongside the mission. Father Cocco, the missionary, once asked a Yanomami why his group gave away all the trade goods it received from him. The reply: "They [interior peoples] do not have them. I am not avaricious. I live close to you. You can get more" (Peña Vargas 1981:64).

Controlling access to a Western provider thus brings major benefits for those who act as trade middlemen.[8] Where Western outposts are established in conjunction with a Yanomami settlement, a new division of labor develops. Outpost villages supply steel tools and other items to villages that lack direct contact with Westerners. In exchange, the middlemen receive a broad range of valuable indigenous manufactures, including bows, quivers, curare arrow points, fish poison, hallucinogenic plants and the grinding stones and blow canes needed for their use, dogs, spun cotton, hammocks, manioc strainers, and even commoditized foodstuffs such as manioc cakes, tapioca, and plantains (Cocco 1972:205, 376–78; Colchester 1984:298; Eguillor García 1984:126; Peters 1973:167–68; and see Ferguson 1993:210–11). But the advantages are not limited to material goods.

Among Yanomami, trade usually involves a delayed reciprocity: one man gives to another on the promise of later compensation. Trade follows conduits of kinship, especially marriage ties (Chagnon 1966:95; Peters 1973:118; Smole 1976:101). A village whose members want to establish or deepen a trading relationship seeks to create marriages with its trading partners. Because of the well-known scarcity of women among the Yanomami, the way to do this is by ceding wives.[9] Wife-receivers incur serious and continuing obligations of support to the wife's family in another village. These obligations are most evident in the relationship of a man to his father-in-law, which is one of authority, and to his brother-in-law, which is one of solidarity—if a solidarity often strained by circumstances. The brother-in-law relationship generally is the most important one serving as a trade conduit (Lizot 1988:539; Peters 1973:71, 118; Shapiro 1972:87–89, 94–97).[10] Saffirio (1985:32) calls women "the most valuable trade-good," for in addition to their value in themselves, they are the capstone of a more secure and generous trading relationship.

As a result of such strategic marriages, there develops a "flow" of brides towards outpost villages from surrounding groups (Albert 1988: 102–103; Chagnon 1966:57–58, 1977:80; Cocco 1972:210–13; Peters 1973:127–29, 132; Shapiro 1972:210–13; Smole 1976:72; and see Ferguson 1993:215). In the three decades after the arrival of "their" mission, thirteen new wives came to live with the Mucajaí Yanomami (one "stolen"), and no Mucajaí women left to marry others (Early and Peters 1990:67–68). At Boca Mavaca, in the six or seven years after settling near Western posts, the Bisaasi-teri acquired "two dozen or so women" from interior trade partners, "while having given or promised only a half-dozen in return" (Chagnon 1977:80). At the founding of the mission of Santa María de los Guaica, the headman of the local Iyewei-teri had but one wife. The next year he acquired a second, making an initial bride payment of one hatchet, one pot, and one machete. He obtained a third wife later, in exchange for allowing her father to move to Iyewei-teri (Cocco 1972:212–13).

At the same time, villages with access to Western manufactures manage to reduce or eliminate the bride service required when one of their men marries a woman from outside, and to force lengthy and onerous bride service when an outside man marries in (Cocco 1972:211; Chagnon 1977:79; Early and Peters 1990:67; Peters 1973:122–29; and see Ferguson 1993:213–15). This is a very serious consideration for Yanomami men, who find years of bride service in another village, surrounded by the bride's kin, an often painful obligation (Chagnon 1974: 13–14; Lizot 1988:538–40; Ramos 1972:152–53). At the Mucajaí mission, all the men who married the thirteen women mentioned earlier were able to do so with short periods of bride service because their in-laws were happy to accept Western manufactures instead (Early and Peters 1990:67). At Boca Mavaca, men who obtained wives from interior villages "cut short" their bride service, but men who married into the mission village were "pressed into very lengthy bride service" (Chagnon 1977:79).

In their exchanges with more remote villages, then, Yanomami who monopolize a source of Western goods gain in the acquisition of indigenous manufactured products, of marriage partners, and of the labor and other support associated with bride service. This flow of persons and realized work effort is potentially measurable; it is what I refer to in chapter 1 as "exploitation." As with exploitation anywhere, terms can be easy or difficult. A rich and beneficent middleman may be extolled for his generosity, even if he is still getting the most out of the deal. But a poor or stingy middleman may provoke, at best, a pronounced ambivalence from his trade partners, and at worst, a hostility that can spill over into war. The tenor of a trading relationship is not confined to its transactions alone, but pervades social interactions as well.

From Exchange to Alliance

The transformation of intervillage exchange implies transformation of political alignments. As Lizot (1976:8–9) puts it: "Thus there grew up two types of community—those holding manufactured goods acquired directly at source, and those (isolated ones) which were deprived of them. The entire map of economic and matrimonial circuits, along with political alliances, was transformed and flagrant imbalances appeared." Trade, intermarriage, and political support are not separate. They are woven together, embedded in a single relationship. Exchanges of goods and people follow established ties of kinship, simultaneously modifying or transforming those ties as a basis for future exchange, and all the while shaping politically actable interests and reacting to political events (Chagnon 1966:94–97, 1977:69–70; Shapiro 1972:114–15, 175; Smole 1976:94–96, 101–102; Ramos 1972:152–59).

But within this complex whole of trade, intermarriage, and political alliance, we can still identify trade as the primary condition, the necessary prerequisite for more developed alliances. "Trade reduces the possibility that one group will attack the other without serious, overt provocation. In effect, it reduces the chance that one group will attribute otherwise unaccountable deaths to the harmful magic of a trading partner. . . . Trade is . . . the first step in a possibly more intimate social relationship: intervillage feasting. . . . When reciprocal feasting eventually results from a long period of trading relations, trade still functions to keep the two groups bound to each other and provides, in many cases, the stimulus to feast" (Chagnon 1967:122).

(The intervillage feast is the Yanomami's main political forum. Making preparations and arranging for the participation of other villages is one of the primary responsibilities of leadership. Most trading is done at feasts, and men negotiate pledges of wives and political support.)

Good (1991:97) shows the fundamental character of trade from another angle: "Among the Yanomami, I knew, a visit is never just a visit. . . . Regardless of whether the formal reason is a funeral or a feast or just a stopover on a longer trip, trade is always involved. You don't just go to visit, and you never come away without trade items of one sort or another, which will be reciprocated later." To put it most succinctly: "There is no alliance without trade" (Lizot 1985:184).

To sum up, four points stand out as relevant for later discussions. First, an alliance is a total social fact (see Mauss 1967). All its different aspects fit together to make up one relationship of many dimensions. Second, the fundamental basis of this total relationship is trade. Other social ties rise upon a foundation of exchange of tangible items. Third, in contact situations, trade is determined—motivationally driven and spatially structured—primarily by the availability and distribution of Western manufactures. Fourth, Yanomami who monopolize sources of Western manufactures are able to use their position as middlemen to obtain local products, women, and labor from more isolated villages.

The Political Character of Alliance

The chapters that follow will show that alliances are sometimes amicable, sometimes more or less neutral, and sometimes strained to the point of breaking into war. What determines the political character of an alliance? Certainly, the whole history of relations between the villages is involved, especially existing kinship ties. But the character of alliances can change radically and fast. In parts II and III, I find the primary determinants of such change to be the prevailing conditions in two areas: the distribution of Western goods, and the ability to apply physical force.

In the early phases of contact with Westerners, the primary benefit of access to sources may be the actual possession of steel tools for a village's own use rather than the ability to exchange them in trade. Even when trade is active, the flow of trade goods two or three villages out from the source may be reduced to mere seepage. Thus there is a tendency towards development of a steep gradient in possessions—for the creation of rich and poor. This new inequality can inspire resentment and tension and, potentially, efforts at extortion or expropriation. Simultaneously, the same inequality creates a countervailing basis for dependency and support. We may safely imagine that the first machete given freely to kinsmen in a neighboring village creates a great sense of obligation to the giver.

As the supply of Western goods at the source increases, middlemen will be able to be more beneficent, trading more and offering easier terms, and perhaps even allowing others direct access to their resident Westerner. They can be rich *and* generous, still extracting women, labor, and local products from their neighbors, but on good terms. The ease with which middlemen trade away Western manufactures is a major factor in determining whether dependent villages are actively supportive or truculent allies. When a trade and alliance relationship is characterized by great disparity in possessions between nearby villages, and when the few and poor-quality Western items provided by middlemen come at great cost, there is the potential for a violent rupture of existing ties.

Whether that violent rupture happens depends on people's abilities to apply force, which itself depends on four interrelated factors—two of them directly linked to the Western presence. First is the political and military support provided by Westerners. It is widely recognized that Westerners in a contact situation often back their favorite "chief" (Ferguson and Whitehead 1992a:13). Resident Westerners make a village more secure from attack: they possess guns, and they are, after all, the geese laying the golden eggs. They also facilitate an effective offense, since with the Westerner "minding the store," a greater proportion of a village's men can leave on a raid without worrying about vulnerability at home (Albert 1988:102; Chagnon 1972a:65–66, 1977:104; Jank 1977:80; Peña Vargas 1981:38–39; Shapiro 1972:33). The medicine and medical care resident Westerners provide means that wounded raiders are more likely to recover (Barker 1959:155, 160–63; Chagnon 1977:122, 133). In the case of established Western posts, the Yanomami generally understand that the resident outsiders themselves are superordinate persons backed by the wealth and power of the outside world (Ramos 1979a:16).

A second and closely related factor in the ability to apply force is the Yanomami's possession of shotguns. The highest concentration of shotguns is usually found around the Western outposts, but they can also spread through trade, as in recent years Brazilian shotguns have been passed to Venezuelan Yanomami villages (Chagnon 1977:149; Good 1984). Shotguns are more likely to kill than are native weapons, and their use in an engagement is often a decisive advantage (see Chagnon 1977:122; Lizot 1985:155). When one side has shotguns, it lowers their expectable costs of war, just as it raises the risk for their opponents. Or as a Yanomami put it (in typically personalistic terms): "When you give a fierce man a shotgun, he becomes ever fiercer and wants to kill without cause" (Chagnon 1977:149). Middlemen with an advantage in guns can get away with more than those who have only native weapons.

A third factor affecting potential force, and thus the political character of an alliance, is the number of active supporters on each side. In all forms of confrontation and violence, the number of men who can be mustered is a major determinant of a group's ability to engage in the conflict and win (Barker 1953:475; Chagnon 1973:134–35, 1977:105, 113–15). Outpost villages may enjoy one form of advantage here: their control over Western manufactures enables them to attract young wife-seekers to settle with them. That other villages are dependent on them for Western goods also gives outpost villages leverage in asking allies for their military support, although acquiescence to such a request is far from assured (e.g., Chagnon 1977:128).

On the other hand, ecological limitations place a ceiling on how many people can live together for long, and this ceiling may be low around long-inhabited outpost villages. (Two of the largest reported Yanomami groups, Patanowa-teri and Mishimishimabowei-teri, are located in the interior, far from the missions.) More isolated villages that share a common interest in breaking the monopoly of current trade controllers may actually have a more secure basis for military cooperation than does a monopolist who calls upon reluctant allies. So although control of Western manufactures may bring numerical support, it is also possible that trade controllers will be outnumbered by actual or potential enemies and thus find themselves in a weak position to dictate the terms of the relationship.

The fourth factor in the ability to apply force is "fierceness." Chagnon (1967:124–26) discusses the Yanomami concept of *waiteri*, which he translates as "ferocity." Others have challenged his interpretation of this concept (Albert 1989:639; Lizot 1989:32–33; Ramos 1987: 286; and see Chagnon 1990a:53). Without entering into this debate over Yanomami semantics, I will define fierceness, without reference to any emic concept, as manifest willingness to enter into confrontations in which one may sustain injury and as the demonstrated ability to inflict violence on others. We may distinguish "normal" from "exceptional" fierceness. The former applies to regular participation in collective violence—that is, simply not being a "coward." But there are also unusually fierce men who are quick to anger and ready to strike. Even one such man can tip the scales in a confrontation.[11] This kind of fierceness may be inversely related to a resident Western presence because exceptionally violent and aggressive men may be found intolerable by Westerners, as Chagnon (1974:195) describes for his experience among the Shamatari Yanomami.

With all these elements going into an alliance—the lure and costs of Western manufactures and the four components of military strength—it is understandable that alliances are very complicated affairs and subject to tremendous variation. Some are stable and pacific, when an abundance of incoming Western manufactures makes for generosity in trade and when the support of resident Westerners and loyal allies, along with a supply of shotguns, ensures local military hegemony. With a strong and expanding Western presence, this penumbra of control can extend outwards through middleman villages along the trade network.

On the other hand, a highly unstable situation exists when a village that possesses many axes and machetes finds itself without Western protection or shotguns, and perhaps is also making stiff exchange demands on more isolated groups that outmatch it in numbers or fierceness. The instability would be aggravated if it arose as part of a retraction of the Western presence, as the flow of Western goods dried up and the backing of Westerners declined. With this turn of affairs, alliances may end or even turn to war.[12]

In this chapter, we have gone from the need for steel and the practicalities of gardens and travel to a structured geopolitical field and multidimensional alliances. We have seen the potential for exploitation in these alliances and the complicated mix of economic and military factors that shape the political character of specific alliances. In chapter 3, we will see how these configurations give rise to actual violence.

3

The Use of Force

In this chapter I turn directly to the use of force as I continue developing the analytical model to be applied later. Even more than in chapter 2, the ethnography of the Orinoco-Mavaca area dominates this discussion as the source of illustrative citations, for the Orinoco-Mavaca is both the best described area and the one with the most observed warfare in recent times. Nevertheless, the model built upon these observations appears valid when tested against less richly described case material from other Yanomami regions.

Violence among Allies

One characteristic that distinguishes the Yanomami from other Native Americans around them is their pounding matches—institutionalized forms of dueling that include chest striking and club fights. These clashes frequently involve groups bound in an alliance, and the matches often occur during feasts. Sometimes headmen arrange them to clear the air of petty animosities in the interest of keeping their groups strong allies. In reports of duels from outside the Orinoco-Mavaca area, they are described as confrontations between a few individuals that remain at a level unlikely to cause serious injury. But in the Orinoco-Mavaca area, they commonly draw in large groups of men and often escalate to more serious forms of fighting (Barker 1953:447–48; Chagnon 1967:114, 132–35, 1977:113–17, 119; Eguillor García 1984:132–34; Migliazza 1972:409; Peters 1973:57, 69–70; Ramos 1972:79–80; Seitz 1963: 139; Smole 1976:235). Chagnon describes the escalatory sequence as a graded series of aggressive activities. . . . The most innocuous form of fighting is the chest-pounding duel. . . . If such a duel is escalated, it usually develops into a side-slapping contest. Occasionally, the combatants will sue for the use of machetes and axes, but this is rare. . . . In some areas the Yanomamo modify the chest-pounding duel in another way: The opponents hold rocks in their clenched fists and strike their adversaries on the chest with an even more stunning blow. . . . Club fights represent the next level of violence (Chagnon 1977:118–19).

The more serious forms of violence can result in deaths (Chagnon 1966: 62), and a death frequently—but not always (Biocca 1971:171–72; Eguillor García 1984:25)—marks a transition to war (Chagnon 1967: 134; Lizot 1989:28).[1]

According to Chagnon (1977:118), chest-pounding matches are "precipitated by such minor affronts as malicious gossip, accusations of cowardice, stinginess with food, or niggardliness in trading." Club fights, on the other hand, are said to result from arguments over women or food theft (Chagnon 1977:119). I could not find confirmation of this differentiation in other ethnographies, and it may be that Chagnon's distinction of precipitating events is overly neat. A serious club fight that he described in detail (Chagnon 1977:109–13) was not reported to have been preceded by any dispute over women; and although an accusation of food theft was made in that case, it was only one of several complaints. Probably a number of perceived offenses combine to give rise to most duels of any kind.

Given the multidimensional or "total" character of alliances described in chapter 2, we might expect many different expressions of conflict to exist within a political relationship. Many sorts of disputes can trigger open confrontation in an already tense situation because any aspect of an alliance can stand for or symbolize the whole, and it is the relationship as a whole that is the real issue. Misappropriations of food or women are serious, provocative acts—much more so than malicious gossip—and they mark the fact that a relationship has already passed from ill will to action. It is understandable that offenses like these would appear more prominent as triggers of the more intense pounding matches.

What is the relationship between dueling and trading? This is a crucial question for which there is little hard information. My hypothesis is that these violent group encounters are used to influence the direction, velocity, and terms of trade for Western manufactures within an alliance. The issue of terms of trade, although not addressed directly in the Yanomami literature, nevertheless must be a concern. Somehow parties must arrive at an understanding, a rough norm, of what constitutes a fair or balanced exchange under existing circumstances. How many curare-coated arrowheads, for example, are equal to a machete? How much spun cotton is worth a cooking pot? The Yanomami place great value on a reputation for generosity (Eguillor García 1984:214–16; Lizot 1991:69; Peña Vargas 1981:64). But what is to be considered generous, and what is stingy? How do standards change when the availability of some item changes? How do terms of trade interact with all the other aspects of the total social relationship that is an alliance?[2] And again, when is force used in this context?

No ethnographer, to my knowledge, has published detailed standards of exchange for Western versus local manufactures among the Yanomami, nor reported how standards change after a violent confrontation between allies. But several general observations from the highly disrupted Orinoco-Mavaca area indicate that there, at least, force does play an important role in setting terms of trade, and that the connection between force and trade has a powerful influence on the alliance relationship as a whole. According to Chagnon (1967:132):

> Chest-pounding duels . . . arise over accusations of cowardice or in response to excessive demands for trade goods, food, or women. The implications of the demands are that if they result in the desired articles and goods, the giver is thought to be lower in status as a political group than the receiver, i.e., one group has coerced the other.

And again from Chagnon (1974:164; emphasis in original):

> Giving does not by definition improve one's status. To give a machete to a man freely without his solicitation will add to the status of the giver. The giver will, all things being equal, be cherished as a generous man. But all things are never equal, and that is the whole point of the relationship between giving and status. To give the same machete to the same man when, for example, he *demands* it "or else" creates a situation latent with status implications that go far beyond the immediate, vis-à-vis relationship with that man.

Or, according to Lizot (1985:184): "In some communities, to declare, 'I will not give anything' or 'I will not give what you are asking' is to risk a clubbing." He goes on to note that the "Yanomami have a passion for barter and bargaining," they "strive for profit," and they push the confrontation in trade "to the brink of rupture" (and see Lizot 1988:554). (Lizot, it should be noted, discounts the utilitarian aspects of such exchange.)

Chagnon (1977:8–9) also notes this brinkmanship in discussing the demands made on him as a provider of Western manufactures.

> It was not as difficult to become calloused to the incessant begging as it was to ignore the sense of urgency, the impassioned tone of voice, or the intimidation and aggression with which the demands were made. . . . I soon learned that I had to become very much like the Yanomamo to be able to get along with them on their terms: sly, aggressive, and intimidating. Had I failed to adjust in this fashion I would have lost six month of supplies to them in a single day. . . . In short, I had to . . . learn how to imply subtly that certain potentially undesirable consequences might follow if they did such and such to me. They do this to each other in order to establish precisely the point at which they cannot goad an individual any further without precipitating retaliation. . . . It was sort of like a political game . . . in which each individual sooner or later had to display some sign that his bluffs and implied threats could be backed up.

Anecdotal support for a connection between force and trade is found in an incident that Chagnon describes in detail (1974:183–95). It was not an actual club fight but rather a chaotic mob confrontation between groups that had been close allies. Headmen stepped in to prevent blows in the supercharged atmosphere. At issue was the distribution of machetes. Chagnon had arrived with fewer trade goods than usual, and his announced plan to give them to men of one village was fiercely opposed by men of the other. Chagnon was threatened with death if he did not accede to the latter's demands.

There appears to be ample evidence, then, in ethnographic descriptions at least from the Orinoco-Mavaca area to support the point that force can be used to influence the terms and direction of trade in Western manufactures.[3]

It hardly needs to be argued that force may be similarly employed to extract wives from allies. Chagnon has consistently stressed the importance of physical coercion in obtaining wives (1966:6–10, 1977: 98, 1988:239, 1990a:52), and to my knowledge, no one has ever challenged the idea that force can play an important role in establishing marriages. It is simply a fact: Yanomami men do sometimes get violent over women, forcibly appropriating women in raids on enemies and in conflicts with allies.[4] How to interpret that fact is another matter. I see it as one expression of the total alliance relationship described in chapter 2 as being structured primarily around the distribution of Western manufactures. Like the exchange of material items themselves, the direction in which wives are ceded and the terms of marriage (bride payments) respond to a combination of the availability of Western manufactures and the ability to apply force.

Ethnographic evidence for the use of force in marriage arrangements again comes mostly (but not exclusively) from the Orinoco-Mavaca area. It is important to situate this violence in broad historical context (Ferguson 1992a; and see part III). Since the 1940s, deaths from disease and violence have shattered marriages and betrothal arrangements throughout the area. Despite a preference for village endogamy, the circumstances of war and trade have put a priority on alliance making, so more marriages have been contracted between villages—over 60 percent in Lizot's sample (1988:539). And while a man can find residence in his wife's village difficult or uncomfortable, an in-married woman may find the absence of supportive male kin positively life threatening, and some run away from the contracted marriage. In an atmosphere where men value belligerence and are ready to resort to violence, and where women are without question the most valuable manifestation of any alliance, it would be surprising if they were exempted from the general instrumental use of violence. For the same reason, we can understand how a group wishing to intimidate or provoke an ally might find no better way of doing so than by grabbing a woman (e.g., Chagnon 1977:125; and see chapter 13).

In this general context, recourse to force can be seen as an aspect of *law*. Violent self-help, a recognized underpinning of countless legal systems around the world, will expectably increase in importance with social disruption and normative strain. Close inspection of Yanomami ethnography indicates that most disputes over women are not simple seizures but are more complex conflicts that revolve around the issue of bride service or around other recognized rights associated with marriage.

Alliance marriages are often negotiated years before a girl is of marriageable age, but the groom will begin providing game, Western goods, and more to his in-laws from the moment of betrothal. If the woman's parents later change their minds and give her to another suitor or otherwise renege on the understanding, their action can lead to a club fight with the groom's family (Early and Peters 1990:39; Eguillor García 1984:83). On the other hand, a suitor may make off with a particular woman, sometimes with her collusion, thus depriving the woman's family of expected bride payments. This event too can provoke a violent confrontation between families, but if other bases of alliance remain viable, a post facto arrangement of compensation will be negotiated (Barker 1953:473–74; Peters 1973:127–28; Shapiro 1972:121–22). Violence can also occur when a negotiated marriage breaks down, when a severely abused woman runs away or is taken back by her brothers (Chagnon 1966:189, 1977:120–22; Cocco 1972:115), or when a husband fails to comply with his bride service agreement (Ramos 1972: 80–81; and see Alés 1984:98).

In all these cases, the outcome depends on the existing relationship between families and villages. Some are talked through without violence; others quickly progress to club fights or even more dangerous actions. One common outcome is a literal tug-of-war over a woman, with the two sides each pulling on her arms (Good 1991:101; Lizot 1988: 541; Smole 1976:76). Shapiro (1972:122) describes one of these and observes: "There seems to be a somewhat formalized aspect to such a contest and both sides may be aware of who is in the right. This does not mean, however, that no real force is used, since the point is to give both sides a chance to show their strength." In such actions, we see a fusion of "political" and "legal"—hardly unusual, as law is so commonly a function of political power.

Chapter 2 ended with a general discussion of the components of force that, along with the availability of Western goods, go into shaping the political character of an alliance. In this chapter, we have so far seen how force can be instrumentally applied within the context of such an alliance, specifically in relation to trade and marriage. When force and extortion predominate over wealth and generosity in setting the political tone, an alliance is in danger of tipping over into war.

From Alliance to War

A death in a club fight or other duel may mark a transition from alliance to war. But wars can begin far more dramatically when invited guests are attacked and slaughtered at a feast. Chagnon (1967:138–39) identifies two correlates of this kind of treachery: it involves groups that have few strong kinship ties, and the attackers often include men from more than one village. Judging from the available cases, I would add one additional (at least frequent) characteristic: such an attack also involves a division within the host village, with some residents opposing the attack and seeking to maintain trading ties.

A treacherous assault at a feast obviously is a more drastic measure than a duel, and indeed, it is more extreme than a raid (Chagnon 1977: 123). None of the cases to be discussed later is described in sufficient detail to allow us fully to comprehend the political complexity of the alliances, factions, and trade relationships surrounding a feast slaughter. But at least three of the four best reports describe situations of fundamentally antagonistic trade interests. In my perspective—etically and behaviorally—the feast slaughter is an attempt to eliminate from the political scene a group that represents a major threat or obstacle to the attackers' trade interests. It can be a very effective tactic. The loss of several fighters or their headman or both generally will neutralize a group militarily until it can reconstitute itself. Emically, such treachery will be rationalized as an extreme measure brought on by some grave offense by the victims themselves.

A change from alliance to war via a feast slaughter, a killing in a pounding match, or even a declaration of the intent to kill is a fairly common occurrence in the cases reported in this book. It is certainly more usual for old allies to go to war than for war to break out between people who previously had no connection to each other. The transformation may result from some change in military balances or the distribution pattern of Western manufactures or from both together. Generally, the historical situations that lead to a shift from alliance to war fall into three broad categories: (1) during a time of Western expansion, some villages suddenly acquire a locally disproportionate amount of Western goods; (2) during a time of established but still limited Western presence, relocations by Westerners (as sources of both manufactures and military support) undercut and destabilize established trade and alliance patterns; and (3) during a time of Western retraction, increasing scarcity of Western manufactures makes middlemen fail to live up to existing obligations to provide such goods to in-laws (wife givers) in other villages. These scenarios will be further elaborated at the end of this chapter.

A killing usually produces a "state of war"—an expectation that at least some members of villages X and Y may try to kill each other in the immediate future. That expectation activates the most compelling of all material interests, the desire to stay alive. I will argue later that the expectation of mortal danger results in a change in movement and visiting, as people try to avoid those seeking to kill them. The expectation of mortal danger typically persists until one village moves away or, less frequently, some kind of peace is negotiated (Anduze 1960:250; Barker 1953:477–78; Eguillor García 1984:133).[5]

In a state of war, fear is compounded by the proverbial "fog of war"—a lack of knowledge about the current location and disposition of an enemy, and uncertainty about his alliances with others. Lack of information is often compounded by rumors of treachery, violence, and witchcraft (e.g., Biocca 1971:160–64), rumors that mirror the underlying tensions in political relationships (Ramos 1979a; and see chapter 6). Indeed, it is the height of diplomacy to convince a potential ally that a third party is planning to attack him (Biocca 1971:185–86; Cocco 1972:115; Early and Peters 1990:67; and see Good 1991:152–53). All this fog can create a situation analogous to the "prisoners' dilemma": both sides may prefer to maintain the peace, but uncertainty about the other's intentions may argue for striking first.

Through fear and fog, a state of war drastically lowers the threshold of violence, and one attack makes another more likely (Ferguson 1992a, 1993). Still, the state of war and its expectations are not self-perpetuating because the massive physical, material, and emotional costs of war act as a form of "drag" against continuing violence. But before looking at factors that work to prevent endless war, we must look at the conduct of warfare proper: the raid.

Raiding

In a state of war, the primary form of violence is the raid. A raid occurs when a group of men enter into the home range of another group with the intention to kill. Before discussing raiding in detail, a capsule description of the practice is appropriate.

Most raids avoid open combat with the enemy. Typically, raiders hide along a trail close by the enemy settlement and ambush people who come out or pass by. They shoot a man or two and then make a hasty retreat, preferably before their presence is even discovered by the men of the community. If the raiders feel unusually secure and the opportunity presents itself, they may make off with unprotected women. Some larger raiding parties are more aggressive, launching volleys of arrows into a shabono. On rare occasions, raiders succeed in routing their enemies, driving them from their village into the surrounding forest. The victors will then loot the settlement and sometimes capture several women. A significant variation on the raid is the ambush on travelers who are passing near a hostile village.

Regional variations on raiding practices exist (Lizot 1988:520; and see parts II and III), but finer details are scarce outside of the Orinoco-Mavaca area. Even within that area, some significant differences are evident. On the south side of the Orinoco, enemy villages are at least two days' journey apart (Chagnon 1967:117), so a typical raid will take close to a week. Raids on more distant enemies can take up to three weeks (Barker 1959:164). But on the north side of the river, raiders sometimes attack enemies who live less than a day's walk away (Lizot 1988:524). Because overland travel in the low-lying Orinoco-Mavaca area is concentrated in the drier months of September through April, raiding tends to take place then too (Chagnon 1966:178–83). The histories in part III indicate that in the Orinoco-Mavaca area, a village may launch two or three raids in a season, but frequency probably varies with a range of local circumstances.

The logistics of the longer-distance raids are not entirely clear. Raiders leave home weighed down with bananas, which slow their movement at first (Chagnon 1967:137, 1977:135; Lizot 1985:182). The goal is for the bananas to last until the attackers reach the enemy village (Chagnon 1977:130). Returning raiders and those on longer raids presumably rely on gathered food (see Lizot 1985:182) or on food collected from the many old gardens scattered across the landscape. Hunting may actually be better while traveling in the deep forest (see Good 1989).

Raiding may be unidirectional. For the Orinoco-Mavaca area, there are several well-described cases in which no retaliatory strike apparently took place within two or three years after an initial killing. If the victims do raid the killers at a later time, they claim that their act is one of revenge for the previous killing. But in these cases, the later violence seems less a continuation of an old grudge than a fresh new conflict.

If raiding continues beyond the initial attack, it will soon cease because one of the parties will move away—either out of raiding range or close enough to one of its allies to make attacks more dangerous (Chagnon 1967:117–18; Hames 1983:407–14; Montgomery 1970: 146). This behavior is quite within the pattern found throughout Amazonia: relocation avoids or ends the danger of war (Ferguson 1989b: 195–96).[6] Consequently, periods of active raiding between two groups are limited—contrary to popular impressions that the Yanomami are constantly raiding each other or that one killing triggers an unremitting cycle of attack and counterattack. Even for the Orinoco-Mavaca area I have been unable to identify any case in which a series of raids clearly extended continuously over more than two travel seasons; even in the ambiguous cases, three seasons seems to be the upper limit. (A state of war, or the fear of attack, may continue indefinitely until there is reason to end it.)

Substantial variation in the size of raiding parties is reported. On the north side of the Orinoco, where enemy villages are close together, there appears to be a distinctive pattern of individual assassins who stalk victims alone. South of the Orinoco, Chagnon (1967:138) puts 10 as the minimum number of men needed to raid, because it is the least number needed to effect a staggered retreat after the attack—the retreat being the most dangerous time for raiders. The need for 10 men, he says, sets a floor of 40 to 45 people for a militarily viable village. One exception in the recent history of his study population was a raid made by 5 men who dispersed after the attack and regrouped later at a nearby base (Biocca 1971:233–35). Larger raiding parties, however, can surpass 40 or 50 men (Chagnon 1977:128–29; Lizot 1985:182), and in one highly unusual attack, the count may have reached 150 (Lizot 1989:28–29). The larger war parties require the participation of more than one village. A multivillage raid is preceded by a feast that binds allies together through ceremonial consumption of the ashes of previous war victims, a mock attack on the enemy, and a final departure ritual (Chagnon 1967:136–37, 1977:128–30).

"The objective of the raid is to kill one or more of the enemy and flee without being discovered" (Chagnon 1977:122; and see Lizot 1988:559). The safest way to do this is to lurk hidden in the forest around the village, waiting for a suitable target to walk by (Chagnon 1977:132; Lizot 1985:182). That there is substantial selectivity in targets is indicated by the fact that headmen are very frequently the victims of raiders (Biocca 1971:37, 56, 185, 194; Chagnon 1977:122; Cocco 1972:112, 398–400; Saffirio 1985:66; Seitz 1963:185). (In war around the world, it is a common tactic to attempt to incapacitate the enemy militarily by killing its leader.)

The danger of being so deep in enemy territory, however, may not allow raiders their pick of targets; a small and vulnerable party had better shoot at the first opportunity.[7] "Most raid victims are shot while bathing, fetching drinking water, or relieving themselves" (Chagnon

1967:137). If raiders do not encounter a suitable target, they may opt to shoot volleys of arrows into the village before retreating (Biocca 1971: 236–41; Chagnon 1967:138, 1977:132). Such an audacious direct attack usually requires a raiding force of men from more than one village (Barker 1953:475).

Retreat can be the most dangerous time for attackers. They are close to the enemy and perhaps his allies, and the victims know the terrain. It is not uncommon for the victims to ambush retreating raiders and kill one or more (Chagnon 1977:122, 133; Lizot 1985:154–55). When "the victims of the raid discover their assailants and manage to kill one of them, the campaign is not considered to be a success, no matter how many people the raiders may have killed before sustaining their single loss" (Chagnon 1977:122). The Yanomami certainly feel the death of one of their own as deeply as would the members of any small, closely knit community.

The Costs of War

Death is not the only hazard that raiders face. Nonfatal wounds may bring great pain and difficult recoveries (Barker 1959:155; Chagnon 1977:133), and sometimes permanent disfigurement (Biocca 1971:230). Long journeys also entail great effort, and raiders sometimes return home sick, hungry, and exhausted (Chagnon 1977:132). The difficulties are both reflected in and compounded by the fact that many raids—three out of four, according to Lizot (1985:183)—do not even engage the enemy (Chagnon 1977:133, 137). Barker describes the effort to attack a distant enemy: "One time they found no one at home. Another time, they got lost, and for lack of food had to return home. Another time the whole group was so sick that they had to return" (Barker 1959:159).

Unsurprisingly, then, there is a marked reluctance to participate in raids (Chagnon 1977:137). Men seek excuses for not joining a raiding party. For example, "Kremoanawe, who has slightly injured his foot, declares he will not participate in the raid. He says: 'I'm in pain; I don't feel like going.' His father answers: 'If it weren't for the snakebite that prevents me from running, I certainly would go. But I can't. Yet one of us should go'" (Lizot 1985:180).

After a war party has left, men begin trickling back. "The raiders had not been gone five hours when the first one came back, a boastful young man, complaining that he had a sore foot and could not keep up with the others. The next day a few more young men returned, complaining that they had malaria and pains in the stomach. They enjoyed participating in the pomp of the *wayu itou* for this impressed the women, but were, at heart, cowards" (Chagnon 1977:130).

A traveling war party is constantly on the alert for omens, and it does not take much of a sign to make them turn back (Lizot 1985:182–83). When near the enemy village the night before the attack, senior men regularly have problems with the younger men: "Most of them are afraid, cold, and worried about every sort of hazard, and all of them complain of sore feet and belly aches" (Chagnon 1977:130). According to Lizot (1985:183, 1988:559), the larger the raiding party, the more likely it is that these kinds of complaints and disagreements over how to proceed will keep the raiders from even carrying out the attack. On the other hand, Chagnon (1966:137) notes that very small parties are especially vulnerable to a failure of will at the last moment.

Those who remain at home during a raid also endure hardship and risk. The absence of so many men leaves a village vulnerable to raids itself (Barker 1959:160–61; Chagnon 1977:132). Men going on a raid in a climate of intense war know that they may return to find family members killed or abducted. Moreover, the decision to raid rather than to maintain an existing peace or to move out of range of current enemies increases the likelihood of being raided in the future. And the possibility of being raided imposes a tremendous cost on villagers.

Anxiety is very high when raids are expected (Chagnon 1967:117; Jank 1977:45–49, 87). "Raids do not occur with much frequency, but their possibility maintains the population in constant fear of them" (Barker 1953:475). A village "acts defensively at all times when there is an active war going on. Only large groups of people can leave the village, and these are well armed" (Chagnon 1977:132; see also Chagnon 1967:137–38). This need for defensive vigilance necessarily makes basic subsistence tasks—gardening, hunting, gathering, even relieving oneself—more difficult.

New labors are called for during wartime. Gardens may need to be established in more defensible locations (Chagnon 1967:119); the choice of garden sites will be restricted by the need to keep them close to the village because vulnerability to ambush increases with distance (Lizot 1980:40). Much work must go into building or repairing a palisade and clearing surrounding vegetation (up to 50 meters out from the palisade) that could give cover to raiders (Anduze 1960:250; Barker 1953:475). More work goes into producing the food needed to feed allies at feasts (Chagnon 1967:114). To maintain a larger fighting force, villages are allowed to grow larger than people would otherwise tolerate (Chagnon 1973:134–35; Hames 1983:423–24; Lizot 1989:29–30), and larger villages tend to be more rent by internal conflict (Chagnon 1966:5). To manage all this effort, along with the requirements of war itself, people cede more daily authority to headmen in wartime than they would put up with during peace (Chagnon 1966:44, 1974:162; Cocco 1972:387; Migliazza 1972:415; Peña Vargas 1981:48; and see Ferguson 1992a:218–19).

These are the expectable costs of war. In chapter 1 I asserted that such costs are too infrequently considered in theorizing about war and that they weigh against the initiation or continuation of raiding. They are why active raiding lasts a short time before one party opts for the considerable effort of moving away from the fray. Given these costs, why do wars start at all? Answering this question requires looking at both prospective costs and benefits in concrete situations.

On the cost side, wars seem to be initiated when the aggressors have good reason to believe they can get away with it. Sometimes they do: many raids are not followed by retaliation against the raiding village. Where retaliation does occur, it can sometimes be seen that the aggressors had hoped to conceal their identity, or they did not expect the victims to be able to mount an effective counterattack. But in Yanomami war, as in all war, things do not always work out as planned. On some occasions, particularly aggressive men may even start a war deliberately, over the strenuous objections of their kinsmen, for reasons to be discussed later.

The Benefits of War

If attacks usually occur when anticipated costs are perceived to be relatively low, what are the potential benefits of deadly attacks on others? In terms of the perspective argued here, what exactly are the situationally structured incentives that lead people to decide on war? In chapter 1, I noted six basic types of strategic objectives, embodying my material motivation hypothesis. Four of these apply to the Yanomami situation: to increase access to a resource by eliminating a competitor; to capture movable valuables; to impose an exploitative relationship on another independent group; and to forestall attacks by others.

Perhaps the most straightforward of these is the second—violent effort to capture movable valuables. But in this case, what valuables?

Readers already familiar with the Yanomami literature may have one answer ready: women. Women are extremely valuable, and the prospect of obtaining one without incurring the normal debts of bride payments would give a man a major additional incentive to raid. The general theoretical significance of woman-capture will be discussed in the concluding chapter of this book. At this point, the issue is whether the objective of capturing a woman is sufficient to explain raiding—and that brings us to what is probably the greatest single misconception about Yanomami warfare.

Contrary to widespread opinion, there is agreement among fieldworkers that the Yanomami do not generally initiate wars in order to capture women.[8] Some men, especially bachelors, hope to have an opportunity to take a woman in a raid, but that is a secondary consideration and definitely not the reason for launching the attack (Alés 1984:97; Early and Peters 1990:94; Eguillor García 1984:134; Lizot 1988:541,559).[9] This point was stated plainly in *Yanomamö: The Fierce People* (Chagnon 1977:123): "Although few raids are initiated solely with the intention of capturing women, this is always a desired side benefit. . . . Generally, however, the desire to abduct women does not lead to the initiation of hostilities between groups that have had no history of mutual raiding in the past. . . . Once raiding has begun between two villages, however, the raiders all hope to acquire women if the circumstances are such that they can flee without being discovered."

In contrast to the widespread overestimation of woman-capture as an incentive to raid, there is an equally great underappreciation of another objective: the plunder of material items, especially Western goods. As will be documented in the historical chapters to come, this incentive is reported frequently from diverse areas and time periods. In its most common form, attacks are aimed at small parties of Westerners, but plunder is also cited as the reason for raids on other Indian populations and among the Yanomami themselves.

But in the wars that have received the most ethnographic attention, especially those of the Orinoco-Mavaca area, the routing of a sizeable village, leaving it open to plunder, is unusual and cannot be taken as an expectable outcome of a raid. In my perspective, the goal of most conflicts is related to the first and third strategic objectives: eliminating a competitor for valuable resources—with "resources" defined broadly to encompass trade—and imposing an exploitative relationship on other independent groups. To understand these objectives requires attention to the ways in which violence, or the threat of it, affects movement through space in relation to sources of Western goods, as discussed in chapter 2. I will argue that raids, attacks on visiting trade parties, and ambushes are tactics directed at improving a group's access to or control over trade in Western manufactures. This occurs in several patterns, which I will describe next. Providing evidence that this model actually explains the behavior of war is the central task of all the historical discussions to follow in parts II and III.

One way to assess the reason for a raid on another village is to look at the most likely outcome of such an action. A likely result of a successful raid is that the victims will move away from the attackers. Most wars are resolved when an endangered group moves out of range, and the Yanomami are certainly aware of this regularity. (On the advent of one raid, a Yanomami said, "We'll make them flee far away from us" [Lizot 1985:155].)

When the targets of a raid or of a surprise attack during a trading visit had been, by virtue of their geographic position, monopolizing access to Westerners or controlling trade in Western manufactures, and the attackers had been less able to get goods because of that monopoly, the forcible displacement of the trade controllers can "eliminate the middleman," open better access to the sources of Western goods, and perhaps allow the victors to establish themselves as middlemen with all the benefits that implies. On the other hand, those in a highly beneficial trade position may, rather than move, respond in kind to attacks from more isolated groups, seeking to force them out of striking range. This response reflects the fourth strategic objective of war, to forestall future attacks by others.

In addition to attacks on villages, there are other forms of violence, usually employed by middlemen but sometimes by those wishing to become middlemen. One is aimed at preventing the establishment of a new garden and settlement at a location that would enhance a rival's position in the trade network. Without specifying context, Eibl-Eibesfeldt and Mattei-Müller (1990:514) call attention to garden destruction as a form of violence often preceding war (and see Barandiaran 1967:39): "The usual procedure is to destroy the tobacco gardens of another group as a warning. If this does not lead to movement, then destruction escalates to staple crops such as bananas and so on, until all out warfare is proclaimed."

Although there are some cases of actual violence along these lines, threats are more typical than actual raids. Few Yanomami would be so reckless as to try to establish a residence and create a garden where they would be exposed to raiding by potential enemies nearby. One expression of this common sense is the Yanomami's noted reluctance to try to "leap frog" past any neighboring village (Chagnon 1973:141, 1974: 75–76).

In another kind of situation, the intended targets are not in a village or trying to establish one but are ambushed while traveling along trails between villages. Given the village-to-village patterning of trails, the practical necessity of using those trails for long-distance travel, and the home-ground advantage in combat, the men of one village can (other things not being grossly unequal) effectively control passage around them, at least sufficiently to make prospective travelers fear for their lives. In this way, the threat of ambush is employed by middlemen to keep more distant groups from bypassing them to approach the source of Western manufactures.[10] Their ability to ambush is one reason why successful middlemen are able to impose the often onerous terms that they do. It is the potential for violence that enforces the unequal alliance. In still other situations, the ambush is a method by which a previously poor group forces itself as a middleman into a going flow of trade. This strategy will be demonstrated most dramatically in chapter 7 by the succession of Yanomami groups that pushed onto the Uraricoera trade route.

In all these situations, the principal benefit of war is to improve access to Western manufactures. The most direct manifestation of this benefit, the simple goal of plunder, applies to only a minority of situations. The other manifestations are attempts to affect intervillage exchange patterns: by making life unlivable for monopolists ensconced in prime locations, thus forcing them to move; by precluding any group from unilaterally improving its position in local trade networks by moving to a better location; and by forcing those who travel for trade to respect the village-to-village organization of commerce. All involve a clear spatial component. In practice, the "state of war" is geopolitical: one's danger of being assaulted by members of an enemy group is directly related to one's location.

Summary

Taking all of the foregoing into account, the theoretical expectations about various forms of attack can be made more explicit. The following scenarios present the general argument developed here, framed in terms of common combinations of historical circumstances (at least for the twentieth century) and indicating the situations of war and peace expected for each.

1. When sources of Western goods are generally absent and no (vulnerable) group has a quantity of them greatly above the local average, no raiding is expected—keeping in mind that in a situation of extreme scarcity, a few machetes are a treasure.

2. When a group has acquired comparatively large quantities of Western goods, whether through trading or raiding, yet lacks any marked military advantage over other Yanomami, villages that lack Western manufactures or obtain them at extreme costs will attack the wealthier group, either for plunder or to drive them out of their controlling position.

3. As an elaboration of pattern (2), when a village with access to Western goods also has the military advantages of contact, such as resident Westerners and shotguns, it may respond to threats from the interior with raids, preserving its own position by driving its attackers away.

4. When a village that is militarily strong also is connected to Western patrons who are unusually well supplied and generous, they will combine these advantages to secure peaceable alliances with all neighboring groups and thus avoid most major violence. The violence may then shift to areas beyond this group of neighbors.

5. Sometimes overlapping with pattern (3), when a village is enjoying the benefits of being a middleman, it will employ violence or the threat of violence to prevent others from undermining its advantage by establishing new gardens and villages in better trade positions, by traveling to trade directly with the Westerners, or by having Westerners come to live with them. This scenario most frequently occurs in relation to some local change in the position of Westerners.

6. When multiple sources of Western manufactures are present and accessible to different groups, so that trade cannot be controlled, and when supplies of Western goods are generally adequate or increasing, there is no incentive to raid.

These scenarios, along with all the other expectations discussed earlier, generate two predictions that are not, to my knowledge, suggested by any existing anthropological theory on war and that may be applied even in situations where there is minimal information. One concerns timing. The model developed here predicts that outbreaks of violence will follow soon after a change affecting the availability of Western goods in an area: a new penetration by Westerners, a shift in the location of sources, or a retraction of Westerners. In the absence of such a change, no raiding is expected. Generally, within one to three years, a new political accommodation will emerge, and if there is no further change in the Western presence, war will end.

The other prediction concerns the direction of violence. As Western manufactures begin to filter into a region, raids (other than for captives) will generally be launched by those more removed from the Westerners against those with better access to the Western goods; the same directionality will be evident in times of withdrawal of sources of Western goods.[11] In situations with a robust Western presence—for example, after the arrival of a well-supplied mission—the direction typically reverses, the common pattern being that an ally of the outpost village attacks more remote groups with the outpost's newly augmented military support. But in all cases, the two sides in a war will be groups with markedly different access to Western goods.

These basic predictions also apply to better described conflict situations, but in those cases we can go beyond simple outlines to study in some detail the politics that go into alliance, factionalism, and warfare. Particularly for the Orinoco-Mavaca area after 1940, multiple historical sources allow finer analysis of the ways in which conflicting interests structured by differential access to Western goods shaped a range of conflict behavior. It is there that the complicated patterning of violence in relation to sources of Western goods can be analyzed; there that the use of force within alliances can be examined in relation to war; and there that the interaction of internal and external village military politics can be explored.

Having stated these theoretical expectations, I must enter several qualifications. First, the scenarios are intended to represent common historical circumstances reported for the Yanomami over the past two centuries, and especially over the past 50 years. There will be, in later chapters, other situations that fit the general theoretical expectations, but in idiosyncratic ways. Second, the scenarios are limited in scope. As I emphasized in chapter 1, there are many other situations known to generate war in other ways among other Amazonian peoples. Even for the Yanomami, these theoretical expectations do not encompass the widespread pattern of raiding for captives that was directed against the

Yanomami by Westerners and their native agents in the first centuries of contact. That kind of fighting, to be discussed in chapter 5, was clearly generated by the Western presence, but not in ways delineated in this model.

It is also theoretically possible—but not predicted by *this* theory—that ancient Yanomami in the Parima highlands practiced war among themselves for other, unknown reasons—although there is no clear evidence on this point. As I have stressed elsewhere (Ferguson 1990b:238, 248), to emphasize the violence-generating impact of Western contact is in no way to deny that completely autochthonous factors may also lead to war. And it is possible that highly acculturated Yanomami with open access to Western goods now have or will develop new forms of interpersonal violence in response to new conditions and conflicts (see Ferguson and Whitehead 1992a:30). Some of the most recent wars of the Yanomami are so different in their contexts and practice that I hesitate to attempt to explain them with this model. As I noted earlier, this model represents the application of a general theoretical perspective to a given ethnohistorical situation; it is not the general theory itself.

Finally, a tenet of the general theory (Ferguson 1990a:31, n.d.*b*) is that all expectations are seen as probabilities. The relationships I posit are strongly determinative of actual processes, but, as in any social phenomenon, when you get down to specific cases there are always other things involved. Density of villages, for example, is a contingency in terms of this model that significantly affects local geopolitics. And there are always exceptions. A significant one can be noted in advance: when a local group first experiences introduced diseases, the inexplicable illness may well be interpreted in terms of preexisting beliefs about witchcraft and thus provoke a strike against the presumed malefactors (Ferguson 1993:224; and see Ferguson 1990b:241).

Qualifications aside, the objective of parts II and III is to show that the vast majority of reported Yanomami warfare conforms to the expectations just outlined. In the concluding chapter, I will argue that the adoption of such a strongly deterministic approach may, perhaps paradoxically, allow us a better understanding of the role of agency in history.

This is my explanation, my model, of Yanomami warfare and, more generally, of Yanomami political history. It is not a simple explanation, but no explanation intended to apply to all historically known cases could be simple. Nevertheless, the model is constructed by the compounding of essentially simple relationships between observable factors.

It is subject to verification by repeated demonstration that actual be-haviors conform to the model's predictions for given contexts, and, conversely, to falsification by demonstration that patterns of violence in delineated contexts regularly contradict its expectations. Verification of the model is the goal of parts II and III.

Before closing this discussion, it is worth repeating a point made in chapter 1. I do not maintain that my logic of violence corresponds to Yanomami conceptions about war in general or to their way of thinking about specific conflicts. With the exception of overt plun-der raids directed against outsiders (Westerners or distant, unrelated, native groups), antagonistic interests shaped by the spatial distribution of Western goods will likely be conceptualized and discussed in terms of moral rights, obligations, and offenses—usually invoking revenge and witchcraft (Ferguson 1992a:222–24)—and in terms of concrete, per-sonal relationships. The closer the social ties, the more moralistic and personalistic will be the emic rationalizations of war.

Thus I have no difficulty seeing the potential compatibility of this model with other approaches that explore indigenous conceptualiza-tions of violence and "the other." I would ask readers interested in such topics to deliberate before deciding that my etic, behavioral ap-proach necessarily contradicts their own perspective. But if contradict they must, my appeal is to the evidence. The remainder of this book is intended to demonstrate that the actual behavior of war corresponds to the theoretical expectations outlined here. If some other cognitive or motivational theory is offered in contradiction to mine, then it must be made to account for the observed historical variations in violence.

PART II

Background and Comparisons

4

Lands, Languages, and Ancient Society

This chapter sets the scene for the historical discussions to follow. It first provides a geographical introduction to the Yanomami area and then discusses the outside world's recognition of the Yanomami as a distinct cultural group, along with what is known or speculated about their origins and prehistoric migrations. A final section draws inferences about the culture of ancestral Yanomami society before its recent contact with Westerners, arguing that without steel, the Yanomami probably were limited in their practice of agriculture and consequently faced greater challenges to subsistence and survival.

Geography

Many discussions of the Yanomami identify their "traditional" homeland as the rugged and inaccessible Parima highlands (map 1), which run approximately 250 kilometers from north-northwest to southeast and cover some 20,000 square kilometers. Most of the region is a moderately dissected plateau dominated by rolling hills at an altitude of 800 to 1,200 meters, with scattered peaks reaching 1,400 to 1,600 meters (Huber et al. 1984:106). Although the Parima does have a pronounced dry season, its typical vegetation is tall rain forest with occasional patches of savanna (Huber et al. 1984:124–32; Smole 1976:199–208).

But the association of the Parima with ancestral Yanomami lands is not perfect. As will be detailed elsewhere, the northern fifth of the Parima was occupied in the eighteenth century by Maku and perhaps others. More importantly, ancestral Yanomami are reported living in several other areas of high country to the east and south of the Parima proper.

The Parima and nearby highlands are surrounded by a network of ancient travel routes, most of them riverine, used by indigenous people, Western explorers, and colonialists. A basic grasp of this network is essential for everything that follows, and so I offer an overview here. Details and documentation can be found in the historical chapters to come.

Western and northwestern approaches to the Parima highlands are dominated by the Orinoco River. The northwestern bounding point of most events discussed in this book is the juncture of the Orinoco and Atabapo rivers. A major travel route went up the Atabapo, over a portage, and down the Guainía River to the upper Río Negro. Above the Atabapo, the Orinoco is joined by the Ventuari, the mainstream of an extensive river system draining a large basin just north of the Parima. The Ventuari and its tributaries have been important indigenous trade routes connected by trails over the high country to northward and eastward flowing rivers. Farther up the Orinoco, the Cunucunuma River provides an alternative entry to that network, connected by trail to the upper Ventuari. These routes are all north of the earliest reported Yanomami territory, but during the twentieth century many Yanomami groups have moved into this area.

Just above the mouth of the Cunucunuma, the Orinoco is joined from the south by a geological anomaly, the Casiquiare canal. Once thought to be mythical, it is an open-water passage connecting the Orinoco to the Río Negro. It has been an important travel route, although passage between the two major river systems was weeks faster via the Atabapo-Guainía route if porters were available. The Casiquiare itself has several tributaries, most significantly the Siapa River. The Siapa drains a large area of mountainous uplands, the Unturán to its north, the Curupira to its east, and the Tapirapeco to its south—hereafter referred to together as the Siapa highlands. These highlands have been a major center of Yanomami residence in the twentieth century, but it has been believed that they arrived in the area only recently. While a relatively recent arrival appears to be true for the ancestors of the current residents, there are consistent references to Yanomami inhabiting these highlands since the last quarter of the eighteenth century.[1] The upper reaches of Siapa tributaries from the Tapirapeco highlands connect by trail to streams flowing into the Río Negro.

Returning to the Orinoco, the Padamo River and its major tributary, the Matacuni, come down directly from the Parima highlands above the Casiquiare on the right bank. Above that, the Ocamo River does the same. The upper reaches of the Matacuni and Ocamo are among the earliest reported locations of the Yanomami. In recent years, Yanomami have moved all the way down to the mouths of the two rivers.

Continuing our tour up the Orinoco, it is next joined by the Mavaca River from the south. The Mavaca area was also outside of Yanomami territory until recently, although there are suggestions of some ancient Yanomami in the highlands east of its headwaters, part of the Siapa highlands just mentioned. The Mavaca was a passageway for Native Americans and some creoles, connecting by trail to the Siapa system and thus to the Negro.

A short distance beyond the Mavaca, the Orinoco is joined by the Manaviche River, which leads into high country just below the Parima proper. Over the past fifty years or so, Yanomami have come to settle in the lowlands along the Orinoco from the Ocamo upwards. Some distance beyond the Manaviche, travel is impeded by a series of difficult rapids, most notably (in ascending order) the Raudal de Guajaribos, Raudal Peñascal, and Raudal Guaica. Some of the earliest reports of the Yanomami have them barring passage into their territory at or below the Raudal de Guajaribos, some distance west of the Parima proper. The Orinoco continues upward into the southern tip of the Parima highlands. One small left-bank feeder of the far upper Orinoco is the Ugueto, which provides overland access to mountain tributaries of the Demini, an effluent of the Negro. All of this rising terrain seems within the range of ancestral Yanomami habitation.

Our tour now jumps down to the Río Negro, a major river that eventually flows into the Amazon. From the Negro's left bank, several rivers lead into the high country between it and the Siapa, a probable area of long-term Yanomami habitation. Perhaps a second wave of Yanomami from the Parima area arrived in these rivers' headwaters early in this century, and some have moved down toward the Negro. Heading downstream along the Río Negro, the main left-bank tributaries are the Cauaburi and its tributary, the Marauiá; the Padauiri; and the Demini with its tributary, the Araçá. They are connected by trail to the Siapa basin.

Much bigger than those rivers is the next tributary of the Negro, the Río Branco. It has been speculated that pre-Columbian Yanomami may have lived around the juncture of the Branco and the Negro. Like the Orinoco and the Negro, the Branco is a major regional trade artery. In its northern reaches, it connects via trails to rivers that flow through the Guianas to the Caribbean. Traveling up the Branco from its mouth, the

Catrimani and Mucajaí rivers come down from the southern Parima. Some very limited information suggests that ancestral Yanomami inhabited their headwaters. Over the past century, Yanomami have moved into their middle and lower reaches.

Farther up the Branco, the Uraricoera River is a major east-west trade route, leading up to the ridge between Venezuela and Brazil, and to the Ventuari trails. Early reports place Yanomami in the highlands along the right bank of the upper Uraricoera, well east of the Parima proper. Above that highland, the Uraricoera is joined by the Parima River, which leads into the highlands and the heartland of ancestral Yanomami settlement. The Uraricoera-Ventuari route also connects up with a number of rivers that flow northward into the Caribbean, including the Paragua and the Caura with its tributary, the Erebato. Over the past century, Yanomami have moved into all these river drainages.

To sum up, Yanomami history is framed by a rough trapezoid of travel routes. To the west are several passages connecting the Orinoco and the Negro. To the south is the Negro itself, and to the east, the Branco. Across the north is a branching network of routes centering on the Ventuari and Uraricoera. All the earliest reports, from the middle eighteenth century onward, situate ancestral Yanomami in relatively inaccessible highlands, although their range was greater than the Parima highlands proper.

A very important fact is that no major travel routes pass through most of the traditional homelands of the Yanomami, with the exception of some smaller trade routes through the Siapa highlands. The Yanomami themselves are quite capable of foot travel throughout the area, of course; but any long-distance travel by other Native Americans or Westerners is much easier and faster if it bypasses the Parima and nearby highlands. On the other hand, from almost all directions rivers and streams lead toward or into these highland areas. If they are inadequate to serve as passages for trade, they were, unfortunately, sufficient to carry slave raiders into Yanomami territory.

The Yanomami as a Cultural Group

Most Yanomami share a distinctive set of culture traits that differentiate them from their indigenous neighbors in north-central Amazonia. Among the diagnostics that enable one to identify Yanomami from early accounts onward are unusually long and well-made bows, reliance on plantains as the cultivated staple, an absence of canoes or other river technology, a bowl-shaped haircut, a wad of tobacco regularly in place under the lower lip, and ritualized consumption of ashes of the bones of the dead. Curiously, the Yanomami were regularly said to be whiter in color than surrounding Indians (e.g., Dickey 1932:283; Humboldt 1889:463–64; Tejera 1877:10–11; cf. Michelena y Rojas 1989: 334–35)—hence their early names "Guahiba blanco" and "Guajaribo blanco."[2] These traits, however, are only the most obvious of a broad range of common characteristics (see Koch-Grunberg 1979 III:239–67; Migliazza 1972:394–447), several of which were once more common in Amazonia (Smole 1976:10–13; Zerries 1955:80–85). Yanomami distinctiveness is in part a function of their having retained more of their ancient culture into the twentieth century.

Westerners have only slowly come to recognize a distinct Yanomami culture. Over the centuries, Yanomami have been referred to by a bewildering variety of names (Kietzman 1967:9–10; Koch-Grunberg 1979 [orig. 1917] III:239–45; Migliazza 1972:5–9, 27–33, 1980:101–104), some of which (e.g., Waika, Maku) are also applied to non-Yanomami. Koch-Grunberg (1979 I:187) is credited with being the first to recognize that the different subdivisions of Yanomami were of one basic culture (Chagnon 1966:46; Colchester 1985a:1), although the similarity of certain subdivisions had been noted by a number of earlier writers. It was only in the 1960s that these people came to be called some variation on "Yanomami," a word that in their language means "person" or "human being" (Anduze 1960; Arends et al. 1967; Chagnon 1966; Wilbert 1963; and see Migliazza 1972:26–27, 1980:101). Contemporary Yanomami recognize a distinction between themselves and non-Yanomami, who are referred to with some variation on "nape" or "naba," which glosses as "stranger" or "foreigner" (Lizot 1988:528; Migliazza 1972:389–90; Smole 1976:14). This self-recognition, however, does not imply any sense of political unity.

The spelling "Yanomami" is one of at least four variations that have been used as a general, inclusive term for all local divisions, along with Yanomama, Yanoama, and Yanomamo, each with its own orthographic variations (Migliazza 1972:26–27, 1980:101; Ramos 1972:3). In a previous paper (Ferguson 1990b), I use "Yanoama," after Colchester (1985a:2), who argues for it "following the accepted scientific practice of using the first reasonable of proposed terms." Since writing that paper, I have become more aware of the inherently political nature of ethnogenesis, and of how demarcating and labeling cultures or ethnic groups is part of a historical process (see Ferguson and Whitehead 1992a:12–15). Therefore, standards of scientific taxonomy seem less relevant than praxis.

In this book, I will use Yanomami as the general rubric because it is the label most commonly used in the campaign to prevent their destruction. The problem with this choice is that Yanomami is also a name applied to one linguistic subdivision. Another label applied to that same subdivision is Yanomamo. For this book, except when quoting other authors, *Yanomami* will denote the entire people, and *Yanomamo*, the linguistic subdivision.

Migliazza (1972) proposed subdividing Yanomami into four geographically distinct languages. With some adjustments and reservations, Migliazza's divisions are broadly accepted by Yanomami specialists (Colchester 1985a:2–3; Comité 1983:34–35; Lizot 1988:489–91). For expository clarity, I will simplify the various names applied to these divisions to Sanema, Ninam, Yanomam, and Yanomamo (map 3). Since geography plays a great role in history, these language divisions correspond to differences in historical circumstances. For that reason—not any possible cultural difference—the language divisions are used as one of the basic structuring principles in this book, the other principle being chronology.

Origins, Affinities, Movements

The origins of the Yanomami people have been subject to considerable speculation, encouraged by a curious genetic anomaly. The Yanomami are unusual in the absence of an antigen, referred to as the Diego factor or Di[a] gene, that is common in other Native American populations. This absence has led some to argue that the Yanomami may be descendants of an earlier wave of migration to the New World—in other words, that their ancestors were among the earliest human inhabitants of the Western hemisphere (Comité 1983:35–36; Layrisse, Layrisse, and Wilbert 1962; Smole 1976:18; Wilbert 1972:4, 14; cf. Lizot 1988:491–92). More recent linguistic reconstructions do not support this idea, although they may not necessarily contradict it.

The Yanomami languages have resisted efforts at broader categorization. Migliazza (1972:25–26, 389) challenges an earlier effort to classify them as Macro-Chibchan and asserts that they still must be classified as "isolated." In a later work, Migliazza (1982:511–12) identifies Yanomami as Macro-Pano-Tacanan. Combining linguistic evidence with archaeological reconstruction of ancient population movements, Migliazza (1982:516–17; also see Spielman, Migliazza, and Neel 1974: 643) speculates that ancestral Yanomami at around 2500 BP lived far to the south and west of their current location, along the lower Ucayali River. Around that time, he postulates, they separated from ancestors of current Panoan speakers, moving down the Amazon mainstream and eventually up the Río Negro and its tributary, the Río Branco. This speculative reconstruction parallels work by Zerries (1955:80–85), whose culture-trait analysis indicates that the Yanomami are of more western origin and are culturally intrusive in the north-central (Guianan) area.[3]

Migliazza (1972:5–12) also points out that place names currently used along the lower Río Branco may be of Yanomami origin, indicating former residence there. He suggests that they may have inhabited an extensive area, perhaps to the Río Negro itself and even beyond the Branco to the east. Migliazza believes there were four westward migrations from the Branco area into the Parima highlands, leading to the contemporary language divisions. His chart (1982:512; also Colchester 1985a:5) has the Sanema separating from the others at about 700 BP, the Ninam separating around 300 BP, and the Yanomamo and Yanomam diverging about 200 BP. In collaboration with genetic researchers (Spielman, Migliazza, and Neel 1974:643), he puts the earliest division (Sanema) as occurring between 600 and 1200 BP, and the most recent (Yanomam-Yanomamo), between 75 and 200 BP.

This posited migration of Yanomami from lower river courses into higher land has been connected (Harris 1977:48; Smole 1976:16) to Lathrap's model of ancient population movements in Amazonia (Lathrap 1970:83, 186–90, 1973). In that model, agriculture evolved along the central Amazon, followed by population growth and radiation outwards, displacing the prior, nonagricultural residents in the process. As Lathrap (1970:77) sees it, the Parima region was bracketed on the east and west by Macro-Arawakan migrations northward along the major rivers from 2500 to 1500 BP.

If Migliazza's reconstruction of ancient Yanomami movements from western Amazonia is correct, their arrival in the Negro-Branco region would have been contemporaneous with these larger population shifts. Since I have been unable to find any historical evidence that places ancestral Yanomami in riverine lowlands prior to their being reported in high country, it is not unreasonable to argue that after arriving in this general area—whenever and from wherever—they were somehow pushed off the rivers, with possibly negative demographic consequences (see Ferguson 1989c:255–57). However, I will argue below that the ancestral Yanomami probably had more connection to the lowlands than did their descendants.

As for the Yanomami's direction of entry into the region, there are problems with Migliazza's scenario of radiation outward from the lower Branco. Albert (1985:35–38) has raised serious objections to Migliazza's toponymic evidence for former Yanomami residence in the lower Branco-Negro area. In the historical materials researched for this book, there is little early reference to Yanomami on any of the Branco's tributaries except the Uraricoera, and, as explained earlier, the Uraricoera is also connected to the Orinoco system.

On the other hand, there are many early reports that place Yanomami in the Orinoco drainage and nearby Siapa highlands. The earliest reported location of the Sanema—of special interest because of their longer linguistic separation—is certainly more consistent with an Orinoco than a Branco origin. All things considered, the possibility cannot be ignored that the ancestral Yanomami spread through the Parima region from west to east, rather than east to west.

Regarding Migliazza's postulated four waves of migration, there are other possible perspectives on the origins of contemporary language divisions. Some authors have questioned whether any actual separation exists between Yanomam and Yanomamo, or whether they instead represent a continuum of dialects (Colchester 1985a:5; Lizot 1988: 489). Furthermore, Albert (1985:51) suggests that the little-studied and linguistically distinctive Yanomami of the Ajarani-Apiaú Rivers in Brazil speak a language intermediate between Yanomam and Ninam.

I would suggest that until historical times, the Yanomamo, Yanomam, and Ninam were part of a more or less continuous chain of residence, interaction, and dialectical variation. In this hypothesis, the creation of the newer Yanomami language divisions was the result of displacements, interdictions, decimations, and long-distance migrations related to the Western intrusion. This hypothesis is speculative, of course, but probably no more so than the Branco radiation hypothesis. And it calls attention to a more general problem: that of inferring a distant Yanomami past from recent observation.

Imagining "Pre-Contact" Society

The widely held assumption that the Yanomami are "timeless primitives" has led many to believe that recent descriptions of their culture represent their highland lifeways over the past few centuries and even before Columbus, unaffected in any major way by the arrival of Europeans (see Ferguson 1992a:200). That belief is unwarranted. Although it is impossible to say with any certainty how ancient Yanomami society was structured, there are strong reasons to believe it was substantially different from its structure in recent years. Examining that possibility will also create a deeper appreciation of why steel has been so critically important in explaining Yanomami political history and war.

Recent archaeological research (Roosevelt 1980, 1987, 1991) indicates that people along some of the fertile floodplains of lowland Amazonia had attained substantial evolutionary complexity long before the arrival of the Europeans. One ethnohistorical study of the Upper Amazon (Golob 1982) indicates that these chiefdoms had extensive peaceful commerce with less complex peoples in the forest.

Closer to the Yanomami region, Whitehead (1989, 1990c, and see 1988a) has documented the existence of complex polities at the center of trade networks in the Branco-Negro-Orinoco region; and there are suggestions of relatively complex societies even where the Orinoco begins its rise into the Parima highlands.[4] Arvelo-Jiménez and Biord Castillo (1989:11–13) argue that recent investigators have failed to appreciate that early reports from the Orinoco region consistently indicate that local groups were integrated in a complex, multiethnic regional system connected by social, political, economic, and religious ties—a system that encompassed southern Venezuela. They and Whitehead (1989, 1992; and see Zent 1993) agree that this pre-Columbian system was destroyed or at least transformed by the disruptive effects of distant European intrusion, long before any European observers arrived on the scene.

Lizot (1988:496) suggests that ancestral Yanomami participated in these larger networks but became isolated from them as a result of the slave raids and epidemics that devastated the region. I concur. The strongest piece of evidence indicating ancient Yanomami integration into regional networks is Humboldt's (1889:462) observation in 1800 that Yanomami of the upper Orinoco came to trade fine-quality green "Amazon stones" at La Esmeralda (on the Orinoco above the Casiquiare) and that they reportedly obtained these valuable items through "traffic with hordes much farther to the east." Amazon stones, in prehistoric times and the first centuries after Columbus, were "one of the principal media of intra- as well as interethnic ceremonial exchange throughout the Tropical Forest area of northern South America" (Boomert 1987: 36). They were even passed between chiefs to seal peace and marriage arrangements. Most Amazon stones came from the lower Amazon River and circulated around the Guiana coast and out through the Antilles. Only a few have been found in the upper Orinoco (Boomert 1987:37–39, 40, 43–44). Ancestral Yanomami who could somehow procure these precious stones would have been in a very good position to participate in the ancient regional trade networks.

Another issue to be considered in the organization of Yanomami society before the twentieth century is that of their subsistence orientation. Specifically, there is a debate about how long the Yanomami have practiced agriculture. In the 1950s, it was thought that the Yanomami had only recently passed from a hunting and gathering way of life (Steward and Faron 1959:434; Wilbert 1963:187–88, 1972:14; Zerries 1955:73). Migliazza (1972:365) attributes the origin of this image to Schomburgk (even though that explorer saw small Yanomami gardens in 1838 [Schomburgk 1841:221]). But Schomburgk only seems to reflect local views about the Yanomami around that time—views that were clearly based on very limited acquaintance (see Bueno 1965: 145; Codazzi 1940 II:48). The weightiest report of Yanomami as neo-agriculturalists comes from Koch-Grunberg (1979 III:250, 257–58), whose interviews in 1911–12 earn him the title of first ethnographer of the Yanomami.

The idea that Yanomami were basically hunters and gatherers fits well with either of two influential anthropological theories about "marginal" tropical forest populations: that they were representative holdovers of an ancient, preagricultural social layer (Steward and Faron 1959:374–78, 434); or that they represented devolved former agriculturalists who had been pushed off the river lowlands by later migrants (see Albert 1985:33–35; Smole 1976:5).

Chagnon (1966:46–49) led a challenge to the idea that the Yanomami had only recently made the transition to agriculture, pointing out the fragile bases of some assumptions and stressing that even early contact reports indicated that the Yanomami did have gardens, albeit small ones. It is Lizot (1977:498–99, 1980:3–7, 1988:506), however, who has become the most ardent champion of an ancient basis for Yanomami agriculture. It appears unlikely that this controversy can be resolved by examination of the ambiguous historical reports. But some inferences about the past may be drawn from Yanomami subsistence as observed in the twentieth century. I will first present evidence about four aspects of recent Yanomami food procurement and then discuss their possible implications.

First, the Yanomami's staple crop is plantains—a staple that is highly unusual, although not unique, among Amazonian societies. It is generally held that plantains are post-Columbian introductions to the New World, although the historical sources leave room for the opposite conclusion too (Holoway 1956; Patiño 1958; Simmonds 1962; Stover and Simmonds 1987:167–68). Recent linguistic research also suggests an ancient presence for plantains in Amazonia (William Balée, personal communication).

Evidence about the antiquity of bananas among the Yanomami is meager and contradictory. Padre Cocco, in a question-and-answer retrospective of his long missionary career among the upper Orinoco Yanomami, asserts that plantains were obtained only toward the end of the last century, by plundering the gardens of neighboring Native Americans (Peña Vargas 1981:25). This is a significant statement from a generally reliable source, but I am aware of no other evidence to support it. On the other hand, Barandiaran (1967:35) makes a persuasive argument for the antiquity of plantains by noting their central place in the mortuary rituals of all Yanomami, including the Sanema, who apparently diverged from the rest centuries before the voyages of Columbus. With so much uncertainty surrounding it, the banana is a questionable basis for any conclusions.

Second, there is the matter of what the Yanomami's staple crop is *not:* a variety of bitter manioc, the staple of most other Amazonian horticulture. This historic lack of manioc cultivation is not for lack of interest; in recent years, Yanomami in contact with bitter manioc producers have adopted the crop with alacrity (e.g., Barandiaran 1967:37; Colchester 1981b:29, 1984:300–302; Good 1984:43; Montgomery 1970: 105). Instead, it would seem that either the ancestral Yanomami never grew manioc or they were compelled to give it up. One reason for giving up manioc would be increased mobility. The standard method of processing bitter manioc to remove its toxins and prepare it as food is a complicated, multistep operation, requiring as basic instruments a large grater board, a long woven press, pots or other containers, and a flat cooking stone or pan. Manioc products are often prepared in quantity and stored. Transporting the necessary tools and stored produce would be difficult for people who frequently travel by foot.

Third, there are questions concerning stone axes and the feasibility of relying predominantly on gardening for food. In chapter 2, I noted that all Yanomami garden clearing and cultivation that has been witnessed by outsiders has been done with steel cutting tools. Some Yanomami are reported to have used stone axes within older informants' memory, but these tools had been found at the sites of long-disappeared people, not made by Yanomami (Barandiaran 1967:29–31; Barandiaran and Walalam 1983:192; Chagnon 1977:24; Cocco 1972:193; Steinvorth de

Goetz 1969:30; Wilbert 1972:30–31). Moreover, I have been unable to locate any report from any Yanomami area that suggests a past ability to make stone axes themselves. Perhaps in the past stone axes were traded in from neighboring peoples, but with the destruction of those peoples after European contact, supply must have become a real problem.

Old stone axes are easily found in certain locations on the far upper Orinoco. In Sanema territory they are less common, but their past importance is suggested by their having remained in use as ritual instruments and by their exemption from the otherwise strict rule of destroying all personal property at death (Barandiaran 1967). Farther from the upper Orinoco, along the Uraricoera, Koch-Grunberg (1979 I:257–58) in 1911 found Yanomami who were completely unfamiliar with a stone ax he showed them. All this evidence suggests that in the past, at least some Yanomami had limited numbers of stone axes; that inference in turn suggests that the Yanomami went through a time when they felled far fewer trees than they have in recently observed agriculture.

With or without stone axes, there is reason to believe that gardening once played a less central role in Yanomami subsistence. Colchester's (1984:302–10) hypothetical reconstruction of pre-Columbian Yanomami subsistence suggests that they could have gardened with stone tools, but with more work and less produce than is possible with steel (and see Carneiro 1979a, 1979b). He concludes that lithic Yanomami would have needed to rely far more on mobile foraging than is the case at present.[5] This tendency toward mobility would be reinforced by the possibility of vegetation-wilting dry spells in the highlands (Huber et al. 1984:109) and, perhaps, by inferior soil conditions in the highlands (Chagnon 1992a:83; Huber et al. 1984:108).

Besides costs in efficiency, productivity, and reliability, another substantial cost associated with intensive gardening is that garden clearing with stone tools relies heavily on burning (Barandiaran 1967:25; Carneiro 1979b:71–72).[6] Burning creates smoke, and one way to find villages in the forest is to climb a tree and look for smoke (Chaffanjon 1986:265; Gheerbrant 1954:167; Gilij 1965 III:96–97). During the times of intensive captive taking, Yanomami within range of raiders would be sending up a beacon every time they started a garden. At those times and places, clearing a garden and remaining near it for prolonged periods would be hazardous. (Bueno [1965:145] reported around 1804 that Yanomami were hard to capture precisely because they were so mobile in the forests.) Together, then, all these factors suggest that Yanomami in recent centuries were much less reliant on gardening and more reliant on hunting and gathering than observed, twentieth-century Yano-mami have been.

Consistent with that conclusion is the fourth aspect of known Yano-mami subsistence practices: their highly developed hunting and gather-ing skills, which have been described in most detail by Good (1983, 1989, 1991) and Valero (Biocca 1971; Valero 1984). Yanomami who have not been sedentized through recent outside contacts spend several months of the year on trek in the forest, and they generally do very well for those limited periods. During a drought in 1972–73, when Yano-mamo of the Siapa River area accidentally destroyed their own gardens by burning, they turned to a fully nomadic life for a time. "Working more than usual, the Indians continued in a state of semi-hunger, but they subsisted" (Lizot 1974:7). It is difficult to imagine long-established agriculturalists such as the Yecuana being able to survive this way.

The Yanomami's traditional reliance on plantains rather than ma-nioc, their tenuous connection to lithic technology, the problems asso-ciated with using stone axes to clear gardens, and their highly developed hunting and gathering skills all point in the same direction: although agriculture may be very old among the Yanomami, they were—before the acquisition of steel tools and the end of slave raiding—probably more reliant on mobile hunting and gathering than any recently ob-served, post-steel Yanomami groups.[7] Barandiaran (1967:35) notes that groups most distant from centers of contact maintained small banana gardens situated at favorite trekking sites, which supplemented wild food. That pattern may have been widespread in earlier times. But varia-tions would be expected—more agriculture or none at all—in relation to ecology, availability of stone (or steel) axes, and local danger of raiders seeking captives.

Their skill on trek notwithstanding, the Yanomami's greater reli-ance on hunting and gathering implies subsistence problems. Generally, hunting and gathering is a difficult way to keep alive in the Amazonian forest (Ferguson 1989c:256; and see Headland 1987). There have been impressionistic indications that the highlands inhabited by Yanomami are relatively poor in both game and gatherable resources (Colchester 1984:294; Vinci 1959:202, 205). Chagnon (1992a:83), after his recent research at higher elevations, confirms this point.

Zent's (1992) detailed study of Piaroa subsistence in another Guiana highland area shows that there may be an inverse relationship between the intensive gardening made possible by steel tools and population pressure on game. Although an extended stay by a sizable group at one garden will diminish local game supplies, a pattern of frequent movement of garden sites may actually augment the number of animals in an area because many hunted species feed on new and old gardens. (Chagnon [1992a:82] estimates that one cluster of Yanomami created more than five hundred gardens over the past hundred years.) And without this reliance on cultivated foods, game animals are required to supply not just protein and fat but also calories, substantially increasing the number of kills needed to maintain adequate nutrition. All things considered, if Yanomami relied more on hunting and gathering in the past, they probably were also more vulnerable to subsistence problems.

Elsewhere (Ferguson 1989c:257) I argue that some ecologically marginal areas in Amazonia have acted as "population sinks"—areas in which population tends to decrease over time—and that the ancestral Yanomami homeland in the Parima highlands is one possible illustration of such a sink. This possibility now seems even more probable to me. My argument then was that during their centuries in the Parima, the Yanomami clearly had not grown at anything like their rate in recent decades, a rate that despite wars and epidemics led to a doubling or more of population over the last century (prior to the most recent decimations). Indeed, overall Yanomami population—as estimated from ethnographic reconstructions of village histories and historical references to geographical expansion—seems to have begun fairly explosive growth only in the later nineteenth century (Albert 1989:637; Colchester 1984: 293; Colchester and Semba 1985:29; Lizot 1977:500; Neel and Weiss 1975 [cited in Harris 1977:49]; Smole 1976:49).

At that time, some Yanomami began to receive more steel tools, although far fewer than their acquisitions in this century. Harris (1977: 50–51) proposed that this development was followed by expansion of gardens, providing the subsistence basis for population growth. This view has been supported by Albert (1989:637) and Colchester (1984: 292–93; cf. Lizot 1988:497) and is consistent with the position developed here.[8] Furthermore, the acquisition of steel may have had an additional impact on one of the most noted aspects of Yanomami growth, their expansion out of the highlands towards the lower rivers. The Parima region has a pronounced dry season (Huber et al. 1984:109), which facilitates burning. Lowland areas such as the upper Orinoco are wetter, and Barker (1953:444) observes that because of the rains (which impede burning), possession of steel was essential for garden construction.

This discussion of Yanomami subsistence practices leads to two conclusions. First, recently observed Yanomami subsistence practices cannot be taken to represent the Yanomami way of life prior to the acquisition of steel, much less prior to the arrival of Europeans. Second, the acquisition of steel tools, with their dramatic increase in efficiency, did not merely mean that life would be easier for the Yanomami. Having been confined to inaccessible highlands and largely cut off from indigenous trade networks by the regional devastation of the seventeenth and eighteenth centuries, Yanomami faced a difficult and uncertain struggle for survival. The acquisition of steel made possible a fundamental shift in subsistence orientation: a greatly increased reliance on agriculture that, in turn, enabled Yanomami population to increase and expand. Thus we can better understand why historically known Yanomami have gone to such lengths to secure supplies of the precious blades.

One final question about the life of ancestral Yanomami: Did they wage war during their times of greatest isolation from the outside world? I find it impossible to answer that question with any certainty. Most of the earliest historical references to Yanomami characterize them as warlike. But those and later reports that mention war between Yanomami communities in the highlands are uniformly associated with periods of expanded Western contact in the area, periods in which raiders or steel tools or both were entering the uplands. Clearly Yanomami war practices have a substantial cultural uniformity that suggests deep roots. But I know of no way to disentangle those roots from the Yanomami's long history of intermittent but critical interactions with the Western world. Moreover, the fact that pre-steel Yanomami subsistence can only be inferred in its very broadest features leaves open any question of possible resource competition among Yanomami during that time.

My own hunch is that before the coming of steel tools, war was limited or even nonexistent between Yanomami communities. This hunch is based on two considerations. First, historically known Yanomami wars are associated with specific circumstances related to Western contact. In the absence of those circumstances, peace prevails. Second, throughout Amazonia, when confronted with hostilities that are building towards open violence, the typical response of people who are not anchored in one place is to avoid violence by moving away (Ferguson 1989b:195–97). A more mobile ancestral Yanomami population would seemingly have been freer to exercise this option than are their descendants. To be sure, my position is nothing more than an educated guess. But it must be kept in mind that the contrary assumption—that isolated ancestral Yanomami did frequently practice war among themselves—is also a guess, without any clear evidence to support it.

5

Early Encounters

The previous chapter contained several references to the impact of slave raiding on Yanomami society. This chapter provides evidence for the extent and intensity of captive taking and other ramifications of the European presence during different periods of colonial expansion, up to a point of maximum European retraction around 1820. Although European activity occurred all around the Yanomami's highland homes, there are only infrequent references to the Yanomami themselves. These scattered reports indicate that Yanomami were at least sometimes directly involved in the broader colonial processes, and they definitely were hemmed in by the danger of slave raids. This chapter also provides a historical baseline for all the regional historical reconstructions to follow.

The First Slave Raids

The areas surrounding the Parima region were spared the most pernicious aspects of Western contact for more than a century after Columbus. Both on the Amazon River and in the Guianas, the Europeans were stalled near the coasts, held back by imperial rivalries, indigenous resistance, and assorted difficult conditions (Hemming 1978; Whitehead 1988a). River colonization expanded sooner along the Amazon than the Orinoco, in the early seventeenth century. Greater European settlement on the lower Amazon was accompanied by an open season on slaving up the large rivers, starting in the 1620s. Slaving increased after 1631, when the region was secured against Portugal's European rivals (Hemming 1978:219, 228). Official punitive slave-taking missions, "rescue" troops who "ransomed" slaves captured by friendly Native Americans, and private slaving parties were all operating along the Río Negro and Río Branco from the 1630s, if not earlier (Hemming 1978:234; Migliazza 1972:359; Wright 1981:121).

To appreciate the devastating impact of slave raiding, one must think beyond the number of people captured. On the basis of extensive ethnohistorical research in the Guianas, Whitehead (1988a:30) estimates that raiders would kill two people for every one they captured. Raiding for slaves could also be expected to polarize local politics, setting off retaliatory attacks and other fighting that would produce still more casualties. Even indirect European contact through raiders (and traders) could cause epidemics, although these seem to become more severe after the establishment of missions or other settlements close to indigenous people. Taken all together, these factors would lead to a breakdown of society—a breakdown that would itself foster more violence. For those who felt the full brunt of the European quest for captive labor, the result was nothing short of genocide.

Thus, by 1650, the huge native settlements seen by the first explorers on the Amazon were already empty (Hemming 1978:322). In 1655, political concessions opened the way for Jesuit missions—a very mixed blessing for Native Americans. The Jesuits opposed the private and government slave expeditions but actively carried out their own raids for "converts," who usually died after no more than a few years at the missions (Golob 1982). In 1657, ransom expeditions brought six hundred captives down from the Río Negro, and in 1658, seven hundred (Hemming 1978:327). The military and the missions (Franciscans and Carmelites after the expulsion of the Jesuits) kept up pressure through the remainder of the century, with missionary control reinforced by new law in 1688 (Boxer 1969:271–92; MacLachlan 1973; Migliazza 1972:359; Pérez 1988:429), although there may have been some frontier retraction during Brazil's severe economic depression in the later seventeenth century (Furtado 1971:32).

On the Orinoco, colonizing efforts remained confined to its lower reaches for a longer time (see Whitehead 1988a). The Spanish did not reach the upper Orinoco until the middle of the eighteenth century. Long before that, however, Europeans on the Guiana coast were buying slaves from native raiders who operated up various rivers leading south (Whitehead 1988a:183). In 1639, the Spanish entered into an agreement for joint slaving raids with Caura River Caribs (Whitehead 1990a:364), which may have put them within striking distance of northern Yanomami communities. Carib trading expeditions in the later seventeenth century, which also captured slaves, took Caribs into and around the Parima highlands (Whitehead 1988a:10).

Very little is known about this first shock wave of European contact to reach the Parima area from two directions. But lack of information does not mean lack of effect. It is possible that ancestral Yanomami were under attack and began to retract farther into the mountains at this time.

The Expansion of Portuguese Slaving

The 1720s saw an intensification of the century-old pattern of slave raiding all around the Yanomami. At the same time, Native American warfare from the Río Negro to the Caribbean became more deeply enmeshed in a complicated imperial rivalry involving Portugal, Spain, Holland, England, and the machinations of rival missionary orders. Each European power had its native allies and used them to further its geopolitical aims (Humboldt 1889:333–34; Whitehead 1988a, 1990a; Wright 1981:132).

For several decades, the Manoa (or Manao), an advanced polity at the center of regional trade networks, had been a major force in the slave trade along the Negro and the Branco. "The Manao controlled virtually all slave traffic from the 1690s through the 1720s and traded for slaves as far afield as the upper Río Negro and upper Orinoco" (Wright 1981: 123). In the early eighteenth century, the price paid for captives by the Dutch in Surinam began to rise slowly, and this trend began to pull in the trade from greater distances. The Dutch bought large numbers of slaves from the Manoa; at some point one of the Manoa's major chiefs was even flying the Dutch flag from his canoe.

In 1722 and again in 1723, some Manoa traveled to Essequibo to trade. They were violently and effectively opposed on these trips by Caribs, who just at that time were becoming dominant as slave traders (Whitehead 1988a:167–68, 1988b:7). Undoubtedly, the growing connection between the Manoa and the Dutch was a factor in the Portuguese war on the Manoa around 1725. The Manoa were decisively defeated, leaving the Portuguese in control on the lower Río Negro and with hegemony over surviving chiefdoms farther up the rivers (Pérez 1988:429–30; Wright 1981:123).

Now in firmer control, and with the Brazilian economy out of its depression, the Portuguese stepped up raiding along the Negro, Branco, and tributary rivers. Slave expeditions reached a peak between about

1737 and 1755. One contemporary in a position to know estimated that some twenty thousand slaves were taken from around these rivers between 1740 and 1750 (Hemming 1978:30; Wright 1981:130–34). Even the distant Uraricoera was the scene of regular Portuguese slave expeditions (Ribeiro de Sampaio 1825:99).

By around 1725, the Portuguese were also traveling over the Casiquiare canal to the Siapa and upper Orinoco to obtain slaves and collect wild products such as puchary laurel and sarsaparilla. These expeditions increased after 1737 (Gumilla 1963:251; Pérez 1988:431; Wright 1981:124–29).

The impact of the slave trade on the peoples of the upper Orinoco area was terrible.[1] The Portuguese took captives themselves, and they induced Native Americans to go to war to obtain prisoners that the Portuguese would buy (Gilij 1965 II:280, 287). Humboldt (1889:427), in the area in 1800, described the Portuguese impact: "The desire of exchanging slaves (*poitos*) for hatchets, fish-hooks, and glass trinkets, induced the Indian tribes to make war upon one another." Of course, the same thing happened all over Amazonia (Ferguson 1990b:240).

Gilij's (1965 I:55) contemporary chronicle portrays the peoples of the upper Orinoco as having been "peaceful" prior to these developments (although one cannot discount the possibility of anti-Portuguese distortion in Gilij's account). The local Guaipunaves, who reportedly came down the Inirida River to establish a heavily fortified site at the important travel juncture of the Atabapo and Orinoco, are noted as a recently intrusive scourge (Gilij 1965 II:57, 188–89; Humboldt 1889:332). Gilij (1965 II:289) cites an estimate by Padre Román that the Portuguese and their Guaipunave allies took more than five thousand captives from the upper Orinoco prior to 1749 (Gilij 1965 II:289). This expanded quest for slaves came to an end around 1756, but during its twenty years or more of full intensity it had a decimating impact on local populations (Humboldt 1889:331–34, 353, 388–89; Wright 1981: 132–33). As Chernela (1993:17–29) discusses, the slave-trade–driven wars also transformed the cultural and political geography of the entire northwest Amazon.

The bloodbath did not spare the Yanomami. In 1759, a Spanish expedition under Apolinar Díez de la Fuente visited some Yecuana living on the Padamo.[2] He found them familiar with streams and passes in the highlands "inhabited by the Guaharibo [Yanomami] Indians" (Michelena y Rojas 1989:171–72). More telling is an excerpt from Díez's diary reproduced in Michelena y Rojas (1989:171; and see Ramos Pérez

1946:393,401): "By interlocution of an Uramanavi Indian, I asked chief Yoni if he had navigated by the Orinoco to its headwaters; he replied yes, and that he had gone to make war against the Guaharibos, who were very brave . . . and who will not be friends with any kind of Indian." Not surprising, under the circumstances. At this time, all the major rivers surrounding the Parima and Siapa highlands to the east, south, and west were avenues for slave expeditions feeding Portuguese demand. And to the north, there was the additional threat posed by the Caribs.

Caribs and Spaniards

In the early eighteenth century, Spanish expansion on the lower Orinoco had been stalled by, among others, the formidable Carib tribes, allies of the Dutch and major procurers of slaves (Whitehead 1988a:104–30). Carib hegemony in the Guiana slave trade increased in the 1720s, after their victory over the Caverre (or Cabre), their enemies on the middle Orinoco (Humboldt 1889:334), and their exclusion of Manoa traders after 1723. In the late 1720s, the Portuguese established an effective presence on the Río Branco, closing out British and Dutch exploration and exploitation of its upper reaches (Migliazza 1972:359–60). Their presence appears to have brought a westward shift in the catchment area for northward-moving slaves. Thus, the main Carib route in the 1730s involved going up the Caura or Paragua River, walking some four days over the mountains, and descending to the upper Orinoco via the Ventuari or Cunucunuma (Ramos Pérez 1946:84).

The Caribs were well armed with sabers and firearms. They traded weapons and other Western goods to Native Americans living near the upper Paragua and Ventuari for captives taken in local raiding (Gilij 1965 II:117; Ramos Pérez 1946:84). Either location was well within striking range of Yanomami in the Parima highlands. Whitehead (1988a: 186–87, 1990b:161–63) estimates the Caribs provided three hundred to four hundred slaves annually to the Dutch around mid-century, and his estimate does not count captives still being taken by the Spanish and their indigenous allies.[3] So the area around the Yanomami was no less sanguinary to the north and northwest than it was in other directions.

All the major rivers that surround and lead into the Yanomami's highlands were channels of violence aimed at procuring captives to trade to Europeans. How far into their territory this raiding went cannot be ascertained. Nor can it be said with empirical certainty that these raids caused Yanomami to retreat farther into the highlands or that they had previously lived in lower lands closer to the main rivers. But there are reasonable grounds to give credence to the Sanema tale that long ago they lived down by a great river and had been chased into the highlands by other people (Colchester 1981b:67–68). My guess is that this event probably occurred sometime before the mid-eighteenth century.

By the 1740s, Spanish strength was on the rise. After decades of neglect, the Crown after the Bourbon Reorganization was actively and capably promoting expansion. The Dutch became less troublesome for Spain as they turned their attention away from commerce with the Indians to sugar production using African slaves as field hands (Whitehead 1988a:105–107, 1990b:159). With less active Dutch support, the Caribs were less able to resist the Spanish, who pressed forward with what Whitehead (1988a) calls "the conquest of Caribana."

After reports of Portuguese *tropas de rescate* (rescue troops) operating on the upper Orinoco had reached the Spanish, Padre Román went to investigate in 1744, thus becoming the first representative of Spanish dominion to reach the upper Orinoco. The Jesuit established friendly contact with the chief of the Guaipunave at Atabapo, and while there he encountered one of the Portuguese troops (Gilij 1965 I:54–55; Ramos Pérez 1946:15, 25; Ribeiro de Sampaio 1825:90–91). Except for this visit, however, the limit of Spanish extension would remain for a while at a mission near the Atures rapids in the middle Orinoco (Ramos Pérez 1946:293).[4]

In 1750, Spain and Portugal signed the Treaty of Limits to establish a border between their colonies. Relations in Iberia were relatively cordial at this moment, and the treaty would allow both states to deal more effectively with the Dutch. Moreover, the Portuguese demand for Indian slaves had been supplanted by a growing reliance on Africans. This shift culminated in 1755, when reforms by the Marquis de Pombal, prime minister of Portugal, officially abolished Native American slavery —although, as will be shown, forcible capture of indigenous people in Brazil would continue off and on through most of the nineteenth century (Hemming 1978:475–82, 1987:30; Wright 1981:134–40).

The Solano Expedition and the Upper Orinoco

The Treaty of Limits was put into effect when José Solano commanded an expedition to the upper Orinoco in 1756. He established a major settlement, San Fernando de Atabapo, near the Guaipunave, after securing their friendship with cutting tools and other gifts. The Solano expedition remained active in the area until 1761, when a new treaty voided the old agreement. During his time there, Solano "reduced" the local natives into 11 new settlements (Ramos Pérez 1946; Tavera-Acosta 1927:202–203). The Solano expedition provides us with our first window into the upper Orinoco, and what life there had become.

Although the Spanish would continue to buy the occasional war captive they encountered (Gilij 1965 II:289), the purpose of the Solano expedition was not to take slaves. Its aim was to establish a firm regional presence by negotiating a local peace and securing the allegiance of native peoples through gifts of Western goods and the promise of protection against outside raiders (Ramos Pérez 1946:295–98, 362). Indeed, the area could scarcely support much more slaving. Once powerful groups such as the Caverre and the Guaipunave were greatly reduced in number. Many other peoples throughout the area were down to a couple of hundred souls, or fewer, or none at all. War, a variety of introduced diseases (including one report of smallpox on the Meta River in 1744 [Tavera-Acosta 1927:26]), and flight to the mountains had left this once populous region largely empty, particularly along the rivers (Gilij 1965 I:133–34, 1965 II:68–76, 279).

Carib penetration close to the Orinoco seems to have been reduced or eliminated by the establishment of Spanish posts at the junctures of major waterways, although apparently Carib raiding continued in the upper Ventuari, nearer to the Yanomami. Solano feared attack not only by the Caribs but also by allied forces of Manoa and Manitivitano, friends of the Portuguese who even had their own artillery pieces (Ramos Pérez 1946:312). That threat is particularly interesting. Although the theoretical model developed in chapters 2 and 3 was developed with specific reference to the Yanomami, events involving the Guaipunave, Manitivitano, and Manoa after the establishment of San Fernando de Atabapo also conform generally to the model's expectations.

As the Spanish were developing their settlement, the Guaipunave chief, Crucero, told Solano that he feared the southern groups would attack. By stressing this danger (and that of the Caribs), Crucero convinced Solano to concentrate troops and artillery at his settlement. At the same time, and without Solano's knowledge, Crucero sent emissaries to both groups, which somehow temporarily ended the threat of their attack (Ramos Pérez 1946:313). Shortly thereafter, both southern groups sent emissaries directly to Solano, asking for permission "to be able to live under the shelter of the Spanish crown." Now described as "friends and relatives" of Crucero's, they were seeking to settle alongside him (Ramos Pérez 1946:313).

In May of 1758, word reached San Fernando that 60 to 70 Manitivitano, armed with guns, would soon arrive. Solano let them know that they would have to submit to the authority of his client, Crucero. As the Manitivitano canoes approached, the Guaipunave took up positions on the walls of the fort and along the beach. A melee ensued that left 14 dead and some 80 wounded; it was ended only by cannon volleys from the fort. Crucero insisted the Manitivitano leave, and the Spanish went along by directing them to establish a settlement at the mouth of the Ventuari (Ramos Pérez 1946:315–16).

Subsequently, Crucero secretly sent out word that others should not attempt to settle near San Fernando, and that they were all his "slaves" (Ramos Pérez 1946:319). But in 1759, the powerful Manoa, being pushed from the Negro, made the attempt anyway. Another fight broke out, which Solano was certain had been provoked by Crucero in order "to remain in preferred position." The Manoa had to accept settlement alongside the Manitivitano at the Ventuari (Ramos Pérez 1946:361–62). Thus, the Guaipunave faced violent challenges to their position surrounding the main source of highly valued "gifts," and they won in large part by virtue of the political and military support of resident Westerners.

San Fernando de Atabapo was far from the homelands of the Yanomami. By dugout canoe, it was about two weeks to the Padamo and Ocamo, which led up into Yanomami homelands, and another week or so to the Raudal de Guajaribos (travel times based on Michelena y Rojas 1989:170; Ramos Pérez 1946:398; Tavera-Acosta 1927:265, 426). However, Solano sent at least three small expeditions to the upper river between 1758 and 1761, the first led by Francisco Bobadilla and the next two by Díez de la Fuente. The second expedition, led by Díez in 1759–60, founded a small outpost at the mouth of the Casiquiare and scouted an additional site upriver below the imposing escarpment of Duida, optimistically believed to be a source of emeralds. In subsequent years, this sporadically inhabited site, La Esmeralda, was often the ultimate extension of Spanish settlement on the Orinoco.

Díez de la Fuente continued to ascend some distance up the Padamo, where he sojourned among the Yecuana ("Maquiritare"). He secured their goodwill with gifts of beads, knives, and liquor, which he found "worked better than all arguments" (Ramos Pérez 1946:392). It was

this stay that produced the report of the Yecuana having raided Yanomami near the sources of the Orinoco, quoted earlier. The Yecuana also
told him that cacao, the substance most sought by the Spanish at this
time, grew best in the area inhabited by Yanomami between the Padamo
and Orinoco. They further agreed to collect cacao for the Spanish. In
their discussions with Díez, the Yecuana displayed a collective decision
making process involving chiefs of several settlements, a form of tribal
political organization that will be seen operating in later events (Ramos
Pérez 1946:325, 389–92).

Díez de la Fuente then continued upriver in search of the sources of
the Orinoco, despite Yecuana warnings that he would be killed. He apparently got as far as the Raudal de Guajaribos, the first Spaniard to
have done so. From the Ocamo to the *raudal,* there were no signs of
habitation at all, nor any signs of trees cut by metal. On this passage,
his Yecuana guides were "dying of fear" of the Yanomami ("Guaribas")
who lived in nearby mountains (Ramos Pérez 1946:396–406).

A second expedition by Díez in 1761 found deserted villages and
other indications of recent local fighting somewhere around the Padamo,
the general area of his visit the year before. This time he was successful in his efforts to get local inhabitants to move to the new Casiquiare
settlement and to La Esmeralda, giving them more metal tools (Ramos
Pérez 1946:409–16).

After Solano on the Upper Orinoco

In 1761, changing Iberian politics following the death of Fernando VI
of Spain voided the Treaty of Limits, and Spanish men and resources
were recalled from the upper Orinoco. The local commander scrambled
to concentrate what little remained at a few critical sites, and most of
the new settlements were abandoned (Ramos Pérez 1946:419–20). The
Guaipunave, apparently disenchanted with their new friends, took this
opportunity to flee into the mountains, where they had to defend themselves against Yecuana raids (Codazzi 1940 II:24–25; Tavera-Acosta
1954:124). (The Yecuana appear to be the dominant indigenous power
on the upper Orinoco from this point on, extending their trading activities from the Spanish at Angostura on the middle Orinoco to the
Portuguese on the Negro and Branco rivers [Coppens 1971:33–35; Migliazza 1980:127].) The sudden Spanish retraction may have emboldened the Portuguese, who stepped up military activities on the Negro

and clashed with Spanish forces there in 1762–63 (Pérez 1988:433–34; Ribeiro de Sampaio 1825:93–94).

In 1764, Spanish activity began to pick up again (see Whitehead 1988a:128). That year Bobadilla led another expedition up the Orinoco, reaching Yecuana and Maku ("Mako") villages, apparently near the headwaters of the Ventuari. His Maku guide brought him to a mountain ridge, where they looked down on a savanna. This apparently puts Bobadilla in the Parima proper (Huber et al. 1984:124–26), the only European I can conclusively place there before the nineteenth century. His guide informed him that Maku lived down there, and they were being continuously raided by Caribs coming over from the Caura to take slaves (Michelena y Rojas 1989:177–78). This confirms that the Carib raids did reach into the Parima itself.

Five years later, a Spanish military expedition set out to end the Carib threat to Spanish territory, massing at La Esmeralda, moving up the Padamo and Cunucunuma rivers, and successfully establishing a military outpost at the juncture of the Erebato and the Caura (Whitehead 1988a:129). Thus 1770 can be taken as the end of Carib raiding in the area around the Yanomami. That does not mean, however, that all raiding ended in the northern Parima; the Caribs' role may have been taken over by the Yecuana—who were Carib speakers themselves (see Migliazza 1980). Gheerbrant (1954:254, 282), citing unspecified "contemporary chroniclers," states that Yecuana were bringing "hundreds and thousands" of captive Yanomami "children to work as slaves for the Dutch of Guiana in the seventeenth and eighteenth centuries." I could not substantiate this claim, but it does not seem out of the question. This trade, if indeed it existed, could have continued until 1810, by which date the British, now in control of former Dutch holdings, were no longer accepting Native American slaves (Whitehead 1990b:164–65).

In 1765, Manuel Centurión, commander of the Spanish expedition against the Caribs, became governor of the Guayana colony. His active leadership led to the founding of some eight towns and about forty smaller native settlements throughout the upper Orinoco–Casiquiare–Negro region. In the same year, San Fernando de Atabapo was refounded with natives from eight nations, along with some fifty or sixty Portuguese deserters. Centurión planned to develop an overland route to the area, and toward that end he established nineteen blockhouses stretching from La Esmeralda to the Caura, which joined the Orinoco below its middle rapids (Pérez 1988:432–33; Tavera-Acosta 1927:362–63, 406–407; Whitehead 1988a:129).

At the time the Spanish treaty expedition was recalled, jurisdiction over native peoples in the area had been given to the Capuchin order (Codazzi 1940 II:78; and see Humboldt 1889:435–36; Whitehead 1988a:129), but the first three missionaries did not arrive until 1765 (Tavera-Acosta 1954:134). The Capuchins quickly found themselves in conflict with Centurión's ambitious plans. Their lobbying at court succeeded in having him removed in 1777 (Tavera-Acosta 1954: 160–62; Whitehead 1988a:129). The year before, a coordinated attack by Yecuana destroyed all nineteen of Centurión's blockhouses in one night (Tavera-Acosta 1927:407). Thus began half a century of Spanish retraction from the upper Orinoco, during which time only three new settlements were founded by the missionaries.

It is clear that Spanish activity in the upper Orinoco was much greater during the period from 1764 to 1776 than it had been under Solano. Detailed information for this time remains limited, but it seems reasonable to expect that the greatly expanded Spanish presence would result in increased interaction with the Yanomami, and there are a few reports that support this inference.

One missionary, José Antonio de Jerez, arrived at La Esmeralda in 1767. He found that the soldiers stationed there had been exploring the surrounding areas, inviting the natives to move to the new settlements. The soldiers estimated that there were some three thousand to four thousand "Guajaribos and Guatapayanes" (the latter not Yanomami) in the area, but "these two tribes had not agreed [to move] because of 'the distance from their dwellings'" (quoted in Cocco 1972:45). De Jerez next went up the Orinoco accompanied by Bobadilla. He encountered stands of cacao "with whose fruit the Guajariba nation maintains itself" (Cocco 1972:45).[5] De Jerez proposed founding a mission to settle and establish commerce with the Yanomami, but there is no indication that this proposal went any further (Cocco 1972:44–45).

Another report concerns a deadly clash between Bobadilla and some Yanomami. There is some controversy over this report, but it appears not to pertain to Bobadilla's expedition of 1764. In my estimate, it concerns an otherwise unknown expedition, sometime between 1764 and 1776. The clash is related by Humboldt, who visited La Esmeralda in 1800. Apparently the story was based on local knowledge some quarter-century after the fact.[6]

According to Humboldt (1889:461), Bobadilla had heard that fugitive African slaves from Dutch territory had entered the area and were living among the natives. African slaves were of such value that Bobadilla mounted an unauthorized military expedition into the far upper Orinoco to try to recapture them. Somewhere below the Raudal de Guajaribos, his camp was entered by "Guaharibos and Guaycas, two warlike tribes, celebrated for the virulence of the curare with which their arrows are empoisoned." The Yanomami "provoked the whites, whom they believed to be without defence. Several of the latter were dangerously wounded, and Bovadilla found himself forced to give the signal for battle. A fearful carnage ensued among the natives."

It is impossible to guess what actually transpired on the basis of this information. The Yanomami action may have been an attempt to bar passage into their lands or to plunder the possessions of the Spanish; or the "battle" could have been an attempt by Bobadilla to obtain Yanomami captives. At any rate, Humboldt (1889:467) notes that because of this encounter, the Yanomami were "more distrustful, and more averse to the inhabitants of the missions." But as we will see, Humboldt's own account shows that their distrust did not prevent the Yanomami from coming out to trade.

Another relevant report is provided by Caulin (1841:74), a source not without its own problems. (His account was written in 1759 and amended for publication in 1779, so the dating of information is uncertain.) Caulin mentions a river that flows into the Mavaca, "in whose headwaters live the nation of the Guariba Indians, white of color like the Spanish."[7] This reported location, one of those indicating long residence by Yanomami in the Siapa highlands, gains significance from the fact that it was known as an area particularly rich in cacao. A map published in 1778 shows "Guahibas blancos" in this area, just beneath the larger label "Pais de los Cacaguayes," which Cocco (1972:36) says refers to "the many plants of wild cacao which there abounded."

Cacao was the primary interest of the Spanish at this time, their "Dorado vegetal" (Ramos Pérez 1946:67–75). The Casiquiare region, gateway to the Siapa drainage, was in 1779 inhabited by almost six hundred "reduced" natives, busily engaged in commercial activities (Pérez 1988:433). Cacao was one of the main concerns of the missionaries there (Wright 1981:165). Cacao, as already noted, was and is a major food for mobile Yanomami. It seems probable that their common interest in cacao would have brought the missionized natives, and Centurión's agents a few years earlier, into active contact with Yanomami.

Administration of the upper Orinoco and upper Negro missions passed from the Capuchins to the Franciscans in the mid-1780s (Wright 1981:164). The rule of the missions has been described (in a hostile source) as lethargic, interested only in mission maintenance, and responsible for letting the region backslide from the advances of previous years (Tavera-Acosta 1927:209, 216–21). But as Wright (1981:174) observes, periods of colonial "decadence" are often periods of indigenous revival, both in numbers and in sociocultural elaboration. And it is clear that the missions played an important role in the renewed development of local travel and trade.

The Casiquiare area was the scene of much activity around 1779. A canoe building operation was begun at Yavita, the Orinoco-side terminus of the portage connecting the Atabapo to the Negro (Wright 1981: 164–65). In 1795, the portage itself was improved (Humboldt 1889: 357). The missions also encouraged gathering of forest products, including resins, gums, oils, puchary laurel, and sarsaparilla. Natives from the Negro collected these items along the Orinoco, after passing over trails to the upper Mavaca River (Humboldt 1889:393–94). To the north, the Yecuana, after their destruction of Centurión's blockhouses, developed and reoriented their trade to connect with the Dutch (and later the British), apparently via Macushi middlemen. That action established a new channel for Western goods, including guns, into the region (Arvelo-Jiménez 1971:18; Cocco 1972:181; Coppens 1971:34, 1981:62).

At the time of Humboldt's visit in 1800, La Esmeralda was a settlement of some eighty people, many of them banished criminals, under the authority of one old officer. Its native residents spoke three languages, with Yecuana dominant. The outpost was a center of indigenous commerce. One Indian was engaged in commercial production of high grade curare, and others collected cane for the manufacture of blowguns (Humboldt 1889:432–35, 439–42, 453).

Humboldt's account (1889:460–63) provides clear confirmation that some Yanomami were involved in this regional commerce. As noted in chapter 4, they were the source of the precious Amazon stones, which they reportedly obtained from others farther to the east. Trading relations along the river seem quite routine. Residents of La Esmeralda were regularly traveling up the Orinoco to the Raudal de Guajaribos or beyond. They reported Guaicas living on a small stream above the Manaviche and Guaharibos on a larger stream, the Gehette (perhaps the Ikari, near present-day Platanal on the opposite bank), both well below the *raudal*. Local knowledge had these Yanomami previously living at the source of the Orinoco, thus suggesting that they had recently moved closer to the area of commerce. Moreover, Humboldt remarks quite matter-of-factly that he actually met both Guaicas and Guaharibos at La Esmeralda.

With all this trading going on, it is certain that limited quantities of metal cutting tools and other Western manufactures were being acquired by some Yanomami at this time. However, there is no hint in Humboldt's account of any warlike activity by Yanomami, other than the claim that they would not allow entry above the Raudal de Guajaribos—and even that claim is somewhat suspect.[8] Local peace is consistent with my theoretical model. Western colonial activity in the area had been relatively stagnant—that is, unchanging—for more than twenty years. The Western goods circulating in the area were carried by slowly elaborated indigenous trade networks, of which local Yanomami were part. Under these conditions, peace is expectable. It may be that some fighting was going on between Yanomami communities in the interior, away from direct sources of goods, but there is no information about that.

But not all Western contact with Yanomami was peaceful in this era. By the time of Humboldt's visit, the missionaries had established a practice of leading expeditions up the rivers into high country to capture natives to populate their settlements—a practice that continued until withdrawal of the missions during the Wars of Independence (Humboldt 1889:335, 346; and see Thomas 1982:21–22; Whitehead 1988a:107, 129).[9] One priest in the region in 1804 quite unapologetically confirms this practice and its targeting of Yanomami. Bueno (1965:145) presents some truly fantastic descriptions of Guajaribos—that they sleep in trees and subsist only on wild roots—but, as Cocco (1972:46) notes, that may be because he only met captive Yanomami children. According to Bueno, the Yanomami are "very timid and untamed [cimarrones]. To be able to catch them they have to be sleeping, because any other way they run far, being so quick and practiced in the forest. The most that is obtained are children, and these for their limited age and experience live in the towns."

Along with the danger posed by mission entradas, the Yanomami had to deal with other predators. The region was inhabited by many fugitive criminals who had been recruited as soldiers during the expansion, as well as the remnants of a wave of prospectors who came in a groundless diamond rush (Humboldt 1889:434). Furthermore, natives were still being ensnared in festering Spanish-Portuguese hostility around the Río Negro (Humboldt 1889:376). Above and beyond these dangers, it is virtually certain, although not specifically reported, that the continuing Western presence in the area was accompanied by epidemics of introduced diseases. In sum, while the upper Orinoco was no longer the pure hell of the 1750s, at the end of the century it was still a dangerous place. Humboldt (1889:291–335, 392) comments on the incredible stretches of river that held no sign of human life. About those few still living in the area, he writes (1889:361): "They mutually hate, because they mutually fear."

The great Wars of Independence from Spain broke out in 1810 and continued with savage ferocity for 15 years. What would become Venezuela suffered perhaps the worst destruction of all, compounded by a series of epidemics and a cataclysmic earthquake in 1812 that destroyed much of Caracas and other cities. Codazzi (1940 II:13) estimates that some quarter of a million people died in these years—approximately one-fourth of the Venezuelan population. The middle Orinoco region was the scene of some of the worst fighting (Tavera-Acosta 1927:182; 1954:189ff.).

The Wars of Independence collapsed the Venezuelan frontier, and the pro-Spanish mission priests who did not flee were expelled by the rebels (Whitehead 1988a:148–49; and see Rausch 1984:167–247; Thomas 1982:22). For this period of maximum European retraction, almost no information is available about the upper Orinoco. It was not completely abandoned, as a few of the main settlements from the previous era still show populations in 1822, albeit diminished: 285 people at San Fernando de Atabapo and 34 at La Esmeralda (Tavera-Acosta 1927:61). It seems possible that the region may even have received new creole residents—fugitives or deserters from the wars—but there is no information on the point. One significant report is that smallpox broke out in the Atabapo–Río Negro area in 1819 (Tavera-Acosta 1927:25–26). But there is no way to know about developments affecting the Yanomami until the renewal of colonizing efforts around 1830. Those developments will be described in later chapters.

Developments along the Negro and Branco

We left developments on the ríos Negro and Branco when we followed Portuguese raiders to the Orinoco in the middle seventeenth century. In the sources available to me, subsequent developments within Portuguese territory are described without the detail available for the Orinoco side, but the general picture seems similar to that described above.

The new source of captives on the Orinoco did not mean that the Portuguese lessened their attention to the Negro and Branco and their tributaries. Indeed, slaving there remained at fever intensity under local "barons" operating with the blessing of Jesuits (Wright 1981:125, 133). One contemporary estimated that twenty thousand slaves were taken from the upper Río Negro between 1740 and 1750, although many if not most of these came from the Uaupés region, outside the scope of this study (Wright 1981:130). "Until about 1750–5, the exploration and systematic depopulation of the Río Branco and upper Río Negro proceeded without interruption. Whole tribes which were prominent in the upper Río Negro region at the time of the first European penetration were gone by the 1760s" (Wright 1981:130–31).

By around 1750, the Portuguese government was interested in establishing greater administrative control over the area, concordant with its aim of delimiting its border with Spanish territory (Wright 1981: 132). Other, more global developments led in 1755 to Pombal's reform laws. These laws officially freed Native American slaves, at the same time taking the administration of indigenous communities away from missionaries and giving it to secular directors (see Hemming 1987:1ff.; MacLachlan 1973:209–22).

Efforts to populate, or, perhaps more accurately, stock these indigenous communities with peoples from the forests continued. At first they came in voluntarily, brought in by "the deterioration of the living circumstances of the Indians in question (due to war, disease, failure in supply of trade goods, etc.), the offer of a haven from whatever hardships were being experienced, together with a reliable source of trade goods, and the cooptation of chiefs as functionaries of the European labor system" (Wright 1981:140; and see Hemming 1987:53–58). The standard attraction procedure relied heavily on the lure of Western goods:

> Scouts were sent out in canoes manned by conscripted Indians, to find out where in the backlands there were Indians who could be persuaded to relocate. With the aid of an interpreter, the military officer would offer the village chief trade goods such as tobacco or fishhooks, in return for some spice. Thus would begin a friendly relationship. [Once official permission to settle was obtained, the] officer would continue the negotiations by offering other trade goods, in return for which the chief might agree to descend the river at a specified future date. (Wright 1981:140–41)

For a few decades in the Negro region, enticement would prevail over force as a method of acquiring indigenous laborers (Wright 1981:141).

Along the middle Río Negro, however, standard procedure was to be overshadowed by extraordinary events.

Portuguese efforts to establish control over this region during the Treaty of Limits period did not go as smoothly as did Spain's, although things started well enough. They established a large military base at Barcelos, near the Deminí, and in 1755, gift-giving Portuguese emissaries had friendly contacts along the middle Negro. But their effort to claim these native lands resulted in military expulsion by the Indians. In 1757, the year Solano was developing his base at San Fernando de Atabapo, the Portuguese garrison at Barcelos mutinied and fled to Peru. Later that year, the Manoa and other natives rebelled against the abuses of colonial administrators, looting and destroying several settlements as they moved downstream. The rebels were narrowly defeated by Portuguese reinforcements in September 1757. The draconian punishments that followed led to the natives' wholesale flight from the river (Hemming 1987: 25–26; Ribeiro de Sampaio 1825:103–104, 110–13).

By this time, the old rivalry between Spain and Portugal had reactivated in the Seven Years War (1756–63). Spanish agents, including Bobadilla, in 1759 used the Portuguese setbacks to cultivate friendship with chiefs along the Negro. (The Manoa, who were seeking to settle at San Fernando de Atabapo in 1759, were among those who had been attacked by Portuguese forces [Ramos Pérez 1946:361].) Spanish moves at this time gave them permanent control of the upper Río Negro, even though a Portuguese offensive in 1762 forced some rollback in their position. The next year, more natives fled Portuguese administration for Spanish territory. As on the Orinoco side, but slightly later, Portuguese expansion was halted (in 1763) after the annulment of the Treaty of Limits (Hemming 1987:26–27, 549; Ribeiro de Sampaio 1825:92–94).

This repeated depopulation and turn toward administrative neglect explains the condition of the river a decade later. Francisco Xavier Ribeiro de Sampaio's (1825:102–109) voyage up the Negro in 1774–75 visited several remaining settlements with mixed native populations, but in general found the river deserted and in a state of "decadence." That condition was no doubt aggravated in 1776 by a particularly bad sequence of epidemics along the middle Negro (Wright 1981:151).

While all this was happening, Yanomami were on the upper courses of rivers feeding into the middle Negro. According to Migliazza (1972: 6), "in 1755, 1774 and 1775 Noronha, Sampaio and Ferreira reported a total of thirty-three tribal names in which appears the denomination *Guahariba* for a group living up the Padauiri, Uaraçá (now Araçá), Uarira (now Marari) and Demení Rivers." (This is the southern range of the area I call the Siapa highlands.) Given the quest to induce natives to descend the rivers and the standard procedure for inducing them, it is likely that these Yanomami obtained steel tools and other goods at this time, especially around 1755.

But there is also evidence that the Yanomami suffered from the Portuguese's subsequent shift to punitive measures or from new diseases or both. Ribeiro de Sampaio, the only one of the sources noted by Migliazza that I could obtain, makes two significant comments. About the Araçá River, tributary of the Demini, he writes (1825:105) that "still in its headwaters exists the remains of the Guariba nation." About the upper Padauiri area, he observes (1825:109): "It was inhabited previously by the Orumanaos, A'nas, and Guaribas. Today however it is believed deserted." This report is the most solid evidence I have found that Yanomami in high country were pushed into even more remote areas by events of the middle eighteenth century.

I could not obtain information about the Río Branco area during the years of the Treaty of Limits. From Ribeiro de Sampaio's reference that about 1774 the Branco was still inhabited by many Carib speakers, armed with Dutch guns, it seems that the Portuguese had neglected this area even more. But this was the time when the Spanish were approaching the peak of their power and increasing their activity around the Paragua (Thomas 1982:20; Whitehead 1988a:129; and above). In 1774, Spaniards crossed from the Paragua to established settlements on the Uraricoera. This move prodded the Portuguese into action, and a large Portuguese force surprised and captured the Spanish in 1775 (Hemming 1987:30–31). Subsequently, the Portuguese moved most of the accessible native inhabitants of the entire upper Branco area to Fort São Joaquim, near the Branco, where they could support the Portuguese and be kept away from the Spanish (Wright 1981:148).

From Fort São Joaquim, expeditions were sent into the hills to "descend" the more remote inhabitants. One report has it that the Yanomami were directly contacted by these missions: "Strenuous efforts were made to persuade chiefs of the Yanomami (then known as Waika) to bring their people down from the forested hills of the Branco-Orinoco watershed. Although a few chiefs and family heads from [the Yanomami and another "tribe"] accepted the blandishments of the white men, most refused to move" (Hemming 1987:32). Hemming bases this description on an unpublished source not available to me, and he does not provide an exact location for it. There is a problem with misidentifying "Waika" in this particular area as being Yanomami, and thus it is possible that the source does not actually refer to Yanomami.[10] There is little reason to doubt, however, that extensive efforts by the Portuguese to contact and attract highland natives provided steel and other trade goods to Yanomami in the headwaters of the Branco tributaries at this time.

For a few years beginning in the later 1770s, Portuguese commerce in the Negro-Branco region increased substantially as settled natives were sent out to extract forest products (Wright 1981:169). In the mid-1780s, penetration of the highland forests increased in a renewed effort to fix and map the Spanish-Portuguese border. This increased European activity led to major new outbreaks of disease among indigenous people throughout the area, often provoking flight into the mountains by settled river populations. With the demand for native labor high, but the availability of natives reaching an all-time low, the Portuguese turned to more coercive measures of "descending" and holding the natives (Wright 1981:149–55).

Between 1780 and 1790, there were several Indian revolts along the Branco. The Portuguese dealt with the rebels lightly at first, with pardons. Reaction turned harsh by the end of the decade. Many natives, even those who had not rebelled, were compelled to relocate out of the region. At the same time, the Portuguese persisted in trying to bring in natives to provide material support for Fort São Joaquim, their bastion against European rivals, and in 1789 they founded cattle ranches along the Rio Branco (Hemming 1987:33–37; Migliazza 1972:362–63; Schomburgk 1841:180, 217). In 1787, Manoel da Gama Lobo de Almada ascended the Uraricoera to the Uraricaá. He did not encounter any Yanomami along the Uraricoera, which was populated by Maku, Guinea, and Porocoto (although he did identify one group [Oayca] on a tributary, which mistakenly has been interpreted as being Yanomami; see note 12).

But beyond their commitment to maintaining a forward presence on the upper Branco, the Portuguese regional presence, like the Spanish, was in decline. The colonialists survived on the basis of indigenous labor, but by the end of the 1780s, there were very few natives left to exploit. Local extractive industries and commerce went into collapse. The provincial capital was relocated down to Barra (Manaos) at the mouth of the Negro in 1790, and by 1795 much of the upper Río Negro was empty of people. The local colonial economic depression lasted into the early 1800s (Wright 1981:172–74). The Portuguese were not to suffer the political implosion of the Wars for Independence; nevertheless, colonial politics on their side of the border also were chaotic from 1808 to

1840 (Worcester 1973:54–83). Local historical information is virtually nonexistent until the late 1830s.

Aftermath

Looking back from the early nineteenth century to about 1620, two distinct periods may be discerned. From around 1620 to 1750, virtually unregulated slave raiding surrounded the Yanomami and at least sometimes reached into their territory. Although extremely little evidence is available about the Yanomami specifically, I believe it is reasonable to infer that this period saw the isolation of the ancestral Yanomami, that they were forced into more inaccessible terrain, and that they were cut off from former connections to regional networks. Virtually no metal tools would be entering Yanomami society at this time. This first period ended with a devastating crescendo of slaving and related warfare.

The second period, from 1750 to roughly 1820, began with efforts by both Spanish and Portuguese colonial governments to establish territorial administrative control. Captive taking continued, but with less intensity, and it was interspersed with times of more commercial interaction. At some times and places, some Yanomami were acquiring limited amounts of Western goods. This period ended with a stepped withdrawal of the European presence through the first decades of the nineteenth century. The respite allowed native populations throughout the region to begin to recuperate and thus barely to survive.

By the end of the eighteenth century, great stretches of the Branco, Negro, Orinoco, and tributary rivers were completely devoid of human life. Legalisms aside, genocide is the appropriate term for the effect of the first two centuries of Western contact. Along the waterways that encompass the Yanomami's highlands, a few small, scattered settlements of "civilized" natives from mixed backgrounds toiled under the uncharitable rule of soldiers, priests, or secular directors. In the highlands above the main rivers, behind protecting rapids, there were pockets of survivors—long-term residents or refugees from the lowlands—most numbering a couple of hundred or fewer. Several such groups will be noted in later discussions; I will briefly mention the main ones here (see Migliazza 1980).

The most populous of the Yanomami's surviving neighbors were the Yecuana. Active raiders and increasingly wide-ranging traders throughout the eighteenth century, the Yecuana persisted in large numbers for two reasons. First, most of their territory was in the mountains beyond impassible rapids, although some were settled along the lower rivers. Second, their political institutions (see Arvelo-Jiménez 1971, 1973), perhaps formed in the crucible of the tribal zone (Ferguson and Whitehead 1992a:12), enabled them to offer coordinated resistance to European enticements to descend, and to expel noxious soldiers. In 1800, the Yecuana dominated the area northwest of the Yanomami, along the Orinoco, Ventuari, Cunucunuma, and Padamo rivers, as well as the country north of the Parima, over the passes and into the Uraricoera drainage.

In the high land near the Ventuari-Uraricoera watershed, into the northern Parima, were the Maku. "Maku" is a term widely used in the northern Amazon; it is applied to an ethnically and linguistically diverse scattering of "backwoods" peoples by the more settled and "civilized" groups of the rivers (see Jackson 1983:148–63).[11] (Along the Río Negro during this century, the Yanomami were called Maku [Seitz 1963:75].) Down the Uraricoera, around a large island in its middle reaches, were the Marakana. Up the Branco's other tributaries were Sapara and Paushiana. Throughout the Negro-Casiquiare area were Bare and Baniwa. The Bare were once a numerous group inhabiting an extensive area (see Pérez 1988). Those who survived became thoroughly integrated into the creole economy. In the upper Mavaca were another still substantial "wild" people, the Mavaca.

In the Parima and nearby highlands, probably a few thousand Yanomami survived. They were not immune to the events going on around them. As we have seen, there are specific reports of some Yanomami being raided and participating in trade, and many other indications of direct or indirect contact with Europeans. But those who remained in the highlands—surely a great majority—were *relatively* insulated from the worst effects. The main travel routes bypassed their homelands, and rivers leading up to them were blocked by rapids and the Yanomami's own resistance. As argued in chapter 4, Yanomami isolated in the highlands would face stark challenges to subsistence and survival. Nevertheless, that relative isolation protected the Yanomami people and culture from extinction.

The survival of isolated peoples in the mountains is not unique to the area around the Yanomami. Across the Guianas, in the highlands that formed the natural division between European empires, a belt of peoples managed to survive while their riverine neighbors became extinct (Colson 1973; Dumont 1976; Henley 1982; Lapointe 1970; Overing Kaplan 1975; Rivière 1984; Thomas 1982; Yde 1965; Zent 1992). These peoples are generally reported to have been engaged in warfare during the time of European expansion, but when the Europeans returned later in the nineteenth century, they were at peace (Ferguson 1990b:242).

The critical difference between the Yanomami and these other, recently peaceful societies, in my estimate, is that the other peoples emerged from their retreat into a physical space criss-crossed by easy travel routes. As we will see in later chapters, the cross-Guiana trade that evolved during the time of European retraction was extremely active, connecting to sources of Western goods at diverse points and transporting them all over the region. We will also see that at a later date, many Yanomami would gain entry to this regional trade system in one way or another (although never again would they be reported to trade Amazon stones). But for the most part, the area where the Yanomami lived was a trade cul-de-sac. Geography protected them, but it also meant that they would lack a developed system for supplying themselves with steel tools and other Western items into the twentieth century. And that, of course, is what I argue to be the basis of their warfare.

6

The Sanema

This chapter is the first of three, each devoted to one of the major linguistic-geographic divisions of the Yanomami. Information for each division is patchy—mostly passing glimpses by early explorers, a few -*teri* (local group) histories reconstructed by ethnographers, and some general anthropological information only for the most recent times.[1] Yet all together, a great deal of information is available. The goal of chapters 6, 7, and 8 is threefold. First, I want to build on the findings of chapter 5 to show that the Yanomami have never been truly isolated and that their lives have been deeply affected by changing historical circumstances. Second, I want to demonstrate that major elements of known Yanomami political history, including alliances and long-distance migrations, clearly represent efforts to improve access to Western goods —a motivation that will thus be established as a paramount political consideration. Third, I want to show that the known incidence of Yanomami warfare conforms to the expectations of the theoretical model developed in chapters 2 and 3, applied to highly varied situations. The following three chapters also establish a broader, comparative context for the more fine-grained discussion of the Yanomamo in part III.

The Sanema language is the most divergent from other Yanomami speech, marking the only division of the Yanomami people that is clearly pre-Columbian.[2] The Sanema homeland in the earliest historical reports appears to be around the headwaters of the Ocamo and Matacuni (see Colchester 1981b:26).[3] They are frequently referred to with some variation of "Guaharibo" or "Shirishana," but both terms are applied to other Yanomami as well. Around 1970 their numbers were estimated at between 1,500 and 2,500; around 1985 they had grown to 3,260, living in about 100 villages (Cocco 1972:29; Colchester 1982:91, 1985b:7; Migliazza 1972:36). In recent years, some Sanema have lived in Brazil, along the Auaris River, but most have lived in Venezuela. Their present range extends from the headwaters of the Padamo and Matacuni rivers in the northern Parima highlands through the Ventuari basin and into that of the Erebato, even reaching the Caura River at the northernmost extent of the range (see map 3). Northern Sanema territory overlaps with that of the Yecuana.

The main thread running through Sanema history is their changing interaction with the Yecuana. The Sanema themselves were beyond direct contact with Europeans until the twentieth century (which also means that there are few historical reports specific to the Sanema until the early 1900s). But the Sanema were not distant from the Yecuana, and the Yecuana were thoroughly enmeshed in the colonial developments that picked up again after about 1820. For the past three-quarters of a century, repeated images of Sanema-Yecuana interaction have appeared in reports: sometimes they are at war; sometimes they are joined in an unequal trading alliance; often the two options alternate in time or are displayed at one time by neighboring groups. These relatively recent examples are discussed in this chapter, but there are hints in earlier material that comparable political options existed as far back as the second quarter of the nineteenth century. Through the Yecuana, the Sanema experienced indirectly the effects of intensifying Western colonialism.

"Civilization" Returns to the Upper Orinoco

Civilization did not return lightly to the upper Orinoco. Its first steps back are not known, but Tavera-Acosta, in his description of the abuses perpetrated against the natives, dates them from 1817. The royalist missionaries had been chased out during the Wars of Independence, and in 1821 control over Native American communities was officially given to secular directors (although the occasional Spanish priest would still pass through the land). The theory was that government-appointed directors would encourage the production of forest products in exchange for tools and clothing. In 1822, the Venezuelan side of the border was, at least, more "prosperous" than the Brazilian side. But corruption and collusion between local government officials and the directors suppressed economic growth and led to great abuses. Natives were ensnared in unpayable debts, parceled out by lots, compelled to work for months without any provision for their families, deprived of their own property, punished brutally, and paid off in liquor (Michelena y Rojas 1989:319–21, 346, 370; Tavera-Acosta 1927:72–73, 169–71, 225–26).

Government efforts to promote development of the stagnant regional economy picked up after the end of the fighting that followed Simón Bolívar's death, and 1832–41 was a time of some growth along the upper Orinoco. The exploited native laborers were extracting and processing more than two dozen products from the forests. Between 1836 and 1839, six new villages were founded (compared with only two from 1827 to 1832), including one started by a Frenchman as far upriver as the mouth of the Mavaca. Censused population in 1838 was roughly a quarter more than in 1822. But by 1841, the steam had gone out of this limited development, and the local elite was still firmly entrenched. An investigator sent by the national government in 1838 complained that in the entire upper Orinoco area, 2,000 *"racionales"* (settled natives) toiled to support "15 egoists"; and that perhaps 3,000 more who had fled into the hills could be brought back and employed if they were to receive decent treatment (Codazzi 1940 III:330–31; Michelena y Rojas 1989:319–21; Tavera-Acosta 1927:61).

This historical moment was also a time of war among indigenous people. Agustín Codazzi, whose inspection tour ending in 1838 provided the first ethnographic survey and population estimates for the upper Orinoco, identified three divisions of Yanomami: the "Quiriscanas" or "Ririshanas" (probably Sanema; see note 2), with a population of 500 in the Parima highlands between the headwaters of the Ocamo and the Orinoco; the "Guaharibos" near the headwaters of the Orinoco; and the "Guaica" who live above the Ocamo, Matacuni, and Manaviche rivers. The last two probably were both Yanomamo.

The Quiriscanas (Sanema) were said to be "ferocious" and "at war with neighboring tribes," but Codazzi does not elaborate. He gives more information, however, about the war of the Yecuana against the two Yanomamo divisions. In 1838, the populous Yecuana ("Maquiritare"), with 3,540 people united in one federation, began to raid the Guaharibo and some Guaica to capture slaves to sell to Dutch traders. Other Guaica were allied with the Yecuana against the Guaharibo (Codazzi 1940 II:20, 26, 44, 48; and see chapter 9). Compared with the Guaica and Guaharibo, the Sanema lived almost next door to the Yecuana. It seems very possible that their reputed ferocity was, in part, a reaction to the depredations of their slave-seeking neighbors.

Amidst this general violence is a report that is the best-known early instance of Yanomami aggression. In January 1839, the explorer Robert Schomburgk, having traveled from the Branco up the Uraricoera, attempted to enter the Parima highlands, the land of the "Kirishana," identified by Cocco (1972:28, 49) as Sanema near the headwaters of the Ocamo. His guides were Yecuana ("Maiongkong"). Schomburgk reported (1841:231):

> In the evening we arrived at the huts of the Maiongkongs, and found them in the greatest consternation, and about to fly from the place in consequence of the massacre of twenty of their tribe by the Kirishana, who inhabit the mountains between the Orinoco and Ocamo, and who had treacherously fallen upon them when on their way to visit them for the purposes of traffic. The same savages had immediately afterwards surprised a Maiongkong settlement only a day's journey from where we then were, and killed every person.

The Yecuana would take him no farther, and Schomburgk had to turn back with them.

This attack by the Sanema has been cited as the first expansionist move of Yanomami against Yecuana (Arvelo-Jiménez 1971:19; Cocco 1972:50). What has not been commented upon is the remarkable coincidence in the event—that it happened at precisely the moment when a European arrived on the scene. From the perspective of the model, the two events are tightly related. Schomburgk, moving slowly upriver into the high country, had been paying the Yecuana with steel and other goods. Probably some tools had preceded him into the Yecuana village whose men just then went to the Yanomami "for the purposes of traffic." That is a very significant phrase. However ferocious some Sanema may have been, the report is that the Yecuana went to them to trade, suggesting already the ambivalent relations between the two so common a century later. My hunch is that the Yanomami attacked because at a time when steel was extremely scarce, the Yecuana had acquired an unprecedented quantity of it. The deadly raid on the Yecuana village would probably have produced substantial booty in Western goods.

In the 1840s and 1850s, creole commerce on the upper Orinoco was controlled by a succession of merchants and officials replaced every couple of years by revolt, riot, assassination, or prosecution. The years 1843–49 saw another burst of growth, with 10 new villages founded— the last new ones until 1873. The 1850s saw a short-lived reform administration accompanied by major public disorders and eventual return to the status quo ante. The continuing brutal exploitation still caused native peoples to flee into the forest and mountains. But the internecine indigenous warfare of 1838–39 did not continue. In 1845, all native peoples of the area were reported to be peaceful (Michelena y Rojas 1989:322–29; Tavera-Acosta 1927:69, 77, 173, 183, 203–204). Perhaps some colonial administrative change had cut off the Yecuana from Dutch slave buyers. At any rate, their attacks of 1838 were, apparently, their last major slave raids against the Yanomami, although more limited captive taking would continue in some areas.

It appears, although the matter is far from clear, that the Yecuana were expanding their trading activities from about 1840 onwards.[4] In the 1850s, highland Yecuana were still insulated from the worst abuses along the river, and this independence enabled them to pursue long-distance trade. In the middle of the decade, small Yecuana communities near the mouth of the Ventuari (Santa Bárbara) and at the first rapids on the Cunucunuma (San Ramón) acted as middlemen for other Yecuana up those rivers and the Padamo, trading out manioc, baskets, birds, resins, oils, and skins (Michelena y Rojas 1989:331–33).

In 1854, the botanist Richard Spruce (1908:407–21) found the Yecuana of La Esmeralda and the Cunucunuma participating in a trading network extending southward over the Mavaca and other routes to the Negro and the Portuguese merchants there; and to the northeast via the Macushi and other routes to the Europeans in the Guianas. Along with this indigenous trade, the Yecuana were producing dugout canoes and a variety of forest products to "trade with the whites," including rubber, the production of which had "only lately begun" (Spruce 1908:411). This beginning was a portentous one. But for the moment, while the Yecuana traded both directly and indirectly with Europeans, they were still poor in Western products. The stock of trade goods described by Spruce (1908:412) consists entirely of indigenous manufactures. Along the Cunucunuma, display of one knife was a sign of wealth (Spruce 1908:414).

In Spruce's discussion of Yecuana trade over the mountains to the Uraricoera and Branco, there is no indication of any danger posed by Sanema, even though some of the Yecuana men he spoke to had known or accompanied Schomburgk on his expedition. Nor is there any other indication of war in the area at this time. Perhaps the Yecuana wars of 1838–39 had driven the Sanema and other Yanomami farther into the mountains. Perhaps some Sanema had established a peaceful niche at the fringe of the regional trade network. But most significant, in terms of my theoretical model, the paucity of Western goods possessed by Yecuana at this time gave the Yanomami little incentive to attack.[5]

The Rubber Boom

The Yecuana's supply of Western manufactures was about to improve. Spruce's (1908:411, 507–508) visit came just after the initiation of rubber tapping in the region. On the middle Orinoco, rubber tapping became a major occupation for northern Yecuana in the 1850s, and they began relocating downstream to establish more direct contact with Westerners (Arvelo-Jiménez 1971:19). On the upper Orinoco, large-scale rubber harvesting began around 1860, when another Frenchman began commercial production at La Esmeralda and San Fernando de Atabapo (Chaffanjon 1986:226; Tavera-Acosta 1927:307).

The rubber boom was a fantastic and tragic epoch of Amazonian history, a time of incredible fortunes and equal depravity (Bunker 1988: 65–75; Hemming 1987:271–362; Taussig 1987). The production of Amazonian rubber increased gradually during the 1840s and was stimulated by a peak in rubber prices in 1853–54. The boom era is often dated as 1870–1920, but its decline began in 1913 with new competition from Asian rubber plantations. During the boom years, the soaring price of rubber sent Westerners and their indigenous agents deep into the forest in search of rubber trees. Unfortunately for scholars, rubber tappers rarely left any accounts of their activities and interactions with Native Americans. Thus, at least in the Yanomami case, there is a great disparity between the known intensity of the Western presence and the little we know about it.

On the upper Orinoco, the rubber boom inflated slowly. The decade after 1862 was a period of intense civil disturbances (Tavera-Acosta 1927:173), perhaps fed by the new money to be made. The middle 1870s were an interlude of reform, government-promoted development, and somewhat more generous treatment for Native Americans. Censused population grew and seven new settlements were founded, the first since 1849 (Tavera-Acosta 1927:65–66, 204–205; Tejera 1877 II:411–12). From an upper Orinoco perspective, 1875–80 marks the beginning of the rubber boom (Cocco 1972:74; U.S. Army Corps of Engineers 1943: 11), although the real peak of the local boom would be delayed until the first decade of the twentieth century.

Despite a renewal of civil disturbances in 1877, which would continue with regularity throughout the boom years, rubber production was now firmly established, especially along the Casiquiare (Chaffan-jon 1986:199).[6] But the three new *pueblos* founded in the early 1880s would be the last new settlements until after 1900 (Tavera-Acosta 1927: 205). The year 1883 began a new period of intensified monopolistic con-trol by local strongmen of all shipping along the upper Orinoco. The first monopoly, "L'affaire Fabiani," ruled until 1886, contributing to two overthrows of local government, four revolts, and assorted combats and pillages. This and later monopolies squeezed the life out of the cre-ole economy (Tavera-Acosta 1927:336).

The explorer Jean Chaffanjon arrived in the upper Orinoco in 1886, just after the fall of the first monopoly, and reported a dismal situa-tion. The Baniwa, until recently the most populous ethnic group along the river, had been so mistreated and exploited that they were fleeing to Brazil, and other natives were heading into the forests and moun-tains. Settlements were abandoned, and Westerners faced an increasing labor shortage. A Bare *comisario* whom Chaffanjon visited had already moved upriver to avoid the press gangs that came out of San Fernando, and he was thinking of going to Brazil. He complained of the tariffs im-posed by officials, the cheating by the merchants, the "fabulous price" they demanded for a hatchet or a machete, and their practice of creating unpayable debts (Chaffanjon 1986:190, 195, 204, 221–22, 230).

The Yecuana had become very active in the rubber trade in the 1860s, moving into closer contact with creoles during that decade (Coppens 1981:24). In 1886 Chaffanjon saw their scattered rubber camps between the Casiquiare and Cunucunuma. But the Yecuana may have learned a lesson by this point, for Chaffanjon also notes that the Yecuana of the Padamo wanted no direct contact with the local whites and traded with them only through intermediaries. The Padamo was at this time the cen-ter of Yecuana habitation, and from there they continued to send expe-ditions to trade with the British in Guiana. An indicator of the Yecuana's overall success in obtaining better access to Western manufactures is that by the time of Chaffanjon's visit they were well known for the num-ber and quality of their shotguns (Chaffanjon 1986:207–208, 226–30, 250, 258).

The recent increase in their stock of Western goods explains the strik-ing change in Yecuana relations with Yanomamo from the Manavichi River area. Around 1880, those Yanomamo raided the southernmost Yecuana communities near the Orinoco in order to obtain steel tools, driving the Yecuana northwards (Chaffanjon 1986:222). Although I suspect similar attacks may have been launched by Sanema, there is no information about them for this time. At any rate, there was a definite change in the tenor of Yecuana-Yanomami relations at this moment. The Yecuana, who terrorized the Yanomami of the far upper Orinoco in 1838, were now reportedly terrified to pass beyond the Ocamo (Chaffanjon 1986:222, 259–64). These events mark the beginning of a broad Yecuana retreat northward, although there is no indication of any raids immediately after those of 1880. Now wary, well armed, and operating farther down river, away from Yanomami lands, the Yecuana would have been much more difficult targets for plunder raiding.

Despite the economic potential of rubber production, growth was stifled over the 1890s by two tightly controlling monopolies (the later one representing British interests), leading to the greatest period of public disturbances yet in 1898–1900. Another brief interlude of political reform in 1900–1902 finally initiated a dramatic expansion of local rubber production, despite a return to political chaos in 1903 (Tavera-Acosta 1927:176–79, 187, 229–30, 308, 336–38). Tax receipts on local trade increased more than tenfold by 1904. Goods imported to the region increased commensurately (Tavera-Acosta 1927:179), as did the population of San Fernando de Atabapo—from 200–300 before 1902, up to some 2,000 by 1908 (Gómez Picón 1978:118–19; Hitchcock 1948: 32; Tavera-Acosta 1927:56). A steamboat with a 20 to 40 ton capacity began to operate in the area (U.S. Army Corps of Engineers 1943:15). Koch-Grunberg (1979 III:378–79) passed along the Casiquiare early in 1913 and found it a center of European activity. He visited one magnate who lived in a great house stocked with fine French wine. But that was to be the last year of very high prices for Amazonian rubber, for prices began to fall in 1914 as a response to competition from Asian plantations (Knorr 1945:10–11).

The year 1913 also marked the beginning of the most violent period on the upper Orinoco since the time of the great slave raids. A seemingly typical merchants' revolt against a typically corrupt governor was led by one Tomás Funes. Funes, however, was unique. In his May revolt, he slaughtered the governor, his family, and others, killing a total of 65 people. Then he imported criminals as henchmen, who murdered anyone who tried to leave the area. Funes himself was killed in 1921 after a battle in San Fernando de Atabapo. During his nine years in power, he murdered between 400 and 800 creoles. His death, the very year rubber prices hit bottom, was followed by the creoles' wholesale abandonment of the upper Orinoco (Acebes 1954:210; Dickey 1932:172–79; Gómez Picón 1978:127; Grelier 1957:47–48; Hanson 1933:579–84; Tavera-

Acosta 1927:200). As Dickey (1932:170, 181) put it, San Fernando de Atabapo "died" in 1921.

Although the peak of the rubber boom brought unprecedented quantities of manufactured goods into the region, it cannot be said to have benefited the indigenous peoples. As native labor became more valuable than ever, each tapper producing something on the order of $100 worth of rubber annually at peak prices (Gómez Picón 1978:127; Tavera-Acosta 1927:88), increasing efforts were made to press Indians into service. Some 2,500 were put to work in the harvest of 1901–1902, up 500 from the year before (Tavera-Acosta 1927:307). With increased Western contact came increased disease. Malaria had become endemic, there were epidemics of pneumonia in 1901 and smallpox in 1903, and syphilis was spreading among the indigenous population. Their numbers were again in sharp decline, and many of their villages were already abandoned. The only main river area where a substantial, settled native population still lived in 1903 was the Casiquiare, the center of rubber production (Tavera-Acosta 1927:24–27, 33, 57–59, 66); and even it was depopulated by 1913 (Koch-Grunberg 1979 III:380). Then came Funes, by far the most brutal in the impressment of native peoples, even in remote areas. He imposed quotas for rubber, and when its price fell, he turned to intensive collection of egret feathers, then a fashion rage worth twice their weight in gold (Acebes 1954:211; Gómez Picón 1978: 133; Grelier 1957:48). "No one counted the number of Indians who had been put to death by him. There may have been several thousand" (Acebes 1954:210–11).

The Yecuana were among the major producers of rubber when Funes seized power (Tavera-Acosta 1903:13; 1927:31). They suffered terribly during his rule. As late as 1959, remote highland Yecuana still feared to let whites enter their villages, remembering Funes. One old man was the sole survivor of an upper Ventuari village that was wiped out on Funes's orders around 1916 (Coppens 1981:30). These decades of exposure to "civilization" severely disrupted and weakened the Yecuana.

> During Funes' incursions the Ye'cuana intensified their internal migrations and divided their villages once more into small groups. Some Ye'cuana were subdued by the invaders and chose to serve as guides into the hinterland of Ye'cuana territory. Others committed suicide before being deprived of their freedom. But the largest number of the population fled and sought refuge in the least accessible areas. (Arvelo-Jiménez 1973:16)

This disruption would make the Yecuana more vulnerable to new aggression by Yanomami. Their weakness was compounded, sometime early in this century, by an apparent interruption of their trade connections across the Guianas, which left them lacking in, and desperate for, shotguns (Colson 1973:9, 32).

The Yanomami themselves came through the rubber boom relatively intact. Their role in rubber production was limited, although there are indications of some contact with tappers. The Yanomami are not included in Tavera-Acosta's (1903:13) list of the peoples engaged in the work, and so presumably they fell into his category of those who "feel an insuperable terror toward these tasks." Their location still largely protected them from impressment, although some no doubt were reached by Funes's men or others.

Along with the terrible circumstances of those who labored in rubber, another factor probably impeded the Yanomami's voluntary participation in rubber tapping. Relatively mobile Yanomami rely heavily on the fruit of the peach palm (*pijiguao;* see Barandiaran 1967:43–47), a cultivated tree that matures in five or six years and then bears fruit for about twenty years (Lizot 1980:34).[7] Yanomami regularly trek to old gardens to collect *pijiguao*. Its peak season of harvest is January and February (Anduze 1960:203; Lizot 1980:34), which happens also to be the best time to tap rubber in the upper Orinoco (Tavera-Acosta 1927: 308). Becoming heavily involved in rubber tapping would have created a major subsistence problem for the Yanomami.

During the peak years of the rubber trade, the Yanomami began intensifying both peaceful and violent contact with the Yecuana across a broad front. For this moment we have direct reports about the Sanema. Koch-Grunberg's voyage up the Uraricoera in 1912 provides the first window into Sanema territory since 1839. Near where Schomburgk had been forced back by the Sanema raid, Koch-Grunberg (1979 I:250) found the Yecuana living "in mortal enmity with their savage neighbors" in the Parima, the "Schirischana." They told him of "struggles ancient and recent," including one fight about a year before in which they had lost "some men" to the arrows of the warriors of the Matacuni. Not all relations with Sanema, however, were violent:

> In the region of the sources of the Matacuni, they say there is one village of tame (*manso*) Schirischana and that they have settled across from the Yekuana, with whom they have friendly relations. They are also exposed to the savage attacks of their tribal

brothers. This report was later confirmed to me by different rubber collectors of the Orinoco and the Casiquiare, who in part knew the village of these "tame Guaharibo" by their own observation. (Koch-Grunberg 1979 I:250)

Koch-Grunberg's report tells us several things. At a time when the Yecuana were receiving probably the most Western goods ever and the Yanomami remained virtually isolated from direct contact with Westerners, some Sanema raided the Yecuana and others adopted a "tame" attitude toward them. The word "tame" clearly suggests the subservient relationship so frequently reported for the Sanema in coming years. That such "tame" Sanema, themselves coming to possess Western goods, are attacked by other, more remote Yanomami is another pattern that will be seen frequently. Koch-Grunberg's report also confirms that rubber tappers were operating at least up to the edge of the Sanema's home ground, suggesting contacts with Westerners as well as Yecuana.

Two additional reports dating from the Funes period come from Rice, a geographer who traveled around the Parima in the 1920s. After exploring the upper Orinoco area in early 1920, he wrote the following report (Rice 1921:333) that indicates the ambivalence in the relationship between Yanomami—apparently Sanema—and Yecuana ("Maquiritares").

The Maquiritares who inhabit the country around the headwaters of the Cunu-cunuma and Padamo are reputed to traffic with the Guaharibos, meeting them once a year or so, when the Maquiritares exchange their old, worn-out iron and steel instruments for hammock thread and small balls of baked clay with which they vary their usual not very extensive dietary. At the present time there is estrangement between the Padamo Maquiritares and the trafficking portion of the Guaharibos, due to marauding and murder of the former by the latter.

Rice's second report describes his travel on the Uraricoera in 1926. There he met some Maku, who occupied a "low place in the scale of Indian nations" (Rice 1928a:214). (The Maku were reported as industrious and allied with the Yecuana about 1903 [Tavera-Acosta 1927: 31].) The Indians related that they had been driven down to the Uraricoera from the Auaris River—the Uraricoera tributary that leads up to the overland trails—because of attacks by the "ferocious warlike Guaharibos" (probably Sanema), sometime after 1914. Rice's reports indicate a general intensification of Sanema pressure on their northern neighbors as the rubber boom faded and Funes came to rely on force alone to obtain native labor. This pressure would become even more intense in coming years, and it parallels developments involving the Ninam Yanomami discussed in the next chapter and the Yanomamo discussed in part III.

After the Fall of Rubber

The date often given for the end of the rubber boom is 1920, but its decline began before that. The price of Amazonian rubber began to fall precipitously in 1914 and went from $2.09 per pound in 1910 to less than $.20 per pound in 1921 (Knorr 1945:10–11). Plummeting prices combined with a scarcity of labor to produce, in the 1920s, a dramatic collapse of both Brazilian and Venezuelan regional economies. In 1927, the provincial capital was moved from San Fernando de Atabapo down the Orinoco to Puerto Ayacucho (Grelier 1957:92). From then on, the middle Orinoco came to replace the upper Orinoco as the main area of Venezuelan activity (Zent 1992).

Hanson (1933:578–92; and see Seitz 1963:30–31), touring the area in 1931–32, reported "radical changes" underway. Forest extraction industries were almost nonexistent, no credit could be had in an economy that functioned on credit, remaining creoles were leaving the area, and capital was already gone. Extremely few Western goods were being shipped in. In 1931, San Fernando de Atabapo was down to 20 creoles, many of them fugitive criminals, and 40 natives (and see Dickey 1932: 168). La Esmeralda consisted of one family, and some other settlements were entirely abandoned.

The collapse of the creole economy, however, was not quite total. As late as 1920, Rice (1921:328, 334) observed substantial rubber processing on the Casiquiare. Ten years later, Dickey (1932:188–94) found, amid a great emptiness along the Orinoco, a village of some eighty Yecuana still engaged in gathering *balata* (another rubberlike gum), as were two creoles (Hanson 1933:580). After the fall of Funes in 1921, a man named Chico González founded the village of Carmelitas some 20 miles up the Ventuari, among the Yecuana and along their main trade route. González developed a reputation for working well with Native Americans, and he and his son would dominate creole commerce above San Fernando for decades (Anduze 1973:322–31; Hitchcock 1948:35). Moreover, the Venezuelan government maintained an administrative eye on the area to prevent the rise of another Funes (Hanson 1933:578).

These exceptions notwithstanding, the Western presence in the upper Orinoco had dropped to its lowest point since the Wars of Independence. As Hanson (1933:588) saw it: "It is probable that the present regression of the region is the most complete in its history since the first advent of the Spanish." It is this brief period of retraction that has been mistaken by contemporary anthropologists as representing long-term isolation of the region. Thus another comment by Hanson (1933: 588) bears a certain irony: "an interesting spectacle is taking place . . . affording an opportunity for some ethnologist to record a brand-new primitive culture in the making."

As noted earlier, times of Western retraction are often times of indigenous revival. The fallen price of rubber meant that "forced labor is no longer a commodity," except for household servants (Dickey 1932: 131; Hanson 1933:584), and the frequency and intensity of epidemics undoubtedly decreased. Thus conditions were favorable for a growth in numbers and social elaboration among people such as the Yecuana. Yecuana trade came to have increasing importance for the upper Orinoco region during this time.

Hanson (1933:588) describes the anxiety caused by the cessation of imports into the area: "Steel knives and machetes are other essentials. The release from rubber slavery does not entirely compensate the Guainía River Indians for the increasing rarity of these goods. On every hand I hear laments—mainly from the women—to the effect that they were civilized people, not savages, and were worried about how they could possibly live now that the white man was withdrawing." Trade from Brazil had been a major source of these goods, and it seems to have been entirely severed (Dickey 1932:171–72; Hanson 1933:583).

Hanson (1933:588) continues to describe how the Yecuana stepped in to fill this void in the trade network, having reestablished their cross-Guiana trade connections: "Even the complete withdrawal of the white man from the region would still permit a certain amount of infiltration of his products by trading from Indian tribe to Indian tribe as shotguns from Georgetown, British Guiana, are being traded clear across unexplored Venezuelan Guiana today, only to emerge on the Ventuari River and be resold to the white inhabitants of San Fernando de Atabapo."

The Yecuana's increased trading appears to have developed soon after the fall of Funes. Rice (1928a:221), traveling on the upper Uraricoera in 1926, found Yecuana traders well stocked with steel, "heavy axes, machetes, and worn-out knives," a sharp contrast to the lack of steel observed by Spruce in 1854. Thus the Yecuana trade route over the mountains came to be a rich artery of steel and other Western goods—the highest concentration in the upper Orinoco.

It is the Yecuana's access to steel, I contend, that explains Yanomami raids at this time. The fighting that, as we saw above, was intensifying between 1910 and 1920 went on until 1940 (Arvelo-Jiménez 1973:15; Colchester 1981b: 26–27, 1985c:47).[8] The Yecuana, weakened by their experience during the rubber boom, were at first unable to resist these attacks: "In the beginning, according to oral tradition, the Ye'cuana fled to the North and Northeastern section of the Venezuelan Territorio Amazonas leaving behind their villages and their fields. . . . They abandoned the sedentary way of life which is linked to a solidly built village. Instead they traveled, and increasing their mobility tried to erase as much as possible the evidence of their presence in a given site" (Arvelo-Jiménez 1973:14–15).

Recent ethnographers inform us about the motives behind the Yanomami raids. The Yecuana had learned by long observation that "the invaders craved for the products of Ye'cuana fields, especially the manioc, and for the industrialized goods which the Ye'cuana obtained through barter with Creoles or Europeans" (Arvelo-Jiménez 1973:15).

From the Yanomami side, we get much the same picture. "The Sanema traded arrows, bows and cotton with the Yekuana for the modern goods but when they could not achieve their ends by peaceful means they turned to violence" (Colchester 1981b:27). And: "The Sanema also raided the Yekuana for women and trade goods causing them to flee their villages on the Ocamo and Matakuni. As the Yekuana withdrew, the Sanema followed in order to maintain trading and raiding contact with them since they were the Sanema's only source of industrial products" (Colchester 1985c:47).

Sanema military expansion came to a sharp halt around 1940. By this time the Yecuana had had almost two decades to recover from Funes's devastation. They launched what may have been coordinated attacks, decisively defeating their Yanomami enemies. A critical element in their victory was their possession of many shotguns (Arvelo-Jiménez 1973: 15; Colchester 1981b:27, 1985c:47). Gheerbrant (1954:157) was given the following account by a Yecuana in 1950: "Ten years ago Kalomera went to war against them. He set out with thirty warriors all armed with guns, and they killed lots of Guaharibos. Not only the men, you understand, but also the women and children. Like that there would be fewer of them later on. Since then they have kept quiet and they don't try to come anywhere near the Ventuari."

Another incident, recalled from sometime during this series of conflicts (Cocco 1972:61), occurred along the Cuntinamo, a tributary of the Padamo. Sanema had been coming down from the mountains to the Yecuana settlements, snatching machetes, clothing, and other items whenever they saw an opportunity. Yecuana men got together ten shotguns and fell upon a sleeping Yanomami encampment. They killed eight, including the Yanomami headman.

Shirishanization

The 1940s witnessed a gradual return of Venezuelans and other Westerners to the Yanomami area. This period of history will be described in detail in relation to better known developments among the Yanomamo in part III. The remainder of this chapter will concentrate on reports specific to the Sanema. These reports are now much more detailed, beginning with the books written by two explorers, Alain Gheerbrant (1954) and Alfonso Vinci (1959), who traveled among the Sanema in 1949–50 and 1953, respectively. In 1958, anthropological research began among the Sanema with an initial brief visit by Wilbert (Lizot 1988:490). These accounts and others by subsequent ethnographers tell us about the variable relationships between Sanema and Yecuana.

After their defeat in 1940, the Yanomami closest to the Yecuana began to shift to a pattern of peaceful but subservient coexistence with their former enemies. This shift was encouraged in 1947, when a Venezuelan air force officer "imported" Brazilian Sanema into Yecuana territory to work on the construction of an air field. That led to a major division of Sanema populations, as many moved far north to this new area between the Ventuari, Erebato, and Caura rivers (Wilbert 1963: 187).[9] From this time on, many groups of Sanema and even Yanomamo would move north to settle close to a Yecuana village. Their coresidence would be on very unequal terms.

The character of this social relationship appears to be quite uniform in reports from different places and different decades (Colchester 1981b: 27; Coppens 1981:67–68, 110; Gheerbrant 1954:142, 196–201; Lizot 1988:573–74; Ramos 1972:10–11, 1979b:3–7, 12–13; Smole 1976: 52; Vinci 1959:178ff.; Wilbert 1963:187–88). It did not favor the Yanomami, who were treated with open contempt, such that Western observers sometimes call them "vassals" and "slaves." They were forced to cede wives for the privilege of social intercourse, and to do all manner of labor obediently—all to obtain worn-down steel and other second-hand Western manufactures. At the same time, the Yanomami adopted many elements of Yecuana culture, notably canoe travel, fishing, and manioc cultivation. This distinctive and frequently repeated pattern has acquired a name, "shirishanization" (Cocco 1972:28).

Arvelo-Jiménez (1971:43) describes the relationship of the Sanema to the Yecuana in regard to labor: "The fact remains that now Guajaribo supply a labour force and engage in hard, unpleasant tasks for the Ye'cuana who in exchange give them second-hand tools and other industrial commodities, or grumblingly supply either manioc roots or the prepared product, cassava." Chagnon and his colleagues (1970:343) are more interested in the pattern of marriages. They explain that the Yecuana's connections to Westerners and their supply of steel tools and other items

> has given them a trading hegemony over the Yanomama, who have remained isolated and thereby avoid direct contacts with outsiders. The Yanomama have traditionally relied on the Makiritare for steel tools. . . . It is for this reason that groups of Yanomama periodically take up temporary residence with the Makiritare; they work for them in order to obtain the necessary and extremely desirable steel tools that make their agricultural economy more efficient. . . . The fact that the Makiritare have a monopoly on steel tools, which they jealously guard, has given them the advantage in the various social relationships that emerge in mixed villages. One way in which this advantage is expressed is that Makiritare men (in mixed villages) demand and usually obtain sexual access to Yanomama women. If intermarriage or semi-permanent co-residence does take place, it invariably involves a Makiritare man with a Yanomama woman.

Lizot (1988:574) describes the monopolistic and status aspects of the relationship: "The Ye'kuana are intermediaries who transmit the industrial goods that the Sanema need. But they are not merely that. The Ye'kuana are also very jealous of their privileged relations with the Sanema and Yanomami, up to the point of energetically opposing those who commit the error of establishing direct dealing with the Sanema."

Many of the observers note the antagonism just below the surface in these unequal and exploitative alliances. That antagonism creates the potential for violent rejection of the relationship. Gheerbrant (1954) details the situation. He found Yecuana traders possessing stores of Western trade goods, from guns to medicines (1954:215), far greater than those Rice had observed a quarter-century before. The Sanema, on the other hand, were said not to possess anything worth having (1954:

200). Sanema were used as porters and treated contemptuously (1954: 196–201). For example, they were paid two boxes of matches and a strip of printed cloth for two days of work hauling 90-pound loads up a mountain (1954:200). Visiting a Sanema village, Gheerbrant found it extremely poor and tumbledown, with "neither hatchets or knives" visible and the residents "pale and emaciated" (1954:307).

Traveling westward on the trade route over the mountains in 1950, Gheerbrant described a situation of "latent warfare" between Yecuana and Yanomami (Gheerbrant 1954:142). While they were contemptuous, the Yecuana traders also feared the Sanema (1954:139). They traveled in groups of canoes that "literally bristled with arms" (1954:185). Gheerbrant did not exaggerate. Later that year, "the Sanema revolted against the Makiritare and declared war without quarter. It was then that different Makiritare sub-tribes united in order to repulse the Sanema, over whom they triumphed in several encounters by the grace of their firearms" (Wilbert 1963:188).

In sum, the relationship between Yecuana and Sanema has all the characteristics that my model ascribes to unequal alliances between Yanomami communities. It is based on unequal access to Western goods. It involves the extraction on exploitative terms of local products, labor, and women. It is a jealously guarded monopoly. It involves clearly unequal positions of social status. It contains within it latent antagonisms that sometimes erupt into open war. And it is maintained by the superordinate military power of the shotgun-owning Yecuana. I doubt that any of these points would be challenged by anyone who has written on Yecuana-Yanomami relations. But no one, to my knowledge, has suggested that this paradigm of unequal alliance could be applied internally within the Yanomami.

Certainly there are major differences between the two situations, corresponding to the very real cultural gap between the two peoples, the absence of prior kinship ties, and the vastly superior military capacity of the Yecuana, based on their tribal form of political organization and, most importantly, on their shotguns. These factors heighten and accent the social distance between Yecuana and Yanomami, making the dominance appear much more categorical. It could be said that in this situation, ethnicity makes a very real difference. In its basic structure, however, the relationship across this cultural or ethnic divide is very similar to unequal alliances we will see among the Yanomami, especially later in part III.

Recent History

The defeats around 1950 ended major Yanomami resistance to the terms imposed by the Yecuana. Subsequently even more Sanema moved north-ward, attaching themselves to Yecuana communities from the Ventuari to the Caura (Wilbert 1963:188). Still, tensions continued between the two peoples into the 1960s and even later (Vinci 1959:190–92; Wilbert 1963:188). Arvelo-Jiménez (1971:42) reports that the last Yanomami attack on a Yecuana party "for the purpose of stealing all the man and his companion had with them was as recently as 1959," and there had been no other incidents during the next ten years.

Steel was still very scarce in some Sanema communities during the early 1950s. Despite the growing contacts between Yanomami and Yecuana, some highland villages had no steel or only a few broken pieces (Gheerbrant 1954:165, 306–307; Vinci 1959:111). Even into the 1960s, the *haowe* ax was still used regularly by Sanema (Barandiaran and Walalam 1983:191), and Barandiaran (1967:32) claims that the most remote Sanema were still limited in their practice of agriculture be-cause they lacked steel. Westerners who entered Sanema territory were at some risk, or at least their possessions were. Around 1950, several groups of woodsmen in the area were stripped of everything, including their clothes, and sent on their way (Cocco 1972:87). That happened to Vinci's party in 1953, but by keeping their heads and being friendly to their captors, they got back their clothes and Sanema cooperation (Vinci 1959:93ff.; also see Gheerbrant 1954:141–46, 170–79).

As Yanomami villages became dependencies of Yecuana communi-ties, violence occurred between these "tame" (*manso*) Yanomami and the "wild" ones still lacking good sources of steel. In fact, the movement of Sanema to settle alongside Yecuana communities was driven, in part, by fear of these raids from the south (Arvelo-Jiménez 1971:43).

Gheerbrant reports that in 1950 seven Sanema groups around the upper Ventuari were "on visiting terms with the Maquiritares" (1954: 223). He describes two wars involving opposed Yanomami groups. One undated combat, perhaps part of the wars reported for Yanomamo around 1946 (Cocco 1972:87; and see chapter 11), was the final inci-dent in a long conflict between Yanomami from "the source of the Ori-noco" and others living "to the south of the Ventuari"—that is, interior groups against those within the Yecuana ambit. The interior group sent a volley of arrows into the village, apparently to no effect. The Ventuari people then managed to kill two of the raiders. "With that the war came to an end" (Gheerbrant 1954:202). By the time Gheerbrant encountered them, the people of the village that came under attack were living well to the north of the raid site. They had moved away from the people who had been raiding them and in the direction of sources of Western goods.

The second war, triggered by the theft of two women, was in progress when Gheerbrant arrived. "The trouble threatened to extend as far as the first of the Maquiritare plantations"—that is, to involve Sanema living near Yecuana. But the Yecuana "wanted peace," and so they "sent off" a Yanomami man who had been living with them to try to "mediate between the two tribes" (Gheerbrant 1954:201). He later reported back that "two of the young men were killed and then the women were returned" (1954:223). This kind of fighting was quite general at the time. "We learned from this that war is endemic among the Guaharibos themselves, and that it is liable to break out again at any minute, always over some dark-skinned Helen" (Gheerbrant 1954:201–202). In my model, such conflicts are expected to erupt between dependent allies and middlemen who have Western goods but lack a military advantage. They may begin as a reaction to excessive demands by the middlemen or as an attempt by the more remote groups to make the middlemen flee.

Vinci, in the area in 1954, also reports hostilities. In one instance, the death of many babies made former "friends" into enemies, each suspecting the other of "the evil eye." No violence resulted, however (Vinci 1959:110). No doubt this account refers to a newly introduced disease, such as invariably accompanies intensified contact and contributes to a diminished threshold for violence. Vinci also reports standing animosity between Yanomami of different locations, which prohibited travel along certain routes (1959:115, 219). One alignment appears to pit Sanema of the mountains, who had established a regular connection to the Yecuana, against more isolated Yanomamo of the Ocamo and Matacuni (1959:219). In these cases, the result was avoidance, not violence. But there were killings.

Vinci, traveling with a party of Sanema whom he paid in trade goods—an incredible windfall for them—entered one Yanomami village where he found four corpses completely enveloped in insects. His Sanema guides told him there were three more bodies elsewhere. Only one had a wound that could be seen beneath the swarming, but other circumstances strongly suggested that these were all homicides and that the killers were men from Vinci's own party who had gone ahead while the expedition was halted.[10] They had a motive, because in all likelihood they would have had to have to turn their precious cargo over to the victims, who may have been established enemies.

Ramos (1972:111–16) also provides historical information for particular Sanema groups that were moving toward the Yecuana during this period. She describes a time of raids, fissioning, and movements, much in contrast to the more stable situation she later encountered. Some of the raiders are identified as Samatali and Kobali, two somewhat shifting referents applied to "wilder" Sanema south of the Yecuana frontier (Colchester 1981b:106; 1982:91; Ramos 1972:14; Vinci 1959:79).

Vinci raises the question of why the Yanomami fight so among themselves. First he explains it as part of their way of life, stimulated by fear and vengeance. Then he adds:

> But apart from fear and the vendettas which grow out of it, there is one native activity which just as easily leads to war: theft. . . . The tribe on the river so-and-so possesses a machete, or a knife—perhaps the result of long bargaining with their neighbours, or, more often, of a highly successful bit of burglary and some skirmishing. After several days' howling and shrieking, an expedition is decided on. It is not certain that a battle will yield the desired utensil or object, but then, it is never certain that a hunt will fill the pot. . . . Even if the encounter produces only negative results, the enemy will henceforth go in fear. (Vinci 1959:123–24)

Later, in reference to a pile of Western goods his party carried, Vinci (1959:186–87) comments: "A store of goods like that would have set in motion every Shirian from the Caura to the Orinoco and enough battles would have been fought over it to destroy the entire race."

Vinci's conclusions are fully supported by Barandiaran and Walalam, based on fieldwork among the Sanema that they began in the early 1960s. "Collective avarice sometimes forces a leader into desperate situations, as, for example, to attack by surprise with his band other groups more favored in elements of first necessity, such as machetes, axes, loincloths or red cloth, glass beads, cooking utensils, etc." (Barandiaran and Walalam 1983:98). And: "The desire to possess some envied object (a machete, a cooking utensil) can degenerate into assault and open war" (1983:103). On two occasions the authors note that the capture of women is also a goal of war, but that it is superseded by the need to flee quickly after seizing steel (1983:102, 191; and Barandiaran 1967:24).

One particular case they describe (Barandiaran and Walalam 1983: 103) illustrates some of the social dimensions and complications of this kind of conflict.

A notable warrior, left his own tribe to reside in a prosperous area and group, maintaining regular contacts with his own people. In every annual visit to his relatives he heaped on them most precious gifts: axes, machetes . . . that they, for their isolation, could not procure for themselves. The warrior died suddenly from snake bite and his people did not receive the expected annual visit. Accusing of the killings the group where the dead man lived, they organized a war expedition with three neighboring groups who had also taken advantage of the generosity of the dead man, decimating the accused group and robbing after setting fire to the village, all of the valuable objects and utensils, but not touching the women and children.

After all this fighting, war by and among the Sanema declined to virtually nothing during the 1960s. This decade saw continuing movement to settle near Yecuana, typically by groups of a few families. Thus an increasing number of Yanomami established a regular supply of Western manufactures and were protected from raiders by their ties to shotgun-armed Yecuana. At the same time, these dependent Yanomami lost their political autonomy, placing themselves under virtual command by Yecuana, who, as we saw in Gheerbrant's account, did not like nearby Yanomami fighting.

For those Sanema still unattached to Yecuana, steel and other Western goods remained in short supply but at least were now coming in through many different sources. Every village associated with Yecuana was a potential source, if an exchange relationship could be initiated. In 1959, those sources were augmented by the first missions among the Sanema, on the Caura and Erebato; and in 1963, by a third mission, on the Auaris at the top of the cross-highland trade route (Migliazza 1972: 389–91). By this time there were other missions close to Sanema territory as well. (No information is reported about political-military developments at the time these missions were founded, or about increased mortality from disease during the period of increasing contact.)

The proliferation of sources of Western goods would reduce the potential for sharply exploitative monopolization of trade between Sanema communities. Thus the Sanema of the 1960s came to appear pacific in contrast to those of decades before, or to the contemporary Yanomamo of the Orinoco-Mavaca area. A missionary among the Sanema at Auaris was perhaps the first to disagree in print with Chagnon's (1968) just-published portrayal of the Yanomami, stating that from what she had observed, they were "anything but fierce" (Montgomery 1970:88).

Sanema villages located near that mission were studied by Kenneth Taylor (1972) and Alcida Ramos in fieldwork from 1968 to 1970. Ramos (1972:9–14, 27, 33) describes the political dynamics of the 1960s. The Sanema settlements centered on the mission and a Yecuana community on the Auaris River. The Sanema community at the mission site was unusually large—over one hundred people. "Most, if not all of them, came to Auaris attracted by the prospect of acquiring trade goods which are provided by the missionaries in exchange for services and food" (1972:10). They received Western goods in relative abundance from the missionaries, but other neighboring Yanomami villages did not enjoy this direct access. Instead, "Western goods reach Kadimani [a village perhaps 10 miles away] only indirectly through trade with other Indians" (1972:38). The Kadimani were in no position to challenge the arrangement. By 1969, most of the adult men at Auaris, both Yecuana and Sanema, had obtained at least one shotgun from the mission.

At the time, the local Sanema were generally at peace, as would be expected with such a stable source of Western goods and such clear military advantages. No raids occurred during Ramos and Taylor's 28 months in the field, up to September 1970.

In October, however, shortly after they left, "there was a raid by the Sanuma on a *kobali* group with four people killed." The raiders were from two communities "with whom we had regular contact" (Ramos 1972:31). At the time, the two villages were negotiating a marriage alliance and the relocation of the more distant village closer to Auaris. That would give the two a more dominating position on the southern approaches to the mission. The "Kobali"—a shifting referent for Yanomami who live some distance to the south—did not at this time visit the mission directly, but traded through Sanema middlemen (Ramos 1972:14, 31, 158–59). It seems probable that this late instance of raiding was somehow related to conflicts over control of this southward trade, although just what the Kobali did to provoke the attack is unknown. Both the timing of the raid (immediately after the visiting Westerners had left) and its direction (middlemen out from a major Western post attacking a more remote group) will be seen to be quite standard.

Ramos (1979a:5–7, 12–13, 16) also describes the situation of the

people around the mission a few years later, about 1974. Some characteristics of the typical Yanomami-Yecuana relationship are seen in material
and labor exchanges and in Yecuana anxiety. But at this time and place,
the missionaries were following a policy of dispensing Western goods
equally to Yecuana and Sanema. In consequence, the Sanema, who had
shotguns that the Yecuana feared, had risen markedly in relative status.
The Yecuana were not satisfied with the Western goods they were receiving from the missionaries, and some men regularly went down the
Uraricoera to Boa Vista to work for a year as ranch hands. One such
trip was the occasion for a rumor that graphically displays many of tensions in Yecuana-Yanomami relations.

A party expected to return from Boa Vista was overdue (Ramos
1979a:8–9, 15). A rumor swept the community that they had been
ambushed while coming upriver, by the same group of Ninam Yanomami that had attacked some Yecuana on the Uraricoera in the 1930s
(see chapter 7). The party eventually arrived unscathed, but as Ramos
(1979a:21) interprets it, the rumor "reflects the anxieties, perplexities,
stereotypes, apprehensions of those who fabricate it in relation to the
human, material and situational elements that enter into its composition. It is in this sense that the ideological character of rumor becomes
most apparent." I would add, for my theoretical purposes, that it reveals
the tensions involved in obtaining Western manufactures: the Yecuana,
undermined by the mission policy of distribution, resentful that this had
made the Sanema more independent, go to great lengths to establish
better sources of Western goods and fear that Yanomami along their
travel route will intercept them with lethal violence. This "ideological
character of rumor" should be kept in mind for later discussions of war
and alliance.

Information on Sanema political history ends at this point.[11] As a
final note, it is appropriate to consider the Sanema's own myth about
"the origin of modern goods," collected about 1980 after steel had long
since become commonplace (Colchester 1981b:67–70). The narrator
explains that Omao, the creator, looked at the ancestors he had created
and found them incomplete. He wanted to give them things—books,
shotguns, airplanes, fabric, clothing, and more. But the ancestors did
not want them; they refused all of Omao's gifts. The narrator continues
(Colchester 1981b:70):

High up in the sky—*m m m m m m m m!* they go flying by.
Things, things they go by! go by! go by! And here are we, us children below.

"O! woe! My ancestors they really make me *angry!*" that is what we say now. "Walking slowly along on the ground—over mountains, along the trails, crossing rivers!—it's all really tiring. And all the while those others go swiftly flying by. And all thanks to our ancestors." That's what we say now, and we are really angry too.

7

The Ninam

The Ninam, also known as Yanam and by other localized labels (Migliazza 1980:102), were first reported in the high country east of the Parima highlands in Brazil, in the mountains along the right bank of the upper Uraricoera, and in the Parima River area. During this century, the Ninam have split into two main divisions, one moving north into Venezuela along the Uraricaá and upper Paragua rivers, the other moving south and east down the Mucajaí (map 3). Ninam of the northern division were the first Yanomami to experience massive direct contact with Westerners in recent years, and they were correspondingly decimated. In 1970, total Ninam population (both northern and southern divisions) was estimated at 350 to 400 people (Migliazza 1972:35, 1980:400); by the mid-1980s it had grown to about 850 (Colchester 1982:91, 1985b:7).

Historical information about the Ninam is of three sorts. First, there are accounts scattered throughout the nineteenth and twentieth centuries of their presence, activities, and migrations along the Uraricoera and into the Paragua watershed. Second, there is oral history from one Ninam population cluster beginning about 1880. Third, there is a detailed study of developments involving that same cluster after a mission was established among them in the 1950s.

The Uraricoera Route in the Nineteenth Century

From the time of Schomburgk's explorations in the late 1830s, there are a series of reports documenting Ninam efforts, both violent and peaceful, to obtain some of the benefits of the indigenous trade passing just north of their highland territory. Before going into those reports, it may be helpful to offer a brief introduction to this repeatedly contested area.

The Uraricoera is a tributary of the Río Branco. About halfway up the Uraricoera is the large Maracá Island; most reports about the Ninam occur upstream from it. Near the western end of Maracá Island, the Uraricoera is joined by a tributary, the Uraricaá (formerly the Uraricapara). The headwaters of the Uraricaá are close to those of the Paragua, a major river that flows northward through Guiana. Farther up the Uraricoera, near a large loop in its course, is the Marutani escarpment and the small effluent called Motomoto. Continuing upstream, the Uraricoera is joined by the Parima River, which flows northward from the Parima highlands. The Parima River in turn is joined by the Auaris, which leads up to the paths connecting to the Ventuari and thus to the Orinoco.

To anticipate myself a bit, the first reports of Ninam come from close to the Marutani mesa. Ultimately, the Ninam come to dominate the Uraricoera and its tributaries from the Auaris down to Maracá Island. Ninam also move northward into the Uraricaá and Paragua areas. A few groups of Yanomam speakers follow behind the northward-migrating Ninam and eventually occupy parts of the upper Uraricoera.

Ninam all along these watercourses take three approaches toward obtaining steel tools and other trade goods: they put themselves in subordinate relationships to Yecuana or other middlemen, they plunder passing traders, and they force their way into the regional trade network as traders themselves. With the limited information available, many of these actions can be connected only in a general sense to changes in the regional Western presence. What is clear, however, is that major acts of war, movement, and alliance making follow the imperative of obtaining steel.

To recapitulate from chapter 5, in the later 1700s the Portuguese reaction to Spanish expansion was to concentrate indigenous people at Fort São Joaquim, near the juncture of the Uraricoera and the Branco, thus depopulating most of the accessible rivers. Some Yanomami may have been contacted and even "descended" during this time, but reports are unclear. The demographic stress on the local population continued until the general reduction of colonial activity in the area in the first decades of the nineteenth century.

When Schomburgk was on the Branco in 1838, the river had not regained its prior level of colonial activity, although military and commercial press gangs made it a dangerous place for indigenous inhabitants. (Schomburgk encountered a gang with 40 Wapishiana and Atori captives taken in night raids after their village was torched [Schomburgk 1841:188–90].) Fort São Joaquim, however, was exceptionally active. Near it were cattle ranches with some 8,000 head of cattle and 500 horses, using 22 local Indians as workers (Hemming 1987:601). After 1839, the fort was also a base for a very ambitious missionary, although his main efforts were directed toward the Wapishiana and Macushi to the northeast (Hemming 1987:339–41). With all this going on, the fort most probably fed some Western goods into the trade system that went up the Uraricoera. As described in chapter 6, the 1830s also saw a significant increase in colonial economic activity on the upper Orinoco. Thus, at the time of Schomburgk's visit, the Uraricoera was a route between two comparatively robust Western centers.

Schomburgk traveled up the Uraricoera and into the Parima highlands until forced to turn back by a Sanema attack on some Yecuana (see chapter 6). Before that, while ascending the Uraricoera close to the Marutani mesa, his party came across a Yanomami ("Kirischana") garden (Schomburgk 1841:221; and Koch-Grunberg 1979 III:239–40). Apparently these Yanomami were recent arrivals on the river, for their homelands were said to be the upper reaches of a small tributary that joins the Uraricoera above Maracá Island. Schomburgk did not actually meet any Ninam, but his description of their subsistence is consistent with the pattern of high mobility and small gardens that I suggested for pre-steel Yanomami in chapter 4. He describes the "Kirischana" as relying primarily on hunting and spending much of their time on long treks. When game was scarce, they fished and ate turtles and caimans. They visited their small gardens in the course of their extended trekking. That they apparently had manioc in their gardens suggests prior contact with Yecuana and perhaps incipient "shirishanization."

Schomburgk reports that the Ninam were locally "dreaded," with a reputation as being "warlike and courageous," ever ready with their poison arrows. The only details he provides are that some Ninam had recently attacked a Yecuana trading canoe coming down the Uraricoera, killing two men. This is the first in a long line of reports of Ninam preying on passing trade canoes. The location of these particular Ninam on the river would give them a greater ability to tap into the currents of trade, in one way or another. Perhaps Ninam raiding was stimulated by an increasing quantity of Western goods passing along the Uraricoera. Later reports will continue the story of Ninam near the Marutani mesa.

The next few years saw greater abandonment by the Portuguese. The Cabanagem Rebellion and its suppression (1835–39) had taken a toll on the economy of the Brazilian Amazon (Hemming 1987:227–37). In its aftermath, the cattle herds around Fort São Joaquim were down to a few hundred head (Hemming 1987:237, 602). The mission there was faltering as well, with few natives left to reduce. In 1849 the missionary sought to bring Yanomami (probably Yanomam) down from the upper Catrimani, but without success. It is not clear whether efforts were also directed up the Uraricoera, but that seems likely. The missionary was removed in 1852 (Hemming 1987:343).

In the mid-1850s, Brazilian colonization of the upper Branco area remained well below that of the later eighteenth century. Fort São Joaquim was the only major settlement, and even it had few inhabitants or contacts with the outside world (Michelena y Rojas 1989:403). The virtual absence of indigenous people along the main watercourses led press gangs farther up remote rivers in 1857–58, capturing men to build cattle roads and young women for a "religious house" in Fort São Joaquim (Hemming 1987:343–44). Again, it is unreported but not unlikely that some of these press gangs had contact with Yanomami. Only after 1866, when an administrative change restricted military press gangs and there were no longer any missions needing converts, were indigenous people relatively safe from being forcibly taken from their homes (Hemming 1987:327).

Echoes of a Distant Boom

As described in chapter 6, Amazon rubber production began to climb in the 1840s and took a jump in 1854. The Río Branco was not a major center of rubber tapping; there were too few *Hevea braziliensis* trees in its forests (Hemming 1987:350). Although some tapping did occur, there is no indication of it on the upper Uraricoera. Nevertheless, the upper Río Branco region did participate, indirectly, in the rubber boom. Around Fort São Joaquim and in the plains along the Branco, the cattle industry expanded during the 1870s to match the increased demand for meat in Manaus. By 1884, there were 32 ranches with 20,000 head of cattle and 4,000 horses. The ranches employed Native Americans, mostly Macushi, but at this time there were still very few Indians along the main rivers, perhaps 250 along 500 kilometers of the Branco (Hemming 1987:350).

As the upper Orinoco economy also picked up during the 1870s, the Uraricoera route now connected two centers of economic expansion.

Moreover, since the 1860s new Anglican missions in British Guiana had been feeding greater quantities of Western goods into the trade network north of the Uraricoera (Colson 1973:9; Thomas 1982:23–24). It seems virtually certain that an increased supply of Western manufactures would be flowing along the Uraricoera in the 1870s. Migliazza (cited in Albert 1985:63–64) suggests that Yanomami in the Parima River area around this time were in direct contact with traders to their north, including Pemon, Macushi, and Purokoto.

But the late 1870s also were a time of intensified Yanomami predation on river traders and the start of their often violent expansion northward into the Uraricaá-Paragua area. An expedition of the Brazilian frontier commission on the upper Uraricoera in 1882 found it still inhabited by Carib-speaking groups (Purokoto, Wayumara, Sapara) and the Marakana. The Uraricaá was inhabited by Awake and Marakana, but local foresters already reported Yanomami ("Guaycas") north of the Uraricoera in the interfluvial area between the Uraricaá and Paragua. The commission found people in the area living in fear of the ferocious Yanomami ("Kirishanas") and Marakana, a fear that had even spread down the Uraricoera to dissuade any would-be colonists from approaching (Albert 1985:61).

There is nothing in this report to indicate that Yanomami had taken over additional river locations in the many years since Schomburgk's visit. That would soon change. Sometime in the decade after 1882, the Ninam scored a major victory in what is recounted as a bloody battle to the west of Maracá Island. The once-feared Marakana were defeated and driven as refugees into the forests (Koch-Grunberg 1979 I:201; Rice 1928b:143).

Two later oral accounts may date to this period of violence. Koch-Grunberg (1979 III:243, 266) reports a history "from remote times" when Yanomami from different highland areas raided Yecuana and others along the Uraricoera and a tributary of the Caura River and frequently attacked the Yecuana's passing trade canoes. The danger was so great that the Yecuana would paddle quietly through Yanomami areas in the middle of the night (Koch-Grunberg 1979 III:243, 266). In 1926, Rice (1928a:214) heard a tradition that Yanomami ("Shirianas") had once pushed a Maku group westward up the Uraricoera to the Parima River. By attacking and plundering those engaged in the regional trade, Ninam undoubtedly acquired steel tools and other goods and drove out some of those ensconced along the main trade route itself.[1]

At this point—the 1880s—an extended history of one Yanomami group enters in, providing additional information and an inside perspective on Ninam raiding and other political relationships during the rubber-boom period. Chagnon and his colleagues (1970) and Peters and Early (Peters 1973; Early and Peters 1990) reconstruct the history of a local group of Ninam who in later years were known as Borabuk.[2] The start of this history is a good place to call attention to a difference between my approach and Chagnon's.

Chagnon and his students have been concerned with mapping the long-distance "macro-moves" of groups, which is a very good thing for the purposes of my study. In explaining these moves, they emphasize the "push" factor of war. The idea that war makes people move is, of course, a basic part of my model. But I believe Chagnon and his students neglect the important "pull" factor of access to Western manufactures, except in a few very general statements.

Borabuk history is a good illustration of this "pull." The reader may observe that in discussing Borabuk efforts to obtain Western goods (with the exception of their dealings with Yecuana), all my references come from Peters and Early, not from Chagnon et al. Although Chagnon et al. (1970:343) present their history with the intention of providing "some idea of the general cultural milieu within which the mating structure operates," that milieu excludes the impact of outsiders: "It should be emphasized that the events we are discussing occurred prior to the intrusion into this region of outsiders, aside from a few expeditions that moved through, so that these events would seem to mirror the traditional pattern of gene flow" (Chagnon et al. 1970:347). The reader may judge whether or not the history of Borabuk fights, fissions, movements, and marriages represents a pattern unaffected by the changing Western presence around them.

In the last quarter of the nineteenth century, the Borabuk's ancestors lived in a village on the upper Auaris River, alongside a Yecuana settlement. As Chagnon's informants recalled (Chagnon et al. 1970: 341–44), their relationship with the Yecuana was typical of the kind of exploitative alliance described in chapter 6. The Yecuana had established sources of Western goods, which gave them "a trading hegemony over the Yanomama" (1970:343). Yecuana men used their advantage to extract brides from the Ninam and have affairs with other Ninam women. The relationship between the two groups was "potentially strained, if not hostile" (1970:343), and the Ninam suspected the Yecuana of witchcraft. In what is estimated to be just before 1900, tensions culminated in a fight in which one Ninam was wounded with a knife.

At this point the Ninam decided to move, but there was disagreement about where to go. They divided, one segment heading east into Venezuela (in 1967, this group was located in the Paragua headwaters). The other segment moved downstream to the juncture of the Auaris and Parima rivers. Early and Peters (1990:17) describe two conflicts from the time when these Ninam were living along the river. One involved a raid on "Wewe," in which two women were captured. Additional women from Wewe and another unidentified group were marrying into the Ninam group around this same time. The other conflict involved Macushi, who reportedly provoked the Ninam by taking a woman and then lost one man in a Ninam raid.

Chagnon et al. (1970:343) describe an internal Ninam fight over a woman around 1910, followed by a second fissioning. Again the dissident faction moved east (in later years they would be called Xiriana), but while they were still in the area they entered into "active hostilities with those who remained behind" (1970:343). Soon afterwards, the progenitors of the Borabuk migrated off the river into the forests to the southeast, a move that marked the beginning of the division of Ninam into northern and southern clusters. Shortly after that, they were hit by a serious epidemic that killed many adult men, a mortality pattern suggesting to Chagnon and his colleagues that the dead were part of an infected trading party who fell ill before they reached home.

Given the uncertainties in this reconstruction, only limited weight should rest on its details. Still, some general correspondences to the theoretical model can be noted. The period of Ninam coresidence with the Yecuana coincided with the latter's increased wealth from the Orinoco rubber industry, and it displayed the tensions typical of such unequal alliances. The fissioning and migration of two successive village segments is consistent with the general movement toward the trade network north of the Uraricoera. It anticipates a pattern that will be seen often in later discussions of movement—that during times of increasing Western penetration, Yanomami villages fission and adopt alternative geographic approaches to the new sources of trade goods. The geographic position of the ancestors of the Borabuk, who remained at the juncture of the Auaris and Parima rivers, was strategic for participation in the trade up those rivers—trade that presumably increased in value with the boom on the upper Orinoco after 1902. (Maku also living on the Auaris in 1911 were known as active purveyors of Western goods brought from both the lower Uraricoera and the Orinoco [Koch-Grunberg 1979 I:266; and see Rice 1928a:213–14].) The Ninam's reported contacts with Macushi, some of whom were seeking wives in this area (see Rice 1928b: 130), reinforce the conclusion that they were active in the river trade.

The overall picture of strained alliances and raiding in several directions is consistent with the antagonisms commonly raised by unequal access to a new influx of Western manufactures. It is roughly coincident with the peak years of the regional rubber boom. The movement of the Borabuk people away from their river location and into a largely uninhabited area sometime after 1910 was probably impelled by the danger posed by so many enemies; but it also came just around the time that Tomás Funes, the tyrant of the upper Orinoco, began to oppress the Yecuana, thus disrupting trade over the Auaris. Yet the reported epidemic indicates that even off the river, the Borabuk people still maintained trading links to some sources of Western goods. The history of the Borabuk people will be picked up again later.

River Traders and Others

The next outside observation of life along the upper Uraricoera dates from the peak of the rubber boom. In December 1911 and January 1912, Koch-Grunberg (1979 I:241–42) visited two Ninam ("Schiriana") groups, one of whom lived by the stream called Motomoto near the Marutani mesa location where Schomburgk had found a Yanomami garden more than 80 years earlier. The Ninam he encountered were more timid than warlike (Koch-Grunberg 1979 I:208–13, 242–43, 257–58). They had recently begun trading with Maku around the Auaris, from whom they obtained all manner of Western goods, albeit in very small amounts.

The Ninam told Koch-Grunberg that steel tools had made it possible for them to construct large gardens, in contrast to what was possible in their recent past.[3] In their gardens grew manioc, but although the Ninam got manioc graters from the Yecuana, otherwise their processing technology was crude. Evidently they had only recently converted to a more agricultural and dependent way of life along the river. Now they lived in fear of attack by the Yanomami of the mountains, where people still lacked enough steel to make substantial gardens. Yet relations with the interior people were not all hostile, as some men from the mountains were in the village during Koch-Grunberg's visit.

This report is roughly contemporaneous with and comparable to the reports of mixed violence and trade just discussed for the Borabuk people. The particular group of Ninam Koch-Grunberg visited were, at the time, taking the shirishanization option. Their situation may also—like that of the Sanema—reflect the pattern in which dependent allies of a supplier of Western goods find themselves under threat from more remote groups lacking in steel.

While all these events were happening along the upper Uraricoera, Parima, and Auaris rivers, other Ninam were taking a more aggressive posture toward trade. Koch-Grunberg (1979 I:204–205, 242–43, 252, 266) describes a Ninam group farther down the Uraricoera who had lived, some years before his visit, on a mountain overlooking the middle Uraricoera near its juncture with the Uraricaá. From there they had launched at least two raids on passing traders, killing several. These attacks made their leader, a man called Kuranai, much feared in the area. But a few years before Koch-Grunberg's visit, Kuranai's people changed their attitude. By then they had relocated to the upper Uraricaá and adopted canoe travel. They were successfully seeking trade connections with Carib speakers and other Ninam along the Uraricoera and, northward from the Uraricaá, with the peoples of the Caroní and Paragua regions, from whom they obtained iron, glass beads, and other items.

These Ninam had managed to do what no Sanema had been able to accomplish: forcibly insert themselves as full participants in the regional trade network. Their success brought them greater benefits than did dependency on the Maku by the Ninam at Motomoto. Although both groups produced the same items to trade—bows, arrows, "sausages" of some dark resin, braided bromeliad fiber, and balls of spun cotton—the Motomoto Ninam seemed to Koch-Grunberg (1979 I:210, 266) to be "more primitive, more poor" than Kuranai's people. The condition underlying Kuranai's achievement was that the middle Uraricoera was largely devoid of settlement, especially after the flight of the Marakana. While the Sanema and upstream Ninam had to deal with Yecuana and Maku in their home range, these Ninam could prey on traders in the middle of a long voyage and could move onto the trade routes without serious opposition.

Kuranai's people were part of the migration by Ninam to the Uraricaá, Paragua, and even Caroní rivers that may have begun in the 1870s but seems to have intensified after the turn of the century. In the process, the Ninam assimilated several small groups of Carib speakers (Albert 1985:63; Cocco 1972:29; Colchester 1985d:61–63; Wilbert

1963:182). There are indications (Albert 1985:63) that the most northerly Ninam pioneers clashed with Maku and Pemon, but by 1927 such clashes were already seen as things of the past. Apparently there were no major conflicts with Pemon during this advance (see Thomas 1982:24–26). The absence of later war reports, the story of Kuranai's people, and the mergers with resident groups all suggest that between about 1910 and 1925, the migrating Ninam generally attained a place within the developed regional trade network, thus obtaining Western goods without the need for violence. As we will see, reports from the mid-1920s suggest that all the Ninam were at peace from the early 1910s to the late 1920s.

Ninam during the Western Retraction

Specific information is almost nonexistent about sources and quantities of Western goods coming into the Ninam area during the years of Western retraction, but some general features can be surmised. By 1925, the rubber boom in Venezuela was well over, the Western presence was drastically reduced, and the Yecuana were just coming out of their disastrous experience with Funes. Brazilian rubber production also had collapsed, and the limited economic activity that followed was at this point almost entirely destructive to the few indigenous people remaining along the Branco.[4]

Probably the richest sources of Western trade goods at this moment were missions lying to the north. In 1915, faced with the expanding influence of Anglican missions in British Guiana, the Venezuelan government instituted the Law of Missions codifying mission rights and responsibilities. In 1921, rules for its implementation appeared. The next year, the government reached an agreement with the Capuchin order that gave the Catholics administrative responsibility for indigenous people in southeastern Venezuela. The first mission under this agreement was founded on the Caroní River in 1922, and others followed (Arvelo-Jiménez 1972:31; Thomas 1982:25–26). This development helps explain the continuing draw of Ninam northward. But from the following account, it seems that commerce originating with the missions still had only limited impact on the upper Uraricoera at this time.

The account comes from Rice's expedition up the Uraricoera in 1924–25.[5] His first encounter was with some of the trading Ninam ("Shiriana"). While working around Maracá Island, he met one of their canoes heading downriver from the Uraricaá and noted that the men in it had the distinctive upper torso musculature of "canoe Indians" (Rice 1928b:129–30). They went on about their business. His next encounter was farther upstream near Motomoto (Rice 1928a:216–17), the area visited by both Schomburgk and Koch-Grunberg. Here Rice saw no steel, but he did see evidence of it in cut marks on tree stumps. Apparently steel tools were too precious to leave out in the open. He also comments on the people's apparent malnutrition. Later, on his return downstream, Rice found the entire community down with a fever, lying in their hammocks with no food (1928c:355).

Rice continued onward to the Parima River, where he met another Yanomami group (Rice 1928c:351–54). Holdridge (1933:382) believes they were Yanomam speakers ("Pairitiri"), who, as mentioned earlier, were to follow after the Ninam as the latter migrated north. In contrast to the others we have seen, these Yanomami had not begun a conversion to the river way of life. They were unfamiliar with being in a canoe, and they brought the explorers plantains, not manioc. (They too appeared to be malnourished.)

Pathways and bridges over streams made Rice suspect this group was linked by trails to the Motomoto people. That would make sense, but the latter would have been very poor providers of steel at this time. That the Parima River people had left visible signs of their presence on the river suggests that they hoped to attract a passing trader. If so, they were well rewarded, for Rice made a substantial distribution of manufactures, starting with a machete, a hatchet, and some clasp knives, all at the direction of a man he took to be the leader. But these Yanomami were still clearly apprehensive about the Westerners and blocked their path when they tried to advance. Their village itself was so well hidden that repeated attempts by the guides could not find it.

On the basis of his experience with Yanomami in 1924–25, Rice (1928c:354) concluded that "the Shirianas are not the fierce and intractable people that legend ascribes them to be, but for the most part poor, under-sized, inoffensive creatures who eke out a miserable existence." (This conclusion is very different from his appraisal of the Yanomamo of the upper Orinoco, as we will see in chapter 10.) In contrast, the Yecuana who operated the length of the Uraricoera appeared to be haughty. Even the Maku, who elsewhere in northwestern Amazonia occupied the bottom of the social scale, here were accomplished traders, contemptuous of the dependent Yanomami (Rice 1928a:210–11, 217–19). There is no indication in Rice's accounts of any ongoing warfare in the area, and certainly no sign that the Yanomami around 1925 were perceived as a threat by river traders. In recent years, there probably had not been concentrations of Western goods worth the risk of an attack.

In the mid-1920s, then, there was substantial inequality in the situations of Yanomami around the Uraricoera. A growing number of Ninam had moved north of the Uraricoera to the Uraricaá-Paragua area and had become part of the general regional trading system. Farther up the Uraricoera, around Motomoto, other Ninam were in worse condition, possessing little steel, being treated with contempt, and suffering from epidemic disease. On the Parima River, at the edge of the Yanomami's mountain heartland, other Yanomami appeared malnourished and may have been in even shorter supply of steel, dependent on the impoverished people around Motomoto.

Our story now reaches the 1930s. By the start of that decade, the Guiana trade had reached such proportions that Yecuana were the main suppliers of Western goods to the upper Orinoco. In the early 1930s, several new government-supported missions were established in southeastern Venezuela and British Guiana (Coppens 1971:12–13, 60; Thomas 1982:26–27), dumping larger quantities of Western goods into the system.

As that trade prospered, so did the Ninam of the Uraricaá area, who were also visited directly by a few Western parties during the 1930s (Albert 1985:72; Comité 1983:45). "They had huge plantations of sweet and bitter manioc, bananas, yams, papayas, sweet potatoes, sugar cane and pumpkin. A few fire arms were found among them" (Migliazza 1972:382–83). On the other hand, they also were suffering from new diseases, "principally malaria, colds, abdominal pains, tooth aches and gonorrhea which they contract from the Macushi" (Migliazza 1972:383). There is no suggestion that these trading Ninam were aggressors in any wars.

Other Ninam—those excluded from the burgeoning trade—were not so peaceable. The 1930s witnessed a resurgence of raids on passing traders, combined with attacks on prosperous Ninam and others by other Yanomami still in the high country. Although these attacks are not described in any detail, they must have been serious, for their result was to drive Yecuana settlements off the Uraricoera and force the Maku of the Auaris area all the way down to the lower Uraricoera, where direct contact with Brazilians and their diseases ultimately led to their extinction (Gheerbrant 1954:338; Migliazza 1980:115).

Migliazza (1980:105) suggests that the newly arrived Yanomam played a role in these expulsions. During the 1930s, Ninam ("Janauperi") of the upper Uraricaá were harried by "continual fights with wild Janauperi of the Parima" (Migliazza 1972:382). In the late 1940s, Yanomami ("Xirianas") and Yecuana ("Mahongons") in the area between the Uraricaá and Paragua claimed to have been driven off the Parima River by other Yanomami ("Jauaperi") (Migliazza 1972:383).

The oral history of the Borabuk Ninam again provides details, this time about two violent conflicts during the 1930s (Chagnon et al. 1970: 341, 344–45; Early and Peters 1990:17–18; Peters 1973:61). One is described by Early and Peters (1990:17–18): "Around 1936, a Maku family was returning upstream after trading with Brazilians. They were noticed by the Ninam, who lured them to the river bank under the pretext of wishing to exchange gifts. The Ninam seized their trade goods, killed the husband and two sons, and took the wife captive."

The other conflict involved a fight with the Yecuana with whom the Borabuk lived while on the upper Auaris. Two versions exist. According to Chagnon and his colleagues (1970:344), sometime around 1930 the Yecuana

> sent a party of workers down the Uraricoera to cut logs and make canoes to trade with the Brazilians in the town of Boa Vista, several days journey further downstream. The members of Borabuk took this opportunity to get their revenge on the Makiritare [who they blamed for their lethal epidemic] and visited the temporary camp on the Uraricoera. They were invited into the hut, and, discovering that they greatly outnumbered the Makiritare, at a signal from Iro, the instigator of the attack, set upon the men and killed many of them with staves.

Their map places this "ambush" in the Marutani area, north of the Borabuk's forest location at the time (Chagnon et al. 1970:341).

In the other version (Early and Peters 1990:18), the Yecuana started the bloodshed by descending the Uraricoera and killing a Borabuk man gathering palm fruit. In return, the Ninam attacked the Yecuana, "killed all the men, took their steel goods, and fled with four women captives" (1990:18). The Yecuana raided the Borabuk in retaliation, and several died on both sides. The last events in this sequence are estimated to have occurred around 1938. It is worth noting that around 1940, coordinated Yecuana attacks using shotguns put an end to Sanema raiding; perhaps something similar happened here.

At any rate, fear of the Yecuana made the Borabuk move farther south to a feeder stream of the Mucajaí. Over the next dozen years or so (the 1940s), they would make several other moves back and forth between the Uraricoera and Mucajaí. During these peregrinations, they were isolated from all other peoples except for one other migrating group of Ninam (see note 3). Borabuk history will be continued later.

At the time of the fighting just described, the Borabuk people had been out of the trade circuit for at least one and possibly two decades. They were extremely short of steel tools. Peters's (1973:193–94) informants recalled the time as one when "sharp pieces of stone [were] attached to sticks by means of bush rope, and were used as axes." The Yecuana victims, in one version, were a tree-cutting, canoe-building party; and the Maku were returning from trading with Brazilians. Both would have been well supplied with steel. The raids reportedly netted the Ninam a quantity of machetes and axes, several of which were still owned and in use as late as 1958 (Peters 1973:61, 136, 194). There is no reason to question that the acquisition of captive women was an additional incentive for their attacks.

Northern Ninam, from Isolation to Devastation

It appears that the wars along the Uraricoera continued well into or even through the 1940s. Gheerbrant (1954:335–39), whose 1950 expedition was a harbinger of the post–World War II wave of Western expansion,[6] stopped at a village of the "Guadema," probably Yanomam speakers.[7] The Yecuana regularly obtained plantains there, and their haughty attitude suggests the typical Yecuana-Yanomami relationship.[8] Gheerbrant took on some Guadema as guides. Further downstream, these men appeared very frightened at passing by the haunts of other, "very mad" Yanomami.

> The Guadema explained to me that the right bank of the river Uraricoera, or Río Parima, around here was inhabited by four groups of Waikas and Waitshas who were at war with the Kaserapis. All the Guadema groups, with the exception of these, had been exterminated by the Kaserapis. On the upper river and into the mountains the Kaserapis had depopulated the whole forest, slaughtering every group, no matter what their race, including the few groups of Maquiratares [who had formerly lived on the Uraricoera]. (Gheerbrant 1954:337)

The Kaserapis were said to live on the left bank of the Uraricoera, not far above Maracá Island and thus not far from the Uraricaá. When

Gheerbrant's party actually passed through Kaserapi territory, he saw one of their trails leading down to the water. "It was an excellent path and quite new. It was obvious that those who had made it were people of a civilization quite different from anything we had met among the Indians to date" (Gheerbrant 1954:338). The Kaserapi called out to the passing canoe, but Gheerbrant's companions frightened them off with drawn arrows—a threat made more impressive, no doubt, by their foreign companion.

Some inferences can be drawn from Gheerbrant's account about Yanomami life along the Uraricoera during the 1940s. Some Yanomami, such as the Guadema, had established a subordinate relationship with Yecuana and were in the process of shirishanization. The Kaserapi were evidently not in such a relationship, yet the manner in which their path was constructed indicates that they had a relatively good stock of steel tools. Their recent enemies in the mountains most probably lacked such quantities of steel, and they may have been the initial aggressors in the reported battles. Although any account of military action provided by an enemy is naturally suspect, and hyperbole is clearly involved in this particular account, there is little reason to doubt that these Kaserapi had raided Yecuana and Yanomami along the river at an earlier time.

The Kaserapi's current location put them in a position to intercept trade on the Uraricoera. Although the open path to the river would seem to indicate peaceful intent, another report from a few years after Gheerbrant's visit suggests that some people called Kaserapi were still obtaining much of their steel through violence. In 1956, on the upper Paragua, manioc-growing, canoe-traveling Ninam, whose trading expeditions went as far as the town of Boa Vista on the Branco, lived in fear of raids by "Kasurapai" from Brazil, who came down some feeder streams to attack trading parties (Cocco 1972:98–99).

In 1958, Ernest Migliazza, of the Baptist Mid-Missions, established a mission near the Xiriana on the Uraricaá (Migliazza 1972:387). That same year, the Unevangelized Fields Mission (UFM) established a mission station along the Uraricoera among the Parime-teri. These were Yanomam speakers, possibly the "Guadema" described by Gheerbrant, and they are discussed in more detail in chapter 8. Very little is written about the Ninam around the Baptist mission on the Uraricaá, although some secondhand information is provided by Chagnon (1966:193–98). He describes the Yanomami near the Uraricoera and Uraricaá missions as having much less warfare than those of the Orinoco-Mavaca area at that time. Migliazza told him that raiding between villages in the area occurred only every four or five years. Conflicts over women were also less intense. However, the one war recounted by Chagnon (1966:197–98) is a war he considers to be one of the clearest illustrations of fighting over women reported for any Yanomami.

As this case is recounted, a group of men from the Uraricaá mission visited another, more isolated village, got the people to bow their heads in prayer, and then suddenly struck and killed the men and took the women. The details of this thirdhand story are unlikely, but the general outline—a mission group staging a treacherous attack on a more isolated group and taking some of the victim's women—is similar to that of political relations soon to be discussed in more detail for the Mucajaí mission around this same time. The Uraricaá mission was closed sometime before 1982 (see Lizot 1988:576), but no further information is available about it. Whatever its level of operation, it was about to be swamped in significance by a massive wave of direct Western contact.

In the late 1950s, gold and diamond rushes on the lower Paragua began to extend into Ninam areas, and in the mid-1960s moved into the center of their region of habitation. Colchester (1985d:63–64; and see Ramos 1979a:4) tells what happened when the Ninam of the Paragua-Uraricaá area attained direct contact with Westerners.

> Apparently there was a "wild west" atmosphere in these temporary towns, since there was a total absence of government authority. Flung from scrabbling poverty to fabulous wealth in a few lucky weeks, the miners drew in a substantial floating population of liquor merchants, storekeepers, prostitutes and gun-runners, that only began to move away again in the mid-seventies. . . . The effects of such a society imposed in the middle of the Ninam and Uruak [one of the groups that merged with the Ninam] were shattering. Economically and sexually exploited, the Indians were also exposed to a host of new diseases and subjected to the abrasive ethnocentrism of the "garimpeiros" and "mineros," to whom the Indians were a lower species of being. . . . However, the Ninam remain keenly interested in mining. Recent estimates suggest that there are still thousands of Brazilian garimpeiros working in the gold fields . . . and these fields continue to be visited by Ninam from Venezuela eager for employment in the mining camps.

In the early 1980s, the Ninam around the Paragua were only "remnants" of their former numbers. Even incorporating the survivors of the

Uruak and Sape and a few Sanema, they numbered only 194 people. Near the Uraricaá, the Xiriana cluster amounted to fewer than 200 people in 1986, and in that year alone seven children died of malaria.

Decades of exposure to miners, missionaries, and government agents had transformed Xiriana life, promoting individualism and undercutting previous patterns of leadership. But by the mid-1980s, the Baptist mission was gone and gold mining had lost its boom quality, settling into regular work for long-resident Brazilians. Ninam came to the settled areas to work and trade but kept their own settlements some distance away. Ninam had learned to produce gold themselves, which increased their autonomy. With distance, income, and time, they had worked out a form of interaction with Brazilian society that left them able to preserve many elements of their own traditions rather than being totally deculturated and assimilated (Lazarin 1988:24–27).

The Borabuk and the Mucajaí Mission

We left the Borabuk people in the early 1940s, isolated from others, wandering between the Uraricoera and Mucajaí rivers. A few years later, between 1945 and 1950, a Brazilian boundary commission party traveling up the Mucajaí left one ax, five machetes, and red cloth hung on trees (Peters 1973:61). This was probably the best deal that had ever been offered these Ninam. "There was much excitement among the Shirishana when they found these goods" (Peters 1973:61–62)—understandably, for by this time they "were depleting their supply of steel tools obtained in previous raids" (Early and Peters 1990:19).[9] This encounter "precipitated the move to the banks of the Mucajaí River, where they hoped to meet the people who made steel tools" (Early and Peters 1990: 19), as well as an exploratory mission toward the Apiaú River (Peters 1973:62).

In 1955 or 1956, a missionary scout plane dropped fishhooks, matches, red cloth, and beads at the new settlement. With that miraculous event, the Borabuk were encouraged in their quest to find a source of Western manufactures, making three long exploratory trips to the east between 1956 and 1958. They had a few brushes with Westerners and on two trips contracted respiratory illnesses that killed several men before they returned home. Nevertheless, in November 1958 the Borabuk met and "warmly welcomed" John Peters and Neill Hawkins, who had come to establish a UFM mission among them (Early and Peters 1990: 7, 19–21, 74–75; Peters 1973:62–63).

Peters (1973:98) conducted missionary work among the Yanomami of the Mucajaí area continuously, except for one year, from 1958 to 1966. In 1972 he returned not as a missionary but as a researcher pursuing a Ph.D. in sociology. His thesis is the only monograph-length investigation of any Yanomami that focuses on "The Effect of Western Material Goods upon the Social Structure of the Family among the Shirishana." It has been followed, recently, by the most detailed demographic study done for any Yanomami group (Early and Peters 1990). This body of work offers extraordinary insight into the way differential access to Western manufactures drives the social and political dynamics around a mission, providing a solid foundation for other discussions of missions in chapter 8 and part III. One lacuna, for my purposes, is that no information is provided on balances of trade for indigenous and Western goods. Developments around the Mucajaí mission will be the focus of the remainder of this chapter.

The missionaries began work on the Mucajaí in 1958. At the time, 121 Ninam lived in two villages, the more distant one moving closer to the mission after its founding. They had been isolated from contact with other Yanomami, the nearest of whom lived four to six days' walk away. By 1987, these same Ninam lived in six settlements and numbered 319 people. Despite bouts with new infectious diseases, they had grown at an average annual rate of 3.5 percent, thanks in large part to the medicine and medical care available from the missionaries. Their local population had also grown because of in-migration of people seeking Western goods and because the local advantages of access to those goods and medicines kept people from fissioning and moving off (Early and Peters 1990:4, 6, 25, 66–67, 72, 81, 95–96).

During their first two years of operations, the missionaries paid large quantities of manufactures to the people of Borabuk for their labor in construction and other services. Subsequently, at the request of Brazilian skin dealers, they arranged for the Ninam to supply animal pelts, until that was banned by law in 1970. In 1962, the people of Borabuk established ties with Brazilians living a three- to five-day canoe trip downstream. Work for these mostly poor Brazilian farmers—who could afford no other help than Yanomami—increased after 1969 and again in 1972, when a farmer with a motor launch began a regular transport service. The Ninam also made and sold canoes to the Brazilians (Peters 1973:48–58, 113–14).

The result of all these contacts was a tremendous increase in the Borabuk's supply of Western goods. When Peters met them in 1958, the only Western goods they had were those obtained from their raids in the 1930s, those left as gifts by the boundary commission, and the few items obtained in their four long searches for Westerners in the 1950s. The total was "three axes, five cutlasses, three knives, one hoe, two old shirts, a cap, and a woman's full length slip" (Peters 1973:136). Within two years of the establishment of the mission, the Borabuk's immediate need for steel tools was filled, and the missionaries began to introduce a range of other goods as payment. In 1972, a tabulation of the possessions of 13 males included 7 shotguns, 16 axes, 28 machetes, 20 knives, 17 aluminum pots, 2 adzes, 6 "metal dirt diggers," 7 "fish line," 17 red loincloths, 18 shirts, and 9 pants or shorts. One family possessed 8 machetes. The total list of new Western goods included 36 different items (Peters 1973:115, 117, 210).

Possession of Western goods became a key to both personal and "tribal" (village) status. The traditional social order, ascribed by sex and age, was upset in favor of one oriented toward achievement as measured in the new merchandise. The most Western goods went to younger men, and sometimes women, who "had a quick grasp of the wants and needs of Westerners" and so were hired "by the missionaries, the Brazilians or visiting botanists or anthropologists" (Peters 1973:149). One young man with exceptional ties to the mission and the Brazilians, and a reputation for generosity with the goods he obtained, was recognized as having precocious status as a leader (here defined as the capacity to tell other people what to do). New kinds of inequality developed. Peters calculates that around 1972, the people of Borabuk had a per capita annual earning, in dollar equivalencies of goods, of $15—far above any of their neighbors. Within Borabuk itself there was a great disparity in earnings, "from a low of possibly $2 for very elderly women, to $80 on rare occasions for young men" (Peters 1973:144–45, 149–51).

Access to Western goods became a crucial element affecting marriage and postmarital residence. Wife givers could ask for and receive Western goods from their in-laws (Peters 1973:71–72). Peters describes one young man who sold a canoe to the missionary for the equivalent of $42. With that, he bought an ax, a knife, a pot, and shirts and shorts—but he kept only the ax and a shirt, giving the rest to his wife's family. Another young man told Peters about his next planned purchases: a pot for his wife, and a pot and knife for his mother-in-law. "Another young man wanted to earn a knife. When asked why he wanted a knife, he responded, 'Because my father-in-law has requested one'" (Peters 1973: 118).

"A potential father-in-law may desire his child to marry a certain individual, because this union will bring him material goods in payment" (Peters 1973:75). Peters goes on to describe how, on his arrival, he was offered "two young, single girls because he had a bountiful supply of pots, pans, knives, cutlasses, and axes. The father-in-law would thus have had a claim to these goods." This giving of Western goods to the wife's family largely, though not entirely, replaced the labor obligations of bride service for those with good access to Westerners.

> Those receiving payment of a pot, axe, cutlass, fish line and hooks, or shot gun and powder are prepared to reduce their expectation in bride service. . . . The one making bride payment also has the ability to reduce the amount of time required for bride service, while still accomplishing the equivalent amount of work. His axe, cutlass and file permit him to cut the trees and brush more quickly. These tools along with the adze help to carve a better canoe more rapidly. The shot gun is more accurate than the bow and arrow. (Peters 1973:125)

A man's obligations to his in-laws begin with the betrothal of the girl or young woman, which may be years before cohabitation starts. "With betrothal the male owes gifts and service to the family of the girl. In the postcontact period the presents consisted of trade goods such as axes, knives, beads, clothing, aluminum pots, and hammocks" (Early and Peters 1990:39). These transactions may not live up to all expectations, and conflict may result.

> If the girl becomes involved with another male, she will be scolded and beaten by her parents and brothers in an effort to maintain the betrothal and its incoming gifts. If this fails, there may be violence between the two families to resolve disputes over return of bridal gifts. Even if there is no question over misconduct, conflicts may arise over the regularity of gifts (Early and Peters 1990:39–40).

Another postcontact change was a sharp increase in village exogamy (Early and Peters 1990:66–67; Peters 1973:74, 126–29). The Ninam's isolation ended with the arrival of the mission, and in the next few years, the people around the Mucajaí mission made contact with seven Yanomami and non-Yanomami villages via the initiatives of the missionaries. "They accompanied the missionary, serving as guides and carriers, receiving Western goods as payments" (Peters 1973:129). Typically the missionaries' companions were young men, "a number" of whom "have purchased non-Shirishana women" (1973:126).

In all cases where Borabuk men took wives from outside their village, the couples broke the otherwise firm rule of uxorilocal postmarital residence and continued to live near the mission (Early and Peters 1990:67; Peters 1973:128). "Exogamous marriage in a society which previously practiced tribal endogamy will bring change in the rule of residence especially when one tribe is considered more prestigious than the other. For example, [if] the bride's parents are from a tribe which has a scarcity of metal tools, they will not be as rigorous in demanding the observance of matrilocality if they desire to receive the valued metal goods as bridal payment" (Peters 1973:126–27; and see Early and Peters 1990:95–96).

At the moment of contact with Peters, the Borabuk had a sharply skewed sex ratio and a pronounced pattern of polyandry.[10] In 1958, of 17 marriages, 14 were or had been polyandrous, and one was polygynous. In 1972, of 38 marriages, 35 were monogamous, one polyandrous, and two polygynous; and three men were noted as "working for" a second wife. This shift was made possible by a major change in the ratio of males to females, from 149 males per 100 females in 1957 and 131 males per 100 females in 1962 to 119 males per 100 females in 1967 and 107 males per 100 females in 1972. The change in sex ratio was the result of several things. A disproportionate number of men died during the period. Peters suspects that there was a decrease in female infanticide. But there was also a net gain of 18 wives acquired from other villages. Eight of these were in arranged marriages involving the transfer of Western goods. Seven or eight more were acquired in two raids (Peters 1973: 76–77, 128, 131–32).

Peace, War, and Fate

The Borabuk were peaceful compared with the Orinoco-Mavaca peoples discussed later, or with their own ancestors. Within the community, verbal duels and fist-pounding matches were frequent but did not lead to more severe or protracted violence—despite the extreme scarcity of women in the early mission years. In the postcontact period, homicide accounted for only five deaths among the Mucajaí people—only 3.8 percent of total deaths—and two of the five killings were actually unconfirmed assumptions about men who went on a trip and never came back (Early and Peters 1990:7, 72, 79–80). The Borabuk, however, after being peacefully isolated since the late 1930s, did participate in four assaults in the three decades after missionization.

The first occurred just a few months after the missionaries' arrival in November 1958, although the Ninam kept quiet about it so that the missionaries did not learn about the raid for years (Peters 1973: 57, 102). In early 1959, passing prospectors informed the Borabuk of the existence of another group, the Marashi-teri, farther up the Mucajaí. At the time, the Borabuk were suffering from recently introduced diseases, "a new and frightening experience." They suspected that the Marashi-teri might be practicing witchcraft and went to find out. The Marashi-teri convinced the visitors that it was not they who were practicing witchcraft but a group called Shiri-teri, located even farther into the highlands, close to the upper Parima River. The Marashi-teri guided the Borabuk to the Shiri-teri village (Early and Peters 1990:65, 67).

"It appears that the Marashiteri were manipulating both groups for their own unknown purposes," for they also warned the Shiri-teri about the hostile intentions of the Borabuk. When the Shiri-teri acted "suspicious and reserved," the Borabuk took it as confirmation of their bad intentions. The two visiting groups attacked the Shiri-teri, shooting one *with a gun,* killing three others, and capturing five women (three for the Borabuk men, two for the Marashi-teri). In the future, the Marashi-teri would become major allies of the Borabuk, one of their two largest suppliers of wives. Eventually, peaceful relations were restored with the Shiri-teri by sending the relatives of the captured women "presents" (Early and Peters 1990:64–68).

The second violent event, also concealed from the missionaries for years, took place in 1968. Borabuk was allied with a local Yanomami group called Aica, which was reduced by disease to a few dozen people in 1959. Initial contact between the two occurred when people from Borabuk accompanied the missionaries on a visit in 1959. Over time, the Aica became Borabuk's other main provider of marriage partners. The Aica in turn established marriage links to a group living on the upper Catrimani. Although some Borabuk met the Catrimani people during a visit by the missionaries in 1961, since then contact had been channeled through the intermediate Aica. Relations were bad between the Aica and the Catrimani people despite their marriage ties.

A raid by Catrimani men killed an Aica who was the brother-in-law of a prominent Borabuk man. The Borabuk suspected the Catrimani people of witchcraft and perceived them as having deliberately insulted the Borabuk with accusations of cowardice—two true rallying cries. The Aica guided some Borabuk men to the Catrimani village, where they were well received. But on the third day of their visit, the Borabuk attacked their hosts, killing eight men and capturing four young women (Early and Peters 1990:64–68).

Two other violent episodes are noted (Early and Peters 1990:68). In both cases, small groups of Borabuk men fulfilled obligations to affinal kin by aiding them in raids on other groups, who again were suspected of witchcraft. In 1970, they helped Marashi-teri against the otherwise unknown Duhun-teri; in 1978, they helped the Parime-teri against the Parahudi. No women captives were taken by the Borabuk. (Indeed, according to Early and Peters [1990:94]: "Female seizure is part of the revenge and provides a spoil for the victor, but it is not the motive for the raid itself.") Early and Peters provide no information about the intergroup relations or situational context for these two later acts of violence, where the Borabuk were secondary participants. But the two earlier acts of war already described illustrate some of the permutations of the theoretical model as applied to real life.

The first assault, against the Shiri-teri, took place not long after the Borabuk finally succeeded in locating themselves near friendly Westerners. Suddenly they were afflicted with unknown diseases, which they initially interpreted through a belief system still unaccommodated to the new lethality. Seeking enemy shamans but unsure about whom to blame, they visited the Marashi-teri, taking a shotgun (apparently borrowed under false pretenses) to demonstrate their military strength and the strength of their connection to the Westerners. The Marashi-teri convinced the Borabuk that it was the Shiri-teri who were practicing witchcraft, manipulating a situation that then led to violence between the mission men and the more distant people.

Seven years later, the Marashi-teri began giving brides to the Borabuk men, and over subsequent years they became one of the two main wife-givers to Borabuk (Early and Peters 1990:64–65)—thus receiving Western goods in return. Because betrothal, which initiates bride payment, can be arranged years before marriage, it seems that the Marashi-teri were contracting to give brides to the women-starved Borabuk not long after their first meeting. It appears, then, that in the context of the first permanent Western move into the area, the Marashi-teri began strategic manipulations that created a beneficial alliance for themselves and an opposition between Borabuk and the Marashi-teri's potential competitors, the Shiri-teri.

In the 1968 attack on the Catrimani people, again the targeted group was the village beyond the ally. Although the ally, the Aica, had been intermarrying with the Catrimani group, the killing of an important Aica man shows that this was a strained alliance. It is not clear what was happening in the general contact situation at this time, especially in the Catrimani area, where big changes had been under way since 1965.[11] One salient fact, however, is that in 1962, the missionaries began to give the Borabuk shotguns. (Previously, they had been allowed to borrow Peters's.) By 1965 every male over 16 years old had one. For several years, ammunition was rationed and costly (Peters 1973:54, 115–16), but in 1968, the limit on ammunition was lifted. "One informant indicated that the acquisition of such large quantities of shot facilitated the raid" against the Catrimani people (1973:54). Thus we have a middle-man village (Aica) being threatened by a more remote exchange partner (Catrimani) but able to quash this threat when their allies at the mission receive a big boost in killing power.

Generally, the Borabuk around the mission enjoyed one of the more stable and peaceful alliances with their neighbors, for several reasons. They had access to the missionary's shotgun from the start—and the fact that they were able to conceal their attacks on two villages illustrates the Yanomami's ability to manipulate resident Westerners. Unlike the situation we will find in the Orinoco-Mavaca area, the main Western presence on the Mucajaí was unitary and stable and allowed the Borabuk the opportunity to earn relatively unlimited amounts of Western goods. The area was inhabited by very few other groups, so the Borabuk could easily afford to be generous as well as strong in relation to the Marashi-teri and Aica. Also, the missionaries made occasional visits to those villages, somewhat equalizing status. A similarly equilibrating factor was the extraordinary scarcity of marriageable women among the Borabuk, so that wife-ceding allies could claim a lot.

Out beyond the allied villages, however—beyond the immediate sphere of mission beneficence and protection—there was violent tension. All four acts of war, including the incidents of 1970 and 1978, involved Borabuk acting with allies against more distant groups with whom the Borabuk had little or no direct contact.

Introductions by the missionaries reestablished Borabuk contacts with people from whom they had separated some half a century before, now known as "Xiriana" and living near the Uraricaá mission. The two groups initiated only sporadic contacts "because of the difficult journey and because the Xiriana have their own sources of trade goods"

(Early and Peters 1990:66). The missionaries also brought about contact between the Borabuk and the Parime-teri, Yanomam speakers of the middle Uraricoera mission. In this case there was substantial interaction with the Borabuk: intermarriage, the acceptance by Borabuk of Parime-teri refugees, and, as noted previously, some military support of the Parime-teri (Early and Peters 1990:64–66). As we will see again in later discussions, such "lateral" alliances are not uncommon between groups both of whom have missionaries present.

Around 1974, the southern Ninam began to feel the effects of an intensified Brazilian presence in the area. That was the year when construction crews for a government highway approached their territory. Ninam prospects were bleak within the development plans. In 1978, along the Mucajaí, the Brazilian government began demarcating huge tracts encompassing Yanomami settlements for clear cutting and conversion to cattle ranching (Taylor 1979:79–80). (I could find no later information on this project.) I will return to the impact of the highway in chapter 8.

As of 1981, the people of the Mucajaí had still avoided many deaths from the epidemics brought by Brazilians, because of the "systematic assistance given to them by a group of missionaries of the Unevangelized Field Missions" (Anthropology Resource Center 1981:2; and Taylor 1979:76). But then gold was found near the Mucajaí Ninam, greatly increasing their direct contact with the outside world. Some Ninam began making routine visits to the district capital of Boa Vista. The Mucajaí community fissioned, with some moving a considerable distance downstream and some relocating to a government Indigenous Protection Service (FUNAI) airstrip (Early and Peters 1990:7, 9).

In 1987, fighting broke out with the gold miners. Three Marashi-teri, one "Mucajaí," and five Brazilian miners were killed. The Brazilian government ordered the missionaries to leave the area. As Early and Peters completed their manuscript in 1988, some 20,000 miners were reportedly streaming up the Mucajaí River (Early and Peters 1990:9). Early and Peters (1990:101) see these years as the start of a third and final phase of Western contact, in which those Yanomami who survive are transformed into a rural peasantry attached to the national society.

8

The Yanomam

The Yanomam, also known as "Yanomama" and by several local terms, numbered an estimated 5,000 in 1978 (Saffirio 1985:38). In the early 1980s, they were censused at 5,311 individuals in 64 villages, all but four of which were within Brazil (Colchester 1985b:7). Migliazza (1982: 512) and his colleagues (Spielman, Migliazza, and Neel 1974:643) argue that the Yanomam language diverged from Yanomamo between 75 and 200 years ago. Others (Colchester 1985b:5; Lizot 1988:489), however, question whether any real linguistic boundary separates the two peoples, who live largely on different sides of the Parima highlands watershed.

The Yanomam language itself exhibits considerable diversity, with perhaps three main dialects (Migliazza 1972:35; cf. Migliazza 1980: 104–105): one in the upper Uraricoera–Parima River area, a second on the upper Parima and Orinoco headwaters, and a third in the Catrimani and Demini river basins (map 3). This current distribution is the result of a radiation outwards over the past century (see Saffirio 1985:40, 91) from a homeland that may have encompassed the upper Parima River and extended southward through the adjacent headwaters of the Orinoco and Catrimani and some of the tributaries of the Demini.

Historical information about the Yanomam resembles that available for the Sanema and Ninam. As with the Sanema, there are very few old reports—fewer, indeed, than for the Sanema. No main travel route like the Uraricoera or Ventuari passes close to traditional Yanomam lands, nor did that area see extensive rubber tapping, so most information about the Yanomam is based on observations and ethnohistorical reconstructions made after 1930. As with the Ninam, we have relatively detailed recent information, including a reconstructed history of the contemporary middle Catrimani people and fairly extensive discussions of political dynamics around a few missions in the late 1950s and 1960s.[1]

Yanomam History through the Rubber Boom

As I discussed in chapter 4, Migliazza believes the Yanomam ancestors remained close to the Río Branco longer than any other Yanomami. If he is correct, they would have been the Yanomami most directly exposed to the slave raiders operating along the Río Negro from around 1630, and it would be that raiding which drove them into the highlands. Correct or not, it seems inescapable that people living near the upper Catrimani would have felt the impact of the intensive raiding coming off the Branco in the 1730s and 1740s. Those Yanomam close to the headwaters of the Orinoco may also have been victimized by the Yecuana raids into that area.

But the difficulty of ascending the Catrimani gave the Yanomam substantial protection. Lobo de Almada's boundary expedition of 1787 found it extremely difficult to proceed over the forty or so rapids along the river, and the limited natural resources he encountered made it not worth the effort. No Yanomami are indicated in the area at that time; the people living along the river were the Arawak-speaking Barauana (Albert 1985:57–58; Lobo de Almada 1861:624, 678–79).

Farther than the Ninam from Fort São Joaquim and the Uraricoera route, the Yanomam were probably more isolated from Western sources of metal during the height of European retraction in the first half of the nineteenth century. But some Western goods came in. As noted in chapter 7, there was an unsuccessful attempt to bring natives—apparently Yanomam—from the upper Catrimani in 1849 to repopulate a waning mission near Fort São Joaquim (Hemming 1987:343). That attempt would have provided a smattering of metal to the highlands. More steel may have been carried in by the Carib-speaking Paushiana, who, during the nineteenth century, came from the Mucajaí to supplant the Barauana on the Catrimani (Albert 1985:58).[2]

Brazilian activity in the area was soon to increase. By the early 1850s, the extraction of forest products was a growth industry gradually extending outward from Barra (Manaus). This growth fueled a substantial increase in the quantity of Western manufactured products passing through Barra to the hinterlands (Herndon 1854:250, 265–68).

The ríos Negro and Branco were visited by seekers of some forty different forest products, including tonka beans, nutmeg, puchary laurel, and palm fibers, as well as indigenous manufactures such as hammocks. This broad-spectrum collecting would soon be dwarfed by the juggernaut of rubber, but it would not disappear. After the fall of rubber, it provided work for scattered people of mixed ancestry, who persevered at the fringe of Brazilian society.

Even the period of the rubber boom is almost entirely devoid of hard information about the Yanomam. Rubber trees were not plentiful around the Branco, and the region's main participation in the boom was through cattle production that extended along the plains south of Fort São Joaquim. Some tapping did occur, and those Yanomam near the headwaters of the Demini probably felt the impact of rubber production on the Negro (see chapter 9). But if any direct contact was made between Yanomam and rubber tappers, it does not appear in the written record. Then again, rubber tappers do not leave written accounts.

Ethnographic reconstructions for the Catrimani Yanomam provide some information about this time. Albert (1985:40–41, 1988:94–95) sees the rubber boom as a period of indirect contact in which the Yanomami connection to the outside world was mediated by small groups of non-Yanomami—survivors of the devastated regional population—from whom they obtained steel tools through trade or war or both. Saffirio's (1985:91) informants at Catrimani mission recalled descending from the Parima highlands around the end of the nineteenth century, moving in as the Paushiana "retreated to the South and became extinct."[3] Epidemics reached the Yanomam, and, as Albert (1988:95) reconstructs them, they were generally interpreted as the work of enemy shamans and often led to war. The transmission of pathogens is a strong indication of exchange networks carrying Western goods.

By 1925, the time of Rice's visits, toward the northern reaches of Yanomam residence, some Yanomam had begun their migration north along the Parima River, following after the Ninam. Toward the southern end of the Yanomam ancestral area, similar moves may have been afoot. Sometime apparently between 1874 and 1885, some Yanomami—either Yanomam or Yanomamo—replaced the Barauana on the upper Araçá River (Albert 1985:56), a tributary of the Demini that may have been an area of considerable rubber tapping (see chapter 9). In sum, there are vague but consistent indications that during the rubber boom, Yanomam moved outward toward areas of economic activity, entering into spaces left vacant by migration and epidemics. In the process, they contracted the new diseases themselves and obtained some Western goods through a variety of contacts with other indigenous people.

Intermittent Contacts after the Fall of Rubber

Contemporary observers report a drastic reduction in the Brazilian population on the Río Negro system after 1910 (Schurz 1925:224). Over half the settlements along the rivers were abandoned by 1922 (Tavera-Acosta 1927:59), as former rubber workers retreated to Manaos. Yet even though the Negro was said to be "now in a state of complete decadence" (Schurz 1925:210), many Brazilians remained in the area. An estimate for 1923–24 counted 75,704 people in Manaos, 20,408 along the Negro, and 7,424 along the Branco. What is more, the Branco at that time, in contrast to the Negro, was just beginning an economic revival driven by *balata* and rubber collecting and cattle ranching. Gathering Brazil nuts would be another active pursuit, but it apparently did not reach the Branco-Negro area until a few years later (Schurz 1925:210, 224–25).

This renewed movement of extractors into the region begins a new phase of intermittent Western contact lasting from 1920 to 1965 (Albert 1988:98–99). The early decades of this phase saw the continuing diminution or even extinction of the scattered indigenous groups located between the Yanomami and the outside world. The main culprit was disease. In contrast to the Uraricoera region from the later 1920s on, there is no evidence that Yanomam of the Branco-Negro area were actively raiding their indigenous neighbors. In 1932, Holdridge (1933: 374, 378) visited some Paushiana on the Catrimani, who gave no indication of Yanomami attacks as they described past residences and showed no sign of current concern about Yanomami. Probably these Paushiana had established stable, socially regulated commerce with the more isolated Yanomam—a relationship undisturbed by any sudden concentration of Western goods.

Relationships with intrusive foresters were not always so smooth. As these comparatively well-supplied extractors moved into the forests in the early 1920s, they came into both peaceful and violent contact with the Yanomam who had moved from the highlands during the rubber boom. There is information about two areas, the Catrimani basin and some tributaries of the Demini. The key source is Saffirio's (1985:95–

100) reconstruction of the history of two closely related groups who, in the 1980s, were living on the middle Catrimani.[4] Between 1920 and 1965, their immediate ancestors moved from the Catrimani to the Deminí drainage and then back to the Catrimani.

My goal is not merely to describe those moves but to explain them. Saffirio's work was guided by Chagnon (Saffirio 1985:xii). Like Chagnon, he is concerned with tracing long-distance "macro-moves," and he concentrates on "push" factors such as war and epidemics. I too see those as reasons to move, but I differ from Chagnon and his students in that I believe the "pull" of access to Western manufactures to be even more essential for understanding long-distance relocations. As we follow Saffirio's history of the middle Catrimani people, I will contextualize it with information about the changing Western presence in the area, in an effort to make the fights, migrations, and fissions more understandable.

Balata collecting on the Catrimani began around 1923, and soon forest workers were all along the river. The first reported attack on them by Yanomam ("Pairitiri") occurred in 1926. Over the following years, there were other attacks, each of which prompted the woodsmen's withdrawal from some section of the river (Holdridge 1933: 374, 376). The violence went in both directions. In one instance in the early 1930s, Yanomam near the Catrimani were "massacred" by woodsmen (Soares Diniz 1969:6). Because of the violence, epidemics, and the falling price of *balata* in the global depression (Holdridge 1933:372), both forest workers and Yanomami left the middle Catrimani practically deserted by the mid-1930s (Albert 1985:57, 71; Holdridge 1933:377–79).

Regarding the Yanomami attacks, Holdridge (1933:376) comments: "In most of the cases brought to our attention it seemed evident, however, that the *balateros* had provoked the attacks." There is no reason to doubt his appraisal (and see Albert 1988:99). It will be seen in part III, however, that at the same time, Yanomamo were attacking woodsmen over a broad area in order to loot their possessions. The two explanations do not contradict each other: accumulating abuses by the woodsmen would make the Yanomami more likely to opt for violence to obtain Western goods.

As Saffirio reconstructs the history of the middle Catrimani people, around 1924 they established a garden in the middle Jundiá River, a tributary of the upper Catrimani, where they worked for *balata* collectors (Albert 1985:57). In the late 1920s, they carried out one of only five raids reported for 57 years of reconstructed history. Saffirio provides no detail about this raid except to say (1985:94) that it was "caused by lack of women." Presumably he refers to raiding noted by another source—Salathé (1932), which I was unable to obtain—as having been directed against other Yanomami ("Waika" and "Jauarys") "in order to get young girls and children to increase their population" (Migliazza 1972:382).

This is one of very few incidents of war reportedly initiated with the goal of capturing women. Since I was unable to obtain the primary source on the matter, I cannot comment further except to note the timing—that this outbreak of raiding occurred shortly after these Yanomam experienced direct contact with the *balata* workers.

From September 1929 to February 1930, the Yanomam were visited by an expedition led by Georges Salathé, no doubt acquiring a local fortune in Western manufactures (Soares Diniz 1969:6). (By this time, their "chief" already had a Portuguese name [Soares Diniz 1969:6].) Soon after the expedition left, many Yanomam died in an epidemic. Rich but reduced in numbers, they moved up a local stream to its headwaters. Even on this high ground, they feared the prospect of being raided by a nearby group and so moved again to the headwaters of the Jundiá (Saffirio 1985:95–99). In this case, the connection of events with the Western visit is more obvious.

Albert (1988:98–99) has investigated the perceptions and reactions of Catrimani Yanomam of this period. In his reconstruction, their first experience with forest workers and new diseases in the later 1920s led to divisions among the Yanomam themselves, with some older men urging a return to the highlands. Their route, however, was blocked by "enemies" pushing them from behind. Salathe, too, relates that his hosts had been forced to move from the Parima highlands to the river by other Yanomam ("Paraitirys") (Migliazza 1972:381; Soares Diniz 1965:6).

To return to Saffirio's reconstruction, these Yanomam moved to the headwaters of the Jundiá around 1931 and remained in the area for about seven years, making three gardens. While there, around the middle 1930s, they were visited by rubber tappers who "offered goods to the Indians in exchange for their helping them to tap the rubber and carry it down to the river. At the end of the work, a fight broke out between the rubber-tappers and the Yanomama during which three men were killed. The Brazilians then fled the area" (Saffirio 1985:96). This seems to have been the last expedition of woodsmen into the upper Catrimani for some time. (The rubber the fleeing tappers left behind was recovered only in the early 1960s [Saffirio 1985:100].) Around 1938 these Yanomam abandoned the area too, moving into the Demini drainage. Their relocations around the Demini system suggest an effort to reestablish ties to sources of Western goods.

Developments near the Demini, 1930 to 1960

There are a few complications that must be noted before I discuss developments in the Demini drainage. In recent years, the Demini itself has been inhabited by Yanomamo speakers while its effluents, the Mapulau and Toototobi, have been inhabited by Yanomam. This may be only a recent arrangement. It usually is not possible, however, to distinguish Yanomam from Yanomamo speakers in the historical reports, so for lack of a better alternative I am projecting recent (post-1950) distributions back to the 1930s. Another problem is that of matching streams in the Mapulau-Toototobi-Demini area on Saffirio's map (1985:99) with identifiable rivers on other maps. These complications combine with the usual ambiguities and gaps in the contact history to make the following discussion especially tentative.

The first information on the area comes from Holdridge (1933: 379–84), who in 1932 found a settlement of some two hundred mestizos on the lower Demini. He said they were residents "for many years" (1933:379), suggesting continuity from the rubber-boom days. They were sickly and living "on the verge of starvation" (1933:384) after the recent collapse of prices for the rubber and Brazil nuts they collected. Holdridge met Yanomami along the Demini who had regular contact with the forest workers. Although I consider them to be Yanomamo speakers, they apparently had an alliance with more "primitive" Yanomam farther upstream. This is indicated by Holdridge's observation of one Yanomam ("Pairitiri") woman and Pairitiri trade goods among the Yanomamo (Holdridge 1933:380–382). He commented: "Specimens of the low material culture of this group [Pairitiri] were obtained by barter"(1933:382).

By the time of Holdridge's visit, Yanomamo along the nearby Araçá had made at least two serious attacks on forest workers (Albert 1985: 55; Holdridge 1933:380–82). We will see in chapter 10 that similar raids were conducted all across the southern Yanomamo frontier in the late 1920s and 1930s, leading to the general abandonment of the left bank of the Río Negro by the close of the 1930s. In 1940, a Brazilian frontier commission party was attacked by Yanomami on the lower Demini. But it is not clear whether there were other clashes with woodsmen on the Demini or whether mestizos ever completely withdrew from it. If so, both the violence and withdrawal were short lived. In 1941 and 1943, other Brazilian frontier commission parties made peaceful contact on the Toototobi and Mapulau—contacts still recalled by Yanomam living on the Catrimani River. After those visits, the Toototobi-Mapalau Yanomam began regularly visiting the camps of rubber and Brazil nut collectors on the Demini and consequently experienced a deadly epidemic around 1945 (Albert 1985:69; Migliazza 1972:383).

The Western presence along the Demini and its tributaries continued to grow during the postwar period. Around 1951, an adventurer named Sotelo "reached that region with many other Brazilians. He bartered axes, cutlasses, knives, fishing lines and hooks in exchange for vines, Brazil nuts, and forest fruits" (Saffirio 1985:97). In 1954, the Brazilian Indian Protection Service (SPI) established a post along the Demini. After 1956, a range of activities picked up along the river, including SPI visits to villages, forest product collection, small-scale farming by mestizos, and visits by missionaries. This trend culminated in 1963 with the establishment of a permanent New Tribes mission among Yanomam of the Toototobi. Sometime in the middle 1950s, an epidemic of apparently massive mortality struck the regional Yanomam population (Albert 1985:70–71).

With this contextual information, we can better understand the events reconstructed by Saffirio (1985:96–99). I have already mentioned that around 1938, with the Catrimani deserted by forest workers, the Yanomam crossed from the Catrimani watershed into the upper streams of the Demini watershed. They were at this location (on an upper feeder of the Toototobi?) at the time of the peaceful contacts with the frontier commission in 1941 and 1943. Around 1944, they moved laterally to other feeder streams (closer to the Demini?), where they would remain for about six years. While there, they "exchanged women" with a "friendly" cluster of villages known as Ama-teri (Saffirio 1985:96) and experienced the visit of the Sotelo expedition. Even though Sotelo's visit was followed by an epidemic, within a year or so (around 1952), these Yanomam moved some 28 kilometers downriver—that is, towards the Westerners. Their next move, apparently in 1953 (this is not entirely clear in Saffirio) put them in an even more strategic location for contact with Westerners coming up the rivers.

At this moment of intensifying Western contact in the early 1950s, these Yanomam made the second of their recorded raids, again, according to Saffirio (1985:94, 97, 99), because of a lack of women. Their targets are not identified. Relations with their allies, the Ama-teri, also changed. In the mid-1950s, they began to fear that the Ama-teri would raid them. This fear led to the move in 1953, but it did not end the conflict with the Ama-teri.

> In about 1957, the Amatheri from Thoothothobi . . . invited them for a feast. During the trip to their host's village, the guests were attacked by a large number of Amatheri. Four men were killed. . . . In retaliation, a few months later, at noon time, the Yanomama attacked some elderly Amatheri working in their garden and killed four of them. Being afraid that they might be raided again by the Amatheri in retaliation, they moved northward and settled in the Sarakasik region. (Saffirio 1985:97)

This flight placed them far away from their enemies on the Toototobi and closer to the Catrimani. A few years later, they moved back into the Catrimani watershed itself, as will be described later. With that migration, Saffirio's information about the Deminí region ends.

All of this behavior is to be expected, according to the model. First, there is a period from the mid-1930s to the early 1950s during which Saffirio's Yanomam were relatively isolated from the outside world and experienced no war. Their movements to and within the Deminí watershed (around 1938, 1944, 1951, and 1953) all put them closer to sources of Western goods. Having made those moves, they conducted one raid, target unknown, and went from good to bad terms with the Ama-teri.

The location of the Ama-teri group of villages is not specified other than that it was on the Toototobi, a center of increasing Western activity through the 1950s. My strong suspicion is that the 1951 and 1953 moves by Saffirio's people somehow undercut a previous middleman relationship between them and the Ama-teri and perhaps even threatened to intercept commerce to the Ama-teri. In 1957, with Western movements into the region intensifying, this threat culminated in the slaughter by Ama-teri. In my model, such slaughters—which typically involve members of several local groups and may go against the interests of some of the hosts—are intended to remove a serious threat to trade interests. If that was the motive here, it worked. The weakened victims fled away from their position of accessibility to the Deminí River commerce and towards the Catrimani.

Developments near the Catrimani, 1948 to 1966

Western contact on the Catrimani lagged considerably behind that on the Demini. The Catrimani was abandoned by Westerners in the mid-1930s, and the first reported return was in 1948, when a group of *balateros* established a camp on a feeder of the lower Catrimani. They made peaceful contact with Yanomam groups who came down from another lower Catrimani feeder, the Xeriana River. Contact continued and intensified. By the late 1950s, three Yanomam communities were located on the lower Catrimani, regularly working for the *balata* gathers. At this time, one village was decimated by an epidemic (Albert 1985:71–71b).

In 1960, an adventurous *balata* collector named Pacheco renewed contact with the Yanomam, or some division of them, on the upper Catrimani. In 1962, Pacheco and his colleagues began extending their gum collecting, and a Catholic missionary, Father Bindo Meldolesi, made contact with Yanomam of the lower Catrimani. In October 1965, Bindo Meldolesi and a Father Calleri established a permanent mission of the Order of Consolata, with an airstrip, on the upper Catrimani at its juncture with the Pacu River (Albert 1985:71–71b; Shapiro 1972: 26; Soares Diniz 1969:6–7). Those events bring us back to the history reconstructed by Saffirio.

We left Saffirio's Yanomam after their war with Ama-teri, as they fled up a stream towards the Catrimani. Aspects of their movements from 1958 to 1965 are unclear (Saffirio 1985:97–100; Shapiro 1972: 26–29), but they involve fissioning, with two or three divisions moving to the upper reaches of Catrimani tributaries no later than 1963 and perhaps as early as 1960. One segment, known as the Hewenahipi-teri, returned to the Jundiá River in the upper Catrimani area, which they had left in the late 1930s. (The Hewenahipi-teri appear to be the group Shapiro calls Kaxipi-teri, who, in her account, seem to be the group that met Pacheco in 1960 and worked for him in 1962.) In 1966, a year after the founding of the Catholic mission, they made the first of three downstream moves that would bring them to the Catrimani River itself in 1978. But by 1967, if not before, they had regular contact with visiting Westerners (Soares Diniz 1969:2).

The other division, called Wakathau-teri, took bolder steps. Between 1962 and 1965, they made two "macro-moves" to and down a stream that feeds into the lower Catrimani—that is, toward the established center of *balata* gathering. In this location they were among the Yanomam most exposed to the incoming Westerners (Saffirio 1985:

97–99; Shapiro 1972:26–28). (In Saffirio's reconstruction, it was the Wakathau-teri who dealt with Pacheco in 1960 and 1962.) Very shortly after the Catholics established their mission along the Catrimani, the Wakathau-teri moved to a spot across the river from the mission. Then, in late 1966, they moved across the river to settle "very close to the Mission Center where they still reside" (Saffirio 1985:100).

These moves were made with such haste that even in 1967 the Wakathau-teri had not yet constructed a collective house (*shabono*) and had to borrow the missionaries' canoe to get food from their gardens across the river. Their haste is understandable. Other, more distant Yanomam were already setting up temporary residences near the mission, in order to work to obtain Western goods (Shapiro 1972:29–33; Soares Diniz 1969:1).

According to Saffirio (1985:97), the Hewenahipi-teri and Wakathau-teri had fissioned "because of a dispute over women and garden produce." In my view, this suggests some broader strain within the original group, perhaps a disagreement about how to approach the Westerners. Behaviorally, the respective actions of the two after fissioning represent alternative pathways toward the Westerners expanding along the Catrimani. The Hewenahipi-teri migrated into familiar lands where the Westerners were known to visit, but still some distance from the major centers of their activity. The Wakathau-teri took a riskier course into unknown land and toward the center of mestizo activity. In 1966, this strategy paid off when they "captured" a mission.[5]

This entire discussion of the period of intermittent contact, 1920–65, has dealt with southern and southeastern extensions of the Yanomam.[6] I have said nothing about Yanomam expansion northward along the Parima River. In fact, very little is known about these groups that was not already mentioned in chapter 7, as these Yanomam followed in the wake of northward-moving Ninam. To recapitulate, Holdridge believes the timid Yanomami met by Rice along the Parima River in 1925 were "Pairitiri"—Yanomam. That area went from peaceful to violent as trading picked up along the Uraricoera route in the late 1920s. The Yanomam were probably involved in the general warfare along the river in the 1940s. By 1950, they may have been reduced to one group along the Uraricoera called "Guadema," who were "shirishanizing" through contact with Yecuana. There is no indication of regular, direct contacts with Westerners until 1958, when the Protestant Uraricoera mission was founded.

Thus, intensification of Western contact on the Uraricoera lagged a decade behind developments on the Catrimani and even farther behind intensifying contact on the Demini. Albert's general assessment of changing political, economic, and migratory orientations among Yanomam would seem to apply to this period of the 1940s and 1950s: "Their networks of political alliance, once oriented towards the Yanomam of the north where they obtained fragments of metal provided by Yekuana (*caribes*), were progressively abandoned. Their migratory trajectory turned towards the south in the pursuit of alliances with Yanomam groups in regular relations with the 'whites,' or of sites closer to those which the latter occupied or frequented" (Albert 1988:98).

Four Missions

In 1957, missionaries visited the middle Uraricoera. In 1958, the Unevangelized Fields Mission (UFM) established a post next to the "Guadema," also known as Parime-teri (Migliazza 1972:387–88; Ramos 1972:26–27), who apparently were a composite of two local groups (Chagnon et al. 1970:348). Little information is available about the impact or operations of what was called Waica Mission. In 1963, it was drawing in Yanomami from at least three other groups (Chagnon et al. 1970:348). Reportedly, raids in the area occurred "only every four or five years" (Chagnon 1966:193). This suggests one or two raids since the founding of the mission, a pattern consistent with the rise of a secure, mission-based hegemon. However, the Parime-teri's political strength would shortly undergo a drastic reduction, and military conflict would intensify correspondingly.

As described in chapter 7, the middle 1960s saw a gold and diamond rush in the Paragua-Uraricaá area, which sucked in Ninam and others (Colchester 1985d:63–64). By 1968, so many Yanomami had moved north that few groups remained near the mission, and the UFM shifted its resources and personnel to another mission. The Uraricoera mission was closed around 1969 (Ramos 1972:26–27), although an airstrip was maintained to permit "sporadic contact" with the Parime-teri. The Parime-teri did not remain near the airstrip for long, however: "since then these Indians moved to an island downriver for purposes of defense against enemy raids" (Ramos 1972:26; and see Montgomery 1970:26, 36, 72, 98). So a mission closes, eliminating its military and political support to resident Yanomam, and those residents are beleaguered. Again, the connection is obvious. Thus beleaguered, the Parime-teri fell back upon a distant ally.

In 1960, the missionaries took some Borabuk Ninam from the Muca-jaí mission to the Uraricoera mission to help lengthen the airstrip as requested by the Brazilian air force. While there, the Borabuk men initiated an alliance with the Parime-teri. With the phased withdrawal from Waica Mission in the late 1960s, the Parime-teri became more dependent on the Borabuk. Intermarriage began in 1968, and in all cases it was Parime-teri who moved to the Mucajaí. (A generation before, the flow was in the opposite direction, as some Borabuk migrated to live with the Parime-teri [Chagnon et al. 1970:348].) They were joined by two families fleeing Parime-teri after a killing within that group. In 1978, in otherwise unknown circumstances, the Parime-teri invoked affinal obligations to secure Borabuk assistance in a raid against the Parahudi, whom they accused of witchcraft (Early and Peters 1990:64–68). Around this same time, it appears the Parime-teri also had "equivocal relations" and some intermarriage with Sanema around the Auaris (Colchester 1981b:116), but no other information is available about this or the more recent history of the Parime-teri Yanomam.

On the Toototobi River at the southern end of the Yanomam range, the New Tribes missionaries were expanding their presence and reaching new groups in the later 1960s. In 1968, they claimed a "breakthrough" when the "chief" of the Yanomam at the mission and some twenty others declared themselves to be Christian (Wardlaw 1966; Wardlaw and Wardlaw 1968). Thus the missionaries were shocked when, in early 1970, some mission Yanomam, along with men from two other villages, raided a Yanomami group to their north in Venezuela. Using shotguns, they reportedly killed eight (although this may be exaggerated) and captured two women. The raid was concealed from the missionaries and only became known to them because the leader of the Christian faction, who had been trying to establish better ties with the victimized group, told the missionaries about it (Wardlaw 1970). Here, as on the Mucajaí and elsewhere, we see the pattern in which a strong mission group with neighboring allies attacks a more distant group—but no other information is available.

In contrast, quite a lot is known about the Catrimani mission founded in 1965, which drew the Wakathau-teri to its side in 1966. The Brazilian government gave the Catholics the authority to restrict movement of outsiders into the area, and they closed it to tappers and other woodsmen (Albert 1988:103; Saffirio 1985:90). This put the Wakathau-teri in the strong position of being connected to the only Western presence on the middle Catrimani.

Two anthropologists, Edson Soares Diniz and Judith Shapiro, worked in the Catrimani mission area in late 1967 and 1968. In their writings, both discuss intervillage relations about two years after the mission's founding. The Wakathau-teri acted as intermediaries in the trade of Western goods from the mission, a role that gave them prestige (Soares Diniz 1969:4).[7]

From data presented by Soares Diniz (1969:3–5, 10–12), we can see several other things that made the Wakathau-teri special. They were relatively exogamous, they had a net gain of several women through exogamous marriages, and they had one of the best male-to-female sex ratios in the area (100:113 versus a regional average of 100:78). Although the Wakathau-teri were only a medium-sized group for this area (32 people when the range was 7 to 45 people per local group), and accounted for only 16 percent of the local population, they also accounted for three out of six local polygynous unions—women from other villages who had been promised to Wakathau-teri men who already had one wife. In sum, the situation appears very similar to the trade-prestige-marriage pattern previously described for the Mucajaí mission.

Shapiro discusses the politics of these changing intergroup relations. She found nearby villages forming new ties with Wakathau-teri and visiting the mission "eager to obtain the axes, machetes, matches and other items" that the priest paid out (Shapiro 1972:29).

> The mission presence constitutes an important additional consideration in the formation of alliance strategies. Groups located at a distance from the mission stations of these respective regions were seeking to establish firmer ties with those living in closer proximity to the new source of material wealth. During my stay in the Catrimani, the headman of the "Pauxiana" village was trying to increase contact with the Catholic mission at Wakatauteri by offering his daughter to the Wakatauteri headman, who—for his part—jealously guarded the exclusive privileges he enjoyed as host to the foreigners. (Shapiro 1972:114–15)

Shapiro also writes:

> Intervillage relations have been affected by the mission: on the one hand, new lines of communication have been opened and alliances established . . . on the other hand, the mission serves as a focus for rivalries, with the Yanomama of Wakatauteri jealously seeking to maintain their privileged position. Furthermore,

the presence of the mission with its firearms has had an effect on warfare activity, making enemy groups more hesitant about entering the area on raids. (Shapiro 1972:33)

Shapiro's and Soares Diniz's observations are especially important in that they describe the extensive changes that occurred within two years of the mission's founding. Bruce Albert worked in the same area from the mid-1970s to mid-1980s. His findings confirm and elaborate those already presented and show how strong and persistent a structuring force was the Catrimani mission.

> The communities closest to the missions assume a regional monopoly of manufactured objects which they obtain in abundance.
> . . . They benefit first from missionary paramedical assistance, and from protection from the risks of intercommunity politics, in which a dissuasive presence is assured them, in the minds of more isolated groups, by the "whites" and their overwhelming power. The "mission communities" thus try to monopolize and to manipulate to their own profit, in the game of intercommunity politics, the material and non-material advantages deriving from the presence of these posts established in their territory. . . . Networks of intercommunity alliance become more polarized and progressively more dense around these mission communities: neighboring local groups attempt to weave with them as many matrimonial ties as they can, in order to arrange, through affinal relations, regular access to the attentions and windfall wealth of the missionaries. (Albert 1988:102–103, translated by Barbara Price)

Finally, Saffirio and Hames (1983:27) add details that further highlight the similarity between developments around the Catrimani mission and those previously described for the Mucajaí mission. Western manufactures were substituted for bride service, and the ability to acquire these goods replaced age and sex as the main basis of social status. In sum, the presence of the mission was as much the central fact of political life in the middle Catrimani area as it was on the Mucajaí and Auaris.

Compared with fighting in some other places of intensifying contact, there has not been much warfare among Yanomami in the area of the Catrimani mission (Saffirio 1985:66–67). Adult male mortality in war is among the lowest reported for any Yanomami: 14 percent (Albert 1989:637). Saffirio's (1985:94) reconstruction shows no raids by Hewenahipi-teri or Wakathau-teri from the time they returned to the Catrimani until the arrival of the Brazilian highway in 1974. Shapiro (1972:170) contrasts the people of the middle Catrimani to the belligerent Yanomamo of the Orinoco-Mavaca area. The primary reason for this contrast, in terms of my model, is the unchallengeable hegemony of the mission village and the relatively unchanging character of contact circumstances.

The mission's ability to limit the entrance of outsiders made it a true monopolist of Western presence, a status it maintained until 1973 (Albert 1988:103; Shapiro 1972:26–27). It stayed put, and it began giving out shotguns soon after its establishment, so that by the early 1970s, 20 percent of local men had one (Saffirio 1985:73). Thus, although Wakathau-teri did not have superior numbers of warriors, they still enjoyed clear and steady military and political dominance. Furthermore, the mission's labor payment system (Shapiro 1972:29–31, 41–42) enabled the Wakathau-teri to earn goods far in excess of their own needs, so they could be generous as middlemen—a generosity made relatively easy by the small size of the local population, only 199 people in 8 local groups (Soares Diniz 1969:3–4). All together, conditions around the Catrimani mission were even more favorable for peace than they were around the Mucajaí mission.[8] This peace would be broken in 1974 when a new Western presence entered the area. But before examining that change, there is another mission to be considered.

This fourth mission takes us into a geographical area not previously discussed—the heartland of Yanomam territory. In 1961, the UFM established a mission at Surucucu in the Parima highlands. The missionaries reached this highland savannah by helicopter, and, after one relocation in 1964, they built and maintained an airstrip in cooperation with the Brazilian air force. By the time of Shapiro's fieldwork in this community in 1968, it had become the UFM's primary mission in Brazil, both in terms of mission staff and the number of Yanomami around it (Shapiro 1972:39–40). It would be the only Western outpost in the area until 1975 (Taylor 1979:48). The first Yanomam people with whom the missionaries had contact, and whose village lay closest to the mission, were the Aikam-teri (Shapiro 1972:41).

Shapiro reports that the mission provided a new basis for social interaction between people of different Yanomam villages, but it also generated new tensions.

The mission also served as a focus for intergroup jealousy. As is the case in the Catrimani, groups with the longest history of contact with the mission were anxious about preserving their privileges. For example, the Mayupateri have as yet been reluctant to spend much time around the Surucucu station since they know that this would displease their Aikam-teri allies. It should also be remembered that, in both the Catrimani and Surucucu areas, groups who come from a distance to work at the mission depend to some degree on receiving food from local villages, a situation that is not particularly appealing to the potential hosts. (Shapiro 1972:43)

Shapiro presents brief sketches of a variety of political relationships that revolved around the mission, the Aikam-teri, and one of the three smaller groups into which the Aikam-teri divided, known as Fenama-teri. These cases illustrate the ambivalence inherent in all political options and the use of force within alliance relations.

One case concerns the Titirimopa-teri, a nearby group that, during Shapiro's stay, sent "steady visitors and workers" to the mission (Shapiro 1972:38, 41). The Titirimopa-teri and Aikam-teri were drawing closer in 1968, propelled by common fear of a hostile group, the Maraxi-teri, who lived four or five days' walk to the southeast. But the deepening alliance was not without mutual distrust and even some club fights. One problem arose when a Titirimopa-teri woman who had been given to the Fenama-teri headman ran away because of the abuse she suffered in her new home. The Fenama-teri let this woman go, perhaps because they needed Titirimopa-teri support too much to press the point.

A second case involves Mayupa-teri, a village that at the time had only infrequent contacts with missionaries (Shapiro 1972:41, 121–22, 177). The Mayupa-teri gave the Fenama-teri one of the latter's two in-married women. Having given a bride, Mayupa-teri would have a claim on a Fenama-teri woman if the two were in an equal, reciprocal relationship. Perhaps that was the thinking behind the elopement of a Mayupa-teri man with a Fenama-teri woman. The Fenama-teri, angered by the absence of any payment for the bride, went to the Mayupa-teri village ready for a club fight. Since the two were otherwise on good terms, they opted, after considerable shouting, for a less dangerous test of strength— a physical tug of war, with the Fenama-teri woman the "rope." The Fenama-teri won, and brought the woman home. The Fenama-teri had demonstrated the number and resolve of their men, establishing that this was not a balanced but an unequal alliance.

A third case involves the Fenama-teri's ties to one of a cluster of villages known collectively as Xite-teri, who were uncontacted by the missionaries until the end of Shapiro's fieldwork (1972:41, 178).[9] One of the Xite-teri villages had given the Fenama-teri the second of their two in-married women. Although the Fenama-teri "are on hostile terms with several of the Xiteteri groups, they do have friendly relations with the one from which she comes and her own father was at Fenama-teri on an extended visit during my stay in the village" (Shapiro 1972: 178). This case illustrates again how raiding and wife-ceding can occur in proximity as alternative strategies for obtaining Western goods. Because Fenama-teri had a population of only around thirty people, its having two in-married wives (not including the Titirimopa-teri woman who ran away) and other marriages under negotiation shows again the marital advantage of being associated with a mission.

Finally, there is the case of Maraxi-teri, the village southeast of the mission that was threatening people closer to the mission (Shapiro 1972:38–39, 41, 147). The Maraxi-teri had never been visited by the missionaries. In unspecified circumstances, some Maraxi-teri men killed four men in an ambush. Another deadly fight is mentioned by Montgomery (1970:147), who visited Surucucu sometime during the 1960s. She refers to the killing of five Parahudi, who lived some distance to the north (and who were raided by Parime-teri in 1978). The aggressors, called Maithas, lived between the Parahudi and the mission, and they blamed the Parahudi for several recent deaths from a new disease.

These killings are the only combat deaths reported for the area, although coverage there is far from complete. Montgomery (1970:26, 85, 88, 111, 140, 146) provides other indications of widespread tension and hostility, including fear of ambushes, pounding matches, suspicions of witchcraft, woman theft, palisaded villages, and village relocations away from enemies. In these characteristics the region bears some resemblance to the Orinoco-Mavaca area described in part III. Shapiro (1972:33, 178–79) specifically contrasts Surucucu with Catrimani as being more conflicted and thus more involved in alliance building. She attributes this to the greater density of settlement in the Surucucu.

As noted in chapter 2, the conflicts outlined in my model can be aggravated by demographic density. More people in an area mean that it takes more Western goods to fill local needs—much more around the Surucucu than around other missions. Around Surucucu there were substantial inequalities even in the most basic goods. Montgomery (1970: 112) notes that some nearby communities were still so short of steel that it limited the size of their gardens and made house building more difficult. Along with the demographic factor, it also appears that the people attached to the Surucucu mission had less access to shotguns than people around the Catrimani or Mucajaí missions, which would have hampered their ability to establish effective hegemony over potential competitors.[10] Finally, there are spatial considerations that may have contributed to political instability, but these are impossible to assess.[11]

The period of missionary dominance ended in 1974, when other outside forces came onto the scene. Although information about the missions among the Yanomam never approaches completeness in terms of the model, there still is more than enough information to support and extend the general point already documented for the Auaris and Mucajaí missions—that the establishment of a Western outpost immediately transforms local political relations. Almost instantly, a mission becomes the center point in all alliances and conflicts, and intervillage relations are driven by actors' desires to improve their access to Western goods from this source.

My discussions of the missions and their effects in this and the previous two chapters will provide a comparative base for more detailed analyses in part III. Many parallels will be evident—as well as one big difference. In the Orinoco-Mavaca area, the frequently changing configuration of the Western presence prevented the development of a stable, nonviolent situation and instead fostered recurrent outbreaks of war.

The Highway and the Miners

In 1974, construction crews for the Brazilian Northern Perimeter Highway entered the middle Catrimani basin. This and subsequent development projects soon resulted in major epidemics and cultural devastation. The ultimate result was to end the political autonomy of the Yanomam in the area, and with it, the possibility of waging war.[12] But the initial impact of the highway was quite different. Initially, the arrival of the road crews led to a sudden burst of raiding.

The best described case involves a group called Opik-teri, who lived not far from the Catrimani mission. After noting that "raids are infrequent in the Catrimani River Basin," Saffirio (1985:66–67; and see Ramos 1979b:13) goes on to note an exception: a raid by Opik-teri against an "unrelated" village (Raynathausu-teri) two days' walk away. A son of the Opik-teri headman had died suddenly, and a shaman blamed the Raynathausu-teri headman and two of his male kin for "the spell that killed his son."[13] About fifteen young men went to raid, killing the three suspects and perhaps another man. That many deaths would greatly reduce the military capability of a small village of about thirty people.

Saffirio sees the underlying interests in this raid as the desire to obtain women. "The Opik-teri were in dire need of women" (1985:66), a condition to be expected in a wife-ceding ally of a mission village. The raiders captured two women, who were given to the young men who did the killing (1985:67). There is no reason to doubt that the possibility of obtaining a wife was an incentive for young bachelors to go on the raid. But they were not the men who identified the "sorcerers" or organized the war party. The timing and geography of this raid suggest another rationale.

The headman's son died in June 1973 (Saffirio 1985:66). The raid, however, did not occur until February 1974 (Ramos 1979b:13). In September 1973, construction of the highway began, reaching the middle Catrimani in January 1974 (Saffirio 1985:99–101). At the time, the victims were living between the raiders' village and the oncoming highway (Ramos 1979b:13, 21). As a result of the raid, the survivors "moved East and settled in an area far away from the Opiktheri" (Saffirio 1985: 67). In late 1974, the Opik-teri moved about 10 kilometers to the north to settle close to the highway, where they manifested "a fascination with the road and all it represented" (Ramos 1979b:21; and see Saffirio and Hames 1983:13–14). In mid-1975, 19 survivors from Raynathausu-teri returned to live with their former enemies along the road (Ramos 1979b: 13)—suggesting the malleability of sentiments of revenge. The timing of the raid and subsequent movements are all consistent with an effort by the Opik-teri to improve access to the intrusive Westerners.

Other raids at this time are mentioned in Saffirio's reconstruction of the history of the Wakathau-teri and Hewenahipi-teri. It will be recalled that in 57 years, only five raids by these people were recorded, including one in the late 1920s and two in the 1950s. The final two "were in revenge for the death by witchcraft of Wara Pata, a famous headman in August/September 1975" (Saffirio 1985:94). No other information is provided. Again we find a remarkable coincidence in timing. After almost two decades without carrying out a single raid (that is, since their retaliation against the Ama-teri around 1957, before the split into the Wakathau-teri and Hewenahipi-teri groups), in the year after the highway arrives these people carry out *two* raids.

This outbreak of raiding was temporary, confined to the period of change when the Catrimani mission's monopoly was being undermined. The new pattern that developed included multiple sources of Western manufactures all along the roadway. A relative abundance of once-scarce items began flowing across overlapping and continuously changing networks of exchange and individual movement (Albert 1988:105; Saffirio and Hames 1983:14–15). These conditions, I argue, are conducive to an end of war, and there is no indication of raiding in the area after 1975.[14] Unfortunately, this date does not signal the beginning of a golden age of peace. On the contrary, the arrival of the road accelerated a process of ethnocide.

One cause of tremendous social disruption was the increase in new diseases (Ramos 1979b:5–33). Initially, the Brazilian government made no effort to vaccinate Indians against expectable infections. When they did provide medical assistance it was grossly inadequate. A measles epidemic struck in June 1974. Rather than have a witness to the continuing abuse and destruction, in February 1976 the government prohibited from the area anthropologist Kenneth Taylor, who had been running an effort to assist the Yanomami. A second measles epidemic, in February 1977, "was so deadly that three villages lost half their population. The dead were so numerous and the survivors so weak that no funeral rites could be performed: the bones of the deceased were left to decay on the forest floor because nobody could take care of them" (Saffirio 1985:20).

The figures are stunning. In settlements near the highway and a FUNAI post without medicines, 22 percent of the population died between late 1973 and mid-1975 (Ramos 1979b:9, 13). Three small villages, recently arrived in the region after migrating eastward for 20 years, suffered death rates of 51 percent, 46 percent, and 30 percent in the measles epidemic of 1977 (Saffirio and Hames 1983:12). Villages closest to the missions avoided such high mortality because of the dedicated efforts of mission personnel, but they still were afflicted with malnutrition, influenza, and malaria—the last having become far worse as a result of massive deforestation for "development" (Ramos 1979b:22–25).

The impact of disease was aggravated by other pressures leading to disorganization and deculturation (Ramos 1979b). Game depletion eliminated meat sharing—a basis for social solidarity—in villages closest to the highway (Saffirio and Hames 1983:35–41). In the Orinoco-Mavaca area, similar mortality and depletions contributed to a lowered threshold for violence (Ferguson 1992a), and thus to a climate of war. But those trends developed over decades, during which time the Yanomamo remained politically autonomous and still highly conflicted over scarce steel tools. In the Catrimani, the disruption of the mid-1970s was not only massive but sudden, and it was accompanied by a reduction in competition between Yanomam for Western goods and by intensified pressure to assimilate into Brazilian society.

Yanomam near the highway quickly became thoroughly entwined in commodity production and dependent on an expanded range of manufactured goods (Saffirio and Hames 1983:15–17). "For the Yanomama the goal of acquiring these goods and customs is to present an image to Brazilians that they are just like Brazilians or *civilizados* and unlike *indios brabos* (wild Indians). In no sense is this goal irrational because the Yanomama realize that if they appear like Brazilians they will be able to interact with them more successfully" (Saffirio and Hames 1983:19).

The residents of Opik-teri along the highway "think of themselves as Brazilian-like people because they wear clothes and thongs, own Brazilian hammocks, smoke cigarettes, speak some Portuguese words, and work at the FUNAI posts, and for settlers. The Yanomama who live far from the highway also think of the Opiktheri as Brazilian-like people. However, the Brazilians still consider them Indians" (Saffirio and Hames 1983:26). Thus the massive disorganization of the mid-1970s led not to intensified warfare but to decreased resistance to assimilation into the lowest stratum of Brazilian society.

Construction work on the Northern Perimeter Highway did not last very long. Shifting development aims and a lack of firm economic foundation brought a halt to construction in 1976 (Pinto 1989:41; Ramos 1979b:5). (There would be additional construction after 1980 [Albert 1988:104].) But this was not an end to government-promoted disruption of the Yanomami. In 1975, the government announced the results of a mineral survey, identifying workable radioactive minerals in the Surucucu area (Taylor 1979:49–51). This announcement prompted a rush of would-be mineral exploiters, *garimpeiros,* into the highland center of Yanomami habitation, where more than 4,500 Yanomami lived within a 150-kilometer radius. The entrance of these prospectors was prohibited by the Brazilian constitution and by law, but no effort was made to turn them back (Anthropology Resource Center 1981:2; Taylor 1979:49–53, 73). Within a year of the government's announcement, some 500 *garimpeiros* had arrived, seeking a big strike or working deposits of cassiterite, a kind of tin (Taylor 1979:53, 58). Within two years, venereal and other diseases were rampant among local Yanomam (Migliazza 1980:105).[15]

Thus, in the Surucucu area as in the Catrimani basin, the old mission monopoly as a source of Western goods ended abruptly, although the *garimpeiros* brought fewer goods than had come with the highway. At first, relations with the *garimpeiros* were good. The Yanomami brought them plantains and yams, which the prospectors bought with Western goods (Taylor 1979:61). But rather quickly, a less happy situation developed. In September 1975, about six months after the first *garimpeiros* arrived, men from the mission village of Aikam-teri killed a member of another native group 32 kilometers to the southeast (the direction of Aikam-teri's enemies in 1968), using a shotgun given to them by *garimpeiros*. Relatives of the victim retaliated in December, wounding an Aikam-teri man with "a home-made 'bullet' fired from a shotgun" (Taylor 1979:61). The parallel to events on the Catrimani is striking. The Aikam-teri, with no previous record of raiding, are embroiled in reciprocal violence with another group within months of the end of their monopoly.

More violence followed. Around April 1976, the Yanomami of the area "began the practice of attacking and sacking the *garimpeiros'* camps, taking clothes, hammocks, cooking pots and, especially, firearms" (Taylor 1979:61). One attack at the end of August left a Yanomami and two *garimpeiros* seriously wounded. Feeling themselves in danger, the *garimpeiros* began to leave the area, and subsequently the government took action to expel those who remained (1979:61–62). No later information is available about violence by or against the Yanomam of the Surucucu region.

Despite steps such as the expulsion of *garimpeiros* in late 1976, Brazilian pressure on the Yanomami continued to increase. For the highlands, the government developed a new plan of mineral exploitation by major national and multinational corporations (Taylor 1979:62–69, 75–90). In the lower areas, around the Catrimani (as around the Mucajaí in chapter 6), plans were set in motion to clear-cut huge expanses of forest for ranching within Yanomami territory. In 1981, a new mineral rush was set off by the discovery of gold, diamonds, and titanium (Wright and Davis 1981). In 1985, the interests of the Brazilian military and national and multinational economic enterprises came together in a new Calha Norte Project. Its plan was to develop an integrated, multi-industry complex capitalized by locally mined gold and linked to aggressive land development, all joined by a regional network of roads (Albert 1990b, 1992:52–54; Lazarin 1988; Pinto 1989:41; Santilli 1989, 1990).

Against these wealthy and powerful interests, a network of anthropologists, missionaries, and other individuals has been working since 1968 to prevent the destruction of the Brazilian Yanomami. Since 1978, efforts have been aimed at the creation of a Yanomami Indian Park to preserve their territory from invasion. The government was reluctant, to say the least, to act on the proposals of the Commission for the Creation of the Yanomami Park (CCYP). For general discussion of these efforts over time, see Albert (1992); CCYP (1979, 1989a, 1989b); Chagnon (1992a:212–16); Davis (1979); Davis and Wright (1981); Ramos (1979b:40); Turner (1991); and Yanomami (1989).

After a brief waning of its influence in the middle 1980s, the Brazilian military in 1987 reasserted its control over development plans for Brazilian Indian lands, including that of the Yanomami. But now their plans were repackaged with attention to the increased international concern over the rain forest and its indigenous inhabitants. Two decrees in 1988, couched in environmental rhetoric, proposed to "protect" Yanomami lands in Brazil in a way that actually opened up 71.5 percent of that land to only slightly restricted development. All the Yanomami in Brazil would be confined to 19 discontinuous zones, a move certain to doom their traditionally mobile subsistence practices and thus to doom much of Yanomami culture.[16]

With this official backing, the *garimpeiro* population operating within Brazilian Yanomami territory swelled to some 40,000 (Albert 1992:38–44). As many commentators have noted, the *garimpeiros'* technique for extracting gold particles from river sediments has dumped massive quantities of toxic mercury into local waters.

As detailed in the sources cited earlier, the combined maladies brought by the *garimpeiro* invasion were devastating in their demographic and cultural impact. The Brazilian government attempted to minimize the bad publicity by banning from the area those who might tell the tale, including missionaries, anthropologists, and reporters (Albert 1992:56). But word did get out, and international pressure on Brazil continued to mount. In 1990, the inauguration of President Collor de Mello marked a significant change in Brazilian policies.

The first year of his administration saw tentative steps to protect the Yanomami and other indigenous peoples of Brazil, but these were held back by stiff Brazilian political opposition. In early 1991, as international pressure reached new heights and appeared more likely to have serious financial repercussions, the Brazilian government took more dramatic steps, initiating a health program and suspending implementation of the previous plan to dismember Yanomami lands. In November 1991, it granted the Yanomami rights to a continuous expanse of land covering some 36,000 square miles. The *garimpeiros* were down to about 7,000 in

June 1991, and reportedly, most were gone by early 1992 (Albert 1992: 61; Chagnon 1992a:216). On May 25, 1992, Collor de Mello ratified the official demarcation of Yanomami lands (Cultural Survival 1992:4).

Thus the Brazilian Yanomami have been given a respite. There are no grounds for complacency, however. Now and for the near future, the greatest danger to Brazilian Yanomami is a very powerful alliance of the military and large-scale mining concerns. As Albert (1992) demonstrates, these groups have become increasingly sophisticated in the use of environmentalist and indigenist rhetoric to deflect international pressure while they position themselves for future advantage. Albert (1992: 56) concludes that this recent history "draws attention to the need for the NGOs [nongovernmental organizations] to monitor the political impact of their campaigns closely in order to thwart governmental manipulation of conservationist concepts, to the detriment of Indian populations and their habitat."

PART III

The Yanomamo

9

The Yanomamo through the Rubber Years: 1820 to 1920

In the next six chapters, the story of Yanomami warfare gets personal. Its general outline will be familiar because it closely parallels the historical situations and Yanomami actions already described. But as the narrative turns to the Yanomamo, the door is open to a more human perspective. Readers will encounter one extraordinary person, Helena Valero, who as a girl was captured by the Yanomami and whose story provides a window into a Yanomamo community during times of maximum "isolation" and then during the disruptive return of outsiders. This same group of Yanomamo is followed up through the time it was studied by Napoleon Chagnon and memorialized as "the Fierce People." I will argue that the presence of Chagnon himself became a major factor in the political developments he described. Readers will learn of many individual visitors and Yanomamo whose distinctive interests and personalities shaped the course of local history, and they will, I hope, come to understand the inside politics of war in a tribal zone.

The Yanomamo are by far the most numerous and best described of the four major divisions of Yanomami. Population estimates put their numbers at 6,000 around 1970 (Migliazza 1972:34), at 9,000 around 1978 (Migliazza 1978, cited in Saffirio 1985:38), and at 11,752 in 171 villages in the early 1980s. Of that last count, 9,564 were in Venezuela and the remainder in Brazil north of the Río Negro (Colchester 1985b:7).

The Yanomamo are also known specifically as Yanomami. As I explained in chapter 4, I use that term to designate the entire family of four languages, but some of the authors I quote in part III use the term in its more restricted sense. In chapter 8 I noted that there is some question whether there is any real division between the Yanomam and Yanomamo languages, or whether they represent a continuum of dialects. Like Yanomam, Yanomamo has internal dialect variations—at least five within Venezuela alone (Smole 1976:52).

The geographical range of the Yanomamo in the early nineteenth century is somewhat difficult to assess. It is generally accepted that they lived in high country from the headwaters of the Ocamo and Manaviche rivers to the headwaters of the Orinoco (see map 3). As I mentioned in chapter 5, however, there are indications that some Yanomami lived east of those locations—closer to the upper Orinoco itself—and to the southeast in what I have called the Siapa highlands. Those areas have been populated during the twentieth century by Yanomamo speakers coming out of the southern Parima area, who found these lands almost entirely uninhabited. The fate of the previous Yanomami dwellers is unknown, as is the language they spoke. For lack of a better alternative, I consider those early inhabitants here, along with the Yanomamo.

The primary focus of part III is on the Yanomamo of the Orinoco-Mavaca area. Centered on the confluence of the Orinoco and Mavaca rivers, this area is, for my purposes, bounded by the Ocamo River to the north, the Raudal de Guajaribos on the Orinoco to the east, and the headwaters of the Mavaca to the south. To the west, uninhabited land stretches to the Casiquiare canal.

The Orinoco-Mavaca area is exceptionally well reported, both historically and ethnographically. Although there remain significant gaps in the information, for certain locales in recent times the descriptions are thick enough to allow a relatively complete and fine-grained analysis of contact, politics, and war, extending even to the motivations and actions of individuals. Thus the Orinoco-Mavaca area provides the opportunity to apply the theoretical model developed in part I in a more thorough and concrete way than has been possible up to this point.

Information varies for other areas of Yanomamo habitation. Relatively little is known about the major population centers in the mountains in the eastern half of the Yanomamo range, and what is available dates to fairly recent times. Within the western half of the Yanomamo range, the people both north and south of the Orinoco-Mavaca area are fairly well described, making for what is certainly the most complete regional coverage of any Yanomami area.

I will present information about these other Yanomamo not just for completeness and comparison but also because it illustrates regional interactions that form the political context of the Orinoco-Mavaca area itself. Through these other Yanomamo, we will see how peace and war in the Orinoco-Mavaca area are connected to developments already described for the Sanema in chapter 6 and the Yanomam in chapter 8. I will pick up the discussion where the historical introduction in chapter 5 left off—around 1820. For the sake of continuity with chapter 8, I will begin with developments along the Río Negro.

The Western Retraction, 1820 to 1870

Slave raids, epidemics, and other repercussions of imperial expansion in the eighteenth century left most of the lowlands from the Río Negro north through the upper Orinoco very sparsely populated. On both sides of the imagined border between the Spanish and the Portuguese, colonial retraction set in late in the century, leaving only a few missionaries to continue their operations and their occasional raiding to populate the missions. During the time of Western retraction, commerce among Native Americans revived and evolved, especially in the area between the Negro and the Orinoco (Hemming 1987:315–18; Humboldt 1889: 393–94; Michelena y Rojas 1989:188, 331–43).

The return of Brazilian nationals to the Río Negro is not described, but outbreaks of smallpox are noted for 1819 and 1844 (Tavera-Acosta 1927:25–26). Developments on the Venezuelan side suggest increased merchant activity along the Negro in the 1830s. The first available description of the river is from Alfred Wallace, who traveled along the Río Negro in 1848, shortly before the beginning of rubber production.

Wallace found many totally or partially abandoned settlements. The Brazilians who remained were "poor and miserable," making what living they could by trading in Brazil nuts, sarsaparilla, dried fish, fish and turtle oil, pitch, palm fibers, and farina (Wallace 1969:113, 163, 167, 174–76, 262–63, 350–52). Wallace provides an impressive list of 65 locally made items, but it is not clear how many of these entered into trading. The extraction and trade of forest products took place within an elaborate system of debt and patronage that reached far into the forests: "These traders give small parcels of goods to half-civilized Indians, or to any one who will take them, to go among the wild Indian tribes and buy up their produce" (Wallace 1969:262–63). For the area between the Negro and the Orinoco, along the Javita portage to the Atabapo and the Casiquiare, Wallace reports a few settlements oriented to the indigenous trading network.

The next report comes from Richard Spruce (1908), who traveled along the Negro in 1851–53. He describes the continuing poverty of the Western settlements on the upper Río Negro and some of the tensions existing between Westerners and natives.[1] The indigenous economy he describes, however, is, if anything, more active than that reported by Wallace a few years earlier—and now it is clearer that it reaches to the Yanomamo. Spruce indicates that local Indians traveled extensively on the Negro's northern (left-bank) tributaries, the Padauiri, Marauiá, and Cauaburi, and up into the highlands. "Persons who have ascended high up the Padauiri, in quest of salsaparilla, assure me they have met Indians from the sources of the Orinoco" (Spruce 1908:354). Those Indians could only have been Yanomami. Neither Wallace nor Spruce gives any indication of warfare in the area, although Spruce specifically notes that a concentration of Western goods could prompt a violent attack (see note 1).

Yanomami just across the Venezuelan border are also reported peacefully trading at this time (Michelena y Rojas 1989:170, 346, 368–70). Michelena y Rojas observes that by the mid-1850s, the Brazilian economy in the region was lagging far behind the Venezuelan.[2] The Río Negro was devoid of cultivators and supported only widely scattered forest collectors. But during the 1850s, the broad-spectrum gathering of forest products developed into a substantial industry, radiating up the Negro from Barra (Manaos). No further information is available about this part of the Negro, however, until after the advent of the rubber boom.

As for the upper Orinoco, what is known about the return of Western activity was presented in chapter 6. As best I can determine, renewed creole activity began, very haltingly, around 1817. The missionaries had been expelled, replaced in 1821 by secular directors, but the brutal abuse and forced labor of scattered indigenous peoples was to continue with renewed intensity. The upper Orinoco remained a dangerous place for Yanomamo in the first decades of the nineteenth century.

Spruce, passing through in 1853, described an encounter that may have occurred in the early 1820s.

> Shortly after the separation of Venezuela from the mother country . . . the Commandant of San Fernando was sent with a considerable body of armed men to endeavour to open amicable relations with the Guaharibos. He reached the Raudal de los Guaharibos with his little fleet of fifteen piragoas. . . . A very

little way above they encountered a large encampment of Guaha-ribos, by whom they were received amicably, in return for which they rose on the Indians by night, killed as many of the men as they could, and carried off the children. . . . Treatment such as this of course is calculated to confirm, and perhaps it was the original cause, of the hostility of these Indians to the whites. The same sort of thing seems to have been practised anciently near the head-waters of all these rivers. (Spruce 1908:355)

Along the Casiquiare, in a Bare village led by a man named Monagas, Spruce met a Yanomamo ("Guaharibo") man about fifty years old, who had been captured by the Bare some thirty years before (or c. 1820–25).

Monagas, with six others, were gathering nuts of Juvia on a river which seems to be the Manaviche, and had gone very far up when they came upon a cleared space in the forest which constituted a pueblo of the Guaharibos. . . . In one house were two young men with three young women. One of the men fled, but Monagas and his companions captured the rest. After binding the captives, they were attacked by a party of returning Guaharibos, but es-caped in the dense forest after killing one of them, and got safely back to their boats. . . . All three women died a few years after-wards of scarlatina. . . . When Monagas revisited the same place two or three years afterwards with several companions hoping to catch more Guaharibos, the pueblo had disappeared. (Spruce 1908:397–98)

The latter half of the 1830s saw a short-lived spurt of colonial devel-opment. Half a dozen new settlements were founded (although in 1842 there were still only about thirty nonindigenous people in the area). Two settlements are of special significance. In 1836, a Frenchman named Francisco Arnaud founded Mauaca, or San Pedro, near the mouth of the Mavaca River—the neighborhood where Napoleon Chagnon would begin his fieldwork 128 years later. Arnaud, a member of the local elite, was probably the same Frenchman ("Arnot") who ran a trade network from La Esmeralda to Barra. Mauaca was populated by some three hun-dred generally "wild" Maguacas.

In 1838, another settlement, Santa Isabel, was organized as a *pueblo* several days' travel up the Mavaca River. Santa Isabel was made up of "Curiaranas," "docile" people who traded to the Río Negro (Cocco 1972:23; Codazzi 1940 II:45, III:330–31; Schomburgk 1841:226;

Tavera-Acosta 1927:63, 167, 203). These two Venezuelan outposts were closer to the traditional homelands of the Yanomamo than any "civilized" settlement before or until 1950. Increased Western contact with local Yanomami seems assured, but there are no direct reports on the subject.

What is clear is that by the late 1830s, creole knowledge about local indigenous people, including Yanomami, had increased immeasurably since the turn of the century. That knowledge is summarized in the report by Agustín Codazzi, whose investigations from 1832 to 1838 produced the first ethnographic survey of the upper Orinoco (Codazzi 1940 II:15). Codazzi (1940 II:48–49) notes the existence of several groups of non-Yanomami around the Casiquiare and Siapa—perhaps 2,000 people, most engaged in trade. He describes two local clusters of Yanomamo: about 1,100 "Guaharibos," who were "bellicose and almost white," living from the Raudal de Guajaribos to the headwaters of the Orinoco and subsisting on fish and game; and about 1,200 "Guaica," said to be "small and white," living near the Guaharibos above the Ocamo, Matacuni, and Manaviche. (A third group, the Quiriscanas, were discussed in chapter 6 as Sanema).

Codazzi is one of the main sources describing the continuing abuses of the accessible natives by a handful of local merchants. Most Yanomamo would have been beyond their easy reach. But in 1838, Yanomamo came under concerted attack from Yecuana of the Ventuari, Cunucunuma, and Padamo rivers. "They make war against the Guaharibos and Guaicas in order to capture Indian boys or girls whom they take to the Demarari to sell, and most commonly to the Dutch, in exchange for metal tools, glass beads, mirrors, etc." (Codazzi 1940 II:26; and see 1940 II:20, 44, 48).

Codazzi (1940 II:48) also reports that some of the Guaicas "are allies of the Maquiritares, and others, of the Guaharibos." This suggests the pattern already described for Sanema and Ninam: some Yanomami establish a subordinate relationship to trading Yecuana, and these groups are threatened by more remote Yanomami.

After about 1838, no more information pertains to the Yanomamo of the upper Orinoco until the 1850s. One commentator reports the entire region to have been at peace around 1845 (Tavera-Acosta 1927:77). In late 1853, Spruce came over from Brazil. He found the area still neglected by Venezuela but traversed by active indigenous trade networks running between the Negro and the Orinoco and from there to the northeast via the Yecuana.

These routes intersected Yanomamo territory at different points. Traders reached the people around the source of the Orinoco via the Padauiri and the upper Siapa (Castanha) River. Regular trade existed with unidentified natives along the upper Orinoco all the way to the Raudal de Guajaribos, and at least one creole had explored the Siapa headwaters. Thus it seems that from both the Negro and the Orinoco, some Yanomamo in the highlands would have been obtaining some metal. Nevertheless, Guaharibos just above the *raudal* were understood by Spruce to be "hostile" and potentially dangerous to travelers (Spruce 1908:353–57, 408).

The hostility of these Yanomamo toward intruders is not hard to understand: "At the season of fruit of [the Brazil nut] tree the Guaharibos descend much below the raudal in order to collect it for food, and at that time the Indians of the Casiquiari, in parties of not more than five or six, lie in wait for them and carry off such as they can lay hold on, making them slaves for cultivating their cunucos. Many Indians on the Casiquiari can show lance-wounds received from the Guaharibos in these expeditions" (Spruce 1908:356).

As late as 1886, an old (Bare?) guide for Chaffanjon (1986:266) told how, when he was young, he, his father, and others were almost killed by "Guaharibo" on the upper Orinoco, a little above the present site of the Platanal mission. As Cocco (1972:50, 159) observes, continuing efforts to capture Yanomamo, even into the 1850s, closed off any possibility of their moving into more accessible lowlands at this time.

For about 1857–59, or a few years after Spruce's visit, Michelena y Rojas (1989:188) reports similar trade routes and confirms that the trade included Yanomamo. He visited the settlement of Santa Isabel, some eight days' travel up the Mavaca from the Orinoco. He met about fifty inhabitants returning from farther upstream, who told him that "[the Guaharibos] were peaceful, that they traded with some of them" (1989:341). Furthermore, he claims that the reported hostility of the Yanomamo near the Raudal de Guajaribos either had been exaggerated or had decreased over a short time. "Also the Indians assured me, that there was no fear whatsoever, with foundation, in going to the Raudal, of being attacked by the Guaharibos; that they had commerce with them and exchanged products, and that they were peaceful. Opinions absolutely contradictory to those which have prevailed up to now" (Michelena y Rojas 1989:170).

Michelena y Rojas (1989:331–46) is another major source describing the continuing abuse of indigenous peoples living close to creole centers—abuse that drove many into flight and left areas such as the Casiquiare almost deserted. After his visit to the trading people of the Mavaca River, he commented (1989:342), "It is not strange that they are tribes who live with more comforts (*comodidades*): that would never happen if they were under the immediate rule of non-Indians." Paradoxically, the Yanomamo of this area may have had more access—though certainly still very limited—to Western manufactures than they would have if they traded through people who lived closer to creole centers.

Almost no information about the upper Orinoco Yanomamo is available for the 1860s; the next reports come from the period of increasing rubber production.

The Rubber Boom, 1870 to 1920

On the Río Negro, extensive rubber tapping began in the 1860s and early 1870s (Wright 1981:321). The tremendous demand for rubber, and the few inhabitants remaining in and around the more remote forests, led the Brazilian government to support the transportation of hundreds of thousands of impoverished Brazilians up the Amazon and its tributaries (Furtado 1971:142–44). How many went near the Yanomamo is not known, but it is reasonable to assume that during the expansionary 1870s, relatively well-provisioned tappers were working close to, if not among, the Yanomamo in the highlands. In the 1870s, production and commerce on the upper Río Negro came under the domination of one man, Germano Garrido y Otero. Unlike Funes later on the upper Orinoco, he earned a reputation of being stern but relatively fair in dealings with natives (Hemming 1987:329).

As I explained in chapter 8, there is very little information about events along the Río Negro during the rubber boom. One detail, however, is highly suggestive of substantial Yanomamo contacts with rubber workers. The upper Cauaburi saw extensive tapping during the boom years (Seitz 1963:18). In 1927, a captive taken by Yanomamo to their village on the upper Cauaburi reported, upon her escape, that their *anciano* chief conversed with her in *geral*, the trade language of the region (Cocco 1972:62–63). That report and the presence of bitter manioc in these Yanomamo's gardens suggest a connection to the rubber trade during its peak years.

Rubber production on the upper Orinoco, along with limited renewal of missionary activity, began around 1860 (Chaffanjon 1986: 226; Tavera-Acosta 1927:231–32, 307). An oppressive and factionalized local elite, however, constricted local production until the early 1870s. Even as late as 1875, indigenous commerce along the Casiquiare seemed largely undisturbed by the rubber industry (Pérez 1988:441). But just at that moment, rubber production entered a new phase of expansion, especially on the Casiquiare, which by the mid-1880s would be the most active area of tapping (Chaffanjon 1986:199).

On the heels of this new phase of economic development came a radical shift in Yanomamo relations with their neighbors in two widely separated locations. "In 1879, some Curiobanas who lived on the Siapa River, tributary of the Casiquiare, were attacked at night by the Guaharibos, who killed the inhabitants and razed the village with the sole aim of obtaining some iron tools. In 1880, the same pretext and the same operation against the Maquiritares of the Ocamo" (Chaffanjon 1986: 222). The "Curiobanas" (possibly Arawak speakers [Migliazza 1972: 374]) are undoubtedly the "Curiaranas" who in 1838 were congregated in Santa Isabel on the Mavaca and who reported trading with Yanomamo in the 1850s. By 1879, Santa Isabel had disappeared, and so had the Curiaranas' peace with the Yanomamo. (Albert [1990a:558], using sources not at my disposal, adds that Yanomamo also fought against the Arawak-speaking Anauyá people in the Mavaca-Siapa area.)

Chaffanjon (1986:259–60) provides more detail about a second raid, along with observations about local political relations as told to him by a Yecuana: "One of the Maquiritares from Iguapo had one of his relatives killed by the Guaharibos in the Ocamo. As they do not have canoes, the braves came from the Manaviche overland, waited for the rivers to fall and surprised several camps during the night, killing men, women and children, stealing everything and disappearing." Chaffanjon goes on to say that both the Yecuana and Curiobana previously had taken Yanomamo wives, and he extrapolates on what that meant (1986: 260):

He also gave me to understand that the Maquiritares of the Ventuari buy Piaroa and Maco Indians. The word "buy" (*comprar*) to me signifies "carry off" (*raptar*). Those of the Cunu-Cunuma and the Iguapo do the same and steal women from whatever tribe. That would be my explanation for those massacres of Curiobanas in the Siapa and the Maquiritares in the Ocamo. The Macos and Piaroas, who are few in number, remain oppressed by the Maquiritares, while the Guaharibos, stronger and more independent, avenge the taking of their children and their mothers.

From my theoretical perspective, two points stand out. First, of course, is timing. After several decades without any reported Yanomamo attacks on their neighbors, war breaks out simultaneously on two fronts, just after a comparative wealth of Western goods begins to flow into indigenous networks.[3] Second is the evident parallel to the standard relationship already seen between other Yanomami and the Yecuana: the latter's control over steel tools enables them to exploit the Yanomami in material and marital ways and thus creates a deep ambivalence and tension in relations between the two. It seems that a similar relationship had also developed between Yanomamo and the Curiobana.

Chaffanjon's interpretation of the attacks as revenge for a form of marriage that verges on abduction is fully compatible with the other reported goal of plundering "iron tools." I think what happened is this: after 1875, both Yecuana and Curiobana began to acquire previously unheard of quantities of Western goods, and they used these to demand more from the Yanomamo, with whom they may previously have had more balanced trade. At the same time, the middlemen were more exposed to the debilitating effects of close contact with Westerners, and they lacked any resident Westerner to back them up. The Yanomamo appear to have had a numerical advantage, and although they lacked the Yecuana's shotguns, they had the element of surprise in their favor. Taken all together, the possibility of plunder came to outweigh the more limited benefits of trickle-down axes parceled out by arrogant in-laws.

The exploitation of accessible natives intensified in the 1880s. A new *comisario* from Caracas scoured the upper Orinoco for native workers. The ambiance of the area can be glimpsed in the fact that the farthest "civilized" settlement on the Orinoco—now pulled back to below the Padamo—was actually the home of two fugitives who had murdered people on the Casiquiare to steal their rubber (Chaffanjon 1986:230, 254, 256). Abuse was forcing the remaining indigenous people to flee into the mountains or to Brazil. Weakened by increased creole depredations, the Yecuana along the Orinoco were in no position to resist the newly aggressive Yanomamo to their southeast.

In the early 1880s, the Yecuana retreated down the Orinoco ahead of the Yanomamo, whose fierceness was at this moment the stuff of local legend. Yecuana traders ceased to travel past the Padamo, and they believed that to go past the Ocamo was to invite an arrow attack from the river bank. The Bare were somewhat more daring, venturing almost to the Mavaca to collect Brazil nuts. Chaffanjon had to suppress more than one rebellion among his quaking guides as he forced them along the Orinoco above the Mavaca. His occasionally dubious observations about this stretch of river have raised questions about his veracity, but there seems little reason to doubt that he glimpsed Yanomamo and many signs of their presence (Chaffanjon 1986:200, 259–80).[4] Above the Manaviche, he examined a trailhead where he found that "the branches had been carefully parted, broken or twisted, but none had been cut. This made me conclude that those savages do not even possess cutting tools" (1986:264). Chaffanjon never made direct contact with Yanomamo, but before departing he left for them quantities of hatchets, fabric, mirrors, necklaces, and other presents.

Between about 1883 and 1902, a variety of local political conditions restrained rubber production from further growth. Even so, the continuation of production at established levels meant a substantial change in the distribution of population. Around 1900, there were said to be 830 nonindigenous people in the area—quite a change from the 30 reported in 1842. On the other hand, the number of recognized indigenous settlements was greatly reduced. Many smaller ethnic groups were becoming extinct, a prospect noted specifically for the Curiobanas and Mavacas who had inhabited the Siapa and Mavaca rivers. Even La Esmeralda was uninhabited. River trade was monopolized by the owners of a few steamboats, and the old trade networks into Brazil had been severed. "Civilized" people—those encapsulated by Venezuelan society—now lived mainly around San Fernando de Atabapo and along the Casiquiare, although there was also a sizable "floating" population.

The majority of rubber workers were Baniwa, Bare, Yecuana, and a few others (Tavera-Acosta 1903:13, 1927:33, 55–59, 66, 261, 334). The Yanomamo were presumably among "the rest [who] are not *gomeros*" (Tavera-Acosta 1903:13). But there are scattered indications that the limited rubber boom (from the later 1870s to around 1902) was already reaching some Yanomamo.

In the 1890s, creoles were familiar with the entire length of the Mavaca and Siapa rivers, which brought them into the Siapa highlands. Along the Siapa around 1900, one of the groups said to "scarcely still exist" (Tavera-Acosta 1903:33) after extended exposure to the rubber business was the "Misatari." In this location, such a name probably refers to a local group or cluster of Yanomamo and perhaps gives us a clue about the fate of the vanished Yanomami of the Siapa highlands. Along the Orinoco, creoles still rarely went past the Raudal de Guajaribos. But the perception of the Yanomamo as a danger had receded or disappeared, and Yecuana and other natives were gathering cacao and

Brazil nuts from as far up the Orinoco as around Raudal Guaica, well within traditional Yanomamo territory (Tavera-Acosta 1903:33, 1927: 243, 259–61, 427–28).

In 1893, an influential Yecuana leader who was familiar with that stretch of river predicted "that one day not so distant his industrious Maquiritares, overcoming the repugnance of the Guaharibos, would amalgamate the tribes and call their neighbors to the table of progress and civilization" (Tavera-Acosta 1927:424–25). In context, this prediction suggests that the Yecuana had already established peace with the Yanomamo by giving them Western goods.

In 1897, one Guillermo Level, who had traveled on the far upper Orinoco, established a new *balata* gathering base at La Esmeralda (Anduze 1960:28)—perhaps the biggest operation yet that far up the river. But this base apparently did not survive the intense political turmoil of 1898–1900, since La Esmeralda was again vacant around the turn of the century. Perhaps there was a brief but sharp economic downturn at this point. If so, it could explain a renewal of Yanomamo raiding, for Yanomamo ("Uahariba") from the headwaters of the Orinoco once again were "making inroads attacking the Maquiritare" (Tavera-Acosta 1927:32).

In chapter 6 I described how the real, explosive boom of rubber production in the upper Orinoco occurred from 1903 to 1912. I found no estimate of how many outsiders moved into the upper Orinoco during those years, but the numbers were considerable. At their peak, the towns of San Fernando de Atabapo and San Carlos on the Venezuelan Río Negro each had about two thousand residents. There certainly was a huge influx of Western manufactures into the region, which were traded to natives in exchange for manioc, *aguardiente* (a liquor), hammocks, and canoes. But disease and continuing exploitation again took their toll on the native population, which by 1913 appears once more to be in sharp decline (Acebes 1954:209; Gómez Picón 1978:118–19; Koch-Grunberg 1979 I:378–80; Pérez 1988:442–44; Tavera-Acosta 1927: 335–36). And that was before the beginning of Funes's reign of terror (1913–21), which devastated the Yecuana and left most of the rivers vacant.

For the years of peak rubber production and the rule of Funes, there are almost no published reports from the upper Orinoco. Yet there are some indications that there indeed was considerable contact between outsiders and Yanomamo. On top of the cacao and Brazil nut collecting already noted as extending up to Raudal Guaica, during the boom years the far upper Orinoco saw new economic activity. A substantial cattle raising operation was begun at La Esmeralda. Tappers commonly reached the Mavaca. What later became the site of the Platanal mission was a tappers' camp (Acebes 1954:242; Steinvorth de Goetz 1969:12).

In later times (1951), Anduze was told that during the period of high prices, some tappers went up the Orinoco beyond Raudal Guaica—but they never came back. Nevertheless, Anduze found the scars left on trees by rubber tappers as far upstream as the rapids called Los Tiestos, above Raudal Guaica, and 60 kilometers or more east of Raudal de Guajaribos (Anduze 1960:41, 96). If tapping reached that far up the Orinoco, it certainly entered Yanomamo territory there and probably on local tributary streams such as the Orinoquito (or Mahekoto ke u), which feeds into the Orinoco between Raudal de Guajaribos and Raudal Peñascal, and which will be described later as a major center of Yanomamo residence.

On the Siapa, where some Yanomami may have been dying out by 1900, "savage" Yanomamo ("Shiriana") were known to residents of the Casiquiare in 1913 (Koch-Grunberg 1979 I:380). Perhaps these were Karawe-teri, Kohoroshiwe-teri, or Shamatari, the vanguard of the Yanomamo who replaced the old residents of the Siapa highlands. And perhaps it was these "Shiriana" who were the Yanomamo responsible for driving Arawak-speaking Mandawaka and Yabaana from the Cauaburi and Marauiá rivers "at the beginning of the 20th century" (Albert 1990a:558–59).

Sometime in this general period, at least one fair-sized expedition of creoles ventured up the Siapa to find the source of the Orinoco. They met a group of Yanomami who, although wary, brought them back to their *shabono* (Acebes 1954:211–13). That action suggests a prior history of some contact with indigenous traders.

The most detailed report about Yanomamo contacts comes from Rice (1921:332–33; and see chapter 6), who explored the upper Orinoco in 1920. Until shortly before then, he reports, Yanomami from unidentified locations had been making annual visits to the Yecuana at the mouth of the Padamo, where they exchanged spun cotton and other items for "old, worn-out iron and steel instruments." But at the time of his visit, this trade had been replaced by Yanomami attacks on the Yecuana, who were increasingly vulnerable because of the assaults by Funes. Around this time, however, one Yanomamo group in the area moved close to some Yecuana villages in order to "enjoy their possible patronage." They were subsequently raided by other Yanomamo and moved away (Cocco 1972:112).

Rice's expedition in 1920 was itself a trauma for some Yanomamo. At the Raudal de Guajaribos, Rice encountered a large party of them. Fearing themselves under attack, his party felt it "necessary to fire to kill" (Rice 1921:340–41). There is no count of the Yanomamo losses, nor is it clear from his account whether he truly was under attack or whether, in a panic, he misinterpreted the belligerent defensive posture often displayed by Yanomami when they meet strangers. Cocco (1972: 60) notes that a more seasoned prospector in the same area a few years later was able to turn a seemingly threatening situation into a cooperative relationship. On the other hand, there is no doubt that many small parties of travelers have been assaulted by Yanomami, especially when bearing steel.

These few scraps of historical information about contacts during the rubber years can be supplemented by recollections from Yanomamo oral history. The ancestors of the Shamatari, apparently living near the upper Orinoco in the vicinity of Raudal Guaica (see Chagnon 1992a: 167; Grelier 1957:map) "had access to steel tools in considerable numbers" (Chagnon 1966:167), but what kind of access is not stated. Ancestors of the Namowei-teri at Wareta, close to the Orinoco near Raudal Peñascal, around the turn of the century were obtaining steel tools from "*algunos 'racionales'*" (Cocco 1972:379)—a term variably applied to creoles, mestizos, and "civilized" Native Americans.

In Wareta, the Yanomamo experienced a major epidemic that was attributed to the magic of enemies who burned Western goods they "surely had robbed" from some tappers (Valero 1984:170). In one incident at Wareta, the Yanomamo mortally wounded a rubber worker and later dug up his body to retrieve the goods they expected to be buried with him (Biocca 1971:136; Valero 1984:173). Members of another Yanomamo group somewhere around the Orinoco were physically abused by woodsmen when they were caught with their hands in the manioc sack (Valero 1984:493).

There is no reason to believe that these few remembered instances were anything out of the ordinary. Given the known extent of rubber tapping, there is every reason to expect that both peaceful and violent contacts between Yanomamo and outsiders were common. Perhaps the most interesting tidbit is the experience of one Namowei band decades later that was pioneering the movement westward on the south side of the Orinoco.

Faced with a deadly epidemic in the late 1940s, these Namowei fled up an unexplored mountain. To their astonishment, they found a major stand of old *pijiguao* trees, the enduring markers of Yanomami gardens.

After some discussion, they concluded that this was the garden of some entirely unknown Yanomami (Valero 1984:311)—more evidence that there were Yanomami in this area who became extinct. *Pijiguao* trees usually take five to six years to mature and then bear fruit for around twenty years (Lizot 1980:34); these trees were still bearing but were recognized as very old. It seems significant that they were found by a group fleeing epidemics that were emanating from points of Western contact. Perhaps this garden was the last stand of Yanomamo victims in the era of Funes.

Yanomamo Politics in the Rubber Years

Yanomamo oral accounts also provide information about their internal politics during the rubber years. Chagnon and others have reconstructed the political history of several "population blocs" of Yanomamo. (A population bloc [Chagnon 1974:71ff.] is a group of villages that share a common origin. The growth and spread of these blocs is itself understood to be a result of the acquisition of steel tools.)[5] Reconstructing these histories is a formidable task (see Chagnon 1974:53–67), and many uncertainties remain. Limited credence must be given to any specific detail.[6] However, these accounts certainly were not collected with an eye toward proving the theoretical relationships I am arguing in this book, so I feel justified in noting the correspondences of reported details to my theoretical expectations.

Chagnon (1966:29, 144–51, 165–71; and see 1992a:167) reconstructs the history of two blocs, Shamatari and Namowei-teri, whom I will refer to simply as Namowei, dropping the suffix to make it clear that the label refers to a population bloc rather than to a particular local group. To start with the Shamatari, the period from about 1875 to 1900 is only dimly recollected, but with one exception it is remembered as lacking in war. Around 1880—the beginning of what I call the limited rubber boom, and roughly simultaneous with Yanomamo attacks on the Curiobana and Yecuana—the ancestors of the Shamatari were raided and consequently moved from the north to the south side of the Orinoco, in the vicinity of Raudal Guaica. As noted earlier, they also received steel tools around this time. Their residence at this location was without reported incident until around 1900, when the Shamatari entered a period of intense conflict, with some six village relocations, five fissionings, and four wars during the years up to around 1910—or roughly coincident with the most expansionary years of the rubber boom in southern Venezuela.

During these chaotic years, the dispersing Shamatari generally moved toward the upper reaches of the Mavaca and Siapa rivers or closer to the center of rubber production on the Casiquiare (see map 4). They continued in that southwesterly direction over the next decade, although there appears to have been less conflict during this time. (The Shamatari may be the "savage Shiriana" noted by Koch-Grunberg as he passed along the Casiquiare.) Cocco (1972:26) asserts that as these Shamatari moved to the southwest, they pushed before them the ancestors of the Karawe-teri and Kohoroshiwe-teri (see note 6), who reached the headwaters of the Marauiá and Cauaburi by about 1920, beginning a new and very active presence on the Río Negro's left bank. (As noted previously, the arriving Yanomamo forcibly displaced the Arawakan residents of those rivers.)

Continuing with Chagnon's reconstruction (1966:146, 149–51), from 1875 to 1900 the ancestors of the Namowei also lived north of the Orinoco at a place called Konata, not far from the place of Shamatari origin. There were no reported wars at that time, and the Namowei are specifically said to have been at peace with the ancestral Shamatari. Toward the end of this period, the Namowei moved into an area vacated by another group, soon to be known as the Wareta-teri, who had been raided. There, war broke out between the Namowei, together with their Shamatari allies, and another alliance of local groups, precipitated by a club fight over a woman. The raiding forced the ancestral Namowei to move, about 1900, to Wareta, home of the Wareta-teri, on the south side of the Orinoco near Raudal Peñascal.

I mentioned earlier that the Yanomamo obtained steel and interacted with collectors and tappers at Wareta. That may be why the Namowei stayed there for some time, from around 1900 to 1910, even though they were required to cede women to the village headman for the privilege of living there. Meanwhile, the Wareta-teri themselves "had their own war" with Shihowa-teri, the other village reported to be receiving steel tools during this period. Then the Wareta-teri headman and two followers were treacherously murdered at a feast in a village to the north. After that blow, around 1910, both the Namowei and Wareta-teri abandoned the site and moved, separately, to the west. They had been driven out of their privileged trade position.

The Namowei settled in a mountainous area, where they acquired the name Namowei, long enough to establish three gardens. Around 1920, some old enemies, the Boreta-teri, began to raid again, and the Namowei moved farther west along the north side of the Orinoco. All told, the Namowei experienced considerably less conflict than the Shamatari over the years from 1875 to 1920, although, as with the Shamatari, the peak of their conflict corresponded to the peak years of rubber production. Of the two groups, it seems that the ancestral Shamatari were exposed to outside contact sooner than the Namowei (Chagnon 1966: 167; and see note 5), and this exposure may be related to their comparatively intense violence.

All these raids and movements conform to expectations of the model. The intensity of war and other political events roughly corresponds to the intensity of creole economic activity. The directionality of raiding cannot always be determined, but mostly it is people more removed from areas of rubber tapping who attack those who are closer to it. The one clear exception involves a war between two local groups who are both reported to be receiving steel and who could have had any number of trade-related reasons to fight. When the victims of raiders move away, even if being forced to abandon one area of contact, they move in the direction of distant but more active Western centers.

The Shamatari and Namowei are the two population blocs that have occupied land to the south of the Orinoco in recent years. To the north, between the Orinoco and the Ocamo, there are three main blocs, called by Lizot (1988:521–24) the Heronapui, the Poreta, and the Uhepeki. The Uhepeki were the progenitors of some local groups that will be prominent in later history, such as the Mahekoto-teri, the Tayari-teri, and the Witokaya-teri. Lizot does not provide historical information, but a village genealogy with dates for the Uhepeki bloc, combined with Lizot's map, indicates that the Uhepeki moved westward between 1880 and 1900, at which time (and again around 1910) the bloc divided into groups heading toward the Ocamo and Manaviche rivers.

Cocco (1972:111–12) and Hames (1979:405–409) provide historical information about another population bloc, the one that moved farthest to the north and west in the vicinity of the Orinoco and became the progenitors of the Iyewei-teri and several groups currently living along the Padamo. Lizot (1988:522) labels this group "Iyewei and Padamo." Cocco places these ancestors around the Orinoquito River about 1880, but near the end of that decade the people migrated to the headwaters of the Manaviche. In this location, they may have been the Yanomamo who were closest to the Yecuana during the time when the Yecuana were acquiring new wealth from the limited rubber boom and were seemingly mending fences with some Yanomamo.

Sometime in the years after 1890, the Iyewei-Padamo were raided by

Namowei; they moved to the northwest but were raided by Namowei again. They then moved farther northwest, arriving around 1910–15 at a site called Teemoba on a tributary of the Ocamo, close to active rubber tapping. While there, hostilities developed with the Uhepeki bloc. According to Cocco, these hostilities included an ax fight, confirming that steel was available at the time. The Iyewei-Padamo then fled north to a rapids on the Ocamo where some Yecuana lived, "to distance themselves from quarrelsome groups and draw closer to the Maquiritares in order to enjoy their possible patronage" (Cocco 1972:112).

From this position, some Iyewei-Padamo men tried to take women from their old enemies, but the Uhepeki responded with arrows, driving them away. They fled far up the Ocamo, well upstream from a settlement of their kinfolk who recently had hived off and allied themselves with the Uhepeki people. That flight bring us up to about 1920. I will continue the history of the Iyewei-Padamo people in chapter 10. All these conflicts and moves are consistent with competition and antagonism over unencumbered access to sources of steel during the years of the rubber boom.

Finally, Fredlund (1982:34–37) provides some information about the Shitari, who presently inhabit the upper reaches of the Ocamo. They say their ancestors crossed over the Parima highlands from Brazil sometime around 1880 and subsequently established alliances with Yanomamo farther down the Ocamo. Of those described here, the Shitari make up the Yanomamo population bloc with the least exposure to the outside world, and, as would be expected, they have had "relatively little warfare . . . over the past 100 years" (Fredlund 1982:37).

The population movements illustrated by Lizot (1988:522) indicate that all the western Yanomamo radiated outward from an area about 80 kilometers east-west by 40 kilometers north-south, north of the Orinoco and framed by the Orinoquito, the upper Manaviche, and tributaries of the Ocamo. During the years of rubber production, they all moved to or down rivers that led to sources of steel—even if they were being forced to flee from others. The paths they took indicate that groups who follow pioneers into Western contact zones are kept from advancing by their predecessors. Thus the Uhepeki bloc, which got an early start from a good location, winds up with most of the river locations along the upper Orinoco. The Iyewei-Padamo bloc is still able to make an "end run" to the north, but the Heronapui bloc is confined to high country between the Ocamo and Manaviche, and the Shitari are restricted to the upper Ocamo.

This pattern is consistent with Chagnon's generalization that Yanomamo rarely attempt to "leapfrog" over villages ahead of them: "Thus, the prior existence of villages at one's periphery constitutes a very real boundary, and all Yanomamo groups, except those at the very periphery, are socially 'circumscribed' in the sense that neighboring villages constitute a barrier as effective as a chain of mountains or a desert" (Chagnon 1974:75–76). I believe the reason this is so is that it would be both difficult and dangerous to try to insert oneself between another local group and its source of steel tools.

The years of rubber production were years of great change along the upper Orinoco—from a time of lethargic creole penetration and extensive indigenous trade, through the limited rubber boom starting in the late 1870s and the height of the boom from 1903 to 1912, to the terrors of Funes and falling production from 1913 to 1921. Changes in any local area may have been even more drastic. In my model, war is the result of a major change in access to Western manufactures—a sudden but spatially restricted influx, a shift in location of sources, an abrupt termination of supply. Sharp local fluctuations in accessibility and other factors identified as shaping the political character of alliances will lead to local political turmoil.

It would contradict my model if, around the upper Orinoco, the rubber years were *not* a time of war, fissioning, and migrations. The one reasonably well-described situation—Yanomamo relations with Yecuana along the Orinoco—is probably typical of the volatility in political relations throughout the entire region: peace in the 1870s, war in 1880, peace in the 1890s, war around 1900, peace in the 1910s, war around 1920. In chapter 10, we will continue to follow the histories of the Yanomamo population blocs and see how the withdrawal of the Western presence around them led first to more violence and then to a fairly substantial interlude of peace.

Before moving on, I must stress that in spite of everything I have just described, the Yanomamo were far less affected by the rubber boom than were indigenous people in the lowlands, or even the Yecuana. While some Yanomami in the Siapa area may have been obliterated, most Yanomamo survived, and relatively intact. Although they moved in the direction of Western activity, they remained on higher ground, still a good distance from the main areas of rubber production, where they were less exposed and less vulnerable. In the fear they sometimes inspired, we can see that contact was on relatively balanced terms. Yanomamo could have peaceful contact and obtain Western goods, but they could also withdraw or even attack. Their ability to "go on the warpath" would be dramatically demonstrated a few years later along the Río Negro.

10

The Yanomamo during the Western Retraction:

1920 to 1940

This chapter encompasses the period after the fall of rubber, when the Western presence around Yanomamo territory was in retraction. Paradoxically, this is also a period for which our information about certain Yanomamo groups is greatly increased. Several ethnographers have reconstructed village histories for this time, and these can be combined with accounts from a truly superlative source of information: the narratives of Helena Valero.

Valero, a mestizo girl, was captured by Yanomamo in 1932 or 1933, shortly after she turned 13. For nearly a quarter of a century, she lived among the Yanomamo in an astonishing odyssey that took her from the Río Negro to the Orinoco and the Ocamo before she finally escaped to San Fernando de Atabapo in 1956. Subsequently, two narratives of her life were independently compiled: *Yanoáma* (Biocca 1971), and *Yo Soy Napëyoma* (Valero 1984). They record a life of hardship and heroism, and—fortunately for the purposes of this book—they tell of the daily life and political history of several Yanomamo groups during the time of Western retraction and return. Through Valero's eyes, we can see how the Yanomami themselves experienced the varying Western presence into the 1950s.[1]

Yanomamo along the Río Negro

The rubber boom assumed major proportions along the Río Negro, but there is virtually no information available about its impact on the stretch of river close to Yanomamo lands. One old Yanomamo was reported in 1927 to have spoken *geral,* the trade language used in the area, suggesting a past history of contact—but that is our only hint. Reconstructions of population bloc movements show the Shamatari and others moving southwest from the Parima area after 1900 and the Kohoroshiwe-teri arriving at the headwaters of the Cauaburi, a tributary of the Negro, around 1920. These groups all seem to have been involved in intense warfare during the peak years of rubber and were still fighting—but less so—during the subsequent decade.

By 1920, rubber production had collapsed. The entire Río Negro entered a severe economic and demographic decline in the 1910s and was thoroughly depressed and stagnant around 1924. But about that time, the new industry of *balata* tapping began to grow, first on the Río Branco and then farther up the Negro. In chapter 8 we saw how this industry led to violent conflict between Yanomam and woodsmen and between Yanomam groups after the mid-1920s and how, by the mid-1930s, the woodsmen had been driven out. A similar sequence of events took place along the Negro.

Between 1926 and 1929 there were several encounters—some violent—between Yanomamo and *balata* collectors along Negro tributaries such as the Cauaburi and Maia, and even close to the Negro itself. Yanomamo raiders killed at least four tappers and captured a woman and child (Cocco 1972:62–63; Comité 1983:45; Seitz 1963:17–18).

Farther down the Negro, the Deminí and its effluent, the Araçá, lead up to high country long inhabited by Yanomamo and Yanomam. There, the Yanomamo had established contact with Brazilians: "Immediately above the first rapid . . . there is a maloka of Shiriana Indians who are in contact with the civilized population farther downstream and some of whom speak a little Portuguese. The chief maintains trade relations with the Uaikas of the forests of the upper river" (Holdridge 1933:380). Reluctantly, this chief guided Holdridge's party to the first of his trading partners. Evidently there were some tensions in the relationship, for the guides insisted that Holdridge's men carry their weapons into the village. The upstream people's initial wariness turned to cooperation when the explorer distributed cloth and steel (Holdridge 1933:380–81).

But there were also deadly conflicts in this area. In 1931, the "civilized settlements of the Araçá were the scene of a spirited attack" by "nearly a hundred persons" who "might have been Uaikas" (Holdridge 1933:380). The upstream people Holdridge visited blamed this attack on other people living ten days' walk to the west-southwest (seemingly the vicinity of the Cauaburi) and noted that they themselves were "at war with the tribe" (1933:382).

From the beginning of the 1930s, Yanomamo repeatedly raided settlements and tapper camps along the Negro tributaries and even down to the big river itself. Raids occurred at least as far east as the Araçá and as far west as the Demití, a small effluent of the upper Negro (not to be confused with the Deminí). By 1935, few Brazilians dared to live in this land, although some had retreated to islands in the Negro. That year, a large party of Yanomamo even tried to attack one of the island settlements during a period of low water, but they suffered many losses as the settlers counterattacked by canoe. A punitive expedition by the settlers killed at least three more Yanomamo and captured six children. But from that point on, the Brazilians' avoidance of this part of the river was so complete that only a few fleeting contacts with Yanomamo occurred for nearly twenty years. The sole exception was the Deminí area, which saw a renewal of mostly peaceful contacts during the early 1940s (Cocco 1972:66–68; Seitz 1963:20).

The raid farthest west, on the Demití, is particularly significant, for it was there that Helena Valero was captured by the Kohoroshiwe-teri in November of 1932 or 1933 (Cocco 1972:104; Fuentes 1984:9). The Kohoroshiwe-teri were mentioned in chapter 9 as possibly being related to the Shamatari and as having been pushed by the latter towards the southwest.

In the early 1930s, the Kohoroshiwe-teri consisted of three local divisions plus some people from other groups (Valero 1984:33, 541), all living around the headwaters of the Cauaburi (Cocco 1972:105). The Kohòroshiwe-teri had recently split off from the Karawe-teri (Valero 1984:43), some years after 1925, while they were living near the upper Siapa (Chagnon 1966:171).[2] Subsequently, they began hunting and then moving long distances to the southwest. Their objective was to find *nape* (foreigners) whose steel tools they could plunder (Chagnon 1966:21; Fuentes 1984:12; Valero 1984:27). By the time of Valero's capture, they had pushed so far that they suffered from a lack of fully developed gardens (Biocca 1971:34, 39, 43, 46).

Perhaps the Kohoroshiwe-teri had grown dependent on steel tools through contacts during the rubber boom. One of their old gardens in the mountains above the Siapa lay close to rich stands of cocoa, *balata,* chicle, and rubber (Valero 1984:61)—all things sought by forest workers coming off the Casiquiare during more prosperous times. At any rate, their subsequent quest for steel and other Western goods was unusually single minded and successful. Their movement southwest brought them closer to Cucuí, the only Brazilian outpost in the area still receiving regular shipments of supplies (Hanson 1933:590), and into an area where woodsmen still worked without fear of Yanomamo ("Macu") (Valero 1984:21–24).

Valero (1984:25–26, 29, 31, 38–39) records substantial plunder brought in during the year or so she spent with the Kohoroshiwe-teri. From her family alone, during the raid in which she was abducted, they took four machetes, three axes, and many pots, along with other articles and manioc. Over their entire career of raiding woodsmen along the Río Negro, the Kohoroshiwe-teri must have acquired dozens of metal tools. Nevertheless, steel was still precious. Valero told Father Cocco (1972: 181) that a man who had a machete slept with it on his chest, and one who had an axe always had it on his shoulder, and when resting would sit on it.

As the Kohoroshiwe-teri moved to the southwest, they were pushed from behind by the Karawe-teri and a Shamatari group, the Matakuwe-teri—both blood enemies of Kohoroshiwe-teri (Chagnon 1966:171; Valero 1984:31, 36). The origin of the Kohoroshiwe-teri's war with the Matakuwe-teri is not described. There had been at least one fight in which at least one Kohoroshiwe-teri woman died. During Valero's stay, there was a nonlethal clash when Kohoroshiwe-teri men ran into a Matakuwe-teri hunting party. The latter group, far from home, was led by Ruwahiwe, whose assassination by some Namowei years later is also described by Valero (1984:36–37). But the threat of the Matakuwe-teri was soon overwhelmed by a more sanguinary reality.

Some months after the clash with the hunting party, visitors from Karawe-teri warned the Kohoroshiwe-teri of an impending attack by their people (one of the informers was given a metal pot). This war was said to have started over insults, and it involved some Karawe-teri men taking women. Having been warned, the Kohoroshiwe-teri moved a few days west (Biocca 1971:31, 34; Valero 1984:43–45)—but not far enough. Karawe-teri raiders routed the Kohoroshiwe-teri at their new home. They slaughtered several children and took many women captive, including Helena Valero. Plunder taking is not specifically mentioned in the account of the raid, but even in their panic the fleeing women did try to hide valuable Western goods in the woods or carry them as they ran (Biocca 1971:32–37; Valero 1984:45–51).[3]

Now it was the Karawe-teri's turn to feel threatened by Kohoroshiwe-teri, whom they feared would retaliate. After debate, some

Karawe-teri decided to accept an invitation to a feast from some allies (the Shekerei-teri) north across the mountains, who themselves feared a raid by the Matakuwe-teri. Valero went with them (Biocca 1971:51– 53; Valero 1984:60–67). Sure enough, the Matakuwe-teri struck the allies' village while most of its men were out hunting. Ruwahiwe, the Matakuwe-teri chief, led a force that killed several men, looted trade goods, and captured some women, including Valero (Biocca 1971:55– 60; Valero 1984:69–71). After that, the Shekerei-teri moved "out of the path of Ruwahiwe" (Valero 1984:74).

Valero was taken by the Matakuwe-teri to the upper Mavaca. They consisted of three local divisions under sons of the "retired" headman, Matakuwe. But she did not stay long, for she was accused of poisoning someone and was shot with a curare arrow. She fled and, astoundingly, survived for seven months alone in the forest, making use of gardens she found. Finally, she turned herself over to a party of Namowei, who had begun visiting the Shamatari to trade, and returned home with them (Biocca 1971:86–107; Valero 1984:91–115). With that event, in roughly 1935 (Cocco 1972:106), Helena Valero moved into the Orinoco area, where her testimony will be picked up later.

Valero's leaving means a sudden shutdown in information for the southwestern Yanomamo front. It seems, however, that the follow- ing decades of increased isolation after the departure of the *balate- ros* were a time of little war. Chagnon's (1966:171–73) reconstruction does not mention any additional conflicts among the Shamatari, the Kohoroshiwe-teri, the Karawe-teri, and others to their south. (Relations to the north are another story.) In 1954, when a missionary from the Negro made contact with southern Yanomamo, there was no indication of recent warfare (see Seitz 1963) although war would quickly resume after his arrival. The missionary found his attempts to travel between villages complicated by residual animosities from past wars, but these were the wars of the 1930s described by Valero (Cocco 1972:96). A Kohoroshiwe-teri headman in 1962 described how, when he was a boy, there had been war with people from the mountains to the north—again an apparent reference to the wars just mentioned (Salazar 1967:154).

But for the years from 1920 to 1935, Valero and others provide enough information about developments among southwestern Yano- mamo to allow a good application of the theoretical model. The Kohoroshiwe-teri arrived above the Negro when rubber had collapsed. Their interaction with the outside world at this time is unknown, but it must have been extremely limited. No specific wars are identified as going on at this point, and at the least, Yanomamo political relations were much more pacific than they would be a few years later. In the mid-1920s, *balata* tappers began going up rivers close to where Yanomamo lived. They met, and Yanomamo began to attack the tappers to take their steel and other goods. Those closest to the Westerners obtained many axes and machetes. Within a few years, political relations between the relatively wealthy Kohoroshiwe-teri and their old allies began to deteriorate, turning to war around the start of the 1930s.

When reasons are stated for these wars, which involved kin or former allies, they are of a personal nature—insults or conflicts over women. But these personal disputes erupt just as the Kohoroshiwe-teri begin to acquire more Western goods. No doubt they traded much of what they took into the interior, but with such limited supplies, they could not possibly even have begun to meet demand. (Valero [1984:35] mentions in passing that because of their plundering, the Kohoroshiwe-teri had many more bead necklaces than the Shamatari.) And plundering was a zero sum game. The victim was not there for a second attack.

By raiding the Kohoroshiwe-teri, their northern enemies could hope to obtain steel and drive their competitors out of their path, making it possible to establish their own gardens closer to the remaining *balateros*. But just as they succeeded, there were no more *balateros* left to plunder. At the same time, around 1935, the flow of Western goods began to pick up on the Orinoco,[4] and the Shamatari began to look in that direction. Along the Yanomamo's southern frontier, conflict may have intensified for a short time after the supply of steel was severed. But with such limited quantities in their possession, the Yanomamo's local inequalities probably would not have lasted long, and geographic position would have lost its importance. The cessation of active warfare is to be expected.

Retraction and Return on the Upper Orinoco

On the upper Orinoco, a tottering creole economy utterly collapsed in the first years of the 1920s. The fall of rubber prices and the terror of Tomás Funes left the area largely deserted after 1921. Hanson (1933: 578–90), passing through in 1931–32, reported the Venezuelan side of the border emptier of people than the Brazilian. Few Western goods entered the region, and those that did were brought in by Yecuana. San Fernando de Atabapo was in ruins, down to 60 residents. Still, some economic activity held on. Chico González was established on the Ventuari, working with Yecuana. By the late 1920s, some Yecuana had developed a sizable *balata*-gathering operation on the river somewhere above San Fernando, and in general they were on an economic and demographic rebound after the depredations of Funes.

What little is known about Yanomami contacts with Westerners in the 1920s centers on the outpost at La Esmeralda in 1929. In that year, the last two "civilized" settlements on the upper Orinoco were La Esmeralda, under retired colonel Emiliano Pérez Franco, and, below it near the Casiquiare, a settlement called Tamatama, under Jesús Noguera. La Esmeralda had developed a bit and was now producing crops and cattle and acting as a center for forest workers who reached as far upstream as the Mavaca. Occasionally it was visited by Yecuana accompanied by "tame" Yanomami (*guaharibos mansos*), a phrase indicating that the standard Yecuana-Yanomami relationship was being played out again along the upper Orinoco in the late 1920s, if not earlier.

But one morning in 1929, the emerald of the Orinoco was surrounded by a large party of Yanomamo from a group that had become the northwestern pioneers of Yanomamo expansion—the Iyewei-Padamo bloc. They had been provoked by the abuse of their women by the colonel's son, who had visited a Yanomamo village while its men were absent. The Yanomamo came "to rob them and not to kill," which they did, sacking the storehouse and retreating. Reinforcements from Tamatama caught up with them, wounded several, and recovered much of the booty. Pérez Franco abandoned the region a few months later (Cocco 1972:64–65). The Noguera family, however, will be heard from again.

In 1931 Herbert Dickey (1932:130–31, 258, 261–64), hoping to reach the source of the Orinoco, had to turn back some distance past the Raudal de Guajaribos (see Cocco 1972:67). An experienced South American explorer, Dickey discounted tales of Yanomamo ferocity against travelers. Somewhere on the upper river he was greeted by a group who called out to him "Guaica"—they knew their outside name. They requested and were given manioc, knives, and machetes. "Nothing but steel cutting instruments were desired" (Dickey 1932:261). The information Dickey inferred from what he saw of the Yanomami and was told by Yecuana contains many errors and distortions. Through the haze, what appears to be described is a strained alliance between the group that greeted Dickey and Yanomamo who lived "far up the Orinoco" (1932:262). Their problems involved disputes over food and women and took the form of club fights and what seem to be a couple of raids. Dickey's hosts denied ever retaliating with raids against their attackers.

The fact that they were by the river, along with their behavior when they saw Dickey, suggests that this particular local Yanomamo group had prior experience with *nape*. But that was Dickey's only contact with Yanomamo in two trips along the Orinoco, though he encountered many signs of their presence (Dickey 1932:262–87). He mentions that they lived in fear of rifle-bearing *balata* hunters (1932:266), so he may have been observed but avoided by other Yanomamo groups.

Yanomamo above the Mavaca probably received very little steel in the years before Dickey's visit. The farthest point reached by people working for Pérez Franco in the 1920s is said to have been Mavaca. It appears unlikely that independent Yecuana would have gone any farther, given the attacks by Yanomami on vulnerable Yecuana parties at this time (see chapters 6 and 7). On the other hand, Dickey's reference to armed *balateros* suggests that some *nape* had been in the area recently and possibly clashed with Yanomamo. The unusually friendly group who came out to greet Dickey 1931 may have obtained a locally unusual amount of Western goods from these visitors, and that could be why they were currently experiencing problems with their former allies upstream.

The early 1930s were unlikely times for much increase in contact between Yanomamo and Westerners along the Orinoco. In 1931, a sudden local credit crisis, in an economy based on credit, began to drive remaining creoles out of the region (Hanson 1933:586–87). In early 1932, Yanomamo again attacked La Esmeralda, immediately after a young German with dreams of colonization arrived there (Hanson 1933:583–84). Direct contact between Yecuana and upriver Yanomamo was also unlikely, since as late as 1935 the Yecuana expressed terror of the Yanomamo (Cocco 1972:70). In 1935, a local guide related that Yanomamo around the Manaviche did not have steel cutting tools (Cocco 1972:71). And as we will see later, the Yanomamo themselves recalled this period as a time of extremely little steel.

But 1935 seems to mark the start of renewed Venezuelan penetration of the upper Orinoco. That year Carlos Wendehake panned for gold just below the Raudal de Guajaribos, and on another journey went ten days' travel beyond that barrier. In the same year, the marqués de Wavrin explored the area. During the 1930s, Luís Vegas went up several difficult watercourses, once reaching well above Raudal Guaica. On a handful of occasions, these men made peaceful contact with Yanomamo and gave them steel tools and other presents (Cocco 1972:70–71, 74). From the inside, Valero's account (1984:114) indicates that *nape* began to travel along the upper river only shortly before she joined the Namowei around 1935.

Farther downriver, some Yanomamo had maintained contacts with Yecuana in the Padamo area and began more actively working with them around the middle 1930s. One Yanomamo man worked for Jesús Noguera in Tamatama for two years. Another "Guajaribo" worked for tappers who were again making camp at La Esmeralda, until, after a dispute with them in 1937, he returned with a large party to plunder all they had (Cocco 1972:6).[5] The late 1930s may also mark the introduction of malaria to the area, for it is reported that fevers killed many Yanomamo around the Padamo (Smole 1976:50). Starting around 1940, the region saw a transition to a more intense level of Western activity, but that will be considered in chapter 11.

The Iyewei-Padamo Bloc

The northwestern Yanomamo who were most directly exposed to the Yecuana and the limited Western presence around La Esmeralda were the people described in chapter 9 as the Iyewei-Padamo bloc, which Hames (1983:405) calls the Haiyamo bloc. To anticipate later discussions, most of the Haiyamo people moved northwest into Yecuana country in the Padamo basin in two often-hostile divisions, each of which continued to subdivide along the way. A third migratory line split off from one of the Haiyamo divisions and headed down the Ocamo (see map 4). They became known as Iyewei-teri, and their residence alongside the Catholic mission at the mouth of the Ocamo marks the northern border of what I call the Orinoco-Mavaca area. Cocco's (1972:110–15) detailed history of the Iyewei-teri line supplements Hames's (1983:406–15) more general reconstruction of movements.

We left the Iyewei-Padamo people in chapter 9 around 1920, living in two antagonistic villages on the middle and upper Ocamo after several bloody clashes with southeastern neighbors during the rubber boom. The next quarter-century—the time of Western retraction—was more peaceful, although not without tensions, and was characterized by a series of fairly long moves toward sources of Western goods.

One line of villages, the Wakawaka sub-bloc, started at a place called

Kareshibowei and moved to five new gardens during the decade from 1920 to 1930. At the second of the five sites there occurred the only reported killings for the entire period covered in this chapter, when Wakawaka attacked some Puunabiwe-teri who were suspected of trying to lead them into a slaughter (Cocco 1972:112–13). The Wakawaka then fled to the northwest, making three gardens and winding up in the headwaters of a lower Ocamo tributary (at a place called Hawaroi) around 1928 (Hames 1983:409–10).

There they temporarily merged with a group from the Shitari bloc whose leader had an established military reputation from the rubber boom wars (Cocco 1972:112–13). (The Shitari were themselves splitting into two geographic divisions around this time [Fredlund 1982: 35].) They stayed in this location for several years, making three gardens. People from this group were among those who pillaged La Esmeralda in 1929 (Cocco 1972:65), which, it will be recalled, followed some years of prior cooperation by Yanomamo with Yecuana and direct contact with Colonel Pérez's family. Thus the move to Hawaroi apparently improved the Wakawaka's access to steel.

While in this area, the Wakawaka developed close ties with the Auwei-teri, but eventually this alliance deteriorated into a bitter pounding match involving a conflict over reciprocity in marriages. Now fearing the Auwei-teri (Hames 1983:409, 410), the Wakawaka moved two gardens north to Mrakabowei around 1940, where they would be closer to Yecuana who were known to have "muchos machetes" (Cocco 1972: 113). This move paid off, because just around 1942, the Wakawaka became famous among Yanomamo for having obtained many Western goods from their "frequent relations" with Yecuana and whites (Valero 1984:245). Sometime in the process of moving about—Hames and Cocco differ as to when—the Iyewei-teri people split off from the Wakawaka sub-bloc.

The other line of movement described by Hames (1983:406–12)— that of the middle Padamo group—is not discussed by Cocco and therefore lacks supplemental detail. In general outline, the timing and direction of events in the Padamo group's history are strikingly similar to those of the Wakawaka's. The Padamo people too moved northwest toward the close of the rubber boom, fleeing enemies. They began the 1920s along the Ocamo at a place called Tokonabowei, downstream from the Wakawaka people. There they spent a decade without any indication of violence. Around 1930, raids by the Madodoi-teri (a Shitari group [Fredlund 1982:35]) to their southeast prompted them to move northwest to the Matacuni, to a site called Apihabowei. They spent another decade there without reported incident, but then again felt threatened by the Madodoi-teri and moved to an effluent of the Padamo around 1940. They were still in this area, at a place known as Kowaci, a few years later when they fissioned into two distinct lines—but that story, and the continuing history of all these northwestern Yanomamo, will be continued in chapter 11.

For all the northwestern Yanomamo, from the post-rubber contraction around 1920 through the gradual intensification of Western penetration in the late 1930s, the only killings that are specifically noted are those of the Puunabiwe-teri by the Wakawaka in circumstances that suggest a spontaneous, unplanned clash (see Cocco 1972:112). It may be more than coincidental that the killers were from a group known to be working with Yecuana in the late 1920s. Of course there could have been other, unreported deaths as well—indeed, the Puunabiwe-teri are known to have been in another lethal clash. Certainly, there are indications of moments of high tension, especially around 1940, when the Western presence in the region began to intensify. But in general, this time and place is a pacific contrast to the years of rubber and to later times of more intensive Western contact.

Hames (1983:419), like his colleague Chagnon, argues that long-distance "macro-moves" are "induced by intertribal raiding."[6] I concur that war can prompt people to relocate, but unlike Chagnon and his associates, I argue that improved proximity to sources of steel is an even more general determinant of long-distance movement. As mapped by Hames (1983:406; and see map 4), macromoves show a consistent pattern of relocation to the headwaters of rivers and then down the rivers towards the sources of Western goods. The indicated village fissionings represent, behaviorally, the selection of different options in approaching these sources. Moreover, in Hames's listing of the causes of 22 macro-moves from 1920 to 1970, only 5 are the results of being raided, and 5 more were caused by fear of raids. In contrast, consideration of access to Western manufactures fits well with all the listed movements, and the information provided by Cocco about the Wakawaka line reveals such access to be the explicit objective behind at least some of their relocations.

Before turning to the Namowei population bloc, I should cite some limited information about other Yanomamo groups living north of the Orinoco. For the area just south of the Iyewei-Padamo population bloc, Valero (1984:437) learned of a war, perhaps during the late 1930s, between the Punabiwe-teri and the Watupawe-teri to their east. At least one man, the father of Valero's second husband, was killed. This war pitted people on the lower Ocamo—that is, those with better access to steel—against people in the highlands of the middle and upper Ocamo. As we shall see, this axis along the Ocamo remained a line of intermittent violence through the 1960s.

"Barafiri" is the name of a dialect of Yanomamo spoken by people who live some 50 miles east of Hames's research area in the Parima highlands. About them, Smole (1976:76, 93, 235, 237–38) makes two references to what is apparently the same event: an intense war between an alliance of Jorocoba-teri and Docodicoro-teri against an alliance of Yoreshiana-teri and Boreawawa-teri. This war is said to have occured "during the 1920s" (1976:93) and "sometime prior to 1935" (1976:235). For the Jorocoba-teri, this would be the only war in their known history. Both date and context are so vague as to preclude any attempt at analysis. However, the possibility of a trade connection is suggested by the fact that around the 1920s the Yoreshiana-teri had been acting as a conduit for a trickle of steel into higher lands.

The Namowei as Valero Met Them

In the 1920s and early 1930s, the Orinoco above the Mavaca had extremely little outside contact, although, as we have seen, some *balateros* and the Dickey expedition did come through. Valero was taken in by the Namowei around 1935 (perhaps early 1936), just as new creole penetration began. Through her eyes we see the Namowei some two decades after the most prosperous years of the rubber boom had ended.

When Valero arrived, the Namowei consisted of five main divisions (Valero 1984:117–18) that periodically joined and dispersed. Three are of limited importance in future discussions: Rashawe-teri, Yaminawe-teri, and Porehipiwei-teri. Two are central: Patanowa-teri and Wanitima-teri. The Wanitima-teri were led by an unusually forceful man named Fusiwe, or Husiwe. This man, who would become Valero's first husband, was a prototypical war leader and an exemplar of the kind of *waiteri* (fierce) woman-taker emphasized in the work of Napoleon Chagnon.

A sixth group typically, but not always, considered as Namowei was the Prararipiwei-teri, who would shortly come to be known as Bisaasi-teri—the people with whom Chagnon began fieldwork in 1964. (When the Namowei were at the place called Namowei, the Prararipiwei-teri were nearby at Morata, and they apparently crossed the Orinoco together [Cocco 1972:111].) One should not imagine, however, that these divisions had fixed memberships. Along with unending mergers and divisions, smaller groups and individuals regularly moved from one larger group to another, or even lived off by themselves. In addition, the dispersed residence pattern was consolidated for defense when there was danger of war (e.g., Biocca 1971:205).

In chapter 9, I described the Namowei as involved in several wars and as moving westward along the Orinoco during the rubber years, winding up at a place called Hahoyaoba around 1920. As their history is reconstructed by Chagnon (1966:151–53), they were there joined by old allies from their previous locations, now divided into two villages: Hasupuwe-teri and Ashatowa-teri. But poor fertility in the area prompted a move across to the south side of the Orinoco, to Patanowa, sometime between 1925 and 1930. Patanowa is located near the upper reaches of a stream that flows into the Orinoco some distance below Raudal de Guajaribos—the same general area inhabited by nineteenth-century Yanomamo who participated in the indigenous trade. Chagnon (1992a:88) characterizes this area, the Shanishani drainage, as a repeated area of settlement for groups heading west and south.

Valero (1984:164, 170, 324, 437–38) provides some information on recent Yanomamo history as she recalls the Namowei explaining it. When matched against Chagnon's account, it appears that Valero collapses several moves over a quarter of a century into one story, "how the Namowei came to live on the south side of the Orinoco." The general picture is that where they once lived, they were "not lacking in anything" (1984:164), but they were continually attacked by enemies (Watupawe-teri and Takowe-teri) who lived high in the mountains.[7]

The one act of aggression Valero actually describes is supernatural in character. The Namowei found some broken and burned pieces of glass, mirror, and fabric. Yanomamo believe that by burning such Western substances a shaman can send the diseases associated with Westerners (and see Valero 1984:38, 158, 470, 506). The Namowei concluded that their enemies had burned these items—which "surely they robbed . . . from the *nape,* who knows where" (Valero 1984:170)—to make them ill. Subsequently, the Namowei fell victim to a deadly epidemic, which, along with raiding, forced them across the river to Patanowa. There they initially suffered from hunger for lack of an established garden, although they did find some food in an old garden of unknown origin.

Understanding developments in the 1930s requires knowledge of the social geography of the Namowei in their new location (see Biocca 1971:99, 120; Valero 1984:131, 141, 151, 156, 158, 167, 197, 252).

Some distance to their east were their old allies, the Hasupuwe-teri (then called Irota-teri) and that group's nearby offshoot, Ashatowa-teri. Farther to the east, apparently close to the Orinoco somewhere past Raudal Guaica, were the Aramamise-teri, relatives of the Shama-tari. (Some Aramamise-teri visited the village of Karawe-teri during the brief time Valero lived there [early 1935?], bringing machetes and other items they had obtained from passing *nape*.)

To the south were Shamatari villages in the Siapa drainage and upper Mavaca. The west was empty to the Mavaca and beyond; much of the lower land in this area is uninhabitable swamp. To the north, downstream and on the other side of the Orinoco, were the Sitoya-teri (soon to be called Mahekoto-teri), and upstream from them, their allies, Yabitawa-teri and Watanami-teri. (Some Watanami-teri were mentioned earlier as temporarily having joined with the Kohoroshiwe-teri above the Río Negro.) Beyond those groups were others, verging into the northern Yanomamo described in a previous section.

During their first years at Patanowa in the late 1920s, the Namowei had no reported enemies and were on good terms with their later foes, the Shamatari (Chagnon 1966:153). But as Valero was told, there was some tension and even violence. Sometime around 1931, a raid and counterraid took place between Namowei and Shamatari (Valero 1984: 119, 123), but she gives no reason for the quarrel. One Namowei and a number of Shamatari were killed, and many Shamatari women were captured, some of whom later escaped.[8]

The Namowei also had conflicts, but no clear bloodshed, with people to their east. Fusiwe captured an Aramamise-teri girl he found bathing in a stream, who became his second wife, and he sought to take women from another group near the Aramamise-teri (Biocca 1971:129, 142). Tensions developed between the Namowei and their once and future ally, the Hasupuwe-teri (Valero 1984:121, 176)—tensions provoked by Fusiwe's making off with a Hasupuwe-teri woman during a feast (she became his third wife) and by the theft of the hallucinogen *yopo* from a garden (see note 15). (The extremely fierce Fusiwe would continue to involve his people in violent conflicts in the future, ultimately to his own undoing. In the conclusion to this book, I will consider Fusiwe as a study in agency.)

But as Valero arrived on the scene, the Namowei and Hasupuwe-teri had reconciled and were just restarting mutual feasting. The Shamatari had sent a peace delegation some time before, saying they would forget revenge and let the Namowei keep the women they took. The two had begun trading, but not feasting.[9] They were friends again, "but not much" (Valero 1984:119). The clash with the Shamatari seems to have occurred shortly after Dickey passed through the area, but I would hesitate to assert a connection or offer any other explanation for these conflicts. Indeed, these particular fights seem to fit better with Chagnon's views on Yanomami warfare than with my own.

These conflicts notwithstanding, the Namowei saw themselves as having lived in peace after the wars that drove them from Konata and Wareta, their residences first north and then south of the Orinoco during the boom years of rubber. Repeatedly, old leaders who counseled against military action during the conflicted 1940s referred to wars they had fought in when they were young, and they warned the new crop of young, belligerent men that they had never experienced real war and so they should not disturb the peace (Biocca 1971:218; Valero 1984:238, 320, 324, 335). For example, as tensions built toward the first serious killings around 1942, one said: "To be killing people, pay attention to how we had to come from Konata, from Wareta, from Namowei, from Hahoyaoba, to now live far from the other Yanomami, and with so much work. Now we are at peace, we should not look for more fights. If we return to make war, we will have to abandon these gardens, leave for other places and start all over" (Valero 1984:227). On one of these occasions (Valero 1984:238), Fusiwe responded by calling the elders cowards.

The time around the 1930s was remembered by the Namowei for its absence of steel—as would be expected, given their relative isolation. Some of Chagnon's (1977:33) older informants recalled having *no* steel when they were young—although this story may be the Yanomamo equivalent of walking seven miles to school—and they spoke of the difficulty of clearing gardens with fire and the stone axes they found. One informant, a man born around 1925, recalled that when he was a young man, his group had only one piece of steel obtained from Yecuana via several intermediaries. Everyone in the village used the piece (Chagnon 1977:14, 34). Valero confirms this kind of shared usage and notes that villages actually grew in size just to preserve access to the common edge (Colchester 1984:296). Axes possessed by some Namowei are identified as having been taken "a long time before from rubber workers" (Biocca 1971:144–45). Little steel means little reason to fight. That situation would change.

Leaving a State of Peace

Soon after Valero arrived among the Namowei (early 1936?), some of them returned from a visit to the Sitoya-teri and Watanami-teri, to whom they traded dogs, "carrying some machete [*algún machete*] which the Sitoya-teri were beginning to receive or rob from some whites" (Valero 1984:124). Perhaps a year and a half then went by without any major political events, during which very occasional contacts with outsiders took place along the Orinoco. But tensions had risen. The Namowei were visited by some men from Aramamise-teri, who warned that other Aramamise-teri and Konabuma-teri (a Shamatari group living in the southern fringes of the Shanishani drainage [Chagnon 1992a:84]) were planning to raid them. The Namowei took this rumor seriously (Valero 1984:141).

Indicative of how unwarlike the Namowei had become, they then did something I have not seen reported anywhere else: they entered into a sustained program of military training and practice. About twice a month, all the men would gather to receive instruction from older men, practice shooting and dodging blunted arrows, and divide into teams that would attack and defend the village (Valero 1984:141).

The aggressive Fusiwe—who had taken Valero as his fifth wife (Biocca 1971:110–38; Valero 1984:125–61)—decided to lead an attack on the Konabuma-teri. He recruited a substantial group of men from all the Namowei divisions and led them to the Konabuma-teri village. But the attack was an almost comic failure, for the hidden raiders were given away when an old man made a lunge for a passing young woman. Fusiwe's disorganized forces took flight, with the Konabuma-teri in pursuit. They did not catch the Namowei only because they did not know who they were or which way they were headed. The only casualty was the lecherous old man, who was hit by a curare arrow but survived, only to face ridicule on his return home. No further clashes followed this event (Valero 1984:142–51).

A similar but far more deadly clash at this same time involved the Namowei's allies, the Hasupuwe-teri. Shortly after a visit to the Namowei in which they had received some steel, they were attacked by an otherwise unknown group, the Oshopiwe-teri, from their east (Valero 1984:151). As Valero explained it to Cocco (1972:387), the Hasupuwe-teri and some allies had been heading toward the Oshopiwe-teri, planning to raid them and training for war as they went along. But during one of their simulated battles near the enemy's home, they carelessly walked into an ambush in which about six of their men were killed—a military disaster.

These two sorties by the Namowei and their Hasupuwe-teri allies show several similarities. Both took place shortly after steel tools began to be given out by the new visitors along the Orinoco. Both went against more isolated groups, both were associated with an unusual level of military training, and both ended in failure, one comic, one tragic. The timing and alignment of enemies fit theoretical expectations, but according to the theory, the initial attack should have come from the isolated groups. The Namowei were expecting just such an attack. Perhaps these two attempted strikes represent an unusually calculated, and maybe insufficiently motivated, attempt at preemption.

In 1938 or 1939, the Namowei invited the Sitoya-teri, Watanami-teri, and Yabitawa-teri to a peach-palm feast (Biocca 1971:119–24; Valero 1984:153–60, 200). At this time the Sitoya-teri, in addition to their contacts with *nape* along the river, had developed ties to another group, the Shawarawe-teri (part of what Hames [1983:411] calls the Haiyamo people), who were living near the Padamo River, and through them obtained Western goods provided by Yecuana. The Sitoya-teri wanted to be better friends with the Namowei. When they came to visit, presumably they brought gifts. What actually happened at the feast is not described, but bad feeling developed for some reason. Coincidentally, at the time of the feast Helena Valero had again fled into the woods. When the invited guests left for home, Fusiwe and some other Namowei men seized upon a pretext—that the visitors might have encountered Valero on the trail and taken her along—to chase after them.

They caught the Sitoya-teri by themselves and took at least seven of their women. (Since the Sitoya-teri lived close by, all but a few of these women shortly escaped back home.) "The Sitoya-teri, cowards, did not do anything. They were very fearful in that time" (Valero 1984:158). As is commonly the case, the Namowei were deeply divided over this extremely provocative move. Some did not participate, and they strongly criticized the aggressors, calling attention to the fact that the Namowei already had to worry about possible attacks from the south. One man warned that the Sitoya-teri were "friends of the white men. They will come with the whites to kill you" (Biocca 1971:124).

But no *nape* was going to risk his neck for the Sitoya-teri. Yanomami canons of revenge notwithstanding, the Sitoya-teri took no retaliatory action at all. Why? In terms of the theoretical model, the Sitoya-teri would have been in a very vulnerable position at this moment: relatively wealthy in Western goods, yet without any real military advantages. They probably already faced a situation that existed in acute form by 1942, in which, threatened by people in the mountains to their north, they desperately needed to secure their southern flank. They simply could not afford to get into a shooting war with the Namowei. On the other hand, if the Sitoya-teri were forced away by such severe provocations, perhaps some Namowei could move into position as "friends of the white men."

For a few years after they took the Sitoya-teri women (1938–41?), the Namowei remained very short on steel cutting tools (Valero 1984:161, 197). They continued to worry about the evil intentions of the Aramamise-teri and especially the Konabuma-teri. But then the Aramamise-teri had a stroke of luck: they were visited by *nape* who gave them tools, clothes, even hats (Valero 1984:167, 169). The Namowei still had not met any *nape* face to face, but they wanted to. Fusiwe and Shamawe, the leader of the Bisaasi-teri, along with some others, set off on a long exploratory hunt closer to the Orinoco where the *nape* passed. Apparently they found a deserted camp or cache, obtaining some machetes but also contracting a nonlethal fever (Valero 1984:169–71).

Some time later, some Namowei went on two long treks to the north side of the Orinoco, but they were frightened back to the south side when they encountered tracks of possible "enemies" (Valero 1984:197–201). As Valero later told Cocco, they went on these trips "with the decided intention of encountering the *nape* and asking them for machetes and axes, but they were also decided to kill them if they said no. . . . They never encountered any whites" (Cocco 1972:376).

There are signs that internal tensions among the Namowei also rose as the Western presence on the upper Orinoco began to intensify around 1940. About this time, two Namowei divisions, the Yaminawe-teri and Wanitima-teri, had a club fight provoked by the theft of tobacco from a garden (Valero 1984:201–203). Other serious quarrels may date to this period.[10] Still, these tensions did not commonly lead to killings. In the 1940s, they did.

11

Maneuvering into War: The Yanomamo, 1940 to 1950

This chapter is the first to concentrate almost entirely on the Orinoco-Mavaca area. That area, as I define it, encompasses the Namowei, the Shamatari to their south, their Hasupuwe-teri allies to the east, and, north of the Orinoco, the Uhepeki bloc (Sitoya-teri and others) and the southern elements of the Iyewei and Padamo blocs. For the years from 1940 to 1950, there is very little information about any Yanomamo except those within this area. Virtually nothing is known about the southwestern Yanomamo overlooking the Río Negro or about those living in the Parima highlands, and the little information available about the Yanomamo to the north of the Orinoco-Mavaca area will be presented after the following reconstruction of local historical context.

Orinoco-Mavaca history is another story. The 1940s saw an unsteady but significant increase in the Western presence in the area, facilitated by the introduction of gasoline-powered motor launches (U.S. Army Corps of Engineers 1943:13) that allowed much greater capacity for movement and supply. For the 1940s, more historical reports become available, anthropologists' reconstructed village histories become more complete and detailed, and above all, Helena Valero continues the story of her life among the Namowei. Taken together, these sources reveal some of the complex maneuvering related to the intensifying Western presence and show how Yanomamo politics culminated increasingly in war.

Civilization Returns, Again

Although to visiting Americans the upper Orinoco economy still seemed moribund in 1942, there are degrees of moribundity. San Fernando de Atabapo was operating as a base for tappers of rubber, *balata*, and chicle, and, most recently, for palm-fiber collectors (U.S. Army Corps of Engineers 1943:19). It had grown from about 60 residents in 1931 to 150 in 1940 (Gómez Picón 1978:118–19). Around 1940, Manuel Butrón came to the upper Orinoco and began to develop a timber trade, which would soon lead woodsmen deep into the Yanomami's forests (Grelier 1957:51). In 1941, Félix Cardona Puig, probably the most experienced of all explorers in Yanomamo lands, traveled to the upper Mavaca (Grelier 1957:108) and, around that same time, to the headwaters of the Padamo and Ocamo (Anduze 1960:38).

Perhaps the most dramatic development, from the Yanomamo point of view, came when Silverio Level—part Yecuana (Cocco 1972:112) and presumably the son of Guillermo Level—and another man built homes near a rapids of the Manaviche River around 1940. They were attacked around 1942 by Yanomamo in perhaps two clashes that left one settler dead and netted the attackers substantial plunder (Cocco 1972:74). The Yanomamo version of this clash will be presented later.

Between 1941 and 1944, a frontier commission was active in the area (Grelier 1957:39), and the U.S. Army Corps of Engineers (1943) arrived to do a survey of the Casiquiare as a possible shipping route. Almost nothing is known about the activities of either group, but the arrival of the Army Engineers most likely represented the greatest infusion of material goods into the local economy since the rubber boom—the sort of largesse, by local standards, that led to cargo cults in other parts of the world. The engineers were supplied by the Rodríguez family enterprise among the Yecuana on the Ventuari River, which at this time had 20 occupied houses along with electrical generators and even refrigeration (Hitchcock 1948:34). Thus 1942–43 represents a substantial, if brief, surge in the Western presence.

After the engineers left, the Rodríguez's post continued to be active during the war years because of its ties to the Rubber Development Corporation (Hitchcock 1948:34). In 1943, international agreements established a high guaranteed price for rubber, but for various reasons this price did not create the hoped-for surge in production of South American rubber. In fact, aggregate production rose only slightly (Knorr 1945:181). I found no specifics for the upper Orinoco area. Whatever its impact, this support for renewed rubber tapping ceased with the end of World War II (Hitchcock 1948:32).

Thus the wartime rubber miniboom—however many new tappers it directed into the forests—did not last long. Hitchcock found the area in the process of emptying out again in 1947, and in that context noted an increase of sightings of Yanomamo in the lowlands (Hitchcock 1948: 35). But this was only to be a lull, not a repeat of the protracted withdrawal of the late 1920s. As the decade progressed, Western penetration increased along three lines.

First, timber workers penetrated deeper into the area's forests. In 1946, Juan Eduardo Noguera, of the Tamatama Nogueras, began searching for valuable trees along the Orinoco, Ocamo, and Manaviche. That year he found an extensive plantain garden visible from the Orinoco and dubbed the site "Platanal." This was a new garden established by the Mahekoto-teri to secure regular Western contact, and it did the job. Noguera began buying plantains and employing Mahekoto-teri men to work for him in his expeditions as far upstream as Raudal Peñascal. Noguera would be a crucial figure in developing contacts with Yanomamo, and he played an important role in all expeditions and mission foundings at least into the 1970s (Cocco 1972:74–76; and see Good 1991:228).

Noguera was not alone. Manuel Butrón had many men working for him by 1950. They had frequent contacts with Yanomamo and even built a shack just above Platanal, where timber that had been floated downstream was cut into boards. Butrón had established a standard exchange rate with the Yanomamo—three bunches of bananas for one machete. The Western goods apparently were brought into the creole economy by a merchant named Fajardo who ran an extensive barter trade covering the entire upper Orinoco. And in 1950, at least one gold prospector was working in the area of Raudal de Guajaribos (Anduze 1960:77–78; Grelier 1957:42, 50–51, 78, 109, 113; Rísquez Ibarren 1962:145).

Not all contacts, however, were peaceful. Experienced woodsmen were well aware that they could encounter serious problems from Yanomamo seeking their trade goods (Grelier 1957:120). Through the later 1940s, Yanomamo would occasionally "steal from the white man but let him go unharmed" (Acebes 1954:217). Several small parties of woodsmen, and even one missionary and his wife, were robbed by Yanomamo and left to walk out of the forest nude (Acebes 1954:217–18; Anduze 1960:40–41; Cocco 1972:87). The Mahekoto-teri did this to one Brazilian woodsman in 1949 (Cocco 1972:374).

This persisting danger may explain why La Esmeralda itself remained uninhabited as late as about 1950 (Gheerbrant 1954:142), a time when San Fernando was a relatively bustling center of some 250 people making a living in *balata* and lumber (Grelier 1957:98). But apparently at least one creole settlement lay close to Yanomami lands: a few whites are recalled by the Yanomamo, but not by anyone else, as living on an Ocamo tributary in the late 1940s. Perhaps fugitives from the law, they left after clashing with Yanomamo around 1950 (Cocco 1972:73). One benchmark of the growing connection between the Yanomamo and creole society comes in 1950, when eight or nine men from Iyewei-teri were brought all the way down to Puerto Ayacucho to meet the governor (Cocco 1972:114). The Iyewei-teri had good ties to the outside world from 1950 onward, if not from even earlier.

A second and ultimately more significant line of contact was the arrival of missionaries, who came into the area on the heels of the woodsmen. In 1937, the Venezuelan government signed an agreement with the Catholic Salesian order to organize missions in the Amazonas Federal Territory, which covered the southernmost part of the country (Arvelo-Jiménez 1971:31). That year, the Catholics established the first mission in over a century among the Piaroa (Zent 1992). But in 1945, before the Salesians could reach the Yanomamo, Venezuela adopted a new constitution that protected religious freedom—thus ending the Catholic monopoly on missions (Thomas 1982:26).

In 1947 Sophie Muller became the first representative of the evangelical New Tribes Mission to reach the upper Orinoco. Others followed quickly. In September 1948 William Northrup, his family, and a Mr. H. Carlson left the new NTM base at San Fernando de Atabapo in search of "new tribes." They were guided by two locals, Domingo Saavedra and Andrés Tovar, "a drunkard," both of whom had declared themselves Christian almost instantly. Northrup and company encountered two parties of friendly "Guajaribo" traveling in canoes around the Padamo or the Ocamo. They then continued upriver for three days, at which time they were greeted by "Guaikas" who, despite their dangerous repuation, took the missionaries to their village and gave them a warm reception (Johnston 1949:8; Northrup 1947:9, 1948:6–7). These were the Mahekoto-teri at Platanal (Migliazza 1972:384). In 1949 the NTM provided them with axes, machetes, knives, and fishhooks (Anduze 1960:225). In September 1950, James Barker and Carlton Hilker established a New Tribes Mission at Platanal (Chagnon 1966:

20; Grelier 1957:115; Migliazza 1972:384). That same year, they made direct contact with Iyewei-teri on the Ocamo (Cocco 1972:114).

The founding of the Platanal mission merits special comment, for it is frequently portrayed as the first significant contact between Yanomami anywhere and the outside world. Obviously, that is not my view. (The family of Juan Noguera, who named Platanal and helped the missionaries settle there, had been dealing directly with Yanomami since at least the 1920s.) But the creation of this mission does represent an important transition to a phase in which Western contact was more sustained, massive, disruptive, and "warrifying" than at any time since the rubber boom. It meant large initial gifts from the missionaries upon their first contact with any group—probably on the order of 25 machetes, 12 axes, and other goods (see Seitz 1963:193)—and then a sustained flow of payments for as long as direct contact persisted.

The third line of Western penetration in the 1940s was less direct but at times more significant: Western contact of varying forms mediated through the Yecuana. As discussed previously, the Yecuana's economic role in the region had been expanding through the 1920s and 1930s. In the first half of the 1940s, the Rodríguez operations and other developments must have poured unheard-of quantities of Western goods into their local trade network. Some goods went to the Yanomamo.

The southward trade routes became very well developed by the late 1940s, as renewed Western activity put more manufactures in Yecuana hands. A visitor in 1951 (Grelier 1957:82, 86–87, 90) described an extensive trade network. The Yecuana themselves avoided going to San Fernando de Atabapo and dealt instead with traveling peddlers. Those who traded with peddlers then traded with more insulated Yecuana, who in turn traded with Yanomami. There were even "itinerant Guaharibo dealers [who] peddle from dug-out canoes" (Grelier 1957:83). In this way even the most remote Yanomami groups were said to receive some trade of Yecuana origin.

But of a broad range of Western goods dispensed by the peddlers, only "hatchets, machetes, knives, threads, and fish hooks . . . reach certain of the Guaharibo Indians, who, for their part, offer nothing but bows and arrows in exchange" (Grelier 1957:90). Not only bows and arrows, however, for according to one Yecuana, "the Waika exchange even women for axes and machetes" (Anduze 1960:225–26).

As in other situations of trade and alliance between Yanomami and Yecuana, the relationship came with the potential for violence. Around

1946, widespread fighting broke out that pitted "Guaharibos" (Yanomami north of the Ocamo), who were allied with Yecuana, against
"Guaicas" from the Ocamo onward (Acebes 1954:217).[1] Fighting continued at least until 1950, when it was reported that "wandering Guaharibo tribes often pillage the Makiritares' plantations . . . and for their
part the Makiritares are not above forcibly carrying off the Guaharibo
women" (Grelier 1957:83). Some spoke of "perpetual war to the death"
between Yecuana and "Waika," even as other "Waika" were drawing
close to the Yecuana and adopting their ways (Anduze 1960:41, 190).

There appears to be a strong spatial element to all this fighting.
The conflicts around 1946 were reported to pit Yanomami north of the
Ocamo against those who lived beyond the Ocamo (Acebes 1954:217).[2]
Around 1951, all the Yanomamo of the Padamo and Ocamo were reportedly living at peace with their Yecuana neighbors (Anduze 1960:385–
86). But the Yecuana could be neighbors only to people on the lower
Ocamo, the upper reaches being exclusively Yanomamo. The "Guaharibo" raiders of the Yecuana, then, probably all came from either the
upper Ocamo or areas to its south and west.

Violence among Yanomamo along the Yecuana Front

Much of this chapter is based on Helena Valero's description of life
among the Namowei during the 1940s. In 1950, Valero fled from the
Namowei and wound up living with Yanomamo in the area between
the Orinoco and Ocamo rivers. During her stay on the north side of the
Orinoco, she learned about wars that had involved these more northerly
groups during the 1940s. One war is very poorly described (Valero 1984:
415–16); it involved Shitari groups up the Ocamo. Apparently they had
several deadly clashes with unidentified enemies. Shitari violence reportedly was carried out by one exceptionally violent man, Kohawe, who
went out to kill enemies all by himself. (He was finally wounded and
caught hiding in a tree, where, roaring like a jaguar, he was shot full
of arrows.) The other war is a more intelligible conflict involving the
Iyewei-teri.

The Iyewei-teri had fissioned off from the Wakawaka sub-bloc sometime in the 1930s, while they were all living in the highlands separating the Padamo from the Ocamo drainage (Cocco 1972:113; Hames
1983:410). Subsequently, the Wakawaka-teri would continue on to the
Matacuni, a Padamo tributary, and the Iyewei-teri would head down
a stream to the Ocamo. (Henceforth the Iyewei-teri are not considered

in Hames's [1983] historical reconstruction.) One reason the Iyewei-teri moved was "to avoid the bothersome contact with the Yeprope-teri, who visited them continuously asking for machetes" (Cocco 1972:113).

In the late 1940s (Biocca 1971:293–94; Valero 1984:437), the Iyewei-teri were in a location that gave them contact with Yecuana. A man named Akawe, who would later be Valero's second husband, joined with some Iyewei-teri men who were going to attack two interior groups—first the Kopariwe-teri and then the Watupawe-teri. Two or three deaths are reported, one of them accidental. The Iyewei-teri actions fit the general pattern of Yanomamo-allied-to-Yecuana conflict with interior Yanomamo. But Akawe claimed to have participated in this war to avenge his father, who had been killed by Watupawe-teri in the 1930s. His mother had saved the father's ashes in order later to feed them to Akawe to cultivate his desire for revenge. Perhaps that is why Akawe, as we will see in chapter 12, grew up to be homicidal.

Piecing all the shreds of information together, it is evident that in the later 1940s there were major tensions leading to wars along the line that extended from the lower to the upper Ocamo. This was a major avenue from the Parima highlands into the lower country where steel was traded, and it was an arena of often violent conflict from the late 1930s through the 1960s. But the other northern Yanomamo—those who arrived in or near the Padamo basin around 1940—appear to have been spared the worst violence.

About these people, Valero (1984:158, 245) indicates that members of the northern sub-bloc were receiving Western goods from Yecuana and trading them to the Orinoco-Mavaca area as early as 1938. The southern sub-bloc received large quantities to trade around 1942. Perhaps these sub-blocs forestalled attacks by being generous with steel, buying off potential enemies, or creating buffers between themselves and interior groups. Or perhaps their long-distance relocations away from their former homes on the Ocamo had put them beyond the reach of envious highlanders, a luxury their Iyewei-teri relatives did not enjoy. At any rate, Hames (1983:409–11) does not report the northern Yanomamo to have been involved in any war during the 1940s. They were, however, riven by intense internal conflict and factionalism.

The more southerly Wakawaka sub-bloc (Hames 1983:410–12) underwent a bitter fissioning around 1947, but there was no killing. At issue was what attitude to take in relations with the Witokaya-teri, and the dispute reached the point of witchcraft accusations. One faction stayed close to the Witokaya-teri, developing strong ties to them. The other, more aggressive faction moved farther down the Matacuni River to Wakawaka.

In the northern, mid-Padamo sub-blocs, intense factionalism led to the killing of the headman of one division in 1945. That event led to fissioning, as the killers' group split off immediately and moved close to a Yecuana village. Their leader "quickly arranged an alliance with the Ye'kwana to protect them from [their former coresidents] by marrying two of his daughters to the Ye'kwana headman" (Hames 1983: 412). Thus these Yanomami experienced destructive rivalries but few deaths. They were "tame Guaharibo"—traders, not fighters—and probably were among the "itinerant Guaharibo dealers" noted by Grelier.

The overall picture for the northern Yanomamo resembles that previously described for the Sanema and Ninam. Chains of trade lead outward from the Yecuana, who use their superior access to Western goods to extract women from Yanomami. Occasionally violence flares between Yanomamo and Yecuana, but more commonly, at a time when the Yecuana are flush with shotguns, it pits Yanomamo who are allied with Yecuana and so possess Western goods against more interior, deprived Yanomamo.

New Tensions along the Orinoco

We left the Namowei around 1940, about two years after they had taken some women from the Sitoya-teri, who had come to feast. Valero had fled into the forest at that moment, but soon she was back with the Namowei. In the next few years, after hearing new reports of *nape* passing along the Orinoco, the Wanitima-teri and Bisaasi-teri made long exploratory hunting trips in search of *nape* from whom they could get steel by trade or plunder. Although they did find some tools, they still had not achieved direct, much less regular, contact with outsiders. The next event occurs in 1941, a year established with certainty by the first airplane overflights of the new boundary commission (Cocco 1972:78; Valero 1984:207).

One day an emissary came from the Sitoya-teri to invite the Namowei to a feast (Biocca 1971:171; Valero 1984:207). The Sitoya-teri by this time had moved their village to a new site nearer to the Orinoco and had taken the name Mahekoto-teri. There they again met *nape* passing upstream, who promised them machetes on their return. The Namowei were suspicious of the Mahekoto-teri's feast offer, fearing it to be a ruse to set them up for revenge for their taking of the Sitoya-teri women. The emissary sought to reassure them: " 'There will not be war on account of women. Women are everywhere; young girls who grow up. Why must we fight for women who are worthless?' The young man continued to speak for a long time; he said: 'The Mahekototeri want to be friends with you again; you have killed no one, they have killed no one. They are sending to tell you to keep their women'" (Biocca 1971:171). But Namowei suspicions persisted, and they did not accept the offer right away.

About a month after this invitation, other people arrived from the north side of the Orinoco. They were Watanami-teri, allies of the Mahekoto-teri. The Watanami-teri had been raided by Takowe-teri, old enemies of the Namowei. The raiders had killed a man and two boys and left the Watanami-teri in such fear that they dared not remain on the north side of the river even to grind the bones of the dead. (This was not the first time Watanami-teri had been attacked by people farther from the Orinoco [Valero 1984:410].) The Namowei took them in for about two months (Valero 1984:207–208).

In this incident we see a tactical element that will be manifested again in several later situations: a group along the north side of the Orinoco, threatened by enemies from the high country farther north, must be able to move to the south side of the river for protection, and that requires being at peace with those who live there. The Mahekoto-teri, too, had such northern enemies, and presumably the Namowei became aware of this situation. Thus the Mahekoto-teri's offer to forswear revenge had a good reason behind it: they could not afford to have enemies to their south. But a few more months passed before the Namowei all joined and traveled slowly toward the Mahekoto-teri village (Valero 1984:209).

The journey was eventful (Biocca 1971:171–76; Valero 1984:209–13). Along the way, one Namowei man killed another with a club, after catching the young man with his wife. Apparently no repercussions followed, showing that a group will not always fission after a lethal club fight. Then another young man sickened with a fever (malaria?) and died. Sorcery was suspected, with the Shamatari as the likely culprits. This death would have major ramifications later. Finally, shortly before the Namowei reached Mahekoto-teri, they were intercepted by a delegation from Kashorawe-teri, a subdivision of the Watanami-teri (Valero 1984:136) living upstream from the Mahekoto-teri. The Kashorawe-teri asked the Namowei to come to a feast in their village instead. Their petition suggests how badly the people along the north shore of the Orinoco needed allies. But the Namowei continued on to the Mahekoto-teri.

On arrival, the reasoning behind the Mahekoto-teri's sincere invitation became clear (Biocca 1971:176–78). The Mahekoto-teri feared that they would be raided by two villages to their north, Shipariwe-teri and Hayata-teri. They also feared these enemies would try to ambush the Namowei—a sensible course for those trying to prevent an alliance. Once safe within the Mahekoto-teri walls, the Namowei were greeted with joy. The headman made sure to prevent any incident involving grievances over the captured women, and he spoke of his desire to be friends.

Fusiwe, a Namowei leader, made it quite clear why he had risked coming: "I have come to you, for you have a machete from the white man; give me a machete that I may carry it with me, for it is very hard work for me to break the tree-trunks with my teeth to make my *shapuno*. You, who are a friend of the whites, have received those necklaces from them; put them round my neck, that the young ladies may say: 'He has been there, where the white men's friend is; on his neck is a beautiful necklace; he has a lovely thing in his ears; he too is becoming a friend of the white men'" (Biocca 1971:178).

From this point on, the Namowei were friends of the Mahekoto-teri and their allies along the north bank, although the relationships still manifested some serious strains (Valero 1984:219–23). Thus the Mahekoto-teri and others eliminated a potential enemy and gained an ally instead. More specifically, they created the possibility of dealing with their northern adversaries by moving to the other side of the Orinoco—a move they would indeed make in response to raids in the 1950s. Such a move would have been impossible while they were on hostile terms with the Namowei.

Around this time—about 1942—two events occurred that cannot be placed in a definite sequence vis-à-vis other events. One involved the Sitoya-teri/Mahekoto-teri, or an offshoot that in later times came to be called Karohi-teri. It was they who attacked Silverio Level's settlement on the Manaviche River around 1942 or 1943 (Cocco 1972:74). In later years, Lizot's informants recalled how they encountered these rubber tappers: "We would watch them through the leaves. In those days we had no metal axes, though a few of us owned some miserable pieces of machete fastened to wooden handles with bowstring. But the foreigners used machetes, axes, and knives: We had never seen so many" (Lizot 1985:3).

At first they bartered with and worked for the *nape*, but this failed to provide enough steel. At the same time, several people died from mysterious new ailments that the Yanomamo attributed to the smoke from the boiling kettles of rubber.

We couldn't stop thinking about the metal tools. . . . We judged them to be miserly with their possessions, and that irritated us. Previously, at night, men of influence and feared warriors had addressed us at length to incite us to stealing: We shouldn't be afraid of these few miserable foreigners, they said. And besides, those vile kettles cause death. (Lizot 1985:4)

This passage is noteworthy for its transparent conversion of material interest into moral terms: the *nape* with Level were stingy; they caused illness; those who did not want to attack them were cowards. These harangues apparently went on for some time, with speakers for both war and peace. Finally, emboldened by the arrival of some Watanami-teri allies, a group of young men decided on direct action. An attempt to make off with *nape* machetes led to a Yanomamo's being shot, but he did not die. A short time later a Yanomamo ambush killed one of the tappers. After this clash, the *nape*—Level and his fellow tappers—withdrew.

The other event is described in both of Valero's narratives as occurring after the Namowei's rapprochement with the Mahekoto-teri, although the two books (Biocca 1971:159–62; Valero 1984:245–47) differ in placing it just before and just after the killing of Ruwahiwe—which we will come to shortly. (To me, this event seems more likely to have been one of the circumstances leading up to Ruwahiwe's death than to have occurred afterward.) Whichever was the case, news came to the Namowei one day that "the Wakawakateri had many machetes" (Biocca 1971:158). The Wakawaka, of course, were one of the groups followed by Hames (1983). At this moment, they were living on the lower Matacuni and "had frequent relations with the Maquiritare and the whites" (Valero 1984:245). Their sudden influx of steel could have come from the boundary commission, the Army Engineers, or both. The Bisaasi-teri and additional men from three Namowei subdivisions quickly decided to make the long trip through unknown territory to ask for machetes.

Evidently they saw the possibility of violence in this encounter. One man who was too afraid to enter the Wakawaka-teri's *shabono* heard their shouted greeting, panicked, and fled all the way home. He told everyone that all the visitors had been killed. Many believed him and were discussing the possibility of a retaliatory raid when the expedition returned, unharmed and loaded down with presents: "many machetes, axes, beads, hammocks, balls of cotton, three aluminum pots . . . they were the first pots which appeared there. Some even brought shirts, white shirts, and they wore them. How funny! One even had a hat.

'Everyone look. I am a *nape*,' they say Hesikakiwe said" (Valero 1984: 247). This extraordinary generosity on the part of the Wakawaka-teri toward a distant, unrelated group is a good example of the "buying off" of potential enemies.

The Plot against Ruwahiwe

Around 1942—months after the rapprochement with the Mahekoto-teri—the first rumblings of a very serious conflict were felt among the Namowei (Biocca 1971:185–201; Valero 1984:223–40).[3] Visitors arrived who passed along a rumor that the man who died from fever on the trip to Mahekoto-teri had been the victim of sorcery by Ruwahiwe, leader of the Matakuwe-teri, also called the Konabuma-teri Shamatari. (We last saw Ruwahiwe in chapter 10, leading raids against the Kohoroshiwe-teri and Karawe-teri on the Río Negro watershed in the middle 1930s.) Shortly thereafter, three of Ruwahiwe's agnates from an offshoot village arrived. They approached Fusiwe and told him the same story.[4] They also claimed Ruwahiwe had recently killed three or four of their own people and that he openly mocked the Namowei. Then they came to the point. " 'It was he,' said the Shamatari, 'and now you must kill him, kill him, kill him.' . . . He repeated that word so many times: '*Shere, shere, shere*'" (Biocca 1971:186). The visitors forswore any intent to take revenge if Fusiwe did kill their brother.

The internal politics of the Shamatari cannot be ascertained from this tale, except to note that they had become highly conflicted just at this moment of increasing Western presence. But one can perceive the visitors' subtext in getting close to Fusiwe and the Namowei. They told Fusiwe that they had been able to convey this news only by telling Ruwahiwe that they were going to the Namowei to ask for machetes with which to clear a new garden, and indeed, they were given three machetes to take back with them (Biocca 1971 188; Valero 1984:225–26). They also asked for and received permission to come and live with the Namowei after the deed was done. Thus they had obtained steel to carry home and the promise of better supply in the future.

Short-tempered Fusiwe believed their story and agreed to do the killing. He told the visitors to tell Ruwahiwe to come for a feast, and that if he brought dogs to trade he would be given machetes and axes and beads. Along with Fusiwe's own Wanitima-teri, the plot was joined by some Bisaasi-teri, led by the equally aggressive Rashawe, and some Tetehei-teri, both of which groups were tightly allied with Fusiwe at this time. The plotters concealed their intentions from the other Namowei. Ruwahiwe, on receiving the invitation, feared treachery but decided to risk the trip in the hope of actually getting the precious steel. The Namowei subdivisions all gathered at the great *shabono* at Patanowa to receive the expected guests.

Ruwahiwe arrived with up to twenty others, mostly men. He was greeted warmly by Repowe, the old and peaceable headman of Patanowa-teri. Repowe at this time had two Shamatari wives, and as the glowering Fusiwe began openly to provoke the visitors, Repowe and other men tried to calm tempers. Despite the palpable tension, the Shamatari continued asking for things and began the formal trading of dogs for machetes—but with Repowe, not Fusiwe. Repowe handed over two machetes and promised an ax as soon as the Watanami-teri gave him one they had promised him.

As the Shamatari squatted in trading, followers of Fusiwe and Rashawe came up behind them. When Ruwahiwe moved to take the second machete, one of the plotters struck him in the head with an ax. In an instant, five other ax wielders struck five Shamatari. The ax blows did not kill, and the plotters opened fire with curare arrows, chasing the Shamatari as they fled into the forest. Ruwahiwe, lurching and staggering, "drunk with curare," was hit with countless arrows of all types.[5] In all, about six Shamatari died.[6] One woman and a child were taken captive.[7]

The assault on the Shamatari visitors outraged those Namowei who had been unaware of the planned treachery. Even his own father condemned Fusiwe. Repowe, furious, came over shouting: "Now you are happy. . . . You killed Shamatari. You never said anything to me. Why did you kill them? Huh? Because they did not give you a dog. That. Because they only gave to me and my son, you killed them out of envy" (Valero 1984:237). Repowe repeated the accusation that Fusiwe killed because he was left out of the trading, but Fusiwe forced him to back down, insisting he had acted only to avenge the sorcery. The Namowei subdivisions then scattered, angry at each other and anticipating Shamatari vengeance.

Repowe's accusations provide a clue about the underlying motives of the Namowei assailants. Repowe was in an excellent position to bring prosperity to his closest kinsmen by acting as a trade middleman. He was on good terms with Mahekoto-teri and Watanami-teri and anticipated more deliveries of metal tools from them. Fusiwe's Wanitima-teri may not have enjoyed such close relations, since Fusiwe had been the instigator behind the taking of the Mahekoto-teri's women a few years before. Even if that unprovoked assault had been "forgiven," it is to be expected that Mahekoto-teri men would deal more willingly and favorably with other Patanowa-teri men than with Fusiwe. So the Patanowa-teri were in a good position to receive a share of future presents handed out by *nape* on the river.

As for the Shamatari, we saw in chapter 10 that they had recently sent word to the Namowei that they wanted to forget old grievances and become friends. "Apparently, trading visits increased in regularity and frequency" in the years just before the slaughter (Chagnon 1992a:2). "Several marriage alliances were developing between the Namowei-teri and one of the Shamatari villages (Konabuma-tedi)" (Chagnon 1966: 152–53). The reason for the Shamatari's new interest in alliance is obvious: the Namowei were obtaining steel, and they sat between the Shamatari and the source of the new goods. But with which Namowei group were the Shamatari establishing these marriage ties?

While Fusiwe had no Shamatari wives, Repowe had two (Valero 1984:161, 232)—although when and how he obtained them is not said. As he demonstrated during the fatal feast, Repowe was prepared to deepen a trading relationship in which steel would be exchanged for hunting dogs, a standard exchange in future years. Fusiwe, in contrast, had led the failed raid against the Shamatari a few years before. Thus we can understand why, as Repowe's accusations imply, Fusiwe might have been left out of this developing trade and alliance. (Fusiwe seems to have concentrated his personal efforts at building trade and marriage bonds with the Hasupuwe-teri [Valero 1984:167, 151, 238, 245], a fact of some significance later.)

Since the Konabuma-teri (Matakuwe-teri) lived close to the headwaters of the stream along which the Patanowa-teri were located (Chagnon 1992a:167), Fusiwe and his allies had reason to fear them as potential competitors for the still very limited supply of steel entering the area. A stronger alliance between the Patanowa-teri and the Konabuma-teri would send Western goods south, away from the Wanitima-teri and Bisaasi-teri, and would at the same time send women to and reinforce the relative political strength of the Patanowa-teri. Even worse, the Konabuma-teri might use this friendship to move into the area. On the other hand, if the plot worked as planned, the connection between the Patanowa-teri and the Konabuma-teri would be severed, and it would be Fusiwe's people who gained the advantage of having Shamatari allies—the plotters and their kin—and probably women too. But the plot only half worked: the result was a severing of all trade links between Namowei and Shamatari for several years.

I do not believe, however, that trade interests were the only factors at work in this instance. The Namowei had just experienced their first death(s) from a new, mysterious illness. While the Yanomami quickly came to recognize the *nape* as the source of new ailments, the earliest deaths were most likely interpreted in terms of traditional ideas about sorcery (see Albert 1988). Fusiwe and others probably believed it when they were told that Ruwahiwe was trying to kill them with magic, especially if they were already primed to believe the worst of him.

Fusiwe's personality must also be taken into account. Even by Yanomami standards, he was an excessively violent man. As we have seen, the slaughter he orchestrated was condemned by most of the Patanowateri, just as some had criticized his earlier assault on the Mahekoto-teri. (When Ruwahiwe's people arrived to trade, even Fusiwe's own wives tried to warn them about his intentions.) Another man might not have agreed to kill Ruwahiwe, which is probably the reason Fusiwe was sought out by the Shamatari plotters.

Individual fierceness is one of the elements I believe determines the political character of intergroup relations. In the concluding chapter, I will say more about the theoretical significance of one man's violent disposition. Here it is enough to refer back to my general characterization of treacherous slaughters like this one: they usually involve a coalition of groups acting against the interests and wishes of others who benefit more from trade than from war. It may also be worth reminding the reader that my theoretical model does not suggest that antagonistic interests in Western manufactures lead to war on the basis of pure economic calculation, but rather that those interests shape moral evaluations and emotional dispositions in a way that rationalizes economically self-serving military action.

Events following the death of Ruwahiwe are not clear. The Namowei went separate ways, so Valero witnessed only some actions (Biocca 1971:202–204; Valero 1984:241–45); her account differs considerably from Chagnon's (1966:153–54, 172) reconstruction. Both Valero and Chagnon agree that after the death of Ruwahiwe, his Shamatari kinsmen attempted retaliatory raids. Chagnon has them killing one person—a Konabuma-teri who was performing bride service among the Namowei! Valero (1984) has the two Shamatari raids turn back without making contact, once because of bad omens and once because they found no one home.

Either way, the Shamatari response was weak. As one of his own people said to Fusiwe: " 'What would they do?' said an old woman. 'All the Shamatari today are afraid of the Namoeteri and are saying that they are about to join up with the Karawetari, for fear of you. You have killed the *tushaua* [leader], who was the most *waiteri;* how can you be afraid of them? Only that timid brother is left behind' " (Biocca 1971:202).

But the Namowei also heard that Ruwahiwe's place as Shamatari war leader had been taken by an able man named Riokowe, leader of the people now called Iwahikoroba-teri (Valero 1984:241). And Ruwahiwe's brothers, Hohosiwe and Sibarariwa, remained a potential threat (Biocca 1971:201).

According to Chagnon (1966:172), the Shamatari did indeed abandon Konabuma at this point, driven away by raiders from three groups: the Aramamise-teri, the Paruritawa-teri—a recently fissioned segment of the Shamatari (perhaps involved in the plot?)—and the Namowei. Valero would have had no direct knowledge about the first two, but she knew about the Namowei, and her account mentions no raids on the Shamatari following the killing of Ruwahiwe. My suspicion, noted in chapter 10, is that the raid Chagnon places in this sequence—a raid in which several Shamatari women were captured—is the same raid that Valero describes as taking place sometime around 1931.

The slaughter of the Shamatari occurred at just the moment—1942 or 1943—when the amount of steel coming into Yanomamo trade networks suddenly surged. It was a time when, as we saw earlier in this section, violence and the fear of violence throughout the Orinoco-Mavaca area reached a level unprecedented in recent decades. But the intensified Western presence deflated to a more moderate level during the next few years—when there would be few, if any, killings in the Orinoco-Mavaca area. Nevertheless, during that time political divisions deepened, setting the stage for even more extensive violence near the end of the decade.

Toward War among the Namowei

During the next four years or so—a lull in Western penetration—some Western goods continued to come into the area, but nothing like the sudden surge of the early 1940s. The Wakawaka-teri still provided goods to the Mahekoto-teri, now including red cloth (Valero 1984:281). Other cloth reached the area from Brazilian boundary commission activities on the Demini (Valero 1984:276). Occasionally a *nape* would pass along the river, giving machetes and knives to those he met (Valero 1984:300). Valero (1984:307) suggests an unusually long absence of any *nape* around 1945–46, just about the time when the least contact would be expected.

The Namowei regularly met with Mahekoto-teri, Watanami-teri, and others from the north bank of the Orinoco to trade. The Namowei gave dogs, which they obtained from Hasupuwe-teri, and cotton and hammocks, which they specialized in producing, in exchange for axes, machetes, bead necklaces, cloth, and even scissors.[8] On one trading visit, a Mahekoto-teri leader gave Fusiwe his only ax, expecting to get another from the *nape* soon. At this time, many Wanitima-teri men had machetes, but others continued to use the *haowe* made from a broken machete blade (Valero 1984:249–50, 252, 281, 284, 301, 311).

But tensions arose in this alliance as the supply of Western goods began to decrease. Around 1944, "the Namoeteri women began to say that the Mahekototeri had many things, many machetes, but that they did not give them away, that when they came, they ate so much and their stomachs were never full. . . . Fusiwe answered: 'It is not true; you women always talk like that, but they have always given us the machetes they had. With those machetes we have cleaned our *shapunos* and prepared our *rocas*'" (Biocca 1971:206). Such complaints, unheeded, can eventually lead to war, and on this occasion the visiting Mahekoto-teri quickly returned home.

The need of the militarily exposed groups on the north bank continuously to reaffirm their alliance with gifts was illustrated when the Watanami-teri visited the Namowei during the brief period around 1945 when no *nape* passed by. The visitors failed to bring the expected machetes, yet they asked for dogs anyway, on the promise of future machetes (Valero 1984:307). "The women said, 'Do not give them dogs. They are not going to bring anything.' 'You like to eat game from my dog,' said Fusiwe, 'but you do not give anything.' The Watanami-teri got a little angry. 'We are not going to come again,' they said. 'If you do not come, better,' responded the women" (Valero 1984:307). This incident shows how a retracting Western presence can generate disputes over unfulfilled expectations in the exchange of Western goods. But in this instance, the retraction was quickly reversed, and so war was avoided.

The middle 1940s were also a time of increasing illness. Fevers, probably malaria, began to strike frequently (Biocca 1971:211–13; Valero 1984:261, 270–72, 308–10). At first only a few among the Namowei died. The Yanomamo now understood that the new illnesses had been introduced by the *nape*,[9] and they developed a standard response of fleeing into deep forest or onto high ground at the first word of an epidemic. Unfortunately, those who carried that word usually brought the pathogen with it. The first really deadly epidemic occurred in what may have been 1945 (Valero 1984:287–300). It spread from the *nape* to the Wakawaka-teri and then to the Mahekoto-teri, and it killed some two dozen or more people among the Namowei.

In chapter 3 I argued that a large number of deaths caused by disease disrupts the social fabric and thus contributes to a climate of instrumental violence in social affairs. Fusiwe's father died in one epidemic (Valero 1984:261); a few years later, when Fusiwe was being provoked to war, he commented, "When my father was alive, he always used to say to me: 'Do not kill.' Now the old man's no longer here" (Biocca 1971:220). When Fusiwe later seemed hell-bent on starting the killing, people said, "He no longer listens to advice" (Biocca 1971:228). Multiply this rupture of restraining influence by dozens of relationships, and one can appreciate the destabilizing impact of so many deaths.

Yet for the moment (c. 1944–47), no war is reported in the area, although the fighting along the Ocamo River, described earlier, may have begun as early as 1946. Under prevailing political conditions, and with very limited quantities of goods coming in, the accumulation of an outstanding quantity of trade goods was unlikely (as is illustrated by the account of the Mahekoto-teri man who gave Fusiwe his only ax), and the passage of *nape* was unpredictable. Thus, the incentive to raid was limited.

Nevertheless, there were rumors and physical signs in the forest that made the Namowei believe Shamatari raiding parties had entered the area, though they never actually attacked (Valero 1984:260–61, 270, 284). Their lack of action suggests they were not trying very hard. The true intentions of the Shamatari cannot be ascertained. The slaughter of their people remained unavenged, but they also remained isolated from sources of Western goods. Any passes they made to the north, toward the Orinoco, may have been for the purpose of seeking out any opportunity they could find, much as the Wanitima-teri and Bisaasi-teri had done in their explorations a few years before.

The year 1946 is a benchmark for the renewal of Western penetration. And it was in that year that Juan Noguera found the new garden the Mahekoto-teri had made along the mosquito-infested bank of the Orinoco. As Cocco (1972:74) reconstructs it, this garden was established after the parent group fissioned and its other division had moved north toward the Ocamo, where it became known as Puunabiwe-teri. (The Puunabiwe-teri were involved in the wars along the Ocamo in the later 1940s, described in a previous section.) The Platanal garden was designed to attract *nape*, and it did. Valero (1984:318) reports one gen-

erous *nape*'s visiting the Mahekoto-teri around 1947. Both external historical sources (Cocco 1972:91) and Valero's narratives indicate regular
commerce between *nape* and Mahekoto-teri and others along the river
thereafter. The details of this commerce relate to a developing conflict
that had its roots in the early 1940s.

At some point, perhaps in late 1943 or early 1944, there was a serious confrontation at a feast hosted by Fusiwe's Wanitima-teri (Biocca
1971:207–208; Valero 1984:252–53). In Biocca's version, this was the
occasion at which the Mahekoto-teri were scared away after complaints
about their stinginess. After they left without trading, and perhaps related to that rupture, an ugly quarrel started among the gathered Namowei when children began throwing firebrands. The Bisaasi-teri guests
were already angry because, they said, they had been slighted in the distribution of maize and meat.[10] Adults were drawn into the children's
quarrel; Fusiwe's temper was again a major factor. The Namowei subdivisions angrily went separate ways.

This incident appears to mark the beginning of the conflict between
Fusiwe and his Wanitima-teri against Rashawe and his Bisaasi-teri,
although it would be years before this ill will led to war.[11] Because of its
start in a dispute over the distribution of meat, along with developments
yet to be described, this war is one that could support the argument for
game depletion as a cause of war—which I will discuss further in the
concluding chapter. But other triggers are also reported for this conflict.
Chagnon (1966:154) has the split start in a bad club fight over a harvest
of peach-palm fruit in an old garden. Subsequently, he wrote (1977:76):
"This split was caused by constant bickering within the group and club
fights over women." All these diverse disputes can be seen as manifestations of a more fundamental conflict of interests—one that was tearing
asunder old ties of kinship and amity, so that any issue could be the start
of a quarrel. But what was the source of the antagonism?

Fusiwe's violent disposition had not only made him enemies, it had
also cost him supporters. Many went to other groups after the killing of
Ruwahiwe, leaving him with about thirty male backers (Biocca 1971:
201). Now, after the firebrand fight, some of his closest male relatives
went off with the Bisaasi-teri (Valero 1984:268).

Fusiwe said he never wanted to get back together with the other
Namowei (Biocca 1971:209), and he took the Wanitima-teri off to visit
the Tetehei-teri, an unusual splinter group of Namowei who, many
years before, had gone off to live apart (Biocca 1971:209; Valero 1984:
255–58). They still maintained relations with other Namowei and with

Fusiwe in particular, because his senior wife was Tetehei-teri (Valero 1984:161). The Tetehei-teri lived in high, flat land west of Patanowa-teri. Their unusual mix of crops, including avocado and bitter manioc, suggests Yecuana influence.[12]

The Tetehei-teri showed Fusiwe a choice garden site about three days' walk away (Biocca 1971:209–10; Valero 1984:258, 300). Because of its thin trees, this appears to have been an old garden, but no Yanomamo had been known to live in the area before. The garden became known as Shihota, and the Tetehei-teri contributed labor and cuttings to get it going. The Yanomami are always making new gardens, but this one was to be especially important. Shihota, as located by Chagnon (1992a:167), was in the upper reaches of Caño Auguey, about 20 kilometers west of Patanowa. This made Fusiwe's people the westernmost of all the Namowei, bringing them almost parallel to the Mahekoto-teri (see map 5). The Shihota site is very important in subsequent political history.

Shortly after starting the garden, Fusiwe opened a direct path down to the Orinoco near Platanal, a trip that could be made in just one (long) day. He and his brothers built a bridge to the other side, and they made the journey to Mahekoto-teri three times during the short period they made use of Shihota (Valero 1984:302, 388). Fusiwe at this time was still calculating how to establish direct contact with whites, and this location put him in a much better position to do so.[13] Not only that, but at Shihota he would also have the potential of becoming a middleman in trade to Shamatari groups. It is this exceptional location for trading, I believe, that made Shihota unusually valuable.

Still, Fusiwe had not severed his ties to other Namowei, and over the next year or so (c. 1945), he would join with them—including the Bisaasi-teri—for major feasts (Valero 1984:268, 275). (Feasting would intensify over the 1940s because proper mortuary custom required collective consumption of the burned and powdered bones of all those who were dying in epidemics [Valero 1984:275, 301].) The Hasupuwe-teri also joined them at one feast, a sign of their deepening alliance with the Namowei. Even though some Mahekoto-teri were also in attendance, the Namowei on this occasion still interceded as middlemen in trade between them and the Hasupuwe-teri (Valero 1984:284).

At the time of these feasts, Fusiwe was openly conciliatory toward the Bisaasi-teri (Valero 1984:268). But the Bisaasi-teri had other plans. Sometime in early to middle 1946, they began clearing a garden for themselves within shouting distance of the Wanitima-teri settlement at Shihota (Valero 1984:301–302). They publicly justified this move by claiming that it was farther away from potential Shamatari enemies, although that reason alone would hardly explain why they went to this particular location. Fusiwe, his men greatly outnumbered by the Bisaasi-teri, kept cool even when he found they had taken cuttings from his garden without asking permission and that they had hunted out all the game along his new path down to the Orinoco. Perhaps a year went by, during which Fusiwe's people and the Bisaasi-teri spent much of their time on trek in the forest, as usual. When Fusiwe returned to Shihota and found that the Bisaasi-teri had again taken food from his gardens, he actually offered to help them with more (Valero 1984:313, 317).

Then the Bisaasi-teri turned to open, flagrant provocation, stealing the Wanitima-teri's tobacco and destroying other crops. When Fusiwe set up a pounding match to clear the air, the Bisaasi-teri men came painted black, as if for war, and concealed stones in their hands when they struck. The match escalated to side slapping with the flat sides of axes, and the older peace leaders had to intercede to urge calm and a return to friendship (Valero 1984:319–21).

The Hasupuwe-teri seized this moment to assert themselves in their alliance with the Namowei groups that now had to worry about the Bisaasi-teri. They contributed to the Namowei's sense of vulnerability by warning Fusiwe that the Shamatari were preparing to attack, at a time when many of his men had not recovered from the pounding match. When some Namowei later went to feast with the Hasupuwe-teri, the hosts took several of their women, although all but one quickly escaped. In their present circumstances, the Namowei were in no position to retaliate (Valero 1984:322–23).

But to return to the central conflict: the Bisaasi-teri did not want to be friends with the Wanitima-teri. They stepped up their provocations and vandalism of Fusiwe's garden. At first Fusiwe's wrath was turned by old Repowe, who reminded everyone about the bad old days and the terrible costs of fighting.[14] But when Fusiwe returned to Shihota on another occasion, he found new Bisaasi-teri destruction. Then they shot arrows into his *shabono*—arrows with fresh curare. This attack was serious, although the arrows were unlikely to kill anyone when fired at random. When the Bisaasi-teri attempted to enter the *shabono*, an enraged Fusiwe led a charge that drove them back—demonstrating that one exceptionally dangerous man can prevail over greater numbers (Biocca 1971:218–23; Valero 1984:323–32).

Now the Bisaasi-teri shouted out their demand: "You must go away; you must leave us this *roca* [garden]; here we must live. Go and live

with the Patanweteri; we must be masters of this place" (Biocca 1971:
224). Greatly outnumbered and virtually unable to leave the confines of
the *shabono*, Fusiwe did leave Shihota under an escort sent to bring him
to Patanowa-teri. Some months passed without incident (Biocca 1971:
225–27; Valero 1984:332–35). "The Bisaasi-teri never came to bother
us. What they wanted they had gotten; to be owners of our garden"
(Valero 1984:335). The conflict seemed to be over.

Then the contact situation changed. In September 1948 the New
Tribes missionaries visited Platanal. The Mahekoto-teri came to tell the
Namowei that many whites had visited and left axes, machetes, and
cloth. They invited the Namowei to a feast (Biocca 1971:227; Valero
1984:335). The arrival of the missionaries in the area signaled the beginning of a much more substantial supply of goods to Mahekoto-teri
and others along the river—a supply that, in the perspective argued
here, made the Shihota location much more valuable.

At this point, Fusiwe's youngest and favorite wife began taunting
him for being afraid of the Bisaasi-teri. When the Namowei left for the
feast at Platanal, Fusiwe announced that he would stay home (Biocca
1971:227–29; Valero 1984:335–37). "Ask for a machete for me too,"
he said. When Repowe asked if he would leave the Bisaasi-teri alone,
Fusiwe replied: "I have no further thought of challenging the Pishaanseteri." "But it was a pure lie," adds Valero (Biocca 1971:228).

A Time of Killing

When the Patanowa-teri left home to go to Platanal, Fusiwe and a few
of his followers went to a small settlement near the Bisaasi-teri, where
a brother-in-law lived. He misled his host about his true intentions, but
his plan was to leave his women there for safety while he went to kill.
His own brothers, however, would not accompany him on this deadly
mission, so he set off with just four inexperienced nephews and his
son-in-law. As they drew near to the Bisaasi-teri at Shihota, they were
almost discovered. Fusiwe decided to shoot the first man he saw, and he
did—even though it happened to be a young man toward whom he felt
very paternal. Fusiwe's companions fled instantly, and they all worked
their way back through trackless forest. The youth shot by Fusiwe died
(Biocca 1971:227–334; Valero 1984:338–42). Thus began the war
among the Namowei—the most serious war involving these people since
the rubber boom. It started within weeks of the first mission contact.

The Bisaasi-teri followed the raiders back to the small settlement from which they had launched the attack (Biocca 1971:234–43; Valero 1984:343–49). They shot at a man who went out to collect honey, then remained for about two days, firing at anyone they could see but only wounding one person. Shortly after they ran out of arrows and went home, an emissary came from Patanowa-teri, telling Fusiwe "that you are too few to be able to fight against the Pishaanseteri, who are so many. Our father sends to tell you to come and live with us, in our *shapuno*" (Biocca 1971:241). They returned to Patanowa-teri to hear a long scolding by old Repowe. Repowe was Fusiwe's father's brother (Valero 1984:262), and by extending protection, he was fulfilling his avuncular obligations. But other Patanowa-teri had had enough of Fusiwe and the fights he started. Other Patanowa-teri had decided that Fusiwe must die.

Shortly after Fusiwe rejoined the Patanowa-teri, they all received an invitation to a feast at Hasupuwe-teri (Biocca 1971: 243–47; Valero 1984:350–54). Fusiwe feared he would be killed during the trip, and he was right. Some Patanowa-teri conspired with the Bisaasi-teri, letting them know when and where they would be traveling. The Patanowa-teri made camp apart from Fusiwe's family and pointed them out when Bisaasi-teri raiders arrived. Early in the morning, Fusiwe was helping his son fix a vine to a basket. Without warning, he was hit in the belly by an arrow with a long bamboo blade, and in the shoulder by a poison arrow.

> The *tushaua* did not utter a shout, only the small boy was shouting with fear. He was standing upright; from that great wound in his stomach, made with a bamboo arrowhead, protruded the long intestine with that yellow fat. He walked a few steps, tried to stand up, but fell. "This time they have killed me!" he murmured. (Biocca 1971:247)

The assassination of Fusiwe did not end the fighting, even though it should have more than satisfied Bisaasi-teri needs for revenge. Instead, the fighting continued for about two years (Biocca 1971:259–65; Valero 1984:364–65, 369–70, 376). The Wanitima-teri, after Fusiwe's death, melded into the other Namowei groups: Yaminawe-teri, Rashawe-teri, and, especially, Patanowa-teri. (In future discussions, I will refer to this cluster of local groups as eastern Namowei, as opposed to the western Namowei of Bisaasi-teri and its later subdivisions.) These eastern groups received strong support from the Hasupuwe-teri. Perhaps two months after Fusiwe died, the Bisaasi-teri ambushed and killed a Yaminawe-teri man in the forest. A few days later, a large party of Hasupuwe-teri arrived, ready for war. The Hasupuwe-teri headman—whose interests in

would be a split decision. What seems certain, in this pattern of visiting, is that by 1949 the Bisaasi-teri had begun to act as middlemen in the
trade of Western goods to the Shamatari, perhaps even before driving
the Wanitima-teri from Shihota. Indeed, Chagnon (1977:102) writes
that before the treacherous feast to come, the Bisaasi-teri "were only
on trading terms with" the Iwahikoroba-teri. Shortly after this meeting
at Shihota, Valero moved north of the Orinoco, and her further reports
about the ensuing carnage are based on what she heard.

In September 1950, Barker and Hilker established their residence at
Platanal. At the time, the Bisaasi-teri were residing at Kreibowei, close
to the Mavaca River. From there, in February 1951 they went to a feast
at Iwahikoroba-teri, their third since Valero had been with them—a
number that indicates very active trade. On February 3, according to one
missionary (Acebes 1954:242), the Bisaasi-teri guests were set upon by
attackers both within and around the Iwahikoroba-teri village. Rashawe
was slain, along with ten to fourteen other men. Six or seven women
were captured, although most of them later escaped back to Bisaasi-teri
(Barker 1959:151–52; Biocca 1971:302; Chagnon 1966:158–59, 1967:
144, 151, 1977:102–103; Valero 1984:432). This is the largest reported
killing ever for any attack on Yanomami by Yanomami.

The Iwahikoroba-teri were not united in this plan. "A few of the
Iwahikoroba-teri refused to participate in the slaughter and even helped
some [Bisaasi-teri] escape" (Chagnon 1977:103). And the Iwahikoroba-
teri did not act alone. In on the assault were also some Shamatari from
the village led by the slain Ruwahiwe's brother Sibarariwa, along with
some Hasupuwe-teri and even some Patanowa-teri (Biocca 1971:302;
Barker 1959:151; Chagnon 1966:158; Valero 1984:432). Just after the
killing of Fusiwe, Valero had heard the Hasupuwe-teri leader propose
enlisting the Shamatari in an attack of this nature (Biocca 1971:283;
Valero 1984:360). Thus, in a sense this attack at Iwahikoroba-teri was
the final and most successful blow by the eastern Namowei alliance
against the Bisaasi-teri.

But why would the Iwahikoroba-teri go along with this plan against
their new trade partners? Revenge for Ruwahiwe's death some eight
years before has limited explanatory value for their actions. Although
the map published by Chagnon (1992a:167) suggests that Iwahikoroba-
teri was a direct outgrowth of Ruwahiwe's people at Konabuma, his
other writings (1966:172–73, 1974:9, 86, 1977:102–103) indicate
that Ruwahiwe's people formed a different group, led by Sibarariwa,
called Mowaraoba-teri (and more recently, Mishimishimabowei-teri).

(Of course, it would be quite normal for people to move between these two entities.) Chagnon (1966:158) says that Sibarariwa's people "persuaded" the Iwahikoroba-teri headman—a man of Aramamise-teri origin (Biocca 1971:281)—to agree to the treachery.

I acknowledge that the killing of some six kinsmen in the 1942 slaughter could be sufficient motivation for Sibarariwa's people to attack, even though they would be killing the people who killed Fusiwe, the organizer of that earlier slaughter. But in my view, the Iwahikoroba-teri would not be persuaded to take such an extreme step, both severing a trade connection and involving themselves in war, unless they themselves had something important at stake. What were their interests at this time? More specifically, what had changed to make them shift from trade to war?

First, the Bisaasi-teri had moved from Shihota to Kreibowei next to the Mavaca River. The Mavaca was a major avenue for commerce in the nineteenth century, and it was probably the scene of rubber tapping during the boom. Its headwaters were explored by Cardona Puig in 1941, and although there is no specific report of *nape* on the Mavaca in the late 1940s, it seems likely that woodsmen and perhaps even missionaries had visited it by 1950.

So, like the Mahekoto-teri before them and many others after, the Bisaasi-teri moved to Kreibowei not merely to get away from their enemies but also to approach a major river, which put them in position to make direct contact with whites. Moreover, from Kreibowei they could circumvent the swamps found in the right angle southeast of the Orinoco-Mavaca juncture (Chagnon 1977:135) as they moved down the Mavaca toward the Orinoco, where they would surely meet *nape*. Indeed, at the time of the slaughter they were already working on another garden at a place called Kobou farther down the Mavaca (Chagnon 1966:159, 1977:103).

The Bisaasi-teri's movements clearly posed a threat to the Iwahikoroba-teri, who were "located on the Mavaca River" (Chagnon 1966: 158) far upstream. The Mavaca is very narrow in places, and ambush is easy (Chagnon 1974:191). As we will see later, whoever controls the downstream areas can control passage upstream. Thus a successful Bisaasi-teri move to Kreibowei or Kobou would effectively eliminate the chances for the Iwahikoroba-teri to make direct contact with whites. And of course, the stakes for all parties took a tremendous leap only a month or two before the slaughter, when the New Tribes Mission was established.

By killing the Bisaasi-teri headman and so many of his men, the Iwahikoroba-teri could reasonably expect the Bisaasi-teri to flee, leaving the Mavaca open. Chagnon (1977:103) describes the Bisaasi-teri predicament: "Kobou was still too new to support the group, and hunger forced them to return to Kreibowei. As this location was well known to their treacherous allies, they wished to abandon it as soon as possible, knowing that their enemies could easily kill the rest of the men and abduct the remaining women." As I will describe in the next chapter, the Bisaasi-teri did abandon the Mavaca temporarily and move in with Mahekoto-teri and others. But they soon returned to the Mavaca, where they effectively prevented any *nape* from traveling up to Shamatari country for nearly twenty years, and where they benefited tremendously from their position as middlemen.

Looking back, the end of the 1940s was a remarkably violent period for the people of the Orinoco-Mavaca area. Tensions had been growing since the *nape* began coming back in 1946, but without lethal violence. Then, in slightly more than two years between 1948 and 1951—beginning some weeks after the NTM missionaries' first visit to Mahekoto-teri and culminating a few months after the establishment of their permanent residence there—some 8 men died in the Namowei raiding and 11 to 15 more in the slaughter at Iwahikoroba-teri. These are the first reported Namowei war deaths (Ruwahiwe's people were not Namowei) since the one reported around 1931. The striking atypicality of this toll of 19 to 23 deaths is revealed in Chagnon's (1966:62) first tabulation of mortality among the Namowei, in which a total of 31 Namowei males are reported to have died in war. In later chapters, we will see that nearly all the remaining Namowei war deaths are accounted for by violence that occurred during the period while Chagnon himself was in the field.

12

The Yanomamo and the Missionaries: 1950 to 1960

In the decade following the founding of the New Tribes mission at Platanal, the Western residential presence on the upper Orinoco went through many changes, but generally it expanded and settled in. For the Yanomamo, the first half of the 1950s were disrupted and violent, but the latter half saw a decline in active warfare. Our understanding of these years is, as always, shaped by the nature of available sources, and these require some preliminary discussion.

When we last saw Helena Valero, after the death of Fusiwe and the outbreak of war between the Bisaasi-teri and the eastern Namowei alliance, she had just fled for her life from the eastern Namowei. She stayed briefly with the Bisaasi-teri and the Mahekoto-teri and then went to live with the Puunabiwe-teri, whose main village at the time was between the Manaviche and Ocamo rivers (see map 4). There she became the wife of Akawe, another exceptionally violent man. She lived in this area until her final escape in 1956. Valero continues to provide some information about the groups south of the Orinoco, but her perspective now shifts to its north.

The politics of this area are different from those south of the Orinoco. More villages lie closer together; most of them are divisions of the Uhepeki population bloc (see Lizot 1988:522). Moreover, there was considerable population flux during the time Valero was there: rapid relocations of villages, splits, fusions, trekking, and extended visiting by individuals and families. So much was happening, roughly simultaneously, that any storyteller would find it difficult to arrange all the events in a linear narrative. Here the role played by the editors of Valero's two narratives may be especially large, although, as always, it is invisible in the texts. One result is increased uncertainty about the accurate sequencing of certain events.[1] On the other hand, more external referents become available now to establish some absolute dates.

Along with Valero's narratives, several other kinds of sources are available. Many Westerners came and wrote about general conditions along the river—especially members of the Franco-Venezuelan Expedition to the source of the Orinoco in 1951. Resident missionaries (Barker 1953, 1959; Cocco 1972) begin to publish material, including sociological descriptions of general relations between villages. Napoleon Chagnon, who arrived in the area in 1964, also provides a good deal of information about political relations in the 1950s. It should be noted with some emphasis that there are other major ethnographic accounts pertaining to this period written in German (Zerries 1964) and Italian (Biocca 1966), neither of which I can read. There is also more information about Yanomamo outside the Orinoco-Mavaca area, which I will discuss in the last section of this chapter. But I will start with an overview of contact history along the upper Orinoco as reported in outside sources.

The New Western Presence

In September 1950, the missionary James Barker and his colleague Hilker established the Platanal New Tribes Mission (NTM). Even though he and other outsiders had been providing the Mahekoto-teri and other groups with Western goods for some time, the founding of the mission assuredly would have been accompanied by a major distribution of presents.

Still, Barker spent his first half-year or so under substantial material limitation. When members of the Franco-Venezuelan Expedition arrived at Platanal in July 1951, they found the missionary without any possessions except the tattered shirt and pants he wore. The Yanomamo had taken everything else and sunk his boat, leaving him unable to travel. Barker felt in danger of losing even his clothing if he walked out of Platanal, and he had visited only one other village so far. At the same time, Barker was reportedly attempting to protect the Yanomamo from the woodsmen who continued to visit Platanal and occasionally robbed them or abused the women (Anduze 1960:42; Grelier 1957: 114–15, 118).

The Franco-Venezuelan Expedition itself was a mammoth affair by local standards. Charged with finding the source of the Orinoco and run under military command, it was certainly the largest Western invasion of the upper Orinoco yet. Its initial airstrip cut travel time between San Fernando de Atabapo and Caracas from a month to four hours. The advance guard reached La Esmeralda in April 1951, clearing another airstrip and establishing a base camp. With DC3s making regular supply runs, personnel quickly climbed to 80 people, including military men, scientists, and many of the woodsmen of the region (Grelier 1957:47–60). The tales they told of Yanomamo attacks dating back to the rubber boom, along with Yecuana stories of recent wars, created an intense fear—a "Guaharibo psychosis"—contributing to the "legend of ferocity of the Waika" (Anduze 1960:41, 62, 190).[2]

A few days after arriving at La Esmeralda, the expedition was visited by a small party of young Yanomamo who had come by canoe from the Padamo. They were given knives and machetes, and left. Three weeks later, a larger party arrived, and from then on many different groups of Yanomamo came and lingered around the base camp. They were given Western goods, which they sometimes demanded with arrows drawn. Some people from the Padamo were already in contact with Yecuana and had had previous dealings with New Tribes missionaries. Some visitors spoke of recent epidemics and wars. The animosity between groups was evident at the camp, and when one group was trading, the others would disappear (Anduze 1960:76–80; Grelier 1957:53–54, 76, 132; Rísquez-Ibarren 1962:70–77).

The expedition began moving up the Orinoco in July and August of 1951. Exploration and associated activities lasted through November, although one small party remained until January 1952. During their passage upriver, expedition members encountered many Yanomamo groups. The first, somewhere above the Ocamo, came out of the forest calling "*shori*" ("brother-in-law")—a gift-giving relationship. The Mahekoto-teri welcomed the explorers. Above Platanal, Yanomamo ran along the riverbank gesticulating for them to stop. They visited villages of some of the Mahekoto-teri's allies upstream. Their generally warm welcome owed much to their standard practice of giving each Yanomamo man a machete and knife, as well as other things such as razor blades, matches, and fishhooks.

The expedition established another base camp at the fabled Raudal de Guajaribos. For about 60 kilometers (linear distance) above the *raudal,* they encountered many Yanomamo, who provided them with food and labor. The natives eagerly accepted gifts and payments but consistently obstructed any attempt by expedition members to walk inland to their villages. Several times, inadequately protected goods were stolen.

Close to the source of the Orinoco, after passing through a very long stretch of apparently uninhabited terrain, the expedition was visited by Yanomamo ("Parejuri") who were familiar with *geral,* the lingua franca of the Río Negro, and who knew the Portuguese words for machete, ax, salt, papaya, coffee, and sugar. (Judging from their location, these people may have had contacts with Brazilians along the upper Demeni and Toototobi.) All together, the expedition may have had direct contact with more than a thousand Yanomamo (Anduze 1960:40, 60, 81, 96, 140, 156, 160, 193, 209; Grelier 1957:80, 111–12, 120, 124–25, 144–48, 163, 180; Rísquez-Ibarren 1962:134–41).

The Franco-Venezuelan expedition introduced hundreds, if not thousands, of steel tools into Yanomami trade networks, although it was a one-time beneficence. But the expedition found a people already connected through trade to the outside world. Western goods had been coming in from Brazil and from the Yecuana and other neighboring peoples, and these goods were rapidly traded into more remote areas by the Yanomamo themselves. The Yecuana by this time were such important suppliers that Yanomamo who had never seen a white person were already "quite familiar with packets of aspirins" (Grelier 1957:87–88). As would be expected in such a situation, they were also familiar with new diseases, and severe influenzas were observed to be at epidemic levels (Anduze 1960:208).

Also as expected, at least in this study, tensions and violence ran high. The first Yanomamo visitors to the expedition's base camp at La Esmeralda were said to be "at war with a neighboring clan" (Grelier 1957:54). Some Yanomami were reportedly antagonistic to the Yecuana, although those of the Padamo and Ocamo were said to be at peace with them (Acebes 1954:242; Anduze 1960:194, 385–86). Anduze (1960: 207) writes: "these indigenies live in constant discord and wars between one faction and another are frequent. Some factions are enemies who have no dealings and can get to the point of fighting with clubs." He further notes (1960:342–43) that the most common sources of enmity are the carrying off of a woman and food theft. The experienced explorer Cardona Puig, however, also warned that "serious conflict" could erupt over Western goods (Grelier 1957:120).

Anduze does not specify the basis of his conclusions, but it seems likely that they derived largely from his observations around Platanal, where he shows some familiarity with the local political situation (1960: 192). Certainly Platanal in its first year as a mission was a place of pervasive conflict.

Hilker (1950) reported intense political discussions going on around the missionaries from the moment they arrived, along with constant efforts to intimidate them out of their trade goods. By early 1952, Barker reported that the hundred or so people who lived around him had split into eight hostile factions, each demanding that he deal directly with it (*Brown Gold* 1952:9). The slaughter at Iwahikoroba-teri occurred in February 1951, and Bisaasi-teri refugees were staying at Platanal. Most significantly, the Mahekoto-teri themselves were attacked between the time the Franco-Venezuelan Expedition first arrived at Platanal in July 1951 and the following November. One child had been abducted and another killed, and the Mahekoto-teri had gone on alert (Grelier 1957: 170). We will see later that this attack was followed by other hostilities. (Anduze [1960:127] makes only one specific allusion to war above Platanal, noting an empty palisaded *shabono* close to the Raudal de Guajaribos.)

The New Tribes mission and the Franco-Venezuelan Expedition opened the door to other contacts. The population of San Fernando de Atabapo grew from about 250 in 1951 to 391 in 1953. Many of the local men who worked for the expedition returned as forest workers. In July 1952, the King Leopold II Expedition visited the Yanomamo (Gómez Picón 1978:118–19; Grelier 1957:98, 183). (Around this time an unknown fever killed several Mahekoto-teri [Barker 1959:153].) The New Tribes presence itself did not grow dramatically in 1952–53. Although Barker remained at the mission, political and other setbacks for the evangelicals in late 1951 curtailed further expansion until 1954 (*Brown Gold* 1953; Gettmann 1954; Wyma 1952).

The Mahekoto-teri themselves became more mobile along the river, adopting the use of dugout canoes. In January 1952, they did not know how to use the one given them by the last party of the Franco-Venezuelan Expedition. By July 1952, they had and were using about a dozen canoes (Anduze 1960:156; Grelier 1957:183). This is a very significant development because canoe travel allows more mobility for trade. The first to adopt canoes in this area were the Iyewei-teri, who learned about them from Yecuana in 1949. By 1954 several groups had them and used them in commerce (Steinvorth de Goetz 1969:134–35).[3] Possession of dugouts also expanded the possibility of fishing, and that is even more important.

It is frequently observed throughout Amazonia that prolonged residence by a substantial village population leads to game depletion, which, if continued, could lead to a deficiency of dietary protein (Ferguson 1989b). Elsewhere I have argued that game depletion is a consequence of the anchoring effect of Western settlements among the Yanomami (Ferguson 1992a:204–206). By the time of the Franco-Venezuelan Expedition, the Mahekoto-teri had been living around Platanal since 1946. There are signs of subsistence resource stress.

Although Platanal was apparently never left empty, people came and went, with total numbers fluctuating between 20 and 150 (Anduze 1960: 206; Grelier 1957:118). Chagnon (1973:139) refers to the early 1950s as an unusually "nomadic" period, but seen in the perspective of Good's (1989) research on traditional subsistence practices, it seems more likely that these absences from Platanal actually represented the Mahekoto-teri's effort to maintain their diet by a resort to trekking (*Brown Gold* 1952:9; Valero 1984:389; and see Grelier 1957:82, 112), and that it was the later sedentism observed by Chagnon that was atypical for Yanomami. Still, they came back to the same place, year after year. At the moment when the Bisaasi-teri were being slaughtered by Shamatari (February 1951), many Mahekoto-teri had gone to visit the Bisaasi-teri because they were short of food (Barker 1959:152). Anduze (1960:203) reports apparent malnutrition and states that their diet was largely vegetal and they ate even mosquitoes. In this situation, expansion of protein resources by increased fishing may have been a nutritional necessity if the Mahekoto-teri were to remain at Platanal.

To return to the chronology of contact, 1954 saw another substantial increase in the Western presence around Platanal. Near the end of 1953, after almost two years of uncertainty about its future, the New Tribes Mission received permission to continue its work in Venezuela indefinitely. It quickly stepped up its proclaimed war against Satanic influence among the savages. In September 1954 there were seven missionaries at Platanal, with regular and adequate resupply, and a new base camp was under construction above Tamatama (map 6). By 1956, two Mahekoto-teri boys were receiving instruction at Tamatama (Gettmann 1954; Landon 1956). From April 1954 until mid-1955, Platanal was also the base for the first anthropologists to visit the area: the German Frobenius Expedition (Zerries 1955). In 1955 and 1956, a boundary commission was again at work in the area (Steinvorth de Goetz 1969:201).

As the Westerners moved in, the Yanomamo moved to meet them. In 1954, the Iyewei-teri, who had been in direct contact with whites since at least 1950, began to clear a new garden at the confluence of the Ocamo and the Orinoco in order to increase their contacts with *nape;* they moved to it the next year (Cocco 1972:114). By the middle of the decade, several Yanomamo groups had moved near the rivers and were in direct, if intermittent, contact with wood cutters, who hired them as laborers and paid for plantains with steel tools (Barker 1959:165; Cocco 1972:18, 32, 108, 117).

In July 1957, the Salesian missionary Luís Cocco received an enthusiastic welcome from the Iyewei-teri at the mouth of the Ocamo. Despite their warnings that he should go no farther lest the savage Waica kill him, he traveled to other river settlements, distributing gifts at each of them. He visited the Mahekoto-teri and the Tayari-teri, a Mahekoto-teri division just then building a garden farther down the Orinoco. He visited the Bisaasi-teri, who at this point were living downstream from Platanal on the south side of the river, and the Monou-teri, a splinter of the Bisaasi-teri residing a short distance up the Mavaca. Returning to the Iyewei-teri, Cocco founded the mission of Santa María de los Guaicas on October 15, 1957 (Cocco 1972:107–109; Peña Vargas 1981:12, 29, 30).

Kindly, though paternalistic (see Peña Vargas 1981:12), Cocco and his colleague Padre Bonvecchio quickly attempted to civilize the Yanomamo by dressing them and making them live in Western-style houses. Anduze, in the area in 1958 to collect blood samples for genetic research, contrasts the Salesians' approach to Barker's less obtrusive style. Anduze found the Iyewei-teri and Bisaasi-teri ill with influenza, and many children had died. Already in that year, three tourists had come to see the "savages," and the priest's assistant was locally notorious as an abusive drunk (Anduze 1973:295, 299–301, 304, 306, 314–19). Thus it is no surprise that tensions developed between the missionaries and Iyewei-teri. In 1959 the latter had gone into the forest, against the missionaries' wishes, and the priests feared they would never return (Vareschi 1959: 161, 169).

But the Salesian mission had an attraction that the Iyewei-teri could not resist. Unlike Barker at the founding of the Platanal mission, the Salesians brought an incredible bounty of Western goods. In a letter written in January 1965, Chagnon (1972a:66) reports that the mission had given out "over 3000 machetes during the last eight years alone." Of these, only about 30 remained in the village, the rest having vanished into their "immense trading network."

By the mid-1950s, malaria had reached epidemic proportions (Chagnon 1966:62). In 1958, the Venezuelan government established a malaria control station at the mouth of the Mavaca (Boca Mavaca). The Bisaasi-teri were invited to move downriver to locate their village alongside the government post, which they promptly did, "hoping to gain access to steel tools" (Chagnon 1966:163).[4] The next year saw an even greater advance—from the point of view of Bisaasi-teri—when the New Tribes Mission moved its main operation, the residence of Barker and an NTM colleague, from Platanal to Boca Mavaca. The evangelical missionaries continued to expand and intensify their activities, developing a circuit tour to prevent backsliding in scattered villages (Landon 1960). Platanal itself was not abandoned; the Salesian Bonvecchio established a mission there in 1958 (Comité 1983:46).

Sometime around 1959, the Bisaasi-teri divided into settlements on either side of the Mavaca—upper Bisaasi-teri and lower Bisaasi-teri—although the two continued to act together in most political matters (Chagnon 1977:78; Eguillor García 1984:23). Upper and lower Bisaasi-teri each had its own resident missionary (Chagnon 1977:151; Cocco 1972:99). The two Biasaasi-teri groups and Monou-teri constitute what I call the western Namowei.

I found no information about the reasons for this relocation of missions, but it seems probable that it had something to do with the developing competition between Catholics and Protestants for the Yanomamo's souls (see Lizot 1976). Similarly, I found only a few references to the operations of Bonvecchio's mission, which may have been a secondary post directed toward maintaining contact with other groups farther upstream. Chagnon (1977:148), however, characterizes the Platanal mission under Catholic supervision as "dormant" and "stagnating in the lethargy of its disinterested sequence of occupants" through the 1960s. If Platanal had been marginalized, Boca Mavaca now became the major site of Western presence on the upper Orinoco. By the end of the decade, several Western outposts were established on the upper Orinoco, all dispensing Western goods and often making visits to other accessible villages. The latter part of the decade is without reports of war.

This, then, is the general history of Western contact on the upper Orinoco from 1950 to 1960. Besides its specific events, it must be understood as a period of recurrent epidemics. Some idea of the toll being taken by new diseases during this period can be derived from Chagnon's initial tally of causes of death among the Namowei up to the mid-1960s. Compared with 31 deaths from warfare, there were 58 caused by "malaria & epidemics," 16 by "dysentery, diarrhea," 15 by "sorcery," and 3 by "chest infections" (Chagnon 1966:62). (The total population of the three major Namowei settlements at this point was 414 [Chagnon 1966: 58].)

Such high mortality from disease, coupled with the fewer but still significant number of deaths in recent wars, necessarily implies major social disruption. I argue elsewhere (Ferguson 1992a) that the disruption attendant upon so many deaths, the prevalence of war in the area, the anchoring effect of Western contact points, and the subsequent depletion of game animals and decline of meat sharing all combine with tensions generated by unequal access to Western goods to create a relatively chaotic state in which instrumental use of violence becomes more normal in interpersonal affairs and the threshold for war is significantly lowered. For the Yanomamo, I see this process as having its roots in the 1940s but taking full effect in the Orinoco-Mavaca area in the 1950s. The following sections examine the political maneuvers and conflicts related to obtaining Western goods in specific times and places—politics that, in this supercharged atmosphere, frequently led to violence.

Mahekoto-teri under Attack

As we saw in chapter 11, the killing of 11 to 15 men at a feast with the Iwahikoroba-teri Shamatari was a stunning blow to the Bisaasi-teri, who already were losing a war of attrition with their eastern Namowei kinsmen.[5] The Bisaasi-teri fled from their Kreibowei garden to Kobou, the site farther down the Mavaca where they had begun a garden. This position was untenable, and the Bisaasi-teri accepted an invitation to move in with the Mahekoto-teri (Chagnon 1966:159, 1977:103).[6] But the Mahekoto-teri themselves were coming and going on treks, clearing gardens, and visiting allies, so the refugee Bisaasi-teri also spent time among neighboring groups such as the Puunabiwe-teri (Biocca 1971: 302–305; Valero 1984:419–20, 433–34).

The Mahekoto-teri needed additional men. In the vanguard of contact with the outside world during the 1940s, the Mahekoto-teri at Platanal in 1950 were trading with woodsmen and being supplied by New Tribes missionaries downstream. As Helena Valero passed through on her flight from the eastern Namowei and Bisaasi-teri, she observed their abundance of machetes and use of fishhooks (1984:389)—and also noted the terrible nuisance of mosquitoes along the river. But the Mahekoto-teri still lacked the military advantages of Western backing. Indeed, the men were still hiding the women against abductions by *nape*, and their headman was trying to keep young men from stealing woodsmen's tools (Valero 1984:390–392). Although their palisade was up (Valero 1984:389), they were still vulnerable to those seeking plunder or trying to chase them away or coerce them into providing more goods. There are suggestions that some of their allies were walking off with their women (Valero 1984:392–93).

Then in late 1950 came the big influx of wealth from Barker's arrival, followed in mid-1951 by the passage of the Franco-Venezuelan Expedition. With the new wealth came war. As noted earlier, between the first arrival of the expedition in July and another pass through in November, raiders killed one Mahekoto-teri child and abducted another. The Mahekoto-teri had gone on alert: cutting down the bridge over the Orinoco, reinforcing their palisade, clearing trees around the *shabono*, posting sentries along paths, and inviting unidentified guests to come feast. Barker "had thrown his shot-gun into the river to save him *from having to take part*" (Grelier 1957:170, my emphasis). The newly arrived Westerner was not being as much tactical help as he could be. The raiders are not identified, but the fact that the Mahekoto-teri cut down a bridge to the south bank of the Orinoco strongly suggests they were Shamatari. The Shamatari had scored a major victory the year before and may have been seeking to move more forcefully into the suddenly well-provided Orinoco area.

In what seems to be early 1952, Mahekoto-teri raided the Shamatari. They were accompanied by Bisaasi-teri and Puunabiwe-teri or Raharawe-teri, some of whom came along in the hope of capturing a woman. The raiders killed an old blind man and fled immediately, but Shamatari defenders mortally wounded one attacker. A few months later, Shamatari caught a gathering party on the south side of the river. They captured five women (two escaped) and killed two men, grossly abusing the corpses—the only instance I know of in which Yanomamo abused the enemy's dead. Shortly thereafter, the Mahekoto-teri and allies went to raid again, but found no one home.

The Shamatari danger made the Mahekoto-teri and Bisaasi-teri cease food gathering on the south side of the river, leaving the once contested Shihota garden site without any owners (Chagnon 1966:160; Valero 1984:433–34). If the Shamatari did intend to clear the way to the river, they succeeded. But the presence of their mortal enemies on the north bank would still make it impossible for them to build a new garden close to the Orinoco.

At the same time, the Mahekoto-teri had to deal with danger from their north. A conflict developed with the Shipariwe-teri (then called Toraemipiwei-teri), a branch of the Mahekoto-teri's own Uhepeki population bloc living in high country some distance to the north (Barker 1959:154–61; Chagnon 1966:160). The Shipariwe-teri had many ties to Ocamo-oriented groups such as the Iyewei-teri, and they also had trade and marriage ties to Mahekoto-teri (Barker 1959:154–55). But in January 1952, a party of men from Shipariwe-teri attempted to make off with a Mahekoto-teri woman. The young woman was subject to a tug-of-war. Finally the Shipariwe-teri men gave up and left, with the Mahekoto-teri shouting death threats after them.

Despite the threats and their loss in a test of strength, some small parties of Shipariwe-teri men continued to visit Mahekoto-teri. No further violence is recorded until October 1953, when the Shipariwe-teri raided. One Mahekoto-teri man was wounded with a poison arrow, but the missionaries successfully treated him. The raiders sustained two wounded. In December 1953, Shipariwe-teri raided again, this time with an ally, Komishibuwe-teri (Barker 1959:156). But the Mahekoto-teri were unreachable: they had camped on the south side of the Orinoco. The missionaries met the raiders and placated them with gifts.

Why did the Shipariwe-teri raid? This outbreak of war was preceded by a conflict over a woman, but it had occurred nearly two years before. During the intervening period, Barker was at Platanal, woodsmen were trading there, and the King Leopold Expedition had come through. The Mahekoto-teri were getting rich, and the Shipariwe-teri had other grievances besides women. Although they traded clay pots to those better connected to the outside (Biocca 1971:309), they were envious of others' supply of Western goods. In what appears to be late 1953—during a period when Helena Valero frequently moved between villages—a Shipariwe-teri shaman was attempting to cure her seriously ill son. As she recalls it (Valero 1984:455–56), the shaman said:

> He will not die. When he has grown, he will be a *nape*. He will be owner of machetes, of axes, of loincloths. He will have much cloth. Then they will not be had only by the Iyewei-teri and Wakawaka-teri who receive them from the Makiritare and from the *nape*. Your child will bring them to us. We too will shine with

cloth while dancing. He will bring us machetes; bring us axes.
We will make a path and he will come to bring us many trade
goods. 'Do not talk that way,' said Poshokomi.

I suggest that the Shipariwe-teri raids against Mahekoto-teri were somehow to improve their supply of Western goods coming from the primary
Western post in the area, Platanal.

The war between Shipariwe-teri and Mahekoto-teri developed in late
1953. Although no warfare between the Mahekoto-teri and Shamatari is
reported for 1953, otherwise it was a time of great tension in the region.
This is illustrated by the map of political relations produced by Barker
in 1953 (Barker 1959:between pages 436 and 437; and see map 5).[7]
Specific parts of this map will be discussed later, but considering it as
a whole, some patterns are apparent. Foremost is the wide network of
hostilities it shows, clearly reflecting a time of general political conflict.

More specifically, the Mahekoto-teri are connected without hostility
to groups closest to them, and a conflict-free line joins them through
intermediaries to the Iyewei-teri, the other source of Western goods.
Barker (1959:316–19) and Valero (Biocca 1971:316–19; Valero 1984:
389, 421, 462, 485) confirm close relationships and frequent visiting
along this axis, with intermediate groups such as the Puunabiwe-teri
being given Western goods by directly contacted groups as they became available. In contrast, the Mahekoto-teri, Iyewei-teri, and their
neighbor-allies are all "hostile" or "very hostile" to villages that are relatively distant from contact points or are separated from those points by
middlemen. Thus there is a variably drawn fault line dividing those with
good access to Westerners from those without good access.

Consistent with this image of general tensions, 1953 was a "bad
time" around Platanal (Barker 1959:153), despite the abundance of
Western goods. There were food shortages, hostile factionalism within
the Mahekoto-teri, and the danger of raiders. A fever killed several
people (Barker 1959:153). With all these hardships, it is scarcely surprising that the Mahekoto-teri and Bisaasi-teri began to quarrel, or that
the Bisaasi-teri began to suspect the Mahekoto-teri of plotting against
them. And the Mahekoto-teri were trying to take women away from the
Bisaasi-teri (Chagnon 1966:160, 1977:103; Valero 1984:434). Barker
(1959:153) reports two violent confrontations over women, one involving a Mahekoto-teri woman misappropriated by Bisaasi-teri, and one
the other way around. The former came close to being a shooting incident; the latter left one man with a serious arrow wound.

The Bisaasi-teri at this point had already begun new gardens (Chagnon 1966:159–60), and during 1953 they moved away from the Mahekoto-teri.[8] In the process, the Bisaasi-teri fissioned into two groups. The smaller group, Monou-teri, will henceforth be a significant independent actor. The other Bisaasi-teri went to a site called Barawa, or Barauwa (Barker 1959:153; Chagnon 1966:160, 1977:103). This relocation, along with subsequent developments among the Bisaasi-teri and Monou-teri, will be discussed in a later section.

Thus 1953, a time of increasing, direct Western contact, was also a time of widespread disturbance. But at least one disturbed relationship was soon patched up. I noted earlier that the Shipariwe-teri raids of October and December 1953 pushed the Mahekoto-teri to the south side of the Orinoco. But Barker's 1953 map suggests that political relations between the Mahekoto-teri and Patanowa-teri, their neighbors to the southeast, had deteriorated seriously since 1950, to the "hostile" stage—perhaps a highly strained alliance. Moving closer to such enemies would entail obvious risks. Perhaps the Shipariwe-teri's threats from the north in late 1953 made the Mahekoto-teri more generous with the Patanowa-teri, to secure their good will. Anyway, something happened, for in September 1954 the Mahekoto-teri were "more or less friends" with Patanowa-teri, even though the latter were still in a latent state of war with Mahekoto-teri's allies, the Bisaasi-teri (Barker 1959:157).

With Patanowa-teri friendly and the Shamatari not heard from in two years, the Mahekoto-teri seemed secure on the south bank of the Orinoco. There they lived in 1954, across from Platanal, feeling safe and able to use the forest again without fear (Barker 1959:156–62). But then members of the Frobenius Expedition came to live at Platanal from April 1954 to mid-1955. Working intensively with the Mahekoto-teri, purchasing large quantities of local crafts for an ethnological collection, and remaining in place even when Barker went downstream (Barker 1959: 160; Zerries 1955:75–76), this expedition created another surge in the foreign wealth coming to the Mahekoto-teri—probably the largest, most sustained supply they had ever had. Predictably, those with a poor supply of Western goods responded quickly.

In September, Shamatari raiders struck without warning, killing one man, abducting four women, and retreating before being detected (Barker 1959:157–65; Chagnon 1966:160–61). It was only with difficulty that the Mahekoto-teri identified the raiders as Shamatari. This attack forced the Mahekoto-teri back to the north bank. There, in December 1954, the Shipariwe-teri raided again, wounding one man, who recovered with medical assistance from the anthropologists. After yet another raid by the Shipariwe-teri, in March 1955, the missionaries not only treated wounds but also gave the residents refuge in the mission house. Sometime during this period, the Mahekoto-teri were also involved in a series of unspecified clashes with the Boreta-teri (Valero 1984:462), another group in the highlands to the northeast.

The public reason for the Shipariwe-teri raids was that a young woman (from Puunabiwe-teri?) for whose family a Shipariwe-teri man had been providing game as bride service had been given to a Mahekoto-teri man instead (Valero 1984:506). Apparently the prior marriage agreement was broken in order to redirect a marriage alliance toward those with better access to Western goods. Although not mentioned by Barker, and perhaps concealed from him by his hosts, the Mahekoto-teri made at least two retaliatory raids on the Shipariwe-teri, killing one person on the first but doing no damage on the second. Then they threatened to send an epidemic against the Shipariwe-teri by burning Western goods (Valero 1984:506). No raids are reported from the north after March 1955. The Mahekoto-teri appear to have won.

To return to the Shamatari problem: after relocating to the north bank of the Orinoco, the Mahekoto-teri called on allies to assist them in retaliating against their southern enemies. The Bisaasi-teri, including the Monou-teri, were now living on the south side of the Orinoco. Although on strained terms with Mahekoto-teri, they had their own interests in killing Shamatari, and they joined in the effort. In late 1954 and early 1955, several raiding parties made the long and dangerous journey into Shamatari country, only to return without having reached the enemy. Not only did the raiders risk death along the way, but their families were exposed to danger while they were gone. Indeed, the last of the Shipariwe-teri attacks—the one in which some of the Mahekoto-teri sought refuge in the missionaries' house—took place while the men were away seeking Shamatari. It is questionable whether they could have taken that risk without the now more formidable presence of the missionaries.

Finally the Mahekoto-teri and their allies located the Shamatari. They destroyed a garden, and then they found what they had been seeking: Riokowe, the Iwahikoroba-teri headman, bathing in a stream with his family. For this incursion, the raiders had recruited Valero's husband, Akawe, who at the time was acting as a bow for hire. Akawe fired a fatal shot into Riokowe. The raiders captured at least one of Riokowe's children, a son, before fleeing. (He was later killed by his captors, for revenge.) The Shamatari pursued, killing one of the raiders but losing two more of their own. After this attack and their serious losses, the Iwahikoroba-teri apparently moved out of the area (Barker 1959: 158–65; Biocca 1971:316–17; Chagnon 1966:161; Valero 1984:469, 485–87).

In sum, the Mahekoto-teri were plunged into intense, violent conflict during the time they hosted the Frobenius Expedition. But the presence of the Westerners now was adding a new dimension to war—an advantage for the mission village that the Shipariwe-teri quickly recognized. An old woman visitor from Shipariwe-teri told Barker: "In her village they didn't like the foreigners, because they were always curing people. When the village wounds someone, they want them to die" (Barker 1959:163). Presumably, the resident Westerners also made the Mahekoto-teri men feel more secure about leaving their women and children to go on retaliatory missions.

Despite their losses, the Mahekoto-teri had won major victories. They had demonstrated that, with their allies, they could successfully strike back over long distances, despite repeated setbacks. Although attacked simultaneously from two directions, they had held their position alongside the *nape* and vanquished their attackers. Militarily accomplished, secure to their south, protected and healed by Westerners, the Mahekoto-teri now had significant advantages over any would-be raiders.

These new circumstances were favorable for the hegemony of Mahekoto-teri. I expect that Mahekoto-teri trade and marriage relations with more isolated groups turned exploitative at this point, but there is no information about those relationships specifically. Active raiding appears to have ceased after 1955, and there would be little collective violence along the Orinoco for nearly ten years. This passage from intense conflict to peaceful coexistence is also seen among groups along the Ocamo, on the northern edge of the Orinoco-Mavaca area.

War and Peace around the Ocamo

Information for this area up to 1956 is provided by Valero. She portrays three local groups—Iyewei-teri, Witokaya-teri, and Puunabiwe-teri—as tightly bound together and continually intermixing. The three groups, however, had different origins. The Iyewei-teri were a branch of the northward-moving "Iyewei-Padamo" population bloc, most of which was now in the Padamo basin. The Iyewei-teri had been moving down toward the lower Ocamo for many years, and by at least 1950 had made direct contact with creoles and missionaries, as well as having established connections to the Yecuana. That year, several Iyewei-teri were brought to meet the governor in Puerto Ayacucho. Thus the Iyewei-teri start the 1950s with exceptional connections to sources of Western goods (Valero 1984:429).

The Puunabiwe-teri and most of the Witokaya-teri were closely related divisions of one branch of the Uhepeki bloc (Lizot 1988:523). But the Witokaya-teri were led by a non-Uhepeki man called Hashowe who, with some followers, had made a succession of moves down from the highlands, staying with intervening groups until they could establish their own gardens. By 1950 this leader had strong marriage ties to Iyewei-teri and Puunabiwe-teri (Valero 1984:402–404). The Witokaya-teri are also reported to have picked up people from Wakawaka-teri when that group fissioned around 1947.

In addition, this "triple alliance" of Iyewei-teri, Witokaya-teri, and Puunabiwe-teri had strong connections to the Mahekoto-teri and the Raharawe-teri, another Uhepeki group located between Puunabiwe-teri and Mahekoto-teri. All together, a chain of strong alliances stretched between the two main areas of contact, Platanal on the Orinoco and the Iyewei-teri on the Ocamo. These alliances were marked by visiting, feasting, trade, intermarriage, and sometimes military support.

When Valero arrived among the Puunabiwe-teri in 1950, the three allies were in fear of raiders from the interior called Ihiteri. There is some question about the raiders' identity, but they were people living up the Ocamo and at higher elevations.[9] This is the same configuration of violence as that of the later 1940s, when lower Ocamo and Padamo groups, receiving new quantities of goods from Yecuana allies, fought with people up and beyond the Ocamo. (One war, it will be recalled, pitted Iyewei-teri against Watupawe-teri and Kopariwe-teri around 1947.) Under these tense circumstances, it is expectable that the Iyewei-teri's direct contacts of 1950—with NTM missionaries and Puerto Ayacucho—would have violent repercussions. When Valero joined them in late 1950, the Puunabiwe-teri were preparing to be raided by the Ihiteri (Biocca 1971:291).

The conflict brewing at this moment well illustrates how changing access to Western goods can produce conflict over both women and moral principles, and how the resulting actions share characteristics of both war and law. In the shorter version (Biocca 1971:292), the Puunabiwe-teri simply seized two Ihiteri women, and the Ihiteri were seeking revenge. But in the longer version (Valero 1984:404), the dispute (*pleito*) is not that simple. The Puunabiwe-teri had long promised two young daughters to men from Ihiteri. The betrothed men had been dutifully providing game to the girls' families for years. But the parents refused to hand over the girls upon demand, and instead gave one of them as a bride to the son of Hashowe, the Witokaya-teri leader. *That* was why the Ihiteri were angry.

From the perspective of my model, the underlying reason for this dispute is clear. During the time when Western penetration of the area remained limited, the Puunabiwe-teri had contracted to give women to groups living farther in the interior on higher ground.[10] But approaching 1950, the benefits for Puunabiwe-teri of a direct Western connection became much more substantial, and that meant ceding women to Witokaya-teri. The immediate contest was "over a woman," and no doubt the Ihiteri, and probably the Puunabiwe-teri as well, felt morally justified in their actions—but it is the changing contact situation that explains why the conflict arose. Comparing the two versions of this dispute also illustrates how a report of an "abduction of a woman" may actually conceal a more complex reality.

But the Ihiteri did not attack- -not right away (Valero 1984:404). It usually takes time to go from alliance to war. Some months passed, as the Puunabiwe-teri developed a new garden closer to the *nape*, ate more manioc, wove hammocks, and got ill (Valero 1984:407–409). Then the Ihiteri attacked, wounding two or more people who were caught outside the palisade, receiving some wounds themselves, and fleeing. The attack appears to have occurred after the Franco-Venezuelan Expedition arrived at La Esmeralda and the new wealth began to flow. In retaliation, Akawe claimed to have stalked up to the raiders' village and fired a killing arrow inside (Biocca 1971:293; Valero 1984:419–21). In this action, Akawe may have been following a local model, for a solo killer was reported in this area some time earlier—Kohawe, whom we met in chapter 11. At any rate, he was building his reputation as an accomplished killer.

The year 1951 was a violent one all over the Orinoco-Mavaca area. But the lower Ocamo, after this one burst of violence, settled into a kind of routine during the next three years or so (late 1951 into 1955). The Iyewei-teri, Witokaya-teri, and Puunabiwe-teri developed new gardens close to the Orinoco, trying to distance themselves from the Ihiteri and draw closer to *nape*. They even cleared paths to the Orinoco to attract Westerners. And Westerners did come to trade and hire workers. A few

Iyewei-teri and Witokaya-teri became particularly associated with outsiders, such that one man came to be called "Nape" and to feel the envy of others.

The three groups kept up their alliance with frequent feasting and visiting. And of course, they experienced more illnesses, of varying strengths. No more raiding is reported until 1955, but in a time of such tensions, it would not be surprising if unreported wars took place (Biocca 1971:313; Valero 1984:421–26, 430, 434–36, 442–43, 459–60, 486, 491, 494–95, 499, 503–505).[11]

We now come to the Frobenius Expedition of 1954–55. The anthropologist Otto Zerries, a member of the expedition, actually visited the new Witokaya-teri garden, guided by local woodsmen up a trail to the Orinoco that the Yanomamo had cleared to attract *nape*. Although some of the Yanomamo talked about attacking the visitors for their goods, they settled for trading plantains for machetes. Many men were given machetes, and they were very happy. Most of these machetes were quickly traded on to Shipariwe-teri and Raharawe-teri (Biocca 1971:312–13; Valero 1984:459–60).

Some time later, around April 1955 (compare Barker 1959:165 and Valero 1984:470), Puunabiwe-teri and others visited the Mahekoto-teri to get more machetes, and there they found that the *nape* had constructed zinc-roofed houses. After loitering around Platanal for about a month, the Puunabiwe-teri returned to their garden. About two weeks later, Ihiteri raiders struck, wounding two (Valero 1984:471–76). Thus the Puunabiwe-teri suffered their first reported raid in four years, just weeks after their second major acquisition of Western goods. A few months later, the Ihiteri made another sortie, without causing any casualties. This was to be their last attack during Valero's stay (Valero 1984: 494).

The Shipariwe-teri played a role in this conflict. They had been intimidating the Puunabiwe-teri and their allies, taking a woman at a feast. A party of the allies accepted a feast invitation from the Shipariwe-teri but backed down from their plan to challenge the hosts to an ax fight. The Shipariwe-teri dissuaded the challengers by invoking the specter of Ihiteri raids (Valero 1984:484). Ihiteri raiders had to pass close to Shipariwe-teri and thus were vulnerable to interception; after the second Ihiteri raid, the Shipariwe-teri told them not to raid again. The three allies needed to keep the Shipariwe-teri's good will. Even so, they all made new gardens closer to or actually along the Orinoco, farther away from both Shipariwe-teri and Ihiteri (Valero 1984:495).

Other conflicts between allies in 1955 were far less muted than this one. Two wildly spreading fights broke out among the three allies, one triggered by a dispute over a woman, the other over meat distribution. Both ended with everyone's going away angry (Valero 1984:496–98). In 1955, a conflict broke out between Witokaya-teri and its allies against Bisaasi-teri/Monou-teri, but that will be discussed in the next section.

Early in 1956, a deadly fever swept outwards from Mahekoto-teri to many of the local villages, including Valero's. But that did not stop the increasingly routine contacts with *nape,* who frequently came to trade and hire Yanomamo workers. Several Iyewei-teri, Witokaya-teri, and Puunabiwe-teri people went to visit the New Tribes base at Tamatama and even to San Fernando de Atabapo (Valero 1984:498–99, 503–505, 508, 524, 527). A violent conflict developed at this time between Shipariwe-teri and Raharawe-teri, the close ally of the Mahekoto-teri. It appears to have involved competition between Shipariwe-teri and Raharawe-teri over who would receive most favored treatment by the Puunabiwe-teri, who at this time were flush with recently earned trade goods (Valero 1984:506–507).

Just around the time of the fever, another conflict developed that suggests some of the new, although transient, tensions that developed among Yanomamo who were reorienting to river trade. In March 1956, the Bisaasi-teri traveled by canoe to the mission base of Tamatama. The Iyewei-teri were incensed that the Bisaasi-teri passed by without stopping—bypassing the middleman—and they set out in pursuit. When they met at Tamatama, the two groups were on the point of violence, but Barker interceded and disarmed them. The next day they left, after the Iyewei-teri traded hammocks and bows to the Bisaasi-teri in exchange for machetes, cloth, matches, and other items (Barker 1959:166–67). This event is something of a milestone in the political resuscitation of the Bisaasi-teri, which we will come to shortly, and it illustrates how monopolization of Westerners by control of passage is much more difficult when travelers use canoes on a broad river.

Helena Valero's final observation for this area—about the circumstances of her escape—provides an unusual glimpse into the way moral values can be manipulated to incite people to war, deliberately concealing a hidden agenda of gaining more Western goods. In this case, unlike all the others, the hidden agenda had to be made known to Valero (1984:517–18), because the scheme revolved around her. Her husband, Akawe, had many enemies and feared some of them were planning to kill him. He also had a frequently displayed desire to obtain Western goods, and he knew that his wife was hoping to flee to the *nape* the first chance she got. So he cooked up a plan.

He addressed the Witokaya-teri and Puunabiwe-teri, calling them cowards because they had only retaliated once for several Ihiteri raids over the years. His exhortations worked. Men from the two villages joined in preparation for a raid, but Akawe dallied, remaining behind. Late in the day before the raiding party was to set out, he arose, and in an apparent rage, painted himself black for war. " 'What are you going to do now?' I asked. 'Look,' he told me in a low voice. 'The men from here are gone. Let us escape'" (Valero 1984:518). And they did: on October 15, 1956, they were brought to San Fernando de Atabapo by Juan Eduardo Noguera (Biocca 1971:319–24; Valero 1984:518–25). At this point Akawe embarked on a remarkable career on the frontier of interaction between Yanomamo and *nape*.

At San Fernando, Valero met Padre Luís Cocco (Valero 1984:529). The priest sent Valero, her children, and Akawe to the Río Negro, where we will see them again. Back on the Orinoco, one year to the day from Valero's final flight, after making a tour of all the river villages, Cocco founded the mission of Santa María de los Guaicas alongside the Iyewei-teri at the mouth of the Ocamo. Iyewei-teri is only about three hours by launch from Boca Mavaca (Anduze 1973:304), whose residents in 1964 would be called "the Fierce People." Yet the Iyewei-teri do not register a single war death from 1957 to 1972 (Cocco 1972:481).[12] Nor is there any indication of their participating in a raid at any time, although they were involved in some confrontations. In short, the Iyewei-teri provide a striking, peaceful contrast to the Yanomamo with whom most people are familiar. Why have the Iyewei-teri avoided war? Three factors explain it.

First, superior military capability. When Padre Cocco arrived at Iyewei-teri in 1957, the headman was growing rice with the intention of using it to buy a shotgun (Cocco 1972:108). He brought the rice when he accompanied the missionaries to Puerto Ayacucho later that year, and there he purchased the weapon (Cocco 1972:119). By 1970, the Iyewei-teri had nine shotguns (Cocco 1972:189). Possessing shotguns when no one else had them, or owning them in superior numbers, gave the Iyewei-teri a military edge—one that would be amplified by the medical care and security provided by resident missionaries.

Second, an unparalleled abundance of Western manufactures allowed the Iyewei-teri to be generous with others. The Salesians were competing with the New Tribes Mission for influence along the river (Lizot 1976), and they gave out astonishing quantities of goods.[13] With an assured supply, the Iyewei-teri made no attempt to restrict the flow of these goods. At one point, Cocco asked a mission man why he so rapidly traded away the goods Cocco gave him. "You can get more," was the reply (Peña Vargas 1981:64).

The Iyewei-teri earned a reputation among local Yanomamo for being both rich and generous, even allowing visitors from distant villages open access to the missionaries. The Iyewei-teri did enjoy the benefits of having their own source of Western goods—they received women from other villages and a multitude of native manufactures—but they apparently did so on "easy terms." Their generosity removed a major reason for fighting and created for them a network of supportive allies (Cocco 1972:210–13, 376–79).

The third factor explaining the lack of war among the Iyewei-teri is the stability of their contact situation. The missionaries settled with a people who had been a point of contact since at least 1950. The mission would remain in that location, and no other major Western residence would be established close to it, for almost two decades. Military dominance and perceived generosity in a contact situation of unusual stability all combined to bring about an absence of warfare directly involving the Iyewei-teri.

But as we have seen in other mission situations, this peace did not extend outward indefinitely. In 1959 or 1960, the Nahibowei-teri, a Wakawaka sub-bloc group living far up the Matacuni, attempted to establish an alliance with Witokaya-teri and Auwei-teri. The Auwei-teri at this time may have lived on the Buuta-u, a tributary of the middle Ocamo (see Smole 1976:58), and were related to the Witokaya-teri (perhaps through the Hashowe subdivision).[14] In the 1940s, those who would become the Nahibowei-teri were bitter enemies of the Auwei-teri. Why were they now willing to become friends?

The answer, I would argue, is that the Auwei-teri were receiving a share of the Salesians' machetes. But at the feast held to formalize the alliance, the Witokaya-teri demanded that the Nahibowei-teri give them two women. When the latter refused, a club fight ensued in which several Witokaya-teri men were injured. The Witokaya-teri/Auwei-teri then raided, killing several men and abducting the two women. Soon afterwards, in 1960, the Nahibowei-teri accepted an invitation to move 30 kilometers west to live next to a New Tribes mission at the confluence of the Matacuni and Padamo (Hames 1983:406, 409–11).

Another conflict around the same place and time shows striking parallels. This one involved the Yepropei-teri, another group of the middle

Ocamo (see Fuentes 1980:6). In 1960, they took a woman from a more remote group, the Hopehi-teri, and otherwise insulted them. But the Hopehi-teri managed to kill the Yepropei-teri headman, despite medical care given to him by a missionary. Hostility between these groups would continue through the 1960s (Cocco 1972:398). Both of these cases illustrate again a pattern discussed in relation to the Mucajaí and Catrimani missions: how middlemen one or two villages out from the point of contact, supplied with Western goods but without the protection of a resident Westerner, become involved in violent conflict with more remote groups, while the mission village itself enjoys relatively undisturbed peace.

The Rise of Bisaasi-teri

Elsewhere in the Orinoco-Mavaca area, the fortunes of the western Namowei—the Bisaasi-teri and their offshoot, the Monou-teri—were beginning to rise. From their low point after the slaughter at Iwahi-koroba-teri, the Bisaasi-teri were back on the road to becoming a major power. It will be recalled that in 1953, the Bisaasi-teri left their tense refuge in Mahekoto-teri and fissioned in the process. The splinter group settled on the Mavaca and became known as Monou-teri. The other Bisaasi-teri moved to a site called Barawa, down and across the river from Mahekoto-teri. Cocco (1972:18) mentions the Bisaasi-teri in his listing of people who established gardens along the river at this time in order to attract Westerners. As demonstrated by his own tour in 1957, the strategy worked.

According to Chagnon (1977:124), the Monou-teri's fissioning off was the result of a club fight over a woman. Nevertheless, the Monou-teri and Bisaasi-teri "remained on good terms with each other" (Chagnon 1966:163) and were actively allied until the reabsorption of Monou-teri into Bisaasi-teri in the mid-1960s. (Villages that divide after club fights over women may remain close allies.) Behaviorally, the movement to two separate gardens represents alternative choices for making independent contact with Westerners. The Monou-teri site was located at some distance from old Shamatari enemies, it could be developed using the garden at Kobou as a base, and it offered control of movement on the Mavaca. Developing the garden at Barawa, which was farther from Kobou, entailed spending more time relying on the dubious good will of the Mahekoto-teri (Barker 1959:153), but it did put the Bisaasi-teri into a position along the Orinoco itself. The ideal choice for acquiring and controlling trade in Western manufactures would have been the juncture of the Orinoco and Mavaca—the later location of Bisaasi-teri—but that was much farther away from both the Kobou and Mahekoto-teri gardens.

The Monou-teri and Bisaasi-teri now began to secure their positions in intervillage politics. They participated in the Mahekoto-teri's successful raid against the Shamatari. Their relations with Mahekoto-teri experienced some tension, but the Mahekoto-teri still joined the Bisaasi-teri at feasts (Chagnon 1977:103). Although active raiding by or against the eastern Namowei and their allies had ceased after 1950, in 1954 those groups were still reputed to be enemies of the western Namowei (Barker 1959:157). In 1955, however, men from both groups attended a feast at Mahekoto-teri (Barker 1959:160). The Patanowa-teri made overtures of peace to both Monou-teri and Bisaasi-teri, and some visiting began after 1955 (Chagnon 1966:76). Marriage negotiations also commenced, and one Monou-teri man "was given two wives by the Patanowa-tedi" (Chagnon 1966:175).[15]

The western Namowei experienced new tensions related to their improving condition. In April 1955, some Monou-teri went to visit Valero's people near the mouth of the Ocamo, for the first time being able to bypass Mahekoto-teri by traveling from their new location. When they left for home, two of Akawe's wives fled with them to escape his brutality. (Barker [1959:165] reports simply that the Namowei "had taken" a woman.) Some Witokaya-teri and Puunabiwe-teri men came after them, and a club fight or a threat to send an epidemic by burning Western goods, or both, made the Monou-teri hand over the women. Bad feeling persisted after the clash (Barker 1959:165–66; Valero 1984:469–70).

About a year later, the Bisaasi-teri were bolder and more mobile, as they passed by the Iyewei-teri in canoes, bound for Tamatama, in the incident described earlier. The transaction at Tamatama demonstrates that by this time, the Bisaasi-teri had become receivers and traders of Western goods, perhaps even better supplied than the Iyewei-teri were before the arrival of the mission the next year.

In 1958, a year after Iyewei-teri's elevation as a mission post, came a comparable advance for the Bisaasi-teri. The government malaria post invited the Bisaasi-teri to move to Boca Mavaca, where they were joined in 1959 by New Tribes missionaries down from Platanal. This rearrangement marks the beginning of western Namowei ascendancy and a corresponding decline in the fortunes of Mahekoto-teri—a shift that would lead to violence in the mid-1960s.

But for a time, peace continued along the Orinoco. No lethal violence is reported along the major rivers after 1955. One cannot rule out that some unreported attacks occurred in this still fluid situation, but there is no suggestion of widespread violence like that associated with the year of the NTM's arrival and the Franco-Venezuelan Expedition, or the year of the Frobenius Expedition. According to Chagnon (1977: 80), "in 1960, the political milieu was quite serene."

The serenity of 1960, however, was interrupted by one act of war (Chagnon 1966:164, 1977:78, 1992a:168). Immediately after the Bisaasi-teri acquired their Westerners, they resumed middleman activity and began developing a new alliance with a Shamatari group, the Paruritawa-teri, who lived on a tributary of the upper Mavaca. The unequal, exploitative character of the alliance will be discussed in chapter 13. For now, the issue is the Paruritawa-teri's cooperation with the Bisaasi-teri in violence against another Shamatari group, the Mowaraoba-teri.

The Mowaraoba-teri were one of the two Shamatari groups that participated in the slaughter of Bisaasi-teri in early 1951. The Paruritawa-teri were not involved in that attack. In 1960, the Bisaasi-teri "persuaded" their new allies to cooperate in a treacherous attack on their Shamatari relatives. The Paruritawa-teri invited the Mowaraoba-teri to a feast, where Bisaasi-teri and Monou-teri men were waiting for them. They killed three of the five Mowaraoba-teri men who came, and abducted all four Mowaraoba-teri women.

Militarily, this attack had terrible consequences for the Paruritawa-teri. "All their other neighbors, allied to the victims of the treacherous feast, relentlessly raided them" (Chagnon 1977:78–79). This raiding made them even more dependent on the Namowei of the lower Mavaca. "By participating in this treachery, the Paruritawa-tedi subordinated themselves to the Bisaasi-tedi and Monou-tedi" (Chagnon 1966:164).

Why would the Paruritawa-teri side with very new friends against their own kin, thus incurring the wrath of their neighbors? Chagnon (1977:78) says no more than that the western Namowei "succeeded in getting them to participate." In terms of my model, the answer is, for the same reason the Paruritawa-teri were developing a new alliance with the western Namowei in the first place: in 1960, the Bisaasi-teri could offer the Paruritawa-teri a regular supply of Western goods, at a time when steel was still extremely scarce among the Shamatari. Of course, in the Paruritawa-teri's discussions preceding the violence, their material interests were probably translated into moral terms invoking sorcery, cowardice, or revenge.

In keeping with expectations, this treacherous attack appears to have involved divisions among those hosting the feast. Some of the Paruritawa-teri continued to supply the Mowaraoba-teri with worn-down steel tools even after the slaughter, and later they actively tried to restore peaceful relations between the groups (Chagnon 1974:8, 1977: 79). Perhaps this was a situation similar to that surrounding the killing of Ruwahiwe, in which one subdivision's success at developing a middleman relationship with a more distant group was destroyed by the treachery of another subdivision. In any case, the outbreak of hostilities up the Mavaca was similar to events happening around the same time up the Ocamo, where the upstream allies of the mission villages became embroiled in war with those farther out.

But what were the interests of the Bisaasi-teri and Monou-teri in this attack? In Chagnon's description, there is no ambiguity: they sought revenge for the slaughter of 1951. Elsewhere I have criticized the concept of revenge as an explanation for war (Ferguson 1989d:564, 1992a: 223–24). In this case, however, the western Namowei had lost 11 to 15 men, which provided an incentive for revenge to an unusually large number of families. Although I suspect there were other considerations involved—as there would be in a similar conflict four years later—I have no trouble accepting that the western Namowei planned this attack in large part for the sake of revenge.

Before moving on to events in other Yanomamo areas, one comment is in order. The reader will have noted the prominence of conflicts over women in the preceding discussions. Such conflicts were unusually prevalent during the 1950s. They occurred within almost every political context and with almost every possible consequence, from quickly forgotten flare-ups between good allies to lingering reasons for vengeance against mortal enemies.

The 1950s have shaped our ideas about the prevalence of fighting over women among the Yanomami. Barker, the man who introduced Chagnon to the Yanomamo, was so impressed by it that he developed his own typology of conflicts over women (1953:474–78). Many incidents from Barker's early years in the field were later recounted by Chagnon to illustrate his argument that the reason Yanomami men fight is competition over women. So I must stress that the kind of conflict reported in this chapter is definitely not "normal" for the Yanomamo. It is greatly in excess of that reported for other Yanomami areas and even for the Namowei before the arrival of the whites. What happened to generate such conflict?

First, the suddenly expanded and intensified Western presence lowered the threshold for violence and made the use of force more common in interpersonal relations. At the same time, so many deaths from disease and war meant that many marriages (including betrothals) had to be rearranged. In the case of the Bisaasi-teri after the killings at Iwahikoroba-teri, a large number of marriage ties had to be constructed all at once in a situation where previous political arrangements had been severely shocked, if not demolished. For a while, then, brute force became a prominent instrument in deciding which women would live where. Chagnon (1966:160) even seems to confirm this interpretation when he writes that "considerable fighting took place among the men when the widows of the Shamatari victims were redistributed to survivors." (As I noted in chapter 11, a similar chain of clashes occurred over Fusiwe's widows.) And along with fights related to demographic disruption, we have seen that some of the most prominent conflicts over women happened when a man who had been doing bride service lost his betrothed to somebody else with a suddenly improved supply of Western goods.

Women are the highest political currency between Yanomami groups, and intermarriage is the highest form of alliance. Increasing strain in intergroup relations can become manifest in many different ways, but prominent among them is conflict over women. Yet such conflicts stand in no uniform relationship to war. Many fights over women do not lead to war; many wars occur without prior conflict over women. To understand both the conflicts over women and the wars, both must be put in historical context—and that means relating both to the intrusive Western presence.

Other Yanomamo during the 1950s

Leaving the Orinoco-Mavaca area, we have information in varying levels of detail about groups to its north, east, and south. For the northernmost Yanomamo, we turn again to Hames's histories. The northern, or middle Padamo, sub-blocs were, by this time, within the Yecuana sphere of influence (Hames 1983:406, 409, 412–13). During the 1950s, their political behavior fell into a pattern that would persist into the 1970s—one of quarrels, fear of attacks, fissions, and movements, all involving attempts to establish ties to Westerners, Yecuana, or other Yanomami attached to Yecuana. No raids or killings are indicated. Disputes and tensions are inherent in unequal exchange, but the greater availability of and options for obtaining Western goods reduced the potential for war between Yanomami. The situation had become similar to that between Sanema and Yecuana at this time (see chapter 6).

In an earlier discussion of groups living along the Ocamo, one division of the Wakawaka sub-bloc, the Nahibowei-teri, was described as getting into a fight with the Witokaya-teri around 1959, then moving to a New Tribes Mission post on the Padamo in 1960, where they became known as Koshirowa-teri. (New Tribes workers had been dealing with Yanomamo on the Padamo and its tributaries since 1956 [Bou 1956; M. Dawson 1960; Johnston 1957].) The Koshirowa-teri would live in peace from the time they moved to the mission (Hames 1983:411). A missionary's account suggests how this peace was bought.

One day in 1960, people from three other subdivisions of the middle Padamo bloc arrived at the mission. They were angry because the mission Yanomamo refused to hand over a bride they had once promised to a man. An escalating confrontation was interrupted by the distribution of mission food but soon boiled up again in a tug of war over, and other brutalization of, the disputed woman. The violence was again suspended when the missionaries handed out matches and fishhooks.

> Then they started a begging session with the folks of our village. The folks from the raiding [sic] villages ask for possessions from the village they go to raid. If they receive them everyone is friendly again. If not, they leave offended and the next time they come the battle is much worse, until it turns into a war with bows and arrows. (M. Dawson 1960:10)

In this case, the visitors got what they wanted. Only the frustrated groom and his brother "left fuming and fussing"—while the disputed bride received first aid from the missionaries. These two men had a legitimate grievance, but the Koshirowa-teri were able to buy off their supporters.

The other Wakawaka division was Wakawaka-teri itself, the group that had obtained so many machetes in the early 1940s. The Wakawaka-teri began the 1950s on the lower Matacuni, an effluent of the Padamo (Hames 1983:406, 409–11). Most of the decade passed for them, as it did for the Nahibowei-teri, without noteworthy event. They began to strengthen their alliance with Yanomamo on the middle Padamo, a well-traveled highway. At the same time, they came to fear both the sorcery of the Kobari far up the Matacuni and the possible bad intentions of the

Witokaya-teri and Auwei-teri. This combination of push and pull culminated in a move to the Padamo itself in 1961.

For the area east of the Orinoco-Mavaca area, a little information is available. A windfall of steel had been given out by the Franco-Venezuelan Expedition in late 1951. Since then, woodsmen and perhaps an occasional missionary kept up contacts around and beyond the Raudal de Guajaribos, and long chains of Yanomamo middlemen also brought some tools to the highlands (Smole 1976:102). But steel must have remained scarce—perhaps rather as it was for the Namowei in the late 1940s. Barker's map (1953; see map 5) indicates peace among those with unobstructed access to the Orinoco but hostilities between them and a couple of groups in higher land to the north. Perhaps even farther into the highlands lived some Yanomamo groups whom we last heard about in chapter 10, when they were chased by war into remote headwaters around the 1920s. Smole's (1976:90–93) historical comments, not intended to be complete, suggest that these groups enjoyed continuing peace through the 1940s and into the 1950s, although at least one local group was involved in war around 1955. Nothing definite here, but nothing that looks unusual.

The best information available is about the southern Yanomamo. It consists of reports written during the early phases of missionization in the middle 1950s, and a second glimpse around mid-1962. Because these two views together illustrate the impact of the missions, and because very little information is available for the years after 1962, I will deal with the southern Yanomamo beyond this chapter's usual cutoff point of 1960.

We left off discussion of the Río Negro in chapter 10, where, by the late 1930s, Westerners had abandoned the north bank because of Yanomamo attacks. I found no information suggesting any return of Westerners during the 1940s. At the start of the 1950s, the middle Negro and adjoining Casiquiare remained largely uninhabited, with very little local commerce (Acebes 1954:209, 231–37; Gómez Picón 1978:61–64). For a few years in the early 1950s, boundary commission expeditions along the Siapa made contact with Yanomamo. Some meetings were peaceful, but in others, the Yanomamo took all the expedition members' possessions (Cocco 1972:87, 374).

It is not known with certainty when Westerners first reentered the middle Negro tributaries such as the Cauaburi, Marauiá, and Padauari. As recounted by Seitz (1963:75, 86, 90), it seems that the Salesian missionary Antonio Gois was the first to renew contacts with Yanomamo, on the upper Cauaburi in 1954, but this rather heroic portrayal may overlook earlier forays by woodsmen. There is little question, however, that Westerners' fears of Yanomamo had persisted since their raids of the 1930s, and penetration by woodsmen came later here than on the upper Orinoco.

Gois's first contacts were with the Kohoroshiwe-teri—the group that had captured Helena Valero two decades before. The Kohoroshiwe-teri immediately wanted to move down to settle at Gois's new mission at Tapurucuara, on the Negro below the Marauiá, but Gois insisted that they first develop gardens at that site. For two years, they descended the river to Tapurucuara to work on their gardens, and Gois went up to visit them. In 1956, Gois learned of other Yanomamo in the nearby Marauiá basin. Although now known by different names (Mokarishiobe-teri and Shamatawe-teri), these were the old Karawe-teri who had abducted Valero from the Kohoroshiwe-teri. The Kohoroshiwe-teri tried to prevent Gois from contacting the Karawe-teri groups, for they did not want him to give them presents. When they saw that he would not be deterred, they acquiesced, and Gois made initial contact in 1958 (Cocco 1972:96).

In January 1957, Helena Valero and Akawe arrived at Tapurucuara on the doleful journey that was her life after escaping from the Yanomamo.[16] Many Kohoroshiwe-teri women and children were living and going to school there. Several months later, two adventurers—Georg and Thea Seitz—came to the mission, drawn by news stories about Valero. They accompanied Padre Gois on a trip up the Cauaburi, where other Westerners were also beginning to penetrate, and they stopped at a village of Gois's "friends" called Araraibo—probably the Kohoroshiwe-teri on the Ariabo tributary. This was a large village, and Gois told his guests how these Yanomamo had expanded it and their gardens with the steel he gave them. Already, there are suggestions of game depletion and a breakdown in meat sharing. Intense alliance building is suggested by Gois's comment that "their brides . . are always fetched from another village" (Seitz 1963:21–22, 90, 96, 100, 141–43, 150, 165).

Then the Seitzes (1963:190, 193) accompanied the missionary when he contacted a new village along the Maia, a middle Cauaburi tributary. These people were called Shamatari but consisted of two groups, the Wawanawe-teri and the Herowe-teri (see Salazar 1967:map), who were moving down from the Maia headwaters.[17] At this first contact, they were virtually without steel. The missionary gave them 24 machetes, 12 axes, 20 aluminum cooking pots, and many other items, and he promised to send more (Seitz 1963:190, 195, 197). Perhaps coincidentally —but probably not—a party of Araraibo men arrived at the Shamatari village seeking women while Gois was there (Seitz 1963:199).

As we will see shortly, it was this priest's deliberate plan to make the Yanomamo dependent upon mission gifts in order to compel them to give up their "sinful" way of life. Seitz provides a detailed account of his dealings and attitudes—an account made all the more disturbing by the author's unconcealed admiration for the man of God. For example, the Padre told the Seitzes: "You see, they are not really human beings— yet" (Seitz 1963:77). Perhaps that belief is what enabled Padre Gois, if the Seitz account is to be believed, knowingly to expose the Araraibo to a man with an active case of measles (Seitz 1963:115, 119, 173–74).

Gois reached these Yanomamo at the end of some twenty years of their isolation. Consistent with the theoretical model, those twenty years seem to have been decades of peace. According to Gois's fellow Salesian, Padre Cocco (1972:96), Gois found his efforts to go from Kohoroshiwe-teri to Karawe-teri impeded by animosities, but these were lingering grudges from the earlier wars described by Valero, now being rekindled by the Kohoroshiwe-teri's fear of losing some of the mission- ary's trade goods. Photographs of villages taken by Seitz in 1957 show no palisades, but brush growing right up to the house structure (Seitz 1963); these are not settlements on war footing. Seitz gives no indication of any active warfare in the area, with one exception, and that involves Valero's husband, Akawe.

From his flight with Valero until his death from pneumonia in 1967, Akawe traveled widely by canoe (Valero 1984:536–537). Early in 1957, the Kohoroshiwe-teri at Tapurucuara mission offered Akawe a wife if he would help them attack the Karawe-teri.[18] (This was during the time when the Kohoroshiwe-teri were trying to prevent Gois from making contact with their old enemies.) Loaded down with goods he had re- ceived from the *nape,* he went off, leaving Valero (Valero 1984:532–33). Not too long after that, Akawe showed up at the mouth of the Ma- rauiá River, leading about a score of Yanomamo who wanted to go to the mission. Apparently he had moved around between villages up in the headwater country, and the group he was now leading was a section of a larger group that had lost its headman to raiders (Seitz 1963:184– 85). Since this group is not identified, little more can be said, other than to note the now familiar pattern in which war breaks out soon after the Western presence increases.

The relatively pacific situation witnessed by Seitz in 1957 did not last. The years from 1960 to 1962 saw clashes with boundary commis- sion parties, missionaries, and others (Salazar 1967:16, 38, 40, 140). The Deminí and Araçá area, east of the Marauiá, became a particular trouble spot. Although it is far from clear, it appears that a German expedition, apparently including Zerries, was working in that area in 1961 or early 1962. By mid-1962, so much fighting had broken out there that the government closed it off to all outsiders (Salazar 1967:31, 38, 183, 224). Around this time, the Kohoroshiwe-teri were "studied" by "Schultes and Holmstedt" (Cocco 1972:100). Most intriguing of all, a "chief" obtained "some shotguns" and chased some missionaries out. This chief was said to be one of Valero's sons (Salazar 1967:40, 93).

In mid-1962, Fred Salazar (1967) toured the same area visited by Seitz. Salazar is an interesting observer, almost a proto-hippie. Many of his assertions are questionable—perhaps misunderstandings, perhaps exaggerations for effect. The latter applies to his claims to be the first to contact villages that in fact had been visited by Seitz. But much else seems entirely consistent with what we know about Yanomami in such contact situations. And he provides a more critical evaluation of the missions' activities than does Seitz.

Although the Salesians had by this time become more careful about spreading infectious diseases, a new wave of prospectors and fugitives had begun to enter the forests. The Tapurucuara mission was competing with a Protestant mission across the river, but the Protestants were not as well provisioned as the Catholics. Many Yanomami children were at the Catholic boarding school (Salazar 1967:63, 72, 114). Salazar (1967:71) comments that the mission "was the perfect place to watch the transition of the Indians from primitive jungle dwellers to caboclos who would eventually populate the miserable river villages and the floating city of Manaus."[19]

By mid-1962, the Salesians had two mission posts in Yanomamo territory: a small one on the Cauaburi and another begun in 1961 on the Marauiá, where Gois now worked out of a two-story building. (There were also a few mission-encouraged Brazilian settlements on these rivers.) At the Marauiá mission, three distinct bands of Yanomamo had settled. The area was already hunted out, and some of the rapidly acculturating Yanomamo lived largely on food provided by the mission. After his initial dispensation of gifts, Gois required his flock to attend mass and either work or trade for his goods. Because there was a marked imbalance of trade goods even among the resident Yanomamo, theft was a serious problem, and several fights with machetes were observed (Salazar 1967:75–76, 128, 133, 138, 213, 222–25, map).

Salazar also visited several Yanomamo villages that demonstrate the variable impact of mission proximity. On the Cauaburi tributary, the Maia, the composite group called Shamatari that was first contacted by

Gois and Seitz about five years before had by now extensive ties to the outside world. They were regularly visited by the Salesians, had many people down in the main mission on the Negro, had hosted the German scientific expedition some six months before, and sometime recently had relocated alongside a government Indian service post. Compared with the Kohoroshiwe-teri, the Shamatari were well provided with cloth and machetes (Cocco 1972:97; Salazar 1967:183, 188). Also in contrast to the Kohoroshiwe-teri, women here "did most of the hard labor and were more subservient. What's more, there were plenty of them. The village was rich in women, the commodity that many of the other villages lacked, the prize for which one village raided another" (Salazar 1967: 188). But no one was attacking the powerful Shamatari, "the lords of the upper Maia" (Salazar 1967:189).

The other group with greatest connection to the missions was the Shamatau-teri, one of the two Karawe-teri groups. A day's walk from the Marauiá mission, visited by Gois, and having a sizable representation at Gois's mission, the Shamatau-teri too were a "strong and prosperous nation" with a relative abundance of women and many young men from other groups residing there (Salazar 1967:222, 228, 230–31).

In contrast to these two groups with solid Western support, the Kohoroshiwe-teri village on the upper tributary of the Cauaburi (probably the group Seitz called "Araraibo") was not doing so well. Despite their head start in contacts with Gois, they were now some distance from the newly established Western outposts. An exceptionally large number of people had consolidated there out of fear of raiders from the north. Their enemies are not identified by name but are said to be those who had previously chased the Kohoroshiwe-teri out of the mountains, back in the time when the current headman was a young boy. (There is no suggestion, however, that they were still at war with Karawe-teri groups who were now associated with the Marauiá mission to their east.) The village was palisaded, and forest had been cleared all around to prevent surprise attacks. The leader had a shotgun, but apparently no ammunition. The children looked sickly and underfed, and one man died of a respiratory problem while Salazar was present. Also during his stay, some kind of violent clash occurred not far from the village, although what really happened cannot be discerned (Salazar 1967:143–44, 148, 152, 154, 158–59, 166–69, 190, 204).

Even farther up the Cauaburi system was another group, the Amaro-kawebue-teri, who were said to have been "decimated" by recent raids. Near the Marauiá, beyond the prosperous Shamatau-teri, lived the other

Karawe-teri group, the Mokarishiobe-teri, who were also being raided, and beyond them, Salazar saw the burned out *shabono* of another group that had just been hit by raiders (Salazar 1967:200, 235, 237). In sum, not only did war break out in this region shortly after the arrival of the missionaries, but the region also quickly fell into the typical pattern of prosperity and security for those closest to the Western outposts and war for those villages one or two steps removed from the Westerners.

In this chapter, building on chapter 11 and all that came before, I believe I have been able to establish quite firmly that Yanomami warfare is tightly connected to changing circumstances of Western contact. The connection is both temporal and spatial. Not every single case of war, but the great majority of cases occur shortly after a major change in the Western presence and involve those who have better access to Western goods fighting those who are more removed from Western sources. Repeatedly we have seen permutations on this pattern. In the next chapter, we will be able to examine more closely the advantages of being a middleman in the Western goods trade, and how those advantages sometimes translate into antagonism and war.

13

The Yanomamo and the Anthropologist: 1960 to 1966

The time frame of this chapter is shorter than those of the others because individual and collective aggression among Orinoco-Mavaca Yanomamo during these six years is described in such detail.[1] That is due to the untiring efforts of Napoleon Chagnon, whose initial field research among the Bisaasi-teri in 1964–66 produced the widely read text *Yanomamö: The Fierce People*. I do not disagree with Chagnon's assessment of the social significance of violence at this moment in time, but I do differ strongly about its relationship to the processes of Western contact.

In the preface to the second edition of *Yanomamö*, Chagnon (1977: xi) claims that the book portrays Yanomamo society "before it was altered or destroyed by our culture." In the prologue or introduction to more recent editions, he asserts that the Yanomamo "retain their native patterns of warfare and political integrity without interference from the outside world" (1992a:1). In the fifth edition, retitled *Yanomamö: The Last Days of Eden*, Chagnon (1992b:xiv–xv) reaffirms that their intense warfare represents the violence of "our evolutionary past," and that which is common among tribal peoples "prior to their contact with the outside world." He dismisses the idea that this violence is a result of Western contact as "the 'bad breath' theory of tribal warfare." (In the foreword to that edition, E. O. Wilson [1992:ix] suggests that "the Yanomamo way of life gives us the clearest view of the conditions under which the human mind evolved biologically during deep history.") Similar statements are found in other of Chagnon's writings (see Ferguson 1992a:199–200).

I assert, instead, that the weight of observations from diverse times and places firmly establishes that there is, at a minimum, a temporal and spatial connection between Yanomami wars and changing circumstances of Western contact. However unaffected by Western contact the Orinoco-Mavaca Yanomamo may have seemed to Chagnon in the mid-1960s, their movements and political relationships had been strongly conditioned by the presence of Westerners since the latest wave of contact began in the late 1930s.

By 1960, the Bisaasi-teri's location at Boca Mavaca had become the center of Western presence on the far upper Orinoco. To recapitulate their most recent history, by the middle 1950s they had reestablished themselves as an independent group and had become important traders in Western goods. In 1958 they moved to Boca Mavaca to obtain the manufactures offered to them by the government malaria station. In 1959 they were joined by two New Tribes missionaries, one each for the upper and lower divisions of the Bisaasi-teri. The closely allied Monou-teri lived a short distance up the Mavaca, the three settlements together making up what I call the "western Namowei."

Shortly after the move to Boca Mavaca, the Bisaasi-teri began to develop an alliance with a Shamatari group living farther up the Mavaca. In 1960, the western Namowei obtained the cooperation of these new allies in a treacherous attack on some old Shamatari enemies, the Mowaraoba-teri. Except for this incident, the political climate of 1960 was "quite serene" (Chagnon 1977:80).

In this chapter, I attempt to demonstrate that the wars and other conflicts of the middle 1960s—those made famous in *Yanomamö: The Fierce People*—are directly connected to changes in the Western presence around Boca Mavaca, including the arrival of Chagnon himself.

Developing and Disintegrating Alliances, 1960 to 1963

The circumstances of Western contact described for the later 1950s continued without major change through 1963. There were now three missions in the area: the Salesians at the mouth of the Ocamo with the Iyewei-teri and at Platanal with the Mahekoto-teri, and the New Tribes missions along with the government malaria station at Boca Mavaca next to the Bisaasi-teri. I found no comment about the activities of forest workers at this time, but their contacts with Yanomami were becoming more regular and routine during the 1950s and probably continued as such in the new decade.

The Yanomamo's movements to be closer to the rivers and Westerners were even more pronounced throughout the 1960s than in the 1950s (Steinvorth de Goetz 1969:24), despite the plague of mosquitoes and other insects close to the water.[2] With more Yanomamo living closer to the rivers, malaria was a serious health problem. Major outbreaks are reported for 1960 (Smole 1976:50) and 1963 (Lizot 1977:503). Specifics are lacking, but generally with such diseases, people in close contact with Westerners and their medicines are less likely to die than those who are exposed to the pathogens and left to fend for themselves—an additional advantage of having a resident Westerner.

Three scientific expeditions passed through in these years, adding to the wide distribution of Western goods. In 1961, Inga Steinvorth de Goetz made her initial visit to the Yabitawa-teri near the Raudal de Guajaribos, although she would not establish regular residence there until late 1965 (Steinvorth de Goetz 1969:54, 91). That same year, Miguel Layrisse and Johannes Wilbert worked somewhere in the upper Orinoco, collecting 140 blood samples (Wilbert 1963:196). In 1962–63, Ettore Biocca led an expedition into the area, briefly visiting the Iyewei-teri, Witokaya-teri, Puunabiwe-teri, Bisaasi-teri, Monouteri, and others (Migliazza 1972:390). Biocca, of course, was the first to record Helena Valero's life history.

Thus the early 1960s were a time of relative stability in Western residence and of multiple sources of Western goods for those close to the major rivers. These conditions are conducive to local peace (although there may have been unreported wars involving more interior groups). However, new political trends had been set in motion that would lead to increasing tensions and sporadic violence, and, in 1964, to a new outbreak of intense warfare in the area.

The late 1950s and early 1960s saw the political fortunes of the Mahekoto-teri and Bisaasi-teri diverge. As the latter rose in prominence, wealth, and power, the former declined. Although Platanal remained a mission post, it was now secondary to Boca Mavaca. Compared with their situation in the middle 1950s, the Mahekoto-teri would have had fewer trade goods to provide to their more remote allies. Probably related to this change, and certainly compounding its impact, two factions split off from Mahekoto-teri in 1960 and 1961, following internal disputes. The new local groups, Shashanawe-teri and Tayari-teri, remained at peace with the parent village (Cocco 1972:399), but the loss of manpower represented by these defections would have significantly weakened Mahekoto-teri militarily.

Political relations between the Mahekoto-teri and Bisaasi-teri cooled at this point, and the two ceased to participate jointly in feasts (Chagnon 1977:103). It is in their relationships with their respective upstream neighbors that the difference between the two becomes clearest. While the Bisaasi-teri were building new alliances, the Mahekoto-teri saw their alliance network fall apart into war.

Upstream from Mahekoto-teri, a series of conflicts developed in perhaps 1961 or 1962 (based on Chagnon 1966:76, 176). Virtually all that is reported is contained in one paragraph concerning the political relations of the Patanowa-teri (Chagnon 1966:156–57). As reported there, the Yabitawa-teri and Kashorawe-teri (segments of the old Watanami-teri, Mahekoto-teri's ally from the 1940s) killed a Boreta-teri man in a club fight. His sister was married to the Mahekoto-teri headman. (The Boreta-teri were Mahekoto-teri's enemies in the middle 1950s, but apparently they had ceded wives and established an alliance since then.) The Mahekoto-teri then began raiding the Yabitawa-teri, and in one raid killed a Patanowa-teri man who was doing bride service, thus antagonizing the Patanowa-teri. Then the Yabitawa-teri seized a woman from the Patanowa-teri, who in return began to raid the Yabitawa-teri, who took refuge with the Kashorawe-teri. The Hasupuwe-teri (formerly the great allies of the eastern Namowei) took the Yabitawa-teri's side and also attacked the Patanowa-teri. Only the Ashatowa-teri (formerly attached to the Hasupuwe-teri) remained friendly to the Patanowa-teri.

This spare narrative can only suggest the deeper political currents at work here, and the details should not bear too much weight without other confirmation. But one thing is clear: a network of alliances was breaking down into mutual hostility. Except for the Boreta-teri, all these groups had been at peace with each other around the middle 1950s, and some of the alliances dated back into the 1940s or even earlier. From what we know about alliances in general, and about the Western contact situation around and beyond Platanal in the late 1950s and early 1960s, it is predictable that these groups would be bound by numerous marriage ties, each accompanied by strong expectations of a continuing supply of Western goods. As the supply of Western goods entering this alliance network diminished along with the diminished Western presence at Platanal, bad feelings, perceived insults, and conflicts over women all would have intensified dramatically.

Political relations upstream from Mahekoto-teri were very different from those developing up the Mavaca. Boca Mavaca in 1960 was a power center. Upper Bisaasi-teri, lower Bisaasi-teri, and Monou-teri each had its own political connections and interests, but the villages could and did act together for common cause (Chagnon 1966:127–29). The Bisaasi-teri had the malaria post and two missionaries—the heaviest concentration of Westerners on the river, at least above Iyewei-teri. Very soon after the Western connection solidified, these western Namowei began to act like a power center.

New alliances developed almost instantly between all three western Namowei villages and a large Shamatari village up the Mavaca, Paruritawa-teri. After the Paruritawa-teri participated in the treachery against the Mowaraoba-teri, they fissioned and moved north to two new gardens they had already begun. The new groups, the Shamatari allies of the western Namowei, were called Momaribowei-teri and Reyabobowei-teri (Chagnon 1966:163–65, 173–74, 1977:78–79). The unequal, exploitative character of these alliances is described by Chagnon around 1966. The basic principles of village-to-village trade, monopolizing a Westerner, and passing along few and worn tools are all clearly operating.

> The Bisaasi-teri would obtain machetes from foreigners like me or the missionaries. When these were worn out, they would pass them on to the first Shamatari group, the Momaribowei-teri, who would wear them down even more before passing them on to their neighbors, the Reyabobowei-teri. By the time the tools reached Sibarariwa's village [the Mowaraoba-teri], they were usually unrecognizable as machetes. Most of them were broken into two or more pieces, and none of them had handles. The Bisaasi-teri did not want me to give my tools directly to the Momaribowei-teri when I went there to visit, and the Momaribowei-teri did not want me to take my tools past them to the Reyabobowei-teri. Each group wanted a monopoly. (Chagnon 1974:11)

In exchange for Western goods, the Shamatari provided the Namowei with spun cotton, curare arrow points (Chagnon 1966:95), clay pots (1977:100), arrows, baskets, hammocks, and dogs (1983:6).[3]

The Namowei villages came to exhibit an inordinate proportion of village-exogamous marriages—53 percent (Chagnon 1972b:272)—and most of these represented women marrying in. By 1966, the two Bisaasi-teri settlements had "managed to acquire two dozen or so women from the Shamatari while having given or promised only a half-dozen in return" (Chagnon 1977:80). (The Bisaasi-teri at the time numbered 136 people [Chagnon 1966:58].) The chain of trading partners demonstrated a "cline in the sex ratio from Reyaboboweitedi to Bisaasi-tedi":

Bisaasi-teri, 0.8 males per female; Monou-teri, 1.1; Momaribowei-teri, 1.2; and Reyabobowei-teri, 1.6 (Chagnon 1966:57–58).

Bride service requirements were similarly skewed. "The [Bisaasi-teri] men who have obtained Shamatari wives have, as well, managed to cut short their period of bride service in the Shamatari village. Conversely, Shamatari men who have been promised women of Kaobawa's group are pressed into very lengthy bride service, sometimes up to three years" (Chagnon 1977:79).

The bride service required of Shamatari men seems to have been particularly difficult. One young man from Momaribowei-teri "was doing bride service to his father-in-law, the headman of the lower group of Bisaasi-teri. . . . As a Shamatari [he] was subject to a considerable amount of ridicule and harsh treatment. . . . Wakarabewa's father-in-law was particularly unpleasant to him. He denied Wakarabewa sexual access to the girl while at the same time he allowed the young men of the natal village to enjoy these privileges" (Chagnon 1974:13–14).

Chagnon does not attribute these inequalities between Bisaasi-teri and the Shamatari to the Bisaasi-teri's relative monopoly over the sources of steel tools. He alludes to a connection between the two at the very start of his dissertation,[4] but later (Chagnon 1977:78–79) he explains this marital inequality as resulting from the vulnerability of the Shamatari allies after they had participated in the western Namowei's attack on Mowaraoba-teri in 1960. (Their participation in that attack itself needs to be explained. I argue, of course, that the Shamatari cooperated in order to improve their access to the western Namowei's trade goods.)

Whatever the case, the kind of marital imbalance reported along the Mavaca is not unusual. Similar imbalances were described elsewhere, in most detail around the Mucajaí mission (Early and Peters 1990; Peters 1973) and in terms of Yanomami-Yecuana relations, but also wherever there is information about exogamous marriages by groups who monopolize a good source of Western goods. The extraction of women by strong trade controllers is the normal pattern.

The Paruritawa-teri's complicity in the western Namowei attack embroiled them in war with more remote Shamatari. They were "relentlessly raided" (Chagnon 1977:79); they fissioned and moved closer to the Orinoco. The western Namowei provided some unspecified support in this conflict, but it was the two offshoots of the Paruritawa-teri who sustained the losses (Chagnon 1977:80). No other details are provided, but again we see a common pattern reported in many other situations:

the villages one or two steps out from new Western settlement are embroiled in wars with more isolated groups.

The Context for War

By 1964, Yanomamo society in the Orinoco-Mavaca area was thoroughly oriented to the Westerners. More than a quarter of a century after *nape* began to reenter the upper river, and nearly fifteen years after the establishment of a resident Western presence, in the face of increasing numbers of woodsmen, scientists, and tourists, all the native groups in the vicinity of the rivers had become dependent, directly or indirectly, on Western providers. While most river groups probably had attained an acceptable minimum of basic possessions, we will see later that even steel tools remained extremely scarce among at least some of the more interior groups (see Steinvorth de Goetz 1969:24, 29).

This dependence was exacerbated in 1964, when local Yanomamo experienced a catastrophic series of shocks. "During eight months of the year 1964, the Yanomama villages missionized by the Salesian fathers and the colleagues of the New Tribes suffered a famine without precedent. Hunger made felt its terrible pangs" (Cocco 1972:176). This hunger came during a memorable drought, which was followed by a flood. The flood led to a major outbreak of malaria, apparently at its worst in August and September (Cocco 1972:481). As Cocco (1972:176) tells it, only massive quantities of mission aid prevented a human disaster.

At Boca Mavaca, Barker was on "furlough," but Derek Hadley and Wallace and Margaret Jank (later to establish a mission in the Parima highlands) were hard at work. By mid-1964, they could see a major impact on the Bisaasi-teri, although not as much as they would have liked.

> Some in this village have shown a real change in their lives recently and the effects of the Gospel are vividly seen in them. This tribe, which was naked and monolingual when our missionaries first arrived among them, has been a difficult one in which to work. Many in this village are still naked and hold to their old culture and superstitions. (Johnston 1964:3)

Sometime during or shortly before 1964, another major event occurred. The Salesians founded a new mission on the Orinoco across from the Mavaca under Pedro Uitervaal (Comité 1983:46). Apparently no Yanomamo came to reside at the mission until 1966, although the missionary was actively trying to lure them. Unfortunately, there is very little information about this mission; much of it is contained in one comment by Chagnon (1977:151): "There was a Salesian (Catholic) mission across the river from Kaobawa's village all during my initial research, but there were no Yanomamo there. It was easy to ignore them at that time for they had no impact on the Yanomamo."

From my perspective, perhaps nothing could be more disruptive of established intervillage political relations than the arrival of a new, beckoning mission. But—I repeat for emphasis—we know little else about this mission and its relationship to the Yanomamo. Both Chagnon (1977:147–51, 154–62, 1992a:208–11, 217–46) and Lizot (1976) have described the crude competition for souls carried out between Catholics and Protestants, and the assaults by missionaries on Yanomamo religion and culture. All the specifics in their descriptions date to 1967 or later, but it is fair to assume that some of these disruptive practices were going on around 1964. Indeed, they were reported as early as 1959 for the Salesians at Santa María de los Guaicas (chapter 11), and the New Tribes missionaries' own writings reveal a frightening equation of Yanomami culture and Satanic influence (e.g., Bou 1956; *Brown Gold* 1952:9).

Thus 1964 was a time of great change and widespread, multifaceted social disruption. Into this context, in November 1964, stepped the young graduate student, Napoleon Chagnon. For 13 months, up through February 1966 (subtracting time spent in Caracas), Boca Mavaca would be his primary residence (Chagnon 1977:1). Although he was introduced to the Bisaasi-teri by James Barker and initially lived in the missionary's hut, Chagnon was largely on his own for his first three months in the field because Barker left and did not rejoin him immediately. The other NTM missionary was downstream recovering from malaria (Chagnon 1977:151, 1983:9–12).

Fortunately for this analysis, Chagnon has been extraordinarily forthcoming and candid about his personal dealings with the Yanomamo. In the following discussions, I will interpret the political and military patterns he describes as being manifestations of an ongoing process of Western contact. Chagnon himself was one agent of that contact, and his presence and actions had a major impact on the course of events. This point is made not to criticize the fieldworker but to explain the warfare. Indeed, I do not know that Chagnon did anything different from any other fieldworkers, except to tell us about it. But in the complicated political context into which he unknowingly stepped, his presence became a factor that cannot be ignored if one wishes to understand the patterning of violence.

Chagnon writes disarmingly of his own naive hopes as he first entered Yanomamo country: "Would they like me? This was important to me; I wanted them to be so fond of me that they would adopt me into their kinship system and way of life, because I had heard that successful anthropologists always get adopted by their people" (1977:4), But to Chagnon's distress, his main significance from the Yanomamo point of view was as a source of steel tools, other items, and various kinds of assistance. Speaking of the isolation and loneliness of fieldwork, he tells of seeking friendship among the Yanomamo.

> All my friends simply used my confidence to gain privileged access to my cache of steel tools and trade goods, and looted me. I would be bitterly disappointed that my "friend" thought no more of me than to finesse our relationship exclusively with the intention of getting at my locked up possessions, and my depression would hit new lows every time I discovered this. The loss of the possession bothered me much less than the shock that I was, as far as most of them were concerned, nothing more than a source of desirable items; no holds were barred in relieving me of these, since I was considered something subhuman, a non-Yanomamo. (Chagnon 1977:8)

After repeated visits into the 1970s, Chagnon (1974:164–65) again discusses the Yanomamo's incessant demands upon him and the implications of extortion and generosity for personal status. He confirms that efforts were made to monopolize him: "Each group wanted me to visit them and only them and resented the fact that I took possessions to other Yanomamo. . . . They publicly defended and justified their desires by accusing their neighbors of chicane and thievery, in some cases while visitors from the villages so denounced were actually present. '*Ba noshi omabou!*' they would say to me—'we want you all to ourselves!' " (Chagnon 1974:164).[5]

It should be kept in mind that when Chagnon arrived in the field in November 1964, he "did not speak a word of their language" (Chagnon 1977:5)—and for the first three months or so, neither of the Protestant missionaries was around to help him (1977:151). In later years, his

Yanomamo friends would reminisce about how easy it was to trick or intimidate him into giving away "vast quantities of valuable goods for almost nothing" (1977:xii).

It seems clear that the Bisaasi-teri were adept at extracting political advantage from his presence. From a letter written while on a visit to Caracas in late February 1965, we learn:

> The village I'm living in really thinks I am the be-all and end-all. I broke the final ice with them by participating in their dancing and singing one night. That really impressed them. They want to take me all over Waicaland to show me off. Their whole attitude toward me changed dramatically. Unfortunately, they want me to dance all the time now. You should have seen me in my feathers and loincloth! They were so anxious to show me off that they arranged to take me to the first Shamatari village so that I could dance with them. (Chagnon 1972a:67)

Dancing in another village is part of politics—one way of displaying strength. The participation of a white man in feathers and loincloth, virtually declaring his identification with Bisaasi-teri in intervillage relations, would represent a major coup. And it was during these first months of Chagnon's fieldwork that the Bisaasi-teri's conflicts with Shamatari and Mahekoto-teri transpired, as we shall see. A month or two after Chagnon wrote this letter, events began to unfold that would lead to his becoming a more independent political agent during the later part of his fieldwork. These events were related to difficulties Chagnon encountered as he pursued his genealogical research.

Chagnon's research objective required the collection of accurate genealogies (1977:10–13, 1992a:19–25). This work was so important that he describes it as a "full-time task [that] left very little time for intensive study of other aspects of Yanomamo culture" (1966:17). Yet collecting genealogies was an exceptionally difficult thing to do, because of the Yanomami's strong aversion to using the name of a living person and their strict taboo against speaking the name of the dead. Chagnon could have been in danger if he inadvertently mentioned the name of someone recently killed, because the Yanomamo "were unable to understand why a complete stranger should want to possess such knowledge unless it were for harmful magical purposes" (Chagnon 1966:17). Chagnon paid informants well for their help, however, so many wanted to cooperate.

What they did was make up comic names and construct ludicrous genealogical relationships. "They invented false names for everybody in the village and systematically learned them, freely revealing to me the 'true' identities of everyone," then "roaring in hysterical laughter" as Chagnon tried to repeat the names (Chagnon 1992a:20). After some five months of this, the deception was revealed to Chagnon during a visit to one of the Shamatari allies, the Momaribowei-teri. Five months of work had to be discarded.

He changed his research methodology, working in private with selected informants and testing and cross-checking responses, and finally he succeeded in developing a core of genealogical relations. Some informants, however, continued to deceive him about the names of the dead, including one old man whose seeming cooperation led Chagnon (1992a: 21) to pay him "quadruple the rate that I had been paying the others"—a pay increase that led to an inundation of would-be informants. But the old man was lying, using the names of deceased ancestors of a village far away. Chagnon learned this from Rerebawa, a young man doing bride service with the Bisaasi-teri, who was to become one of Chagnon's main informants and friends. Rerebawe revealed the deception at a moment when he was angry at the Bisaasi-teri and in a mood to insult them.

When Chagnon learned of this deception, he changed his research method a second time (1977:12):

> Thereafter, I began taking advantage of local arguments and animosities in selecting my informants. . . . I began traveling to other villages to check the genealogies, picking villages that were on strained terms with the people about whom I wanted information. I would then return to my base camp and check with local informants the accuracy of the new information. If the informants became angry when I mentioned the new names I acquired from the unfriendly group, I was almost certain that the information was accurate.

Chagnon (1977:9) also describes the way he approached the other villages he visited, in a discussion of the constant demands to provide Western manufactures:

> I made regular trips to some dozen different villages in order to collect genealogies or to recheck those I already had. Hence, the intensity of the begging and intimidation was fairly constant for the duration of the fieldwork. I had to establish my position in some sort of pecking order of ferocity at each and every village.
> For the most part, my own "fierceness" took the form of

shouting back at the Yanomamo as loudly and as passionately as they shouted at me, especially at first, when I did not know much of their language. As I became more proficient in their language and learned more about their political tactics, I became more sophisticated in the art of bluffing.

Chagnon tells us, "I had to become very much like the Yanomamo to be able to get along with them on their terms: sly, aggressive, and intimidating" (1977:9). But while he was behaving more like a Yanomamo big man in his interpersonal relations, his other actions—his quest for the taboo names of dead ancestors, his moving back and forth between antagonistic villages, and, above all, his being the source of Western goods that every village wanted to monopolize—created a very different and "un-Yanomami" context for his behavior. Chagnon thus became something of a wild card on the local political scene. (Probably the same could be said for the resident missionaries, but their activities are not described.)

During Chagnon's first fieldwork, the group that monopolized him most of the time—the group regularly in position to relieve him of his trade goods—was the Bisaasi-teri. In addition to Chagnon, the Bisaasi-teri also dominated access to the government malaria station and the two NTM missionaries. One can understand why, with all these sources of Western goods already at hand, the Bisaasi-teri might not want to relocate to the "vacant" Catholic mission across the river. (As soon as Chagnon left, however, some did move across.) But the Bisaasi-teri could hardly be indifferent to another group's moving in. Such an event might involve the loss of a dependent ally, and it could lead to the creation of a strong competitor for Western favors. The Bisaasi-teri had an effective veto over prospective residents: it would be extremely difficult, if not impossible, to establish a garden right across the river from hostile neighbors who had long since learned how to use canoes.

The Bisaasi-teri taken as a whole were a fairly large group, about 136 people (Chagnon 1966:58). They probably could field 40 fighters on a good day, and more with Monou-teri (population 66) added in. This would be a good-sized force, yet it could have been easily matched by the larger groups such as the Patanowa-teri (population 212) or by an alliance. Although they did have the advantages of resident Westerners, the Bisaasi-teri at this time did not have any shotguns of their own (Chagnon 1983:57). Thus their superlative trade location was out of proportion to their military strength—although their wealth gave them the means to enlist allies. Altogether, the Bisaasi-teri were in a very favorable position but not immune to intimidation.

The preceding discussion provides context for the three distinct conflicts involving the Bisaasi-teri. These conflicts are of particular importance because they constitute the bulk of the violence detailed in all five editions of Chagnon's *Yanomamö*. They are the Yanomami wars that everyone knows about. By far the most serious of the three was a shooting war with the Patanowa-teri, along with related factional maneuvering, that spanned the entire time of Chagnon's fieldwork. Because of its complexity, I will discuss it last. The other two conflicts were more episodic: one involving enemy Shamatari up the Mavaca, the other a severe club fight with the Mahekoto-teri. Both transpired within Chagnon's first months in the field.

The Shamatari Conflict

In the vicinity of the upper Mavaca in early 1964, there were four Shamatari villages. Two of these, Momaribowei-teri (population 85) and Reyabobowei-teri (population 77; Chagnon 1966:58), were subordinate allies of the Bisaasi-teri and Monou-teri—the ones who helped them attack other Shamatari in 1960. The other two Shamatari groups were old enemies who had slaughtered Bisaasi-teri in 1951: the Iwahikoroba-teri and Mowaraoba-teri. The latter, who around this time began to be called Mishimishimabowei-teri, had been victims of the western Namowei in 1960.

In 1964 the Mishimishimabowei-teri moved from the Siapa region to the Mavaca headwaters (Chagnon 1966:173, 1974:14). As we have seen in many previous cases, a move to a headwater is often a prelude to a move downriver toward a source of Western goods. (A division of the Mishimishimabowei-teri did just that about a decade later [Chagnon 1992a:222–23].) What is more, Mishimishimabowei-teri was "staggeringly large by Yanomamo standards," with about four hundred people around 1967 (Chagnon 1977:153). It would have been a formidable military power. Sometime during 1965, "rumors reached the Bisaasi-tedi that Iwahikoroba-tedi had split into two factions, both moving down the Mavaca River" (Chagnon 1966:169). Thus, both enemy Shamatari groups appeared to be moving closer to the rich sources of Western goods at Boca Mavaca, even though that meant moving toward danger.

Why take the risk? Both the enemy Shamatari groups were in desperate need of steel, to judge from what Chagnon found when he finally made contact with them a few years later. In 1968, one subdivision of Mishimishimabowei-teri—some eighty people—had "two of the most miserable 'axes' I have ever seen. They had been worn down by years—perhaps decades—of heavy use and were about one third the size they had been when they were manufactured" (Chagnon 1983:39). Even later, the Iwahikoroba-teri were using one "extremely dull and badly worn machete of a type that I had seen only in Brazil: their steel tools came from Brazilian villages via a long trading network" (Chagnon 1974:176–77). This combination of material need, group size, direction of relocations, and past record of attacks must have made the Shamatari expansion down the Mavaca a worrisome prospect for the western Namowei around Boca Mavaca.

When Chagnon made contact in 1968, the Mishimishimabowei-teri knew all about him, down to minute details. They had sent messages to him in 1965 and 1966, asking him to come visit. They wanted the steel tools he gave as gifts (Chagnon 1977:79, 1983:38). Although Chagnon apparently never received those messages, he made the first of several unsuccessful attempts to contact these villages in September 1965 (Chagnon 1966:169). In fact, it was Chagnon's intent "from the very beginning" of his fieldwork to go on from Boca Mavaca to study the less directly contacted Shamatari (Chagnon 1974:6).

The Bisaasi-teri reaction to this intention was thoroughly predictable: "The Bisaasi-teri were justifiably aggrieved that my objective to live with the Shamatari would ultimately lead to a lack of supply of steel tools, so they incessantly advised me *not* to go to the Shamatari villages" (Chagnon 1974:7). They used every stratagem possible to thwart Chagnon's efforts to ascend the Mavaca to the Iwahikoroba-teri or Mishimishimabowei-teri (1966:169, 1974:11–15, 1977:152–53, 1983: 32). They told him the Shamatari would murder him, they refused to act as guides, or they simply turned back once a journey had begun. These tactics successfully obstructed Chagnon's plans until 1968.

Thus, in 1964–65 the western Namowei faced two dangers: that powerful enemy Shamatari would come down the Mavaca, and that Chagnon would go away up the Mavaca. Both possibilities gave the Bisaasi-teri and Monou-teri reason for antagonism against these Shamatari. (Remaining feelings of revenge for the 1951 slaughter would make killing them feel justified and good.)

The interests of the Reyabobowei-teri and Momaribowei-teri seem more complicated, and perhaps divided. Given their recent history, they certainly had some reason to fear the approach of the Mishimishimabowei-teri. Both were against Chagnon's traveling to visit them: "Most of the men in the two contacted Shamatari villages tried to prevent me from going by telling horrible tales of the treachery that awaited my visit, describing how the Shamatari will kill me. The truth of the matter is that they know that I will bring the uncontacted Shamatari machetes and axes that might otherwise be given to them" (Chagnon 1977:79).

Quite in tune with that opposition, both groups were themselves acting as middlemen in trade with the Mishimishimabowei-teri, providing them with "a small, but constant trickle of badly worn steel tools" (Chagnon 1974:9–11). The Reyabobowei-teri especially were in the process of renewing better relations with the other Shamatari, something the Bisaasi-teri tried to prevent by "chicane, threat, and intimidation" (Chagnon 1977:79).

Military action came in two reported events. The first took place soon after the Mishimishimabowei-teri moved to the Mavaca headwaters: "Monou-tedi and Momaribowei-tedi sent a raiding party against them at this location about the time I started my field work, and killed one man" (Chagnon 1966:173). The second event followed shortly. In mid-January 1965 (Chagnon 1972a:65), some Reyabobowei-teri had reestablished good ties with the Mishimishimabowei-teri, whom they invited to a feast. When this became known, men from Bisaasi-teri, Monou-teri, and Momaribowei-teri prepared to ambush the feast party, in cooperation with other Reyabobowei-teri. Friendly Reyabobowei-teri, however, warned off the approaching Mishimishimabowei-teri, and no violence occurred (Chagnon 1966:174, 1977:79, 104). As usual, planned treachery at a feast involved divided interests within the host village and the cooperation of allied groups.

This attempted ambush illustrates the military advantages of having a resident Westerner. The Reyabobowei-teri village was far from Boca Mavaca. The planned attack would require most of the Bisaasi-teri men to leave their village and families for some time—which could be dangerous, with old rivals such as Witokaya-teri just down the river. Chagnon describes the situation:

> The men were gone almost two weeks. All during this time, those who remained behind flocked to my mud hut at dawn and remained in it the whole day, not permitting me to leave. Every hour or so they asked to see my shotgun. I soon discovered that they were frightened and suspected that the Widokaiya-teri were going to raid them to abduct women. . . . I, unknowingly, guarded

the women and children by day with my shotgun, while the [few remaining] men did the same at night with their own weapons. (Chagnon 1977:104)

(The true nature of Chagnon's duty was unknown to him at the time because he had been misled about the nature of the Bisaasi-teri expedition. In a letter from the field dated January 22, 1965, he explains: "About ninety percent of the men are inland trading with the Shamataris. There go all my axes and machetes!" [Chagnon 1972a:65].)

In sum, the enemy Shamatari, in desperate need of Western goods, posed a threat to the western Namowei and at least some of their Shamatari allies: they threatened their dominance of the lower Mavaca, their established trade relationships up the Mavaca, and their monopoly of Chagnon as a source of the desired goods. With this raid and attempted ambush, the western Namowei and their allies demonstrated their resolve and capacity to project force at a distance against the enemy Shamatari. The latter would risk their lives if they started a garden farther downstream. The western Namowei had reemphasized an effective state of war, the perception of which persisted for a few years without any further violence (Chagnon 1977:101). By taking these aggressive measures, the western Namowei and their allies successfully forestalled direct contact between enemy Shamatari and Westerners until 1968.

Chagnon (1966:174) sees these actions as a continuation of western Namowei efforts to obtain revenge for the 1951 slaughter. I see the raid and the planned ambush of the Mishimishimabowei-teri as directly related to the immediate contact situation. These acts served to protect the western Namowei's privileged position in the trade of Western goods, and the attempted ambush—at such distance and with so many men—was made possible by Chagnon's having recently returned to Boca Mavaca with his shotgun.

The Clash with the Mahekoto-teri

The second major conflict that took place during Chagnon's initial fieldwork developed just as the Bisaasi-teri were trying to pull off their ambush, and it involved tensions among the groups located along the Orinoco itself. In it, the Mahekoto-teri applied muscle to upper Bisaasi-teri—the village headed by Kaobawa, where Chagnon spent most of his time (1977:13). The men of upper Bisaasi-teri were supported at critical moments by men from lower Bisaasi-teri (1977:110, 113). The Monou-teri apparently did not provide support in this case. Their main worries, as we shall see, were up the Mavaca and east to the Patanowa-teri, not along the Orinoco.

Upper Bisaasi-teri was also supported by the Karohi-teri, "a small but dependable ally" (Chagnon 1977:105). The Karohi-teri, a branch of the Uhepeki bloc who, in the 1950s, were called Raharawe-teri (Lizot 1988:523) and were closely allied with Mahekoto-teri, lived on the Manaviche River, easily accessible from the Orinoco just above Boca Mavaca. They began to receive direct visits from missionaries and scientists after about 1963 (Lizot 1971:40). Karohi-teri was the natal group of Rerebawa, a young man who was doing bride service in Bisaasi-teri and who became one of Chagnon's principal informants and friends (1977:11–12, 16–17, 93). Rerebawa continued to visit Karohi-teri, no doubt bringing with him substantial amounts of Western goods. Thus the Karohi-teri had a community of interests with Bisaasi-teri.

Mahekoto-teri, it will be recalled, had been the major contact center on the Orinoco since the late 1930s, but had declined relative to the Bisaasi-teri after 1958. During the 1960s, the once strong alliance between the two cooled to occasional trading (Chagnon 1977: 103). Mahekoto-teri had also lost strength through village fissionings and had lost allies in fighting upstream around 1962. Yet it still was a relatively large group with at least one small but dependable ally—its former enemy, the Boreta-teri (Chagnon 1977:105). Though relatively strong, the Mahekoto-teri's access to Western goods was limited. After the Catholics replaced the Protestants at Platanal, the mission "lay dormant for a number of years, stagnating in the lethargy of its disinterested sequence of occupants until about 1970" (Chagnon 1977:148). That is the context, now to the event.

In mid-January 1965, while the men from Bisaasi-teri were away trying to ambush the Mishimishimabowei-teri and Chagnon was left guarding the women, an unidentified party of Yanomamo men arrived at Bisaasi-teri "hoping to trade" (Chagnon 1977:104). When they learned that few of the men were present, they became exceptionally demanding. Chagnon treated the men for malaria and colds, ferried them across the river, and made arrangements to visit their village. These visitors spread the word about the situation at Bisaasi-teri, and a few days later a large party of men left Mahekoto-teri for Bisaasi-teri (Chagnon 1972a:66).

The Bisaasi-teri men returned to find that the Mahekoto-teri and some Boreta-teri had set up camp nearby. Faced with this fact, upper Bisaasi-teri invited them to feast. The guests arrived, a hundred strong, a week early and expecting to be fed—the first of several obvious provocations (Chagnon 1977:104–109). After the feasting, as is the custom, trading began. Each side felt the other was taking advantage (1977: 111–12). The Mahekoto-teri were not happy, and they proceeded to violate etiquette by not leaving when they were obliged to. The Bisaasi-teri served notice that if they did not leave, they would face a chest-pounding duel. After more maneuvering, that is what transpired (1977:113).

The two sides were about evenly matched, with either 60 (Chagnon 1977:113) or 25 to 30 (Chagnon 1972a:67) men each. But Bisaasi-teri had fierceness problems: many of its men were not joining in. That put more strain on those who did meet the challengers, and it soon became clear that Bisaasi-teri was losing. The match escalated to more painful side slapping. The hosts' position deteriorated as more men were disabled by injuries. Finally, the desperate Bisaasi-teri were thrown back into their living quarters, with their arrows ready to fire at the oncoming Mahekoto-teri. Chagnon, at this point, was actually in the house structure, crouched behind the line of bowmen. Having thus beaten their adversaries, the Mahekoto-teri slowly withdrew (Chagnon 1977: 113–17).

There were additional violent clashes involving some of these same groups, but the timing and identity of opponents is often unclear.[6] With so much uncertainty, about all that can be said is that for the Bisaasi-teri by late 1965, these additional conflicts contributed to a deteriorating political situation and reduced military support from some allies.

As to why this particularly brutal confrontation and the later clashes occurred, the sources are limited. One missionary at the time believed that the Mahekoto-teri set off to capture Bisaasi-teri women while the men were away (Chagnon 1977:104), but there is no indication that any such attempt was made or that any other conflict over women took place. Chagnon himself (1977:117) seems to see this duel as a routine test of strength that just happened to get out of hand.

From my perspective, the underlying interests in this clash are more obscure than in the case of the enemy Shamatari. The contrasting trade positions of Mahekoto-teri and Bisaasi-teri are clear, but there is no information on the direction, intensity, or terms of trade between the two prior to the club fight. How the western Namowei were using their superior trade position in relation to the Mahekoto-teri is unknown. Still, the timing of the conflict strongly suggests that it was stimulated by the new source of wealth represented by the still empty Salesian mission and the arrival of Chagnon. The clash was set up when the Mahekoto-teri heard that it was momentarily possible to approach Chagnon without Namowei interference; the violence itself was triggered when the Bisaasi-teri tried to make them leave.

Alliance and War with the Patanowa-teri

The only actual shooting war observed by Chagnon began the very moment he arrived at Boca Mavaca in November 1964 and continued with varying intensity for the duration of his stay. "This particular war got started the day I arrived in the field, (cause: woman stealing), and it is getting hotter and hotter," wrote Chagnon (1972a:68) on April 17, 1965. The initial clash occurred at the feast so dramatically portrayed in the opening of *Yanomamö* (Chagnon 1977:5). This was a protracted and complicated conflict involving the interaction of war (described in *Yanomamö* [Chagnon 1977:124–37, 1992a:191–204]) and internal factionalism (described mainly in Chagnon's thesis [1966:183–88]).

The initial feast was intended to be a major occasion—the culmination of a new alliance between Patanowa-teri and Kaobawa's village, upper Bisaasi-teri. This was the first time one had hosted the other at a feast since their antagonistic split around 1948, although their state of war had lapsed after both participated in a Mahekoto-teri feast in 1955. After 1955, the Patanowa-teri secured an alliance with the Monou-teri by ceding women to them (Chagnon 1966:176, 1977:125). Why cultivate Monou-teri? As will be demonstrated in two incidents described below, the Monou-teri controlled the trails by which the Patanowa-teri could approach Boca Mavaca. This spatial hegemony, I argue, enabled the Monou-teri to operate as an exploitative middleman. Thus it is no surprise that Monou-teri did not join in when the Bisaasi-teri feasted the Patanowa-teri: if the two established a new relationship, it could enable the Patanowa-teri to bypass the Monou-teri middlemen.

The Patanowa-teri at this point were already involved in wars with their eastern and northern neighbors in the decaying network of alliances farther up the Orinoco. They needed allies (Chagnon 1966:176, 1977:125). But the Bisaasi-teri were too far from that fighting to be of much help in combat. Furthermore, as we will see, the prospective alliance with Bisaasi-teri carried with it the risk of serious trouble with the Monou-teri. All together, this prospective alliance would be of questionable military value to the Patanowa-teri if they remained in their current location.

The timing of the feast suggests that it was related to the establishment of the Salesian mission across the river (not with the arrival of Chagnon, who actually came the day after the conflict began). The

Patanowa-teri may have been seeking Bisaasi-teri cooperation in a move to that mission, or they may have been seeking to move in with upper Bisaasi-teri. Either move would have augmented the military manpower of the Bisaasi-teri and probably given them additional wives, and would have placed the Patanowa-teri out of striking range of their eastern neighbors. (A group of Patanowa-teri did move in with Namowei at Boca Mavaca less than two years later.) It is also possible that the Patanowa-teri were simply negotiating a standard, dependent trade alliance with Bisaasi-teri, although the lack of unimpeded passage between their villages makes that seem less likely. In any possible variation, the general character of alliances makes one thing certain: more Western goods would be going to the Patanowa-teri via the Bisaasi-teri.

Such a change would represent a threat to Monou-teri interests. If a substantial number of Patanowa-teri relocated to Boca Mavaca or managed to circumvent Monou-teri as a supplier of Western goods, it would reduce Monou-teri's middleman advantages, as well as reducing Bisaasi-teri's need of them as an ally. Thus the Monou-teri had good reason to sabotage this incipient alliance, and they seized an opportunity to do so (Chagnon 1966:176–77, 1977:125).

Some Monou-teri men "discovered a group of seven Patanowa-teri females outside the main village and could not resist the temptation: They forcefully took them back to Monou-teri" (Chagnon 1977:125). The Patanowa-teri went after them, armed with clubs, and recovered five women. Then the Monou-teri threatened to ambush the Patanowa-teri on their way home, demonstrating their geographic control of the approaches to Boca Mavaca. The Patanowa-teri had to leave immediately to avoid ambush, but before leaving, they pledged to continue their efforts to develop stronger ties with the Bisaasi-teri, regardless of what developed with the Monou-teri. Thus the threat to Monou-teri's position persisted.

Indeed, the threat may have gotten worse. Around this time, the Patanowa-teri began to cultivate the old garden site at Shihota (Chagnon 1966:181–83, 1977:127). This was the location once fought over by Fusiwe and Rashawe, from which the Bisaasi-teri around 1949 developed trade to the Shamatari and subsequently jumped to the Mavaca. A repeat of either development by the Patanowa-teri would be consistent with their deepening ties to upper Bisaasi-teri, and either would weaken the position of the Monou-teri.

The Patanowa-teri were also encouraged to move west to Shihota because that would distance them from their eastern enemies—the

Hasupuwe-teri and others. A move to Shihota would thus follow the standard practice of moving away from one's enemies and at the same time getting closer to the source of Western goods. If the Patanowa-teri succeeded in establishing themselves at Shihota, the Monou-teri, outnumbered by Patanowa-teri males by three-and-a-half to one, would be hard pressed to oppose them. The Monou-teri prepared for war, clearing a new and more defensible garden across the Mavaca (Chagnon 1966: 178).

The upper Bisaasi-teri then took a step that clearly displayed their feelings in this conflict. They took one of the abducted Patanowa-teri women away from the man who claimed her, with the understanding that she might go back with the Patanowa-teri the next time they visited. In the face of this open affront, the Monou-teri had little choice but to challenge the upper Bisaasi-teri men to a club fight, in which Monou-teri was "thoroughly trounced" (Chagnon 1966:178–79).

It was in this context that Monou-teri took a risky and ultimately costly step: "After they had cleared the large trees from their new garden site, they raided the Patanowa-tedi in the last week of January 1965, and succeeded in killing Bosibrei" (Chagnon 1966:178).[7] According to Chagnon (1977:125) the reason for this raid was that the Monou-teri headman, Damowa, "was angry because the Patanowa-teri had recovered so many of their women." I believe there were more strategic considerations involved.

By raiding the Patanowa-teri at this moment, the Monou-teri could hope to deter them from moving to Shihota. The Patanowa-teri were harried by old enemies to their east and north, so the Monou-teri could reasonably expect that they would avoid a new war to their west. If they followed standard practice, the Patanowa-teri would move away from all their enemies, southward toward their only active ally in the area, the Ashatowa-teri. That is exactly what the Patanowa-teri did, but only temporarily. They also kept visiting Shihota (Chagnon 1966:182, 1977:127). And what the Monou-teri obviously did not anticipate was how swift and deadly Patanowa-teri retaliation could be. In the first week of March, Patanowa-teri raiders crossed the Mavaca. They found Damowa, the fierce Monou-teri headman, outside his new garden and killed him with a volley of arrows (Chagnon 1966:179, 1977:126). (Although Damowa was accompanied by his two wives, the Patanowa-teri made no effort to capture them.)

The killing of Damowa left the Monou-teri without military leadership. When Damowa's wives reached the Monou-teri camp with word of the attack, the others fled into the forest rather than give pursuit. "For a while there was no leadership whatsoever in Monou-teri" (Chagnon 1977:126). A headman is the capstone of a residential group. The killing of Damowa at such a crucial moment created a complex and unstable political situation—a real crisis. Dealing with that crisis involved all the other political conflicts going on at the same time, and it is at this moment we see most forcefully how complex—how "unprimitive"—Yanomami politics can be.

Damowa was killed in early March. Recall that by early February, the Bisaasi-teri had to contend with threats from both enemy Shamatari up the Mavaca and belligerent Mahekoto-teri up the Orinoco (see note 6). They were in need of any military supporters they could get. So it is understandable that the upper Bisaasi-teri headman, Kaobawa, stepped into the leadership vacuum (Chagnon 1966:179–80, 1977:126). Apparently "furious" about the killing of his classificatory brother, he "assumed the responsibility of organizing a revenge raid" (Chagnon 1977: 126). The recent rift between his group and the Monou-teri was patched up, and in late March the Monou-teri were allowed to move into Bisaasi-teri for protection while they continued to develop their new garden. An incipient line of fission within upper Bisaasi-teri also closed up in this dangerous time, as all moved into a new, well-fortified *shabono* that the Monou-teri helped construct (Chagnon 1977:127). Thus Kaobawa made himself the leader of a large number of men, well prepared for war.

Now Kaobawa faced a delicate political situation. He had accepted public responsibility for avenging Damowa, but his political interest up to this point had been to develop a relationship with the Patanowa-teri. As will soon be seen, that interest did not change. Only some rather exceptional luck allowed Kaobawa to follow through on both accounts.

Kaobawa prepared to raid the Patanowa-teri but delayed until just before the rains began, to minimize the chance of retaliation. The warriors left Bisaasi-teri on April 21, 1965, returning on May 2 (Chagnon 1966:180–81, 1977:128–33). If Kaobawa were to participate in killing any Patanowa-teri, an alliance with them would be much more difficult to accomplish. Thus it was fortunate that after the raiding party set out, pains in his lower torso forced him to turn back, with his brother, before reaching the Patanowa-teri. Arriving home, they "staggered into the village, nearly dead from exhaustion." Who could blame them for turning back, being hardly able to walk? It was another stroke of luck that while returning, they happened to find a dugout canoe that Kaobawa's son-in-law happened to have concealed along their route (Chagnon 1977: 132–33).

After Kaobawa turned back, the raiders continued on their mission. They encountered a Patanowa-teri at the Shihota garden and killed him. Retreating, they were overtaken and ambushed by Patanowa-teri, who severely wounded one of the raiders. Chagnon helped nurse him back to health (1966:181, 1977:133).

With this raid, "Kaobawa felt that he had satisfied his obligation to avenge Damowa's death. The Monou-teri, however, wanted to prosecute the war further and continue raiding" (Chagnon 1977:133)—even though they were now ahead in the body count, two to one. The two groups had different interests because the Monou-teri were still threatened by the Patanowa-teri, while upper Bisaasi-teri still wanted to develop ties to them.

From after the killing of Damowa in March until late April, the Monou-teri had been living largely off of others' gardens. They had failed to pursue the raiders who killed Damowa or to raid on their own, and they were standing in the way of the alliance that Kaobawa was intent on developing. Soon they were "being treated like pariahs by their allies" (Chagnon 1977:128). So, just after the raid Kaobawa organized, the Monou-teri returned to their new garden, "as the jungle separating their village from the Patanowa-tedi is inundated at this time of the year and cannot be traversed" (Chagnon 1966:180). But if the Monou-teri did not take decisive action soon, their viability as an independent group would be in real jeopardy. They had the high-water time of May and June to think about it.

Fortunately for the Monou-teri, before the 1965 rainy season came to a close, Chagnon discovered the genealogical frauds perpetrated by the Bisaasi-teri and moved into his more aggressive and independent phase of fieldwork. Around the end of the rainy season—which probably means around mid-June (Chagnon 1966:181)—a small Monou-teri raiding party, only ten men, prepared to raid the Patanowa-teri (Chagnon 1977:134–37). Chagnon was staying at Monou-teri at the time, and his presence would give the village some protection while its men were away.

But he was a more active participant than that. The night before the raid, during the ceremonial mourning for the slain Damowa, Chagnon writes, "I allowed them to talk me into taking the entire raiding party up the Mavaca River in my canoe. There, they could find high ground and reach the Patanowa-teri without having to cross the numerous swamps that lay between the two villages" (1977:135).

This assistance gave the Monou-teri a significant advantage. Because of the impassable swamps, the intended victims would not be taking the precautions of a village expecting raiders. Canoe transport also allowed the raiders to start the trip with an "enormous supply of plantains" (Chagnon 1977:135). This was "the only time Yanomamo ever expressed gratitude to me," wrote Chagnon (1977:135).

As it turned out, the raiders could not locate the Patanowa-teri, and they returned in about a week. Altogether, the Monou-teri did not change anything with this raid, except perhaps to lessen their reputation as cowards. But equally, it demonstrated that they would scarcely be able to carry on a war with the powerful Patanowa-teri all by themselves. They would need allies, despite Kaobawa's unwillingness to fight. On June 20, the Monou-teri moved back into Bisaasi-teri (Chagnon 1966:181). At this point, the internal politics of upper Bisaasi-teri come to the fore.

Factionalism and War

Prior to this conflict, upper Bisaasi-teri had been divided into two factions living in separate *shabonos* a few yards apart (Chagnon 1966: 129, 183–84, 1977:127). Kaobawa, "who had many relatives in both Patanowa-tedi and Monou-tedi," led the larger faction; Paruriwa, "who had no consanguineal relatives in Patanowa-tedi, but many in Monou-tedi," led the smaller (1966:184). As head of the largest kin group in the village, Kaobawa was the "acknowledged leader of the entire upper section of Bisaasi-tedi, including Paruriwa's group" (1966: 184), although the latter was a man of some influence. When Koboawa refused to lead any more raids, he left "a political vacuum within Bisaasi-tedi, as the Monou-tedi were demanding military aid from them. Paruriwa seized upon this as his opportunity to advance his prestige, and after the middle of 1965 initiated several raids against the Patanowa-tedi without the support of Kaobawa" (1966:184–85).

The rivers fell early in 1965, and Paruriwa's first raiding party left Bisaasi-teri on July 10. His men were accompanied by Monou-teri men and some others from Momaribowei-teri and Reyabobowei-teri. They found that the Patanowa-teri had gone to stay with their allies, the Ashatowa-teri, and decided to turn back, to the displeasure of the

Monou-teri (Chagnon 1966:181–82, 1977:133–34). Paruriwa would lead raids, but his heart was not in it. "As Paruriwa was not related to the slain Monou-tedi headman (consanguineally), his participation in the war is best seen as an expression of his attempt to advance his status" (Chagnon 1966:185).

Commensurate with his new leadership role, Paruriwa began to act like a headman.

> After the middle of the year, Paruriwa began to emerge as leader in his own right, and began duplicating many of the activities normally the prerogative of the village headman. Thus, when Kaobawa initiated a feast for members of an allied village, Paruriwa duplicated his efforts by sending out his own hunters to provide meat for the guests, and furnished an equal amount of cultivated food, which he disposed of from his own section of the village. Normally, the headman sends out the hunters and disposes of the cultivated food from his own house. Paruriwa, by duplicating Koabowa's efforts in these activities, announced that he was a headman. (Chagnon 1966:184)

He had little success, however, in getting others to accept his claim: "Visitors from other villages consistently sought out Kaobawa as Bisaasi-tedi's headman during the feasts and the trading after the feasts, no matter how much effort Paruriwa spent in emphasizing his own role in the feast" (Chagnon 1966:185). Could it be that Kaobawa had more Western goods to trade?

Paruriwa also sought Chagnon's recognition. "He wanted to be the village leader and privately told me to address him as the headman" (Chagnon 1977:94). "He constantly reminded me that he was a 'big man', as if I would fail to notice this" (Chagnon 1966:185). But there was a great difference between Chagnon's close relationship with Kaobawa—"the wise leader" (1977:14), "the quiet unpretentious headman" (1983:125)—and his antipathy for Paruriwa, "a very cunning, treacherous fellow" (1977:94). Kaobawa is portrayed as "unobtrusive, calm, modest, and perceptive," while Paruriwa is "belligerent, aggressive, ostentatious, and rash" (Chagnon 1977:96). In time, Kaobawa became one of Chagnon's principal informants and friends (1977:13–14). Chagnon's association with Kaobawa would have important consequences in the next event in this sequence.

In July 1965, Kaobawa sent his brother-in-law to the Patanowa-teri to inform them that his group did not intend to raid them anymore

(Chagnon 1966:186–87, 1977:93–94). The emissary returned with two older Patanowa-teri people—a sign of trust. They carried the message that a delegation of men would follow, and it arrived a few days later. Paruriwa's group was visiting the Witokaya-teri at this time. When he heard about the meeting going on at Bisaasi-teri, Paruriwa and a group of Monou-teri men rushed back, "intending to murder the three visitors" (Chagnon 1966:186). Kaobawa warned Paruriwa that he was prepared to defend the visitors with force.

> A crisis developed out of this situation, and for a whole day Paruriwa and his Monou-tedi supporters debated the wisdom of their plan. Finally, Paruriwa decided to desist from the murder. . . . The Monou-tedi who were to participate in the murder of the three visitors were enraged because Paruriwa failed to execute the plan, and they returned to Monou-tedi to recruit a raiding party, hoping to intercept the visitors on their way back to Patanowa-tedi. (Chagnon 1966:186–87)

"Their plan failed," Chagnon adds in a footnote, "as I took the Patanowa-tedi back to their village part way in my boat, and we went the remainder of the way on a trail the Monou-tedi could not reach" (1966: 187). He did this after Kaobawa, realizing the danger of ambush on the return trip, "visited me that night and asked me to take the visitors back to their village" (Chagnon 1977:94). (Chagnon had wanted to visit the Patanowa-teri anyway.) Without in any sense implying that Chagnon should have let these men be ambushed, it must be recognized that his action was a significant political event. In a crisis, Chagnon had sided with Kaobawa in his effort to develop ties to the Patanowa-teri, and he had provided a means of transport that neutralized the Monou-teri's trump card, their dominance of the footpaths between Boca Mavaca and Patanowa-teri.

Before continuing the narrative of events at Boca Mavaca, I must digress to the strategic situation of the Patanowa-teri at this moment. When the travel season began in July 1965, Patanowa-teri found itself besieged from all directions but the south (Chagnon 1966:182, 1977: 41, 127). After the Monou-teri and Bisaasi-teri raided them, their three old enemies to the east began to raid with increased intensity, although their interests in doing so are opaque. The western Namowei's Shamatari allies and several other unspecified groups also sent raiders, until the number of enemy villages reached about a dozen.

Many of them joined the hostilities because they knew that the Patanowa-teri could not defend themselves against a host of enemies. The new belligerents, therefore, stood a good chance of abducting women while being relatively immune to punitive raids. They could also discharge obligations to their allies by supporting their raids against the Patanowa-teri without exposing themselves to great danger. (Chagnon 1977:41)

In this instance, my perspective does not differ from Chagnon's. The costs of joining one of many raiding parties were unusually low. Young bachelors dreaming of capturing a wife, encouraged by their fathers who saw the political benefits of participation, no doubt swelled the number of raiders. But it should be noted that this was an extremely unusual level of hostility for the Yanomami. With one late exception discussed in chapter 14, I know of no other case in which so many villages raided one village at the same time. The Orinoco-Mavaca area was an extraordinarily violent place in 1965.

The raids against Patanowa-teri reached high intensity by July, the month in which Paruriwa led the aborted raid and the Patanowateri emissaries visited Bisaasi-teri (Chagnon 1966:182–83, 1977:127). Overall, the Patanowa-teri were raided "at least twenty-five times while I conducted my fieldwork" (Chagnon 1977:127). They suffered about eight deaths. Nevertheless, strategically they were winning the war.

They managed to drive the Hasupuwe-teri across the Orinoco in July, and they continued to raid it until "their fierce ones were all dead, and nobody was interested in prosecuting the war any further" (Chagnon 1977:127). Another factor encouraging the Hasupuwe-teri to move away from the war may have been renewed outreach by an order of Catholic brothers who, in early 1966, were urging the Hasupuwe-teri to settle closer to the river in order to "enjoy the goods of civilization" (Steinvorth de Goetz 1969:74). In any case, as time passed, the war in the east died down. This left the Patanowa-teri, who had continued to use the Shihota garden site, free to concentrate on the Monou-teri.

That brings us back to Boca Mavaca, in July of 1965. Paruriwa had made a claim to be the village headman but had backed down from Kaobawa. Chagnon had sided decisively with Kaobawa and the Patanowateri. The next few months are rather murky, but they were not good ones for the Monou-teri. It seems that they undertook no raids from Boca Mavaca against the Patanowa-teri between the one led by Paruriwa on

July 10 and the following November.[8] After the July raid, the Monou-teri alternated between their old village, their new garden, and Bisaasi-teri. The Patanowa-teri began stepping up their incursions to the Mavaca, and "signs of the Patanowa-tedi raiders were found numerous times at the old site of Monou-tedi" (Chagnon 1966:182). Although there is no indication that the Monou-teri were actually attacked by Patanowa-teri raiders, the prospect of a Patanowa-teri move to the Mavaca was now all the more credible.

While the Monou-teri were fearfully trudging from place to place, Paruriwa, at upper Bisaasi-teri, embarked on a new course of action. Because of his political defeat by Kaobawa, "Paruriwa decided to move away from Kaobawa's group" (Chagnon 1966:186), and he began to build a house on the other side of the river. But he did not move away until Chagnon had gone: "Shortly after I left the field, Paruriwa and his group separated from Kaobawa's and moved across the Orinoco" (Chagnon 1966:185). In a chapter added to the 1977 edition of *Yanomamö*, Chagnon (1977:151) adds a crucial detail: "The Salesian priest across the river had taken advantage of the fact that a fission was developing in Kaobawa's village and that Paruriwa . . . was emerging as a strong leader in the dissident faction: he lured Paruriwa and his group across the river with generous gifts of outboard motors, shotguns, and other desirable trade commodities." [9] Thus fissioned upper Bisaasi-teri.

I reconstruct Paruriwa's changing interests this way: Before being faced down in July, he hoped that by putting himself at the head of the Monou-teri, in addition to his own Bisaasi-teri faction, he could replace Kaobawa as leader of upper Bisaasi-teri and be treated accordingly. Then he would dominate several rich sources of Western goods: the resident NTM missionary, the malaria station, Chagnon, and the unoccupied Catholic mission across the river. After backing down from Kaobawa and in the process both losing the Monou-teri's allegiance and seeing Chagnon act in support of Kaobawa, he knew his plan' would fail. At this point he began work on his house by the mission, but he held off moving while Chagnon remained in upper Bisaasi-teri, in the meantime allowing the priest to make him generous gifts.

But Paruriwa's interests would still be jeopardized if the Patanowa-teri vanquished the Monou-teri and followed through by moving toward Boca Mavaca. Thus Paruriwa rallied available forces against Patanowa-teri, inviting the Monou-teri to come and stay in his section of Bisaasi-teri (Chagnon 1966:187). "By early November, the Monou-tedi had begun raiding the Patanowa-tedi with great frequency, supported by members of Paururiwa's group. Paruriwa himself sent three raiding parties against the Patanowa-tedi between November and February, all of which included men from Monou-tedi" (1966:187). (Since Chagnon [1977:134] elsewhere tells us that the Monou-teri and Bisaasi-teri launched a total of six raids during his time in the field, and this narrative has already discussed four, I take it that three was the total number of raids sent against the Patanowa-teri during this period; see note 8.)

One of the raiding parties, apparently the last one, made up of Monou-teri, some Patanowa-teri defectors, and presumably some of Paruriwa's followers, finally managed to kill a Patanowa-teri man (Chagnon 1966:189). This is the first reported death in the war since April, and apparently it was the last.[10] By sending raiders at them, Paruriwa demonstrated to the Patanowa-teri that they would still be risking their lives to come to the Mavaca and gave himself breathing room to follow through on his plans.

After so long at war, tensions and factionalism were high among the Patanowa-teri (Chagnon 1966:188–89, 1977:120). It will be recalled that the Patanowa-teri were made up of a few major divisions (the eastern Namowei) that had united for defense. The alliance was now coming apart. A month before Chagnon left the field, a fight developed over a woman. It escalated out of control until the headman killed another man by spearing him with a sharpened club. The dead man's faction was then "ordered to leave the village before there was further bloodshed" (Chagnon 1977:120).

The Patanowa-teri headman was a close agnatic kinsman of Kaobawa, and so presumably his faction was involved in the negotiations for an alliance. The faction that was ordered to leave went to live with its relatives in Monou-teri and with the Bisaasi-teri (those linked to Paruriwa's faction?). From there it participated in raids on its former co-residents, the Patanowa-teri. "The hosts, of course, took several women from the refugees" (Chagnon 1977:120). Shortly after the defectors' arrival, Chagnon left the field, and Paruriwa moved his followers to the mission.

This lengthy discussion of the politics involved in the war with the Patanowa-teri has relied entirely on data provided by Chagnon. Our narratives have been different: he presented data as ethnographic illustrations of many different points, while I have brought them together into one unified political history. We have little or no substantive disagreement about what happened. Where we differ is over why these events occurred when, where, and how they did. Chagnon explains the war as having been initiated and carried along by emotional impulses. The war begins when some men cannot resist the temptation to capture a vulnerable group of women, and it escalates to raiding because a headman is angry that most of the women were taken back. The war continues out of rage and desire for revenge, and it is complicated by a factional struggle within Bisaasi-teri that is motivated by a quest for social status.

My point, in contrast, is that all these events display a pattern—one consistent with the demonstrated pattern of all Yanomami warfare—in which actors employ force instrumentally in order to enhance their access to and control over Western goods. From my perspective, the Westerners themselves are significant political actors. I have focused on the role of Napoleon Chagnon, but only because he writes about himself. There is virtually no information—only the few crucial bits that I have noted here—about the activities of the missionaries or malaria workers. But I should emphasize here that the presence of the empty mission was itself probably as or more significant than Chagnon's presence in affecting the course of events.

14

The Yanomamo, 1966 to 1992: Acculturation Accelerates

Material for this final chapter on the Yanomamo is rather unruly for narrative purposes, with weaker information about some of the main groups of previous chapters and substantial accounts about other areas. Some of the best description comes from more remote areas, probably because initial contacts with deep forest groups are more likely to be reported than are increasingly routine interactions with visibly acculturating people along the rivers. As all the different areas come momentarily into view, they provide a composite picture of increasing Yanomamo contact with Westerners on a regional level. Because of both the gaps in local histories and the evident connection of local events to regional processes, I have organized all discussions in this chapter around one unified chronology rather than discuss groups outside the Orinoco-Mavaca area separately, as I did in earlier chapters.

The Last Quarter-Century of Contact

From the middle 1960s onward, the Western presence on the upper Orinoco intensified and radiated outward. By 1965, an airstrip was being operated by the Salesian mission on the Ocamo—some 70 kilometers beyond the Esmeralda airstrip—and it became a gateway for more Westerners and supplies (Steinvorth de Goetz 1969:8, 11). Ethnographic research continued. In late 1966, Inga Steinvorth de Goetz (1969; Cocco 1972:101–102) began her sojourns along the far upper Orinoco, from the Raudal de Guajaribos all the way to the river's source, and later along the upper Ocamo. She returned to the region for months at a time into at least the 1970s. In January 1968, anthropologist Jacques Lizot began an unusually protracted stay among the Yanomami. He would live with the Karohi-teri and Tayari-teri, with visits to several other villages, for much of the time until at least the late 1980s (Lizot 1971:32, 1976:6, 1989:34).

Napoleon Chagnon ended his original fieldwork in February 1966. He returned for one- and four-month visits to the upper Orinoco in 1967 and 1968, prior to the publication of *Yanomamö: The Fierce People* (Chagnon 1977:1). Since then, he has returned regularly to the area, except for a period from 1976 to 1985 (Chagnon 1992b:144), spending about 49 additional months with Yanomami (1992a:8). Except for an occasional comment or footnote, however, Chagnon has written little more about the political events he witnessed during his initial fieldwork. In terms of historical descriptions of war, the fifth edition of *Yanomamö* (1992b:182–238) remains substantially unchanged from the first edition (1968:97–137).

From late 1968 through 1972, Chagnon (1974, 1977:1, 152–54, 1983:30–41) extended his geographic research area, focusing on the Mishimishimabowei-teri, one of the "enemy Shamatari" groups up the Mavaca. He often returned as part of fairly large expeditions that included biomedical researchers and a filmmaker (Asch 1972, 1979, 1988). On an expedition arriving in April 1975, he was accompanied by Robert Carneiro and William Sanders and by graduate students Eric Fredlund, Kenneth Good, and Raymond Hames (Good 1991:22). Good (1989:5, 1991) has maintained frequent contact with villages around and beyond the Raudal de Guajaribos up to the present.

Of far greater consequence for the Yanomamo, however, was the growth of missionary activity. In 1966, a Catholic brother named Iglesias, operating out of Platanal, was dealing with groups in the forest beyond the Raudal de Guajaribos. He invited the Hasupuwe-teri "to move to a place closer to the Orinoco, so that they could thus enjoy the goods of civilization" (Steinvorth de Goetz 1969:74). They quickly did so. By 1967, the Catholics already had begun taking a few Yanomamo children into a boarding school near Puerto Ayacucho and to their trade school in Caracas (Chagnon 1977:159), beginning an intensified direct assault on Yanomami culture. Although little is reported about life around the main mission posts, the march toward assimilation appears to have continued unabated. In 1971, the headman of the Iyewei-teri—a leader among the Yanomamo in commercial farming of plantains—was even taken to Rome to meet the Pope (Chagnon 1977:144).

In what appears to be late 1967 or early 1968, New Tribes missionaries from the Orinoco trekked up to a savanna in the Parima highlands, where they cleared a landing strip. There they began a new mission in a previously "isolated" area (Alès and Chiappino 1985:80–81; Jank 1977:20–25). A couple of years later, this mission served as anthropologist William Smole's research base (Smole 1976). Developments in the areas of new direct contact will be shown to have followed familiar patterns. But in the areas of established contact with the river missions, the acculturation process would enter a qualitatively different and more destructive phase in the decade after 1965.

Looking back from the mid-1970s, both Chagnon (1977:145–51, 154–62) and Lizot (1976) provide scathing assessments of missionization. One indictment is the missions' disregard for the epidemiological consequences of intensifying contact. Chagnon (1992a:240–41) tells of one incident—and Lizot (1976:25, 33) supports this account—when he was working with a biomedical research team in 1968, vaccinating groups in a race against a spreading and very lethal epidemic of measles. Chagnon passed through Platanal while the Mahekoto-teri were away, to discover a Brazilian employee of the mission sick with the disease. He urged the missionaries and the government Indian Commission physician to remove the man before the unvaccinated Mahekoto-teri returned. They didn't, and the Westerners abandoned the village after the epidemic broke out, "leaving the Yanomamo to fend for themselves" (Chagnon 1992a:241).

The Mahekoto-teri lost 11 people, according to Cocco (1972:417), or about 25 percent of their population, according to Chagnon. Numerous other villages around the area of mission activity—including the Hasupuwe-teri and Shipariwe-teri—suffered in this epidemic, with death rates of 20 percent to 30 percent. Generally, in this and other epidemics, when Yanomamo at a mission became sick, more would recover through the missionary's care than would survive in villages with only occasional outside contacts (Chagnon 1977:146, 1992a:241; Cocco 1972:176, 417; J. Dawson 1964:2).

Nevertheless, the missionaries' attitude toward the Yanomamo remained about what it was in the 1950s: the Yanomamo were not quite human (Chagnon 1977:151, Lizot 1976:5). Most of the missionaries were determined to place religious conversion above all else. Chagnon wrote (1977:151), "I once put a hypothetical question to a Protestant missionary as follows: Would you risk exposing 200 Yanomamo to some infectious disease if you thought you could save one of them from Hell— and the other 199 died from the disease: His answer was unequivocal and firm: Yes."

Some improvement in medical care after 1968 is credited to the efforts of nursing nuns and the malaria service workers—including one of Helena Valero's sons (Good 1991:43). On the other hand, the increasing number of outsiders in the region in the 1970s led to increasing respiratory infections, and severe malaria outbreaks occurred despite government efforts (Lizot 1976:24–26, 30).

Another charge is that the missionaries gave or loaned out shotguns, ostensibly for hunting, which actually were used in war. Although Chagnon (1977:122) once noted that "the missionaries are very cautious about loaning the Yanomamo firearms, knowing that these would be used in the wars," more recently he has emphasized a history of missionary laxity and unwillingness to accept or act on reports of raiding using shotguns, a practice that the Yanomamo "assiduously conceal" from the missionaries (Chagnon 1992a:220). The missions, however, were not the only source of shotguns and ammunition; they were also given out by expeditions, scientists, employees of the government malaria station, and others (Misioneros 1991:28–29). Whatever their source, the proliferation of shotguns contributed to more violence.

The headman of Iyewei-teri was the first local Yanomami to acquire a shotgun, in 1957. No Yanomamo around Boca Mavaca owned a shotgun when Chagnon began his fieldwork in 1964 (Chagnon 1983:57), but borrowed shotguns were used in a fight north of Bisaasi-teri late during that fieldwork. Shotguns became more common from then on, coming from local sources and from trade out of Brazil, where they were frequently obtained from woodsmen (Chagnon 1977:149; Cocco 1972:189). By 1970, there were at least 25 shotguns in the area, which had been used in seven killings (Cocco 1972:189). By 1975, there were 40 shotguns (Chagnon 1983:57), and one man alone had used his to kill "at least three people" (Chagnon 1977:149). Around that time, the paths leading from Brazilian Yanomami villages through the Siapa to the upper Mavaca became known as "the trail of the shotguns" (Misioneros 1991:28).

The possession of shotguns dramatically tips the scales of military capability and can significantly lower the threshold for war. Chagnon goes so far as to say, "Some of the raids in which shotguns have been used were conducted only because the raiders had a new superior weapon and wanted to try it out—the possession of the gun *caused* wars where none previously existed" (1977:149). While I would question whether possession of a shotgun is ever the only reason for a raid, it certainly can be the deciding factor in a tense situation.

The first half of the 1970s saw a further intensification of the assault on Yanomamo culture, with major changes in government policy and mission activity. In 1970, the Venezuelan government announced its project CODESUR—Commission for the Development of the South or, colloquially, Conquest of the South—aimed at economic development, geographic integration, and cultural assimilation of its wild southern region, including the lands of the Yanomami (Zent 1992:chapter 3). In 1971, the CODESUR project cleared an airstrip at Platanal (Chagnon 1977:148) and lengthened the one on the Ocamo to accommodate large planes (Cocco 1972:110). Census and border commission parties went up the Ocamo and part of the Siapa (Cocco 1972:110; Lizot 1974, 1988: 110). This spurt of activity brought a "tremendous amount of goods and services" into southern Venezuela, but it was short-lived; CODESUR was "basically abandoned by 1975" (Frechione 1990:121).

Even greater changes were in store on the religious front. In the competition for souls, the Catholic missionaries had the considerable advantage of acting, by contract with the government, as secular authorities for the area (Chagnon 1992a:217; Lizot 1976:22). Sometime between 1970 (Cocco 1972:26) and 1975 (Lizot 1976:36), the New Tribes Mission abandoned its post at Boca Mavaca, conceding the field to the Catholics. The New Tribes Mission did not retire, however; it built a new landing strip and mission ("Koyowe") on the Orinoquito, a tributary of the far upper Orinoco, and continued its mission efforts in the Parima highlands (Alès and Chiappino 1985:80; Lizot 1976:36, 1988:577).

Around 1971, a new and more active administrator took over the Salesian mission at Platanal. This priest

> embarked on a vigorous campaign to promote tourism and civilization with a passion that would have embarrassed the Conquistadores. A tour agent in Caracas soon had a fleet of sleek speedboats there and the priest kept him supplied with ample quantities of gasoline. He also built a number of guest houses to accommodate the visitors and soon the mission was a booming tourist center. Direct flights from Munich and other European cities were advertised in 1973, stopping briefly in Caracas for a

changeover to a small twin-engine craft that would fly them directly to the Yanomamo village of Mahekodo-teri on the Upper
Orinoco, and into the Stone Age. (Chagnon 1977:148)

The tourism peaked between 1972 and 1974. In 1975, Chagnon found
some forty Brazilians living at Platanal and working in support of the
tourist operation. But some restriction of tourist entry began that same
year.

In 1972, the Catholics opened a new boarding school at La Esmeralda (Lizot 1976:19). They aggressively recruited children down to age
six or seven (Chagnon 1977:159). Lizot (1976:19) portrays the recruitment as nothing less than kidnapping. Parents, however, "were 'com-
pensated' for their temporary losses by well-calculated gifts" (Chagnon
1977:159). Conditions and treatment at the school were provoking
widespread avoidance of it by mid-1975 (Lizot 1976:20–22). But many
stayed on. At the boarding school, the children saw their own culture
undermined in various ways, and they were taught the basics of becoming non-Yanomami (Chagnon 1977:159–60; Lizot 1976:20–21).
In 1975 Lizot (1976:16) wrote: "The great projected intention is to
place at the head of these communities young Indians who have been
educated in the religious boarding-schools and trained in obeisance." In
the 1980s, that goal would become a reality.

This direct assault on Yanomamo culture, however, was only the tip
of the iceberg. By around 1975, some eight to ten villages in the area
had regular, direct contact with Westerners (Chagnon 1983:57), and the
people's lives were well on their way to transformation (Chagnon 1977:
148–49; Lizot 1976:8–9, 13–18). New hunting patterns and larger
populations had wiped out accessible game and even some fish. Trade,
marriage and alliance patterns, material production, and internal leadership were by now obviously shaped by dependency on the Westerners.
Communal residence broke down into nuclear huts as theft of Western goods became a major social problem. Thus the missions' teachings
only contributed to what was a situationally inescapable crisis in values
as Yanomami came to mime the *nape*.

In 1975, the Catholic missions went through an internal reform
(Comité 1983:50–52; Peña Vargas 1981:14). Older missionaries, including Cocco, were replaced by a new breed whom Lizot (1988:577)
found to be more open-minded about retention of aspects of Yanomami
culture. Sister María Isabel Eguillor García describes Catholic efforts
since 1976 as aimed at conserving the Yanomami's culture while pre-

paring them to interact with and represent their own interests in the outside world (Eguillor 1991). But Chagnon—who in recent years has become involved in an open conflict with the Salesians—is critical of what he portrays as the assimilationist policy of the missions and their continuing efforts to induce remote groups to relocate closer to the missions.[1] He illustrates the latter with an event from around the mid-1970s, when the Salesians at Boca Mavaca persuaded a segment of the Mishimishimabowei-teri to relocate farther down the Mavaca, where the Catholics established a satellite mission called Mavakita (Chagnon 1992a:223, and see Chagnon 1993b).

At this moment—1976—historical information about the Orinoco-Mavaca Yanomamo declines precipitously. One reason is that from 1976 to 1985, Chagnon, usually one of the best sources of contextual information, was denied permission in Venezuela to work with the Yanomami (Chagnon 1992b:144, and see 1983:204). I found almost no information for the years from 1976 until the early 1980s, and most of what there is pertains to one war against the Tayari-teri. One intriguing item, however, is a 1980 count of possessions among the Cinc-teri, an offshoot of the Bisaasi-teri named for their zinc-roofed houses (Eguillor García 1984:24–25, 236). It indicates that Western goods remained in short supply in the late 1970s: the quantities of key possessions (axes, machetes, knives, pots) are only slightly higher per family than they were in a relatively isolated interior group around 1969 (Lizot 1971:45).

The lack of information is even more complete for other Yanomamo areas. I found extremely little about conditions on the north bank of the Río Negro, although it appears that mission-induced acculturation was proceeding apace, and by the mid-1980s animal trappers were entering Yanomamo lands (O'Hanlon 1990:147). Hames's (1983) reconstruction of Padamo Yanomamo history contains almost nothing about changing contact circumstances and ends in 1976. Two Protestant missions on the Padamo were still operating in the early 1980s (Comité 1983:48). In the Parima highlands, at some time prior to 1980, the New Tribes Mission established a second, occasionally staffed satellite post ("Parima A") to the southeast of the mission ("Parima B") they had created in the late 1960s. In 1982, the Venezuelan government began to establish its own presence, including medical stations, in this area (Alès and Chiappino 1985:81).

Somewhat more extensive information documents the erosion of the "isolation" of the Siapa River groups. Boundary commission parties, including Lizot (1974), had visited several villages near the river in 1972 and 1973 (Chagnon 1992a:210). In late 1976, Ken Good (1991:86ff., 105ff., 167ff.) trekked overland to make first direct contact with groups in the upper Siapa, where he would return on several later occasions. According to one local recollection, the Venezuelan Ministry of Mines sent a party into the lower Siapa around 1978, and some Italian botanists went there around 1981 (O'Hanlon 1990:152). In 1982, Good (1991:167ff.) participated in a government census of the Siapa area by helicopter, landing in one village.

Around 1985, the adventurer O'Hanlon (1990:143–53, 164–65, 211–17) visited a Brazilian living at the juncture of the Siapa and the Casiquiare. A group of Yanomamo had relocated close by in order to trade, and their degree of acculturation suggests this was a relationship of some years' standing. They knew how to use canoes and had traveled as far as La Esmeralda. O'Hanlon's own journey brought him into contact—first contact, he believes—with a related group living on the Emoni, a tributary of the lower Siapa. Of course, along with these incidents of direct contact, all the villages around the Siapa had long-established lines of communication and trade that stretched to the Orinoco and the Río Negro (Chagnon 1992a:210; Lizot 1973:8–9; and see map 2).

Information about the Orinoco-Mavaca area picks up again around 1983. The Western institutional presence was now very substantial. Along with the malaria post, Catholic missions—each with an airstrip, dispensary, and school—continued at Platanal, Boca Mavaca, and Boca Ocamo, and there was a school at the satellite station of Mavakita (Comité 1983:48). Around Boca Mavaca, the center of the Catholic sphere of influence, the Yanomami population was growing and at the same time dividing into smaller clusters: 4 settlements in 1976 had grown to 7 in 1983, with a total of 422 people spread out over 7 kilometers of river shore (Eguillor García 1984:26–28, 44). In 1985, the number of settlements had grown to 12, and the population to around 500 (Good 1991:250)—more than double the 1968 population at Boca Mavaca (Chagnon 1992a:222).

By 1983, a web of administrative control was forming over the Orinoco-Mavaca area. In addition to the often imperious Yecuana government agents (Comité 1983:53), a new breed of Yanomamo, trained in the boarding schools, began to emerge as leaders. Backed by missionary and government officials and operating over large areas, these highly acculturated young men aggressively pursued their own self-aggrandizement (Chagnon 1992a:217–18, 224; Good 1991:182, 211, 225).

In the mid-1980s, the Salesians organized most of the river settlements into a cooperative: Shabonos Unidos de los Yanomamo del Alto Orinoco (SUYAO) (Bórtoli 1991; Chagnon 1992a:218–19; Guzman 1991). SUYAO's stated goals were to develop mutual assistance in production, commercial activities, acquisition of goods, transportation, and credit; to promote indigenous cultural values; and to encourage local capital formation (Bórtoli 1991:52).

According to Chagnon (1992a:223–26), the Salesians continued their efforts to attract remote groups. In 1985 and again in 1987, these efforts prompted two Shamatari groups to relocate farther down the Mavaca. Their new locations left these people more exposed to infections yet still too distant for effective medical care by the understaffed missions. A curve of mortality is apparent in recent epidemics, in which the intermediate groups have about four times the deaths of those who are under direct mission care and three times the deaths of those isolated from the missions. As of about 1990, however, according to one Venezuelan medical authority (Botto 1991:11), "probably no communities exist which are 'uncontacted' by viral, bacterial and parasitic agents."

The late 1980s saw a new round of shotgun proliferation along the Orinoco. In 1989, SUYAO began stocking them. Chagnon (1993b) asserts that until 1991, it was Salesian "policy" to "attract converts by offering shotguns." Chagnon links this policy to an increase in war in the late 1980s. Unidentified mission villages, well armed with shotguns and now having another tactical advantage in possessing motorized canoes, began attacking unspecified, more isolated groups (Chagnon 1992a: 219–20). A similar increase in shotguns and shotgun killings is noted for Brazilian mission areas from the middle 1980s onward (Chagnon 1992a:221; O'Hanlon 1990:147).

The missionaries of the upper Orinoco, not surprisingly, tell the story differently. They claim that they tried to collect all the shotguns at one time, but the Yanomamo would not go along with the effort. Multiple sources of guns and ammunition, including Brazilian woodsmen, made control very difficult. And in repeated assemblies called by SUYAO, Yanomamo asked questions like, "All who come here have shotguns, they hunt. . . . Why can't we have them?" (Misioneros 1991:28–32).

In the area around Boca Mavaca, by the late 1980s, the missions' separate areas of control had merged and overlapped into one continuous area. The increasingly fragmented local Yanomamo population was ever more thoroughly enmeshed in commodity production and consumption. A flow of Yanomami strangers passed through to work, to beg, or to steal Western goods. Mission-trained Yanomami political leaders and teachers carried the missions' influence into more distant villages. The Yanomamo around Boca Mavaca were becoming "peasantized" (Chagnon 1992a:209, 221–22).

The year 1989 was a critical one for the Venezuelan Yanomami. Medical care, despite fine plans, suffered from a pronounced lack of support. Malaria cases in the encompassing Venezuelan federal territory of Amazonas jumped dramatically—nearly fivefold by 1990, compared with the 1984–88 average. Infection with onchocerciasis (African river blindness) stood at 90 percent in some Parima communities and 49 percent at Platanal. Many other medical problems were severe (Botto 1991; Hoariwë 1991; Landaeta 1991; Mondolfi 1991; Perret and Magris 1991; Urdaneta 1991). But that was not all.

A gold rush that had begun in Brazil in 1987 began to spill over the border as thousands of *garimpeiros* crossed into Venezuela. The main point of penetration was around the Orinoco headwaters—a short hop from the Mucajaí and Catrimani rivers, where the Brazilian gold rush was most intense. Some prospectors—how many is not clear—entered the Siapa basin.

Caracas began to worry about its southern border and soon made a major governmental about-face. After ignoring for several years a proposal by pro-indigenist organizations to establish a protected area for Venezuelan Yanomami, just after the *garimpeiro* invasion a new government "eco-development" agency began work on a proposal for an Upper Orinoco–Casiquiare Biosphere Reserve. On August 1, 1991, President Carlos Andrés Pérez signed a decree setting aside a reserve of some 32,000 square miles (Arvelo-Jiménez and Cousins 1992:10, 12; Briceño 1991; Chagnon 1992a:211, 215).

In January and February 1992, Venezuelan armed forces made extensive efforts to remove Brazilian *garimpeiros* from Venezuelan Yanomami territory, and the government announced plans for new military bases along the border (Brooke 1992). It is not clear how many bases have been established, but in 1992 there was a National Guard contingent at Platanal (Chagnon 1992a:231) and at least one other in the Parima highlands (Bórtoli 1993). The future role of the military, along with most other policy dimensions of the Biosphere Reserve, remained to be defined as of early 1992 (Arvelo-Jiménez and Cousins 1992:13; Chagnon 1992a:215). It is on those details that the Venezuelan Yanomami's future hangs. As I noted in chapter 8, governments polishing their international image have learned to manipulate ecological and indigenist rhetoric to cloak plans of military and commercial development.

A final historical event once again involves Napoleon Chagnon. In 1990 and 1991, using Venezuelan air force helicopters, he led multidisciplinary scientific teams into the Siapa basin. In the field for a total of six months, the expeditions visited several Siapa Yanomamo villages, and plans exist for continuing research in the area (Brooke 1991; Chagnon 1992a:81–82). These most recent research visits produced important new information on variations in Yanomami warfare, which I will discuss in the last section of this chapter.

This work also led to a very public controversy over access to the Yanomamo, which has grown more heated in the wake of the 1993 massacre of Yanomami by Brazilian *garimpeiros*. Chagnon (1992a:217–43, 1992b:255–89, 1993a) portrays this conflict as mainly between himself and the Salesians. Elsewhere (1993b), he accuses the Salesians, anthropologists, and others of opposing him because of their prejudice against sociobiology. The Salesians (Bórtoli 1993; Misioneros 1991) and the Venezuelan press (in a packet of articles distributed anonymously at the 1993 meetings of the American Anthropological Association) portray the controversy as pitting a broad coalition of Venezuelans and others not primarily against Chagnon but against his associate in the Siapa project, the politically connected Charles Brewer Carías. Brewer Carías is, among other things, a gold miner, and his opponents maintain that it is inappropriate for him to be in a position of power in the Siapa basin.

This conflict colors information about military developments among the Yanomamo, especially from the late 1980s on. But for now, my narrative returns to 1966 and the Patanowa-teri war that we left at the end of chapter 13.

The Bisaasi-teri: 1966 and Beyond

In the previous chapter, I described how an attempted alliance between Bisaasi-teri and Patanowa-teri led to a war between Monou-teri and Patanowa-teri and to related factional maneuvering around Boca Mavaca. By late 1965, the Patanowa-teri had neutralized the danger once posed by enemies to their east, and they were intensifying pressure on the Monou-teri. In response, perhaps three raids were launched against the Patanowa-teri by a heterogeneous lot, including some recent defectors from Patanowa-teri itself. In early 1966, the body count was two or three Patanowa-teri killed versus one death for the Monou-teri. When Chagnon returned to visit the Monou-teri, apparently in early 1967, he wrote, "The war was still being conducted, but on a lesser

scale" (1968:137). If any raids had occurred after early 1966, they did
not produce any deaths on either side, and the score remained two or
three to one against Patanowa-teri. "Hence, the Monou-teri, at least for
the time being, came out ahead" (Chagnon 1968:137).

If, as many have suggested, Yanomami warfare is truly carried out for
the sake of vengeance, the implications of this imbalance in deaths are
clear. Near the end of the 1968 edition of *Yanomamö*, Chagnon makes
a testable prediction about the role of revenge: "The Patanowa-teri will
not cease raiding them until they kill at least one more Monou-teri, but
then the Monou-teri will be obliged to avenge this death when it occurs"
(1968:137).

I have found no indication in any source that active raiding in
this war continued beyond 1967. In the next edition of *Yanomamö*,
(Chagnon 1977:137), Chagnon adds a footnote to his prediction that
reverses the blood debt: "The Bisaasi-teri were still trying to avenge
Damowa's death in 1975 and were actively raiding the Patanowa-teri."
In the most recent edition, Chagnon (1992b:238) has deleted the statement about the Monou-teri's coming out ahead and the Patanowa-teri's
being obliged to raid for revenge.

The wars ended because the situation at Boca Mavaca had changed
in many ways. Paruriwa's faction from upper Bisaasi-teri had moved
into the once empty Catholic mission shortly after Chagnon left—thus
filling the political vacuum and eliminating a major source of instability.
Whether the Patanowa-teri continued to negotiate an alliance with Kaobawa's group is unknown. By 1966, however, the Patanowa-teri had
been weakened by their internal fight and fission and by the stepped-
up raids by Monou-teri and its allies. My suspicion is that these events,
along with the weakened position of Bisaasi-teri, put an end to the alliance plans. At any rate, the Patanowa-teri were about to focus their
alliance intentions on the Mahekoto-teri.

The Bisaasi-teri were weak for several reasons. Kaobawa's rival,
Paruriwa, had become an independent, mission-supported headman,
thus splitting the upper Bisaasi-teri forces. Chagnon no longer lived with
them, taking away a major source of upper Bisaasi-teri's wealth, military
security, and status. After 1968, the Bisaasi-teri had no choice but to accept Chagnon's deepening relationship with former "enemy Shamatari."
Upper and lower Bisaasi-teri were on worsening terms, although over
what is not indicated. "Just before I returned," Chagnon writes, "there
was a club fight involving all of the villages: The Upper Bisaasi-teri and
Reyabobowei-teri fought, as a group, against the Lower Bisaasi-teri and
Momaribowei-teri" (1977:80).

The Bisaasi-teri still had external enemies, too. In 1966, they were involved in a pounding match while attending a feast given by Witokaya-teri (Cocco 1972:399). The hosts brutally pummeled the visitors with stones hidden in their fists. A few months later, the Bisaasi-teri invited the Witokaya-teri and some Iyewei-teri to a feast, where they did the same thing to their guests. Fortunately, Cocco tells us, this conflict dissipated without other, more serious fighting.

The severely divided and still threatened Boca Mavaca people had become more reliant on their respective Shamatari allies, who thus gained political clout. When Chagnon returned in 1967, "the situation had changed appreciably. There were many more Shamatari men living in the group because they had been given women; that is, the exchanges were more balanced" (Chagnon 1977:80). This change shows up in data on the intervillage migration history of people living around Boca Mavaca in 1983 (Eguillor García 1984:56). Of those who arrived between 1959 and 1968, 66 were male and 78 female. Of those who arrived between 1969 and 1983, 47 were male, and 34 female. After around 1967, it seems, the Bisaasi-teri were no longer able to demand women from would-be trade partners. In this deteriorating political situation in 1968, Monou-teri broke up, and its members became part of the Bisaasi-teri villages (Chagnon 1974:127).

Thus, between 1966 and 1968, the empty mission was occupied, the western Namowei blockade keeping *nape* away from "enemy Shamatari" was broken, the Bisaasi-teri no longer monopolized such an extraordinary fount of Western goods, and their middleman relationship with "ally Shamatari" had turned less exploitative. In addition, new supplies of Western goods were reaching villages along the Orinoco farther upstream. All together, other groups had less reason to fight the Bisaasi-teri, and the Bisaasi-teri were less able to impose their interests on others.

As Boca Mavaca went into relative decline, the center of hostilities apparently shifted up the Orinoco. Unfortunately, information about these obviously complicated conflicts is so limited that understanding of them remains very poor.

One serious conflict centered on the Tayari-teri and Mahekoto-teri (Cocco 1972:399–400). As Cocco describes it, the trouble began in 1967 when a pounding match between Mahekoto-teri and Tayari-teri resulted in the deaths of two young men from the latter group.[2] Tayari-teri called on its allies, the Karohi-teri and Makorima-teri, and together they raided Mahekoto-teri. (It will be recalled that the Mahekoto-teri suffered terribly during the measles epidemic of early 1968, and that sometime that year, Karohi-teri became Lizot's main research site.) The raiders managed to wound the Mahekoto-teri headman, but his son then killed the Makorima-teri headman with a shotgun blast.

Over the next year or so, the Tayari-teri alliance, now also supported by Witokaya-teri, raided Mahekoto-teri perhaps three times. Mahekoto-teri was supported by its allies, Shashanawe-teri, Boreta-teri, and Patanowa-teri. But this alliance did not actually raid Tayari-teri until 1969, when six close kin of the Mahekoto-teri headman ambushed and wounded the Tayari-teri headman. He too recovered, and this is the last reported incident in the war.

About the same time as this conflict, the Mahekoto-teri and Patanowa-teri became involved in another, one phase of which was caught on film. In early 1968, the Patanowa-teri were living at an inland location "to escape its myriad enemies." They were reached by Chagnon's colleague, the filmmaker Timothy Asch, accompanied by a young missionary and three guides. By radio, Chagnon persuaded the Patanowa-teri headman "to move back to an old garden near the Orinoco River where the genetics expedition could work with them and we could take film" (Asch 1972:11). Chagnon and Asch wanted to film a feast, and after about two weeks with the Patanowa-teri, they got one when the Mahekoto-teri came to visit (Asch 1972:7, 11). This event is the subject of Chagnon and Asch's film, *The Feast*.

This feast suggests that the Patanowa-teri by 1968 had reoriented their alliance hopes from the Bisaasi-teri to the Mahekoto-teri, their enemies only few years earlier. More than just becoming friends, at this feast the two groups discussed a raid on a common enemy whose identity is not provided. In the film, we are told that this raid did occur. From Asch's (1972:17) description, the raiders were to set out immediately after the feast itself. After that raid, it seems, another clash occurred, for Chagnon reports that one of the Patanowa-teri leaders seen in *The Feast* "had his head blown off with a shotgun shortly after we completed the film" (1977:149).

Although the target of the Patanowa-teri/Mahekoto-teri raid is not identified, I suspect it was the Hasupuwe-teri, who in 1967 had relocated close to the Orinoco to attain greater contact with the Platanal missionaries and Steinvorth de Goetz (1969:74, 87). Lizot (1985:154–55) provides an undated report describing a joint raid against Hasupuwe-teri by Mahekoto-teri and Patanowa-teri. One Hasupuwe-teri man was killed, after first being wounded by a gun that had been given by a missionary to a Mahekoto-teri man. Prior to this, it is said, the raids against Hasupuwe-teri had "practically ceased" (see chapter 13). Lizot's informants predicted revenge raiding by both sides, but no lethal violence is reported along the river for several years after 1968.

This sequence of conflicts appears to be as complicated as that of 1964–66, but there is far less information about it. Basic chronology is murky and detailed analysis impossible. To sum up and speculate: in 1967, the Mahekoto-teri were aggressively trying to elevate their political position, acquiring for themselves a reputation as the most politically shrewd and militarily formidable group in the area (Cocco 1972:400). The killing of two Tayari-teri men in the pounding match during 1967 was one step along that path.

Early in 1968, brought together in cooperation with the Chagnon expedition, the Mahekoto-teri and Patanowa-teri joined as allies in war. Their target may have been the Hasupuwe-teri, who at this time were enjoying the favors of newfound Western friends and drawing off Western goods that otherwise might have been given to Mahekoto-teri and its allies. Then the Mahekoto-teri were hit by measles. Thus weakened, and with enemies to their east, the Mahekoto-teri became momentarily vulnerable. The Tayari-teri and their allies—perhaps bolstered by the arrival of Lizot, although the date of his arrival is uncertain—pressed their raids against the Mahekoto-teri, their rivals and enemies of 1968. By 1969, the Mahekoto-teri had recovered enough strength to retaliate.

After the Mahekoto-teri's raid on the Tayari-teri, Cocco (1972:400) notes a decline in tensions. This observation is supported by a tabulation of deaths kept at Boca Mavaca starting in 1969, in which no war deaths are recorded for 1969 through 1972, two war deaths appear in 1973, and then none again for 1974 and 1975 (out of a total of 73 deaths during this time) (Flores et al., cited in Colchester and Semba 1985:26).

According to Lizot (1971:41), in 1969 the village of Ihirubi-teri, a relatively isolated group farther up the Orinoco and several hours' walk inland, suffered the "only deadly raid in the region." Around the time of this raid, Lizot was working with the Ihirubi-teri in order to make a comparison with the more acculturated Karohi-teri with whom he lived. He notes that the Ihirubi-teri had to move from camp to camp around their two gardens because they feared enemy raids. Lizot does not provide other specifics, but the connection between visits by a gift-giving Westerner and attacks by other Yanomami who are not so favored is a suggestive coincidence.

After 1968, no major changes in the Western presence are recorded for a few years. My theoretical expectations are that a new accommodation to the contact realities would take place, and war would diminish or cease, just as it did after the middle 1950s.[3] In addition, this was the time when Western influence began to become more pervasive and controlling along the upper Orinoco. Western goods had become more common and were available from multiple sources. The missionaries had also become more involved in attempting to mediate conflicts (Cocco 1972:400), although it is not clear what impact they had (see Cocco 1972:398).

These years of peace did not signal the end of violence along the rivers once and for all. But later conflicts begin to look very different from "traditional" Yanomami warfare. Nor did this period signal the end of war in some interior areas where Western goods were still rare. In the next two sections, I will deal with conflicts attendant upon the contact experience in more remote areas, before returning the narrative to the Orinoco-Mavaca area in the middle 1970s.

Up the Orinoco and into the Parima

This section deals with two distinct areas: the stretch of the Orinoco above the Raudal de Guajaribos, and the area around the New Tribes mission in the Parima highlands. The first is known through the work of Steinvorth de Goetz (1969), who began her periodic investigations on the far upper Orinoco in November 1966. She quickly met the Hasupuwe-teri, who had moved closer to the river at the encouragement of the missionary, Brother Iglesias. She distributed many Western goods, and the Hasupuwe-teri soon began work on another garden even closer to the river (1969:87).

In early 1967, farther upstream, Steinvorth de Goetz met the Guarocoawe-teri, a seemingly timid and relatively isolated group. They had heard of beads but did not possess any. The Guarocoawe-teri were reputedly "enemies" of other groups downstream, and only a man from even farther downriver would agree to guide Steinvorth de Goetz to them. She gave them many axes and machetes, and the Guarocoawe-teri did not want her to leave. They refused to guide her upstream, where they said other enemies lived (Steinvorth de Goetz 1969:90–92, 108, 110, 113). It is not clear from her account, however, whether these "enemy" relationships reflect active warfare, strained alliances, or simply efforts to detain the party. In this situation, any possibility would fit with antagonism over access to Western goods.[4]

It seems that tensions were high along other river passages up into the highlands. In what appears to be early 1968,[5] New Tribes missionaries set out on foot to reach highland villages with measles vaccine.

On the way they passed through a palisaded village whose inhabitants seemed prepared to kill them for the goods they carried (Jank 1977:12–18). But this hike is more significant for what happened next. Reaching a savanna in the Parima highlands, the missionaries cleared an airstrip. Shortly thereafter, Derek Hadley, Wally and Margaret Jank, and others returned by plane to begin the new Parima mission. The nearest Yanomamo gave them a big welcome (Jank 1977:10, 20–25).

Some time after the mission was established, William Smole (1976) arrived to begin his fieldwork in the area. His work describes something of the social history and current situation as of the late 1960s. This part of the Parima highlands was extremely remote, from an outsider's perspective, but certainly not entirely insulated from the outside world. Steel tools had been filtering in since the 1920s (Smole 1976:237), and the inhabitants certainly would have begun receiving more since the Western presence on the Orinoco and Ocamo picked up after 1950. Substantial Western contact was established with some savanna groups several years before the mission got there (Jank 1977:10)—perhaps in 1964 (Smole 1976:236)—when some otherwise unidentified Brazilians built an airstrip on the savanna, thinking it was located in Brazil (Alès and Chiappino 1985:80). They departed before the missionaries arrived.

One group on the savanna when the missionaries arrived was the Niyayoba-teri, residents of the general area for several decades. Before the arrival of the mission, they had received steel tools from their kinsmen the Yoreshiana-teri, another interior group located between them and the Orinoco. Around 1961, the Niyayoba-teri moved from the forest to the edge of the savanna. (Yanomami generally do not establish villages on the resource-poor savannas.) While there, they became involved in a war with several other groups. In what may have been 1966, the Niyayoba-teri and three other local groups—210 people in all—moved into one large *shabono* on the savanna itself, for purposes of defense. This settlement, called "José's village" by Margaret Jank, would be the group with the closest ties to the mission (Jank 1977:10, 25; Smole 1976:74, 92–93, 102).

Across the savanna were the Jorocoba-teri, or "Miguel's village." They too had long lived in this general area. Unlike the Niyayoba-teri, they had "not been involved directly in warfare for a generation" (Smole 1976:76). There is one report of strained relations with the Yoreshiana-teri—the middlemen to the Niyayoba-teri—around 1964, but that had been patched up a few years later (1976:93–94, 236). In the next valley to the southeast was a group of villages, including one called Mayobo-teri, that had not been involved in any war since around 1955. These

"Balafili Valley" groups (Jank 1977:8) had kinship ties both to the Niyayoba-teri and to other groups farther to the southeast. The more southeastern groups had been the Niyayoba-teri's enemies in the mid-1960s war. When the missionaries arrived, animosity between the two remained high, but the Mayobo-teri and their neighbors were neutral in the conflict (Smole 1976:90, 93–94, 235).

That is the basic geopolitical layout at the moment of the founding of the mission. With only this information, there is no way to understand the conflicts that apparently took place in the middle 1960s. It is known that a substantial Western presence—an airstrip—came and went sometime during this period. It could well have been a factor in the wars, but the information is so vague that not even a temporal link can be established. What happened after the New Tribes mission was established, however, will be familiar to anyone who has read this far.

As the missionaries saw it, the Yanomamo were practically jumping for joy at their return, shouting: "My brother has come to live with me! My brother has come to give me things! Axes to chop trees! Machetes to clear my garden! Clothing in which to dance!" (Jank 1977:25). Immediately the newcomers were bombarded with an unending stream of demands, thefts, and intimidations (1977:29–32). The Niyayoba-teri cluster quickly established its monopoly over the Westerners and their goods. This maneuver is dramatically illustrated by one missionary's account of what happened when the threat of raiders forced the Niyayoba-teri cluster to go on trek.

> Our contact with Miguel's people [Jorocoba-teri] had been sporadic because of a vague animosity that existed between his village and the people on the big savannah, but once they realized we were alone, they began to appear with increasing regularity. They apologized for having neglected us, and they explained that José had warned them against coming too often. The problem did not seem to be entirely because of the hard feelings between the two groups. Apparently, José had filed a claim on us! . . . [He claimed] undisputed ownership of us all. We did our best to persuade them that we were public property. (Jank 1977:50)

Soon afterward, a man from the Balafili Valley appeared at the mission. He stayed for two days, trying to arrange a way for his relatives to come work in exchange for knives or machetes. He left as soon as the Niyayoba-teri returned, but the Niyayoba-teri still became angry that the missionaries had entertained outside visitors (Jank 1977:52–54).

"They resented the fact that we had extended visiting and trading privileges to other people. . . . The jealousy of some drove them to test our loyalty by impossible demands for time and attention, and it resulted in bitter accusations that we always had time for other people, but not for them. Others repaid our infidelity by stealing everything they could lay their hands on and shouting insults" (Jank 1977:54–55).

Similar scenes were repeated anytime the Niyayoba-teri cluster went on trek—something the missionaries discouraged because of the "thievery, gossip, and immorality" into which they lapsed outside the mission environment (Jank 1977:85). "On one occasion, they returned to find that their gardens had been raided. Knowing that visitors often moved in to claim our time and trade goods in their absence, they laid the blame on Miguel's people" (Jank 1977:86). To settle things, they invited the Jorocoba-teri to a feast, at which a rather severe pounding match passed from fists to machete and ax slapping (1977:86–87).

On the other hand, when the Niyayoba-teri later hosted new friends from another area, the Jorocoba-teri came and harangued and intimidated the visitors all night, making them leave the next morning (Jank 1977:157–58). And when a relatively distant group did begin to receive direct visits from missionaries, that group resolutely attempted to prevent the missionaries from dealing directly with any group farther on (1977:72).

The people with direct access to the missionaries actively developed new trading connections to villages around them, with the missionaries' encouragement (Jank 1977:88–90, 156, 193–95). No information is presented about balances in trade, but it is clear that those located at the mission had a decisive advantage in marriage arrangements. About half the men had more than one wife, even though fights over women were common. The Niyayoba-teri cluster had 44 adult males to 54 adult females, a rather extraordinary "surplus" in contrast to the Jorocoba-teri, who had 20 males to 20 females (Smole 1976:72, 174–78).

About a year after the founding of the New Tribes mission, a war developed between the Niyayoba-teri and groups to their southeast—enemies from the conflict of the mid-1960s. Raiders, ostensibly seeking revenge for a witchcraft death, wounded two, but had two of their own killed as they fled. Constant fear of raiders made life miserable for the Niyayoba-teri group near the mission, compelling them to go on trek in the forest. Hoping to establish peace as well as spread the gospel, a missionary made an initial visit to the neutral groups between the raiders and the savanna but could not reach the enemy villages. Shortly after his return to the savanna, raiders struck again, killing one man who was out hunting (Jank 1977:41, 47–49, 72–74). Apparently, this was the only death suffered by the Niyayoba-teri cluster during the period from mid-1968 to mid-1970 (Smole 1976:74, 233).

In response, the Niyayoba-teri sent out a raiding party that killed one man. Soon afterward, the missionaries succeeded in visiting the enemy village, whose residents urged them to return with more goods. Within a few months of that visit, raiders hit the Niyayoba-teri two more times, wounding two teenagers in one attack and killing a guest from another area in the second. But during this same time, the missionaries were continuing their efforts to establish regular, direct contact with the enemies and other nearby groups. By late 1969, their persistent effort had broken the Niyayoba-teri cluster's monopoly, and visiting back and forth started to become routine. Once guaranteed access to Western goods, the enemies immediately accepted the missionaries' proposal that they stop the war. The Niyayoba-teri palisade fell into disrepair (Jank 1977: 68–69, 80, 84–85, 87–90, 92–93, 131–33, 160–67, 195).

Only scraps of information are available about this area after 1970. A second NTM mission ("Parima A") was established farther to the southeast, near the Niyayoba-teri's former enemies. Otherwise, the Western presence in the area was very stable: "From 1968 to 1980 . . . the mission centre was the only point of contact with the outside world for a large number of the Yanomami of the central Parima" (Alès and Chiappino 1985:80–81). Anthropologists Catherine Alès and Jean Chiappino take credit for breaking the NTM's local monopoly with their arrival in 1980, and that monopoly was further undermined in 1982 by the founding of a major government health center with "abundant cargoes of food and goods" (1983:81).

In 1980, groups from the Parima A area went to war against groups such as the Niyayoba-teri around the Parima B mission. The war began over food theft, which led to a club fight where one man died. The war claimed three victims over the next two years (Alès 1984:103). The apparent coincidence of a new Western penetration accompanied by renewed warfare is suggestive, but without better information, no more can be said.

Contact and Conflict on the Upper Mavaca

It will be recalled that from the start of his fieldwork Chagnon had intended to travel on to live in the Shamatari area and had made his first effort to reach it in 1965. This and subsequent efforts were stymied by the Bisaasi-teri and other groups between Boca Mavaca and Mishimishimabowei-teri, who did not want to give up the advantages of possessing Chagnon and acting as middlemen. When he finally made contact in 1968, he was guided by a twelve-year-old boy—"something of an outcast"—born in Mishimishimabowei-teri and raised in Momaribowei-teri, who was visiting Bisaasi-teri (Chagnon 1974:18ff.).

There is no indication of violence between Mishimishimabowei-teri and the Boca Mavaca groups after the events of late 1964 and early 1965. Nevertheless, relations had been so bad up to this point that any rapprochement would seem to have been impossible (e.g., Chagnon 1983:31). Not so. Once Chagnon had established contact with the Shamatari, men from Bisaasi-teri would regularly accompany him when he went upstream. Despite Mishimishimabowei-teri's being the home of the main attackers in the slaughter of Bisaasi-teri in 1951, Chagnon's companions "were able to ignore these men as individuals when they developed friendly ties with Moawa's group" (1974:172).

When, in 1972, however, Chagnon announced that he would not return to Mishimishimabowei-teri after a fight with its headman, Moawa, Chagnon's companion, Rerebawa, grew to "hate Moawa overnight, recalling the treachery of 25 years earlier when Moawa's village had tricked the Bisaasi-teri and had killed, among others, the brother of his wife's father. Now he remembered these things well and decided, after all, that the Shamatari were a bunch of unmitigated bastards, treacherous to the core" (Chagnon 1974:194). One could not ask for a better illustration of the political flexibility of revenge.

Mishimishimabowei-teri and Iwahikoroba-teri both remained desperately poor in steel at this time, possessing very few and extremely worn blades obtained via chains of middlemen from Boca Mavaca or Brazil. The former group had been sending invitations to Chagnon since 1965 (Chagnon 1974:35, 176–77, 1983:39). By 1968, Chagnon had become an even wealthier provider of Western goods than he was during his initial fieldwork. Working now in collaboration with a multidisciplinary biomedical investigation, he had to be able to visit remote villages and very quickly collect blood samples.

> One unfortunate consequence for my continuing anthropological interest in many of the villages was that I was identified by the Yanomamo as an inexhaustible fount of goods. Thus, to assure the complete cooperation of entire villages for some of

our studies I had to give goods to men, women, and children. The positive effect was that the "team" could visit villages like Mishimishimabowei-teri with me and in three days have all the material and data they came for. The negative effect was that all my subsequent visits to this village were disappointments to the Yanomamo because I did not come with equivalent quantities of goods. (Chagnon 1974:165)[6]

Thus, to the Yanomamo, Chagnon must have seemed not only rich but also erratic. Perhaps this perception explains the increasingly direct physical measures they applied in efforts to control Chagnon's distributions of goods.

Mishimishimabowei-teri was in the process of fissioning in 1968. Just before Chagnon made contact, the gargantuan old village had divided in two still large villages—about 250 and 150 inhabitants, respectively—located a few hours' walk apart. For the next several years, village size and composition fluctuated as individuals and small groups moved back and forth between the two villages or went off on their own (Chagnon 1981:491–92). There are no indications of any major confrontations between the subdivisions during the first few years of Chagnon's fieldwork with the Mishimishimabowei-teri. That situation changed in 1971.

In that year, while Chagnon and his film colleague, Asch, were staying in the main village, people from one of the recently fissioned segments were visiting and refused to leave when they should have (Chagnon and Bugos 1979:218–21). The visitors were closely tied to a faction within the main village. These kinsmen encouraged the visitors to stay permanently. Because increased numbers would give them greater leverage over everything that went on in the village, this encouragement constituted a challenge to the dominant factions, of or allied to Moawa. A tense situation came to a head as a minor quarrel over some plantains escalated chaotically. It almost turned deadly when two men appeared ready to attack with an ax and a machete. But when more and older men joined in, it settled into a hostile standoff. Some of the visitors left the next day. (This is the incident seen in the film *The Ax Fight*.)[7] As we will see shortly, a similar confrontation occurred the next year.

Also in 1971, Chagnon attempted and finally succeeded in making contact with the other Shamatari village, Iwahikoroba-teri (1974:172–73). Predictably, both the Bisaasi-teri and the Mishimishimabowei-teri —even though the latter were allied to Iwahikoroba-teri—were eager to prevent this contact and, as usual in these situations, told Chagnon he would be killed if he went there. Chagnon decided he would have better luck leaving from Bisaasi-teri. On his first attempt, he was guided by an old woman who had been captured from Iwahikoroba-teri many years before. They could not find the village, and turned back. Having thus established the seriousness of his intentions to reach Iwahikoroba-teri, Chagnon had to leave the area for "the next several weeks" to assist his colleagues in the Ocamo River basin.

When he returned, the political leaders of Bisaasi-teri seemed to have had a change of heart (Chagnon 1974:174–75). Now Rerebawa and three other men agreed to guide him. After progressing about a day's journey beyond where he had turned back with the old woman, they began to see signs of Iwahikoroba-teri activity. But that day, Chagnon "began to react violently to an insect bite, or a toxic plant, or wild food that I had eaten." He became too ill to move, and the expedition halted. The next day, his camp heard the sounds of Iwahikoroba-teri hunters nearby. His guides spoke in whispers, but Chagnon called out and drew the hunters' attention. The men asked if he was Shaki (Chagnon's Yanomamo name), and when told that he was, they helped bring him to their village.

The Iwahikoroba-teri were willing to let Chagnon's colleague take blood samples and otherwise cooperate. Chagnon was working with previously compiled genealogies when he learned that, "as luck would have it, the husband of the second person on the list had been killed by Bisaasi-teri raiders only a few weeks before my visit, and the Iwahikoroba-teri were very angry that I knew their names" (Chagnon 1974:177). Bad luck, indeed.

People from Bisaasi-teri and Iwahikoroba-teri had not met "eye to eye" for "many years" prior to 1970 (Chagnon 1974:173). That year, a number of Bisaasi-teri men accompanying a party of Mishimishima-bowei-teri ran into Iwahikoroba-teri hunters. Rather than fight, they exchanged goods, and the Iwahikoroba-teri extended an invitation for them to visit. Yet a year later, after Chagnon had demonstrated his determination to reach Iwahikoroba-teri, the Bisaasi-teri raided them. From the perspective of the model, this raid seems to have been an attempt to drive the Iwahikoroba-teri away and thus foreclose the possibility that Chagnon would go live with them.

But since Chagnon had made contact, and the Iwahikoroba-teri had cooperated, if sullenly, the problem for both the Bisaasi-teri and Mishimishimabowei-teri remained. Chagnon did not go back to Iwahikoroba-teri, however, because of what he was told when he returned to the field the next year (Chagnon 1974:178–79). His friend Rerebawa told Chagnon that he had been told by Dedeheiwa, a leader of one of the Mishimishimabowei-teri groups, that while Chagnon was sleeping in Iwahikoroba-teri, its headman and two of his brothers had been creeping up on Chagnon's hammock. They intended to crush his skull but were scared off when Chagnon shined his flashlight around the village. Since then, they had vowed to kill him the next time he came. Chagnon was "shaken badly" by this tale and decided not to go back to Iwahikoroba-teri.

Back in Mishimishimabowei-teri in 1972, trouble was brewing (Chagnon 1974:167–72, 1992b:38). Over the course of Chagnon's visits, there had been a "gradually accelerating feeling of strain with Moawa" (1974:168), the very aggressive headman of the main village, who Chagnon claims "had killed twenty-one people" (1992b:38)—an incredible number. At issue was the distribution of the anthropologist's Western goods. Chagnon describes in great detail Moawa's increasingly belligerent efforts to have them or at least control their distribution. He wanted them all, even to the point of demanding all of Chagnon's eye medicine (Chagnon 1974:169). Other villagers complained, but Moawa was fierce, and the leader of the largest faction.

Matters finally came to a head in 1972 (Chagnon 1974:183–86). Chagnon had returned up the Mavaca temporarily short of trade goods. His plan was to pass through the Moawa's village of Mishimishimabowei-teri and collect blood samples in the split-off village led by the old headman Sibarariwa. But when he arrived, Sibarariwa's entire village was visiting the main village for a joint mortuary ceremony—normally a moment of great solidarity among participants. When Moawa greeted Chagnon, he saw that Chagnon had only 15 machetes and few other items. Chagnon told him that all of these were to go to Sibarariwa's village. Moawa opened up the bundle and began examining the machetes.

> His face turned solemn at the third repetition of my intended disposition of the machetes he was examining; he looked at me coldly and then, bluntly, informed me that the machetes were to be distributed to the men *he* designated, and *none*—repeat, *none*—were to be given to people in Sibarariwa's group. They were thieves and liars, he said. (Chagnon 1974:186, emphasis in original)

The mortuary service was held the next morning (Chagnon 1974: 188–91). Chagnon planned to begin his work in the afternoon. Tensions rose. Screaming fights broke out among the women, the hosts yelling at the visitors to go home. The men were deep in their drug states, but they still staggered forth to keep the women from striking each other with firewood. "It was one of the most volatile situations I have ever been in," wrote Chagnon (1974:189). Deciding to take the blood samples as quickly as possible and leave, he set up his equipment and "was surrounded by about 200 pushy, impatient, angry, shouting people, each determined to get a particular item of which I had very few to distribute" (1974:191).

While Moawa watched, Chagnon began taking blood samples from men Moawa had designated. When the headman went away, Chagnon switched to those Moawa had sought to exclude. He explains that he had to select these men "very carefully":

> From my knowledge of past fights and disputes in the group when Sibarariwa and his section lived in the same village with Moawa, I knew who the men were that had stood up to Moawa and defied him. I began calling them, in turn, knowing that Moawa would be less able to prevent me from giving my machetes to these men without a fight. . . . I quickly sampled the important men and paid them with machetes very quickly. I was down to one machete when Moawa learned what I had done.
>
> He trotted over in a rage and stared in disbelief at the single machete. He glared at me with naked hatred in his eyes, and I glared back at him in the same fashion. . . . He then raised his axe to strike and I saw how white his lips and knuckles were. Moawa hissed again: "Either you give that machete to that man over there, or I'll bury this axe in your head." (Chagnon 1974: 192–93)

Under the circumstances, Chagnon complied.[8]

Chagnon finished his work and left the next day. He had resolved never to return to Mishimishimabowei-teri "so long as Moawa lived there" (1974:193), but he did not say so at first.

> Only after I returned to Mavaca did I let my feelings be "officially" known. I told the Bisaasi-teri that I planned never to return to Moawa's village. Nor would I go to visit the Iwahikoroba-teri. I was tired of having people threaten to kill me. I was alarmed at how close some of them had come. I told them that I would do "the same" to Moawa as he did to me, should he ever venture to come to Mavaca to visit. By the time this information got to him

it undoubtedly had acquired embellishments and exaggerations that characterize the growth of Yanomamo and all other rumors. I hope this was the case, and that Moawa will think twice about coming two weeks by trail to visit the villages at the mouth of the Mavaca River. (Chagnon 1974:195–96)

Only the broad outline of events is known for some Shamatari from this point onward. In 1972, the Momaribowei-teri, spurred by the increased tensions in the upper Mavaca, made a very long move to the mission center at Tamatama on the Casiquiare, although they later moved back. (In 1964, Piaroa Indians had moved several hundred miles up the Orinoco to settle alongside the New Tribes missionaries at Tamatama [Johnston 1964:11].) The Reyabobowei-teri similarly made a long move, five days to the south (Chagnon 1974:14, 27, 32, 181–82). In the mid-1970s, the Salesian missionaries persuaded a segment of the Mishimishimabowei-teri to break off and move down the Mavaca river, where they became known as Haoyabowei-teri. The Salesians then established a satellite mission post ("Mavakita") close by, and from this base began extending their own direct contacts to other Shamatari upstream (Chagnon 1979:123, 1992a:222–23).

This increased contact with groups who were still too far from the main mission to receive medical care led to a great increase in mortality. An unidentified Shamatari village that began sending men down the Mavaca "to obtain machetes" in 1972 was struck in 1973 by an upper respiratory infection carried back by a trade party. Forty percent of the village population died, including virtually all the children (Chagnon 1977:147). The largest village in the area, presumably the main Mishimishimabowei-teri village, was also hit by this epidemic (Chagnon and Melancon 1983:59). The missionaries say they first heard of the deaths in Mishimishimabowei-teri a few months after Chagnon left there, suggesting that Chagnon's party was as likely a source of the infection as any other (Misioneros 1991:21).

Besides the epidemic, some shooting wars were going on somewhere during the early 1970s. Chagnon's mortality data for 1970 through 1974 indicate nine war deaths among all the people he studied (Melancon 1982:42). Since the Orinoco appears to have been mostly quiet at this time, presumably most deaths were among the Shamatari. It is consistent with my model for wars to continue longer in the more remote areas that were just beginning to experience direct contact.

From the Mid-1970s Onward

Along the Orinoco, the relative peace that had prevailed since 1969 came to an end in the mid-1970s. In 1975, the Bisaasi-teri were "actively raiding the Patanowa-teri" (Chagnon 1977:137), and "at least two Patanowa-teri were killed with shotguns, including Komaiewa, the headman" (Chagnon 1983:189). In the mortality statistics kept at Boca Mavaca, one war death is reported for each of the years 1976, 1977, and 1979, and three for 1978 (Flores et al., cited in Colchester and Semba 1985:26). Kenneth Good also witnessed a war at the start of his fieldwork in 1975.

Good went to the field with two other graduate students of Chagnon's. After a month in another village, and accompanied at first by a senior colleague, Robert Carneiro, Good went to live with the Hasupuwe-teri on April 1, 1975 (Good 1989:4, 1991). There is little information about the Hasupuwe-teri from about 1968 to 1975. In the early 1970s, a violent internal fight led some people to move to another village. Around 1973, Chagnon visited the Hasupuwe-teri. Around 1974, they fissioned, and those who continued to be called Hasupuwe-teri retained 119 people. At the time of Good's arrival, they were located some 15 to 20 linear kilometers above the Raudal de Guajaribos and were developing a new garden about a half-day's walk from the river (Good 1989:4, 6, 1991:24, 206). Although they were occasionally visited by a malaria team (Good 1991:28) and others, they remained comparatively isolated in 1975 relative to the situation from Platanal downriver.

In his initial fieldwork, Good stayed with the Hasupuwe-teri for two years, during which time he accompanied them on travels south and began his research on the Siapa River groups. Good would return on nine separate visits up to 1988, for a total of 68 months in the field. He spent most of his time near the Orinoco but several months in the Siapa area, and he eventually married a Yanomamo woman (Good 1984:1–2, 1989:4–5, 1991). Good has only begun to publish his extensive research findings, however, and both contact and war histories are limited in his currently available works.

Good's description of his relationship with the Hasupuwe-teri reveals the texture of such contact situations. He and Carneiro were warmly welcomed: "Having an outsider come to live with them was regarded as a kind of windfall from heaven, an endless source of trade goods—machetes, cloth, aluminum pots, fishhooks, axes" (Good 1991:

28). They quickly became the center of attention—the subjects of un-remitting scrutiny and never-ending demands for trade goods. "The strangers had an incredible amount of material things, most of which they had never seen before, a simply astonishing collection of exotic goods. . . . Bob Carneiro and I were the biggest attraction they had ever seen" (Good 1991:31).

Good was gradually assimilated into the social order of the village, becoming a fictive consanguine to one of its two divisions and an "affine" to the other. But jockeying for his trade goods never ceased (Good 1991: 79–80, 120).

> As I got to know the village situation better, I realized that there was a kind of subtle competition for my friendship between the two sublineages that made up the Hasupuweteri—the winners of course thinking they would have an easier time getting trade goods from me. . . . At the beginning [the leader of one division] had tried to bully me, demanding goods, not just for himself, but for visiting headmen, as if I were his private resource. He stopped that soon when he saw that I could be just as aggressive as he was. Before long we became friends, though it was a friendship built on respect rather than on good chemistry. (Good 1991:79)

Good has strongly criticized Chagnon's image of Yanomami "fierce-ness." In his long experience in the field, he instead "was struck by how harmonious Yanomama life actually was" (Good 1991:69, 327). One war, however, did break out against former allies, very soon after Good and Carneiro arrived (Good 1991:44–46).

At first, Good was living in a hut along the river about a third of a mile from the Hasupuwe-teri *shabono*. Every morning people would come down the trail to begin their day's observation of the anthropolo-gist (Good 1991:29–30). In mid-April, the villagers were walking down the path to Good's hut (he had just been joined by a malaria team) when they were ambushed by raiders from Kashorawe-teri. One man was lethally wounded.

The Kashorawe-teri were a downstream group long associated with the Yabitawa-teri, who had contacts with *nape* dating back to the 1940s. "Until recently the Hasupuweteri and Kasharaweteri had traded and visited with each other, enjoying friendly relations" (Good 1991:45). But then the latter had gone to a feast hosted by the Hasupuwe-teri, where they became insulted by the relative paucity of food prepared for them. Arguments developed, and some of the hosts "hid their guests' canoes" (Good 1991:46). (The Hasupuwe-teri, above the Raudal de Guajaribos, had not adopted canoe travel when groups farther downstream did. In 1975 they still lacked even a single canoe [Good 1991: 29].) It was these insults that the raiders intended to avenge.

No doubt the Kashorawe-teri did feel insulted. But the timing of their attack suggests an ulterior motive: to separate former trade dependents from their new source of wealth. Further details are lacking, but this first raid appears to have initiated a flurry of raiding and counterraiding (Good 1991:46). Good remained in active contact with the Hasupuwe-teri, however, and judging from his general descriptions of Yanomami peaceableness, it seems that this was the only war for some time.

The same early 1975 expedition that brought Good to the Yanomami brought Eric Fredlund to the middle Ocamo village of Hotoba-teri, which would be his base for about 15 months (Fredlund 1982: 37, 45). Fredlund (1982:32) found that the relocation of villages down from headwater areas toward the rich source of Western goods at the mouth of the Ocamo, which had begun, according to him, after 1954, was continuing in the 1970s, even though it brought greater exposure to malaria. The village of Auwei-teri, mentioned in chapter 12 as an ally of the Witokaya-teri, made a particularly long move downstream (compare maps in Smole 1976:56 and Fredlund 1982:34; Fuentes 1980:6).

Fredlund provides almost no information about his fieldwork situation or political relations among the local Yanomamo. The Shitari bloc he studied had been insulated from direct contact with Westerners until recently. Consistent with that insulation, Fredlund contrasts the "relatively little warfare reported in the Ocamo River Basin over the past 100 years" with the situations described by Chagnon for the Namowei and Shamatari, and he notes that comparatively few middle Ocamo people had died in war (Fredlund 1982:37). This statement, however, probably refers to conflicts between groups within the area, since, as I described in previous chapters, middle and upper Ocamo groups were raiding lowland groups from the late 1940s onward.

On the other hand, Fredlund does note signs of conflict in the area during his stay. While the men of Hotoba-teri were out hunting, two men from a neighboring village attempted to rape a Hotoba-teri woman and were only prevented from doing so by Fredlund's intervention. The people of Hotoba-teri were attributing illnesses to sorcery by a more distant Shitari village. Sometime in 1975, the first village north of the Hotoba-teri raided another village farther to the north, killing one man (Fredlund 1982:34, 37, 42, 70). All these events are consistent with often-observed patterns subsequent to the establishment of a new Western presence in an area.

The third graduate student of Chagnon's to begin work with the Yanomamo in 1975 was Raymond Hames. Hames, whose historical reconstructions I have cited extensively, worked in the Padamo area among Yanomamo connected to Yecuana villages. No lethal violence had been reported for those groups since 1960 or even earlier. But there too, tensions rose during the 1970s. In 1972, one village in the Waka-waka sub-bloc fissioned after several members died of malaria (Hames 1983:411). Sorcery accusations that "implicated the missionary in the witchcraft" were accompanied by other rearrangements; and in 1976, one village fused with another in anticipation of an attack by a third.

Among the villages of the middle Padamo sub-blocs, relations were also growing strained at this time (Hames 1983:413–14). In 1975, a club fight held in one village somehow led to the deaths of five men, including two participants from Iyewei-teri and the headman of one of the sub-bloc villages. As of 1976, several villages were living in fear of raids (Hames 1983:414–15; and see Chagnon and Hames 1979:912).

The 1975 fighting around Hasupuwe-teri and in the middle Ocamo appears similar to conflicts described in so many other situations of increasing contact in remote areas. The sudden intensification of tensions and violence in the Padamo area is more problematic. Certainly there were important changes in the Western presence in that area from the early to mid-1970s, which could account for a rise in antagonisms— the growth of mission schools, the reorganization of Salesian mission policy, the development and then collapse of CODESUR.

The problem is that these Yanomamo had already gone so far to adapt to both Westerners and Yecuana that it is questionable whether my model, developed to explain war among relatively "traditional" Yanomami, can be applied to them. Good and Lizot (1984:134) discuss the situation at Hames's main field site, Toropo-teri, and conclude that "the conditions at this community (as well as its extreme geographic marginality) have so drastically altered this group of Yanomami that they cannot legitimately be represented as Yanomami society."

A similar caveat should apply to the shotgun attacks launched by Bisaasi-teri against Patanowa-teri in 1975, which I noted at the start of this section. The intensifying changes of the first half of the 1970s affected all those directly exposed to the missions and other Westerners. It was around 1975 that Kaobawa of the Bisaasi-teri moved his group away from the missions to their old garden site (Barawa) on the Orinoco because there were too many foreigners around the mission trying to control the daily life of his people (Chagnon 1977:160). Malaria was also rampant at this time, with 33 deaths attributed to it at Boca Mavaca for 1975–76 (versus a more usual 6 deaths from 1977 through June 1979) (Flores et al., cited in Colchester and Semba 1985:26). In unknown ways, the genesis and practice of violence in areas of high contact from the mid-1970s onward may no longer fit the model developed in this book.

The social panorama at Boca Mavaca continued to change during the late 1970s and early 1980s, as described by Sister María Isabel Eguillor García of the Catholic missions (1984:26–28, 54–56, 93–95, 233, 236). Around 1982, the Western settlement there consisted of about a dozen buildings and an airstrip. New Yanomamo leaders emerged, local groups fissioned and fused, and Yanomamo from distant places appeared in increasing numbers. One telling indicator of change is a pronounced shift from virilocal to uxorilocal postmarital residence. Yet despite the increased Western presence, the number of Western goods possessed by an average family at the local village of Cinc-teri, according to Eguillor García (1984:236), remained only slightly greater than that of the isolated village of Ihirubi-teri and well below the number owned at the village of Karohi-teri around 1969 (see Lizot 1971:45).

That all of these changes were producing commensurate changes in social conflict is illustrated by the last well-described war in the Orinoco-Mavaca area (Chagnon 1988:991, 1990b:98–101; Eguillor García 1984:25–26; Lizot 1989:28–29). The principal opponents were the Bisaasi-teri and the Tayari-teri. Chagnon had not been in the field at Bisaasi-teri since 1975. Tayari-teri was Lizot's current location. The two anthropologists differ considerably, and with feeling, over what occurred in this fight, but it is Eguillor García who provides the most complete account. She dates the start of hostilities to November 1977, when a fight during a feast hosted by the Witokaya-teri resulted in the deaths of some Karohi-teri and Tayari-teri. The Musiu-teri, one of the groups into which the Bisaasi-teri had divided, were implicated.

For the next two years, tensions remained "half latent" (Eguillor García 1984:25), manifested in verbal and some physical abuse between Bisaasi-teri and Tayari-teri people. Lizot (1989:28) describes the building tension as a "product of impertinent speeches, insults, brickbats, provocations, garden thefts, and the arrogant attitudes of certain leaders of Tayari." When a group of Bisaasi-teri were camping near the Tayari-teri and went to ask them for plantains, the village children pelted the

headman with mud balls and sticks, while their parents stood by. Shortly
thereafter, when Tayari-teri came to see the Salesians at Boca Mavaca,
they in turn were pelted with chunks of concrete (Chagnon 1990b:99).

In March 1979, the two groups met at Tayari-teri, intending to settle
their animosity with a pounding match. But events got out of hand,
and two Tayari-teri men were killed. Quickly, the Tayari-teri raided and
wounded or killed one Bisaasi-teri person. In November, they caught
a young man from Bisaasi-teri out fishing and left him riddled with
arrows (Chagnon 1990b:100; Eguillor García 1984:25; Lizot 1989:
28). During the following weeks, the Bisaasi-teri made several attempts
to attack the Tayari-teri, but the latter had temporarily moved inland
(Chagnon 1990b:100). At the same time, the Tayari-teri consolidated
their alliances with "all descendants of the Sitoya-teri group" (which
would include the Mahekoto-teri, although this is not specified); and
"in their pride that they could not be defeated," they attacked an upper
Ocamo group called Klawoi-teri, burning their *shabono* and abducting
five women (Eguillor García 1984:25).

Up to this point, the fighting does not seem to be unusual. But what
happened next is without precedent. A great alliance of fourteen local
groups—the six current divisions of the Bisaasi-teri, four Shamatari
allies, the Klawoi-teri, the two Iyewei-teri divisions, and the Witokaya-
teri (Eguillor García 1984:25)—planned coordinated attacks on the
proud Tayari-teri. They came by motorized canoes on two consecutive
days, about 150 men each time, with shotguns and gasoline to set fire to
the Tayari-teri residence (Lizot 1989:29). Never before had Yanomami
mounted such a massive, overpowering assault. In the fierce battle, six
(Lizot 1989:29) or seven Tayari-teri men were killed and about a dozen
wounded, one woman was captured, and the village was completely
looted. The survivors fled to nearby allies, including the Mahekoto-teri,
and "Tayari disappeared from the Yanomami geographic map" (Eguillor
García 1984:26).[9]

The Boca Mavaca groups prepared for retaliation by the survivors
and their allies, which came in two raids in early and mid-1981. One person was wounded in the first, and Kaobawa's daughter and son-in-law
were killed in the second (Chagnon 1990b:101; Eguillor García 1984:
26). (The three or four Bisaasi-teri casualties in this war are the only
war fatalities reported for the Boca Mavaca groups since before 1968
[Eguillor García 1984:53].) Although Kaobawa's followers wanted revenge, they could not get others to go along. Eguillor García (1984:26)
observed of the situation: "Some begin to get tired. Others are already

fed up with fighting and satisfied with what they have gotten. There is discord, and not even the ashes of the young couple, divided between the allies, brings unity to the discussions."

Lizot (1989:30) notes a "brusque descent of warlike activities, based on a strong activation in the process of acculturation" since around 1983 (although Chagnon [1990b:101] reports that some Bisaasi-teri a few years later still hoped to attack the Mahekoto-teri for revenge). By the end of the decade, the acculturation process had proceeded so far around Boca Mavaca that many local Yanomamo had given up communal living, partly because of problems of theft, and were well along the road to "peasantization" (Chagnon 1992a:221–22).

Farther up the Orinoco, in areas more removed from the center of Western activity, violent conflict continued to run high during the 1980s. Near the end of that decade, Lizot (1989:29) notes that some time before, the Patanowa-teri were involved somehow in a massacre at the Kashorawe-teri village, in which a "great quantity" of men were killed and women captured. He attributes this act to revenge for a killing long ago, and he notes that the Patanowa-teri fissioned soon afterward. (Eguillor García [1984:54] mentions that a large number of Patanowa-teri moved to Boca Mavaca around 1982, but it is not clear whether this is the fissioning referred to by Lizot.)

Good (1991:208, 247, 298, 322) refers to growing tensions above the Raudal de Guajaribos in 1984, which broke out into reciprocal raiding involving the Hasupuwe-teri and a related group against a downstream enemy known as Konaporepiwe-teri, apparently in 1985. In the summer of 1985, Good (1991:287) encountered some Poreweteri (Steinvorth de Goetz's Porepoi-teri?) who had been moving down toward the Hasupuwe-teri area. Recent raids on them by unnamed enemies had killed several, causing them to split up and flee. Lizot, living among the Karohi-teri in 1988, observed that "at the moment in which I write these lines, all of the communities of the mountains are at war against each other" (1989:32). While it is expectable in terms of my model that war would pass to once relatively isolated groups as the effects of a deepening Western presence spread outward from the Orinoco-Mavaca center, I would again enter a caution here. By the 1980s, so much had changed and so little information is available about the impact of those changes that unanticipated factors may be involved even in the conflicts farther up the Orinoco.

Political relations and conflicts up the Mavaca River during the 1980s show a similar mix of "standard" and new elements. Missionary inducements to relocate led a large division of the Iwahikoroba-teri to move closer to the Haoyabowei-teri and the Mavakita mission around 1984–85, where they became known as Washawe-teri. In 1987, the Kedebabowei-teri, a group closely related to the Mishimishimabowei-teri, were persuaded to move downstream and begin commercial production of manioc. The missionaries established a school among them, and in 1988 a young man was killed in a club fight "over accusations of theft of the 'school food'" (Chagnon 1992a:222–25). Both these groups subsequently suffered very high mortality from diseases: they were close enough to the missions to catch illnesses, but still beyond the ability of missions to provide critical medical care (Chagnon 1992a:223–24).

In the late 1980s, men from the more acculturated mission villages suddenly began attacking some of the more remote groups. The proliferation of shotguns among the former now combined with possession of motorized boats to give the mission groups the ability to travel far to raid others and to outflank anyone who dared to raid them (Chagnon 1992a:219). Once again, the political manipulation of revenge is evident: "Significant numbers of Yanomamo in the remote villages are being shot and killed by raiders from mission villages who, now that they have an arms advantage, invent reasons to get 'revenge' on distant groups, some of which have had no historical relationships with them" (Chagnon 1992a:220).

Some of these raids occurred up the Mavaca. Around early 1990, a remote group called Hiomota-teri was raided by "friendly" neighbors who had just formed an alliance with a shotgun-owning mission group. Two men were killed and seven women abducted, because, as it was explained, the Hiomota-teri had "failed to deliver dogs they had promised" (Chagnon 1992a:220). Judging from the date and the number of people killed and captured, this appears to be the same incident Chagnon mentions in a separate footnote, in which "a splinter of the Patanowa-teri" (the "friendly" neighbors?) joined with raiders from the Boca Mavaca mission to attack a "remote village that was becoming friendly with the Patanowa-teri" (Chagnon 1992a:190). Later that year, "two more Hiomota-teri youths were shot and killed in broad daylight while visiting a village near the Salesian satellite mission at Mavakita" (Chagnon 1992a:220), probably the village of the Washawa-teri (1992a:225).

While Chagnon was visiting the Washawa-teri in early 1992, a rumor spread that the Yanomamo comisario from Mavakita was planning to raid them with shotguns. Chagnon believes his own presence and shotgun may have scared off the attackers. Instead, the comisario went to harass the Kedebabowei-teri, recently weakened by an epidemic that killed 21 people, before returning with his followers "to his mission redoubt at Mavakita" (Chagnon 1992a:224–25).

With these few facts, in-depth analysis is not possible. But along with the new elements—fighting over mission food stores, motorized canoe transport, and the structured military inequality associated with unequal possession of shotguns—an old theme can be discerned. Those who have stronger connections to the mission posts at Boca Mavaca and Mavakita, along with their allies such as the Patanowa-teri splinter group, direct violence at others who are attempting to get closer to the missions—the Washawe-teri, the Kedebabowei-teri, and the Hiomota-teri.

The new bout of raiding apparently extended even into the remote Siapa basin. As I discussed in the historical overview earlier, direct but sporadic contact with some Siapa River groups began in the 1970s and continued during the 1980s. It is not clear to what extent the Siapa groups experienced direct contact with *garimpeiros* after 1987, but a substantial Western presence was established in the area during 1990 and 1991, when Chagnon and other researchers were transported in by Venezuelan air force helicopters (Chagnon 1992a:81).[10]

Chagnon was struck by the "startling difference" in warfare and violence from that in the Orinoco-Mavaca area. The relatively isolated Siapa people were "sedate and gentle," with smaller villages, less elaborate alliances and feasting, and fewer abducted women (Chagnon 1992a: 85–87).[11] Chagnon attributes this contrast to ecological differences—a hypothesis I will come back to in the concluding chapter. I attribute it to the historical absence of Westerners in the area and to the fact that the Siapa basin, since the 1950s, had been a low-contact zone between two high-contact zones, the Orinoco and the Negro. There were no "more isolated" people to attack them from behind as they received Western goods via well-developed exchange networks.[12]

This peaceful existence was being threatened, however. Along with his general observations, Chagnon (1992b:6) also notes that war was "still common" in the Siapa area. And after discussing the killings of the Hiomota-teri men near the Mavaca, he adds the following paragraph.

I was further angered and depressed to discover a number of recent shotgun killings in yet other extremely remote villages I have recently started working in, villages that are many days' walk from the mission groups that are now raiding them, the traveling distance being greatly reduced by the use of motorized canoes for at least some portions of the trip. Particularly disturbing is the large number of shotgun killings of Venezuelan Yanomamo in isolated villages in the Siapa Basin by Brazilian Yanomamo who have obtained large quantities of guns from mission posts like Abaruwa-teri. The circumstances surrounding these shotgun killings are well outside the traditional patterns of Yanomamo warfare. (Chagnon 1992a:220–21)

In September 1991, Chagnon's colleague Charles Brewer Carías told a *New York Times* reporter that during the preceding year, 21 "wild Yanomami" had been killed by shotgun-using "mission Yanomami" (Brooke 1991).

In these recent wars, the impact of Western contact is obvious on the face of it. That mission Yanomamo attack villages where Westerners are trying to develop a new presence is consistent with the explanation of warfare developed in this book. But beyond that broad observation, much remains unknown. We have no information about the economic and political relationships between aggressors and victims. The situation is unique: a major new Western presence suddenly drops from the sky, and there are seemingly unprecedented long-distance strikes out of the missions. Moreover, the polemical character of Chagnon's recent writings about mission activity cannot be overlooked. Because of all these factors, it would be imprudent to say more.

15

Explaining Yanomami Warfare:

Alternatives and Implications

In this book I have attempted to compile what is reported about Yanomami history and explain its main events by reference to a coherent
structure of theoretical propositions. One overarching proposition is
that the Yanomami's practice of war—along with such political matters as long-distance migrations, the splitting of population blocs during
those moves, and the interrelated domains of trade, intermarriage, and
political alliance—is primarily determined by local articulation with
agents and aspects of European expansion.

As the Yanomami entered known history in the middle of the eighteenth century, they were keeping to the high country, surrounded on all
sides by hunters of humans to feed the colonial slave markets. With the
formerly complex societies of the region obliterated, and with no travel
route passing through their homelands, the Yanomami remained less exposed to the ravages of Western contact than were peoples of lower and
more accessible terrain. After mid-century, episodic expansion into the
region by a semblance of colonial government mitigated the slave hunting, although in places it continued for at least another century. But
now there also were peaceful contacts and opportunities to trade, and
through them, to obtain steel tools.

After the mid-1700s, the Western presence waxed and waned. It collapsed in the decades around the turn of the nineteenth century, returned
at low levels during the century's middle decades, and then exploded
during the rubber boom. The collapse of the boom by 1920, followed

by the global economic depression, led to a spasm of Western retraction that is often mistaken for absolute, unbroken isolation. The initial penetrations by the most recent wave of Westerners began at different times in different places, but in the 1950s contact picked up all around and began to spread out from new points in the highlands. At some times in some places, massive contact and sociocultural disruption set in, and acculturation proceeded toward "peasantization" or cultural extinction.

The theoretical model developed in part I of this book is intended to apply to Yanomami situations beginning at the time when outside raiding for captives ended and trading began, and ending with the onset of acculturative transformation. The effort to substantiate the model's validity with historical information in parts II and III has been lengthy and detailed, so a summary of the model is probably now in order.

It begins with the significance of steel. Steel tools are crucial means of production that, along with other Western manufactures, have been avidly sought by many, if not all, Yanomami. The problem is one of supply: Western manufactures have been scarce and unequally distributed. Improving access to them has involved three options, each with its own drawbacks. First, Yanomami can relocate their villages closer to source points, which may require the considerable effort of starting a new garden at long distance and perhaps draw the violent opposition of others. Second, people can move as individuals or families into another village with a better established supply—but they do so at the sufferance of residents who may demand a bride for the privilege. Third, a group can develop trade with a village that has good access, but again, this option may require securing goodwill with brides or other offerings.

The third option brings up the matter of intervillage economic organization. Constrained by the practicalities of travel, trade strongly tends toward stepped transactions along chains of neighboring villages, except where Yanomami have adapted to canoe travel along the broader rivers. Villages with resident or regularly visiting Westerners try to monopolize access to them and thus to their trade goods. Accomplished monopolists assure themselves a supply of goods for their own use and a surplus they can trade to more remote groups. Those who trade out Western manufactures receive considerable benefits in return: indigenous manufactures, wives, labor, and political and military support. A growing dependence on Western products thus creates a potential for sharply exploitative exchange and thus for an often pronounced ambivalence between trade partners.

Trade is the foundation of a unitary alliance relationship that is interwoven with considerations of marriage, political understandings, and status. In a multidimensional alliance of this sort, any part can stand for the whole. Thus, in a severely strained relationship, a trivial slight may be sufficient grounds for a fight. Women, the most valuable "item" of exchange and the capstone of the alliance, are frequently of central concern in times of strain, and men's disputes over them frequently trigger violent clashes.

The political character of an alliance—how people get along—is shaped by two factors: the availability of Western goods, which makes for "generous" or "stingy" trade partners, and the ability to apply force. That ability is determined primarily by four elements: direct support by Western backers, possession of shotguns, numbers of militarily able men, and exceptional fierceness of individuals. The first two correlate with direct access to a source of Western manufactures, but the last two may favor more remote groups. Different combinations of factors produce a range of possibilities and lead to changes over time that can include passage from alliance to war.

Force can be applied within an alliance through duels of varying intensity. In relatively good relationships, carefully managed chest poundings can clear the air of animosities. But in a politically charged atmosphere, pounding matches can escalate to include large numbers of men who menace each other with clubs and axes, or worse. When the violence turns deadly, it can mark the transition from alliance to war. Duels can be precipitated by various affronts because, as I just noted, any one can stand for the whole alliance relationship. The application of force in a duel is a means of affecting the terms of that relationship. The terms may be those of the exchange of women, of the balance, direction, and velocity of trade in Western versus indigenous products, and of relative status. A more violent shift from alliance to war results from a treacherous slaughter of guests at a feast. These comparatively rare events involve complicated political positionings and come about at moments of sharp contradiction in trade interests.

The shift from alliance and trade to war occurs in three general situations: when recent Western expansion into an area leads to a new, marked inequality in possession of Western goods and therefore to unsettled exchange relationships; during times of established but still limited Western presence, when shifts in the positioning of Westerners destabilizes recently developed exchange and alliance patterns; and during periods of Western retraction that creates scarcities of manufactures among more dependent people and an inability by Yanomami suppliers to live up to expectations to provide Western goods. Stability in the contact situation generally leads to a reestablishment of peaceful, albeit often strained, relations of trade and alliance.

Once a state of war exists, the expectation of danger, combined with informational limits and uncertainties, can push groups toward preemptive raiding. A period of intense raiding and counterraiding may ensue, or raids may be unidirectional. Active wars rarely last longer than two years because one side will move out of range. A frequent tactic is to kill a headman and thus militarily incapacitate his group. The human costs of war are great: death, pain, disfigurement, emotional loss, arduous and dangerous journeys, much labor, and unpleasant living circumstances. For these reasons, people seek to avoid war, and active warfare cannot be prolonged.

Generally, a war is initiated when the aggressors have reason to expect that their costs will remain relatively limited. The benefits that can outweigh such limited costs include an improved supply of Western manufactures and the corollary advantages it brings. In some efforts, supply is improved directly, through plunder. More often, the strategic rationale is to affect intervillage economics by eliminating, preserving, or inserting a middleman in a trade network.

When Western manufactures are in short supply everywhere, or when they are available in abundance from multiple sources—so that in either case there is relative equality in possession of them—no raiding is expected, according to the terms of this model (although other sources of conflict could certainly develop). Raiding is predicted to occur when there is a general scarcity of steel but marked local inequalities in possession. The standard pattern is that more isolated groups raid better connected villages when the latter do not have the political and military advantages provided by a resident, armed Westerner. This direction of raiding is typically reversed as Western outpost villages establish military hegemony; then violence often occurs out beyond the first dependent allies. Other strategic uses of violence are to prevent a group from establishing a new garden in a location that would harm the aggressors' trade interests, and to keep people from more remote groups from attempting to bypass middlemen and approach the sources directly.

The expression of all these posited relationships displays several major variations, as well as seemingly endless local permutations. Across much of the northern range of their territory, Yanomami entered into war or subordinate alliances, or both, with non-Yanomami who had better access to sources of Western goods. The main version of this pattern joined the Sanema with the Yecuana, but Ninam, Yanomamo, and even some Yanomam were drawn to these options as well, and others besides Yecuana sometimes assumed the dominant position. In this pattern, the ethnic disjunction between unequal allies adds a categorical element absent in intra-Yanomami relations, but otherwise the structure of the relationship is quite similar to that of relationships between dominant and dependent Yanomami groups (see Ferguson n.d.c).

Farther east, a critical difference in geography gave rise to another major variation. Ninam and later Yanomam lived close to the trade artery of the Uraricoera and the huge trade network to its north. Some local groups became dependent allies of established traders, while others pirated passing trade goods. When this violence forced the few peoples remaining on the rivers to leave, the Yanomami moved in, joined the trade system, and promptly gave up raiding. Farther south, several groups of Yanomam and Yanomamo experienced another distinctive pattern in the decades after the rubber boom, first working for and then raiding and looting *balateros* and other woodsmen.

The year 1950 marks the beginning of the missions and other outposts of resident Westerners. The missions provide a sample of cases for comparison, and information about local intervillage relations is often exceptionally good. As these situations have been described, the Yanomami's efforts to control the sources of Western goods seem uniform, but the political-military relations that developed around the outposts varied considerably. This varying political character was shaped by the quantity of Western goods flowing from source points, by the ability of different groups to apply force, and by the stability or instability of the Western presence.

In all the major pattern variations, however, violence extends outward from the areas where Western goods are first received. The center of contact itself may pass into largely nonviolent, if still antagonistic, political relations, but those who obtain goods through trade, service, or ceding women often find themselves attacked by other Yanomami farther out. When Yanomami subordinated themselves to Yecuana, the "tame" villages were frequently attacked by *bravos* to the south. When Yanomami broke through the Uraricoera into the Guiana trade network, they were raided in turn by the "wild" people of the mountains. When some more southern local groups became wealthy in steel by working for or plundering woodsmen, they were assaulted from behind by others. And around so many of the missions, war was recorded between the outpost monopolists' allies and those farther away—although, dealing from strength, the mission group's allies were more likely to be the aggressors than the victims. All this fighting is what constitutes the internal warfare of the Yanomami.

The Orinoco-Mavaca area—the main focus of part III—lay at the extreme end of the spectrum of violence, in contrast to the relatively peaceful Mucajaí and Catrimani mission zones and even the nearby Iyewei-teri. Sporadic contacts along the Orinoco from the late 1930s were linked to increasing tensions and outright warfare. Starting in 1950, a major Western "invasion" occurred, but no secure Western support for any group existed during its first years, and warfare reached a high pitch. Over all these years of antagonism and high mortality from disease and war, local society was disrupted and destabilized, making the instrumental use of violence common and lowering the threshold for war.

Nevertheless, stabilization of the Western presence was soon followed by Mahekoto-teri hegemony and a return to peace after the mid-1950s. Subsequent changes in the Western presence in the late 1950s led to new tensions and actual warfare in areas of marked retraction. Around the juncture of the Orinoco and Mavaca rivers, tensions were brought to a boil by the arrival of new Westerners in 1964. But again within a few years, the new situation was accommodated and wars ended. The worst violence then passed outward to more remote areas experiencing new contacts.

Comparing the Orinoco-Mavaca area between 1937 and 1968 to other places and times, its periods of warfare were not necessarily the most protracted and intense periods of violence ever experienced by the Yanomami. The slave raids of the mid-eighteenth century and the rubber boom of the late nineteenth and early twentieth centuries may have produced as much or more bloodshed in some areas. But the wars of the Orinoco-Mavaca area certainly were the worst of any well-reported situation, and we have extensive and detailed information about them. These Yanomami truly were fierce people, but that fierceness was not an expression of Yanomami culture itself.

The form of explanation employed in this book is not like most anthropological theorizing on war. The application of the model is historical: it maps the actual occurrence of war and other major developments against discernible interests in regard to the contact situation. The model interlocks with another approach (Ferguson 1992a) that can be applied only to situations with unusually complete reporting. In the article just cited, I posit that the broad disruptions of Western contact have fostered reliance on violence in interpersonal affairs and lowered the threshold at which conflict turns to war.

My causal, deterministic approach to history is hardly the current style. It is also true that not every case fits the theoretical expectations and that many individual wars could just as easily be explained by other theories. But when one considers *all* Yanomami wars, clear exceptions to the pattern are few and the evidence in support of the theory is strong. Ultimately, the test of any theory is how well it explains the facts in comparison with other theories. In the following sections, I contrast my approach to the other major theories that have been offered to explain Yanomami warfare.

The Protein Hypothesis

One major line of explanation has come to be known as the protein hypothesis (see Chagnon 1983:81–89; Chagnon and Hames 1979, 1980; Gross 1982; Hames and Vickers 1983:12–18; Harris 1984; Sponsel 1983). Actually, there are several linked hypotheses, which I have discussed individually in two previous publications (Ferguson 1989b, 1989c). Readers interested in the details of the theories and in the pan-Amazonian evidence are referred to those works. In this discussion, I will stick to the main points and the Yanomami situation.

It was Jane Bennett Ross (1971) who initially proposed that Yanomami warfare was an adaptive response to the limited availability of nutritionally necessary game animals. The general hypothesis, however, has been argued most persistently by Marvin Harris (1974, 1977, 1979, 1984). The basic structure of the theory begins with the observation that it is the male's role to provide meat. As Siskind (1973b) suggested on the basis of her work among the Sharanahua, culturally patterned expectations require that men provide meat to women who provide sex. Game is depleted by hunting, and hunting pressure is a function of village size and the length of time spent in one location. As local game availability declines and hunters experience diminishing returns for their effort, male competition over women intensifies, leading to fighting within groups and raiding between them. Thus—the theory goes—game depletion leads to conflicts over women, which lead to war.

The fact that war makes Yanomami groups move apart from each other is interpreted as having two adaptive consequences: the no-man's-land between enemies acts as a kind of game preserve, allowing animal populations to replenish themselves; and people in flight may pioneer new or long-unused territory where game is more abundant. A related hypothesis was first proposed by Divale (1970) and elaborated by Divale and Harris (1976): by fostering a male supremacist ideology, war among the Yanomami leads to a devaluation of females, a preference for male babies, and a pattern of female infanticide. Divale and Harris suggest that female infanticide, so induced by war, is a primary means of population regulation in band and village societies.[1]

In one earlier paper (Ferguson 1989b), I examined the first half of this theory—that a limited game supply leads to warfare. After reviewing data from all over Amazonia, I concluded that although there is much evidence to support aspects of the model, there are also reasons why it is inadequate as a general explanation of Amazonian war. Diminishing returns for hunting effort do beset larger, settled villages, and decreasing hunting success is accompanied by a variety of tensions along gender lines. But the typical result is that people move, not that they go to war.

Regarding the Yanomamo specifically, the question of game availability and protein consumption in the Orinoco-Mavaca area has been bitterly contested, without anyone's presenting definitive evidence (see Ferguson 1992a:205). No one disputes that by the mid-1970s, game was almost entirely depleted in the areas most exposed to hunting by mission groups, but it is not clear when diminishing returns and decreasing supply initially set in. I believe they began within a very few years after any Western outpost anchored a local Yanomamo group in one place. Chagnon and Lizot may disagree with me about this timing, but we are all in accord that game depletion is not an expectable result of subsistence practices of Yanomami who are not stuck to a Westerner.

Good's fieldwork (1989, 1991) among a less settled group demonstrates that unanchored Yanomami regularly move around in hunts and between gardens. Helena Valero's two narratives (Biocca 1971; Valero 1984) provide abundant confirmation. Moves respond to a variety of considerations, game availability being a significant one. These movements seem to prevent depletion and ensure a generally adequate supply of meat, without recourse to war. Good (1989:135–40) also describes how a decline in meat sharing in a larger village led to decreased solidarity and tendencies toward fission, without suggesting that a fissioning is predictably followed by war.

Reviewing the case material compiled in this book, there are instances where indications of local game depletion are reported before a turn to war. Certainly the most significant case is the conflict between Fusiwe's people and Bisaasi-teri over the Shihota location (chapter 11), in which quarrels about meat distribution and animosity over local game depletion are reported. In Chagnon's reconstruction of this conflict, fighting over women is also involved. This one important and unusually well-described case thus demonstrates the full theoretical sequence: (1) problems with game supply, (2) followed by fighting over women, (3) followed by war. But the Shihota case is the only one I know of in which the full sequence is indicated, and even this case of conflict, when considered in full, is more thoroughly and securely explained by considerations of access to Western goods.

In my view, game depletion in areas around Western outposts is an important factor leading to diminished reciprocity and encouraging the instrumental use of force, thus helping to lower the threshold for war. Conflicts related to game and garden produce can also provide the trigger for war between two groups who already have a strained relationship—as can insults, suspicions of witchcraft, or disputes over women. Game depletion can be a contributing factor, but only that, in the occurrence of war. It does not explain why actual warfare breaks out in certain times and places.

In another paper (Ferguson 1989c), I considered the second half of the protein hypothesis—its posited adaptive effects—again using data from all around Amazonia. Although buffer zones and population relocations do result from war, it is not clear that these provide major adaptive advantages that could not also be attained without war. Moreover, war may force populations to concentrate for defensive purposes, and this nucleation may itself lead to less efficient exploitation of game resources.

All these observations appear to be applicable to Yanomami warfare. It has been documented repeatedly that wars end when one group moves away from another. It seems only common sense that sometimes those in flight will enjoy better hunting in their new location, and that a no-man's-land between blood enemies will witness an increase in local game. But there is no evidence that either of these considerations plays a crucial role in the Yanomami's adaptation to their natural environment. Moreover, long-distance movements into new territory, although often spurred by the "push" of war, are much more often motivated by the "pull" of sources of Western goods. And when people have to put up with a diminished game supply in order to preserve access to Western goods, they learn to cope. In sum, there is only a very tenuous relationship between game depletion, war, and movements that increase game availability.

Regarding the postulated adaptive effect of increased female infanticide, the issue is more complicated. Divale (1970:175) attributes his formulation of the model to a reading of Chagnon, and Chagnon's own descriptions (1967:139–41, 1972b:273–74, 1973:134, 1975:96) repeatedly state that there is a circular relationship among warfare, preference for male children, female infanticide, a scarcity of adult women, conflict over women, and war.[2] What Divale and Harris (1976) do is relate the competition over women to game scarcity and extend the argument to postulate consequences of population regulation.[3]

In my previous paper (Ferguson 1989c:254–255), I argued that evidence, though far from conclusive, does support an association of female infanticide with times of active warfare among the Yanomami—although perhaps not the exact association postulated by Divale and Harris. On the other hand, the evidence does not indicate that such female infanticide leads to stabilization of population, which, as discussed in chapter 4, has been growing rapidly in recent years. My current research found additional support for the existence of preferential female infanticide and its association with times of war. Eguillor García (1984:50–51) documents that the practice does exist in the Orinoco-Mavaca area. Without reference to time period, she reports that of 482 live births, 15 males and 24 females were killed.

Early and Peters (1990:133–37), working around the Mucajaí mission, produced the most comprehensive demographic study done for any Yanomami group. Although they criticize what they see as an exaggerated emphasis on female infanticide, their own analysis tends to support Divale and Harris's position. First, they confirm that "preferential female infanticide is practiced precisely to hasten another pregnancy and birth, hopefully a male" (1990:136–37). This is in keeping with the Divale-Harris proposition that war encourages female infanticide by elevating the preference for male children. Second, their data show that women make up only 22.6 percent of the cohort born between 1914 and 1943 (1990:20–21), a period in which this group was involved in several wars (see chapter 7). The cause of this imbalance is not known, but it is consistent with Divale and Harris's expectations. Third, the study population appears to have been shrinking prior to contact in 1958, a fact clearly linked to the extreme scarcity of women (Early and Peters 1990:19–23, 140), which in turn supports the posited population control function.

Overall, there is a great deal of evidence that the integrated propositions that make up the "protein hypothesis" deal with genuine relationships. Where it is weakest, however, is precisely as an explanation of the occurrence of warfare.

An Eye for an Eye?

Despite their disagreements on many topics, Lizot (1991:68–70) and Chagnon (1988:986) coincide in emphasizing revenge as an explanation for Yanomami warfare.[4] Lizot's explanation invokes Mauss and Lévi-Strauss; it claims that Yanomami fight in the spirit of reciprocity, giving blow for blow. I do not question that Yanomami see war this way. It is part of my model that material interests are converted into moral terms, and always, "they started it."[5] But how can reciprocity explain the change from peace to war and war to peace? How can it explain spatial and temporal variation in the history of conflicts?[6] Lizot's response seems to be that it does not have to, because war and peace are fundamentally the same thing—merely alternative modalities of the fundamental, underlying reality of the spirit of reciprocity. I remain unconvinced that war and peace are essentially the same.[7]

Chagnon (1979a:87, 1988:985–87) avoids these more obvious problems because he argues that wars start over other issues—mainly women—and are (only) continued for revenge. His larger theoretical point is that seeking revenge may confer a reproductive advantage on an individual or a group of kin because a reputation for ferocity may deter others from attacking or attempting to take advantage of them.

Revenge is frequently cited as a cause of "primitive warfare," but its value as an explanation is questionable (Ferguson 1984b:39–40, 1988c:ii–iii). I distinguish revenge—a desire to strike back at someone who has wronged you—from retaliation—a counterstrike against an enemy intended to deter future attacks. In some, but not all, political circumstances, retaliation is a sensible tactic. When a group is retaliating, or even when it is initiating new hostilities, it will use the rhetoric of vengeance to rationalize action and mobilize support (Ferguson 1992a: 223–25). Along with other moral themes, especially those of witchcraft and bravery or cowardice, revenge can be used to persuade others to adopt a course of action. I believe, however, that Black-Michaud's (1975:50) generalization—"whatever the rules relative to passive solidarity, the taking of vengeance always tends everywhere to be the affair of the close agnates of the victim rather than the group as a whole"—applies even within the highly interrelated local groups of the Yanomami.

Except where many different members of a local group have similar losses to avenge—such as after the Shamatari's killing of as many as 15 Bisaasi-teri men (chapter 11)—a blood debt alone will generally not lead to war. In a great many cases reported in this book, perhaps even a majority, a killing is not followed by any counterraid within the next few years. Chagnon probably would not restrict the time frame that narrowly: "Vengeance motivation persists for many years" (Chagnon 1988:986). The only case he cites to substantiate that claim, however, is the 1975 raid by Bisaasi-teri on Patanowa-teri, supposedly intended to avenge the 1965 killing of the Monou-teri headman. This is the case discussed in chapter 14, where it was pointed out that Chagnon had originally stated that the blood debt went in the opposite direction—that it was the Patanowa-teri who needed vengeance. Thus the actual behavior is the reverse of what was specifically predicted in earlier publications.

Moreover, I found numerous incidents described in the literature in which a claimed need for revenge was obviously manipulated. The demand for vengeance can be trumped up, as when the Monou-teri needed to avenge the Patanowa-teri's repossession of five of their own women (chapter 13). It can be forgotten and then suddenly remembered when politically convenient, as it was by Chagnon's friend Rerebawa regarding the Shamatari (chapter 14). It can even be fabricated out of whole cloth, as happened during recent raids by mission Yanomami on the Yanomamo of the Siapa region (chapter 14).

Chagnon makes the general point that physical revenge may be sought for an imputed sorcery killing, so that "even in the absence of active military contest, Yanomamo groups constantly generate mutual hostility" (1972b:259). A sorcery accusation, of course, is virtually a "strain gauge" (Marwick 1970) for the tenor of relations between groups, a point Chagnon (1977:118) makes himself.

In my view, the Yanomami control revenge; they are not controlled by it. For people other than the victim's very closest kin, revenge is a real but highly malleable motivating factor. There are frequently many dormant reasons for seeking revenge, and if none exists, some can be made up. They come to the fore in conflict situations because that is one way to frame materially self-interested actions in moral terms. Vengeance is "good to think" and good to persuade.[8] But a focus on vengeance will not elucidate why wars happen. Nor do I think that those who take revenge are doing themselves a reproductive favor. That point, however, will be considered in a later discussion.

Fighting over Women

There is no question that Yanomami men on many occasions fight over women; there is no doubt that such fights sometimes lead to war. What is in dispute is the theoretical significance of this fighting and, in particular, its utility in explaining war. Chagnon, of course, is most closely associated with the position that Yanomami go to war over women (e.g., 1968:123, 1992b:112–14). In his doctoral thesis, after noting a shortage of sexually available women resulting from female infanticide, polygyny, and postpartum sex taboos, he offers the hypothesis: "The frequency of intra-village fighting and intervillage warfare co-varies with the frequency with which males may legitimately satisfy sexual desires" (Chagnon 1966:2).

From the middle 1970s onward, Chagnon's position became encompassed within his evolving sociobiological perspective, in which Yanomami fighting was seen as a form of sexual selection—part of a broader process of competition for mates aimed at maximizing inclusive fitness (Chagnon 1979a:87–89, 1983:86, 1987:29, 1990b). Chagnon acknowledges that men will compete and fight over material resources when they are scarce, but he argues that when resources are abundant, men will compete and fight over women and reproductive success. It is the latter situation, he maintains, that applies to the Yanomami (1979a: 87, 103–104, 1979b:375–77, 401, 1980:123, 1981:507, 1990b:82).

In a previous paper (Ferguson 1988b:151–52), I questioned whether there is evidence to support Chagnon's (1980:123) proposed inverse relationship between material resource scarcity and (1) polygyny and (2) fighting over women, either among the Yanomami or elsewhere. In the discussion to follow, I will consider first some other questions related to the connection between war and fighting over women, and then the issue of whether aggressive Yanomami men actually do increase their reproductive success.

It is my impression that the anthropological and general publics misunderstand Chagnon's position. Judging from countless conversations, I believe most people think Chagnon's argument is that competition between men is the cause of raiding to capture women. But Chagnon (1977:123) asserts that raids are *not* initiated in order to capture women, although once raiding begins, that possibility is an additional incentive. Rather, Chagnon's central theory (1979a, 1982:305, 1988:986) appears to be that competition over women within a local group leads to fissioning, and fissioning frequently leads to war between segments.

Certainly such sequences of events do occur. But recently fissioned villages go to war only in some cases, and local groups often divide without any hint of a major fight over women. Thus Chagnon's most detailed theoretical discussion can apply only to some fraction of reported wars. To that number could reasonably be added cases where intermarriage between villages is followed by a fight over women that leads to war. But most such conflicts concerning marriage do not result in war, and I suggest they might more appropriately be considered as the operation of law. Even judging from the most inclusive number of cases, for many Yanomami wars we have no indication of any conflict over women antecedent to the outbreak of violence.

In a recent summary exposition, Chagnon's expectations about behavior are framed very broadly: "I am simply arguing that conflicts of reproductive interests occur commonly in band and tribal societies and that these often lead . . . to intergroup conflicts that we traditionally consider to be warfare" (1990b:82). Whether conflicts over women should necessarily be considered "conflicts of reproductive interests" will be discussed below. But if I understand Chagnon's position correctly, all he predicts about behavior is that in the multiple and complicated interpersonal and intergroup relations that precede the outbreak of war, it is common to find reports of a fight between men over women. As an empirical generalization, this prediction cannot be disputed. But it still applies only to some cases of war, and even in those cases it is typically only one of several antecedent grievances.

Consider the two cases Chagnon picked to illustrate his position. One (Chagnon 1990b:96–97, 104) involves a disputed reclassification of potential marriage partners in 1960, which eventually led to a village's fissioning. (The reclassification is apparently the incident described in Chagnon 1977:87, but which fissioning it refers to is not clear.) After fissioning, the two divisions had other, similar quarrels, and a rape in 1986 led them to the brink of war. But instead of going to war, they dissipated their hostility in a club fight. Chagnon (1990b:97) concludes that "*if* a 'war' develops" (my emphasis) then it would be "misleading to argue that reproductive striving is irrelevant to understanding the development of that war." The other illustrative case (Chagnon 1990b: 98–101) is the incident that took place around 1979 when the old Bisaasi-teri headman, Kaobawa, was pelted by Tayari-teri children, an insult that was followed by war (chapter 14).

In his discussion, Chagnon (1990b:101) states that neither of these two conflicts can be attributed to one isolated provocation—that they are "continuations of smouldering antagonisms that originate in a multitude of previous acts," including seductions, male competition over females, insults, status testing, and a desire for revenge. He concludes that "it is relatively easy to relate all of these variables to reproductive striving" because, he claims, a village that fails to respond aggressively to any slight will be victimized and lose women.

Neither of the two cases Chagnon chose to exemplify his theory provides any support for a posited connection between fighting over women and war. In the first, a disputed marriage reclassification a quarter-century earlier is said not to be "irrelevant" to a war that could have happened (but didn't) in 1986. In the second case, a war did erupt after a series of insults, but none of the sources describing this war refers to any conflict over women having been involved. As Lizot, who was there, points out (1989:28): "The element 'competition to obtain women' is totally absent in the initiation of the hostilities and the development of the crisis."

Thus the operative point in Chagnon's exposition becomes that it is "easy" to relate any and all fighting to "reproductive striving," because aggressive behavior itself is believed to have a reproductive payoff. I will consider that issue in a moment. For the current issue—whether Yanomami warfare can be explained with reference to fighting over women—the two cases Chagnon has selected in fact make opposite points: disputes over women can occur without leading to war, and wars can occur without any triggering dispute over women.

My own position regarding men fighting over women has several components. In an earlier comparative study (Ferguson 1988b:148–52), I noted that regardless of what causes war, the Yanomami stand out among Amazonian societies for the political prominence of their fighting over women, and I suggested several underlying features that may be responsible for that distinction: the unusually limited basis for female cooperation in an economy reliant on plantains rather than bitter manioc; the existence of strong fraternal interest groups in some areas; and the ideological reinforcement associated with unusually intensive warfare. In my article on "warrification" of the Orinoco-Mavaca Yanomami (Ferguson 1992a), I identified additional factors: the atypical number of marriages between villages, which make women more significant as political symbols and leave them more subject to abuse; and the high number of deaths from disease and war, which in an otherwise disturbed environment encourage the instrumental use of force to decide marriage arrangements. (Ramos [1979c:186] emphasizes that the picture of male dominance presented by Chagnon does not apply to Yanomami in other areas.)

In this book I have been concerned with marriage primarily as the capstone of a total relationship between groups. The tone of that relationship is determined in part by each group's ability to apply force, but also and more fundamentally by the distribution of Western goods. From my perspective, it is the total relationship that is at issue in any fight. In a good relationship, many things can be overlooked. In a bad one, any dispute can trigger violence. The detonator may be food, status, or sorcery, but fights will frequently be "over women" because exchanged women are the ultimate medium of alliance.

Striving for Reproduction

A further difference between my position and Chagnon's is that I do not accept the presumption expressed in his sociobiological writings that conflict over women is in itself evidence that male behavior is motivated by "reproductive striving." Men may fight over women for reasons other than maximization of inclusive fitness. Yanomami women may be part of a contract between groups who have definite expectations about trade and political support. Women are laborers, and their value may increase when they have the option of working for missionaries. They are sex partners—a role quite distinct from that of being a mother. Obviously, sex leads to reproduction, but what Chagnon is (or at least was) arguing is that reproductive success in itself is a goal with a direct impact on individual behavior.

The proposition that people deliberately act in ways that maximize their inclusive fitness is the most distinctive and debatable point in human sociobiology. Chagnon (1987:29) holds that "Yanomamo males are tracking their environment with their own fitness interests at stake," and they "manipulate and adapt to [this environment] in striving for reproductive success and maximal inclusive fitness." In earlier work (Chagnon 1979a:128; Chagnon and Bugos 1979:223), Chagnon held this motivation to be unconscious but strongly determinative—comparable to the effect of gravity on a falling rock or to planetary motion. In recent theoretical statements (1988:985, 1990b:79, 81), he argues that there are two kinds of resources people strive for, two kinds of human effort, two kinds of competition: somatic and reproductive.

Thus there is no ambiguity in the hypothesis Chagnon has advanced for over a decade: a desire to maximize inclusive fitness is itself a major factor shaping Yanomami behavioral decisions. Yet in a rejoinder to me (Ferguson 1989d), Chagnon (1989b:567–68) introduces an entirely different proposition: "I maintain that it is useful and legitimate to investigate the possibility that material gain might possibly be turned into reproductive benefits . . . that is, I am interested in ultimate (reproductive) consequences, not just proximate (immediate material gain) consequences." This distinction between ultimate and proximate goals is very different from distinguishing between alternative goals, and it gives rise to a completely different set of theoretical expectations and understandings.

I find nothing to argue about in the proposition that individuals tend to their material self-interest and that in evolutionary perspective, such self-interest has a generally favorable impact on reproductive success.[9] But it remains very much in question whether aggressive behavior itself can be seen as a reproductive strategy (see Moore 1990), even among the Yanomami.

The main evidence for aggression's having a reproductive payoff appears in Chagnon's (1988) controversial article in *Science*. In that piece, Chagnon asserts that *unokai*, men who have undergone the purification ritual for killers, have considerably more wives and children than do other men. His position was immediately challenged by Albert (1989: 638, 1990a:559–60) and Lizot (1989:33), who claim that the status of *unokai* is not an accurate marker of men who have killed. Chagnon (1990a:49–50) replies that the way he collected the data, it is. I leave this argument to those with the necessary linguistic competence and field experience.

My own dispute with Chagnon (Ferguson 1989d) has been about whether his statistical data show that *unokai*, as Chagnon defines them, really do have greater reproductive success (and see Albert 1990a:560–61). These are the only published data relevant to his claim that taking revenge is adaptive because those who do so are less likely to be attacked, and to his more sweeping claim that a demonstrated willingness to fight contributes to reproductive success by deterring the aggression of others.

The way in which Chagnon has characterized his findings in recent publications is not, I believe, what his statistics show. Chagnon (1990b: 95, and see 1992a:205, 1992b:239–40) claims his research demonstrates that *unokai* have more than three times as many children as non-*unokai of the same age*. His data, in contrast, show that this 308-percent difference in number of children is derived from the total sample, *not* broken down by age. This is a significant distinction. His table, divided into four age categories, makes clear that "success" in both killing and reproduction is associated with age: younger men are less likely to have killed or had children. As I have pointed out previously (Ferguson 1989d:564), in the two older age categories—which include 86 percent of all *unokai*—the number of children reported for *unokai* men shrinks to 140 percent and 167 percent of the number reported for non-*unokai* men. Differences of such magnitude could still represent a substantial reproductive payoff for "killers," but closer examination calls that inference into question.

In my previous critique (1989d), I raised three questions about Chagnon's data and inferences. One was that these apparent differences in *unokai*'s reproductive success might represent a spurious correlation. As Chagnon (1988:988) notes, all the headmen in the sample are in the *unokai* category. An exceptional tendency toward polygyny by political leaders, with or without war, has been an axiom of Amazonian ethnography for at least half a century.[10]

This is the only one of my three points that Chagnon seriously addresses in his rejoinder (1989b:566). Reanalyzing the statistics with headmen factored out, he reports that there remains a statistical relationship at the 0.05 level of significance in all but one age category. He concludes: "I would not care to argue, given these data, that living *unokais* among the Yanomamo have *fewer* offspring than non-*unokais*." This assertion of a statistically significant relationship between *unokai* status and marital and reproductive success is a far cry from the claim that *unokai*, "compared to same-age non-*unokai*, have over twice as many wives and over three times as many children" (Chagnon 1990b: 95). But if Chagnon's reanalysis supports my point that the inclusion of headmen skewed the results, it still does not establish that aggressive men have even a marginal statistical advantage in reproduction, because of other problems with the data.

My second objection (Ferguson 1989d:564) is that some of the apparent correlation of *unokai* status with higher numbers of wives and children may be a result of covariation with age *within* the four age categories. A 40-year-old man, for example, is more likely to be *unokai* and to have more children than a 31-year-old man. Chagnon's (1989b:568–69) response is that precise estimates of age are impossible, and so lumping people into categories is necessary.[11] Perhaps so, but that does not address the problem. Given that the correlation is drastically reduced by factoring out headmen, this additional source of potential bias raises the question whether any relationship, even a statistical one, really exists.

The third problem is the most serious. For reasons Chagnon does not explain, his data on reproductive success (1988:989) do not include "living children whose fathers are dead." I question the impact of participation in a killing on the likelihood of being killed (Ferguson 1989d: 564): Does the average *unokai* live and breed longer than the average non-*unokai*? After compiling the case material presented in this book, I emphasize this question even more (and see Albert 1990a:560–61).

Most of the men identified as war leaders were killed in war, including Ruwahiwe of the Konabuma-teri, Fusiwe of the Wanitima-teri, Rashawe of the Bisaasi-teri, Riokowe of the Iwahikoroba-teri, Kohawe of the Shitari, and Damowa of the Monou-teri. People were expecting Helena Valero's second husband, Akawe, to be killed before he fled to the world of the *nape* (Valero 1984:471). Moreover, at least one of Riokowe's children was killed by his enemies, and Valero had to flee to prevent the same from happening to Fusiwe's children. Only Kaobawa's rival, Paruriwa, seems to have prospered after leading several raids, and he did so by securing the support of the Salesians and obtaining a shotgun. All this evidence suggests that unusually active leaders in violence could lose so many reproductive years that it would diminish their lifetime reproductive success.

In his response, Chagnon (1989b:566) acknowledges that this is an important issue and adds one new item of information and inference. He claims that one headman—Moawa of the Mishimishimabowei-teri, now dead from unknown causes—had killed an extraordinary number of people (21 or 22) and left no living children. He concludes: "Being *excessively* prone to lethal violence may not be an effective route to high reproductive success, but, statistically, men who engage in it with some moderation seem to do better reproductively than men who do not engage in it at all." In short, adding in deceased men and their offspring could lower the *unokai*'s measured reproductive advantage; it is certainly within the realm of possibility that *unokai* men would be found to have fewer offspring than non-*unokai*.

Chagnon (1989b:566) states that he now has the data to address this question, collected during fieldwork that he carried out after completing the *Science* article, and "as my schedule permits, I will publish them." He reassures us that "while I have not completed the analysis of these new data, my impressions of how they are shaping up give me little reason to believe that my initial suspicions [that *unokai* are not at greater risk of violent death] are wrong" (1989b:566). At the time of this writing, over four years have passed and the new data have not yet appeared in any publication with which I am familiar. When they do, it may be possible to begin to answer the question of whether killing another person has the effect of increasing the lifetime reproductive success of Yanomami men. That question cannot be addressed with the information provided so far. At present, there simply are no data that substantiate the claim that aggressive behavior is associated with reproductive success among the Yanomami.[12]

A Demographic Pump?

In recent fieldwork in the highlands of the Siapa region, Chagnon (1992a:82–86) found that in contrast to the warlike peoples of the Orinoco-Mavaca area, the Siapa people were gentle and sedate. They also differed in several of the correlates of war, having smaller villages, less elaborate alliances and so less feasting, and fewer marriages based on abduction or coercion. When there was coercion, highland women went to lowland men.

To explain this contrast, Chagnon invokes ecological differences in altitude, terrain, and the fordability of local rivers. The lower lands near the Orinoco are said to be richer in "game animals, plants for food, construction and manufactures, and well-drained easily cultivated lands for gardens" (Chagnon 1992a:83). In the mountainous areas, it is much more difficult and costly just to keep alive. On the other hand, the wider Orinoco and lower Mavaca and Siapa rivers are difficult to cross, so Yanomamo generally avoided settling there until the advent of the missionaries. "These low, flat areas in regions where the rivers are small and easily crossed are the regions that Kaobawa's people—and many other groups—appear to have preferred as settlement locations for the past 150 or so years; and these areas are dotted with hundreds of long-since abandoned gardens—more than 500 of them" (Chagnon 1992a:83).

According to Chagnon, it is competition for prime resource land that explains the political tone of the lowlands.

> Groups that live in the lowlands have to be large and bellicose in order to control the large, desirable, and wide-open ecological niche they live in. They seem to keep their neighbors at a comfortable distance by adopting an extremely bellicose strategy that entails frequent raiding and chronic attempts to either abduct

women from their neighbors or coerce weaker neighbors into ceding more women than they ultimately "repay" via marriage alliance agreements. To be effective at this, they must maximize village size. (Chagnon 1992a:87)

The problem, as he explains it, is that for other reasons, villages tend to fission after reaching a certain size. In the local atmosphere of violent competition, the new, smaller groups have three options: they can live close together to maintain an advantage in numbers; they can move into more marginal highland zones; or they can pioneer into vacant lowlands. The second option is the most relevant for Chagnon's recent observations. He posits a repeated pattern in which groups are pushed out of optimum areas such as the Shanishani drainage, longtime home of the Patanowa-teri. The Shanishani area is said to have functioned as a kind of "demographic pump" (Chagnon 1992a:88), spewing groups westward and southward through the Siapa region.

This argument represents a surprising turn to cultural ecology after Chagnon's years of sociobiological theorizing. It does not invoke reproductive competition, and although it contains no suggestion that war may be related to differential access to Western goods, Chagnon's new approach does include many points that are convergent with positions I have argued in this book.

Chagnon (1992a:89) acknowledges the "possible" role of sources of Western goods in pulling Yanomamo southward across the Siapa River. He acknowledges (1992a:86) an inequality in relations between people in areas of greater exposure to Westerners and those in the more isolated hills—an inequality that involves a unidirectional ceding of women. He acknowledges (1992a:209–10) that the most isolated Yanomamo appear to be the most peaceable. He describes (1992a:220) a recent wave of wars that pitted mission groups against "wild" groups. And he posits a "demographic pump" (1992a:88) that sounds very much like an idea I proposed in an earlier paper (Ferguson 1989c:255), following Steward and Lathrap—the idea of a prehistoric "population pump" whereby war pushes people from prime lowland resource zones into mountains and other marginal areas.

There is, however, one seemingly insurmountable problem in applying a model of pre-Columbian population movements to the historical Yanomami. Whether or not the Yanomami of the past 150 years "preferred" to live in low, flat areas, where they *actually* lived until recently was not in the low flatlands but in the Parima and Siapa highlands.

Chagnon's proposed pump, pushing Yanomami from lowlands into highlands, may fit certain local situations during the twentieth century, but as a general process, population movements have been from higher to lower ground.

Another evidentiary problem confronts the suggestion that people in the lowlands are warlike while those in the highlands are peaceable. That frequently is the case because lowland groups are usually more exposed to Westerners, and the highlanders are more isolated. But we have seen numerous instances where groups with greater exposure to sources of Western goods are pushed farther into low country by attacks from more isolated groups from higher elevations. On several occasions, war has broken out between highland groups after a Western presence was established there; and several lowland groups, under facilitating circumstances, are reported to have been quite peaceable. Thus the lowland/highland dichotomy is less adequate as an explanation of war than are circumstances of access to Westerners.

Emics and Agency

The point of this book has been to understand why war happens. Not war as a quality of a species, not war as an abstract cultural pattern, but war as actual practice: war in which real people die at particular places and times. My explanation is a highly deterministic model applied to observed behavior. But real wars are not carried out by models. What about the real people? Have they no say in what happens? And if my model is right, why has no Yanomami ever offered it as an explanation of why he fights?

Several years ago (Ferguson 1984b:38–42), I called attention to the many problems involved in eliciting emic statements about the motivations that lead to war, and I advocated instead an approach that infers motive from action—an etic, behavioral approach. But the question of the Yanomami's stated reasons for war deserves a direct answer.

One answer might be that the Yanomami do not want the *nape* to know why they fight. It is well documented that they are skilled at misleading outsiders—witness their concealing deadly raids from missionaries who loaned them shotguns, or their countless tales of ferocious killer Waikas upstream, or their five months of comedy at Chagnon's expense over the fake genealogies. All Westerners among the Yanomami experience their nearly overwhelming demands for manufactured goods; those demands cannot be concealed. But how would missionaries and other well-meaning Westerners react if their local friends explained that people were being killed over them? Revenge, fights over women, and witchcraft, on the other hand, are all acceptable as local culture— something the stranger is there to study or reform.

Although deliberate manipulation of outsiders may be one reason why Yanomami do not offer conflict over Western goods as an explanation of their fighting, I would not push this too far. Helena Valero's two narratives provide an insider's perspective on some wars and show that the Yanomamo do not talk in terms of my model even among themselves. Indeed, if one read those two accounts and nothing else, one would probably see Napoleon Chagnon's views on war as more accurate than mine. Valero's husband Fusiwe—unusually polygamous, highly aggressive, ready to respond violently to perceived insult—is virtually the Chagnonian ideal. But his behavior does conform to the patterns I have argued and documented, and there are indications that his real motives for war remained unspoken.

Fusiwe began wars without any reported reference to differential access to Western manufactures. He justified the killing of Ruwahiwe as revenge for sorcery. But after the slaughter, his kinsman Repowe accused Fusiwe, in the logic of the concrete, of killing the Shamatari because he was left out of the trading of machetes for dogs. Later, when Bisaasiteri provocations and his youngest wife's jibes goaded him into starting a war, Fusiwe lied about his intentions to his own people, while Valero and others openly speculated that he was pursuing some hidden agenda.

But the most revealing incident in Valero's narrative occurs with her second husband. Fearing for his own safety and wanting the largesse of the *nape,* Akawe goaded other men with accusations of cowardice, inciting them to take revenge on the Shitari. It was a sham—a ruse to give himself and Valero an opportunity to flee to the whites. The only reason Valero learned of the deception was because she was part of the plot.

The position advocated here is that material interests are converted into moral points for public discourse. Everyone knows the existing circumstances and what may be at stake. But basic interests, even matters of life and death, can only become realities in a social world. Everything else in life is piled on top of those basic interests: family, politics, status, and, above all, a value system. To behave as a pure "economic man," openly and rationally weighing costs and benefits to decide on war, oblivious to this highly textured social reality, would be, in a word, crazy.

Public discussion invokes collective values to persuade, to put pressure on those with mixed feelings, to make someone's self-interest seem an expression of moral principle. In the process, unadorned material interests are put into an idiom of normative behavior—an essential step toward any course of social action but especially one in which a person may be called upon to kill a relative or former friend. But any political discourse, however well argued, will persuade others to accept the risks of war only if the message is consistent with the listeners' self-interests.

I strongly suspect—without any means of proving it—that proponents of moral arguments believe in the morality themselves, at least to some degree. Perhaps this is how culture works in general. There are comparatively few people, I believe, who think of themselves or their actions as deliberately "bad," no matter how reprehensible others may find them. Morality, well cooked, provides the means for translating "need" or "want" into "right." Because actions in war often grossly violate established norms of behavior, the pressure to rationalize must be great. Combine these points with the idea that when a total relationship is at issue, any component can stand for the whole, and the dialogues recounted by Valero—along with the explanations given to anthropologists—make perfect sense.[13]

Is there any role for agency in understanding Yanomami warfare? Yes, at two levels. If by agency one refers to individual human beings making choices that shape the course of history, rather than simply acting out the forces that work through them, this study allows some specification of its scope. Again, Helena Valero provides the necessary details.

Valero tells us that Fusiwe personally, though not alone, initiated three violent conflicts: the early failed raid against the Shamatari, the slaughter of Ruwahiwe's party, and the war against the Bisaasi-teri in which he died. Fusiwe was able to do this because of a combination of situation and structure. The situation was the rising antagonism associated with the times. As danger increases, others listen more closely to the man with the aggressive personality—the war leader. The structure was his position as headman of the Wanitima-teri. He had supporters to lead into war. The equally aggressive but junior Akawe, in contrast, had the situation but not the structure. He traveled from group to group, a bow for hire by anyone who would feed him or offer him a wife.

What difference did Fusiwe make? In my view, there was a strong probability of war involving the Namowei at this time, just as war was breaking out all over on the other side of the Orinoco. But the enemy and alliance pattern could have gone very differently. Around 1948, Fusiwe, virtually on his own, started the war between the eastern Namowei and the Bisaasi-teri at Shihota. Had the more peaceable Repowe prevailed, the eastern Namowei might have reestablished peace, perhaps by ceding women to the Bisaasi-teri as the Patanowa-teri did later. Maybe then the Namowei as a group would have found themselves going to war against others, such as the Hasupuwe-teri. The underlying structure of antagonisms made some warfare highly likely, but it remained for political leaders to actualize the possibilities.

Agency can also be identified on another level: that of indigenous people's actively shaping their collective history. The Yanomami are not passively molded by contact with the outside world. They have aggressively pursued their own interests. They have shaped a political milieu in response to the intrusive Western presence, which itself is largely beyond their control. Indeed, one could say that along the banks of the Orinoco, it was the Yanomamo who made contact with the outside world, rather than the reverse. That the result of Yanomami maneuvering is often quite terrible for themselves is no surprise, given the circumstances they face and their fallibility as human beings.

Some Broader Implications

In this final section, I will attempt to apply more broadly some of the themes developed in this book, starting with the issue of how anthropologists approach their subject matter. Although it is fashionable to decry scientific approaches and causal theories in the study of culture, and although cultural materialism is derided in particular, the view of Yanomami politics developed here grew out of an application of the cultural materialist principle of infrastructural determinism (see Ferguson n.d.*b*). That theory directed me toward steel tools—items the culture of anthropology has somehow relegated to insignificance. And although this study might be perceived as similar to other recent challenges to established ethnographic portrayals, it is no exercise in reflexive contemplation of our own discourse. It is, rather, a reaffirmation of the value of the comparative method.

One of the biggest problems facing anthropology today is a lack of strong theory, comparatively applied. The protein hypothesis—although I disagree with it as an explanation of war—has been a tremendous stimulus for research, and our understanding of Amazonian ecology is much richer because of it. A criticism of this book, I feel sure, will be that the author did no fieldwork among the Yanomami. But as the persevering reader will now appreciate, a huge amount of material is already out there, all based on firsthand experience. What has been done with it? Helena Valero's narratives are incomparable ethnographic sources, but no one has made serious use of them. Anthropology is filling warehouses with information. Can we not use this accumulating knowledge to generate better theory?

My hope is that the theory developed in this study could be part of a more comprehensive understanding of war. The model I develop and apply to Yanomami warfare is an application of a more general approach, tailored to the particulars of the case. There are a vast range of "warrifying" situations in tribal zones (Ferguson 1990b; Ferguson and Whitehead 1992a), and my present model would require major modification if it were applied to any but the most similar of them. With other applications of the general approach, it would be possible to better understand major parameters and permutations in war situations. It might even be possible to work toward a general understanding of social conflict, spanning the spectrum from war to witchcraft accusations and on to revitalizations, ethnic violence, class conflict, and revolution. A distant ideal to be sure, but any progress toward it would be commendable in a world facing a constantly changing and seemingly worsening panorama of violence.

Another issue arises from the different superlatives that can be applied to the Yanomami as a case study. Although I have stressed the role of Western contact, it is nevertheless true that the Yanomami have been more isolated from Westerners longer than any other large group of Native American people. They stand as the end point—the outer limit—of the post-Columbian, New World tribal zone. For others with more history of exposure to Westerners, the impact of Western presence should be even greater than that described here.

The Yanomami have also acquired in popular and some anthropological literature a reputation for being the most warlike people on earth. This study shows how misleading such statements can be. Some Yanomami in some places and times have been extremely warlike, but most Yanomami in most places and times have been peaceable. And the violent periods, I have argued, are caused by circumstances introduced by intrusive Westerners. Considering the Yanomami's "most remote" status, analysts should proceed with caution in alleging that any observed warfare among nonstate peoples anywhere is a purely indigenous pattern.[14]

For another superlative, the Yanomami are one of the "simplest" societies for which warfare has been well described. Contrary to some recent thinking, I see no contradiction between historical explanation and evolutionary comparison. My teacher Morton Fried (1967, 1968) developed his evolutionary theory in connection with an investigation of the postcontact generation of tribes. Evolutionary comparison, as I understand it, does not presume any people to be pristine, unchanged survivors of the Stone Age. Rather, it uses ethnographic description to explore the implications of organizational or other features associated with different levels of societal scale and complexity.

The Yanomami show us war at its smallest and with the least amount of political structuring piled on top. The political process of Yanomami warfare—all its discussion, deception, alliance building, military recruitment, and so on—is probably our clearest window on how war is carried out in any situation where people live in small, shifting groups without any basis for fixed or authoritative leadership. Although it is my position both for the Yanomami and in general (Ferguson 1989b:197, 1993) that war is an infrequent occurrence among small, relatively mobile groups who have not been destabilized by a tribal zone, to whatever extent war was waged by such groups in the distant past, it was probably waged something like this.

Yet at the same time, Yanomami fighting, when we look beyond the paint and feathers, seems not unlike war as practiced the world over. A contemporary military analyst, made appreciative of the practicalities of Yanomami existence, would have no problem understanding the logic and practice of their warfare. Thus the Yanomami as a case argue against the idea, framed by Turney-High (1971) but accepted by many anthropologists, that "primitive" and "civilized" war constitute two qualitatively distinct categories. On the other hand, Yanomami warfare is very different in that its small scale allows it to be studied in its full social context, within which major permutations can be compared. That goal is far beyond the reach of even the most massive research projects directed at modern warfare.

I have argued (Ferguson 1984b:1–2) that it is the possibility of developing a more complete theoretical picture that constitutes anthropology's greatest potential contribution to understanding the human problem of war. In that spirit, several inferences with contemporary relevance may be drawn from the Yanomami case. First, war is not a natural state of affairs for human societies. It is not the normal condition, leaving peace the state that needs to be explained. Yanomami do not go easily into war or stay there long, although their proneness to war does vary with local history. It took several years for the Bisaasi-teri and eastern Namowei to go from peace to war.

Second, war is not self-perpetuating. The costs are too high. But war can be self-reinforcing. In combination with other pressures toward violence, war itself lowers the threshold for war and puts into positions of greater influence men who are prone to use military force. From a regional systems perspective, the introduction of war may select out the possibility of nonviolent resolution of antagonisms (see Ferguson 1990a: 29, 1993). In sum, opting for war makes future war more likely, but something else is always involved.

Third, there is nothing in any of the accounts of war between Yanomami communities to suggest the "tribal loyalties" so frequently invoked by pundits trying to explain this or that conflict in the modern world. Indeed, the in-group amity/out-group enmity often posited by ethologists and sociobiologists seems here a most fickle sentiment, when amity and enmity regularly shift within the same social universe. The Yecuana-Yanomami relationship exemplifies how cultural differences that coincide with fundamental material antagonisms can provide definition to existing hostility, but only that. The cultural differences are not the cause of the conflicts.

Fourth, a "negative image of the other," sometimes suggested as that dimension of war on which anthropology can shed some light, is itself merely an expression of conflict, not its cause. Thus the eastern Namowei, already pushed to the brink of war, decided that the Bisaasi-teri were not true Namowei after all, and that is why they caused so much trouble. But this recategorization was to explain what was already happening. Any attempt to understand why war occurs that takes negative images of the enemy as its main focus is putting the cart before the horse.

Fifth, war is bad business. I argue that war is initiated because those who decide on war think they will be better off fighting than not. Yet it does not always work out that way for the decision makers. When the total costs for everyone involved are tallied up and compared with possible outcomes of conflicting interests in the absence of war, war's net effect is destructive, any possible adaptive benefits notwithstanding (see Ferguson 1989c:258).

Sixth, understanding war requires close scrutiny of those who make political decisions and what their interests may be in a given situation of war or peace. This requires an understanding of the dynamics of political process, which in turn requires attention to levels of evolutionary complexity. In relatively egalitarian societies like the Yanomami, almost every man can make up his own mind whether to fight, based on his own evaluation of circumstances. At the other end of the evolutionary scale, in states, decision-making ability is very unequal: men can be compelled to go to war, and interests in any political situation will vary according to a person's position within the structure of stratification.

Seventh, and finally, when studying decision makers, it should be remembered that they often lie. They conceal their true motives. They skillfully employ commonly held values to make their favored course of action appear to be a moral imperative in the interest of everyone in their society. But perhaps more insidious than plain manipulation is that decision makers may very well come to believe their own self-serving justifications. Critical examination of any moral claim by any political leader justifying war is always in order.

Afterword

Yanomami history only slowly gains ground from mystery. Their situation in the pre-Columbian social universe and the first effects on them of the new Western presence are entirely unknown. What is known is that Yanomami have suffered a variety of exogenous afflictions for at least 250 years. Now they face new threats. Civilization is spreading its tendrils throughout the entire Yanomami habitat. *Nape* penetrate the deep forests. New diseases reach more remote areas, and Yanomami die from illnesses that could be easily treated or prevented. Along different contact fronts, "peasantizing" survivors assimilate into the lowest levels of Venezuelan and Brazilian society. The future of the Yanomami people and culture is in jeopardy.

Throughout my work on this book, I have been acutely aware that the words I write may be used and misused in the political debates over establishing legal protection for the Yanomami (see Booth 1989). I hope to have made clear the distortion inherent in the appellation "fierce people" and the hollowness of the idea that Yanomami are so violent they ought to be separated from each other in small "island" preserves. The Yanomami are not intrinsically violent. Their wars arise out of the circumstances of Western contact—circumstances that can be changed.

But contact with *nape* will not stop. Yanomami do not want it to stop. Participating in an international conference on the Yanomami, Marcus Colchester (1991:15) wrote:

> It is essential that the Yanomami desire for exchange, barter and commerce not be ignored by those who plan their future. An idealization of the Yanomami as a self-sufficient people who maintain themselves on the margin of all contact with white society is as dangerous for their future as the opposed vision that

they constitute backwards people, obstacles for progress who must be integrated into modern society for their own good.

Even more recently, in early October 1993, Fiona Watson, a Survival International anthropologist who has worked with Yanomami, was quoted in *El Diario de Caracas:*

> The ideal would be that the Yanomamis would decide what it is that they want, but they cannot remain totally isolated. They want, up to a certain point, to integrate themselves into white society but maintaining their ancient customs, without feeling assimilated and having proprietorship over the lands where they live.

The issue is whether the Yanomami will have enough geographical protection soon enough to allow them to develop their own accommodation to the outside world, or whether that world will simply come crashing in. Time to adjust and the ability to maintain distance from areas of major Western settlement or activity creates the possibility of conserving much of Yanomami culture, although substantial change appears inevitable (Eguillor 1991; Lazarin 1988:25). Tribalization—the formation of unifying political structures to deal with external relations—is possible, even likely (Ferguson 1992a:226). But that opportunity will exist only if current efforts in Brazil and Venezuela succeed in defining and demarcating Yanomami lands and limiting access by outsiders.

Health care is just as important as land. Contact with *nape,* as the Yanomami have long known, is accompanied by exposure to new diseases. An estimated 1,500 Yanomami died of malaria and other illnesses in Brazil during the big gold rush of 1987–90 (Brooke 1993a). This catastrophe could have been prevented. Inoculations, distribution of basic medicines, elimination of health hazards associated with river mining and deforestation, screening of visitors for transmittable illnesses, and a system for emergency response to epidemics are all achievable and necessary.

But along with land and health care, friends of the Yanomami must confront the issue of Western goods. Without a rational plan for making these available—a plan cognizant of the political implications of distribution—we will see Yanomami continue to get them anyway they can, sometimes with terrible consequences. An unwanted illustration of this fact arose during the final editing of this book.

In August 1993, newspaper headlines began telling of a massacre of up to 73 Yanomami by Brazilian *garimpeiros* (Brooke 1993b, c, d, e). More careful investigation, including interviews with survivors by Bruce Albert (1993:3–7; CCPY 1993:1), concluded that about 16 Yanomami were actually killed and that the violence occurred over the border in Venezuela, where the Brazilians were mining illegally.

The killings began in mid-June, when four or five young men were shot to death in one treacherous assault by *garimpeiro* hunting companions. The Yanomami of Haximu-teri responded with two raids on miners' storehouses, killing at least one miner and wounding two others. A group of *garimpeiros,* encouraged by owners of river mining rafts and led by hired guns, set out to exterminate the 85 people of Haximu-teri. They found only the most defenseless of them, temporarily alone at a forest camp. The miners slaughtered and mutilated about 12 people— almost all of them old people, youths, or infants—and then shot up and burned the Haximu-teri *shabono.* The Yanomami were stunned by the brutality of the *nape* raid.

What led up to this slaughter will seem familiar to readers of this book. Albert (1993:1–2) describes the "gold mining trap" that recurrently snares Yanomami: when the first few *garimpeiros* enter an area they court Yanomami with seemingly generous gifts. As more miners come in, the balance of power changes and the intruders become less solicitous. Just at this point, their presence begins to have a major impact on local conditions: game is depleted, rivers are polluted, and new diseases reach epidemic levels. The Yanomami, now hooked on a regular flow of Western goods, medicine, even food, come to be seen as a nuisance by the *garimpeiros.* Tempers flare over demands for Western goods, and violence is a common result. That is what happened with the Haximu-teri—the killings grew out of an exchange relationship gone bad.

The immediate responses to this massacre should be a concerted effort to bring the killers to justice and new vigilance in stamping out illegal mining operations in Yanomami territory, both of which appear to be under way at the time of this writing (November 1993). But a long-term solution must include a system of supply and distribution of basic Western goods, along with essential medical care—a system that will not strongly encourage the Yanomami to move toward the major rivers and Western outposts and that will not create the kinds of inequalities and monopolies that foster violence.

How this could be done is a question that must be left to those with experience in the field, including many dedicated Brazilians, Venezuelans, and others who in recent years have labored to obtain recognition and respect for Yanomami land rights, to bring vaccines and other medicines into remote villages, and to help Yanomami develop their own institutions of political representation. The relationships described in this book may provide some guidelines for avoiding political disruption and violence, but any such system will have to be developed on the ground, in tune with current realities. People at a distance who are concerned about the Yanomami can help by supporting the international groups that support them. These groups include Amanaka'a Amazon Network, New York; Cultural Survival, Cambridge, MA; and Survival International, London.

Finally, it is worth repeating a caution from the preface to this book. I have set out to explain the underlying structure of vital interests shaping practical political decisions about war, alliance, trade, relocation, factionalism, and population fissioning—and only that. The richness of Yanomami culture and, more pointedly, their own conceptions of war and their own way of imbuing the past with meaning are incidental concerns for this argument. But that cannot be so for anyone who wishes to understand the Yanomami as a people. Yanomami culture is a complex tapestry that global citizens should treasure. The Yanomami may be the descendants of the first people to enter the Western hemisphere; the events discussed in this book are just one part of their story.

Important

Notes

Chapter 1

1. Although the Yanomami are known as a male-dominated society, women are by no means passive or lacking in political voice. As the detailed accounts in part III show, women often exercise great influence in important political decisions.

2. Robarchek (1989) claims that materialist explanations of war are incapable of addressing the question of motivation in war. That criticism would have been generally valid up to the mid-1970s. Since that time, however, there has been a shift in materialist research to deal with the question of motivation in war (see Ferguson 1984b:35). This shift, the general move away from homeostatic systems explanations, and my own emphasis on motivation were made clear in a School of American Research Advanced Seminar in which Robarcheck and I participated (Haas 1990).

3. Decisions for war involve weighing potential costs and benefits. If, for some reason, decision makers are able to initiate a war with assurance of no major risks to themselves, then the hypothesis of necessary material gain may not apply (cf. Hallpike 1991).

4. This is one point of overlap with sociobiology. Sociobiological arguments frequently present data intended to show people acting "as if" they were pursuing reproductive success. I remain unconvinced (see chapter 15). Just to be clear, my argument in regard to this point differs from sociobiological arguments in two important ways. First, unlike the entirely hypothetical human "reproductive striving," the material motivations I invoke as explanatory are abundantly documented as being very real. One may argue that Amazonian people seek to maximize inclusive fitness, but it is impossible to deny that they are driven to obtain steel tools. Second, my motivational hypothesis is tested systematically against all known cases of war, rather than merely illustrated with supportive case material.

5. It would be more accurate to speak of iron or steel cutting tools. Earlier tools were more likely to be made out of iron, but the two are not distinguishable in available reports. (Nor is there any way to distinguish quality of manufacture, which surely varied greatly.) For simplicity, I lump all metal tools as steel tools.

6. As this book was going to press, I received a copy of a new article by

William Denevan (1992) that advances the proposition that the slash-and-burn gardens described by so many ethnographers are made possible by metal tools and that "shifting cultivation, as an ancient practice in Amazonia, seems to be a myth. There is no evidence for it" (1992:161).

7. The implications of the Maku are somewhat obscure. Their subservience to more settled riverine horticulturalists is associated with both an inequality in access to Western manufactures and a differential reliance on agriculture versus hunting and collecting. Speculatively, it may be that exchange of garden produce for forest products itself structures a form of social inequality, and this kind of inequality may have existed in ancient times.

8. This has been suggested by Thomas (1972:15) in regard to other peoples close to the Yanomami: "Thus the relatively capital-intensive Pemon, as middlemen, exploit their western neighbors, the Makiritare, at least as far as any kind of labor equivalence is a measure of value." (See also Colson 1973:54–55.)

Chapter 2

1. Lizot (1976:13) describes dramatic regional game depletion on the upper Orinoco, Mavaca, and Ocamo, but he says this process began only in the mid-1960s (some fifteen years after the first mission was established in that region). Elsewhere (1988:503), he says that game began to decrease only after some six or seven years of shotgun hunting. This stands in sharp contrast to quantitative and other studies from all over Amazonia (Ferguson 1989b:188–91), which repeatedly document diminishing returns for hunting efforts commencing within a few years of the establishment of a fairly large and fixed settlement. Lizot (1977: 508–12) has published figures showing more than adequate game supplies for one small and one medium-sized village over short observation periods, but he has not, to my knowledge, presented longitudinal data relating game intake to village size and time spent in one place.

Early and Peters (1990:114) report some reduction in game availability around the long-established Mucajaí mission, but never to the point of its being a real subsistence problem. The total Yanomami population in that area, however, is small, starting at 121 in 1958 and reaching 319 by 1987. Surrounded by a vast expanse of uninhabited forest, and relatively free of war, those 319 people reside in six locally dispersed and frequently relocated villages (Early and Peters 1990:4–7). I have argued for a causal linkage between an absence of warfare, smaller village size, and resilience of game supplies (Ferguson 1989b:185–86, and see 1992a:213). Thus, the fact that this population has only minor problems with game depletion is entirely consistent with theoretical expectations.

2. An "ancient" Sanema Yanomami man in the relatively acculturated Caura basin once scolded some younger men, showing them a stone ax: "This stone axe belonged to my father and my grandfather.... I have used it along with fire to fell trees. You do not know what it is to fell or cut a tree. Pum! pum!... a chop here, another chop there, and your tree has already fallen. We needed several days to chop down one single tree. You all are bums [vagos]" (Barandiaran 1967:25).

3. One measure of the significance of the introduced items is a report of their exemption from the generally strict rule of destroying all possessions at a person's death. Peters (1973:139) reports that exceptions "are made in regards to the costly Western goods such as an axe or shotgun. Such items may be hidden for a few months and then used again."

4. There is reason to be concerned about, and even to condemn, some missionaries' direct assault on indigenous belief systems (see Chagnon 1977:147–51; Lizot 1976; chapter 14). But it is worth noting, as well, that missionaries with extensive experience among the Yanomami have concluded that Yanomami come to the missions only for Western goods, and they rarely, if ever, develop genuine interest in the religious teachings (Early and Peters 1990:95–96; Migliazza 1980:105; Peña Vargas 1981:24; and see Dickey 1932:28). Religious change is not the main effect of the missions.

5. Detail on rate of payment is extremely limited. In an area of increasing contact on the far upper Orinoco around 1950, the going rate was one machete for three stalks of bananas (Cocco 1972:91). A couple of years later, a young man who returned from about a month's work at a mission post farther down the Orinoco returned with one machete, two shirts, one mirror, two combs, and several fishhooks (Valero 1984:508). At a highland mission around 1970, payment was one machete or ax for four or five stalks of bananas (Jank 1977:68). Around the same time, another mission along the Mucajaí River was paying a shirt, trousers, ax, or machete for three to five days of work, a large metal pot for six to ten days, and a shotgun for two months (Peters 1973:125).

6. An important change occurs when Yanomami shift to canoe travel on the wider rivers. This has happened in only a few instances, which are described in the historical chapters of this book. The implications of this infrastructural change are not clear. In the Orinoco-Mavaca area (see chapter 12), it appears that although there may remain some danger in paddling past hostile intermediate villages, river travel nevertheless brings more flexibility in movement.

7. One adventurer among the Yanomami and their neighbors commented about such warnings: "Anyone who has the least idea of Indians will know how much faith to put in their tales that they themselves are so good and the other tribes 'over there' so bad: precious little" (Vinci 1959:110).

8. Because information about the functioning of middlemen in the Western goods trade is extremely sparse, I will use the term in a rather general sense. I am certain, however, that additional information would reveal major variations in forms and practices of middleman activity. There are probably several different types of middlemen.

9. Two factors are involved in the relative scarcity of marriageable women: female infanticide and polygyny. Female infanticide is discussed elsewhere (Ferguson 1989c:253–55) and in chapter 15. Another factor that affects perceived scarcity of sexually available women, and thus encourages polygyny, is a postpartum sex prohibition while the mother is nursing, generally lasting from two to four years (Early and Peters 1990:43; Eguillor García 1984:49). Eguillor García (1984:83–84) also observes that men want plural wives because their female offspring are used to secure the important allegiance of sons-in-law. The

possibility of acquiring more wives, however, is limited by the requirement of providing game for so many mouths. The introduction of shotguns has enabled some men to procure more game, and so support more wives.

The actual extent of polygyny varies greatly, in some areas even being superseded by polyandry (Early and Peters 1990:106–107). An unsubstantiated observation from the Orinoco-Mavaca area at the start of its direct contact phase suggests very infrequent polygyny—only one known case (Anduze 1960:246). A man named Fusiwe, however, had five wives in the late 1930s; and Ruwahiwe—son of Matakuwa, or "Shinbone," renowned as progenitor of a highly unusual number of descendants (Chagnon 1979:379)—had four or five wives (Biocca 1971:9, 75; Valero 1984:79). More recently for this area, Lizot (1989:31) puts polygyny at about one in ten marriages; and Eguillor García's 1983 survey (1984:84) shows 16.7 percent polygynous families, with six particularly influential men having two, two, three, four, five, and five current wives, respectively.

10. According to Chagnon (1966:92–93), "The brother-in-law *(shoriwa)* tie is the key link in alliances between local descent groups, both within and between villages. . . . *Shoriwa* implies a set of obligations and duties between the speakers. One can depend on his *shoriwa* for material goods and gifts, and a request for such items from a shoriwa is not easily denied. . . . The Yanomamo use this term for foreigners as well. . . . [They] address the missionaries with this term hoping to maximize their chances of obtaining desirable manufactured goods such as machetes and axes. . . . [A] conversation between two shoriwa is punctuated frequently by these constant reminders that each owes the other goods, services, and respect by virtue of the fact that they stand in wife-giver/wife-receiver relationship to each other. . . . One who has actually given a sister to the other's group has an advantage, in a trading sense, as he can more legitimately claim goods from the wife receiver."

11. The most detailed information about exceptionally fierce men is scattered throughout two narratives of life as a captive among the Yanomami (Biocca 1971; Valero 1984), notably in descriptions of two men, Fusiwe and Akawe. Fusiwe's violent disposition enables his small band to rout a larger group in a club fight. As tensions develop between two villages, one courts Fusiwe as a formidable ally but is unable to restrain his rage, and Fusiwe and a few followers precipitate a war (Biocca 1971:196–244). (As Cawte [1978:116–17] argues, in very small groups in conflict-laden situations, one individual, belligerent beyond social control, may precipitate broader violence.) Fusiwe's bellicose actions ultimately lead to his isolation and death (Biocca 1971:196–244), a fate that frequently awaits unusually aggressive leaders (Lizot 1988:556).

12. Lévi-Strauss (1943) noted the alternation of commerce and war, seeing them as two sides of one relationship of reciprocity. To bring in the factors discussed here does not contradict that perspective but can take it further, explaining why a relationship goes from one form of reciprocity to the other.

Chapter 3

1. The Orinoco-Mavaca area also seems extreme in interpersonal violence outside of formal duels—not only men against men, but also men against women (Biocca 1971:167–70; Chagnon 1966:189, 1977:81–84; Cocco 1972: 213, 216; Lizot 1985:71), women against men (Biocca 1971:132, 306), and women against women (Chagnon 1974:190, 1977:132). Certainly interpersonal violence occurs within other Yanomami groups, and probably some of its prominence in the Orinoco-Mavaca area is a reflection of the interests of its ethnographers (see Ramos 1987). But I argue elsewhere (Ferguson 1992a) that this truly is an area of unusual interpersonal violence, a result of those same factors that impel men to go to war and of a secondary cultural adjustment—a heightened valorization of belligerence necessitated by the atmosphere of war.

2. Some indication of the complex and changing factors that go into setting terms of exchange is evident in Padre Cocco's reflections after living 17 years with the relatively peaceful Iyewei-teri Yanomamö:

> The value of the things is relative to the need which they have for them, on the ease with which they are obtained, on the friendship which exists between the parties, on the generosity which is supposed to prevail over material interest. Thus, they are capable of handing over a machete for a few leaves of tobacco; handing over an axe for a little bit of *yopo*. In the past for an axe they gave up to a woman. The missions have made more accessible the products of our technology. (Peña Vargas 1981:37)

3. It merits stating again that the role of force in trade will vary according to circumstances. Some outpost villages can afford to be so generous that force is unnecessary; some more isolated villages can engage in entirely mutualistic, noncoercive trade relationships. Even at the edge of the Orinoco-Mavaca region, Good (1991:214) reports that trading, though "intense," is "never carried out by intimidation." Most significantly, Good makes this point in contrast to one incident he witnessed, when a Yanomami man with strong Western connections came upstream carrying a shotgun and jiggling four cartridges in his hand, and then openly used that edge in demanding arrowheads and feathers from the visibly frightened headman of Hasupuwe-teri. In this case, the intimidation did not work, because the Hasupuwe-teri headman was supported by Good, who was known to have his own shotgun.

4. The extent to which men forcibly take wives from allies apparently varies. Lizot (1988:540) argues that it is rare, and he presents data from an area marked by extensive violence showing that only 0.9 percent of wives were taken by force from allies. Chagnon has not, to my knowledge, presented comparably specific information. In a tally of marriage types in *Yanomamö: The Fierce People* (1977:73), "alliance and/or abduction" is presented as one undifferentiated category. But in a recent work, Chagnon (1990a:51) writes: "The minimal amount of 'abduction' in current marriages among the members of the villages I study is approximately 17 percent, far higher than the rate in the area Lizot has been studying." He goes on to discuss "the possibility of acquiring additional mates by coercion, force, or, in simple terms, abduction," and explains

that most "abductions" are not captives taken on raids but women taken from allies. His statement suggests that for Chagnon the use of any "coercion" or "force" in establishing or maintaining a marriage is enough to classify the marriage as an "abduction," a broad definition that may account for some of the difference between his estimate and Lizot's data.

5. Even during active wars, some individuals closely bound by kin ties to "the enemy" may remain apart from the fray and thus keep open a potential diplomatic channel between hostile villages (Lizot 1988:558–59). Also, diplomatic messages may be carried by old women, who are never targeted in war and so are able to travel anywhere (Biocca 1971:236; Eguillor García 1984:133).

6. On a similar principle, one of the main tactics for dealing with enemies during a cycle of raiding is temporarily to vacate the usual habitation, going on trek or visiting relatives in other villages (Chagnon 1977:126–27; Good 1991: 153; Jank 1977:45–49, 87; Lizot 1988:552). Generally, more mobile groups are less likely to be hit by raiders (Barandiaran 1967:39).

7. An illustration of this is found in the exceptionally small raiding party mentioned earlier. The raiders wanted to kill the enemy headman, but the first person to come out of the enemy village was a young man with strong ties to the attackers. Fearing discovery if they tarried, they shot him anyway, and later wept bitterly over his death (Biocca 1971:231–34).

8. Saffirio must be noted as an exception to this near unanimity. Discussing the infrequent wars among the Catrimani basin Yanomami, he writes (1985: 66), without explaining the basis for his conclusion: "*Even though it was rarely stated by my informants,* in the past the abduction of women was the paramount reason for a raid" (my emphasis).

9. Chagnon has not, to my knowledge, presented a tally of how many marriages are a result of abductions on raids. In Lizot's (1988:540) sample, only 0.8 percent of marriages involve women captured on raids. The Mucajaí Yanomami, during several decades prior to contact, had obtained five and lost at least two women in raids; after contact, they obtained seven to nine women of marriageable age in two attacks (Early and Peters 1990:22, 67–68, 92–93).

In a previous article (1988b:150), I implicitly accepted Helena Valero's statement that "perhaps about fifty" women were captured in one rout (Biocca 1971:38). I would like explicitly to retract that idea now. More likely, Valero's statement reflects the hyperbolic memory of a very frightened young girl. In any case, the number of women who were actually kept by the raiders was about four (Valero 1984:53, 55).

10. In a commentary on his map of Yanomami village locations and political relations, Barker (1953:435) observes how the latter affect movement and thus his mission's ability to hire different Yanomami as workers: "If a group of Waikas were contracted to do certain tasks, they could be disposed to work well in certain areas, but without doubt they would refuse to enter into areas inhabited by their enemies."

11. The directionality prediction does partially overlap with expectations growing out of other explanations of war, notably Vayda's (1961) model of expanding agriculturalists and Chagnon's (1973) model of social circumscription (see Ferguson 1989b:186). Those arguments suggest a consistent pattern of military pressure pushing outwards from a demographic center. If the sources of

Western goods constituted a consistent circle around Yanomami territory, the predictions would be indistinguishable. But that is not the case: Western goods enter Yanomami trade networks from many points, sometimes from missions located in the heart of their traditional territory. Local conflict patterns respond to the actual location of the sources rather than exhibiting a consistent centrifugal tendency.

Chapter 4

1. In the late eighteenth century, for example, reports and maps based on Spanish and Portuguese explorations note "Guaharibas blancos" (see note 2) and "Guahibas blancos" in the highlands above the Siapa, Mavaca, Padauiri, Araçá, and Demini rivers (Cocco 1972:35–36; Migliazza 1972:6). Cocco believes these designations refer to Yanomami who were trekking from the Parima to gather cacao in the region, rather than to village settlements. That is possible, although speculative, and it implies a much longer trek than has been observed for Yanomami. Moreover, many other historical references put the Yanomami in the same place throughout the nineteenth and into the twentieth century; and the recognized "boundary" of Yanomami territory around 1800 was the Raudal de Guajaribos, located midway between the Parima and Unturán highlands.

I believe the reason these reports have not received current recognition is that the twentieth-century Yanomami groups who inhabit the area are known to have arrived recently from the Parima region. In other words, if there were Yanomami living there in the past, they seem to have disappeared. The most plausible explanation, to me, is that there were Yanomami living in the area in the past, but they were decimated, pushed back, or assimilated into other Yanomami or non-Yanomami groups over the course of history. Or, perhaps some day Yanomami will be found who will claim that their ancestors lived in this area.

2. Migliazza (1972:6) states that "Guahariba" is a Brazilian word for howler monkeys, frequently used to designate isolated, "backward" Native Americans and applied to Yanomami in the headwaters of the Río Negro feeder streams since the third quarter of the eighteenth century.

3. While Migliazza's (1982) reconstruction would seem to contradict the genetic argument that the Yanomami are survivors of a prior wave of settlers, that is not necessarily so. By analogy with ethnographically observed peoples, we can imagine that if Yanomami ancestors were politically dominated by more complex polities, Yanomami women would marry into the dominant group, but not the reverse—thus preventing Yanomami acquisition of genetic material. The dominant polity could also have had linguistic influence on the Yanomami, which, two thousand years later, might be taken as evidence of common origin. All this is purely speculative, of course, but it does raise a more substantial point: that if, indeed, the Yanomami are genetically distinctive, it does not necessarily indicate, as some have understood (Smole 1976:18), that they have been isolated from other peoples all this time.

4. By the time any literate observer approached the far upper Orinoco, populations already had been decimated (see chapter 5). Although there is no direct observation of native population density or settlement size, there are indications

that relatively complex societies once existed there. Although there is no fertile floodplain in the area, rectangular patches of bamboo in the forest suggest more intensive earlier methods of farming (Lizot 1980:41, 47). Furthermore, extensive surface remains of pottery clearly unrelated to that of the Yanomami are found even above the major rapids, along with what may be the remains of a major stone ax manufacturing center (Anduze 1960:96, 210; Grelier 1957:129–30, 139, 144). Three radiocarbon dates for pottery found near the Mavaca River range from 940 to 1450 A.D., plus or minus 170 years for the more recent date (Wagner and Arvelo 1986:694–95). That leaves open the question of whether the makers of those pots lived there until the intensification of the slaving wars.

5. Hames's (1989:73) calculations support Colchester's reconstruction. Zent's (1992) detailed study of the impact of steel on the subsistence practices of traditional Piaroa, who live in high country north of the Yecuana, also supports Colchester's conclusions.

6. Valero (1984:183) describes a case of garden clearing in which the group had only a couple of pieces of steel. It involves much breaking of vegetation by hand and pulling down partially cut trees with vine ropes.

7. Smole (1976:199–211) has suggested that the large patches of savanna found scattered throughout the Parima highlands are the result of past Yanomami gardening, which would imply more extensive long-term reliance on agriculture than I have suggested. Huber et al. (1984:130, 132, 135), however, present evidence that these savannas are natural in origin, and they fail to confirm Smole's hypothesis that burning of forest land for gardens leads to its conversion to grassland. They do observe that the savannas of the southern Parima, where the Yanomami traditionally lived, are ecologically impoverished in comparison to savannas in the northern Parima. That may indeed be a result of Yanomami burning to clear trails (or for purposes of burrow hunting [Zent, personal communication]), but probably not for garden construction, because Yanomami avoid living in the relatively infertile savannas unless induced to settle there by the establishment of a mission.

8. Lizot (1988:496–97), who has long opposed Harris's ideas (see Lizot 1977), disputes the role of steel tools in the Yanomami's demographic expansion, arguing that growth began well before their acquisition of steel, an occurrence he places around 1900. But steel was reaching some Yanomami groups long before 1900, and Lizot provides no alternative explanation for the observed population growth. Moreover, Lizot's position on the impact of steel is ambiguous. He asserts (1980:7) that there has been no expansion of Yanomami garden size in the past 50 years (a questionable assertion), but he also notes that gardens may have grown larger with the gradual acquisition of steel tools: "We can assume, without great risks of error, that the introduction of metal tools, by facilitating work, permitted an extension of garden surfaces, a lesser dependency on wild resources, a sedentization undoubtedly greater, and, sometimes, a concomitant demographic push" (Lizot 1980:8–9).

Chapter 5

1. For further details and discussion of events to be described for the upper Orinoco, see Cocco (1972:37ff.).

2. The Yecuana, whose name is spelled in various ways, are Carib-speaking Indians also known as Makiritare and Maiongong. They are the Yanomami's most populous indigenous neighbor, and they currently share territory with northern Yanomami in Venezuela and Brazil. Yanomami-Yecuana relations are discussed in the historical chapters.

3. Whitehead (1988a:186–87) argues that most slave raids involved the capture of one or two people by a small band of men, rather than major attacks carrying off hundreds at a time. Thus raiding could be "subcontracted" to smaller groups living farther up rivers. The real profits were in the control of the slave trade. Carib or Dutch middlemen were "paying two hatchets, two machetes, some knives and glass beads for captives on the Orinoco and receiving some ten axes, ten machetes, ten knives, ten bags of beads and other general trade goods from the Dutch buyers" (1988a:187).

4. In 1750, the fortified mission at this site, San Juan Nepomuceno, came under attack—although it is not entirely clear who started the shooting—by what seems to be a coalition of the Portuguese's allies from the region between the Orinoco and the Negro, including Baniwa, Manitivitano, and Guaipunave. The native forces numbered about two hundred—noted by Gilij as large for this depopulated area—and came on in controlled formations. They were repelled by cannon fire, and after looting surrounding buildings, made an orderly and covered retreat (Gilij 1965 III:118–20; Pérez 1988:431–32).

5. De Jérez (in Cocco 1972:45) says the Yanomami preserve cacao for later in the year, something which, as Cocco notes, no recently observed Yanomami do. This may be one sign of greater reliance on gathering in the past.

6. Humboldt's account was dismissed by Michelena y Rojas (1989:190), who, like Tavera-Acosta (1927:382) believed no clash occurred. Ramos Pérez (1946:380) found no external evidence to support Humboldt and declared himself uncertain about the account's factuality. Ramos Pérez supports Michelena y Rojas's claim that the fight could not have happened where Humboldt said it had during Bobadilla's 1764 expedition, because that expedition did not go there. Humboldt (1889:461), however, did not say the clash took place on that expedition, but only that it happened while Bobadilla was in command of the Spanish military post at San Carlos on the Río Negro. Bobadilla was reported to be still in the area in 1775 (Tavera-Acosta 1927:203). While Humboldt may have been confused about some points of local history, I find it hard to believe that he would fabricate such a story entirely. I think the fight did take place, probably sometime between 1764 and 1776.

7. Humboldt (1889:463) confirms that the people Caulin called "Guaribas" were Guaharibos, that is, Yanomami.

8. Michelena y Rojas (1989:187) argues that Humboldt was seeking an excuse for not having reached the source of the Orinoco. ("How could we hope to pass a point where the commander of the Río Negro, Don Francisco Bovadilla, was stopped [?]" [Humboldt 1889:467].) Although Humboldt claims "no

white man has been able to penetrate" beyond that point (1889:461), that assertion is contradicted on the next page when he mentions that the missionary Gonzales "had visited those countries" (1889:462).

9. Humboldt (1889:346–47) described a raid farther down the Orinoco:

In 1797 the missionary of San Fernando had led his Indians to the banks of the Río Guaviare, on one of those hostile incursions which are prohibited alike by religion and the Spanish laws. They found in an Indian hut a Guahiba women [sic] with her three children (two of whom were still infants), occupied in preparing the flour of cassava. Resistance was impossible; the father was gone to fish, and the mother tried in vain to flee with her children. Scarcely had she reached the savannah when she was seized by the Indians of the mission, who hunt human beings, like the Whites and the Negroes in Africa. The mother and her children were bound, and dragged to the bank of the river. The monk, seated in his boat, waited the issue of an expedition of which he shared not the danger. Had the mother made too violent a resistance the Indians would have killed her, for everything is permitted for the sake of the conquest of souls (la conquista espirituel), and it is particularly desirable to capture children, who may be treated in the mission as *poitos*, or slaves of the Christians.

The subsequent escapes of the mother, and her ultimately fruitless efforts to be reunited with her children, provide one of the most moving and heroic narratives encountered in this literature (Humboldt 1889:347–49, excerpted in O'Hanlon 1988:135–36). (Also see Gilij [1965 III:96–97, 104–106] for an enthusiastic endorsement of similar raids and such comments as "between the reductions and the forests there is the same difference as between the barracks and the battlefield" [1965 III:116].)

10. In 1787, Lobo de Almada (1861:676) identified "Oaycas" as inhabiting the Majari and Parimé rivers. This has been read as meaning "Waikas" (Yanomami) on the Parima River, close to the Parima highlands. But the Parimé is actually a different river, a smaller stream closer to the juncture of the Uraricoera and the Branco, and these Oayca are a Carib group (Albert 1985:42; and see Koch-Grunberg 1979:243; Migliazza 1972:362–63).

11. *Maku* is Arawakan for "son-in-law"; just as *poito*, which is frequently translated as "slave," means "son-in-law" in Carib (Colchester 1982:93; and see Whitehead 1988a:181–83). The father-in-law/son-in-law relationship is the most authoritarian kinship relationship in a great many Amazonian societies (see Ferguson n.d.*a*).

Chapter 6

1. As this and subsequent chapters approach the present day, more information will be presented about specific Yanomami local groups. In Yanomami languages, these groups are identified with some variation on the suffix "-teri," meaning "dwellers of" or "inhabitants of" (Migliazza 1980:103). For simplicity,

I have standardized all linguistic and orthographic variations to this one form, except in direct quotes.

2. Usually, it is impossible to match historical references to linguistic characteristics and divisions within Yanomami. Past identities are reconstructed from contemporary locations and what is known about historical movements.

3. There is an intriguing but ambiguous reference in Humboldt (1889:465) to "fair-complexioned tribes" related to those he observed at La Esmeralda—seemingly a reference to Yanomami—living in the area between the Padamo and Ventuari and the Erebato and Paragua. That is close to the center of current Sanema occupation, well north of the generally accepted limit of ancient Yanomami lands. Humboldt could, however, be referring to non-Yanomami peoples.

4. After the withdrawal of the Solano expedition in 1761, the Yecuana became known for their long-distance travel to sources of Western goods (Arvelo-Jiménez 1971:18; Cocco 1972:181; Coppens 1971, 1981:62; Migliazza 1980: 127). Around 1840, Yecuana were traveling from the Cunucunuma to Georgetown via the roundabout route of the Casiquiare, Negro, and Branco rivers (Coppens 1981:62). In the mid-1850s, a Yecuana "capitán" on the Cunucunuma had visited the British at Georgetown via both the Cunucunuma and Padamo and the Orinoco and Caribbean coast (Michelena y Rojas 1989:332). Direct visits to the British continued at least into the late nineteenth century (Chaffanjon 1986:258).

But somehow over time, the Yecuana came to rely less on long-distance expeditions to European sources and more on shorter trips to native middlemen who carried Western goods. (A similar transition may have occurred among the Pemon.) As early as the 1840s, Akawaio and others transported large quantities of Western goods into the region northeast of the Yecuana to trade to more interior groups, reaping a substantial profit for the effort. This trade increased after the establishment of missions in British Guiana in the 1860s. As the trade system developed, Western goods would find their way to Yecuana via subdivisions of the Pemon. Yecuana trading through Macushi and Piaroa middlemen is also reported. The Yecuana became specialists in the production and trade of dugout canoes and, especially, manioc graters, as well as middlemen for products such as curare from the Piaroa. Once the trade chain was established, Yecuana attempted to bypass middlemen only on rare occasions (Colson 1973: 9–10, 16, 18, 27–32, 60; Coppens 1971:36–38; Thomas 1982:23–24).

5. On the Cunucunuma, Spruce's visit was the occasion for a feast involving several Yecuana communities, at which a brawl occurred (Spruce 1908:417). Fighting among local allies is common when bearers of gifts visit "isolated" groups.

6. Between 1877 and 1914, local governors in the provincial capital of San Fernando de Atabapo did not last long. Six were prosecuted, nine died "tragically," ten died of illness, and twenty-four were overthrown or fled from organized movements or crowds, usually led by rival merchant cliques. One consequence of this turmoil is that local records were repeatedly destroyed (Tavera-Acosta 1927:180, 188). If that had not happened, we might know much more about the Yanomami today.

7. Commenting on this dependence on *pijiguao,* Barandiaran (1967:47) suggested calling the Yanomami "the People of the Peach Palm." One wonders how anthropological debates about the Yanomami would have been affected if this name had been adopted rather than "the Fierce People."

8. The wars of the 1920s and 1930s are not described in any detail. From general principles of Yanomami warfare, it is probably safe to assume that their raids were neither coordinated nor continuous. More likely they occurred in clusters: some during the height of the rubber boom, as Yecuana came to possess many Western goods; some during the time of Funes, as the supply of Western goods decreased and the Yecuana became militarily vulnerable; and some during the period of resurgent trade of Western goods through Yecuana connections.

9. The Sanema expansion in turn led to a separation of the Yecuana of the Cunucunuma from those of the Ventuari, for the Yecuana feared to travel through the Sanema zone now between the two rivers (Wilbert 1963:188).

10. The circumstances that make it seem like a raid in an existing climate of war are these: a new "stockade of thorny palm, freshly piled up for some defensive purpose . . . [and] an insuperable obstacle for bare Indian feet" (Vinci 1959:212); some destruction of the house structure; the careless disposal of the bodies within the village; and, above all, the behavior of Vinci's Sanema bearers. Vinci himself suspected they were involved in this attack, which occurred one day ahead of him along his established line of travel. That suspicion does not seem unwarranted, for his guides had mysteriously halted the expedition two days before, gone off with all their arrows, and then returned with no arrows, animatedly acting out a battle for their kinsmen. Because the victims' village was deserted when the Vinci party arrived, his guides were able to pass through it and remain with their source of Western goods (Vinci 1959:208–209, 212).

11. There is one relevant later report that in the early 1980s, some Yecuana obtained a new basis for dominating Yanomami. A few more acculturated Yecuana had obtained official positions, and these politically connected individuals acted in a prejudicial manner toward Sanema (Comité 1983:53).

Chapter 7

1. At this point it is appropriate to note the detailed ethnohistorical research on Brazilian Yanomami carried out by Bruce Albert (1985, 1988). His thesis is that the period from 1720 to 1920 was a time of indirect contact between Yanomami and the outside world. The channels of contact ran through a few dozen small "ethnies" (peoples or ethnic groups), speakers of Carib, Arawak, or isolated languages, that survived the demographic assaults of colonialists by retreating to the middle courses of many rivers leading toward the Yanomami. Albert (1985:65–66) argues, quite reasonably in my opinion, that Yanomami in the highlands obtained steel tools and perhaps new cultigens by trading with or raiding these peoples. It is also appropriate at this point to acknowledge that much of my information on the early history of Yanomami in Portuguese-Brazilian territory is based on Albert's (1985:51–75) research and on the more general overviews provided by Hemming (1987) and Migliazza (1972). I have a

limited ability to read Portuguese and therefore have not pursued those historical sources the way I have the Spanish.

2. Calling these people "Borabuk" is actually an oversimplification. Early
and Peters (1990:19) identify two groups as giving rise to the Ninam living
around the Mucajaí mission from the 1950s: the Borabuk and the Kaserapai.
These two villages were in parallel migration with some intermarriage during
the 1940s. They merged after settling along the Mucajaí River in the 1950s. But
their histories are not distinguished in Early and Peters. Therefore I treat them as
one and refer to them as Borabuk, following the usage in Chagnon et al. (1970).

3. They told him (Koch-Grunberg 1979 I:258) that before then they had no
steel and obtained their food from gathering in the forest, as other Yanomami in
the mountains were still doing. It is not clear whether they were saying they had
no gardens, or just smaller gardens, similar to those reported by Schomburgk.
At any rate, they were completely unfamiliar with how to use a stone ax, which
Koch-Grunberg showed them.

4. Koch-Grunberg, referring to the Roraima area in the east, wrote in his
diary in 1924: "The Indians of Río Branco are close to their end. Those who escaped influenza, which killed entire malocas, are now being liquidated for ever
by balata-gatherers, gold prospectors or diamond seekers" (quoted in Hemming
1987:362).

5. At least two other parties made contact with Yanomami along the Uraricoera during this period: in 1922, two Brazilian traders accompanied by some
Macushi visited the middle Uraricoera; and in 1927, officials inspecting the
frontier got as far as the Parima River (Migliazza 1972:380–81).

6. Another harbinger was a Brazilian boundary commission party around
the Uraricaá in 1947–48, which was attacked by some Yanomami and made
peaceful contact with others. They tried to persuade the friendly ones to come
down the Uraricoera to settle near ranches, but only three individuals did so
(Migliazza 1972:383–84).

7. That these "Guadema" may have been Yanomam speakers is suggested by
the term *warima*, which means "in-law" in the Yanomam language (Migliazza
1980:104). It is similar to the name "Walma," later applied to the Yanomam of
the middle Uraricoera mission (Colchester 1981b:116).

8. The Yecuana spoke of these Yanomami: "The Guademas are not so much
like monkeys as the others are. . . . They have canoes and they plant cassava—
in fact they're almost men" (Gheerbrant 1954:335).

9. As unspecific as this report is, it is perhaps the firmest estimate available
about how long steel tools last among Yanomami. Based on this case, I would
hazard a guess: under heavy use, steel tools do not provide cutting edges for
more than 25 or 30 years. Of course, life span would respond to many factors,
and the Borabuk situation is far from the heaviest use possible. In many cases,
25 years is probably an overestimate.

10. The Borabuk are a confirmatory case for a subhypothesis of the "population pump and sinks" argument (Ferguson 1989c:255–58), previously noted
in chapter 4: that groups displaced by war from river zones could suffer demographic decline. Informants emphasize that in the past, they had been much
more numerous. Disease alone cannot account for that decline. A major factor

was the Borabuk's severely skewed sex ratio, itself a result of some selective female infanticide and the vagaries of births in such a small group. In 1958, only 36.4 percent of the total population was female, and only 22.6 percent of the population aged 15 to 44 years was female (Early and Peters 1990:19–23). Early and Peters (1990:140) reach the conclusion that the often assumed stability of ancient populations may be illusory, masking a pattern in which some groups grow while others shrink to the point of extinction.

11. The Catrimani region is discussed in chapter 8. Here it is sufficient to note that 1965 marks the beginning of a permanent Catholic mission on the upper Catrimani and the cessation of a long-established pattern of mission visits to Yanomami of the Apiaú and Ajarani rivers (Albert 1985:71–71b). It is not known how the Catrimani village that the Borabuk attacked was affected by these nearby developments.

Chapter 8

1. This chapter will also contain information about the Yanomami recently living near the Apiaú and Ajarani rivers. As noted in chapter 4, Migliazza (1980: 104) tentatively classifies these people as speaking a dialect of Ninam, but he notes that they may actually speak a distinct, fifth language. Albert's limited linguistic investigation of these groups seems to confirm their distinctiveness, and he suggests calling their language Yanowami. Most of them remained relatively isolated from direct contact with Westerners until the mid-1980s, when clandestine mining began in that area (Albert 1985:51–53). Since their geographic location places them closer to the historical events affecting the Yanomam than those affecting the Ninam, the little information that is available will be presented in this chapter.

2. As Albert (1985:58) points out, there is no indication of any hostilities between Paushiana or Barauana and Yanomami. While this could be nothing more than a function of the relative paucity of reports, it is also true that in this general area there is no indication of any early reputation for ferocity, as is reported for many other Yanomami groups. The relative isolation of the upper Catrimani area may have been accompanied by relative peace.

3. In a possibly parallel move, some Yanomami are reported to have migrated by the late 1920s from between the Catrimani and Mucajaí rivers to the area south of the Ajarani (Albert 1985:58). Perhaps these people were the ancestors of the linguistically distinctive Yanomami of the Ajarani-Apiaú rivers area.

4. Saffirio (1985:89–104) reconstructs the history of two villages, Wakathau-teri and Hewenahipi-teri (which fissioned around 1962), part of a nine-village "population bloc" inhabiting the middle Catrimani area in the 1980s. Wakathau-teri lived alongside the Catrimani mission. I noted earlier that the earliest recollections of Saffirio's informants have their ancestors coming down from the mountains in the late nineteenth century. More specific information starts only in the mid-1920s.

5. Shapiro (1972:28–29) also notes what seems to be another group, the

Prauki-teri, that split off from this stock and moved toward the Branco itself.

6. The little information available about the linguistically anomalous Yano-mami of the Ajarani and Apiaú rivers fits the general picture. After 1950, they had sporadic contacts with Catholic missionaries. These contacts became more regular from 1962 to 1965 and then fell off again (Albert 1985:71b). In 1964, Migliazza (1972:35) was told by people of the lower to middle Ajarani that the people of the upper Ajarani were their enemies.

7. In regard to internal politics, the missionaries endorsed individuals as group chiefs and made gift distributions only with their approval. These designated chiefs treated others as subordinates (Shapiro 1972:31; Soares Diniz 1965:9).

8. Under these circumstances, however, we might still expect to see some violence breaking out one or two villages away from the mission, between middlemen once removed and more distant groups, as described for the Auaris, Mucajaí, and Surucucu missions. It may be that similar raiding did happen here and is just not reported in my sources. But it may be a genuine contrast, and if so would merit more investigation to ascertain further reasons for this relative peaceableness.

9. When the missionaries made their initial visit to Xite-teri, they found the people "suffering serious consequences of a whooping cough epidemic which had reached Surucucu via the usual trade and communications networks" (Shapiro 1972:41).

10. This difference in the distribution of shotguns is not reported as such, but is inferred from a 1975 report that a raid by the Aikam-teri followed their obtaining a shotgun from a *garimpeiro* (Taylor 1979:61).

11. A possible factor in the military balance is village location. Yanomami avoid establishing gardens in savannas, and it seems (Montgomery 1970:71), although this is not entirely clear, that even the Aikam-teri villages were some distance away from the mission itself. That distance would have weakened their control of the space around the mission. Also, the mission changed its location in 1964, moving westward and closer to Yanomam settlements (Shapiro 1972: 40). No other information is provided, but a similar move by a mission in the Orinoco-Mavaca area contributed to political instability in that area.

12. The linguistically anomalous groups of the Apiaú and Ajarani rivers were also severely disrupted by the arrival of the highway, but as usual, little else is known (Anthropology Resource Center 1981:2; Taylor 1979:75ff.).

13. There was a grave epidemic in Catrimani in 1973, but not its first. Another had come through in 1967 (Albert 1988:103), and of course several major epidemics occurred during the period of intermittent contact.

14. In 1975, the Brazilian National Indian Foundation (FUNAI) increased its involvement with Yanomami. It prohibited the sale of shotguns and ammunition to the Indians, so that by 1981 there were few working shotguns remaining in Yanomami possession (Saffirio 1985:73). By that date, however, war by the Yanomam around Catrimani was over.

15. By the late 1970s, onchocerciasis, or African river blindness, had been introduced to the Deminí (Migliazza 1980:106), adding to the panoply of health hazards spreading among the Yanomami.

16. One rationale offered to the Brazilian public for this proposed archipelago of Yanomami reserves was that separating local groups would keep them from making war on each other (Yanomami 1991). It was such political manipulation of the Yanomami's image of fierceness in Brazil that led some anthropologists to criticize Napoleon Chagnon's portrayals of the Yanomami (Albert 1989; Carneiro da Cunha 1989; cf. Chagnon 1989a, 1992a:90).

Chapter 9

1. The Brazilian forts were manned by criminals, many of them murderers. They would regularly impress local people as unpaid laborers, mainly as rowers for the long trips downriver and back (Spruce 1908:293–94). Farther up the Negro at San Carlos, the Venezuelan border outpost, local people were clearly hostile to the two resident whites, and there was fear of an uprising. One native warned Spruce of a plan to kill him and the other whites. He explained why: "As with my little stock of merchandise I found myself the richest merchant in San Carlos, pretty pickings were calculated on in the sacking of my house" (1908:350). Spruce and the two Brazilians sat up all night with shotguns, and no attack occurred.

2. Michelena y Rojas (1989:404–406) also claims that Brazilians were still making strikes into remote areas to obtain captives, in contrast to the Venezuelans at this time. But his strongly pro-Venezuelan sympathies must qualify this report.

3. Tejera (1877 II:10–11) reports that "Guaica" were "staunch enemies of the Guaharibos." That may apply to this time period. There is no basis indicated for this assertion, however, and in other respects it reads so much like Codazzi (1940) that I suspect it reflects that author's description of conditions at an earlier time.

4. The main problems with Chaffanjon are his false claim to have reached the source of the Orinoco and his apparently deliberate distortion of river widths to support his claim. Beyond that, he produces a drawing of a Yanomamo house that charitably can be called fanciful. On the other hand, his illustration of a Yanomamo bridge is very authentic, and the first one published, to my knowledge. Even skeptics accept that Chaffanjon passed some distance above the Raudal de Guajaribos, although falling far short of the source of the Orinoco (Grelier 1957:36–38; Perera, in Chaffanjon 1986:280; Tavera-Acosta 1927:424).

5. Several researchers have shown that clusters of a dozen or more contemporary settlements may be traced back to a single village a century ago. It is this apparent growth in the number of descendant local groups, rather than any direct estimate of early population numbers, that is the main basis for inferring a Yanomami population explosion during this time. As discussed in chapter 4, most observers credit this rapid population growth to the acquisition of steel tools. Regarding the cases at hand, for instance, Chagnon (1966:167) notes that the Shamatari bloc had grown more than the Namowei-teri bloc, and explains: "Presumably the size of the populations involved is a function of their agricultural potentials, and the Shamatari apparently expanded earlier than the

Namowei-tedi because they had access to steel tools sooner." (He also notes that the Shamatari had the advantage of expanding into completely empty territory.)

6. For example, in Chagnon's (1966:171) most detailed account of the history of the Shamatari bloc, the two groups known as Karawe-teri and Kohoroshiwe-teri split off from their Shamatari relatives as recently as 1925. But in a later discussion, after more research, Chagnon (1974:75, 86) is less certain of any phylogenetic relationship, and if one does exist, he places the split sometime well back into the nineteenth century.

Chapter 10

1. Generally, Valero's narratives have stood the test of time as an accurate source about the Yanomamo. Aspects of Yanomamo life and culture that were published first in Biocca's Italian edition have since become standard elements of the ethnography, although with some discrepancies that have been attributed to the editor (Fuentes 1984:10; Lizot 1988:495). Valero's descriptions of historical events are verified by other reports. Because these two books are such essential sources for me, additional commentary on their value and problems is warranted.

To start, there are the problems inherent in translation. The translation of kinship terms in particular makes it difficult or impossible to ascertain genealogical relationships between individuals.

Both books are presented as continuous, first person narratives, without clarification about how Valero's words were elicited and edited. Biocca (1971:9–11), who recorded Valero sometime in 1962–63, refers to repeated questioning about particular episodes, and mentions "steering the narrative towards those aspects which I considered most important," without saying what those were. There is even less information about the preparation of *Yo Soy Napëyoma*. Renato Agagliate is listed as compiler, and Emilio Fuentes, as editor. Apparently, Fuentes began with a manuscript, although he did have extensive conversations with Valero (Fuentes 1984:15). The actual recording appears to have been done prior to 1972 (Cocco 1972:104).

Recurrent markers of interviewer presence are Biocca's regular estimates of the number of people involved in a particular occurrence and Valero's regular estimates of elapsed time between events (both in very round units). Other interviewer influences would be less obvious. One potential bias is especially significant for my purposes: I suspect that in both works the interviewers were more interested in traditional lifeways than details of indirect acculturation. Thus, references to steel tools occur only in the context of relating a specific event or dialogue. Neither book contains any mention at all of the quantity of tools present in a village at a particular time. Indeed, some of the most telling observations by Valero about the general availability of steel come not from either of these books but from her longtime patron, Padre Cocco.

Comparing the two works for historical purposes, there are some significant differences between them, but generally the two strongly confirm each other in their descriptions of events. When Valero's accounts differ from descriptions of an event in other sources, I take Valero to be authoritative, especially when she was an eyewitness.

For the most part, the two sources present events in identical sequence. Significant discrepancies in sequencing will be noted as they arise. *Yanoáma* is shorter and much less complete than *Yo Soy Napëyoma*. It concentrates on more dramatic incidents and leaves out much of the quotidian subsistence activities, most notably the frequent trekking to gather and hunt. This editing makes the Biocca version unusable for estimating elapsed time. *Yo Soy Napëyoma* can be used, with caution, to date events. By matching references in the narrative to a few externally known dates, keeping track of statements indicating approximate passages of time, and noting references to seasons and seasonal activities, I have been able to put together a rough chronology. It must be acknowledged and stressed, however, that a good deal of "jostling" had to be done to make everything fit. The dates I assign to events described by Valero must be taken as approximations. Most could be off by a year either way, sometimes more.

Valero's own perspective and biases must be considered. Her recollections of her first year or two among the Yanomamo appear somewhat jumbled and given to hyperbole, in contrast to later discussions. Although she ultimately adjusted to life among the Yanomamo, she was an unwilling captive who never ceased trying to escape. She was repeatedly and brutally abused—beaten, burned, and wounded by arrows perhaps half a dozen times. The other wives of her two husbands, Fusiwe and Akawe, were also abused, but not to the same extent. As Valero was regularly reminded, she had no male kinsmen to protect her.

Valero was raised and remained Christian. Perhaps it is this that accounts for a complete absence of any discussion of sexual activities, although many of the female war prisoners she mentions surely were raped. Because she is a woman, Valero was not centrally placed to describe the long political negotiations that went on between men. Finally, towards the end of her captivity, the years of stress may have taken a psychological toll, for she reports several supernatural occurrences as fact.

Having said all this, I would add my own subjective evaluation that Valero is an exceptional and honest reporter of life among the Yanomamo. She never became Yanomamo, but she knew them and respected them as individual human beings, some noble, some savage. With the qualifications noted, her words can be trusted. And more than providing us with data, as important as those data are, the life of doña Helena is an extraordinary testimony to human perseverance and to a mother's love for her children. Perhaps some day a dramatist will tell her story to a wider public.

(At the time of this writing, *Yo Soy Napëyoma* is available from Fundación La Salle de Ciencia Naturales, Apartado 1930, Caracas 1010-A, Venezuela.)

2. One of the more significant discrepancies between Valero (1984:33, 43) and Biocca (1971:27–29) is that the latter (and see Chagnon 1966:21–22) says that the antagonistic split of Kohoroshiwe-teri from Karawe-teri occurred after they returned from their joint participation in the raid that captured Valero. In *Yo Soy Napëyoma*, on the other hand, the two were already established enemies, and the Karawe-teri did not participate in the raid that captured her. Perhaps

the split had occurred, but some Karawe-teri continued to associate with their Kohoroshiwe-teri kinsmen, which would not be unusual. Also associated with the Kohoroshiwe-teri at this moment were some Watanami-teri, who at a later time returned to live with their kin close to the Orinoco (Valero 1984:541–42).

3. As portrayed by Valero, this attack on the Kohoroshiwe-teri by the Karawe-teri is probably the most brutal act of war ever reported for any Yanomami. This may be partly due to the Karawe-teri's seemingly extraordinary success in routing the Kohoroshiwe-teri. But I also suspect these descriptions may reflect some of the terror inspired in young Helena at the time and perhaps embellishments encouraged by those she talked to later. For example, the slaughter of children, and specifically the act of taking them by the feet and bashing their heads against rocks and trees (Biocca 1971:35), is never reported for Yanomami anywhere else, but it is one of the most commonly recounted vignettes in captivity narratives.

4. The year 1935 was one of increased creole activity on the far upper Orinoco, the impact of which was quickly felt at great distances. In the brief time Valero was with the Karawe-teri, they were visited by a man from Aramamise-teri, closer to the Orinoco (Chagnon 1966:170), who came with machetes, tins of manioc, and a dyed hammock obtained from whites—apparently Brazilians—who passed along the river (Biocca 1971:99). (Woodsmen commonly crossed frontiers.)

5. There is also an isolated report of Yanomamo attack on *balateros* on the Siapa in 1934 (Cocco:1972:67). Perhaps the raiders were Shamatari.

6. Hames (1983:419) discusses macromoves as if they were single relocations. But as noted in the previous discussion of the Wakawaka sub-bloc, Cocco reconstructs many smaller moves as having occurred. In the two macromoves covered by Cocco (1972:408–410), between Karishibowei and Hawaroi (27 kilometers), there were four intermediate gardens, and between Hawaroi and Mrakabowei (15 kilometers), there were five, although the first three remained in the vicinity of Hawaroi. I suspect similar intermediate steps existed within other macromoves.

7. The Watupawe-teri are members of the Heronapui population bloc (Fredlund 1982:34; Lizot 1988:522), which was noted in chapter 9 as being geographically locked out of good access to sources of steel all across the western front. In chapter 11, they will be seen again to be pressuring Yanomamo in the Ocamo basin.

8. I believe this is the raid that Chagnon (1966:154) reconstructs as having occurred after the killing of Ruwahiwe, which resulted in fourteen specifically named woman captives, three of whom escaped. Valero does not indicate any Namowei raids on the Shamatari at that later time, but she does state (1984:123) that all the Shamatari women living among the Namowei during her time with them were from this one earlier raid.

9. Valero (Biocca 1971:130) mentions that Shamatari traded dogs (perhaps of Brazilian origin) for cotton, which the Shamatari lacked and the lower-altitude Namowei cultivated in abundance. With the Irota-teri (Valero 1984:176), the Namowei traded cotton for the hallucinogen *yopo*, which grows better in higher terrain.

10. It may have been at this point that the Bisaasi-teri were involved in a serious club fight with other Namowei, triggered by a disagreement over the distribution of meat from a joint hunt. There were some bad feelings, but the grievances were officially resolved (Biocca 1971:142–46).

Another undatable conflict involves the Hasupuwe-teri (Biocca 1971:154–58). Some Namowei were invited to feast. While there, however, they were harassed by what seems to be a faction within the Hasupuwe-teri that did not want to invite the visitors in the first place. Tension crackled in the air as Fusiwe warned: "We are in this world to avenge ourselves; if you do it to me, I will do it to you" (Biocca 1971:158). Women were in danger; an attempt to trade collapsed. The Namowei warily left and returned home. There was no violence.

Chapter 11

1. As Cocco (1972:87) points out, there are evident misunderstandings in this report, and Acebes's suggestion of a general retreat southward by a broad coalition of Guaica is without foundation.

2. There appears to be an accepted usage at this moment of "Guajaribo" for all Yanomamo and Sanema from the Ocamo northward, and "Guaica" for all Yanomamo south of the Ocamo (Barker 1953:map; Grelier 1957:73, 109).

3. Both Valero and Chagnon (1966:152–53, 1992a:1–3) describe those events. The accounts in Valero's two narratives are very similar, but they differ in many respects from Chagnon's reconstruction, most significantly in regard to timing. Chagnon originally dated the events to around 1940, but he currently places them around 1949. Valero has them occurring within the period bracketed by airplane overflights (1941–43). My guess is late 1942, possibly early 1943. Generally, I will adhere to Valero's eyewitness accounts, with their compelling attention to detail.

4. Chagnon (1992a:2) reports that several children died among the Bisaasi-teri at this time, and their deaths also were attributed to the Matakuwe-teri/Konabuma-teri. These deaths are not mentioned in Valero, but she was not living with the Bisaasi-teri subdivision.

5. This is the version in Valero (1984:234). In Biocca (1971:194), Fusiwe himself starts the slaughter by coming up and contemptuously throwing machetes in front of the Shamatari. A sense of the scene is provided by Valero's description (Biocca 1971:197) of the removal of Ruwahiwe's body from the center of the village:

> Then those who had killed him took lianas and tied the dead body. So they dragged it out; you could hear the arrows which went tr, tr, trr as they scraped along the ground. The *tushaua* [leader], sitting in his hammock, watched. The designs on that bloody body were still perfect; the ornaments had stayed in the ears and on the arms. No feather had fallen on account of the arrow-shots.

6. In an odd twist, one of the dead was the very man who had incited Fusiwe to kill Ruwahiwe. Inexplicably, from the Namowei conspirators' viewpoint, he

had gone against instructions and accompanied the trade party. His behavior prior to the violence suggests extreme depression. Fusiwe decided to kill him also because he feared from this odd behavior that he would later seek revenge (Biocca 1971:192; Valero 1984:230–37).

7. Again, Chagnon (1992a:1–3) differs on many of these details. For instance, he has Ruwahiwe arrive and die alone, and there is no mention of the conspiracy or the lure of trade machetes. Chagnon writes (1992a:3): "Thus began the war between the villages of Bisaasi-teri and Konabuma-teri," which was still continuing many years later when he arrived in the field. While I do not see this and subsequent conflicts as one continuous war, I agree that this event does mark the transition to a time in which war becomes common.

8. Clay suitable for pots is found only in certain areas (Valero 1984:199, 372). At this time the Namowei were getting pots both from the Hasupuwe-teri and Watanami-teri (Valero 1984:284, 300).

9. Fusiwe explained it thus: "Last night I dreamed of so many white men, all clothed and with a cloak over them; when they shook the hood, smoke came out, and that smoke entered into us. When the whites undress, they leave the illness in their clothes. We die because of Shawara-wakeshi; it is the whites. White men cause illnesses; if the whites had never existed, diseases would never have existed either" (Biocca 1971:213).

10. Note 9, chapter 10, mentions an undated conflict between Fusiwe's people and the Bisaasi-teri over the distribution of meat from a joint hunt (Biocca 1971:142). In Biocca, this incident is separate from and earlier than the firebrand fight (1971:207), but it could be that it actually pertains to the sequence of events described in Valero (1984:252).

11. Chagnon's (1966:154–58, 1977:76–77) spare reconstruction of this hostile fissioning and war differs in many respects from the events described by Valero. As with the earlier killing of Ruwahiwe, I will rely primarily on Valero's eyewitness accounts.

12. Although the Tetehei-teri ate much bitter manioc, they did not have the standard Amazonian processing technology, using instead a much cruder method to extract the toxin. They are the only group described by Valero to rely so much on manioc at this time. This small group is also unusual in being organized around a core of female kin. In another work (Ferguson 1988b), I follow the argument of Robert Murphy (1956, 1960) that intensive manioc production exerts pressure toward uxorilocality, and that uxorilocality is also associated with internal peace. The Tetehei-teri are noted as enjoying an unusually peaceful existence (Valero 1984:255–56).

13. Fusiwe around this time said he would send Helena and their son to live among the whites when the boy was older, so that "always you will send me machetes" (Valero 1984:288).

14. Repowe's speech reveals the Yanomamo's own conception of the costs of war, and the fact of its absence for some time:

Oh my son, you must not shoot. You have two male children; one is growing up, the other has only recently appeared. Why do you think of killing? Do you think that killing is a joke? If you kill today, tomorrow your sons will be alone and abandoned. When a man kills, he often has to flee far off, leaving his children behind him, who weep for hunger. Do you not yet know this? I know it, because I am old. When we used to live on the other side of the great river, we used to fight with the Kunatateri, who had killed one of us. We fled, carrying with us the bones of the man who had been killed, on the journey we found no bananas and so much time passed before we could prepare the banana pap for the ashes. We ate only *inaja,* the fruit of *balata:* sometimes not even that. Your father wept with me and you yourself, who were then a child, used to weep for hunger. So would you now wish to do the same? (Biocca 1971:218)

Nevertheless, in an interesting illustration of the social distancing that accompanies conflict, old Repowe at this point said that the Bisaasi-teri, who had been included as Namowei in many previous contexts, were not really Namowei after all, but Morota-teri, and that was why they caused trouble (Valero 1984: 324).

15. This flight was part of a series of confrontations related to the disposition of Fusiwe's four living wives (Valero 1984:363, 380). Conflicts over women, so prominent in many descriptions of Yanomami, are often associated with deaths of husbands, and those deaths increase through disease and war during times of increased contact.

16. When Fusiwe saw the young man, toward whom he felt paternal, coming along the path, he reportedly thought, "I must kill him; he is Rashawe's brother. When this young man is dead, then Rashawe will be quite right to bear me a grievance" (Biocca 1971:234).

Chapter 12

1. Two major occurrences that are firmly dated, the slaughter of Bisaasi-teri by Iwahikoroba-teri (chapter 11) and the arrival of the Franco-Venezuelan Expedition, are reversed in Valero (1984:421, 432).

2. The expedition's first contact with "Guaharibo" actually came before San Fernando de Atabapo, when expedition members met a group who had established a garden along the Orinoco. These otherwise unknown people, who were cultivating manioc and making pots to trade across the river to Piaroa (Grelier 1957:96), might rival the Mahekoto-teri as being in the vanguard of Yanomami contact with outsiders around this time.

3. Valero (1984:503, 505, 511) confirms the Iyewei-teri lead in this area and describes some of the difficulties another group encountered in its initial efforts to build and use canoes.

4. Some idea of the kind of relationship that existed between the Bisaasi-teri and the malaria service personnel can be gleaned from the following comment by Chagnon (1983:15–16), who is discussing the circumstances of his own field-work a few years later: "So persistent and characteristic is the begging that the

early 'semi-official' maps made by the Venezuelan Malaria Control Service (Malarialogía) designated the site of their first permanent field station, next to the village of Bisaasi-teri, as Yababuhii: 'Gimme.' "

5. Bisaasi-teri men visited the Puunabiwe-teri to demand aggressively that they hand over Valero and her children, whom the Bisaasi-teri needed because they had lost so many men to raiders. Valero's husband, Akawe, was ready to give her up, but then refused when his brother argued that to do so might give the impression of weakness (Valero 1984:410).

6. According to Chagnon (1967:152), the Bisaasi-teri made a retaliatory raid on the Shamatari before moving in with the Mahekoto-teri. That would have been a major accomplishment, since they had lost their leader and a dozen or so other men. But the events Chagnon associates with this raid—killing the Shamatari headman, rescuing some abducted women, and capturing a boy—are said by Barker (1959:163–65) to have happened "much later." In Valero (Biocca 1971:316–17; Valero 1984:485–86), this raid occurs after she meets Zerries, making it 1954 or 1955, and part of the later Mahekoto-teri–Shamatari war.

7. This map contains a wealth of information, but some qualifications are necessary. First, geography off the Orinoco mainstream was poorly known at the time, so positions are very approximate. Second, no information is provided as to the map's construction. Thus the difference between "hostile" and "very hostile" is not explained, and the currency of conflicts is not indicated. Third, things changed rapidly after 1953. By 1955, for instance, Iyewei-teri, Witokaya-teri, and Puunabiwe-teri had all moved to the west, close to the Orinoco, and the pattern of current animosities was quite different. Finally, comparing Barker's spellings with those I have adopted illustrates some of the difficulty involved in matching reports of particular local groups from different sources. Some group appellations, such as "Liakoatedi," are entirely different from those I use and can only be matched up, sometimes, by context. Others may represent changes over time. In particular, the Kashorawe-teri and Yabitawa-teri are new groups formed out of the old Watanami-teri (Valero 1984:136), ally of the Mahekoto-teri in the 1940s.

8. The date 1953 is based on comparison of Chagnon (1966:146, 163), Barker (1959:153), and Valero (1984:434), but undoubtedly the move was a process over time. Barker's 1953 map shows Bisaasi-teri as an independent village on the Orinoco. Its location conforms to Barauwa on Chagnon's map (1977:43).

9. Valero refers to these enemies as "Ihiteri" (e.g., Biocca 1971:291) and "Hii-theri" (e.g., Valero 1984:404). In the latter citation, she specifies that Hii-theri is a collective term including the local groups Potomawe-teri and Komishibuwe-teri. I take the label to be the same term Fredlund (1982:35) transcribes as "Shitari": "a term used by groups living in the Ocamo basin to refer to people living upstream or at higher elevations in the Parima Mountains." That would include the two groups indicated as "very hostile" to Valero's people in Barker's 1953 map, Konabuma-teri and Watupawe-teri. In what I estimate to be late 1953 or 1954, the Watupawe-teri are identified as current enemies of the Puunabiwe-teri (Valero 1984:469).

Because in earlier discussions I have followed Fredlund, who assigns the term "Shitari" to specific clusters of villages (much as Chagnon does with the similarly shifting referent "Shamatari" [see Lizot 1988:527–28]), I will restrict that spelling to those villages and use "Ihiteri" to refer to the often unspecified interior enemies of Valero's people.

10. As Yanomamo began to move from highlands to lowlands, resource variation by altitude may have become a more important basis for trade. For instance, arrow cane and the hallucinogen *ebene* both grow better at higher altitudes (Fredlund 1982:33; Valero 1984:158).

11. During this time, around 1954, another dispute over a woman occurred, this one involving the daughter of the Witokaya-teri headman. She was betrothed to Valero's husband, the fierce Akawe, but she ran away with an Iyewei-teri man. Akawe's sardonic comment (Valero 1984:461) is instructive about relationships between access to Western manufactures, betrothals, and fierceness: "Hashowe likes that son-in-law more than me. He likes him for the red cloth which he brings to stop up his asshole and for the beads he gives to Oshewei to conquer her." But as it turned out, Akawe's reputation and bluster—he publicly beat a dog to death—led to the return of the young woman (Biocca 1971:299; Valero 1984:461–66).

12. Cocco (1972:393) estimates that among some 2,000 Yanomami with whom Salesian missionaries had contact between 1957 and 1972, a total of about 25 died from violence. A large part of that total can be accounted for by the wars of the mid-1960s, described in chapter 12.

13. A complete tabulation of goods distributed by the mission from 1960 to 1971 is presented in chapter 2. In another discussion, Cocco says that from the mission's founding up to 1978, it distributed more than 10,000 machetes, more than 2,000 axes, and close to a million fishhooks (Peña Vargas 1981:37).

14. The locations of both the Auwei-teri and the Yepropei-teri are known only from maps using information dating to 1970–75.

15. This is one of only a few indications of Patanowa-teri's ceding wives in order to establish alliances. It appears to have been a frequent practice, however, unless there is some other explanation for the fact that, in the mid-1960s, they had one of the most skewed sex ratios in the area—122 males to 90 females (Chagnon 1966:58).

16. Valero was rejected by her brothers, who were ashamed of her past. She was almost abducted again by some Kohoroshiwe-teri at the Tapurucuara mission. Then she went down to live in poverty in Manaus (where some 50,000 people lived in a "floating city" reputed to be one of the worst slums in the world [Salazar 1967:28].) In the early 1960s, she worked with various missionaries and scientists. In 1971, she was invited to return to the Ocamo region by Padre Cocco (Biocca 1971:325–29; Valero 1984:531–38). As of this writing, she still lives there (Ken Good, personal communication).

17. Cocco (1972:97) suggests that the Wawanawe-teri may be an offshoot of the Iwahikoroba-teri Shamatari, who fled southward from the Mahekoto-teri/Bisaasi-teri raids of the mid-1950s. This illustrates both the persistent "steel poverty" of the Shamatari and the interconnectedness of developments throughout the region.

18. Akawe's homicidal accomplishments would make him valuable to in-

experienced warriors planning an attack; his travels and his wife made him valuable as a broker to the outside world. In contrast to her attitude toward her first husband, Fusiwe, Valero was contemptuous of Akawe, who only stopped abusing her when she nearly choked him to death (Valero 1984:492,516). Unfortunately, it is not unusual for such self-serving individuals to act as brokers between indigenous peoples and Westerners.

19. Salazar (1967:76) relates the following dialogue with Padre Gois about dealing with the natives. After stressing that the missionary must never appear afraid or undecided, Gois continued:

"At the same time you must show generosity; give them food, clothing, tools, medicine."

"And in return?"

"In return they attend mass, send their children to the mission school, and settle down around the mission to learn to live like Christians."

"What if they don't cooperate?"

"Then I stop giving them gifts. If they want them badly enough they come around. Eventually they learn to value the rewards of a civilized life."

Chapter 13

1. Partly because of the shorter time period covered by this chapter, there is very little to report about other Yanomamo. In the south, as noted in chapter 12, Brazilian Yanomamo armed with shotguns were raiding more isolated villages in Venezuela—an expectable development in that extending contact situation. In the north, villages in Hames's (1983:409–14) middle Padamo sub-bloc continued their tense but not violent shuttling around Yecuana country. The New Tribes missionaries (M. Dawson 1961; Dye 1962; Johnston 1964:3) also reported much sublethal violence, often directed against women. They had opened a new mission on the Cuntinamo, and in 1962 the local groups around them were in hostile confrontation. In 1964 a severe malaria outbreak caused many deaths throughout the area. One missionary (J. Dawson 1964) speculated that the epidemic was sent by God in answer to missionary prayers, to make the Yanomamo, who were becoming increasingly indifferent to Bible teachings, lose faith in their shamans and trust the missionaries who cured them.

One violent incident to the north of Bisaasi-teri is reported by Chagnon, involving two unidentified villages, both with strong connections to different missions (1977:120–22). The fighting was triggered when a woman fled her cruel husband, and it escalated even though she returned to him. This clash includes several unusual elements: it went from clubs to a spear fight; the "home" side was driven from the village, after which the "visitors stole all the hammocks, machetes, and cooking pots they could find" (1977:122); and each side had borrowed, under false pretenses, a shotgun from the missionary. One headman was shot in the face—the first such use of a shotgun reported for the area. With many months of care by the missionaries, the headman recovered.

2. Chagnon (1977:161), noting the Yanomamo's traditional avoidance of the large rivers and their recent movement toward them "because of the allure of exotic trade goods," comments: "No Yanomamo would tolerate the discomfort of living near the bug-infested rivers unless there were powerful incentives, such as trade goods, to attract them there."

3. I have been unable to locate in Chagnon's essays any explicit statement that Western goods go in one direction in this alliance, and indigenous products, in the other. He implies that this is so, however, in a published letter written a few months after his arrival in the field: "Some villages specialize in making one or another object; others who have special sources of access purvey axes or machetes and pots to the rest" (Chagnon 1972a:66). The two-directional relationship is also implied in the captions of two photographs from the same scene: "Kaobawa trading his steel tools to Shamatari allies" (Chagnon 1974:facing 11), and "Kaobawa, headman of Upper Bisaasi-teri, trading with his Shamatari allies for arrows, baskets, hammocks, and dogs" (Chagnon 1983:6). Furthermore, Cocco (1972:205, 376–78) and Lizot (1976:8–9), each with long experience in the Orinoco-Mavaca area, describe this economic specialization as characteristic of exchange involving villages with direct access to sources of Western manufactures. Chagnon is by no means unusual in not providing specific information on this point. On the contrary, it is rare to see it discussed by anthropologists unless the work is focused specifically on the process of acculturation.

4. The text of this comment reads: "In some cases, the disposition of desirable trade goods may affect the balance in the exchange of women between two villages. In general it may be said that, when one village is allied to another which can provide it with more military assistance and desirable trade goods than the former can give to the latter, an imbalance in the exchanges of women will follow" (Chagnon 1966:6–7). Note that this comment does not specify Western trade goods, and in context, the stress is placed on the military rather than the trade dimension.

5. On the other hand, the perception of him as the source of coveted goods is what enabled Chagnon to work in so many villages. As he describes his first meeting with the headman of the previously uncontacted village of Mishimishimobowei-teri in 1968:

> I called to him: "Father-in-law! I have come to your village to visit you and bring *madohe* [trade goods]. Is it true that your people are poor and in need of machetes?" I could hear the whispers of excitement around us after I spoke. "Yes! We are poor in machetes." . . . I concluded by telling him that I would give him the cooking pot I had with me and one of the knives in the morning, and that I would bring him a big gift on my next visit. This visit was primarily to discover if they were friendly and if they were in need of steel tools, as the rumors said—a story I always tell when I visit a village for the first time. One must always imply that he has many more possessions *back home* and intends to bring them on his next visit, provided the people are friendly. (Chagnon 1974:29)

6. "Shortly after" the Mahekoto-teri's assault on the Bisaasi-teri, the latter's Karohi-teri allies lost two men in a pounding match with some unidentified ene-

mies who concealed stones in their fists (Chagnon 1983:167). The Karohi-teri also became embroiled in a protracted conflict with Mahekoto-teri, involving some raiding, but its timing and connections to other events are unclear (Lizot 1985:81, 141). Such problems would leave the Karohi-teri less able to offer military support to anyone else. Also, sometime in 1965, the Bisaasi-teri had another chest-pounding duel with the Tayari-teri (Chagnon 1990b:99), allies of the Mahekoto-teri. Finally, a "club fight" in an unidentified village in 1965 somehow brought the Bisaasi-teri and Mahekoto-teri close to a state of war. Some time after that clash, the two would have a rapprochement and begin trading again, albeit on strained terms (Chagnon 1977:117).

7. The date, again, is January 1965, not January 1966 as given in all five editions of *Yanomamö* (e.g, Chagnon 1977:125, 1992b:222).

8. This conclusion is based on Chagnon's statement that "the Monou-teri and Bisaasi-teri raided against the Patanowa-teri six times while I lived with them" (1977:134). My count is seven: the first raid by Monou-teri in late January 1965; the raid organized by Kaobawa in late April; the solo raid by Monou-teri, tentatively dated to June; the raid led by Paruriwa in July; and three more attributed to Paruriwa between November and February 1966 (Chagnon 1966: 187). Whatever the reason for this discrepancy, it indicates that no raids by Monou-teri or Bisaasi-teri occurred between July and November.

9. The continuation of this quote demonstrates plainly that the support of a Westerner and control of his trade goods were the basis of political success.

I saw Paruriwa in 1967 when I stopped to greet the priest: he was proudly bearing a presumptuous Spanish title, beating his chest with his fist, urging me to pay attention: "Me Capitan! Me Capitan! Me Capitan!" He swaggered off after I acknowledged that he was a leader now, carelessly shouldering a rusty 16-gauge shotgun, barking commands to his followers in the three or four Spanish words he had learned during the year, a shadow of the man I had last seen, dwarfed in the raggy and tattered pants that marked his new status and guaranteed in that status by *his* monopoly on the priest's trade goods. (Chagnon 1977:151, emphasis in original)

10. Looking back on the war, apparently from the vantage of early 1967, Chagnon observes that the Monou-teri had killed two men and captured two women, while the Patanowa-teri had killed only one, Damowa (Chagnon 1977: 137). But with the two Patanowa-teri losses in the January and April raids, this last killing would make three Patanowa-teri deaths. I cannot explain this discrepancy. The two women apparently are those taken at the feast in November. No other women are reported captured in the raids.

Chapter 14

1. Chagnon (1992a:219, 235–39) describes himself in a growing conflict with the Salesian missionaries and the Yanomamo associated with them. He attributes their opposition to two things: his interest in causes of death, which

document the impact of diseases and shotguns coming through the missions; and his practice of freely dispensing trade goods in nonmission villages, which deprived the missionaries and mission Yanomamo of their leverage over more isolated groups. (For another account of the missions' attempt to monopolize contact and the dispensation of health care as a means of securing control over Yanomami, see Alès and Chiappino [1985].)

2. Details of this initial incident resemble those of an event described in a footnote to the third edition of *Yanomamö* (Chagnon 1983:167), in which the Karohi-teri, rather than the Tayari-teri, are said to have lost two men in a pounding match with an unidentified neighbor (see note 6, chapter 13). They may be the same event.

3. This shift toward peace after 1968 may explain why Lizot presents a much less violent portrait of the Yanomamo than Chagnon, even though their main research sites and times were close together and even though, as Lizot (1989:30) has recently confirmed, the war mortality in their populations is comparable (24 percent versus 30 percent of adult male mortality). Chagnon arrived in the field in 1964 at the start of a few years of unusually intense violence. All the information in his initial monograph came from that period, and those descriptions remain, with only minor revision, in editions two through five. Lizot arrived in 1968, near the end of this time of war, and his writing reflects his long exposure to more peaceful times.

4. On another visit in early 1969, far up the Orinoco, Steinvorth de Goetz encountered the linguistically distinctive Porepoi-teri. They had formerly been in contact with Brazilians, but since at least 1967 had been moving toward the Orinoco (1969:141–42, 146). The deepening Western presence along the river in the 1960s was drawing groups from far away.

5. The primary source for the Parima mission, Jank (1977), contains almost no dates. My time estimates are based on passing comments about elapsed time or time of year, starting with the measles epidemic of early 1968.

6. The extent of Chagnon's fame is indicated by an incident from 1972. While visiting a village in Brazil, one of his biomedical colleagues "casually mentioned my Yanomamo name, Shaki, in front of a Yanomamo. The Yanomamo immediately and excitedly demanded to know where I was and if I were going to visit them. This Yanomamo village was many miles away from any Yanomamo village I had ever visited" (Chagnon 1983:38).

7. It is also the incident analyzed for its reproductive implications in Chagnon and Bugos (1979). They conclude that "members of each team are more closely related among themselves than they are to their opponents, i.e., that mutual supporters are more closely related genetically among themselves than they are to the individuals of the group they are opposing" (1979:225). Since these two groups came from two distinct kin-based factions, that is not surprising. If the analysis had been done on any of the cases described in this book in which one group defects and joins with another to fight against their own kin, a very different result might be found.

8. Chagnon's explanation of the conflict between Moawa and himself, and of similar conflicts between Yanomamo, is that they were about status (1974: 194).

9. Lizot had been living with the Tayari-teri, but his location and disposition during these hostilities is not mentioned in any of these sources. Such information might be helpful in understanding this highly unusual war and the events leading up to it.

10. Chagnon's missionary adversaries assert that the large number of visitors this brought to the Siapa region—scientists, military men, reporters, and tourists—may have exposed these remote groups to diseases, with no one remaining to provide medical care between visits (Misioneros 1991:20).

11. O'Hanlon (1990:143) traveled to the lower Siapa from the Río Negro around 1985. Up until his arrival there, his travelogue is replete with references to Chagnon's descriptions of Yanomami belligerence. The peaceable situation he encountered took him by surprise. He comments (1990:217): "Maybe Chagnon just happened to have picked a particularly violent set of societies, disturbed, too near mission stations, over-aggressive, confused."

12. In 1973 Lizot (1974:8–13) found Siapa groups to the south of Hasupuwe-teri to have a great many hafted pieces of steel and other Western goods. Two censused villages also had a pronounced shortage of women (61 males to 50 females, and 38 males to 24 females, respectively). I expect some of their absent women went to establish alliances with the sources of their steel.

Chapter 15

1. All this theorizing relied heavily on Chagnon's first portrayals of the Yanomami and their wars, including the prominence of conflicts over women. Thus Chagnon (e.g., 1983:86, 1992a:95) misrepresents the protein hypothesis by claiming it denies that Yanomami fight over women. This assertion is contradicted by numerous clear statements of his opponents' theory (see Ferguson 1989b:180). The debate between advocates of the protein hypothesis and Chagnon is not about whether Yanomami fight over women, but about what theory best explains that fighting.

2. After his turn to sociobiology, Chagnon (Chagnon, Flinn, and Melancon 1979:308–309) dropped all reference to this circular relationship, as well as his previous claims that sex ratio at birth could not be accurately determined. He began to argue instead that Yanomami had a live-birth ratio of about 129 males to 100 females. After considering various reasons for doubting this proposal, I concluded (Ferguson 1989c:254) that "unless strong new evidence is presented to support the skewed-ratio-at-birth hypothesis, it can be rejected."

In his recent work, Chagnon (1992a:93) claims that he stopped publishing about female infanticide after 1985 because some Venezuelan politicians wanted to use his findings to prosecute Yanomami for murder. That claim does not accurately reflect the development of this debate, as just described. It does, however, confirm that even Chagnon has dropped the sociobiological skewed-ratio-at-birth hypothesis. While I certainly sympathize with his ethical dilemma, his silence now obviously does not help resolve the scientific questions.

3. Chagnon (1992a:96) again misrepresents his opponents' position when he asserts that they claim "a woman will kill her own newborn to make the

jungle more productive in monkey protein for future members of the group." Regarding the motivation for female infanticide, advocates of the protein hypothesis merely took Chagnon at his word.

4. It is worth noting that for all their differences, Lizot and Chagnon (1974: 77, 1977:163) agree on another fundamental—and empirically unsupportable —assumption: that warfare "is endemic *among all primitive peoples*" (Lizot 1979:151, emphasis in original).

5. But I do not agree at all with Lizot's (1991:62) dismissal of the often outrageous demands for Western goods that permeate trade dialogues as being nothing more than figures of speech to remind the other of the necessity to exchange.

6. In another discussion, Lizot (1989:31–32) makes several points with which I am in complete agreement: that a variety of motives go into any war, that the final incident that leads to a war may be merely the detonator in a relationship gone bad, and that understanding war requires close examination of village histories and intervillage relations. What Lizot does not offer is any key to explaining major variation in those histories and relations, or why they sometimes get to the point of violent detonation.

7. In a footnote to this discussion, Lizot (1991:72) levels several criticisms at a manuscript version of my paper "A Savage Encounter" (Ferguson 1992a). One is that I approached my study with a theory already elaborated. In a broad sense, that is true, although the general theory was critically reevaluated and specified through examination of Yanomami case material. But it is difficult to understand how Lizot can mean this as a criticism when his own approach is a straightforward application of the ideas of Mauss and Lévi-Strauss. Lizot also accuses me of selective presentation of data and ignoring contrary information, although he offers no specifics. I do not accept the criticism in regard to that article, and it certainly cannot be said of this book, which applies my theory to every single case of Yanomami warfare that I could find.

8. The idea that "tribal" peoples make war for revenge seems to be part of the broader conceptual divide implicit in our dichotomies between simple versus complex, nonstate versus state, and, especially, primitive versus civilized war (see Turney-High 1971). It would sound ludicrous to suggest that World War II was a continuation of World War I for the sake of revenge, but if the scale were reduced to the Yanomami level, that characterization probably would be applied. The role of revenge in the conflicts of nonstate people may actually be analogous to the "sense of history" in modern societies and equally subject to political manipulation.

9. Chagnon (1989b:567) challenges me to clarify whether I believe that "humans are designed by natural selection to make choices that generally increase their material benefits." I do (see Ferguson 1984b:37–38). But no one could possibly doubt that humans are motivated to maintain the resources and safety needed to survive, whereas it is entirely hypothetical that they are motivated by an unconscious reproductive striving. My skepticism is directed to the proposal that this hypothetical motive would confer sufficient additional reproductive advantage to be maintained by natural selection in our biogram against the relentless drift of mutation.

10. Chagnon (1989b:568) claims that I "seriously misrepresent" the facts

when I say (Ferguson 1989d:564), "It is a commonplace in Amazonian ethnography, at least since Levi Strauss' (1944) famous article, that headmen have more wives and more children." He counters (Chagnon 1989b:568), "If that knowledge is widespread, it cannot be based on very much empirical evidence." I will concede half the point: ethnographers have been more interested in leaders' plural wives than the number of their offspring. But on the matter of leaders' polygyny, I repeat, the fact is so routinely reported that it is merely a commonplace. Clastres (1987:32) for instance, comments that the ethnographic literature for lowland South America documents that "nearly all these societies, whatever their type of socio-political unity and demographic size, recognize polygamy; and almost all of them recognize it as the usually exclusive privilege of the chief."

11. Chagnon (1989b:566) states that I assume that "offspring production by men is a simple function of aging, that is, that all men produce the same number of offspring if they live to be the same age." This is another of Chagnon's straw men. What I do say on the point is that "as a young man matures, he is . . . more likely to have more children," an elementary observation that is obvious in Chagnon's own data.

12. Chagnon attributes to me other positions that I do not hold. He claims that I dismiss his theory as wrong simply because it is sociobiological (Chagnon 1990a:49). Of course that is an invalid way to argue, although Chagnon makes just that kind of judgment against anthropologists who have not adopted new biological models (1990b:78, 1992a:93; Chagnon and Hames 1980:347). He asserts (1990b:89) that I assume all human populations are approaching their carrying capacity. My stated position (Ferguson 1990a:32) in that same volume is the opposite: "It is certainly not inevitable that human populations expand until they are stopped by scarcity of some crucial resource." Chagnon (1992a: 91–92) claims that materialist models in general focus on the level of the group and ignore individual-level strategizing. As I discuss elsewhere (Ferguson 1984b: 35–38), that criticism was valid up to the mid-1970s, but no longer. Certainly my theory in this volume is much more concerned with individual strategizing than with the essentially group-selection model Chagnon has most recently presented.

Chagnon claims that during a conference we both attended at the School of American Research in 1986, I made "a statement to the following effect: 'I don't understand why "you sociobiologists" keep bringing in reproduction. After all, if you have enough to eat, reproduction is more-or-less automatic' " (Chagnon 1989b:567, my emphasis). An endnote (1989b:569) adds: "His comments were both tape-recorded and heard by the some dozen or so other participants in the symposium." Shortly thereafter we are told: "The assumption 'when people have enough to eat reproduction is more-or-less automatic' is a serious defect in his approach" (1989b:567). As presented, that is a silly statement. I could not remember or imagine saying it, so I obtained the tapes of the discussions of our two papers in order to check. I found no such statement. What I did ask Chagnon to explain was what the calculation of inclusive fitness added to an understanding of behavior, compared to the material variables I stress, and that is the way the seminar chairperson describes this debate (McCauley 1990:2–6).

13. What I am suggesting is that Yanomami do something similar to what

anthropologists do. Anthropologists frequently acknowledge that an intense demand for Western goods characterizes their immediate environs, but they leave that aside in the ethnography to concentrate on "more interesting" cultural norms. Yanomami too direct their attention to more elevated cultural levels.

14. Knauft (1993:1186) takes exception to this position and cites interior New Guinea as an area in which ethnographic documentation reveals warfare "not appreciably influenced by state societies." As Whitehead and I note (Ferguson and Whitehead 1992a:6), "highland New Guinea . . . seems to offer some of the best material for relatively pristine warfare," yet even there, exogenous influences may be ignored at some peril.

For instance, Salisbury (1962), one of the earliest anthropological fieldworkers in the highlands (in 1952) and the author most concerned with the impact of steel tools, notes attacks aimed at plundering goods introduced by explorers in 1933 (1962:114). More significantly, during World War II, when outsiders were largely absent from the Siane area but steel tools were filtering in through exchange networks, "three large wars occurred in the central Pira Valley, in which villages were burned and clans exiled," compared with only four burnings on a smaller scale during the previous 25 years. He adds in a footnote: "The same trend has been remarked for other areas following first contact with Europeans, not merely in Highland New Guinea but throughout the Pacific. Wars on the scale seen in 1938–45 would have rapidly devastated the whole Siane area" (Salisbury 1962:118–19).

The year 1933 is not the earliest date that the external world impinged on life in the New Guinea highlands (see Feil 1987). The point here is not to disregard or minimize local sources of conflict, but to argue that they should be considered in relation to possible stresses associated with state expansion. Clearly, cases will exist in which such stresses are insignificant or even nonexistent, but that conclusion cannot be *assumed* to be true, as it typically has been.

References

Acebes, Hector
1954   *Orinoco Adventure*. Garden City, NY: Doubleday.
Albert, Bruce
1985   Temps du sang, temps des cendres: Représentation de la maladie, système rituel et espace politique chez les Yanomami du sud-est (Amazonie Brésilienne). Doctoral thesis, Université de Paris X, Nanterre, France.
1988   La Fumée du métal: Histoire et représentations du contact chez les Yanomami (Brésil). *L'Homme* 28(2–3):87–119.
1989   Yanomami "violence": Inclusive fitness or ethnographer's representation. *Current Anthropology* 30:637–40.
1990a   On Yanomami warfare: Rejoinder. *Current Anthropology* 31:558–63.
1990b   Développement Amazonien et sécurite nationale: Les Indiens Yanomami face au projet Calha Norte. *Ethnies* 11–12:116–27.
1992   Indian lands, environmental policy and military geopolitics in the development of the Brazilian Amazon: The case of the Yanomami. *Development and Change* 23:35–70.
1993   The massacre of the Yanomami of Hashimu. Manuscript.
Alès, Catherine
1984   Violence et ordre social dans une société Amazonienne. *Etudes Rurales* 95–96:89–114.
Alès, Catherine, and Jean Chiappino
1985   Medical aid, shamanism and acculturation among the Yanomami of Venezuela. In *The Health and Survival of the Venezuelan Yanoama*. M. Colchester, ed., pp. 73–90. Copenhagen: Anthropology Resource Center/ International Work Group for Indigenous Affairs.
Allman, William
1988   A laboratory of human conflict. *U.S. News and World Report*, April 11, pp. 57–58.
Anduze, Pablo
1960   *Shailili-Ko: Relato de un naturalista que también llegó a las fuentes del río Orinoco*. Caracas: Talleres Gráficos Ilustraciones.
1973   *Bajo el signo de Mawari*. Caracas: Imprenta Nacional.
Anthropology Resource Center
1981   *The Yanomami Indian Park*. Boston: Anthropology Resource Center.

Arends, T., G. Brewer, N. Chagnon, M. L. Gallango, H. Gershowitz, M. Layrisse, J. Neel, D. Shreffler, R. Tashian, and L. Weitkamp
1967   Intratribal genetic differentiation among the Yanomama Indians of southern Venezuela. *Proceedings of the National Academy of Sciences* 57:1252–59.

Arhem, Kaj
1981   *Makuna Social Organization: A Study in Descent, Alliance and the Formation of Corporate Groups in the North-Western Amazon.* Uppsala Studies in Cultural Anthropology, no. 4. Stockholm: Uppsala University Press.

Arvelo-Jiménez, Nelly
1971   *Political Relations in a Tribal Society: A Study of Ye'cuana Indians of Venezuela.* Cornell University Latin American Studies Program Dissertation Series, no. 31. Ithaca, NY: Cornell University Press.
1972   An analysis of official Venezuelan policy in regard to the Indians. In *The Situation of the Indian in South America,* W. Dostal, ed., pp. 31–42. Publications of the Department of Ethnology, University of Berne, no. 3. Geneva: World Council of Churches.
1973   *The Dynamics of the Ye'cuana ("Maquiritare") Political System: Stability and Crisis.* Copenhagen: International Work Group for Indigenous Affairs, no. 12.

Arvelo-Jiménez, Nelly, and Horacio Biord Castillo
1989   Introducción. In *Exploración oficial,* by F. Michelena y Rojas. N. Arvelo-Jiménez and H. Biord Castillo, eds., pp. 11–26. Iquitos, Peru: IIAP-CETA.

Arvelo-Jiménez, Nelly, and Andrew Cousins
1992   False promises: Venezuela appears to have protected the Yanomami, but appearances can be deceiving. *Cultural Survival Quarterly,* Winter:10–13.

Asch, Timothy
1972   Ethnographic filming and the Yanomamo Indians. *Sightlines,* Jan.–Feb.: 6–12, 17.
1979   Making a film record of the Yanomamo Indians of southern Venezuela. *Perspectives on Film* 2, August 1979, pp. 4–9, 44–49.
1988   Collaboration in ethnographic filmmaking: A personal view. In *Anthropological Filmmaking,* J. Rollwagen, ed., pp. 1–29. New York: Harwood Academic Publishers.

Aspelin, Paul
1975   *External Articulation and Domestic Production: The Artifact Trade of the Mamainde of Northwestern Mato Grosso, Brazil.* Cornell University Latin American Studies Program Dissertation Series, no. 58. Ithaca, NY: Cornell University Press.

Balée, William
1988   The Ka'apor Indian wars of lower Amazonia, ca. 1825–1928. In *Dialectics and Gender: Anthropological Approaches,* R. Randolph, D. Schneider, and M. Díaz, eds., pp. 155–69. Boulder, CO: Westview Press.

Bamberger, Joan
1979   Exit and voice in central Brazil: The politics of flight in Kayapó society. In *Dialectical Societies: The Gê and Bororo of Central Brazil,* D. Maybury-Lewis, ed., pp. 130–46. Cambridge, MA: Harvard University Press.

Bancroft, Edward
1769   *An Essay on the Natural History of Guiana in South America.* London: T. Becket and P. A. De Hondt.

Barandiaran, Daniel de
1967 Agricultura y recolección entre los Indios Sanemá-Yanoama, o el hacha de piedra y la psicología paleolítica de los mismos. *Antropológica* 19:24–50.

Barandiaran, Daniel de, and Aushi Walalam
1983 *Los hijos de la luna: Monografía antropológica sobre los Indios Sanemá-Yanoama.* Caracas: Editorial Arte.

Barker, James
1953 Memoria sobre la cultura de los Guaika. *Boletín Indigenista Venezolano* 1(3–4):433–89.
1959 Las incursiones entre los Guaika. *Boletín Indigenista* Venezolano 7(1–4): 151–67.

Bennett Ross, Jane
1971 Aggression as adaptation: The Yanomamo case. Manuscript.

Biocca, Ettore
1966 *Viaggi tra gli Indi Alto Rio Negro—Alto Orinoco*, 4 vols. Rome: Consiglio Nazionale delle Ricerche.
1971 (Ed.) *Yanoáma: The Narrative of a White Girl Kidnapped by Amazonian Indians.* New York: E. P. Dutton.

Black-Michaud, Jacob
1975 *Cohesive Force: Feud in the Mediterranean and the Middle East.* New York: St. Martin's Press.

Blick, Jeffrey
1988 Genocidal warfare in tribal societies as a result of European-induced culture conflict. *Man* 23:654–70.

Boomert, Arie
1987 Gifts of the Amazons: "Green stone" pendants and beads as items of ceremonial exchange in Amazonia and the Caribbean. *Antropológica* 67:33–54.

Booth, William
1989 Warfare over Yanomamo Indians. *Science* 243:1138–1140.

Bórtoli, José
1991 Solidaridad e intercambio: Bases para la autogestión. *La Iglesia en Amazonas* 12(53):47–52.
1993 Reflexiones sobre un artículo de N. Chagnon en *New York Times*, "Covering up the Yanomamo massacre." Manuscript.

Botto, Carlos
1991 La situación de salud de la población Yanomami. *La Iglesia en Amazonas* 12(54–55):11–15.

Bou, James
1956 Why did you wait? *Brown Gold* 14(6):2–5, 11.

Boxer, C. R.
1969 *The Golden Age of Brazil, 1695—1750.* Berkeley: University of California Press.

Briceño, Nelson
1991 Contribución de la iglesia en Amazonas a la creación de la Reserva de Biosfera en el area Yanomami. *La Iglesia en Amazonas* 12(54–55):48–50.

Brooke, James
1990 In an almost untouched jungle, gold miners threaten Indian ways. *New York Times*, Sept. 18, p. C1.

1991   Venezuela befriends tribe, but what's Venezuela? *New York Times*, September 11, p. A4.
1992   Venezuela's policy for Brazil's gold miners: bullets. *New York Times*, February 16, p. A20.
1993a   Brazil is evicting miners in Amazon. *New York Times*, March 8, p. A7.
1993b   Miners kill 20 Indians in the Amazon. *New York Times*, August 20, p. A10.
1993c   Attack on Brazilian Indians is worst since 1910. *New York Times*, August 21, p. A3.
1993d   Questions raised in Amazon killings. *New York Times*, August 29, p. A14.
1993e   Gold miners and Indians: Brazil's frontier war. *New York Times*, September 7, p. A4.

Brown Gold
1952   Tribes of Venezuela and Colombia. *Brown Gold* 9(12):8.
1953   Frontiers for Christ. *Brown Gold* 11(7–8):3–11.

Bueno, P. Ramón
1965   *Tratado histórico*. F. de Lejarza, ed., pp. 95–185 (published with *Conversión de Piritu*). Caracas: Biblioteca de la Academía Nacional de la Historia.

Bunker, Stephen
1988   *Underdeveloping the Amazon: Extraction, Unequal Exchange, and the Failure of the Modern State*. Chicago: University of Chicago Press.

Cannon, Aubrey
1992   Conflict and salmon on the interior plateau of British Columbia. In *A Complex Culture of the British Columbia Plateau*, B. Hayden, ed., pp. 506–24. Vancouver: University of British Columbia Press.

Carneiro, Robert
1979a   Tree felling with stone ax: An experiment carried out among the Yanomamo Indians of southern Venezuela. In *Ethnoarchaeology*, C. Kramer, ed., pp. 21–58. New York: Columbia University Press.
1979b   Forest clearing among the Yanomamo, observations and implications. *Antropológica* 52:39–76.
1983   The cultivation of manioc among the Kuikuru of the upper Xingú. In *Adaptive Responses of Native Amazonians*, R. Hames and W. Vickers, eds., pp. 65–111. New York: Academic Press.

Carneiro da Cunha, María Manuela
1989   Letter to the editor. *Anthropology Newsletter* 30(1):3.

Caulin, Antonio
1841   *Historia corográfico, natural y evangélica de Nueva Andalucía*. Caracas: George Corser.

Cawte, John
1978   Gross stress in small islands: A study in macropsychiatry. In *Extinction and Survival in Human Populations*, C. Laughlin, Jr., and I. Brady, eds., pp. 95–121. New York: Columbia University Press.

CCPY (Committee for the Creation of the Yanomami Park)
1979   Yanomami Indian Park, proposal and justification. In *The Yanoama in Brazil 1979*, A. Ramos and K. Taylor, eds., pp. 99–169. Copenhagen: Anthropology Resource Center/International Work Group for Indigenous Affairs (no. 37)/Survival International.
1989a   The threatened Yanomami. *Cultural Survival Quarterly* 13(1):45–46.
1989b   Brazilian government reduces Yanomami territory by 70 percent. *Cultural Survival Quarterly* 13(1):47.

1993　　Brazil and Venezuela step up efforts to investigate massacre. *CCPY Update* 72, September 28, pp. 1–6.

Chaffanjon, Jean

1986　　*El Orinoco y el Caura.* Joelle Lecoin, trans. Caracas: Editorial Croquis.

Chagnon, Napoleon

1966　　Yanomamö warfare, social organization and marriage alliances. Ph.D. dissertation, University of Michigan. Ann Arbor, MI: University Microfilms.

1967　　Yanomamö social organization and warfare. In *War: The Anthropology of Armed Conflict and Aggression,* M. Fried, M. Harris, and R. Murphy, eds., pp. 109–59. Garden City, NY: Natural History Press.

1968　　*Yanomamö: The Fierce People.* New York: Holt, Rinehart, and Winston.

1972a　　Untitled letters from the field. In *The Human Condition in Latin America,* E. Wolf and E. Hansen, eds., pp. 65–69. New York: Oxford University Press.

1972b　　Tribal social organization and genetic microdifferentiation. In *The Structure of Human Populations,* G. Harrison and A. Boyce, eds., pp. 252–82. Oxford: Clarendon Press.

1973　　The culture-ecology of shifting (pioneering) cultivation among the Yanomamö Indians. In *Peoples and Cultures of Native South America,* D. Gross, ed., pp. 126–44. Garden City, NY: Doubleday.

1974　　*Studying the Yanomamö.* New York: Holt, Rinehart, and Winston.

1975　　Genealogy, solidarity, and relatedness: Limits to local group size and patterns of fissioning in an expanding population. *Yearbook of Physical Anthropology* 19:95–110.

1977　　*Yanomamö: The Fierce People,* 2nd ed. New York: Holt, Rinehart, and Winston.

1979a　　Mate competition, favoring close kin, and village fissioning among the Yanomamö Indians. In *Evolutionary Biology and Human Social Behavior: An Anthropological Perspective,* N. Chagnon and W. Irons, eds., pp. 86–132. North Scituate, MA: North Duxbury Press.

1979b　　Is reproductive success equal in egalitarian societies? In *Evolutionary Biology and Human Social Behavior: An Anthropological Perspective,* N. Chagnon and W. Irons, eds., pp. 374–401. North Scituate, MA: Duxbury Press.

1980　　Highland New Guinea models in the South American lowlands. In *Working Papers on South American Indians #2: Studies in Hunting and Fishing in the Neotropics,* R. Hames, ed., pp. 111–30. Bennington, VT: Bennington College.

1981　　Terminological kinship, genealogical relatedness, and village fissioning among the Yanomamö Indians. In *Natural Selection and Social Behavior: Recent Research and New Theory,* R. Alexander and D. Tinkle, eds., pp. 490–508. New York: Chiron Press.

1982　　Sociodemographic attributes of nepotism in tribal populations: Man the rule-breaker. In *Current Problems of Sociobiology,* King's College Sociobiology Group, eds., pp. 291–318. Cambridge: Cambridge University Press.

1983　　*Yanomamö: The Fierce People,* 3rd ed. New York: Holt, Rinehart, and Winston.

1987　　Male Yanomamö manipulations of kinship classifications of female kin for reproductive advantage. In *Human Reproductive Behavior: A Darwinian*

Perspective, L. L. Betzig, M. Borgerhoff Mulder, and P. W. Turke, eds., pp. 23–48. Cambridge: Cambridge University Press.

1988   Life histories, blood revenge, and warfare in a tribal population. *Science* 239:985–92.

1989a   Letter to the editor. *Anthropology Newsletter* 30(1):3, 24.

1989b   Response to Ferguson. *American Ethnologist* 16:565–70.

1990a   On Yanomamö violence: Reply to Albert. *Current Anthropology* 31:49–53.

1990b   Reproductive and somatic conflicts of interest in the genesis of violence and warfare among tribesmen. In *The Anthropology of War*, J. Haas, ed., pp. 77–104. School of American Research Advanced Seminar Series. Cambridge: Cambridge University Press.

1992a   *Yanomamö*, 4th ed. Fort Worth: Harcourt Brace Jovanovich.

1992b   *Yanomamö: The Last Days of Eden*, 5th ed. San Diego: Harcourt Brace Jovanovich.

1993a   Covering up the Yanomamo massacre. *New York Times*, October 23, p, A21.

1993b   Anti-science and native rights: Genocide of the Yanomamö. *Human Behavior and Evolution Society Newsletter* 2(3):unpaginated.

Chagnon, Napoleon, and Paul Bugos

1979   Kin selection and conflict: An analysis of a Yanomamo ax fight. In *Evolutionary Biology and Human Social Behavior: An Anthropological Perspective*, N. Chagnon and W. Irons, eds., pp. 213–38. North Scituate, MA: Duxbury Press.

Chagnon, Napoleon, and Raymond Hames

1979   Protein deficiency and tribal warfare in Amazonia: New data. *Science* 203:910–13.

1980   La "hipótesis proteica" y la adaptación indígena a la cuenca del Amazonas: Una revisión crítica de los datos y de la teoría. *Interciencia* 5(6):346–58.

Chagnon, Napoleon, and William Irons, eds.

1979   *Evolutionary Biology and Human Social Behavior: An Anthropological Perspective*. North Scituate, MA: Duxbury Press.

Chagnon, Napoleon, and Thomas Melancon

1983   Epidemics in a tribal population. In *The Impact of Contact: Two Yanomamo Case Studies*, K. Kensinger, ed., pp. 53–78. Cambridge: Cultural Survival, no. 11/Bennington, VT: Working Papers on South American Indians, no. 6.

Chagnon, Napoleon, M. Flinn, and T. Melancon

1979   Sex-ratio variation among the Yanomamö Indians. In *Evolutionary Biology and Human Social Behavior: An Anthropological Perspective*, N. Chagnon and W. Irons, eds., pp. 290–320. North Scituate, MA: Duxbury Press.

Chagnon, Napoleon, James Neel, Lowel Weitkamp, Henry Gershowitz, and Manuel Ayres

1970   The influence of cultural factors on the demography and pattern of gene flow from the Makiritare to the Yanomama Indians. *American Journal of Physical Anthropology* 32(3):339–49.

Chernela, Janet Marion

1983   Hierarchy and economy of the Uanano (Kotiria) speaking peoples of the middle Uaupés basin. Ph.D. dissertation, Columbia University.

1993   *The Wanano Indians of the Brazilian Amazon: A Sense of Space*. Austin: University of Texas Press.

Clastres, Pierre
1989   *Society against the State: Essays in Political Anthropology*. New York: Zone Books.

Cocco, P. Luís
1972   *Iyëwei-teri: Quince años entre los Yanomamos*. Caracas: Librería Editorial Salesiana.

Codazzi, Agustín
1940   *Resumen de la geografía de Venezuela* (3 books). Caracas: Biblioteca Venezolana de Cultura.

Codere, Helen
1950   *Fighting with Property: A Study of Kwakiutl Potlatching and Warfare 1792—1930*. New York: J. J. Augustin.

Colchester, Marcus
1981a   Ecological modelling and indigenous systems of resource use: Some examples from the Amazon of south Venezuela. *Antropológica* 55:51–72.
1981b   Myths and legends of the Sanema. *Antropológica* 56:25–127.
1982   Languages of the Orinoco-Amazon watershed: Some comments on Migliazza's classification. *Antropológica* 57:91–95.
1984   Rethinking Stone Age economics: Some speculations concerning the pre-Columbian Yanoama economy. *Human Ecology* 12:291–314.
1985a   Introduction. In *The Health and Survival of the Venezuelan Yanoama*, M. Colchester, ed., pp. 1–11. Copenhagen: Anthropology Resource Center/International Work Group for Indigenous Affairs, no. 53.
1985b   (Ed.) *The Health and Survival of the Venezuelan Yanoama*. Copenhagen: Anthropology Resource Center/International Work Group for Indigenous Affairs, no. 53.
1985c   Medical aid among the Venezuelan Sanema (northern Yanoama). In *The Health and Survival of the Venezuelan Yanoama*, M. Colchester, ed., pp. 45–57. Copenhagen: Anthropology Resource Center/International Work Group for Indigenous Affairs, no. 53.
1985d   The Venezuelan Ninam (north eastern Yanoama): Their health and survival. In *The Health and Survival of the Venezuelan Yanoama*, M. Colchester, ed., pp. 59–72. Copenhagen: Anthropology Resource Center/International Work Group for Indigenous Affairs, no. 53.
1991   Economías y patrones de uso de la tierra en los Yanomami. *La Iglesia en Amazonas* 12(53):10–17.
n.d.   The Yanoama at war: Subsistence, sovereignty, and social change in an Amazonian society. Manuscript.

Colchester, Marcus, and Richard Semba
1985   Health and survival among the Yanoama Indians. In *The Health and Survival of the Venezuelan Yanoama*, M. Colchester, ed., pp. 13–30. Copenhagen: Anthropology Resource Center/International Work Group for Indigenous Affairs, no. 53.

Colson, Audrey Butt
1973   Inter-tribal trade in the Guiana highlands. *Antropológica* 34:6–70.

Comité para la Creación de la Reserva Indígena Yanomami
1983   *Los Yanomami Venezolanos*. Vollmer Foundation, Inc.

Coppens, Walter
1971   Las relaciones comerciales de los Yekuana del Caura-Paragua. *Antropoló-gica* 30:28–59.
1981   *Del canalete al motor fuera de borda.* Caracas: Fundación La Salle, Instituto Caribe de Antropología y Sociología, no. 27.
Cultural Survival
1992   Yanomami land demarcated. *Action for Cultural Survival* July/August:4.
Davis, Shelton
1979   Yanomamo park proposal: A critical time for Brazilian Indians. *Anthropology Resource Center Newsletter* 3(4):1.
Davis, Shelton, and Robert Mathews
1976   *The Geological Imperative: Anthropology and Development in the Amazon Basin of South America.* Cambridge: Anthropology Resource Center.
Davis, Shelton, and Robin Wright
1981   Preface. In *The Yanomami Indian Park,* unpaginated. Boston: Anthropology Resource Center.
Dawson, Joe
1964   A Guaica report. *Brown Gold* 22(6):2, 11.
Dawson, Millie
1960   Guaica raiders strike again. *Brown Gold* 18(8):6, 10.
1961   Life in a Guaica village. *Brown Gold* 19(2):4–5.
Denevan, William
1992   Stone vs. metal axes: The ambiguity of shifting cultivation in prehistoric Amazonia. *Journal of the Steward Anthropological Society* 20:153–65.
Dickey, Herbert Spencer
1932   *My Jungle Book.* Boston: Little, Brown.
Divale, William
1970   An explanation of tribal warfare: Population control and the significance of primitive sex ratios. *New Scholar* 2:173–92.
Divale, William, and Marvin Harris
1976   Population, warfare, and the male supremacist complex. *American Anthropologist* 78:521–38.
Dumont, Jean-Paul
1976   *Under the Rainbow: Nature and Supernature among the Panare Indians.* Austin: University of Texas Press.
1978   *The Headman and I: Ambiguity and Ambivalence in the Fieldworking Experience.* Austin: University of Texas Press.
Dye, Dorothy
1962   Guaica report. *Brown Gold* 20(8):10.
Early, John, and John Peters
1990   *The Population Dynamics of the Mucajaí Yanomama.* San Diego: Academic Press.
Edmundson, George, ed.
1922   *Journal of the Travels and Labours of Father Samuel Fritz in the River of the Amazons between 1686 and 1722.* London: Hakluyt Society.
Eguillor García, María Isabel
1984   *Yopo, shámenes y hekura: Aspectos fenomenológicos del mundo sagrado Yanomami.* Vicariato Apostólico de Puerto Ayacucho: Librería Editorial Salesiana.

Eguillor, María Isabel
1991   La escuela Yanomami, modelo de interculturalidad. *La Iglesia en Amazonas* 12(53).
Eibl-Eibesfeldt, Irenäus, and Marie-Claude Mattei-Müller
1990   Yanomami wailing songs and the question of parental attachment in traditional kinbased societies. *Anthropos* 85:507–15.
Emmanuel, Arghiri
1972   *Unequal Exchange: A Study of the Imperialism of Trade.* New York: Monthly Review Press.
Farabee, William
1918   *The Central Arawaks.* The University Museum Anthropological Publications, vol. 9. Philadelphia: University of Pennsylvania.
Feil, D. K.
1987   *The Evolution of Highland Papua New Guinea Societies.* Cambridge: Cambridge University Press.
Ferguson, R. Brian
1983   Warfare and redistributive exchange on the Northwest Coast. In *The Development of Political Organization in Native North America,* E. Tooker, ed., pp. 133–47. Proceedings of the American Ethnological Society, 1979. Washington: American Ethnological Society.
1984a   A reexamination of the causes of Northwest Coast warfare. In *Warfare, Culture, and Environment,* R. B. Ferguson, ed., pp. 267–328. Orlando: Academic Press.
1984b   Introduction: Studying war. In *Warfare, Culture, and Environment,* R. B. Ferguson, ed., pp. 1–81. Orlando: Academic Press.
1988a   How can anthropologists promote peace? *Anthropology Today* 4(3):1–3.
1988b   War and the sexes in Amazonia. In *Dialectics and Gender: Anthropological Approaches,* R. Randolph, D. Schneider, and M. Díaz, eds., pp. 136–54. Boulder, CO: Westview Press.
1988c   Introduction. In *The Anthropology of War: A Bibliography,* with L. Farragher. Occasional Paper no. 1. New York: The Harry Frank Guggenheim Foundation.
1989a   Anthropology and war: Theory, politics, ethics. In *The Anthropology of War and Peace: Perspectives on the Nuclear Age,* D. Pitt and P. Turner, eds., pp. 141–59. South Hadley, MA: Bergin and Garvey.
1989b   Game wars? Ecology and conflict in Amazonia. *Journal of Anthropological Research* 45:179–206.
1989c   Ecological consequences of Amazonian warfare. *Ethnology* 28:249–64.
1989d   Do Yanomamo killers have more kids? *American Ethnologist* 16:564–65.
1990a   Explaining war. In *The Anthropology of War,* J. Haas, ed., pp. 26–55. School of American Research Advanced Seminar Series. Cambridge: Cambridge University Press.
1990b   Blood of the Leviathan: Western contact and warfare in Amazonia. *American Ethnologist* 17:237–57.
1992a   A savage encounter: Western contact and the Yanomami war complex. In *War in the Tribal Zone: Expanding States and Indigenous Warfare,* R. B. Ferguson and N. L. Whitehead, eds., pp. 199–227. Santa Fe: School of American Research Press.
1992b   Tribal warfare. *Scientific American* 266 (Jan.):108–13.

1993　The general consequences of war: An Amazonian perspective. In *Studying War,* S. Reyna and R. Downs, eds., pp. 85–111. New York: Gordon and Breach.

n.d.*a*　Relations of production, politics, and war in Amazonia. Manuscript.

n.d.*b*　Infrastructural determinism. In *Science, Materialism, and the Study of Culture: A Reader in Cultural Materialism,* M. Margolis and M. Murphy, eds. In press.

n.d.*c*　Dangerous intersections: The local and the larger in African violence. Prepared for *Paths of Violence: Destruction and Deconstruction in African States.* G. Bond and J. Vincent, eds.

Ferguson, R. Brian, with Leslie Farragher

1988　*The Anthropology of War: A Bibliography.* Occasional Paper no. 1. New York: The Harry Frank Guggenheim Foundation.

Ferguson, R. Brian, and Neil L. Whitehead

1992a　The violent edge of empire. In *War in the Tribal Zone: Expanding States and Indigenous Warfare,* R. B. Ferguson and N. L. Whitehead, eds., pp. 1–30. Santa Fe: School of American Research Press.

1992b　(Eds.) *War in the Tribal Zone: Expanding States and Indigenous Warfare.* Santa Fe: School of American Research Press.

Fock, Niels

1963　*Waiwai: Religion and Society of an Amazonian Tribe.* Copenhagen: The National Museum.

Frechione, John

1990　Supervillage formation in the Amazonian terre firme: The case of Asenöña. *Ethnology* 29(2):117–131.

Fredlund, Eric Victor

1982　Shitari Yanomamö incestuous marriage: A study of the use of structural, lineal and biological criteria when classifying marriages. Ph.D. dissertation, Pennsylvania State University. Ann Arbor, MI: University Microfilms.

Fried, Morton

1967　*The Evolution of Political Society: An Essay in Political Anthropology.* New York: Random House.

1968　On the concepts of "tribe" and "tribal society." In *Essays on the Problem of Tribe: Proceedings of the 1967 Annual Spring Meeting of the American Ethnological Society,* J. Helm, ed., pp. 3–20. Seattle: University of Washington Press.

Fuentes, Emilio

1980　Los Yanomami y las plantas silvestres. *Antropológica* 54:3–138.

1984　Introducción. In *Yo Soy Napëyoma: Relato de una mujer raptada por los indígenas Yanomami,* pp. 9–19. Caracas: Fundación La Salle de Ciencias Naturales, no. 35.

Furtado, Celso

1971　*The Economic Growth of Brazil: A Survey from Colonial to Modern Times.* Berkeley: University of California Press.

Gettman, Karl

1954　The venture in Venezuela. *Brown Gold* 12(5–6):6–8.

Gheerbrant, Alain

1954　*Journey to the Far Amazon.* E. Fitzgerald, trans. New York: Simon and Schuster.

Gilij, Felipe Sálvador
  1965   *Ensayo de historia Americana* (3 books). Trans. and preliminary study by A. Tovar. Caracas: Biblioteca de la Academía Nacional de la Historia.
Gillin, John
  1936   *The Barama River Caribs of British Guiana.* Papers of the Peabody Museum of American Archaeology and Ethnology, Harvard University, vol. 14. Cambridge, MA: Harvard University Press.
Goldman, Irving
  1963   *The Cubeo: Indians of the Northwest Amazon.* Urbana: University of Illinois Press.
Golob, Ann
  1982   The upper Amazon in historical perspective. Ph.D. dissertation, Department of Anthropology, City University of New York.
Gómez Picón, Rafael
  1978   *Orinoco, río de libertad,* 2nd ed. Bogotá, Colombia: Banco de la República.
Good, Kenneth
  1983   Limiting factors in Amazonian ecology. Paper prepared for the symposium "Food Preferences and Aversions," Cedar Key, Florida. October.
  1984   Demography and land use among the Yanomamo of the Orinoco-Siapa block in Amazon Territory, Venezuela. Manuscript.
  1989   Yanomami hunting patterns: Trekking and garden relocation as an adaptation to game availability in Amazonia, Venezuela. Ph.D. dissertation, University of Florida.
Good, Kenneth, with David Chanoff
  1991   *Into the Heart: One Man's Pursuit of Love and Knowledge among the Yanomama.* New York: Simon and Schuster.
Good, Kenneth, and Jacques Lizot
  1984   Letter to *Science,* Appendix 3.2 in M. Harris, Cultural materialist theory of band and village warfare: The Yanomamo test. In *Warfare, Culture, and Environment.* R. B. Ferguson, ed., pp. 111–40. Orlando, FL: Academic Press.
Gregor, Thomas
  1977   *Mehinaku: The Drama of Daily Life in a Brazilian Indian Village.* Chicago: University of Chicago Press.
Grelier, Joseph
  1957   *To the Source of the Orinoco.* H. Schmuckler, trans. London: Herbert Jenkins.
Gross, Daniel
  1982   Proteína y cultura en el Amazonia: Una segunda revisión. *Amazonia Peruana* 3:127–44.
Gumilla, P. José
  1963   *El Orinoco ilustrado y defendido.* Caracas: Biblioteca de la Academía Nacional de la Historia.
Guzman, Antonio
  1991   SUYAO: La organización Yanomami. *La Iglesia en Amazonas* 12(53):46
Haas, Jonathan, ed.
  1990   *The Anthropology of War.* School of American Research Advanced Seminar Series. Cambridge: Cambridge University Press.

Hahn, Robert
1981   Missionaries and frontiersmen as agents of social change among the Rik-
        bakca. In *Is God an American? An Anthropological Perspective on the
        Missionary Work of the Summer Institute of Linguistics*, S. Hvalkof and
        P. Aaby, eds., pp. 85–107. Copenhagen: International Work Group for In-
        digenous Affairs.
Hallpike, C. R.
1991   Review of *The Anthropology of War*, J. Haas, ed. *American Anthropolo-
        gist* 93:964–65.
Hames, Raymond
1979   A comparison of the efficiencies of the shotgun and the bow in neotropical
        forest hunting. *Human Ecology* 7(3):219–52.
1983   The settlement pattern of a Yanomamö population bloc: A behavioral
        ecological interpretation. In *Adaptive Responses of Native Amazonians*,
        R. Hames and W. Vickers, eds., pp. 393–427. New York: Academic Press.
1989   Time, efficiency, and fitness in the Amazonian protein quest. *Research in
        Economic Anthropology* 11:43–85.
Hames, Raymond, and William Vickers
1983   Introduction. In *Adaptive Responses of Native Amazonians*. R. Hames
        and W. Vickers, eds., pp. 1–26. New York: Academic Press.
Hanson, Earl
1933   Social regression in the Orinoco and Amazon basins: Notes on a journey
        in 1931 and 1932. *The Geographical Review* 23:578–598.
Harner, Michael
1973   *The Jívaro: People of the Sacred Waterfalls*. Garden City, NY: Anchor
        Books.
Harris, David
1971   The ecology of swidden cultivation in the upper Orinoco rain forest, Vene-
        zuela. *The Geographical Review* 51:475–95.
Harris, Marvin
1974   *Cows, Pigs, Wars and Witches: The Riddles of Culture*. New York: Ran-
        dom House.
1977   *Cannibals and Kings: The Origins of Culture*. New York: Random House.
1979   The Yanomamo and the cause of war in band and village societies. In
        Brazil: Anthropological Perspectives, Essays in Honor of Charles Wagley,
        M. Margolis and W. Carter, eds., pp. 121–32. New York: Columbia Uni-
        versity Press.
1984   A cultural materialist theory of band and village warfare: The Yanomamo
        test. In *Warfare, Culture, and Environment*, R. B. Ferguson, ed., pp. 111–
        40. Orlando: Academic Press.
Headland, Thomas
1987   The wild yam question: How well could independent hunter-gatherers live
        in a tropical rain forest ecosystem? *Human Ecology* 15:463–91.
Hemming, John
1978   *Red Gold: The Conquest of the Brazilian Indians*. Cambridge, MA: Har-
        vard University Press.
1987   *Amazon Frontier: The Defeat of the Brazilian Indians*. Cambridge, MA:
        Harvard University Press.

Henley, Paul
1982 *The Panare: Tradition and Change on the Amazonian Frontier.* New Haven: Yale University Press.

Herndon, W. Lewis
1854 *Exploration of the Valley of the Amazon,* part I. Washington, DC: Robert Armstrong.

Hilker, Carlton
1950 Guaika Indians of Venezuela. *Brown Gold* 8(7):9.

Hitchcock, Charles
1948 *La región Orinoco-Ventuari, Venezuela: Relato de la expedición Phelps al cerro Yavi.* Caracas: Ministerio de Educación Nacional Dirección de Cultura.

Hoariwë, Itilio
1991 Los Yanomami y los problemas de salud. *La Iglesia en Amazonas* 12(54–55):21–22.

Holdridge, Desmond
1933 Exploration between the Río Branco and the Serra Parima. *The Geographical Review* 23:372–84.

Holmberg, Allan
1969 *Nomads of the Long Bow: The Siriono of Eastern Bolivia.* Garden City, NY: Natural History Press.

Holoway, M.
1956 *Bananas.* Washington, DC: Pan American Union.

Huber, Otto, Julian Steyermark, Ghillean Prance, and Catherine Alès
1984 The vegetation of the Sierra Parima, Venezuela-Brazil: Some results of recent exploration. *Brittonia* 36(2):104–39.

Humboldt, Alexander von
1889 *Personal Narrative of the Travels to the Equinoctial Regions of America, during the Years 1799—1804,* vol. II. T. Ross, trans. and ed. London: George Bell and Sons.

im Thurn, Everard
1967 *Among the Indians of Guiana.* New York: Dover Publications.

Isaac, Barry
1977 The Siriono of Eastern Bolivia: A reexamination. *Human Ecology* 5:137–54.

Jackson, Jean
1983 *The Fish People: Linguistic Exogamy and Tukanoan Identity in Northwest Amazonia.* New York: Cambridge University Press.

Jank, Margaret
1977 *Culture Shock.* Chicago: Moody Press.

Jank, Wally, and Margaret Jank
1970 Guaica warfare. *Brown Gold* 27(9):6, 10.

Johnston, Kenneth
1949 Venezuela ripe for harvest. *Brown Gold* 6(10):6–9.
1957 Venezuela then and now. *Brown Gold* 15(1):6–9.
1964 Open season in Venezuela. *Brown Gold* 12(2):2–3, 11.

Kietzman, Dale
1967 Indians and culture areas of twentieth century Brazil. In *Indians of Brazil in the Twentieth Century.* J. Hopper, ed. and trans., pp. 1–50. Washington, DC: Institute for Cross-Cultural Research.

Kloos, Peter
1977   *The Akuriyo of Surinam: A Case of Emergence from Isolation.* Copen-
        hagen: International Work Group for Indigenous Affairs, no. 27.
Knauft, Bruce
1993   Review of *War in the Tribal Zone. Science* 260:1184–86.
Knorr, K. E.
1945   *World Rubber and Its Regulation.* Stanford: Stanford University Press.
Koch-Grunberg, Theodor
1979   *Del Roraima al Orinoco,* 3 vols. E. Armitano, ed. Caracas: El Banco Cen-
        tral de Venezuela.
Kracke, Waud
1978   *Force and Persuasion: Leadership in an Amazonian Society.* Chicago: Uni-
        versity of Chicago Press.
Kroeber, Clifton, and Bernard Fontana
1986   *Massacre on the Gila: An Account of the Last Major Battle between
        American Indians, with Reflections on the Origin of War.* Tucson: Uni-
        versity of Arizona Press.
Landaeta, Jesús Toro
1991   Problemática y soluciones de la situación sanitaria en el Territorio Federal
        Amazonas: El caso malaria. *La Iglesia en Amazonas* 12(54–55):4–8.
Landon, Dave
1956   Life among the Guaicas. *Brown Gold* 13(9):2, 10.
1960   Guaica progress. *Brown Gold* 17(9):4.
Lapointe, Jean
1970   Residence patterns and Wayana social organization. Ph.D. dissertation,
        Department of Anthropology, Columbia University.
Lathrap, Donald
1970   *The Upper Amazon.* New York: Praeger.
1973   The "hunting" economies of the tropical forest zone of South America:
        An attempt at historical perspective. In *Peoples and Cultures of Native
        South America,* D. Gross, ed., pp. 83–95. Garden City, NY: Natural His-
        tory Press.
1982   La antiguedad e importancia de las relaciónes de intercambio a larga dis-
        tancia en los trópicos húmedos de Sudamerica precolombina. *Amazonia
        Peruana* 4(7):79–97.
Layrisse, Miguell, Zulay Layrisse, and Johannes Wilbert
1962   Blood group antigen test of the Waìca Indians of Venezuela. *Southwestern
        Journal of Anthropology* 18:78–93.
Lazarin, Marco
1988   Brazil: Calha Norte project and mining prospecting—two aspects of the
        same invasion. *IWGIA Newsletter* (International Work Group for Indige-
        nous Affairs, Copenhagen) 55/56:17–30.
Lévi-Strauss, Claude
1943   Guerre et commerce chez les indiens de l'Amerique de sud. *Renaissance* 1:
        122–39.
Lizot, Jacques
1971   Aspects économiques et sociaux du changement culturel chez les Yanō-
        mami. *L'Homme* 11(1):32–51.
1974   El río de los Periquitos: Breve relato de un viaje entre los Yanomami del
        alto Siapa. *Antropológica* 37:3–23.

1976   The Yanomami in the Face of Ethnocide. Copenhagen: International Work
        Group for Indigenous Affairs, no. 22.
1977   Population, resources, and warfare among the Yanomami. Man 12(3/4):
        497–517.
1979   On food taboos and Amazon cultural ecology. Current Anthropology 20:
        150–51.
1980   La agricultura Yanomami. Antropológica 53:3–93.
1985   Tales of the Yanomami: Daily Life in the Venezuelan Forest. Cambridge:
        Cambridge University Press.
1988   Los Yanomami. In Los aborígines de Venezuela, vol. 3, W. Coppens with
        B. Escalante, eds., pp. 479–583. Caracas: Fundación La Salle de Ciencias
        Naturales.
1989   Sobre la guerra: Una respuesta a N. A. Chagnon (Science, 1988). La Igle-
        sia en Amazonas 44 (April):23–34.
1991   Palabras en la noche: El diálogo ceremonial, una expresión de las relaciónes
        pacíficas entre los Yanomami. La Iglesia en Amazonas 53 (June):54–83.

Lobo de Almada, Manoel da Gama
    1861   Descripção relativa ao río Branco. Revista trimestral do Instituto Histo-
            rico, Geografico e Etnografico do Brasil 24:617–83.

Lumsden, Charles J., and Edward O. Wilson
    1983   Promethean Fire: Reflections on the Origin of Mind. Cambridge: Harvard
            University Press.

McCauley, Clark
    1990   Conference overview. In The Anthropology of War, J. Haas, ed., pp. 1–
            25. School of American Research Advanced Seminar Series. Cambridge:
            Cambridge University Press.

MacLachlan, Colin
    1973   The Indian labor structure in the Portuguese Amazon, 1700–1800. In
            Colonial Roots of Modern Brazil: Papers of the Newberry Library Confer-
            ence, D. Alden, ed., pp. 199–230. Berkeley: University of California Press.

Mauss, Marcel
    1967   The Gift: Forms and Functions of Exchange in Archaic Societies. I. Cunni-
            son, trans. New York: W. W. Norton.

Maybury-Lewis, David
    1974   Akwē-Shavante Society. New York: Oxford University Press.

Melancon, Thomas
    1982   Marriage and reproduction among the Yanomamö Indians of Venezuela.
            Ph.D. dissertation, Pennsylvania State University. Ann Arbor, MI: Univer-
            sity Microfilms.

Metraux, Alfred
    1963   Tribes of eastern Bolivia and the Madeira headwaters. In Handbook of
            South American Indians, vol. 3, J. Steward, ed., pp. 381–463. Washing-
            ton, DC: Smithsonian Institution, Bureau of American Ethnology.

Michelena y Rojas, Francisco
    1989   Exploración oficial. Nelly Arvelo-Jiménez and Horacio Biord Castillo, eds.
            Iquitos, Peru: IIAP-CETA.

Migliazza, Ernest
    1972   Yanomama grammar and intelligibility. Ph.D. dissertation, Indiana Uni-
            versity. Ann Arbor, MI: University Microfilms.

1980   Languages of the Orinoco-Amazon basin: Current status. *Antropológica* 53:95–162.
1982   Linguistic prehistory and the refuge model in Amazonia. In *Biological Diversification in the Tropics*, G. Prance, ed., pp. 479–519. New York: Columbia University Press.

Milton, Katharine
1984   Protein and carbohydrate resources of the Maku Indians of northwestern Amazonia. *American Anthropologist* 86:7–27.

Misioneros (Un grupo de misioneros del alto Orinoco)
1991   Consideraciones a un documento de Charles Brewer Carías. Pamphlet. Caracas: Editorial don Bosco.

Mondolfi, Alejandro
1991   Problemas de salud de las comunidades Yanomami del alto Orinoco. *La Iglesia en Amazonas* 12(54–55):16–17.

Montgomery, Evelyn Ina
1970   *With the Shiriana in Brazil*. Dubuque, IA: Kendall/Hunt Publishing.

Moore, John H.
1990   The reproductive success of Cheyenne war chiefs: A contrary case to Chagnon's Yanomamo. *Current Anthropology* 31:322–30.

Morey, Robert, and John Marwitt
1975   Ecology, economy and warfare in lowland South America. In *War: Its Causes and Correlates*, M. Nettleship, R. D. Givens, and A. Nettleship, eds., pp. 439–50. The Hague: Mouton.

Morey, Robert, and Donald Metzger
1974   *The Guahibo: People of the Savanna*. Acta Ethnológica et Linguistica no. 31. Vienna.

Murphy, Robert
1956   Matrilocality and patrilineality in Mundurucu society. *American Anthropologist* 58:414–34.
1960   *Headhunter's Heritage: Social and Economic Change among the Mundurucú Indians*. Berkeley: University of California Press.

Murphy, Robert, and Buell Quain
1955   *The Trumaí Indians of Central Brazil*. Monographs of the American Ethnological Society, no. 24. Seattle: University of Washington Press.

Murphy, Robert, and Julian Steward
1956   Tappers and trappers: Parallel processes in acculturation. *Economic Development and Cultural Change* 4:335–55.

Myers, Thomas
1974   Spanish contacts and social change on the Ucayali River, Peru. *Ethnohistory* 21:135–57.

Neel, James, and K. Weiss
1975   The genetic structure of a tribal population, the Yanomamo Indians. *American Journal of Physical Anthropology* 42:25–52.

Netting, Robert M.
1974   Kofyar armed conflict: Social causes and consequences. *Journal of Anthropological Research* 30(3):139–63.

Nimuendajú, Curt
1967   *The Apinayé*. Oosterhout N.B., The Netherlands: Anthropological Publications.

Northrup, William
  1947   News from Venezuela. *Brown Gold,* Oct./ Nov.: 8–9.
  1948   Another new tribe contacted. *Brown Gold* 6(7):6–8.
Oberem, Udo
  1985   Trade and trade goods in the Ecuadorian montaña. In *Native South Americans: Ethnology of the Least Known Continent,* P. Lyon, ed., pp. 346–57. Prospect Heights, IL: Waveland Press.
Oberg, Kalervo
  1953   *Indian Tribes of the Northern Mato Grosso, Brazil.* Smithsonian Institution, Institute of Social Anthropology, Publication no. 15. Washington, DC: U.S. Government Printing Office.
O'Hanlon, Redmond
  1990   *In Trouble Again: A Journey between the Orinoco and the Amazon.* New York: Vintage Books.
Overing Kaplan, Joanna
  1975   *The Piaroa, A People of the Orinoco Basin: A Study in Kinship and Marriage.* Oxford: Clarendon Press.
Patiño, Victor Manuel
  1958   Plátanos y bananos en America equinoccial. *Revista Colombiana de Antropología* 7:295–337.
Peña Vargas, Camila
  1981   *El P. Luís Cocco: Ejemplo de evangelización Salesiana en Venezuela.* Caracas: Librería Editorial Salesiana.
Pérez, Antonio
  1988   Los Balé (Bare). In *Los aborígenes de Venezuela,* vol. 3, W. Coppens with B. Escalante, eds., pp. 413–78. Caracas: Fundación La Salle de Ciencias Naturales.
Perret, Monique, and Magda Magris
  1991   Programa Parima-Culebra '86: Historia, evolución y resultados. *La Iglesia en Amazonas* 12(54–55):18–20.
Peters, John Fred
  1973   The effect of Western material goods upon the social structure of the family among the Shirishana. Ph.D. dissertation, Western Michigan University. Ann Arbor, MI: University Microfilms.
Pinto, Lúcio Flávio
  1989   Calha Norte: The special project for the occupation of the frontiers. *Cultural Survival Quarterly* 13(1):40–41.
Price, David
  1981   Nambiquara leadership. *American Ethnologist* 8:686–707.
Ramos, Alcida
  1972   The social system of the Sanuma of northern Brazil. Ph.D. dissertation, University of Wisconsin. Ann Arbor, MI: University Microfilms.
  1979a   Rumor: The ideology of an inter-tribal situation. *Antropológica* 51:3–25.
  1979b   Yanoama Indians in northern Brazil threatened by highway. In *The Yanoama in Brazil 1979,* A. Ramos and K. Taylor, eds., pp. 1–41. Copenhagen: Anthropology Resource Center/International Work Group for Indigenous Affairs (no. 37)/Survival International.
  1979c   On women's status in Yanoama societies. *Current Anthropology* 20:185–87.

1987   Reflecting on the Yanomami: Ethnographic images and the pursuit of the exotic. *Cultural Anthropology* 2:284–304.
1990   *Ethnology Brazilian Style*. Universidade de Brasília, Instituto de Ciências Humanas, Série Antropologia no. 89.
Ramos, Alcida, and Kenneth Taylor
1979   *The Yanoama in Brazil, 1979*. Copenhagen: International Work Group for Indigenous Affairs (document 37).
Ramos Pérez, Demetrio
1946   *El Tratado de Límites de 1750 y la expedición de Iturriaga al Orinoco*. Madrid: Consejo Superior de Investigaciónes Científicas.
Rausch, Jane
1984   *A Tropical Plains Frontier: The Llanos of Colombia 1531—1831*. Albuquerque: University of New Mexico Press.
Ribeiro de Sampaio, Francisco Xavier
1825   *Diario da viagem da capitania do río Negro*. Lisbon: Typografia da Academia.
Rice, A. Hamilton
1921   The Río Negro, the Casiquiare Canal, and the upper Orinoco, September 1919–April 1920. *The Geographical Journal* 58:321–44.
1928a   The Río Branco, Uraricuera, and Parima, part 2. *The Geographical Journal* 71:209–23.
1928b   The Río Branco, Uraricuera, and Parima, part 1. *The Geographical Journal* 71:113–43.
1928c   The Río Branco, Uraricuera, and Parima, part 3. *The Geographical Journal* 71:345–56.
Rísquez-Ibarren, Franz
1962   *Donde nace el Orinoco*. Caracas: Ediciónes Greco.
Rivière, Peter
1969   *Marriage among the Trio*. Oxford: Clarendon Press.
1984   *Individual and Society in Guiana: A Comparative Study of Amerindian Social Organization*. Cambridge: Cambridge University Press.
Robarchek, Clayton
1989   Primitive warfare and the ratomorphic image of mankind. *American Anthropologist* 91:903–20.
Roosevelt, Anna
1980   *Parmana: Prehistoric Maize and Manioc Subsistence along the Amazon and Orinoco*. New York: Academic Press.
1987   Chiefdoms in the Amazon and Orinoco. In *Chiefdoms in the Americas*, R. Drennan and C. Uribe, eds., pp. 153–84. Lanham, MD: University Press of America.
1991   *Moundbuilders of the Amazon: Geophysical Archaeology on Marajo Island, Brazil*. Orlando: Academic Press.
Roth, Walter
1985   Trade and barter among the Guiana Indians. In *Native South Americans: Ethnology of the Least Known Continent*, P. Lyon, ed., pp. 159–65. Prospect Heights, IL: Waveland Press.
Saffirio, Giovanni
1985   Ideal and actual kinship terminology among the Yanomama Indians of the Catrimani River basin (Brazil). Ph.D. dissertation, University of Pittsburgh. Ann Arbor, MI: University Microfilms.

Saffirio, Giovanni, and Richard Scaglion
    1982   Hunting efficiencies in acculturated and unacculturated Yanomama villages. *Journal of Anthropological Research* 38:315–27.

Saffirio, John, and Raymond Hames
    1983   The forest and the highway. In *The Impact of Contact: Two Yanomamo Case Studies,* 1–52. Cambridge: Cultural Survival, no. 11/Bennington, VT: Working Papers on South American Indians, no. 6.

Salathé, Georges
    1932   Les Indiens Karimé. *Revista del Instituto de Etnología de la Universidad Nacional de Tucuman* 11/12:297–316.

Salazar, Fred, with Jack Herschlag
    1967   *The Innocent Assassins.* New York: E.P. Dutton.

Salisbury, Richard
    1962   *From Stone to Steel.* New York: Cambridge University Press.

Santilli, Márcio
    1989   The Calha Norte project: Military guardianship and frontier policy. *Cultural Survival Quarterly* 13(1):42–43.
    1990   Projet Calha Norte: Politique indigéniste et frontières nord-Amazoniennes. *Ethnies* 11–12:111–15.

Schmidt, Sabine
    1990   Conflict and violence at the local level: A world-system perspective. *Zeitschrift fur Ethnologie* 115:13–22.

Schomburgk, Robert
    1841   Report of the third expedition into the interior of Guyana. . . *Journal of the Royal Geographical Society of London* 10:159–267.

Schurz, W. L.
    1925   The distribution of population in the Amazon valley. *Geographical Review* 15:206–25.

Seitz, Georg
    1963   *People of the Rain-Forests.* A. Pomerans, trans. London: Heineman.

Semba, Richard
    1985   Medical care and the survival of the Yanomami of southern Venezuela. In *The Health and Survival of the Venezuelan Yanoama,* M. Colchester, ed., pp. 31–43. Copenhagen: Anthropology Resource Center/International Work Group for Indigenous Affairs, no. 53.

Shapiro, Judith Rae
    1972   Sex roles and social structure among the Yanomama Indians of northern Brazil. Ph.D. dissertation, Columbia University.

Sharp, Lauriston
    1974   Steel axes for Stone Age Australians. In *Man in Adaptation: The Cultural Present,* 2nd ed., Y. Cohen, ed., pp. 116–27. Chicago: Aldine.

Simmonds, N. W.
    1962   *The Evolution of Bananas.* London: Longmans.

Siskind, Janet
    1973a   *To Hunt in the Morning.* New York: Oxford University Press.
    1973b   Tropical forest hunters and the economy of sex. In *Peoples and Cultures of South America,* D. Gross, ed., pp. 226–40. Garden City, NY: Natural History Press.

Smole, William
    1976   *The Yanoama Indians: A Cultural Geography.* Austin: University of Texas Press.

Soares Diniz, Edson
  1969   Aspectos das relações sociais entre os Yanomamö do río Catrimâni. *Bole-tim do Museu Paraense Emilio Goeldi* 39:1–18.
Spielman, Richard, Ernest Migliazza, and James Neel
  1974   Regional linguistic and genetic difference among Yanomama Indians. *Science* 184:637–43.
Sponsel, Leslie
  1983   Yanomama warfare, protein capture, and cultural ecology: A critical analysis of the arguments of the opponents. *Interciencia* 8(4):204–10.
Spruce, Richard
  1908   *Notes of a Botanist on the Amazon and Andes,* vol 1. A. Wallace, ed. London: Macmillan.
Stearman, Allyn MacLean
  1984   The Yuqui connection: Another look at Siriono deculturation. *American Anthropologist* 86:630–50.
Steinvorth de Goetz, Inga
  1969   *Uriji Jami! Impresiónes de viajes Orinoquenses por aire, agua y tierra.* Caracas: Asociación Cultural Humboldt.
Steward, Julian, and Louis Faron
  1959   *Natives Peoples of South America.* New York: McGraw Hill.
Stocks, Anthony
  1983   Native enclaves in the upper Amazon: A case of regional non-integration. *Ethnohistory* 30:77–92.
Stover, R. H., and N. W. Simmonds
  1987   *Bananas,* 3rd ed. New York: Longman Scientific and Technical/John Wiley and Sons.
Taussig, Michael
  1987   *Shamanism, Colonialism, and the Wild Man: A Study in Terror and Healing.* Chicago: University of Chicago Press.
Tavera-Acosta, Bartolomé
  1903   *El caucho en Venezuela.* Caracas: Empresa Washington.
  1927   *Rionegro: Reseña etnográfica, histórica y geográfica del territorio Amazonas,* 2nd ed. Maracay: Imprenta del Estado.
  1954   *Anales de Guyana.* Caracas. (Publisher not listed.)
Taylor, Anne-Christine
  1981   God-wealth: The Achuar and the missions. In *Cultural Transformations and Ethnicity in Modern Ecuador,* N. Whitten, ed., pp. 647–76. Urbana: University of Illinois Press.
Taylor, Kenneth
  1972   Sanuma (Yanoama) food prohibitions: The multiple classification of society and fauna. Ph.D. dissertation, University of Wisconsin. Ann Arbor, MI: University Microfilms.
  1979   Development against the Yanoama, the case of mining and agriculture. In *The Yanoama in Brazil 1979,* A. Ramos and K. Taylor, eds., pp. 43–98. Copenhagen: Anthropology Resource Center/International Work Group for Indigenous Affairs (no. 37)/Survival International.
Tejera, Miguel
  1877   *Venezuela pintoresca e ilustrada* (2 books). Paris: Librería Española de E. Denné Schmitz

Thomas, David John
1972   The indigenous trade system of southeast estado Bolívar, Venezuela. *Antropológica* 33:3–37.
1982   *Order without Government: The Society of the Pemon Indians of Venezuela.* Illinois Studies in Anthropology, no. 13. Urbana: University of Illinois Press.
Turner, Terry
1991   Major shift in Brazilian Yanomami policy. *Anthropology Newsletter* 32(6): 1, 46.
Turney-High, Harry
1971   *Primitive War: Its Practice and Concepts,* 2d ed. Columbia, SC: University of South Carolina Press.
Up de Graff, Fritz
1985   Jívaro field clearing with stone axes. In *Native South Americans: Ethnology of the Least Known Continent,* P. Lyon, ed., pp. 120–22. Prospect Heights, IL: Waveland Press.
Urdaneta, Luís
1991   La salud Yanomami. *La Iglesia en Amazonas* 12(54–55):9–10.
U.S. Army Corps of Engineers
1943   *Report on Orinoco—Casiquiare—Negro Waterway Venezuela—Colombia—Brazil,* vol 1.
Valero, Helena
1984   *Yo soy Napëyoma: Relato de una mujer raptada por los indígenas Yanomami.* Caracas: Fundación La Salle de Ciencias Naturales, no. 35.
Vareschi, Volkmar
1959   *Orinoco arriba: A través de Venezuela siguiendo a Humboldt.* Caracas: Lectura.
Vayda, Andrew
1961   Expansion and warfare among swidden agriculturalists. *American Anthropologist* 63:346–58.
Vickers, William
1981   The Jesuits and the SIL: External policies for Ecuador's Tucanoans through three centuries. In *Is God an American? An Anthropological Perspective on the Missionary Work of the Summer Institute of Linguistics,* S. Hvalkof and P. Aaby, eds., pp. 51–61. Copenhagen: International Work Group for Indigenous Affairs.
Vinci, Alfonso
1959   *Red Cloth and Green Forest.* James Cadell, trans. London: Hutchinson.
Wagley, Charles
1983   *Welcome of Tears: The Tapirapé Indians of Central Brazil.* Prospect Heights, IL: Waveland Press.
Wagner, Erika, and Lilliam Arvelo
1986   Monou-teri: Un nuevo complejo arqueológico en el alto Orinoco, Venezuela. *Acta Científica Venezolana* 37:689–96.
Wallace, Alfred Russel
1969   *A Narrative of Travels on the Amazon and Río Negro,* 2nd ed. New York: Haskell House Publishers.
Wardlaw, Keith
1966   Rio Demini excerpts. *Brown Gold* 24(4):2.
1970   Trouble at Tootobobi. *Brown Gold* 27(11):6–8.

Wardlaw, Keith, and M. Wardlaw
1968   Uaica breakthrough. *Brown Gold* 25(12):6–8.
Whiffen, Thomas
1915   *The North-West Amazons: Notes of Some Months Spent among Cannibal Tribes.* London: Constable and Co.
Whitehead, Neil Lancelot
1988a   *Lords of the Tiger Spirit: A History of the Caribs in Colonial Venezuela and Guyana 1498—1820.* Providence, RI: Foris Publications.
1988b   The lords of the Epuremei: An examination of the transformation of Amerindian trade and politics in the Amazon and Orinoco, 1492–1800. Paper presented at the 46th International Congress of Americanists, Amsterdam, July.
1989   The ancient Amerindian polities of the lower Orinoco, Amazon and Guayana coast: A preliminary analysis of their passage from antiquity to extinction. Paper prepared for Wenner-Gren Symposium no. 109, "Amazonian Synthesis: An Integration of Disciplines, Paradigms, and Methodologies," Nova Friburgo, Brazil. June.
1990a   Carib ethnic soldiering in Venezuela, the Guianas and Antilles: 1492–1820. *Ethnohistory* 37(4):357–85.
1990b   The Snake Warriors—Sons of the Tiger's Teeth: A descriptive analysis of Carib warfare ca. 1500–1820. In *The Anthropology of War,* J. Haas, ed., pp. 146–70. School of American Research Advanced Seminar Series. Cambridge: Cambridge University Press.
1990c   The Mazaruni pectoral: A golden artefact discovered in Guyana and the historical sources concerning native metallurgy in the Caribbean, Orinoco, and northern Amazonia. *Journal of Archaeology and Anthropology* 7:19–38.
1992   Tribes make states and states make tribes: Warfare and the creation of colonial tribes and states in northeastern South America. In *War in the Tribal Zone: Expanding States and Indigenous Warfare,* R. B. Ferguson and N. L. Whitehead, eds., pp. 127–50. Santa Fe: School of American Research Press.
Whitten, Norman
1976   *Sacha Runa: Ethnicity and Adaptation of Ecuadorian Jungle Quichua.* Urbana: University of Illinois Press.
Wilbert, Johannes
1963   *Indios de la región Orinoco-Ventuari.* Caracas: Fundación La Salle de Ciencias Naturales.
1972   *Survivors of Eldorado: Four Indian Cultures of South America.* New York: Praeger.
Worcester, Donald E.
1973   *Brazil: From Colony to World Power.* New York: Charles Scribner's Sons.
Wright, Robin Michael
1981   History and religion of the Baniwa peoples of the upper Río Negro valley, 2 vols. Ph.D. dissertation, Stanford University. Ann Arbor, MI: University Microfilms.
Wright, Robin, and Shelton Davis
1981   Massive gold rush in Yanomami territory. *ARC Bulletin* 4, January, pp. 3–4.

Wyma, "Mel"
  1952   Days of grace in Venezuela. *Brown Gold* 10(5–6):6–7.
Yanomami, Davi Kopenawa
  1989   Letter to all the peoples of the earth. *Cultural Survival Quarterly* 13(4): 68–69.
  1991   A Yanomami leader speaks: A message from Davi Kopenawa Yanomami. *Anthropology Newsletter,* September, p. 52.
Yde, Jens
  1965   *Material Culture of the Waiwai.* Copenhagen: National Museum.
Yost, James, and Patricia Kelly
  1983   Shotguns, blowguns, and spears: The analysis of technological efficiency. In *Adaptive Responses of Native Amazonians,* R. Hames and W. Vickers, eds., pp. 189–224. New York: Academic Press.
Zent, Stanford
  1992   Historical and ethnographic ecology of the upper Cuao River Wōthɨhā: Clues for an interpretation of native Guianese social organization. Ph.D. diss., Department of Anthropology, Columbia University.
  1993   Ethnic fluidity and open ecological spaces in native Guiana. Paper presented at the 92d annual meeting of the American Anthropological Association, Washington, DC.
Zerries, Otto
  1955   Some aspects of Waica culture. *Proceedings of the 31st International Congress of Americanists,* pp. 73–88.
  1964   *Waika: Die Kulturgeschichtliche Stellung der Waika-Indianer des Oberen Orinco im Rahmen der Völkerkunde Südamerikas.* Munich: Klaus Renner Verlag.

Index

■ **R. BRIAN FERGUSON** is an associate professor of anthropology at Rutgers University. Raised in Albany, New York, he has lived on Manhattan's upper west side since 1969 and received his undergraduate and graduate degrees from Columbia University. He is a contributor to the 1990 School of American Research Advanced Seminar volume *The Anthropology of War* (Cambridge University Press) and is co-editor, with Neil L. Whitehead, of the 1992 Advanced Seminar volume *War in the Tribal Zone* (SAR Press). His current work includes a study of the evolution of the New York City police and a comparison of contemporary "cultural conflicts" and disintegrating states.

■ Author photograph by Leslie Farragher